STUDIA POST BIBLICA

VOLUMEN QUARTUM DECIMUM

STUDIA POST-BIBLICA

ADIUVANTIBUS

J. BOWMAN . J. HOFTIJZER . T. JANSMA . H. KOSMALA
K. H. RENGSTORF . J. COERT RIJLAARSDAM
G. SEVENSTER . D. WINTON THOMAS
G. VAJDA . G. VERMES

EDIDIT

P. A. H. DE BOER

VOLUMEN QUARTUM DECIMUM

LEIDEN
E. J. BRILL
1969

A HISTORY OF
THE JEWS IN BABYLONIA

IV. THE AGE OF SHAPUR II

BY

JACOB NEUSNER

Professor of Religious Studies
Brown University

LEIDEN
E. J. BRILL
1969

For Eli Ephraim

TABLE OF CONTENTS

III Babylonian Jewish Government (I):
   The Rabbi as Administrator 125

IV Babylonian Jewish Government (II):
   The Rabbi as Judge 183

V The Life of the Schools. 279

LIST OF MAPS

PREFACE

The age of Shapur II, 309 to 379, corresponds to far more than the period of a single generation of Amoraim. The sayings of Rav and Samuel pertained mainly to the years of Ardashir and Shapur, and those of their chief students, to the age of Shapur I's sons and heirs through the death of Hormizd II. Shapur II, however, outlived three generations of Amoraim, the third, fourth, and fifth. In such a long period, sufficient changes in academic life and thought may well have taken place to justify a different procedure from that followed in volumes II and III. While I have reviewed the political events of the entire reign of Shapur II, I have concentrated upon the social and cultural-religious history of only the third and fourth generations of Amoraim. In the next volume of this study, I hope to treat the fifth, sixth, and last generations of Amoraim. The data warrant this procedure, for the third and fourth generations seem to me to coalesce, like the fifth, sixth, and last ones, into a meaningful and coherent division. The Amoraim whose sayings form the foundations of this volume are R. Joseph b. Ḥiyya (d. 333),[1] Rabbah b. Naḥmani (d. 330), Abaye (d. 338), Rava b. R. Joseph (d. 352), Naḥman b. Isaac (d. 356), and their chief contemporaries. Of these, R. Joseph and Rabbah, and their disciples, Abaye and Rava, were the most important. As heads of schools, their sayings predominated in the traditions handed on in this time. I have, on the other hand, omitted R. Naḥman b. Jacob (d. 320), to whom much of vol. III was devoted, and R. Papa (d. 376). It seemed to me that R. Naḥman was important in the earlier period, as a leading younger contemporary of the disciples of Rav and Samuel. R. Papa similarly seemed to play a more central role in the last years of Shapur II. As far as dates go, however, one might have just as well preferred to include both with the Amoraim of the middle of the fourth century.

Few new issues have been raised in this volume. I have continued to apply the same questions and methods as seemed fruitful earlier, particularly in vol. III. Indeed, this study must be regarded as a close continuation of its immediate predecessor. I have tried to test the notions and theses of vol. III against the data of the following two generations. I could find no better way of proceeding. The sayings of

---

[1] The dates are R. Sherira's, and I have no way of verifying them.

the fourth century masters differ little from those of the late third
century ones. They are mostly contained in legal sayings and discussions, and offer only limited amounts of historical data. Yet those
data were awaiting examination in a detailed and comprehensive
manner, and I could see no more useful task for myself than to undertake that examination. In all, I am still trying to clear away the under-
brush, to find out little more than what came first and what came
afterward. What are the chief political events, the main governmental
institutions, the most obvious social, religious, and cultural developments, revealed by our one-sided and extremely limited sources. I believe it is worthwhile to study new material in pretty much the same
way that earlier material was studied. I set forth certain fundamental
lines of investigation, which from vol. II led directly to what I think
are the new issues and ideas of vol. III. These have here to be extended
to, and tested against, later data. No progress has been made in the
historical evaluation of the sayings. The Talmud is primarily the work
of the last period it represents, namely, of the late fourth and fifth
century masters, and the subsequent editors. It was then put into its
present form. Only when we have reached the history of that last
period can we begin to estimate with some confidence the motives and
conditions which put the corpus of sayings into its present form. We
can, making allowance for these, then argue back, with some hope of
success, from the present form to the earlier material. So this study
essentially preserves the provisional framework of discourse evident
in the former ones.[1]

I have not integrated the Jewish data into the account of Shapur II's
political and religious history. These data wholly pertain, quite naturally, to what happened to the Jews, and are reviewed in Chapter One,
sections iv-xi. In my view, had I included them in the broader survey
of Shapur's times, I should have conveyed a distorted and false impression. It would have seemed to the reader that what was really most
important about Iran, including Babylonia, from 309 to 379 was the
local, parochial history of that part of the Jewish community we know
about through the academic records. Emperor Julian seems to me to
have paid far more attention to Byzantine, particularly Palestinian
Jewry, than Shapur II did to the Jewish communities of his empire.
Arsacid times were no more; the Jews were not now a formidable

---

[1] This is essentially the argument of "In Quest of the Historical Rabban
Yoḥanan ben Zakkai," *HTR* 59, 1966, 391-413. See also vol. III, pp. ix-xxi,
which serves to introduce this volume as well.

factor in Sasanian dynastic life. They were not important in the politics of the empire, nor in military affairs, and certainly not in the religious and cultural life of the Iranians. They took a mostly passive part in international politics. Shapur's religious advisers were concerned mainly with the Christians, who suffered terrible persecutions, and with various heretics within the Mazdean tradition, but not with the Jews, who, I think, were mostly left alone. So it seemed to me appropriate to treat the Jews apart from the general history of the empire.[1]

I confess to a strong bias in favor of Shapur II. While trying to preserve an open mind, I have found very little persuasive evidence that he harmed the Jewish community, and it may be that my general bias in his favor has affected this judgment. The evidences are presented for the reader's own evaluation.

After the usual review of the external setting of Babylonian Jewish history, in Chapter One, and of the internal political institutions of Jewry, in Chapter Two, I have devoted most attention to the relationship between the rabbis and the ordinary people. If our data had reached us from other sources, or if we had some independent accounts of Babylonian Jewish culture in addition to the Talmud, further issues would surely have been susceptible of close study. All our literary sources, however, derive from rabbinical schools, which preserved their own, but no other, records for posterity. Our glimpses into the life of Babylonian Jewry reach us, therefore, through the prism of the academy. These perceptions have, moreover, been affected directly or indirectly by the perspective of later Judaism. The normative and correct version of Judaism was long believed to be that of the Babylonian Talmud and its cognate literature from Palestine. This essentially theological judgment takes for granted the claim of the rabbinical schools to preserve "the whole Torah" and so to constitute the repository of divine revelation. History and theology have therefore combined to determine the ways in which ancient texts will be interpreted not merely for religious, but also for scholarly purposes. The result is that the history of the Jews in Babylonia in Parthian and Sasanian times has been categorized as "Talmudic history" or "the Talmudic period."[2] It has been written until now mostly in terms of the personalities of the schools, their legal and theological ideas, and the comments of medieval authorities upon their literature. So Talmudic history constituted a category of literary studies. We need now to dis-

---

[1] Compare vol. III, pp. 1-7.
[2] See vol. III, pp. xii-xx.

tinguish, however, between history and theology, and also between the
history of the Jews and Judaism and the history of the rabbinical
academies and writings.

The history of the Jews in Babylonia seems to me to consist of more
than what a handful of great men said and did. It requires much attention to the life of a large community. In Chapter Three, close study
is given to the role of the court in other than narrowly legal affairs, and
to evidence of the rabbi's influence in various aspects of ritual life. In
Chapter Four, the court's legal activities and consequent power to
govern Jewish community affairs are assessed. These Chapters corre-
spond to vol. II, Chapter Eight, and vol. III, Chapters Four and Five.
Chapter Five continues the effort, begun in vol. II, Chapters Four,
Five, and Six, and vol. III, Chapter Three, to describe the cultural and
religious significance of the schools. While we may not yet know
precisely how reliable are the attributions of various sayings to the
great masters, we have factual evidence about the schools from their
own carefully redacted traditions.

I realize that the emergent picture may trouble the Jewish reader,
particularly if he has paid much attention to Talmudic literature as it
is taught in Jewish schools and synagogues. It may prove difficult for
him to accept what I believe is the fact that "Torah" was a source not
only of law and ethics, but also of magic in a great many modes. Indeed, while most people are aware that magical sayings are contained
in Talmudic literature, only few have taken seriously the fact that the
leading rabbis were also presented as men preeminent precisely because of their magical powers, *and* that their magical powers were believed to be a *direct* consequence of their mastery of "Torah." If the
data in vol. III, Chapter Three, have not sufficed to persuade the reader
that this was the case, I hope that those presented here may do so. The
common modern distinction between "religion" and "magic," or between "true religion" and "science," on the one hand, and "magic,"
"superstition," and "folk religion," on the other, has very little basis
in the phenomena themselves, as we shall see. It is one thing to say that
the rabbis were masters of the advanced sciences of their day, including
astrology and various methods of healing, protection from demons,
and the like. That fact has been widely recognized. It is quite another
to say, as is asserted here, that the rabbis in their schools exhibited no
greater awareness of any distinction between what is now commonly
called "magic, superstition, and folk religion," on the one hand, and
what is now commonly called "true religion and advanced science," on

the other, than did the ordinary people. They certainly offered a perfectly candid distinction between Torah and "magic." "Magic" was what other people did. "Torah" was what they knew and what empowered them to do supernatural feats, including the resurrection of the dead, the creation of men, communication with the heavenly court, angels, demons, and the dead, as well as more commonplace ones, such as making rain and driving away demons. I have tried in Chapter Five to explain why they held such convictions about themselves.

We must remember that the stories we have are those the Talmudic editors chose to tell. They were not embarrassed by magical data, but eager to report how the great masters performed theurgical wonders of all sorts. Whatever philosophical distinctions have been made in later times between magic and theology are data of the medieval and modern history of Judaism and of religion generally. If so, the distinction recognized by the rabbinical schools is an equally important datum, and it should not be set aside in favor of those which proved more acceptable to philosophical theology as it took shape in medieval and, more especially, modern times. I am guided by what Professor Thomas Kuhn wrote in connection with Galileo's refutation of Aristotle, "We like to forget that many of the concepts in which we believe were painfully drummed into us in our youth. We too easily take them as natural and indubitable products of our own unaided perceptions, dismissing concepts different from our own as errors, rooted in ignorance or stupidity and perpetuated by blind obedience to authority. *Our own education stands between us and the past...*"[1]

Four important issues are not treated here at all. First, I have made no effort to ascertain the origins of various magical beliefs and practices. I believe questions of origins are important, but not decisive when attempting to describe the actuality of the schools and their culture. Second, I have not paid attention to the content of the law. To stress that this is not a work on the history of Jewish law, I have omitted the substance of the decisions in various court cases, reporting only the circumstance in which the case arose or apparently came before the rabbi. In doing so, I mean to underline the importance of legal study in its own right and make it clear that so narrow a framework as defines this volume leaves no place for speculation on the history and development of Jewish law. (I have as yet discovered no grounds to suppose that much that happened outside of the schools made signifi-

---

[1] Thomas S. Kuhn, *The Copernican Revolution. Planetary Astronomy in the Development of Western Thought* (N.Y., 1959), pp. 95-96. Italics supplied.

cant impact on the formation of the law inside of them. Doubtless future studies will provide more adequate basis for that widespread supposition.) Third, I have paid only brief and superficial attention to the content of Scriptural exegesis (in Chapter Five, section xiii). This is not a work of text-commentary or criticism. I am not a qualified philologist and so cannot offer new information on the meanings of specific words or even sentences in *agadic* passages. Many such passages are cited, of course, in the context of a historical discussion. To my knowledge, I have not contributed to the illumination of any one of them. Fourth, and most important, I have not yet turned to important and central questions of the history of the traditions shaped in the rabbinical academies and now preserved in the Babylonian Talmud. It is not that I do not think it an important question for historians to work out. On the contrary, I think it too important to deal with here and now, for it requires consideration not of one period alone, but of the formation of the Babylonian *gemara* as a whole over a period of three hundred years.[1]

Originally I supposed that if one separated the various sayings attributed to the several masters by generations, he might discover signs of development, change, growth—in other words, the raw data of history. To the present time, I regard the enterprise as mostly a failure. It is true that we can recover some historical and political materials of interest. I had hoped, however, that we might be able to trace the development of legal and theological ideas, if not in great detail at least in some general way. I thought that we might thus detect changes of mood, or uncover different topics of discussion characteristic of one period and not of another, and that it would be possible to relate such changes of interest or of stress to larger political, economic, sociological, or religious questions. So far, I have seen very few significant changes of any sort. The literature presents a timeless and immutable visage, as if very little innovation took place over a century and a half among many different people in various circumstances. Whether or not the

---

[1] For some remarks on the literary contributions of the fourth-century masters, see especially S. Funk, "Das literarische Leben der babylonischen Juden im vierten Jahrhundert," *MGWJ* 50, 1906, pp. 385ff. and I. Y. Halevy, *Dorot HaRishonim*, III, pp. 480-504. On the attribution of Kallah Rabbati to Rava, see J. Rabbinowitz, in A. Cohen, ed., *The Minor Tractates of the Talmud* (London, 1965), Introduction, p. v, and compare the remarks of M. Friedman, A. Aptowitzer, and M. Higger, cited by Rabbinowitz. Without systematic study, we have no means of evaluating such attributions as this one. Broader methodological issues require prior consideration. See also Y. N. Epstein, *Mavo le-Nusah HaMishnah* (2nd ed., Jerusalem-Tel Aviv, 1954), pp. 369ff., and I. Y. Halevy, *Dorot HaRishonim*, II, 480-494.

schools actually were so static, their intellectual life so unvarying, their concerns so remote from the vicissitudes of society and history, I cannot say. Reason suggests that times changed and people changed with them. The evidence as I now comprehend it suggests otherwise. So I have tried to describe the apparently static phenomena of the school, the rabbi, and the court as they emerge from data pertaining to the middle fourth-century masters. I cannot now specify important details in which these phenomena would radically have differed from one place or age to another. It seems clear to me that we shall have to place greater stress upon the history of the rabbinical academies. Perhaps through such an history we may uncover the insights which so far have eluded me in the search for the history of the Jewish community as a whole.

Since I have specified problems I have not satisfactorily confronted, I hope it will not seem pretentious to note the broader disciplines to which I here try to contribute. These are history, sociology of religion, and history of religions. Chapters One and Two are purely historical in method and orientation. Chapters Three and Four focus upon data relevant both to history and to the sociology of Judaism. Chapter Five is shaped by the concerns of history of religions, though it is not an essay in the history of religions. I have offered a number of comments appropriate to the comparative study of religions, both in vol. III (pp. 95-126 and 192-194) and below. Historians of religions, however, normally do not concentrate upon a particular tradition, but generally pursue broader issues, cutting across many religious traditions. I have learned much from Professors Jonathan Z. Smith, University of Chicago, Geo Widengren, Uppsala University, Carsten Colpé, Göttingen University, Willard G. Oxtoby, Yale University, Hans H. Penner, Dartmouth College, and Morton Smith, Columbia University, whose various researches have exerted profound influence on my understanding of specific problems in studying the history of religions in late antiquity. So while retaining an abiding, indeed predominate interest in the study of history and in historiographical issues, I find as a historian working with sources of a primarily religious character that the discipline of history of religions provides a most fruitful and promising set of issues, inquiries, and perspectives. So narrowly limited a framework of time and space as mine is not, however, the best setting for demonstrating the value of *religionsgeschichtliche* methodology for the study of Judaism. The researches of Professors G. G. Scholem and R. J. Z. Werblowsky, Hebrew University, should be consulted as far more significant exemplifications of that value than I am able to offer.

I have translated some texts, but more often have cited with minor alterations the translations of the Babylonian Talmud edited by I. Epstein and published by Soncino Press, London. These are generally cited in the names of individual translators where they appear. In general, I translated texts of importance for narrowly historical questions, while those of the group of translators directed by Dr. Epstein seemed more than satisfactory for purposes of illustration or citation elsewhere. These I have checked against the original printed text, and against variant manuscript readings when available in Rabinowicz's *Diqduqei Soferim* (now including Gittin, in the excellent edition of M. S. Feldblum). However I have made only very minor alterations in them. Where I have translated texts myself, I have noted differences from the Soncino translators. I have gladly consulted all existing translations. They have made historical study far easier, and even at points where I have differed, have proved interesting and illuminating. I may have presented too many examples of cases, but preferred to err on the side of excess.

Research for this study began during my tenure as Faculty Fellow at Dartmouth College. Substantial research expenses, including typing of manuscripts, photocopying articles and parts of books, were paid by the Committee on Research at Dartmouth College. Other expenses were paid by grants from the Penrose Fund of the American Philosophical Society. My thanks to these institutions for their generous support.

Professor Michael Avi-Yonah, Hebrew University, graciously obtained permission to reproduce the copyrighted map appearing below, p. 184, from his Atlas. Professor W. W. Hallo kindly gave permission to reprint, in revised form, my translation of Chapters XIII and XIV of Škand Gumanik Vičar, which originally appeared in the *Journal of the American Oriental Society* ("A Zoroastrian Critique of Judaism," *JAOS* 83, 3, 1963, pp. 283-294, and "Škand Miscellanies," *JAOS* 86, 4, 1966, 414-416). I wish once again to express my indebtedness to Professor R. N. Frye, with whom I studied the Škand material, and who guided my translation, and to the critical text of Professor P. J. de Menasce, on whose text, translation, and commentary my effort was entirely based.

My beloved teacher, Professor Morton Smith, provided extensive criticism and comment, of invariably great value. His remarkable generosity with both his learning and his time, his constant admonitions and encouragement, and his friendship sustain me. He read the manuscript in an earlier draft, and while he is by no means responsible for my deficiencies in method and learning, he certainly shares whatever credit accrues for any contributions to learning I may have made. Professor Baruch Levine and Rabbi Gerald Blidstein offered many helpful comments. Professor Jes P. Asmussen kindly read Chapter One, and corrected mistakes of both fact and judgment. He also brought to my attention important monographs on Iranian Christianity and Mazdaism which I might otherwise have missed.

My brother-in-law, Dr. Elihu D. Richter, M. D., M. P. H., provided interesting information on diseases endemic to Iraq. My brother, Frederick D. Neusner, Assistant Attorney-General of the State of Connecticut, explained several legal terms and categories. Rabbi David Goodblatt corrected the typescripts and proof, and made many useful suggestions. My understanding of the historical task has often been enriched in conversations with Professors Yoḥanan Muffs, Richard T. Vann, and Avrum Udovitch.

Former colleagues in the Department of Religion at Dartmouth College have made a formidable contribution to my intellectual growth. If my interests have broadened to include aspects and issues of the study of religions formerly unknown or unclear to me, it was on their account. From each of them I learned something. From all of them I learned for the first time the satisfactions of life in community based upon concern for scholarship. Special thanks are due to Professors Robin Scroggs and Wayne Meeks, the latter now of Indiana University, who helped me to understand the achievements of New Testament scholarship; and to Professors Fred Berthold jr. and David Kelsey, the latter now of Yale University Divinity School, who taught me to recognize, understand, and respect the theological enterprise in its own right, and so to distinguish history from theology.

The less tangible contributions of my wife Suzanne, and sons, Samuel Aaron and Eli Ephraim, no less important to me, do not require specification. They know what they have given. No words can ever contain my gratitude.

No one shares the burden of my deficiencies, except the reader.

JACOB NEUSNER

Providence, Rhode Island
1 Elul 5728
25 August 1968

LIST OF ABBREVIATIONS

To the list of abbreviations provided in vol. II pp. xxi-xxii should be added the following

I. Journals

BJRL   = Bulletin of the John Rylands Library
DOP   = Dumbarton Oaks Papers
HR   = History of Religions
JRS   = Journal of Roman Studies
Pat. Or. = Patrologia Orientalis
YCS   = Yale Classical Studies

II. Talmudic Literature

Kil.   = Kila'im
Tem.   = Temurah

III. Biblical Books

Koh.   = Kohelet *corrected to* Qoh. = Qohelet

IV. Other Abbreviations

Vol. II   = A History of the Jews in Babylonia, II. The Early Sasanian Period.
Vol. III = A History of the Jews in Babylonia, III. From Shapur I. to Shapur II.
Vol. V = A History of the Jews in Babylonia, V. Later Sasanian Times.

CHAPTER ONE

THE AGE OF SHAPUR II
309 TO 379

I. SECURING THE THRONE AND THE FRONTIERS

Shapur II proved worthy of his illustrious forebear's name. Unlike Shapur I,[1] he found no ordered and stable government when he took power. He did not enjoy the advantage of a quick and smooth succession, nor did he inherit the leadership of a strong army. On every side foes pressed in, by contrast to the secure position of Iran in 241. Yet Shapur II imposed his will upon his empire and prevailed against all his enemies. While his successes on the battlefield do not compare favorably with those of Shapur I, he won his wars. Through diplomacy, he achieved what had proved too difficult for Iranian armies over the generations, namely, possession of Nisibis and predominance in Mesopotamia, Armenia, and the Caucasus. He was a brilliant leader, a shrewd politician, an effective administrator, a brave and selfless soldier, an emperor of grand dignity and poise, surely the greatest leader of his times. Our very brief review of his reign cannot possibly do him justice. It scarcely suffices merely to call the age by his name.

When Hormizd II died in 309, his son, Hormizd III, assumed that he would succeed, but the nobility had other ideas and imprisoned him. Discovering that one of Hormizd's wives was pregnant, and hearing from the astrologers that it would be a male, the grandees proclaimed the embryo to be the king of kings of Iran and Non-Iran. They went further, and held the royal diadem over the mother's womb. In a few months, Shapur II was born, crowned king at his birth. In his times, Byzantium was ruled by Galerius, Constantine, Constantius and Constans, Julian, Jovian, Valentinian I, Valens, Gratian, and Valentinian II. He proved to be the equal of them all. But during his first years, some must have doubted the throne would survive long enough for him to inherit it. In the time of his minority, powerful lords assumed the regency but proved unable to hold the state together or even to protect its frontiers. On the contrary, the incursions of Arab raiders

---

[1] See vol. II, pp. 1-10, 39-52.

proved a grievous problem. They generally came down the Euphrates from the north or up from the Persian gulf, but occasionally struck straight out across the desert to ravage the rich territories of Babylonia and Khuzistan.[1] As in Parthian times, when cuneiform records tell how the people again and again hid in the fields to escape marauders from the desert, so now life was unsafe, and everyone suffered. A local Mesopotamian sheikh, Thair, even attacked Ctesiphon, took the city by storm, and captured a member of the royal family. In the east, the Kushans took the occasion of weakness at the center to reestablish their former power. Presumably the local grandees likewise exploited the possibilities of the unsettled times. So through his minority, generally thought to be the sixteen years from 309 to 325, Shapur II reigned over a disintegrating empire.

When he assumed the responsibilities and power of government, he proceeded methodically to reestablish stable and peaceful conditions, first at home, and then on the eastern frontiers. Finally in the disputed Mesopotamian marches he resumed the struggle with Rome and attempted to retrieve the disastrous situation bequeathed to him in consequence of Narseh's peace of 298. It was a sensible and necessary procedure. He could scarcely undertake frontier campaigns if his rear was endangered. He could hardly hope for popular support and for the regular collection of taxes to finance his wars abroad if at home people were unable to rely upon his protection for themselves and their property. So he turned first of all to subjugate northeastern Arabia and the Persian Gulf and to reestablish a secure frontier on the central and southern Euphrates. The record of his campaigns, preserved in Arab legend, reports a policy of harsh repression. Tabari and other Arab authors mention his victorious expeditions against the Arab tribes and his occupation of Bahrain on the Persian gulf. According to Tabari, he supposedly pierced the shoulder-blades of Arab prisoners to prevent their making war again. His victories in the south were intended not only to protect the "heart of the Iranian Empire," namely Babylonia, but also to assure that for the future, no similar problems would recur. The Arabs recalled later on that he acted with exceptional cruelty. He next turned to operations against the Kushans, smashed their armies, and annexed their territories to Iran as a new province to be governed by Sasanian princes residing at Balkh. During his Roman campaigns he had from time to time to suspend operations whenever an invasion of Little Kushans and Chionite Ephthalites threatened the eastern

---

[1] On contemporary Jewish traditions relating to the Arabs, see below, p. 44.

marches. In every case he was able to pacify the nomads, generally by settling them on Kushan territory as confederates and by hiring them to furnish troops for his western campaigns. As soon as he could, he turned to the west. In 337 or 339 he began a campaign which continued, with long intervals of truce, for more than twenty-five years, until the great peace of 363, in which he won all that he wanted and more. As I said, he began the reconquest of the west only after he had taken control of the interior and then the east; he suspended it only when he had to. It was the grand obsession of his reign. Though often defeated on the battlefield and disappointed in sieges, sometimes hard-pressed even in his home territories around Ctesiphon, he never gave up the struggle. Unlike Narseh, he was not disappointed or humiliated so as to give up in defeat, though he suffered defeat. Unlike Shapur I, he never sought to reach beyond the limits of his resources. He knew precisely what he wanted, namely, the restoration of the Iranian position in Armenia and Mesopotamia. And he succeeded.[1]

The twenty-five years of Iranian war with Byzantium were marked by five major campaigns including four Persian offensives, and involving attacks on, or sieges of, Nisibis, in 337, 346, 348, and 350, sieges of Amida and Singara in 359 and 360, respectively, and finally, the aggressive invasion of Julian in 363. The utter rout of Narseh in 297-8 had left the Romans in complete control of Mesopotamia, masters of Nisibis in the west and of five provinces across the Tigris in the east. The road to Ctesiphon lay open through Adiabene. To the north Armenia was securely in Roman hands. Persian power had in effect been driven back to the Iranian plateau, and the Sasanian hold upon

---

[1] On the early years of Shapur II, the following proved most helpful: A. Christensen, *L'Iran sous les Sassanides* (1st ed., Copenhagen, 1936), pp. 229-230; George Rawlinson, *The Seventh Great Oriental Monarchy* (London, 1876), pp. 143-8, on the Arab campaigns, pp. 145-7; R. Ghirshman, *Iran* (Baltimore, 1954), pp. 296-7, especially on the eastern campaigns; and T. Nöldeke, trans., *Tabari*, pp. 52-9, especially on the Arab wars, pp. 53ff. According to Nöldeke, p. 51 n. 3, Hormizd II had several other sons. On Shapur's mother, 'Ifra Hormizd, see below, pp.35–39. The reference to Parthian times is based upon conversations with Professor Abraham Sachs, who has not yet published his very important discoveries in cuneiform sources relating to Seleucid and Parthian times. On the coins of Shapur II, see especially Robert Göbl, "Aufbau der Munzprägung," in Franz Altheim and Ruth Stiehl, *Ein Asiatischer Staat* (Wiesbaden, 1954), pp. 107-11. On the eastern campaigns, see also R. Ghirshman, *Iran: Parthians and Sasanians* (London, 1962), p. 317. See also F. Justi in *Grundriss der Iranischen Philologie* ed. Wilhelm Geiger and Ernst Kuhn (Strassburg, 1896-1904), II, pp. 521-5. Note also Arthur Vööbus, *History of Asceticism in the Syrian Orient* (Louvain, 1960), II, p. 38, who says that in 337 Shapur's forces invaded some of the trans-Tigrene provinces, basing his date upon Aphrahat's *Fifth Treatise* (of which more below, pp. 20–27).

Babylonia was tenuous. In succeeding decades the consequences were catastrophic. Rome was quite satisfied with what she had and remained peaceful, a benign lion enjoying her spoils. But the centripetal forces always pulling at the Persian empire from the fringes proved so powerful that great territories fell away, as in the east, or proved barely tenable, as in Babylonia itself. So the wise settlement of 298, in which Diocletian treated with honor the claims and needs of Narseh, nonetheless proved too sweeping and one-sided. Iran could not stand upon so shaken a foundation, even though Rome had no intention whatever of upsetting her. It seemed to Shapur II absolutely necessary to resume the struggle ignominiously broken off a generation earlier. He did so, as I said, as soon as he was able. His preliminary purpose was to recover the five provinces ceded in 298, and regain control of Nisibis if possible. He would thus restore the territorial integrity—as he saw it—of the Iranian empire.[1] But his larger purpose was to regain superiority in Armenia Major. In Roman hands, Armenia was an ever-open highway of invasion, where the powerful Persian cavalry could hardly hold its own. In Iranian hands Armenia was a buffer, a great wall against aggression from the West. Shapur II proceeded stage by stage. When he was finally ready, he began with a quick razzia against Armenia, in 335. The Armenian nobles appealed to Rome, and Constantine intervened, sent an army, and drove out the Persian marauders. In May of 337, Constantine died. By summertime, Shapur had laid siege to Nisibis.[2] Rawlinson attributes the eagerness of Shapur to the presence in Byzantium of a dangerous rival to the Persian throne, an older brother.[3] Had Constantine and Constantius no plans whatever for intrigues against the Sasanian throne, however, Shapur would still have made war.[4]

---

[1] Including, of course, Babylonia, which the Sasanians always regarded as an Iranian and *not* a Non-Iranian province. Since the capital was there, it was a reasonable judgment on their part, even though the majority of the population could not have been of Iranian descent. Indeed, Professor Jes P. Asmussen points out that from Achaemenid times, it was so regarded.

[2] I follow the chronology of Vööbus and especially N. H. Baynes, "Athanasiana," *Journal of Egyptian Archaeology* 11, 1926, p. 66. Christensen cites also P. Peeters, "L'Intervention politique de Constance II dans la Grande Arménie, en 338," *Extr. des Bull. de la Classe des Lettres de l'Acad. Royale de Belgique*, 5e série, vol. 17, 1931.

[3] *Op. cit.*, p. 149.

[4] For the course of Persian-Roman relations between 337 and 379, I have followed Rawlinson, *op. cit.*, pp. 151-254; Christensen, *op. cit.*, pp. 230-35; Ghirshman, *Iran*, pp. 317-20; Nöldeke, *Tabari*, pp. 55-67; R. N. Frye, *Heritage of Persia* (N.Y.-Cleveland, 1963), p. 215; Justi, *op. cit.*, pp. 189-92; N. H. Baynes,

Prospects of the summer, 337, could not have seemed unpromising. In place of a great general, grown old on the battlefield, Shapur faced a young and untried heir, who actually held only one-third of his father's empire. The forcible conversion of Armenia to Christianity by Trdat and Gregory the Illuminator was resisted by many who were attached to the old religion. A discontented faction developed, therefore, ready to make an alliance with any foreign power willing to reestablish the ancient cult. Obviously Byzantium would not cooperate. After the death of Trdat in 314 strong government ceased in Armenia, and, according to Faustus, Shapur was already able to recover Media Atropatene well before the new war. So matters looked favorable at the outset of the quarter century of war. Shapur overlooked one detail which in the end was to thwart each of his offensive operations: his army remained woefully weak in engineering and siege-operations. That made all the difference. On the contested frontier, any well-situated, well-constructed fortress could impede the progress of an invasion. Without adequate means of subduing the many walled cities of Mesopotamia, Shapur wasted his precious time and gold in long and heart-breaking sieges of one town after another, only in the end to be forced by the winter rains to retreat to his capital. Shapur's invasion of 337 proved inconsequential. Constantius was able to restore his position

---

"Constantine's Successors to Jovian: And the Struggle with Persia," *Cambridge Medieval History*, I, pp. 55-86; Louis Dillemann, *Haute Mésopotamie*, pp. 290-2; on the treaty of 363, pp. 218-223, on the trans-Tigrene provinces, pp. 210-11. Note also Freya Stark, *Rome on the Euphrates* (London, 1966), pp. 312-356. The many biographies of Julian contain full accounts of the Persian campaign. I found most useful Louis Dillemann, "Ammien Marcellin et les Pays de l'Euphrate et du Tigre," *Syria* 38, 1961, 1-2, pp. 87-158. In general, I have tried to avoid all disputed issues in this brief summary, but rather to provide a simple account following the accepted histories. See also Andrew Alföldi, trans. by H. Mattingly, *The Conversion of Constantine and Pagan Rome* (Oxford, 1948); Jacob Burckhardt, trans. by Moses Hadas, *The Age of Constantine the Great* (N.Y., 1956); G. P. Baker, *Constantine the Great and the Christian Revolution* (N. Y. 1930); J. Bidez, *La Vie de l'Empereur Julien* (Paris, 1930); Norman H. Baynes, "The Early Life of Julian the Apostate," *JHS* 45, pp. 251-254; N. H. Baynes, "Rome and Armenia in the Fourth Century," *English Historical Review* 25, 1910, pp. 625-643; Ernst Honigmann, *Die Ostgrenze des byzantinischen Reiches von 363 bis 1071* (Brussels, 1935); Ernst Stein, *Geschichte des spätrömischen Reiches I. Vom römischen zum byzantinischen Staate* (Vienna, 1928); E. A. Thompson, *The Historical Work of Ammianus Marcellinus* (Cambridge, 1947). The sources of the war of 363 are Ammianus Marcellinus, books 23-25, and passages in Zosimus, Malalas, and Libanius (Speech Eighteen); I followed Rawlinson's summaries of the latter three sources. Note also Edward Gibbon, *The History of the Decline and Fall of the Roman Empire*, ed. J. B. Bury (London, 1896), II, pp. 227, 265, 267, 270, and for Julian's invasion, pp. 487-528; and S. Funk, *Die Juden in Babylonien* (Berlin, 1908), II, pp. 78-93.

in Armenia, to win over some of the Mesopotamian Arabs, and to fortify the trans-Tigrene cities. In 338, Shapur resumed the struggle. His cavalry swiftly overran the open country, and, as was the Persian custom, burned crops and villages and slaughtered cattle and people. But a quick raid would accomplish nothing. The great city of Nisibis, commanding the region, had to be taken. Situated on the Mygdonius River, an effluent of the Khabur, and about sixty miles from the Tigris, Nisibis was a powerful fortress. The first siege, in 338, lasted sixty-three days, and the city held. Christian chroniclers preserved the record of miracles done by its bishop, St. James, in the defense. Through the next decade or so, the Persians moved at will upon the plains, which their mobile cavalry effectively controlled, but struck no decisive blow anywhere.

In 341 Shapur resumed his intrigues against Armenia, with good result. He tried to put on the throne a friendly monarch, and succeeded in placing in power Arsaces, scion of the cadet Arsacid line which had controlled Armenia for over a century after the Sasanian revolution in Iran itself. It was a substantial victory, one of many Shapur won through diplomacy. He thus achieved great influence in his enemy's flank. In 346, he again attacked Nisibis, besieging the city for three months. In 348, he called out a vast army, including allies and merce-naries, and moving out of Adiabene, advanced toward Nisibis. Con-stantius was stationed near Singara, but did not fight at the river or on the plain between the Tigris and the mountains for fear of the Persian horse. He planned a defensive campaign in the foothills. Shapur thus chose his position, set archers on the hills, and then advanced upon the Romans. The Persian view of the battle was that it was a victory. They held that they merely pretended to retreat to draw their pursuers along the plain to their fortified camp. There the horse and archers were ready. The Iranian horse-charge was thwarted, but when the legions burst into the camp, they scattered in search of booty. Then as the sun set, the Persians surrounded the camp and slaughtered the disorganized foe. A Roman account could have reported the battle of Singara some-what differently. "Letting" the enemy take one's camp seems an ex-pensive enticement. The Romans could have explained, therefore, that they had won a victory, but the Persian horse remaining in the neighbor-hood succeeded in killing some stragglers scattered for looting. In any event the "victory" at Singara had no significant result. That the Persians could not follow up their "success" strongly suggests, Pro-fessor Morton Smith comments, that the Roman account would thus have been mostly correct. Shapur returned home. In the campaign of 350, he again besieged Nisibis, a final, desperate attempt. He brought with him allies from India and their elephants. In early summer, he crossed the Tigris, took a number of minor fortifications, and marched north against the city. He began with the usual futile procedures, battering the walls with rams and sapping them with mines. He finally hit upon a novel plan. The Mygdonius, swollen with melting snows, had covered much of the plain on which Nisibis was located. Shapur built an embankment on the lower part of the plain, so as to form a deep lake around the town, which crept ever closer to the walls. He then built a fleet of vessels, put his artillery on them, and attacked the city. The walls were weakened by the water, and in one part, they collapsed for a space of one hundred and fifty feet. The troops rushed in, first heavy cavalry, then elephants. But the rush soon became a slogging struggle through the mud. The horses were entangled, and the elephants sank down. Shapur called the retreat, and the archers kept up a rapid fire against the breach to prevent repairs. But by the next morning, the wall was six feet high. Shapur gave up the siege soon afterward, more than three months' work having gone to waste. He had no choice, because of troubles in the Caspian region and on the Oxus.

The apparent failure of Shapur produced one predictable consequence: Arsaces of Armenia had to make his peace with Byzantium. This he did by marrying the daughter of an imperial official. A formal alliance was made. From 350 to 357, Shapur could do little about it, being busy in the east. By the latter year, however, he had made peace in the east, extending his influence, though we have no details of how he did it. In 357-8 he engaged in negotiations with Constantius. The Romans, knowing his preoccupation in the east, and aware of Constantius's troubles in the west, opened negotiations through the satrap of Adiabene. Shapur responded with great pride and dignity, especially so since by then he had successfully concluded his eastern campaign. The letter of Shapur follows, in John C. Rolfe's translation of Ammianus Marcellinus (17.5.3-8):

> I, Sapor, King of Kings, partner of the stars, brother of the sun and moon, to my brother Constantius Caesar offer most ample greeting. I rejoice and at last take pleasure that you have returned to the best course and acknowledged the inviolable sanction of justice, having learned from actual experience what havoc has been caused at various times by obstinate covetousness of what belongs to others... I shall

state my proposal in brief terms... That my forefathers' empire reached
as far as the river Strymon and the boundaries of Macedonia even your
own ancient records bear witness; these lands it is fitting that I should
demand, since... I surpass the kings of old in magnificence and array
of conspicuous virtues. But at all times right reason is dear to me...
And therefore it is my duty to recover Armenia with Mesopotamia,
which doubledealing wrested from my grandfather [= Narseh]. That
principle shall never be brought to acceptance among us which you
exultantly maintain, that without any distinction between virtue and
deceit all successful events of war should be approved. Finally, if you
wish to follow my sound advice, disregard this small tract, always a
source of woe and bloodshed, so that you may rule the rest in security,
wisely recalling that even expert physicians sometimes cauterize, lance,
and even cut away some parts of the body, in order to save the rest
for sound use... This assuredly I declare, that if this embassy of mine
returns unsuccessful, after the time of the winter rest is past, I shall
gird myself with all my strength and with fortune and the justice of
my terms upholding my hope of a successful issue, I shall hasten to
come on...

Shapur thus referred to the settlement of Diocletian, seeing it as
untenable. He said he could never acquiesce, nor could any Persian
emperor, in the results of an "unjust" war. The Persians had not held
Thrace since 479 B.C., so the "injustice" was Shapur's own invention.
He knew Diocletian regarded the settlement as honorable and reasonable, and he too was master of these virtues. He refrained, after all,
from demanding all which history recorded as "his own." He did not
demand the shores of the Aegean Sea, but "only" the highlands of
Armenia. Thus he offered what was to his mind a fair settlement. But
it represented a unilateral rejection of the sixty-year-old treaty. He
would sign over what he might have claimed without much right, in
favor of what he did not then hold but wanted to recover. Constantius
took a different, more reasonable and just position:

> This covetousness of yours, always unbending and more widely
> encroaching, I vehemently reprobate. You demand Mesopotamia as
> your own, and likewise Armenia, and recommend lopping off some
> members of a sound body so that its health may afterward be put on a
> firm footing...

Reviewing his initiation of negotiations, an act of general goodwill,
Constantius then informed Shapur the true state of affairs. He too was
newly strong:

> For at this time, when the sequence of events... has beamed in
> manifold form upon us, when with the overthrow of the usurpers, the

whole Roman world is subject to us, it is absurd and silly to surrender what we long preserved unmolested...

Shapur then prepared to attack.

He was strengthened by the adherence of a Roman official, Antoninus, who took refuge in Persian territory from the demands of creditors and informed the Persians about the disposition of the Roman army. He was well received and given a hearing. He urged Shapur to make an immediate attack, striking directly for Syria (like Shapur I a century ago), for the emperor was fighting on the Danube, and the Roman east was barely defended. He advised the emperor to ignore and bypass the Mesopotamian fortresses, cross the Euphrates, overrun Syria, and devastate the west. Shapur, however, was unable to bypass the Roman army of Mesopotamia, then sitting on the banks of the Tigris. He crossed the river, and found his enemy in process of destroying forage, evacuating indefensible towns, and falling back upon the line of the Euphrates. The Euphrates itself prevented a crossing, for it was in full flood. Shapur then marched northeastward from Zeugma toward Amida. He defeated the Romans in a battle near Amida and besieged the city. He first took two nearby fortresses, treating the captives with great respect, and so attempting to ease the surrender of Amida. When, however, he approached the walls of the city to demand surrender, the defenders ignored his royal rank and peaceable mission, and threw spears and stones at him. He was outraged at what he regarded as sacrilege and ordered immediate attack. The siege drew on, lasting for seventy days. It came time to give up or make one final effort. Shapur pressed the assault, bravely fighting in the front ranks. After three bloody days, the wall gave way, and the Persians occupied the city, slaughtering everyone they found. Exasperated by the losses of the prolonged siege, Shapur allowed the carnage. He claimed as his own subjects all captives who came from the trans-Tigrene provinces, for he had never accepted the loss of that territory. These he had massacred. Many others were sold as slaves. The victory of 359 was an expensive one, however, and Shapur retired across the Tigris. Through the winter he restored his forces and gathered stores for the next attack.

The new attack was directed against Singara, which was vigorously defended. Within a brief time the city fell. The Persians this time bypassed Nisibis, and proceeded to Bezabde on the eastern bank of the Tigris. It was chief city of one of the five provinces ceded by Narseh and had been well fortified by Rome. Shapur invited surrender but was disappointed. Finally he took it after a long siege. Shapur then carefully repaired the defences, intending to hold the city. Other fortresses offered little resistance, but, held up at Birta, Shapur returned home. So in the campaigns of 359 and 360, Shapur had achieved notable successes. Amida, Singara, and Bezabde were now his. The adaptable Armenians, seeing the way matters were developing, began to reconsider their Byzantine alliance. Constantius prevented an outright revolt, but it was clear that only a major victory over the Persians would retain Armenian loyalty for Rome. Constantius and Shapur both proceeded cautiously, the former ever more respectful of the enemy, the latter now satisfied, for the moment, to keep what he had won. Shapur engaged in elaborate maneuvers, all on the eastern side of the Tigris, and by the autumn of 361, had withdrawn to the capital. The two never met again, for Constantius died toward the end of 361. His successor, Julian, kept the peace for two years.

In 363, Julian resumed the war,[1] mounting a grand invasion, in the manner of Trajan, down the Euphrates. It was his greatest undertaking as emperor on the battlefield, and his last. In the winter of 362-3 he made preparations, gathering ships and armaments. Julian received offers of assistance of various semi-independent Arab tribes, promptly rejecting them, saying that Rome would give, not receive, aid. At the same time he commanded Arsaces to join him. Julian proceeded to the Euphrates, crossing near Hierapolis and proceeding to Carrhae. Two roads led southward, one by the line of the Tigris, the other down the Euphrates. Alexander and Trajan had chosen the former, Cyrus, Avidius Cassius, and Severus, the latter. The Tigris could be used only if Armenia was friendly. Julian chose the Euphrates, sending some units down the other way, through Armenia into Northern Media, with orders to join him before Ctesiphon. With the main army he left Carrhae on March 26, 363, and proceeded by Nicephorium. There he received the submission of the Arab chieftains and met his fleet, which was to carry the provisions, weapons, and armament. He proceeded to Circesium, at the junction of the Khabur with the Euphrates. Until now, he was in Roman territory. Here he made his arrangements for the invasion. On April 7 he crossed the Khabur on a bridge of boats, and continued his advance along the Euphrates, with the fleet hanging by. In a few days, he had reached Dura-Europos, then in ruins, and four days more brought him to Anthan (Anat, Anatho). The Persian garrison surrendered, and he burned the fort. Eight miles below he came to

---

[1] On his effort to win the friendship of the Jews of Palestine, Mesopotamia, and Babylonia, see below, pp. 27–35.

another island fortress where the garrison remained quiescent: if Julian won, they promised they would join him. Meanwhile they made no trouble, nor did he. It seems plausible that Shapur had given orders to his outlying fortresses to permit the Romans easy passage ever deeper into Iranian territory and to preserve their force for later use if necessary. Falling back, Shapur thus traded space for time and strategic advantage. So as Julian proceeded, the great fortresses each made the same arrangement. Julian in effect advanced with Persian connivance, leaving in his rear a great danger should he fail in the attack. He came after five days to Hit, which had been deserted by the soldiers. The Romans slaughtered all civilians they found, mostly women and children. The army moved further, still not meeting opposition. The Persians had not even burned the fields, and forage was plentiful. At Hit, the plain ended, and the army entered the low alluvium of Babylonia. Here the Persians showed themselves and their strategy. They would harass the enemy in quick hit-and-run attacks, taking advantage of their powerful cavalry to wear down the enemy. Having enticed Julian deep within their land, they now scorched the earth before the aggressors. So the Romans marched on, with the Persian horse cutting off stragglers and threatening wherever and whenever they could. The Romans reached Piruz-Shapur, a strong island fortress surrounded by a double wall. But the walls were made of bitumen, and the Romans were able to break them with the ram, take the city, and slaughter the inhabitants. Julian proceeded down the Euphrates, passing the latitude of Ctesiphon, to the Royal Canal. (See Map I.) The Persians had opened the dikes, and the fields were flooded. Now in the midst of the richest part of Babylonia, the Romans saw palm trees loaded with dates and vineyards extending as far as the eye could see. Nearing the Tigris, they came upon a city abandoned by its Jewish inhabitants, which the soldiers burned, and then to Maiozamalcha, which they took. Only the Tigris stood between Julian and Ctesiphon. Still the Persians offered no systematic resistance. Julian reached the western suburb, Seleucia, now known as Coche. He wanted to transport his army across the river, however, and found the fleet would be able to approach to the city only from below. He could not send the fleet into the Tigris below Seleucia while the army occupied the right bank of the river above it; the fleet would then have to force its way against the current through the length of the hostile city. He therefore made a cut from the Royal Canal into the Tigris above the city by restoring a canal which had been dammed by the Persians. The old channel rapidly filled, and the fleet was brought into the Tigris above Seleucia. Now the Persians appeared in force, intending to contest the crossing. Julian waited out the night, and then forced a crossing against stout resistance. The Persians retreated into Ctesiphon. The gates were closed. A regular siege appeared in prospect. So Julian had brought his army to the walls of Ctesiphon, gaining rich spoils and massively destroying the heartland of the defender.

Julian surely intended to take the city. But when he contemplated his task, he realized the formidable problems facing him. Ctesiphon was full of troops. It was strongly fortified. Julian had done no perceptible damage to the Iranian armies, which were entirely intact. He had never even faced Shapur II in battle. Behind him lay a bleeding land, cleared by foe or friend of all its produce and unable to support a retreat. For all he knew, an army of relief might appear at any time, leaving him to fight on two fronts at once. Ammianus describes the decision:

> Having held council with his most distinguished generals about the siege of Ctesiphon, the opinion of some was adopted, who felt sure that the undertaking was rash and untimely, since the city, impregnable by its situation alone, was well-defended, and besides, it was believed that the king would soon appear with a formidable force.

Without securing Ctesiphon, Julian could scarcely proceed deeper into enemy territory. He could hardly remain before Ctesiphon. So the only issue was, In which direction to retreat? He determined to burn the fleet and move north along the Tigris. The land was intact and able to support an invading army. Within two hundred fifty miles lay Kurdistan, in Roman hands. But to get there, the great Persian army, maneuvering in its home territory and on the best possible terrain for its cavalry, had to be eluded. No important town had been lost to Iran. No unit had been decimated. Shapur had followed the best possible policy: harassment but not commitment. On June 16, the Roman withdrawal began. Within a day the Persians set out in pursuit. No longer was the army held back. The horse engaged, and Julian found himself surrounded by enemies, in front of him engaged in destroying the forage, behind and beside him attacking stragglers. At Maranga he gave battle, no longer able to elude the pursuers. The Persians attacked on horse; the Romans retreated to their camp, and the Persians withdrew. Their battle would be won for them by heat, hunger, great distances, and disease. On June 26, the camp was struck, and the army moved across the hot plain, with the Tigris on its left and some hills on the right. Near Samarra the Persians attacked again,

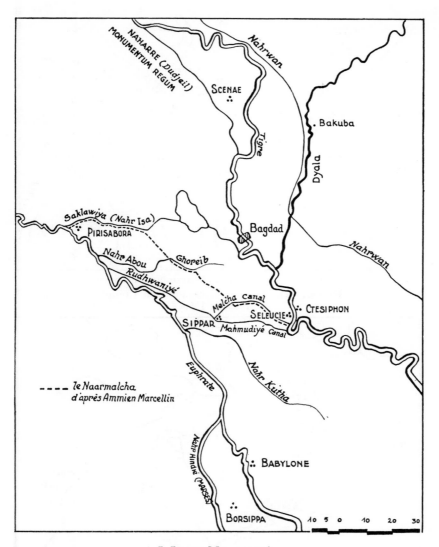

I. Lower Mesopotamia

Source: Louis Dillemann, "Ammien Marcellin et les Pays de l'Euphrate et du Tigre." *Syria* 38, 1961, 1–2, p. 155.

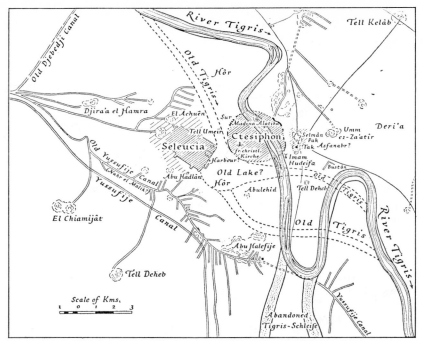

II. Map of the District around Ctesiphon and Seleucia

Source: Oscar Reuther, "The German Excavations at Ctesiphon" *Antiquity* 3, 1929, p. 135.

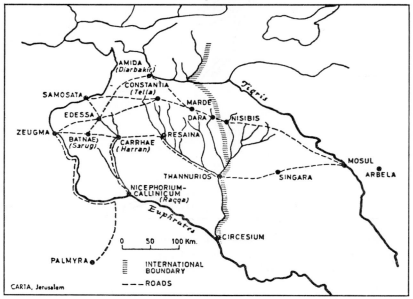

III. Northern Mesopotamia

Source: J. B. Segal, "The Jews of Northern Mesopotamia before the Rise of Islam," in *Studies in the Bible Presented to M. H. Segal.* Vol. XVII, *Publications of the Israel Society for Biblical Research*, ed. J. M. Grintz and J. Liver (Jerusalem. 1964), p. 36.

at first at the rear. Julian hastened to the relief of the rear guard, only to hear that the van was also engaged. He was moving to the front, when the Persians made their main attack upon his right center. The Persians' sudden attack caught him half-armored, and he was wounded by a javelin and brought back to camp. There he died in the evening. Both sides suffered grievous losses, but the Romans had lost their emperor, and the Persians, only generals. The Romans called it their victory. It hardly mattered. Jovian, elected by the troops to succeed Julian, led the troops to battle on the next day. By nightfall he reached Samarra. For four days more, the Romans retreated along the Tigris, moving slowly and under constant pressure from the Persians and their Arab allies. At Dura on the Tigris, eighteen miles north of Samarra, the Roman troops pled with Jovian to cross the river. The frontier, they thought, was not far. Jovian allowed the enterprise to proceed. Shapur unhappily witnessed the preparations for escape. He could not hope to have his troops swim the Tigris. He had brought no boats, and would have to build a bridge. The Persian engineers were hardly so adept as the Romans. It would take time. But time was at that instant just what Shapur lacked—time and good engineers.

Within hours, Shapur opened negotiations with the Romans, whose peril seemed to them considerable. They did not know what foes they would meet in the next two hundred miles. The Arab allies of Persia were on the other side of the river. So out of fear, they agreed to negotiate. Shapur could hardly lose, for now time worked in his favor, and whether it passed in conference or upon the battlefield hardly mattered. The Romans received the terms of peace: the return of the five trans-Tigrene provinces, and surrender of Nisibis, Singara, and other strongholds. Jovian managed to win Persian approval of one clause: the inhabitants of Singara and Nisibis were to be allowed to evacuate their cities. Shapur made one further condition: he was to have a free hand in Armenia. The treaty was concluded, and scrupulously observed by both sides. The Romans made their escape. The Persians had won a tremendous victory. Shapur had gained everything he had set out to get a quarter of a century earlier. He had lost nothing. Ammianus says it would have been better to fight ten battles than to give up. But the Roman army retreated, now supplied by the Persians, and the stipulated provinces were quietly surrendered, the inhabitants not being allowed to resist the Persians. Nisibis was deserted by her Christian population. So in 363, Roman power was driven out of Mesopotamia. Shapur had lost every battle that was not a draw. But he won the war by his acute sense of strategy. Fighting like the Russians in 1812 and again in 1941-3, he had given up as much ground as the enemy could take, rendering it ever more useless, and then, when the aggressor found himself hopelessly trapped deep inside hostile territory before a stronghold he could hardly hope to win, Shapur unleashed so vigorous a guerilla action, accompanied by mobile attacks whenever possible, that the enemy was compelled to come to terms. It was Shapur's most brilliant campaign, and his utilization of every possible resource, but especially climate, time, and space, wins the admiration of the ages. Nisibis was the handsomest prize of all. Three times besieged, in 338, 348, and 350, attacked in 346 as well, she fell to a verbal demand of surrender, just as Shapur originally had intended so long before. Amida, Carrhae, and Antioch lay open. Not for two centuries did the Romans recover influence in Mesopotamia. Shapur attacked prudently, defended brilliantly, and all the time knew just what he wanted. He restored Persia to the powerful position established by Ardashir and Shapur a century earlier. Indeed, not much more than a century had passed between the capture of Valerian and the surrender of Jovian.

Only Armenia remained to be subjugated. Shapur II invited Arsaces to visit. Moses of Xorene records the friendly letter received by the Armenian court. Arsaces was promised safe-conduct. He came, forthwith was blinded, chained in silver, and consigned to oblivion. Shapur then advanced on Armenia and Iberia, in both places setting up his own officers instead of the pro-Roman nobles. After a protracted campaign, he left his own men in charge. During these campaigns, Shapur II deported large numbers of Armenians, both Jews and Christians, to Isfahan and Susiana, as part of his effort both to strip Armenia of its economic and demographic resources and to enrich Iran. According to Moses Xorenaẓi, 95,000 Jewish families and 92,000 Christian families were deported from Artašat, Vagharšabat, Yerovandašat, Sarehaven, Sarišat, Van in Dosp, and Nachdšavan. Whether the statistics are accurate or not we cannot say. Beyond doubt is the fact of the deportations, which were meant to weaken the foe and strengthen the empire.[1] When it seemed that the Romans were interfering in Iberia, Shapur collected a large force, and in 371 crossed the frontier and attacked the Roman force. The war dragged on a few more years.

---

[1] See vol. III, pp. 339-354, and especially the excellent discussion of Geo Widengren, in "The Status of the Jews in the Sassanian Empire," *IA* I, 1961, pp. 134-139.

Valens hoped only to maintain some Roman influence in Armenia and Iberia. Shapur permitted negotiations to continue. In 376 peace was made. Both powers agreed to abstain from further interference in Iberia and Armenia. It was a stand-off. But Shapur was left with considerable influence in Iberia, Georgia, and Armenia, much more than he had at the outset of his long reign. Shapur died in 379 or 380.

ii. The Mazdean State-Church under Shapur II

A monarch such as Shapur II was likely to make his mark on Mazdean religious tradition. He was well aware of the conversion of Constantine. Like him, Shapur established a strong state-church. He allegedly recognized the Mazdean faith as that of the state; like Constantine at Nicea, determined what would constitute orthodoxy; and like Mani, produced a written body of Scriptures to serve as the measure of orthodoxy. In the fourth book of the Denkart, we read (in Zaehner's translation[1]):

> The King of Kings, Shapur[2] son of Hormizd summoned men from all lands to an unprejudiced (?) disputation to examine and investigate all creeds. After Atūrpāt had been vindicated by the consistency of his argument, he issued a declaration before all those representatives of the different sects, doctrines, and schools in this wise: "Now that we have seen the Religion upon earth, we shall not tolerate false religions and we shall be exceeding zealous." And thus did he do.

Zaehner sees the Denkart tradition as indicating an "orthodox" reaction under Shapur II against Zurvan. Atūrpāt, who is often cited in the Pahlavi books, was credited with preserving the classical dualism of the faith, against the creeping monotheism of the Zurvanites. He was supposedly subjected to an ordeal, emerged victorious, and thus was able to see to the acceptance of his doctrine. So, Zaehner holds, the Denkart reference indicates the "purification" of Mazdaism in the time of Shapur II. Atūrpāt is credited with a collection of "wise sayings" or a *handarz*. By submitting to the ordeal, he obtained acceptance of his doctrine. Zaehner cites a later passage:

> Through the submission of Atūrpāt son of Mahraspand of goodly Fravahr to the ordeal of molten brass and through his victory in argu-

---

[1] R. C. Zaehner, *Zurvan, a Zoroastrian Dilemma* (Oxford, 1955), p. 7.

[2] I have preserved the transliterations used elsewhere in this volume, rather than Zaehner's more accurate ones.

ment the disputing parties of all Xuanīras were confounded during the
reign of His Majesty Shapur King of Kings son of Ohrmazd.[1]

He identifies the doctrine of Atūrpāt with that adopted after the end
of Sasanian rule, that is, the dualism which holds that two primeval
spirits, Ohrmazd and Ahriman, existed without beginning, separate
from and opposed to each other, alongside the principles of good and
evil, light and darkness. Zaehner concludes that the "Zoroastrian
Church" before Shapur II possessed no fixed dogma. What then of
Kartir's work as defender of the faith? Zaehner holds that the Magi
were all-powerful, and encouraged the cult of fire, water, and cattle,
and incestuous marriages. That was the sum of Kartir's doctrine.
Zaehner says, "Kartir, in fact, is interested in reviving the characteristic
aspects of Zoroastrian religious practice which were almost certainly
common to Mazdeans and Zurvanites; he does not appear to be interested in the formulation of doctrine. He depicts himself as an enthusi-
astic religious imperialist—putting down alien religions at home and
seeking to establish the national cult in alien sections of the empire,
yet bringing the Iranian 'devil worshippers' and heretics back into his
fold and expelling the obdurate."[2] We know little of Kartir's own
religion. Zaehner holds that Kartir's time was a period of religious
confusion, in which Mazdean orthodoxy first tasted victory. Under
Shapur II, "the high water mark of orthodox Mazdeanism" was
reached. The achievement of Atūrpāt "was built on the foundation laid
by Kartir." In Shapur II's reign, "uniformity was enforced within the
Church and other religions were heavily and savagely chastised." So
Zaehner.[3]

J. Duchesne-Guillemin and others have interpreted the relevant texts
quite differently. Duchesne-Guillemin says[4] that Mazdaism seems to
have been strongly tempered by devotion to Anahita and to Zurvanism.
The heads of the Christian martyrs were offered to Anahita. Shapur
founded a temple to the waters, that is to say, to Anahita, which would
manifest a religious policy tending to unite the local cult to a church

---

[1] Zaehner, p. 12. See also *Škand Gumanik Vicar* 10:70, in the translation of
P. J. de Menasce (Fribourg, 1945), p. 119, 1. 70:

Enfin, elle reçut confirmation lors de l'ordalie par effusion de plomb fondu
subie par le Bienheureux Atūrpāt i Mahraspandān sous le règne de Bag Šāhpur,
Roi des Rois, fils de Ohrmazd, lors d'une controverse avec nombre d'hérétiques
divers.

[2] *Ibid.*, p. 25.
[3] See also his *Dawn and Twilight of Zoroastrianism* (London, 1962), pp. 176, 187.
[4] *La Religion de l'Iran Ancien* (Paris, 1962), pp. 283ff.

which was in process of organization. So he says that the official religion was largely eclectic. Shapur persecuted the Christians for not worshipping not only the sun, moon, and fire, but also Zeus, Nanai (a Mesopotamian goddess identified with Anahita) Bel and Nabo. Mary Boyce points out, moreover, that there is no evidence that Atūrpāt was "orthodox."[1] Geo Widengren credits Shapur II with the assembling of the holy scriptures.[2] He regards Tosar as a legendary figure and supposes that the formation of the state-church was the work of Atūrpāt and Shapur II. Shapur II was seen as Magus and God.[3] We note, finally, the view of H. S. Nyberg[4] that Shapur II established "the Zoroastrianism of the Magi" as the official religion of the empire. Then a book was produced, like Mani's and for much the same purpose, the Avesta as we have it. Nyberg says that Zoroastrianism had to have its own sacred scriptures. The legend of its earlier transcription was an effort to outdo the Manichaeans.[5] Other discussions of Mazdaism under Shapur II include Christensen's and Molé's.[6]

I am not persuaded by Zaehner's interpretation of the data. Boyce's view, that Atūrpāt was not demonstrably "orthodox," and Duchesne-Guillemin's, that from late Achaemenid times Anahita remained an important figure, seem to me decisive. As to the alleged assemblage of holy books or their composition under Shapur II, W. B. Bailey points out that as late as the ninth century, no single account of the transmission of the texts had uniformly been adopted. He notes that in 377, Basilios stated that "the Magians had no books, nor masters of dogma, but the sons learned from the fathers," and he stresses that the Moslems thought the Zoroastrians had no claim to be called a "people of the book."[7] It seems to me that Bailey's arguments are quite weighty. Bailey says that Shapur II "checked the non-conformity of his time, assisted by Atūrpāt-i Mahraspandan,"[8] and it seems to me that is all we can say for sure. It is true that he persecuted the Christians, but the reason was political, not narrowly religious, and certainly had nothing

---

[1] "Some Reflections on Zurvanism," *BSOS* 19, 1957, p. 307.

[2] *Die Religionen Irans* (Stuttgart, 1965), pp. 253-255.

[3] *Ibid.*, p. 316.

[4] *Die Religionen des Alten Iran*, trans. H. H. Schaeder (Repr. Osnabrück, 1966), pp. 404ff., esp. pp. 414-419.

[5] *Ibid.*, p. 427.

[6] Christensen, *op. cit.*, p. 137, pp. 509-513, M. Molé, *Culte, Mythe, et Cosmologie dans l'Iran Ancien* (Paris, 1963), pp. 63-64, 280, 351f., 403.

[7] W. B. Bailey, *Zoroastrian Problems in the Ninth Century Books* (Oxford, 1943), pp. 162-169. See also vol. II, p. 16 n. 3.

[8] *Op. cit.*, p. 156.

to do with an effort to force Mazdaism or any other single cult upon the entire empire[1]. Shapur II probably did not persecute the Jews.[2]

III. THE CHURCH OF SAINTS AND MARTYRS

At the turn of the fourth century, the chief priest of Seleucia-Ctesiphon was Papa b. Haggai, the first known *Catholicos* in the capital. Christianity had been well established for over a century in parts of the Iranian Empire, in particular in Adiabene and in other Iranian lands now held by Romans.[3] Its numbers had been greatly augmented by Shapur's deportations of 260, and were to be again by Shapur II in consequence of his several western campaigns and the great deportations from Armenia. A number of Babylonian Christians also had come from the Jewish community.[4] Papa now led the organization of an independent Iranian church.[5] He saw himself as the leader of the movement for a strongly centralized and self-sufficient polity. Being in the capital provided obvious advantages. Like the exilarch, he was the natural representative of the Christian community before the Court. Higgins says that he doubtless laid it down as a condition for obtaining favors from the court that the bishop concerned should acknowledge his supremacy.[6] But Papa aroused strong opposition. He appealed to Antioch for support and got it. But, Higgins notes, "He exercised his new powers...so arbitrarily and tyrannically as to alienate everybody, not only the hierarchy but even his own clergy and faithful." At a dramatic confrontation with his enemies Papa laid his hand upon the sacred Scriptures and was forthwith paralyzed. This sign from heaven ensured the election of his arch-enemy, Simeon bar Sabba'e. The same troubles recurred, however, in his time. Labourt supposes that the

---

[1] The persecutions of the Christians began with the campaigns against Rome, and were probably brought on by the quite correct view of the Court that the Christians sympathized with Constantine and Constantius. But from the conversion of Constantine and the recognition of Christianity as the most favored religion of Rome, until the outbreak of war between Iran and Rome, almost three decades, Christians were not mistreated. So I do not suppose that Christianity was threatened along with all non-Mazdean religions and cults, as part of an effort to wipe out such "foreign" faiths.

[2] See vol. III, pp. 8-11, and below, pp. 35-56.

[3] See vol. I, pp. 166-169; II, pp. 23-25; III, pp. 12-16.

[4] Vol. III, pp. 12-14, 26-29.

[5] On the work of Papa, see J. Labourt, *Le Christianisme dans l'Empire Perse* (Paris, 1904), pp. 21-27.

[6] Martin J. Higgins, "Chronology of the Fourth-Century Metropolitans of Seleucia-Ctesiphon," *Traditio* 9, 1953, pp. 45-100, p.95.

hostile remarks of Aphrahat's Homily on the Church of Seleucia in fact
were directed against Simeon bar Sabba'e. So the bad temper and
highhandedness of Papa characterized his successor as well. The situation of the Church proved not unfavorable during Shapur's minority
and in the first years of his active rule. The conversion of Armenia in
301, Constantine in 311, and Georgia in 330, and the Roman recognition of Christianity as the most favored religion, at first caused *no*
difficulties whatever. When Constantine allegedly wrote a letter to
Shapur II, he reflected on very satisfactory treatment of Christians in
Shapur's lands. But in Shapur's mind, Constantine's letter must have
raised grave doubts about the loyalty of the Christian minority.
Eusebius gives the text as follows:

> By keeping the divine faith, I am made a partaker of the light of
> truth; guided by the light of truth, I advance in the knowledge of the
> divine faith... This God I invoke with bended knees, and recoil with
> horror from the blood of sacrifices, from their foul and detestable
> odors, and from every earth-born magic fire ... For he who is Lord of
> all cannot endure that those blessings which in his own lovingkindness
> and consideration of the wants of men he has revealed for the use of
> all should be perverted to serve the lusts of any. His only demand from
> man is purity of mind and an undefiled spirit ... Imagine then with
> what joy I heard tidings so in accordance with my desire, that the
> fairest districts of Persia are filled with those men on whose behalf
> alone I am at present speaking, I mean the Christians. I pray therefore
> that both you and they may enjoy abundant prosperity, and that your
> blessings and theirs may be in equal measure; for thus you will ex-
> perience the mercy and favor of that God who is the Lord and Father
> of all. And now because your power is great, I commend these persons
> to your protection; because your piety is eminent, I commit them to
> your care. Cherish them with your wonted humanity and kindness, for
> by this proof of faith you will secure an immeasurable benefit to both
> yourself and us.[1]

Eusebius represents the letter as Constantine's reply to an invitation
to form an alliance which had come from the Ctesiphon court. If so,
it was a disaster. Shapur was even now devoting great efforts both to
checking non-conformity and to the establishment of a single, orthodox, Mazdean faith. His deepest concern was the recovery of the lost
provinces in the Upper Tigris valley. To be told that the Christians,
many of whom lived in Adiabene and to the north, were subject to the

---

[1] Trans. Ernest Cushing Richardson, in *Select Library of Nicene and Post-nicene
Fathers*, Second Series, vol. I (Grand Rapids, 1961), pp. 543-544. See also *Aphra-
hat's des persischen Weisen Homilien*, trans. by Georg Bert, (Leipzig, 1888), pp. 69-88.
I know of no English translation of the complete homilies of Aphrahat.

special protection and concern of the Empire's most feared and hated enemy could hardly have pleased so proud an emperor as Shapur. Nor could it have done the Persian Church any good at all. Indeed, even if the letter was not genuine, we should expect severe difficulties for the Christian community. When the Iranian armies fought, they fought a Christian state. The Roman emperor advanced accompanied by priests, and in some cases, portable churches, just as Shapur came surrounded by Magi. When Iranian diplomacy struggled for support in Armenia, its efforts were thwarted by the Christian character of the government there, which now (though not for long) saw in Byzantium, and not in Ctesiphon, its natural ally.

The conversion of Constantine must have had still another consequence for Iranian Christianity. Now the Christians perceived a vision of a truly blessed circumstance: the state and the church might unite in the service of one God. As Gavin says, "A state under Christian rule, with the Church fully recognized and supreme in her own domain, was the only ideal worth living for."[1] Gavin notes that in Homily 23 Aphrahat seems to despair of seeing such an ideal realized in his day. In any case, the local Christians must have hoped that what had happened through a miracle in the West might also take place by similar means in the East, so that the whole civilized world would come under the rule of God and the church. Rome was the Christian state. Her monarch took counsel with the bishops; indeed at Nicea he had acted like Shapur and Aturpat in their own country. The 5th Homily of Aphrahat provided a glimpse into the Christian mind of the day. There he assured the faithful that it was God who decided what would happen and who brought on the wars of the age. All who glory will be humbled, he said, providing appropriate Scriptural citations. He quoted Dan. 8:20-21, to prove that from the time that the two horns of the ram were broken until now were six hundred forty-eight years, that is, to the year 336-7. Thus, he said, "Therefore as for the ram (the King of Media and Persia)—its horns are broken." And then, "O Ram, whose horns are broken, rest thou from the beast and provoke it not, lest it devour thee and grind thee to powder." He added, "O thou that art exalted and lifted up, let not the vaunting of thine heart mislead thee, nor say thou, 'I will go up against the rich land and against the powerful beast.' For that beast will not be slain by the ram, seeing that its horns are broken..." But of Rome: "And of the fourth beast he said that it was exceedingly terrible and strong and mighty, devouring and crush-

---

[1] Frank M. Gavin, *Aphraates and the Jews* (Toronto, 1923), pp. 29-31.]

ing and trampling with its feet anything that remained. It is the kingdom of the children of Esau..." Further, "Therefore this Kingdom of the children of Esau shall not be delivered up into the hand of the hosts that are gathered together, that desire to go up against it, because the Kingdom is being kept safe for its Giver, and He Himself will preserve it. And as to this that I wrote to thee, beloved, that the Kingdom of the children of Esau is being kept safe for its Giver, doubt not about it, that that Kingdom will not be conquered. For a mighty champion Whose name is Jesus shall come with power, and bearing as His armor all the power of the Kingdom...." So he concluded, "And even if the forces shall go up and conquer, yet know that it is a chastisement of God; and though they conquer, they shall be condemned in a righteous judgment. But yet be thou assured of this, that the beast shall be slain at its appointed time..."[1]

Since by "the kingdom of Esau," both Jews and Christians understood Rome, it is difficult to see how the Persian government enjoyed much loyalty among the Christian community. The sage of the church, regarding Rome as the guardian of the heavenly kingdom to come, assured the Christians that the children of Esau will not be given to the 'forces now gathered which are coming up against it.' Roman power had not yet conquered Persia because Rome did not carry in their midst 'him by whom victory was to be won.' That is to say, Valerian was not a Christian. But Constantine and Constantius were. Now that Rome was Christian, God's plans would indeed be fulfilled. Rome was a fit instrument for God's work, and Luke 14.11 made this clear. So in 336-7, Aphrahat assured the church that Persia was certainly doomed to defeat at the hands of Rome. It was a perfectly natural hope, and none can condemn it. Aphrahat and the Christians who shared his faith quite reasonably expected that God, who ruled history, would very soon complete his plan. Even now half of the world was under Christian rule. Who could suppose that the other half would long remain pagan? So with the armies of Constantine and Constantius marched the victorious Jesus. Before the walls of Nisibis Shapur was bound to meet disappointment. By now, it was a largely Christian city. God surely would not give his faithful into the hands of his enemies.

That was all well and good for the Christian to believe, especially when Shapur failed at Nisibis. But returning from his campaigns of 337 and afterward, Shapur must have seen things from a rather different perspective. Christians opposed him. The bishop of Nisibis strengthen-

---

[1] Trans. John Gwynn, in *ibid.*, XIII, pp. 352-362, *passim*.

ed the hands of the besieged. The Christians of the Persian Empire hoped that the Romans would defeat their own government. However laudable from their perspective the reason for that hope, the Sasanian regime could never have accepted such a subversive attitude. It had not mistreated the Christians up to now, despite their international connections. It had preserved them in peace and protected their lives and property. Indeed, it had behaved with greater tolerance than had the Christian government across the Tigris toward non-Christians in its power. Shapur's response was not long delayed. He decreed that the Christian community pay double the normal head-tax. The decree served two good purposes. First, it enlarged the revenues available for his future campaigns, which were very expensive and involved cash payments to the eastern mercenaries and tribes. Second, if paid, it would serve to demonstrate the real feelings of the Christians. They might thus show that they were loyal to the Iranian Empire and eager to support its wars.

There was only one problem. The Christians could scarcely afford the tax, nor were they in any mood to pay it. They were generally poor people—at least Simeon bar Sabba'e so informed Shapur, and I think it was probably the truth; many were nuns and monks possessing no property. Moreover they regarded Shapur's wars as those of the devil, and the victory of Byzantium as the triumph of Christ himself. Whether or not they could pay the double-tax, they hardly believed it proper to do so, since they expected the imminent establishment of God's rule in Persia itself—for the ram had, in Aphrahat's words, charged south (against the Arabs), north and west (against the Roman-held positions in the Mesopotamian valley), and was now to be devoured by the lion. Simeon bar Sabba'e informed Shapur II that he could not pay the taxes demanded of him and his community. It was a courageous gesture, and courageously did Simeon bar Sabba'e meet his martyrdom. So began, probably on Sept. 14, 344,[1] a very long period of persecution, sometimes ferocious and sometimes quiescent, of forty years, during which time the Seleucia-Ctesiphon church gave up choosing bishops, since election to the office was merely a prelude to a glorious death.

Suffering was widespread, not at all limited to the capital. In Adiabene, Beth Garmae, Khuzistan, and many other provinces in which

---

[1] I have found no convincing refutation of Martin J. Higgins, "Date of Martyrdom of Simeon bar Sabba'e," *Traditio* 11, 1955, pp. 1-17. Higgins gives the date as Sept. 14, 344, the first day of the great slaughter. See also his "Aphraates' Dates for Persian Persecution," *Byzantinische Zeitschrift* 44, 1951, pp. 265-271. The conventional date is Good Friday, 341.

Christians were settled, the local Mobads, supported by the satraps, organized slaughters of believers. Particular wrath was directed against the monastic communities, whose poverty was one of the reasons that it proved so difficult for the Christians to pay the tax. The Mobads offered nuns the choice of marriage or death, and the monks, of worship of the emperor and the sun, or death. The hagiographical literature preserved the memory of popular, not merely governmental outrages against the Christian community. Not before the time of Yazdegerd, at the end of the fourth century, did the church find peace. The persecutions were generally localized. In Seleucia and a few places in the north, Christians were actually hunted down. The general procedure, however, was neither constant nor regular. Sometimes the martyrs were denounced by Jews or Zoroastrians. Occasionally, other Christians, or members of Christian families, were involved. The bishop of a village in one place was denounced to the king by his nephew, Labourt points out. A satrap or marzeban or village chief might take the initiative and imprison clergy, religious, and lay people. Most often it was the Zoroastrian clergy, in particular the lower clergy, who took the lead. The accused were imprisoned many months, even years. They were questioned and given an opportunity to renounce Christianity. The chief intention was to induce the accused to apostatize. Those who remained loyal to the faith were tortured and given over to fiendish forms of execution. Some were cut into two; others were chopped up limb by limb. In some instances the Christians were forced to slay one another. Decapitation was common. Not many could have apostatized, for the question of the reconciliation of apostates to the Church never appeared as a serious problem when the Church was permitted to reorganize. In the north things were worst of all, for the king or important officers of state often passed through Adiabene, a province full of churches and monasteries. But throughout the Iranian Empire it was a difficult time for Christians.[1]

---

[1] See especially Labourt, *op. cit.*, pp. 45-82; J. M. Fiey, *Assyrie Chrétienne* (Beyrouth, 1965), I, pp. 43-47; Arthur Vööbus, *op. cit.*, I, pp. 209-258; Victor Langlois, *Collection des Historiens Anciens et Modernes de l'Arménie* (Paris, 1880), I, pp. 203-310, in particular pp. 273-275, on the ravages and deportations after 363 in Armenia; Paulus Peeters, "Le 'Passionaire d'Adiabene,'" *Analecta Bollandiana* 43, 1925, pp. 261-304, on the death of Simeon bar Sabba'e, p. 266 n.; Paulus Peeters, "La Date du martyre de S. Symeon, archevêque de Seleucie-Ctesiphon," *Analecta Bollandiana* 56, 1938, pp. 118-143; A. Christensen, *op. cit.*, pp. 261-268. Martin J. Higgins, "Chronology of the Fourth-Century Metropolitans of Seleucia-Ctesiphon," *Traditio* 9, 1953, pp. 45-100, dates the synod against Papa in 314/5, and the death of Papa in 327; Simeon's dates were 327 to 344, when he was

Aphrahat says (Demonstration 21 :1) that the Jews rejoiced at the persecution of the Christians. The Chronicle of Julianus and Bar Hebraeus preserved traditions that in the time of Julian, Edessan Christians staged a massacre of Jews.[1] On both sides, feelings ran high.[2]

martyred. Then there was a vacancy to some unknown date before Shapur's death. Shahdost, metropolitan from 344/5, was also martyred. The dates of Barbashmin are unclear. A long vacancy followed Shapur's death as well, probably for twenty years. He says (p. 84) that Shapur's persecutions were so severe that "a bishop of Seleucia-Ctesiphon survived so brief a time in office that the Christians felt it useless any longer to elect one."

See also Felix Haase, *Altchristliche Kirchengeschichte* (Leipzig, 1925), pp. 94-111; Georg Hoffmann, *Auszuge aus Syrischen Akten Persischer Martyrer* (Leipzig, 1880), *passim*; Geo Widengren, "Stand und Aufgaben," *Numen* 2, 1955, p. 119; N. Pigulevskaja, *Les Villes de l'État Iranien aux Époques Parthe et Sassanide* (Paris and The Hague, 1963), pp. 169-173.

Vööbus (I, p. 228), points out that whatever his policy toward local Christians, Shapur II nonetheless deported to his empire many thousands of Christians, and the end result ironically was the establishment of many churches, including those in Istakhr, Ardasher-Khvarreh, and Bih Shapur. He holds that the main thrust of the persecutions was against the ascetics. It may be that our knowledge, based upon the monastic records, tends to overlook the suffering of lay-Christians and to preserve the record of monastic suffering in disproportionate degree.

[1] See Ernest A. Wallis Budge, trans., *The Chronography of Gregory Abu'l Faraj ... commonly known as Bar Hebraeus* (London, 1932), I, p. 61; and Michael Adler, "The Emperor Julian and the Jews," *JQR*, o.s. 5.1893, p. 621 n. 5.

[2] See especially S. Funk, *Juden in Babylonien*, vol. II, pp. 56-65, on Jewish-Christian relations. On Jewish complicity in the persecution of Simeon bar Sabba'e, pp. 50-51, and vol. III, p. 11. Professor Jes P. Asmussen kindly called my attention to the important research of Gernot Wiessner, *Untersuchungen zur Syrischen Literaturgeschichte I: Zur Märtyrerüberlieferung aus der Christenverfolgung Schapurs II, Abhandlungen der Akademie der Wissenschaften in Göttingen, Philologisch-Historische Klasse*, 3rd series No. 67, Göttingen, 1967. Wiessner's is the first form-critical study of the oriental martyrologies. Wiessner divides the martyrologies into the 'Syro-Persian martyrology of Simon's circle, or of the Khuzistan Province' (pp. 40ff), and the 'Syro-Persian martyrology of Adiabene' (pp. 199ff). In the former is a tradition that the Persian queen was a Jew (pp. 45ff. 78-9, 87-8, 156, 180-2), which supposedly facilitated the Jews' effort to instigate persecutions of the Christians. Wiessner says that this tradition refers to the friendship toward 'the Jews' of 'Ifra Hormizd the mother of Shapur, and cites the several Talmudic passages noted below. His judgment of the story about the emigration of Jews from Babylonia to rebuild the Temple (cited below, p. 32) is as follows: "Diese Nachricht des Simon-Martyriums hat in der sonstigen Überlieferung keine Parallele. Es wird jedoch unrecht sein, an ihrer Historizität zu zweifeln, da die Unruhe der Juden, die eine Aufrichtung des Tempels und des jüdischen Reiches erwarteten, schon vor dem Bemühen Julians um den Temple bezeugt ist und durch dasselbe einen ungeheuren Aufschwung bekommen haben wird..." (P. 46 n. 2). Wiessner repeatedly takes it as a fact (p. 181) that there were close ties between the Jewish community and the Persian court.

I find it regrettable that in so learned and sophisticated work as this, references to the Jewish community and its history rely entirely on Graetz (e.g. p. 183 n. 2) as if Funk, Obermeyer, and others had not made significant scholarly advances in the last century.

Hagiographical traditions report that Jews in some places actually instigated the persecutions against the Christians. Hostility between Jews and Christians was already old and general. Presumably Jews would take advantage of the new policy to make trouble for the Christians. It was, however, a Sasanian persecution, mounted by the state with Mazdean church cooperation for political reasons, and ended by the state when it chose. Nothing other minority groups did could have brought on such a disaster, and nothing they did could have ended it. Yet, after a certain point, nothing the Christians did mattered very much either. There is absolutely no hint of Christian treason in 363, when the Roman armies stood at the gates of Ctesiphon. In no place in his narrative does Ammianus Marcellinus refer to Babylonian Christian cooperation with the invading armies. The Christian hopes for Byzantine success were based upon theological expectations alone, and produced no political or military result. The local Christians did nothing effectual to subvert Persian government, though in Roman cities they fought with special courage against Iran, as was quite natural. Once the persecution was unleashed, it took its own course, and whether originally issued for good reason or not, Shapur's decrees were obeyed long after the original provocation had been forgotten. Sozomen attributed Shapur's persecution to Jewish and Magi influence, and as to the episodes when the mob took over, he was probably right. But the persecution was first of all Shapur's understandable reaction to defeat by a great Christian power, to his Christian subjects' obvious satisfaction at his defeat, and perhaps also to his feeling of encirclement by the Christian powers of Armenia, Iberia, and Georgia, as well as Rome.

IV. JEWRY IN BYZANTINE PALESTINE

Only against the background of Byzantine treatment of the Jews of Palestine and the Roman Diaspora shall we be able to assess the policies of the Sasanian government toward Babylonian Jewry. We shall therefore briefly survey the well-known facts about Jewry in the Byzantine Empire during the fourth century.

After the battle of the Milvian Bridge Constantine enriched the church with privileges and money. He associated with priests and bishops, some of whom had been imprisoned only recently. So Christians now found themselves, as if in a dream, basking in the favor of the government which short years earlier had persecuted them. The government fostered Christianity. The soldiers of the army were made to repeat a monotheistic prayer. The emperor commended his religion to his subjects as forcefully as he could. Early legislation on the Jews was not unbearable.[1] Proselytism was prohibited, and slaves bought by Jews could not be circumcized. Ordinary people could not have suffered much from such rules. Converts to Christianity had to be left alone. But synagogue officials were confirmed in their immunity from the expensive curial duties. At Nicea, on the other hand, when he promulgated the edict on the date of Easter, Constantine denounced the wickedness of "the Jewish people who had murdered Jesus." Constantius II, his son, made the circumcision of a slave a capital offence; forbade the Jews to buy slaves of gentile origin; and almost certainly subjected Jewry to discriminatory taxes.[2] As A. H. M. Jones says, "Christianity added theological animus to the general dislike of the Jews, and the numerous diatribes against them, in the form of sermons or pamphlets, which Christian leaders produced, must have fanned the flames. It is surprising, indeed, that the emperors, most of whom shared the popular view, maintained such moderation in their legal enactments: the language of Constantine, for instance, in his laws, and even more in his letter on the date of Easter, is strangely at variance with his quite restrained and fair-minded enactments."[3] Later on, in 614, however, the Jews rejoiced at the Persian conquest of Jerusalem, acting much as did the Christians in Persia, and for similar reasons.

If there was a Palestinian Jewish revolt against Constantine, Eusebius did not mention it. A persistent tradition holds that there were revolts against both Constantine and Constantius, but Juster examined the evidence and arguments in regard to the former, and holds that it probably did not take place.[4] In June, 351, the Jews of Diocaesarea (Sepphoris) allegedly massacred the local Roman garrison. In consequence, the Jews were massacred and the city was destroyed, as were Tiberias, Lydda, and other Jewish towns of Palestine where the revolt took hold, according to some traditions. Avi-Yonah[5] points out that three factors would have aided the rebels, unrest in the Western part of the empire, the weakness of the emperor Gallus, and the approaching Persian invasion. The leader of the Jewish forces, Patrick, supposedly hoped that the internal difficulties of the Roman government would

---

[1] A. H. M. Jones, *The Later Roman Empire* (Oxford, 1964), pp. 92-93. See the view of S. Lieberman, cited below, p. 31 n. 3.

[2] *Ibid.*, pp. 944-947.

[3] *Ibid.*, p. 948.

[4] Jean Juster, *Les Juifs dans l'Empire Romain* (Paris, 1914), II, pp. 196-198.

[5] M. Avi-Yonah, *Bimei Roma uVizantion* (Jerusalem, 1952), pp. 124-130.

lead to easy success. But the rabbis did not share his hopes, and the rebels were a small group without much widespread support.[1] Besides the three cities, about fifteen villages were supposedly destroyed, but most of Jewish Palestine remained intact, Avi-Yonah says.[2] The Roman-supported Jewish rulers, not having participated, were not punished, and Jewish government remained undisturbed, as did the rabbinical academies. Indeed, the rabbis permitted the Jews to bake bread for the Roman troops both on the Sabbath and even on Passover, and so enhanced the chances of reconciliation. By 352 the *alleged* rebellion was fully put down.[3]

When Emperor Julian came to power, his favor toward the Jews came as a refreshing respite. Whatever his motives—whether out of love of Judaism or hatred of Christianity—the Jews enjoyed a period of imperial grace. Julian declared a general religious amnesty. All religions were to be equally tolerated. In practice, pagan cults were fostered, Judaism tolerated, and Christianity, deprived of its former most-favored status, suffered humiliation. (Julian's attitude toward Judaism as a religion, while interesting, is not relevant here.[4]) Julian's motives seem to have been mixed. Some have held that he favored Judaism because of a generalized fondness for ancient institutions; or because it was the enemy of Christianity, which he hated; or because he held it was a genuine faith, close in spirit to Neo-Platonism. Adler points out,[5] in addition, that Julian hoped to win over to his side the Babylonian and Mesopotamian Jewries, in preparation for his contemplated invasion of 363. It seems to me that, knowing the history of Trajan's invasion, and aspiring to the encomium *Parthicus*, Julian could not have ignored the lessons of 115-117, when Jews behind the Roman lines revolted in Northern Mesopotamia, possibly in Palestine, and throughout the Roman diaspora, rendering Trajan's position ex-

---

[1] If there was such a revolt at all! See Lieberman, cited below, p. 31 n. 3.

[2] *Op. cit.*, p. 127.

[3] For the sources on the revolt against Gallus, see Juster, *op. cit.*, II, p. 197, n. 1. See also M. A. Tannenblatt, *Peraqim Ḥadashim le Toledot Ereẓ Yisra'el uBavel beTequfat HaTalmud* (Tel Aviv, 1966), pp. 168-184, who provides a discussion of rabbinic sayings relevant to the war.

[4] Michael Adler, "The Emperor Julian and the Jews," *JQR* o.s. 5., 1893, pp. 591-651, offers a thorough account of Julian's attitude toward Judaism, his citations of the Septuagint, his plans in connection with rebuilding the Temple, and the like. See also the learned critique of Adler by J. Vogt, *Kaiser Julianus und das Judenthum* (Leipzig, 1939). Much has been written on this subject, and a full summary, to 1893, will be found in Adler's article, which must, however, be read in the light of Vogt's comments. See also Avi-Yonah, *op. cit.*, pp. 130-146.

[5] *Op. cit.*, p. 619.

tremely difficult. That the Jews of the fourth century were unable to
mount a similarly dangerous rebellion he could not have known. It was
sufficient to see to it that they had no reason to do so. Reversing the
policy of Constantius and Gallus Caesar, he freed them from special
taxes, and promised that upon his safe return from Persia, he would
undertake the rebuilding of the Jerusalem sanctuary. Adler holds that
that project was never begun, and rejects the various Christian miracle-
stories which explain why, when the temple was actually under construction, the emperor had to order the builders to desist. Wright and
Graetz say that it *was* begun, but given up because of earthquakes.[1]
As to the authenticity of the letter *To the Jewish Community*, Wright holds
that it was consistent with attitudes expressed elsewhere, and regards
it as substantially genuine.[2] J. Vogt denies its authenticity on linguistic
grounds. Juster notes that it is the very friendly tone of the letter which
caused some scholars to question its authenticity and says that this is
no argument. He notes that Sozomen, no apologist for Jewry, already
cites the letter, and he asks, What Jew would have been able to commit
such a forgery so near the time of Julian?[3] The text, in Wright's translation, is as follows:

> In times past, by far the most burdensome thing in the yoke of your
> slavery has been the fact that you were subjected to unauthorized
> ordinances and had to contribute an untold amount of money to the
> accounts of the treasury. Of this I used to see many instances with my
> own eyes, and I have learned of more, by finding records which are
> preserved against you. Moreover, when a tax was about to be levied
> on you again I prevented it, and compelled the impiety of such obloquy
> to cease here; and I threw into the fire the records against you that
> were stored in my desks; so that it is no longer possible for anyone to
> aim at you such a reproach of impiety. My brother Constantius of
> honored memory was not so much responsible for these wrongs of
> yours as were the men who used to frequent his table, barbarians in
> mind, godless in soul. These I seized with my own hands and put them
> to death by thrusting them into the pit, that not even any memory of
> their destruction might still linger amongst us. And since I wish that
> you should prosper yet more, I have admonished my brother Iulus
> [Hillel II] your most venerable patriarch, that the levy [in support of
> the patriarchate] which is said to exist among you should be pro-
> hibited, and that no one is any longer to have the power to oppress the
> masses of your people by such exactions; so that everywhere during

---

[1] See also Wilmer Cave Wright, trans., *The Works of the Emperor Julian* (London
and N. Y., 1923), I-III, III, xxi-xxii.

[2] *Op. cit.*, p. xxii.

[3] *Op. cit.*, I, pp. 159-160.

my reign you may have security of mind, and in the enjoyment of
peace may offer more fervid prayers for my reign to the Most High
God, the Creator, who has deigned to crown me with his own immacu-
late right hand. For it is natural that men who are distracted by any
anxiety should be hampered in spirit, and should not have so much
confidence in raising their hands to pray; but that those who are in all
respects free from care should rejoice with their whole hearts and offer
their suppliant prayers on behalf of my imperial office to Mighty God,
even to him who is able to direct my reign to the noblest ends, according to my purpose. This you ought to do, in order that, when I
have successfully concluded the war with Persia, I may rebuild by my
own efforts the sacred city of Jerusalem, which for so many years you
have longed to see inhabited, and may bring settlers there, and together with you, may glorify the Most High God therein.[1]

The reference to the patriarch Hillel, Τὸν ἀδελφὸν ῎Ιουλον, Τὸν αἰδε-
σιυώτοτον, in the same language as that to Constantius—ὁ ἀδελφός—,is,
to be sure, striking. Given the loyalty of the patriarchate in suppressing
a supposed rebellion only a decade earlier,[2] and the memory of what
had happened in Palestine when the patriarch, Gamaliel II, was unable
to do the same, Julian may well have spoken warmly of Hillel. However, I find it more striking still that he removed the ἀποστολή, that is
to say, the tax paid by Jews for the support of the patriarchate itself.
Jews must indeed have hated the patriarchate and objected to paying
a tax in its support, if the emperor, seeking to win their favor, should
annul that tax. So however pleased Hillel may have been—if the letter
is genuine—by the kindly reference to him, he could not have been
wholly delighted with the contents of this rescript. That the tax was in
support of the patriarch is, I think, clearly indicated by the words τὴν
λεγομένην εἶναι παρ᾿ ὑμῖν ἀποστολήν, that is to say, the government
does not collect the tax, but it is "said to exist among you." So Julian
said he prevented the imposition of discriminatory taxes, and the Jews
were to be freed from an additional and apparently highly unwelcome
obligation to the patriarchate.[3]

---

[1] Wright, op. cit., III, pp. 177-181.

[2] For I think the rabbis did consistently side with the Roman government,
even in the times of Constantius. Both Lieberman and Avi-Yonah hold this view.

[3] On the emigration of Palestinians to Babylonia in this period, see Y. I.
Halevy, Dorot HaRishonim, II, p. 481; on the decrees of Constantine and conse-
quent emigrations, II, pp. 467-473. On the revolt in Sepphoris, see also H. Graetz,
History of the Jews (Philadelphia, 1952), II, p. 179.

S. Lieberman, "Palestine in the Third and Fourth Centuries," JQR n.s. 36, 4,
pp. 329-370, in particular pp. 329-336, (and see Baron's critique of his view, op.
cit., p. 398, n. 11), holds that there were no outright persecutions of the Jews in
Palestine during this period, and examines the evidence which suggests to others

Geo Widengren[1] calls attention to the passage cited by Oskar Braun[2] which tells of a massacre of Jews who wanted to emigrate to Palestine to build the Temple. Widengren gives the text as follows:

> After twenty four years when Constans and Constantius, the sons of Constantine the Great, had died, Julianus was the ruler of the Romans. And at once when he was a ruler he sacrificed to the idols. In order to stir up the Christians and to convict the words of Christ of

a contrary view. He holds that the traditions on a rebellion against Gallus, found in Jerome, Socrates, Sozomen and others, cannot be correct, for the contemporary rabbinic literature does not say a word about the destruction of the cities of Tiberias and other places. The Talmud only states (y. Yev. 16:2) that the people of Sepphoris were sought in the days of king Ursicinus, and disguised themselves, but the destruction of the city is not mentioned. Lieberman concludes that the Jews led by Patricius attacked Sepphoris's Roman garrison. "This Patricius might have been a heathen Roman officer whom the Diocaesarean Jews preferred to the extremely cruel Gallus, who, like the emperor, was a devout Christian ... in 353 Ursicinus was summoned by Gallus ... to sit as judge in the trials of high treason." Ammianus Marcellinus, on his staff, gave a detailed account of these trials, and mentioned neither a Jewish revolt nor Patricius. So, Lieberman says, "The revolt in Diocaesarea and 'king Patricius' were probably too insignificant to be mentioned. Thus, the rebellion of the Jews against the *Roman Empire* (in 353) is a possible figment of imagination of later writers. We have instead a local insignificant incident of a Roman usurper supported by some of the Diocaesarean Jews. ... The incident had no serious consequences for the community in general, because the majority of the Jews were not involved. ... At any rate it is quite clear that neither the Patriarch nor the rabbis were involved in any action against the Roman empire during the third and fourth centuries."

In fact, Lieberman denies there were religious persecutions. He says that Constantine and Constantius began to curtail certain Jewish rights, but the Jews were not forced to transgress their laws. "Moreover, rabbinic literature of the time does not refer to the limitations of Jewish rights imposed by the first two Christian emperors. These decrees had probably very little, if any, practical application in Palestinian localities thickly inhabited by Jews. ... In places inhabited either by Jews or by heathens the religious policy of the Christian emperors remained more theoretical than practical."

Nevertheless, Lieberman does stress that the reign of Constantius was a difficult time, because of heavy collection of taxes and the exploitation of the people—"not only as provincials, but also as Jews."

In Avi-Yonah's account of the revolt of Gallus, I have been impressed by the archeological evidence concerning the destruction of Beth She'arim and part of Sepphoris, following Baron's view of the matter. Moreover I find it difficult to take seriously the argument that because the rabbis did not refer to a historical incident, therefore it did not happen. The rabbis were not chroniclers, nor was their literature history. They failed to mention many noteworthy events in Babylonian Jewish history, including in this period Julian's invasion and the destruction of the Jewish town referred to by Ammianus Marcellinus. Nonetheless, Lieberman's judgment must always be reckoned with, and therefore my brief summary follows the main lines of his article.

On Julian and the Jews, in addition to the works cited above, note also Graetz, *op. cit.*, II, pp. 596-598.

[1] *IA* I, 1961, p. 133, n. 2.

[2] *Ausgewählte Akten Persischer Märtyrer* (Munich, 1915), pp. 13-15.

falsehood which he prophesied on the devastation of Jerusalem ... he ordered the Jews in his whole Empire to go up to Judaea and rebuild Jerusalem and the Temple, and to bring the sacrifices in accordance with the decree of the Law. Many went up actually and started to dig out the groundworks of Jerusalem. Meanwhile there came an imposter to the land of the Persians and proclaimed to the Jews saying, "It is the time of return appointed by the prophets and I have been ordered by God to proclaim to you the return. You shall go up!" That imposter came also to Maḥoza in Bet Aramaya and deceived myriads of Jews. They left and went out from Maḥoza because of the hope of return and they went away three parasangs from the town. However when the matter was known to Shapur he sent his troops who killed many thousands of them.

Widengren accepts this account at face value. He says that from this incident we see that the Jews were "not as happy as they in general have been depicted." The account appears in the *Martyrium des Simon bar Sabbae*, one of twenty-nine Syrian martyrologies originally published by Assemani and Bedjan, and presented as above by Braun. It is difficult, Braun says, to answer the question, Who was the editor of this collection? Braun points out that the collector did not witness the early martyrdoms, but he did see the last ones. So Braun states (p. xii):

> Die Möglichkeit, dass diese Sammlung tatsächlich auf Maruta von Maiparkat zurückgeht, der wahrscheinlich schon im Jahre 399, sicher im Jahre 408 als römischer Gesandter am persischen Hofe weilte, im Jahre 410 der Synode von Seleucia präsidierte und zahlreiche Märtyrerreliquien aus der Verfolgung Schapurs in seine Bischofsstadt zurückbrachte, muss zugegeben werden.

If the account dates back to the first quarter of the fifth century, it represents at least as ancient literary testimony as any in our hands concerning fourth-century Babylonian Jewry. The story is consistent with other Christian sources in holding that emperor Julian actually did undertake the construction of the Temple in Jerusalem. There is, however, no independent source showing that he "ordered" the Jews to do so. The "miracles" which prevented it were obviously meant to serve Christian theological purposes. This story is part of the same fabric of anti-Jewish polemic: Julian and the Jews attempted to prove that the prediction of Jesus was false but were miraculously prevented from doing so. The precise specification of Maḥoza, on the other hand, is striking, and makes it likely that the story of what happened there, while exaggerated, may not be a complete invention. The Jews who left were followers of a false prophet, if not a false Messiah. Therefore rabbinic literature ignored them, and contained no word of regret for their fate. Shapur had them massacred because, as his Armenian policy showed, he was well aware of the value of artisan population, and had no intention of letting a large number of people escape to the enemy. In the balance, therefore, I think the story must reflect an actual event, because of its fairly early redaction and because it seems to me plausible and accurate in an important detail. So I suppose that messianic fervor led to an attempted emigration from Maḥoza, and that the Iranian government put a stop to it.[1]

Julian's immediate successor, Jovian, renewed the edicts of toleration. Valens (364-78) who followed was an Arian, and protected and favored the Jews, as did Valentinian I (364-75) in the west. So to the end of the reign of Shapur II, Jewry in the Roman Empire enjoyed favorable circumstances.

What is important for Babylonian Jewish history is the fact that the first Christian Byzantine emperors and Julian "the apostate" did not persecute the Jews in their empire. The Christian emperors proved on the whole moderate and whatever their private opinions, did not enact legislation which significantly distressed the Jews. Julian moreover made every effort to win their support. So from the perspective of Babylonian Jewry no cause existed for opposing the Roman forces when they reached the Jewish towns and villages of the region. The Roman armies brought destruction, but not upon the Jews alone. The Jewish communities did nothing to oppose them, any more than did others in the region. Whatever their opinions of the empire that had in earlier times destroyed the Temple, Babylonian Jewry could not have seen any threat to its existence in the campaign of 363. On the other hand, it had no good reason to oppose the Iranian forces. So it probably kept to a position of passivity. The situation in Northern Mesopotamian Jewry must have differed, for the local Christian populations and Jewish communities hated one another. I should imagine, therefore, that the efforts of Shapur to recover the trans-Tigrene provinces and to seize the Roman fortresses in the northern plains would have had considerable Jewish support. Yet in the accounts of Shapur's campaigns we find no evidence that local Jews aided him, as did others, either through intelligence or by means of subversion within the walls. In general, therefore, both sides seemed to want to neutralize the possible hostility of the Jewish communities, but in neither case would it have been a

---

[1] See A. Marmorstein, "The History of the Jews in Palestine in the Fifth Century C.E.", in Hebrew, in *A. M. Luncz Volume*, ed. I. Press and E. L. Sukenik (Jeruslem, 1928), pp. 41-50.

major or dominating motive. Neither would have wanted to give the
Jews any reason to rebel or go over to the enemy. But both had far
more important matters to tend to. The Jews were not an important
factor in fourth-century international politics, but all they really could
have wanted, as Gog fought Magog, was to be let alone. It suited both
Iran and Byzantium to do so.[1]

v. 'IFRA HORMIZD AND THE JEWS

Our examination of the traditions on the political situation of Babylonian Jewry begins with 'Ifra Hormizd, "mother of King Shapur,"
who supposedly befriended the Jews and served their cause at court.
We shall first consider the traditions about her, and then assess their
usefulness.

Four stories relate that the queen-mother presented to rabbis three
gifts and one question:

> 'Ifra Hormiz the mother of Shapur the king sent a purse of denarii
> to R. Joseph. She said, "Let them be for the performance of a great
> commandment." R. Joseph sat and considered, "What is a great
> commandment?" Abaye said to him, "Since R. Samuel b. Judah taught,
> 'One may not levy charity from orphans even for the redemption of
> captives,' one may infer that redemption of captives is a great command-
> ment."
> (b. B.B. 8a-b)

> 'Ifra Hormiz the mother of Shapur the king sent four hundred
> denarii to R. Ammi [in Palestine] and he would not accept them. She
> sent them to Rava, and he accepted them on account of keeping peace
> with the government. R. Ammi heard and was angry. He said, "Does
> he not accept the teaching of the Scripture, 'When the boughs thereof
> are withered they shall be broken off, the women shall come and set
> them on fire' (Is. 27.11) [The meaning is, 'When the gentiles have ex-
> hausted their merit, then their power will be broken, and charity adds
> to their merit']." And Rava—? On account of the peace of the king-
> dom. And R. Ammi—for the same reason should have accepted them?
> [He was angry] because he ought to have given the money to the
> pagan poor. But Rava did give it to the pagan poor? R. Ammi was
> angry because they did not complete the report to him.
> (b. B.B. 10b-11a)

> 'Ifra Hormiz mother of Shapur the king sent an animal sacrifice
> [קרבנא] to Rava. She sent word to him, "Offer it up to Him for the
> sake of Heaven." Rava said to R. Safra and R. Aḥa b. Huna, "Go and

---

[1] Compare vol. I, pp. 23-30, 58-97; vol. II, pp. 27-52, 64-72, 119-125; vol. III,
pp. 17-24.

put forward two [pagan] young men [of the same age], and see where the sea has thrown up alluvial mud, and take new twigs and make a fire with a new flint and offer it up for the sake of Heaven."

(b. Zev. 116b)

'Ifra Hormiz mother of Shapur the king sent blood to Rava. R. 'Ovadyah was sitting before him. He smelled it and said to her, "This is a blood of lust." She said to her son, "Come see how wise the Jews are." He said to her, "Perhaps it is like a blind man on a window [a lucky accident]." She went and sent him sixty kinds of blood, and all he identified except the last one, which was lice blood and he did not know it. Fortunately, he sent her a comb which kills lice. She said, "Jews! In the inner chamber of the heart you live!"   (b. Nid. 20b)

The fifth story is of a different sort altogether:

A certain man was judged liable to the lash in the court of Rava because he had intercourse with a gentile [lit. Samaritan] woman. Rava had him lashed and he died. The matter was heard in the court of Shapur the king. He wanted to punish Rava. 'Ifra Hormiz the mother of Shapur the king said to her son, "Have no dealings with the Jews, for whatever they ask of their Master he gives to them." He asked her, "What would it be?" She replied, "They pray for mercy and rain comes." He said to her, "That comes because it is the normal time for rain, but let them ask for mercy now in the summer season [lit.: in the Tammuz cycle] and let rain come." She sent to Rava, "Concentrate and beg for mercy that rain may come." He prayed for mercy but rain did not come. He prayed before Him, "Lord of the world, 'Oh God, we have heard with our ears, our fathers have told us; a work you did in their days, in the days of old' (Ps. 44.2). But we with our own eyes have not seen it." Rain came until the gutters of Maḥoza emptied their water into the Tigris. His father came and appeared to him in a dream and said to him, "Does anyone trouble heaven so much? Change your place!" He changed his place [for sleeping], and next morning he found that his bed was cut with knives.   (b. Taʿanit 24b)[1]

As to the name 'Ifra ('YPR'), Nöldeke finds the name unclear, and no other sources report Shapur's mother's name as 'Ifra Hormiz(d).[2] His father's name of course was Hormizd. The Nestorian Chronicle[3] records a tradition that Shapur's mother's father was a Jew; that Simeon bar Sabbaʿe had converted her to Christianity; and that this was one of the reasons for the persecution of Simeon and the Church.

The stories of 'Ifra Hormizd's gifts to R. Joseph and Rava are of two

---

[1] See also b. Ber. 56a for an echo of the story about Rava's arrest.

[2] Nöldeke, *Tabari*, p. 52, n. 1; see also p. 68, No. 1. Compare F. Justi, *Iranisches Namenbuch* (Hildesheim, 1963), p. 141 col. a.

[3] *Patrologia Orientalis*, IV, pp. 297-298.

different kinds. The first two were told as the occasion for discussion of a legal issue, in the first case, "What is a great commandment?" and in the second, "How would one rabbi justify declining a gift from the government, while another justified accepting it?" The second story appears to be the least credible, for I think it unlikely that the queen-mother would have had sufficient information about the Palestinian rabbis to send a gift to R. Ammi. That someone gave a purse of denarii to a very important Babylonian rabbi seems to me quite plausible.

The third and fourth stories, while different from one another, are preserved in a more narrowly historical framework; that is to say, in neither case is a legal discussion attached to, or caused by, the participation of 'Ifra Hormizd. The gift of an animal sacrifice to Rava has its parallel in the gift by an Arab of an animal sacrifice to Rav Judah in the preceding generation.[1] The consultation about the meaning of a vaginal excretion does not appear unlikely, since the rabbis achieved a widespread reputation for their expertness in interpreting just such phenomena. But why a non-Jew should inquire I cannot say. The point of the story was that the rabbis were supernaturally powerful, and should not be trifled with. This is the message of the story about how the queen-mother saved Rava from her son's punishment. We know that the Sasanians, as soon as they took power, checked up on Jewish courts which administered physical punishment, and the case in which the prohibition was reported is similar to the one before us. R. Shila ordered lashes for a man who had intercourse with a gentile woman, and later murdered him because he suspected him of intending to inform the Sasanian authorities of Shila's contempt for them.[2] What is important in this story, however, is the belief of the queen-mother in the supernatural power of the rabbis, who could pray and bring rain, just as they could interpret the most subtle natural phenomena. The point, it seems clear, is that the magical effectiveness of the rabbis' prayers and their wonderful knowledge of physiology won the admiration of the queen-mother, whose gifts to R. Joseph and Rava, including not only money but also an animal sacrifice, would have been a natural result. These traditions preserve a memory that Shapur II's mother did believe the Jews were supernaturally powerful, therefore tried to win their favor by giving them gifts of money and animal sacrifices, and even warned her skeptical son against interfering in their affairs.

These are unusual traditions, since no similar stories in relation to

---

[1] Vol. III, pp. 30-31, and below, pp. 63-64.
[2] Vol. II, pp. 32-33.

earlier times were told. The third and fourth stories, about the animal
sacrifice and the blood consultation, included details that played no
particular role in the narrator's mind. The instructions to the two men,
cited by name, and the presence of R. 'Ovadyah do not contribute to
the point of the story. No legal issue is settled through retelling this
legend as a precedent. I should suppose that these two stories have a
substantial basis in fact. But what that fact actually was we shall not
likely uncover. A gift from the court, perhaps from some minor official's wife (or slave-girl for the matter) could as well have been
characterized as a present from the queen-mother herself.

The story about 'Ifra Hormizd and her respect for the rabbis'
miracle-working power similarly rings true—but only in a generalized
way. That Rava got into trouble with the Persian government for a
miscarriage of justice in his court is most reasonable; that the queen-
mother thereupon warned her son not to get involved is not. Shapur
II had great bureaus of state to oversee such petty affairs, and I find it
hard to believe that he himself would have engaged in a discussion of
what happened in the millet court system, or of whether or not the
Jews were good magicians. Rather, I take it as a fact that some miscarriage of justice occured. The Sasanian government intervened. Rava
was not punished. A story was invented replete with details of heavenly
response to prayers for rain, mysterious messages through dreams, and
angelic punishment of a rabbi for bothering the heavenly court too
much. So I do not see how the fifth story can be used for historical
evidence, though as we shall see,[1] it reveals much that is of interest to
the historian of religion.

I should suppose therefore that the first two stories and the fifth
are of little historical use, but the third and the fourth indicate that
someone at the court of Shapur II believed the Jews were good magicians and physicians. That does not prove that the Jews had a friend at
court, only that the rabbis' reputation as people possessing supernatural
power was taken seriously. If, as it seems, they enjoyed such a reputation
at the court of Shapur II, it would have stood them in good stead in
such troubled days as were at hand. No other source preserves the name
of Shapur II's mother as 'Ifra Hormizd, which suggests either that the
rabbinical academies had no very good traditions on the subject, or
that some other 'Ifra Hormizd, later on called "mother of Shapur the
King," was involved. But I do not think the king's mother figured in

---

[1] Below, Chapter Five.

whatever actual events underlay these stories.[1] In the end, it is the absence of corroborative evidence which must be decisive. It is not impossible that the queen-mother, always a powerful figure at oriental courts, should have had an interest in Judaism and have sent presents, sacrifices, and problems to the most prominent rabbi. Origen was consulted by an empress. Nor is it incredible that a capital charge against an important judge in a millet court should have got to Shapur, and that, if it did, his mother might have put in a word to protect the rabbi. Without further confirmation—especially of the name of the queen-mother[2]—we cannot suppose, however, that these stories actually took place as the rabbinical accounts say.

VI. SHAPUR'S TAXES AND THE JEWS

The only story which relates to government persecution of Jews specifically explains the reason: tax evasion. There are two questions concerning taxes: first, did the Jews try to evade them? Second, were the rabbis obligated to pay them?[3]

The latter issue affected the entire Jewish community, for taxes were levied by communities, according to the number of people listed as belonging to them. If the rabbis did not pay their share of the community's tax, others would be obligated to pay a larger portion. But so far as the government was concerned, it hardly mattered, so long as the required revenues were forthcoming from each community. On the other hand, the Christians were persecuted specifically because they were unwilling and unable to pay the heavy war levies after 337, and they were unable to do so in part because a large number of Christians had subjected themselves to vows of poverty and hence did not own possessions to begin with. Were a similar situation to prevail within Jewry, the government would have on its hands two considerable,

---

[1] Wonder-working exploits of the rabbis were, as here, rarely cited when matters of state were at issue. If they were magicians, it did not help them to overcome either the government or the exilarchate, and indeed such stories were not told when legal or administrative issues were at hand. See vol. II, pp. 274-287, in particular p. 282, and vol. III, pp. 317-338.

[2] Note in this connection that in E. Benveniste, *Titres et Noms Propres en Iranian Ancien* (Paris, 1966), pp. 27-50, "Reines et princesses," no germane, corroborative data will be found. It is of interest that in his discussion of *chiliarch*, pp. 67-71, Benveniste makes no reference whatever to the Talmudic *gezirpati*; though he does refer to biblical material, specifically in this section, he seems not to have seen Talmudic evidences.

[3] On the taxes see Widengren in *IA* I, 1961, pp. 149-154, and below, p. 85. There we shall consider the evidence about the liability of rabbis to the poll-tax.

uncooperative communities, So the court of Shapur could not ignore
the issue of whether rabbis, and many were so designated by this time,
had to pay the head tax, the corvée, and other levies. The fact is that
some rabbis did try to evade taxes by actually denying they were Jews
and affirming they were "worshippers of fire." The relevant story is as
follows:

> Rava stated, "A disciple of the rabbis may say, 'I am a servant of
> fire and do not pay the poll-tax.'" What is the reason? It is said only to
> drive away a lion.
>
> (b. Ned. 62b)

The rabbinical commentators explain that since God is designated a
consuming fire (Deut. 4:24) it is not exactly a lie. The Sasanians, however, would not in any circumstance have considered it the truth. We
shall return to this matter below (pp. 85-91).

That tax evasion was a serious problem for the government is illustrated by the following:

> ...Abaye replied, "Do you speak of Dura deRe'uta? There the fields
> belonged to people who hid themselves and did not pay the land tax
> (tasqa') to the king, and the king decreed that whoever paid the land-
> tax might enjoy the usufruct of the land."
>
> (b. B.B. 54b)

The case under discussion was the purchase, later disputed, of a field
from a gentile. It suggests that it was not uncommon for gentiles as
well as Jews to attempt to avoid the taxes as best they could. So I think
it is clear that tax evasion was not a minor problem.

Another difficulty was the attempt to bribe court officials. One recalls
that R. Yohanan, upon hearing of the coming of the Magi to Babylonia,
took comfort in the thought that they accepted bribes.[1] In this period,
we have the following story:

> "Then my anger shall be kindled against them in that day, and I will
> forsake them, and I will hide my face from them" (Deut. 31.17). R.
> Bardela b. Tavyumi in Rav's name said, "Anyone to whom 'hiding of
> the face' does not apply is not one of them...." The rabbis said to Rava,
> "The master is not among those to whom 'the hiding of the face'
> applies..." He said to them, "Do you know how much I send in secret
> to the court of Shapur the King?" Even so, the rabbis set their eyes
> on him. Meanwhile the Court of Shapur the King sent and plundered
> him. He said, "This illustrates the teaching of R. Simeon b. Gamaliel,
> 'Wherever the sages set their eyes, there follows either death or
> poverty.'"
>
> (b. Hag. 5a-b)

---

[1] Vol. II, p. 28.

Whatever the criticism of Rava implied in the rabbinical gesture of disapproval, what is important here is his admission that he sent bribes to the court of the emperor. That he was eventually punished—we do not know for what specific crime[1]—merely illustrated the efficacy of rabbinical disapproval. Rava's former prosperity, perhaps in a time of trouble, seemed to indicate that God favored him, so 'the hiding of the face,' that is to say, the worldly suffering which indicated divine disapproval, did not apply to him. His reply was that he was saved only by the bribes he sent to the court. The rabbis' view was that whoever did not share the divinely-visited troubles of the community, as Rava obviously did not, could not share its eventual glory.

The death of Rabbah, conventionally dated at 330, was specifically described as a consequence of persecution on account of tax-invasion:

> R. Kahana said that R. Ḥama son of the daughter of Ḥama told him that Rabbah b. Naḥmani died on account of persecution. Informers testified against him at court. They said, "There is a certain man among the Jews who keeps twelve thousand men of Israel from paying the royal head-tax a month in the summer and a month in the winter. They sent a royal messenger [PRYSTQ' = parastak] after him, but he did not find him. He fled from Pumbedita to 'Aqra', from 'Aqra' to 'Agma', and from 'Agma' to Shehin, and from Shehin to Zerifa, and from Zerifa to 'Aina' deMayim, and from 'Aina' deMayim to Pumbedita. In Pumbedita he found him. The royal messenger happened upon the hostel of Rabbah. They brought him a tray, gave him two cups,[2] then removed the tray. His face was turned backward. They said to him [Rabbah], "What shall we do for him? He is a royal messenger." He said to them, "Bring him a tray and give him one glass, then remove the tray and he will be healed." They did so and he was healed. He [the agent] said, "I am quite sure that the man I seek is here." He searched and found him. He [the detective] said, "I shall leave here. If they kill [that man =] me, I shall not reveal him, but if they torture me, I shall reveal him." They brought him [Rabbah] before him. He led Rabbah up to a chamber and locked the door before him. He [Rabbah] prayed and the wall broke down. He fled to 'Agma'. He was sitting on the trunk of a palm and studying. In the heavenly academy they were [then] arguing thus, "If a bright spot precedes a white hair, it is unclean, and if the white hair precedes the bright spot, it is clean. When in doubt, the Holy One blessed be He says it is clean, and the entire heavenly academy say it is unclean. Who will decide the matter? Let Rabbah b. Naḥmani decide it, for Rabbah b. Naḥmani said, 'I am unique in laws relating to leprosy and tents.'" They sent a messenger after him. The angel of death could not come near him, because his

---

[1] As to the "arrest of Rava," b. Ber. 56a, I do not think the passage relevant to political history.

[2] A way of calling demonic punishment.

mouth did not cease from his studies. Meanwhile a wind blew and caused a rustling in the branches. He feared that was a band of cavalry. He said, "Let my soul die, but let me not be given into the hand of the government." While dying, he said, "Clean, clean!" A heavenly echo went forth and said, "Happy are you, Rabbah b. Naḥmani, that your body is clean and your soul went forth in clean- ness." A slip of paper fell from heaven into Pumbedita, [on which was written], "Rabbah b. Naḥmani has been summoned to the heavenly academy." Abaye and Rava and all the rabbis went out to attend to him, but they did not know his place [where his body was lying]. They went to 'Agma' and saw birds hovering and overshadowing [the corpse]. They said, "So he is there." They mourned for him three days and three nights. A slip of paper fell, "Whoever holds aloof [from lamenting] will be under a ban." They mourned seven more days. A slip of paper fell, "Go home in peace." On that day, a hurricane lifted a Tai[1] who was riding a camel, from one side of the Papa canal to the other. He said, "What is this?" He was told, "Rabbah b. Naḥmani has died." He cried, "Lord of the World! The whole world is yours, and Rabbah b. Naḥmani is yours. You are Rabbah's and Rabbah is yours. Why do you destroy the world!" The storm subsided.

(b. B.M. 86a)

What shall we make of this account? For our study of rabbinical religion[2] it will provide many hard facts. But what facts can we make use of for critical historical purposes? R. Sherira stated that the two months of the Kallah assemblies were Adar and Elul, and during that time, the absence of those attending Rabbah's lectures caused a drop in revenues. Obermeyer[3] discussed the various sites, all in the vicinity of Pumbedita, to which Rabbah allegedly fled. But whatever minor details may be accounted for, the fact is that a story about prayers which break down doors and walls, conversations in the heavenly academy, the prevention of the angel of death's work through incessant repeating of one's lessons, letters sent from heaven to Pumbedita, and the like— such a story lays no claim whatever to concrete historical reliability. All we may say is that an account full of miraculous and incredible events rests upon the tradition that Rabbah got into trouble with the government for causing mass evasion of taxes. But whether or not Rabbah actually did so—by intent or otherwise—I cannot say. The story of Rabbah's death on account of "religious persecution" has been widely discussed.[4]

---

[1] See below. pp. 44-45.
[2] Below, Chapter Five.
[3] *Die Landschaft Babylonien*, p. 237.
[4] See for example Salo W. Baron, *Social and Religious History of the Jews*, II, pp. 243, 413 n. 25.

Graetz's account was quite naturalistic; a serious charge was brought against Rabbah:

> by means of Rabbah's discourses during the Kalla months, his 1200 students had been induced to evade the poll-tax.[1]

Rabbah's death, Graetz said, was caused by "fright at the rustling of the wind in the trees." He casually bypassed all the details of heavenly interference in Rabbah's life processes. The corpse was "covered over and hidden by birds." (That they were vultures, as was common in Zoroastrian Babylonia, is never suggested.) So Graetz ignored or rejected some miracles, but reported, even created others. The text cited above does not say that Rabbah had *induced* his students not to pay their taxes, but rather, through the *Kallah*-lectures, students *happened* not to be at home when the tax-collectors came by. Rabbah had no intentional part in the matter, according to the account. M. Beer and E. E. Urbach, who most recently have discussed this passage, simply do not comment upon those miraculous details which in the story itself seem to be taken for granted.[2]

In any event, I do not find in the above story sufficient proof that the regime of Shapur II persecuted the Jews as a community, nor is there any persuasive evidence that Rabbah himself died in a "religious persecution."[3] I think Rava's saying that one may lie to the government about one's religion represents more valuable evidence, which receives corroboration from the saying that he had bribed officials at Shapur's court, but was apparently made to pay for it. It is quite clear that Jews, among others, did try to evade the heavy taxes imposed by the Sasanians. Rava, in particular, held that the rabbis were not supposed to pay the taxes required of them by civil law. Rava himself resorted to deceit and bribery to avoid payment. Ordinary people probably did likewise, without offering theological or exegetical reasons for their action.[4] I should imagine that later on Shapur II did everything he could to enforce tax-collections, and that the story about Rabbah's flight and death may have a foundation in that fact. What actually happened to Rabbah we do not know. Afterward rabbis recalled—at the very least—that he had died on account of mass tax evasions, as had

---

[1] Graetz, *History*, II, p. 580.

[2] In *Tarbiz* 33, 3, 1964, pp. 247-258, in particular pp. 255-257 and 33, 4, pp. 349-357, as well as E. E. Urbach in *Tarbiz* 34, 2, 1965, pp. 156-161, and below, pp. 100-102.

[3] Since Rabbah allegedly died in 323, Shapur II was in any case twelve or thirteen years old, and not in control of the government.

[4] For an earlier example of mass tax-evasion, see vol. III, pp. 24-27.

Simeon bar Sabbaʿe. But no persecution of the Jews followed. Sasanian government wanted taxes, not lives, except in the case of the Christians, and for special reasons. So if a rabbi was punished for lying or evading taxes, it would have been exemplary, and not universal, punishment. Since no evidence suggests any further difficulties, I should conclude that the Jewish community learned its lesson and paid its taxes. Coming on the eve of Shapur's active years, the incident would have sufficed to insure future compliance.[1]

VII. SHAPUR'S WARS AND THE JEWS

Whether or not the Jewish community faced a hostile government in the age of Shapur II, the Jews certainly suffered along with everyone else in Babylonia on account of the great wars of the day. We shall here consider how the insecurity of Shapur's minority, the movements of armies in Babylonia, and the devastating invasion of 363 were reflected in Talmudic traditions.

The Arab Incursions: The Tai invasions which weakened the government between 309 and 325 were intended mostly to seize goods or captives. The latter were then ransomed to their families. Redemption of captives was a great commandment, Rava said.[2] Things reached such a state that the rabbis ruled Nehardeans, who lived near the frontier, were permitted to carry weapons on the Sabbath.[3] A case involving the captivity of Jews came to Abaye;[4] Levi b. Darga ransomed his own daughter;[5] an Arab woman brought *tefillin* to Abaye for ransom:

> A certain woman of the Tai tribe brought a bag of *tefillin* to Abaye.
> He said to her, "Give them for a few dates a pair." She was angered

---

[1] The motive of the story-teller, R. Kahana, is not obvious to me. R. Ḥama may have wanted to emphasize some particular detail. I find most striking the account of Rabbah's death as an act of the heavenly court in its pursuit of its studies. The magical power of the rabbi as well as the respect of heaven for rabbis' learning are, of course, commonplace themes; so the story is part of a vast corpus of legends about the rabbis as amazing men, who enjoy special connections with the world above—even to the extent of receiving letters from heaven. But if Rabbah died because the heavenly court needed him to report his traditions about purity laws, then one can hardly say he died on account of a religious persecution! If the story is a composite, however, I cannot discern its segments.

[2] b. B.B. 8b, and above, p. 35.

[3] b. ʿEruv. 45a, Ket. 23a, etc. See H. Z. Hirshberg, *Yisraʾel BaʿArav* (Tel Aviv, 1946), p. 42, and p. 281, n. 52.

[4] b. B.M. 39b.

[5] b. Git. 45a.

and threw them into the river. He said, "I should not have cheapened them so much in her eyes."

(b. Git. 45b)

A more serious case involved the seizure of land:

> Certain [Tai] Arabs came to Pumbedita and forcibly seized land. The owners came before Abaye. They asked, "Will the master examine our deeds and write duplicates, so that if one deed is forcibly taken away, we shall hold the other in our possession..."
>
> (b. B.B. 168b)

The presupposition of the request was that the Arabs might eventually be driven out, and the owners might thereupon recover their land. Without a deed, it would prove difficult, especially if in the meanwhile the Arab land-grabber were to sell to a third party. The case that came to Abaye suggests that the Arab incursions proved particularly trying in his day, for it was not merely a matter of ransoming an individual or recovering a bag of *tefillin*. The Arab tribes were sufficiently powerful to take and hold a section of Babylonia not far from the royal capital. The inevitable result of the desert raids was the disruption of normal agricultural life.[1] To Rava came a case which indicates how serious a problem was posed by famine:

> Rava was [in the beginning] of the opinion that famine is not like war ... But he changed his mind, for a certain woman came before him with the claim that her husband had died in famine, [and therefore she should be permitted to remarry]. "You have done well in saving yourself, since it would not occur to anyone that he would survive on the little bit of flour you left for him." [His intent was to find out whether she had witnessed his death, or was merely transmitting hearsay evidence.] She replied, "The master also understands that in such a circumstance one cannot survive." So he changed his mind and ruled that famine is worse than war...
>
> (b. Yev. 114b)

Military Occupations: With the increased efficiency of Shapur's government, armies were mustered, and campaigns began in Babylonia. So in place of the unsafe conditions which prevailed during his minority, the local residents had to undergo the discomforts resulting from the presence of large armed forces. Evidence of what this meant is seen in the following:

> An army once came to Pumbedita. Rabbah and R. Joseph fled from the town, and R. Zera met them on the road. He said to them, "Fugitives! Remember the olive's bulk...."
>
> (b. Ḥul. 46a)

---

[1] See also b. B.B. 45a, the seller must help a Jewish purchaser recover property from a gentile who has seized it. On the Tai festivals, see b. A.Z. 11b and Obermeyer, *op. cit.*, p. 234.

Since both rabbis died well before 363, the army was an Iranian, not
a Roman one. The rabbis fled not because of hostile action, but because
of the inconvenience of an occasional military occupation; and the
incident was only remembered as the context for an exchange of legal
opinions about an abstruse matter. Rava similarly gave instructions to
the people of Mahoza about removing before Passover the leaven
belonging to troops billeted in their homes.[1] He gave orders about
how to carry the apparel of the troops to the baths on the Sabbath.[2] He
also referred to the possibility that a general, coming to town, might
requisition food prepared for a wedding feast.[3] So the mobilization of
Shapur's armies led to a certain amount of dislocation in Babylonia.
On the other hand, the early years must have been yet more difficult,
and ordinary people may have preferred to carry the soldier's garments
to the bath house rather than to lose their fields or their families, to
the Arab raiders.

Extreme difficulties followed in the wake of Julian's invasion. The
Persian defense involved destruction of dikes and flooding of fields.
Major waterways were dammed up to prevent the Romans from using
them for their fleet. The Roman army burned many smaller towns and
villages along its path, including much of central Babylonia where the
vast majority of Jews lived. Adams points out that future Sasanian
investment consequently was to be mostly in the Diyala basin, rather
than in the more threatened region between the Tigris and the
Euphrates.[4] Ammianus Marcellinus refers to one Jewish town destroyed by the invaders:

> In this tract, a city which, because of its low walls, had been abandon-
> ed by its Jewish inhabitants, was burned by the hands of the angry
> soldiers.[5]

There followed the siege and storming of Maiozamalcha. Near
Pumbedita, Piruzsabur (later, Anbar) was besieged and taken after a
three day siege (XXIV 2 9-22), but most people were able to flee, and
few were taken prisoner.[6] Graetz identifies Birtha with the unnamed
city which the Roman troops burned to the ground.[7] He also says that

---

[1] b. Pes. 5b.

[2] b. Shab. 147b.

[3] b. Ket. 3b.

[4] Robert McC. Adams, *Land behind Baghdad. A History of Settlement on the Diyala
Plains* (Chicago, 1965), p. 70.

[5] XXIV, 4, 1.

[6] See Obermeyer, *op. cit.*, p. 219. Pumbedita was nearby.

[7] II, p. 602. A. Musil. *The Middle Euphrates* (N. Y. 1927), p. 241, says we do
not know what town this was.

Maḥoza was identical with „Maoga-Malka," but I am unable to explain his reason.[1]

The silence of the Talmudic sources on Julian's invasion is striking. Not a single source can be found to testify to Jewish opinion on the matter, nor do we have evidence of very much suffering, though the people certainly did suffer in the invasion. The main consequence was, however, the necessity to rebuild the towns, for the people fled from them before the Roman armies came near and returned as soon afterwards as they could. Hence I should suppose that it was a difficult spring and summer in 363. What is most significant is the unreliability of Talmudic materials for the history of the Jewish community. It indicates that the final collectors and editors were not concerned about historical reminiscences, which must have survived, but only about other matters mainly pertaining to events and opinions within the academies.

The War of 363: We do not, therefore, have much evidence about Jewish opinion on the Persian-Roman wars. On the one hand, the Jews under Byzantium were not severely persecuted, and before the invasion Julian had removed an aggravating tax. So I do not think the Jews behind Julian's lines had much reason to hope for his defeat, and I doubt that they did. On the other hand, no good reason existed for Babylonian Jews to oppose Shapur II, who had not generally persecuted them or restricted the free exercise of their religion in any way. Their view of Rome, hostile for centuries, could not have been rendered favorable in the brief time of Julian's rule, particularly not by a destructive invasion. A code message had reached Rava some years earlier—we do not know exactly when—which informed him that the Romans would not let the Palestinian Jews intercalate the calendar.[2] Lieberman explains, however, that since the Romans were not concerned with the practice of intercalation, but rather with the procedure, the reason was not "religious persecution." Rather, the government generally looked askance at the solemn public meeting which was required, and especially at times of

---

[1] *Ibid.*, compare Obermeyer, *op. cit.*, p. 178, n. 6, who rejects this identification. He says he believes that Maogamalka is to be identified with Nahr al Melik of Arabic times. Y. I. Halevy, *Dorot Harishonim*, II, p. 496 identifies the synagogue of "Romans" in Maḥoza with Jews who came in the invasion of Julian and remained. He is wrong; the passage he cites, b. Meg. 26b, refers to Rava, who died long before the Roman invasion. Moreover, Obermeyer, p. 179, identifies the "Roman" Jews as coming from Rumakan, near Maḥoza, and having no connection either with Syria or with Byzantium. On Be Kokhe, see Obermeyer, p. 108, and n. 40.

[2] b. Sanh. 12a.

hostility it objected to the dispatch of messengers to the Jewish diaspora.[1] Whatever the Romans' reasons, however, the Babylonian Jews
could not have been won over to the Roman side upon hearing that
"yon Edomite" did not permit the rabbis to meet to add an additional
month to the year. Abaye and R. Nahman b. Isaac cited Scriptural
verses (Hos. 2:8, Lam. 3:9) to indicate that the direct route from
Palestine to Babylonia had been closed, but the brief discussion contains no hint that the Romans had closed the roads in their day.[2] R.
Nahman b. Isaac cited Gen 25:23 to prove that when Caesarea flourishes,
Jerusalem does not, and vice versa. R. Papa was told by Rava that King
Shapur was to be eclipsed by Caesar, as was proved by Dan. 7:23, "It
(the fourth beast) shall devour the whole earth, and trample it down
and break it to pieces."[3] R. Joseph said that Dan. 7:5, "And behold
another beast, a second, like to a bear" refers to the Persians, "who eat
and drink greedily like the bear, are fleshly like the bear, have shaggy
hair like the bear, and are restless like the bear."[4] Rava said that Israel
was destined to be saved in the seventh (Sabbatical) year, which fell,
in this period, in 312, 319, 326, 333, 340, 347, 354, 361, and 368, but I
see no relationship whatever between Rava's saying and the events of
the day. For exegetical reasons the rabbis supposed that the Romans
were the stronger of the two empires, but that did not indicate they
hoped for a Roman victory. Indeed, no discussion unequivocally
related to the actual events of 363.[5] Christian, but not Jewish, traditions
recorded renewed messianic yearnings, as might be expected in a
crisis.[6] Some may have hoped to see the restoration of the Temple in
Jerusalem, as Julian promised.

The Jews suffered in the wars of Shapur, but on the whole, they
cannot be said to have borne more severe trials than any other group.
If a Jewish town was destroyed, so were a great many inhabited by

---

[1] *JQR* n.s. 36, 4, pp. 331-332.

[2] b. R.H. 23b.

[3] See b. A.Z. 2b, the scripture refers specifically to Rome.

[4] b. A.Z. 2b, b. Qid. 72a. Other rabbinic sayings on the Persians included the
following: b. 'Eruv. 29b-30a, R. Joseph said that the Persians eat roasted meat
without bread; b. Ket. 48a, R. Joseph said that the Persians wear clothes when
they engage in sexual intercourse; b. Shab. 94a, R. Adda b. Mattenah said to
Abaye that the Persians ride swathed in garments and so are like bound men; b.
Ber. 26a, Rava on the Persians' privies.

[5] That no comment was made about an invasion through one's own lands is
simply incredible. Rather, whatever was said in the schools about the invasions
and wars did not concern the later collectors, who were not interested in reports
of the consequent sufferings.

[6] See vol. II, pp. 52-57.

non-Jews. If the Jews were troubled by the Arab invasions across the lightly-defended frontier, especially in the years of Shapur's youth, so too were non-Jews. The times were difficult, but the government was doing what it could to retrieve the situation, and except for the terrible invasion of 363 and the occasional inconveniences caused by the mobilization of armies in the area inhabited by Jews, the ordinary people must have preferred the years of Shapur's strong rule to anything that had gone before for close to a century. Shapur brought peace to Babylonia, and by his astute, if costly, retreat of 363, he insured peace for centuries afterward.

VIII. SHAPUR AND THE JEWS

Two stories relate alleged conversations between Shapur II and rabbis:

> Shapur the King said to R. Ḥama, "How do you prove from the Torah that one must bury the dead?" He was silent and did not reply. R. Aḥa b. Jacob said, "The world is given into the hands of fools. He should have said...."
>
> (b. Sanh. 46b)

> Mar Judah and Ba'ti b. Tuvi were seated before Shapur the King. An *etrog* was brought before them. He cut and ate a piece, cut and gave a piece to Ba'ti b. Tuvi. Then he went and stuck the knife into the ground ten times, cut a piece, and gave it to Mar Judah. Ba'ti b. Tuvi said, "And is that man [I] not a son of Israel?" He replied, "Of him I am certain, of you I am uncertain..."
>
> (b. A.Z. 76b)[1]

These stories do not reflect an atmosphere of hostility. The question to R. Ḥama was natural for a Zoroastrian, who regarded burial as an abomination; the behavior with Mar Judah and Ba'ti b. Tuvi indicated that the emperor was supposed to be careful to respect the legal requirements of Judaism for a person who was loyal to them. So the only traditions directly pertaining to Shapur II preserve a picture of a respectful, if skeptical monarch. Like the traditions on 'Ifra Hormizd and Shapur II, they suggest little animosity against the Jews or Judaism. Whether or not any such conversations took place I cannot say. On the one hand, the Jews did live in the territories near the capital, so it is by

---

[1] In vol. II, p. 70, I cited this passage with erroneous reference to Shapur I. Professor A. Weiss kindly called that error to my attention. Mar Judah was a fourth-century master.

no means impossible for the emperor to have known about their religious practices and inquired about their basis. On the other hand, the
stories seem to me to stress the importance of, in the first case, knowing
how to prove Scriptures require precisely what the Jews actually do;
in the second, recognizing that even the mighty emperor honors those
who follow the rabbis' rulings. In the absence of other evidence,
stories of this sort do not prove that the emperor really had such
conversations with rabbis. What is important about them, therefore, is
the *absence* of ill-feeling toward Shapur. The first story suggests that if
an adequate Scriptural basis for the practice of burial could be cited,
then Shapur would have permitted the practice. This further suggests
that Shapur respected the Sacred Books of the Jews, and would not
demand violation of their laws. These suggestions may not be correct,
but at any rate the rabbinical academies did not preserve stories reflect-
ing Shapur's hostility toward the Jews.[1] Nor do I think the 'Ifra
Hormizd traditions preserve a contrary view, for in them, her credulity
(faith) in the rabbis' magical powers is merely contrasted against
Shapur's skepticism, but no hostile attitude on his part toward the
rabbis or toward the Jews as a group was implied.[2]

A number of traditions, however, refer in general terms to persecutions of Jews and Jewish hatred of the Persians. In the former
category are the following:

> R. Beroka of Khuzistan used to frequent the market at Be Lapat [the
> capital] where Elijah often appeared to him. Once he asked, "Is there
> any one in this market who has a share in the world to come?" He
> replied, "No." Meanwhile he caught sight of a man wearing black
> shoes and who had no thread of blue on the corners of his garment,
> and he exclaimed, "This man has a share in the world to come." He ran
> after him and asked him, "What is your occupation." The man replied,
> "Go away and come back tomorrow." Next day he asked him again,
> "What is your occupation?" And he replied, "I am a jailer, and I keep
> the men and women separate, and I place my bed between them so that
> they may not come to sin; when I see a Jewish girl upon whom the
> gentiles cast their eyes, I risk my life and save her...." He further asked,
> "Why have you no fringes, and why do you wear black shoes?" He
> replied, "That the gentiles among whom I constantly move may not
> know that I am a Jew, so that when a harsh decree is made I can inform
> the rabbis, and they pray, and the decree will be annulled." He further
> asked him, "When I asked you, 'What is your occupation,' why did
> you say to me, 'Go away now and come back tomorrow'?" He answer-

---

[1] Compare vol. II, pp. 27-39, 64-72, and vol. III, pp. 17-24.
[2] Above, pp. 35-39.

ed, "They had just issued a narsh decree, and I said I would first go and acquaint the rabbis of it so that they might pray to God...."

(b. Taʿanit 22a)[1]

Rava said, "If a pagan said to a Jew, cut grass on the Sabbath and throw it to the cattle, and if not I shall kill you, let him be killed but not cut it..."

(b. Sanh. 74b)

The latter passage contains a difficult reading, which Jacob Levy has interpreted to mean that Rava referred to giving Persian priests braziers and coal shovels for personal pleasure but not for religious worship.[2] So according to Levy, Jews were forced to contribute to the fire-cult. The story from Khuzistan refers casually to "evil decrees," but we do not know what they were. All we know is that the rabbis were believed able to influence Heaven to abrogate them, and a Jew who masqueraded as a gentile in order to be able to inform them and so mobilize their supernatural powers was highly praised on that account. But what sort of decree would be known to the local jailer before it would be announced to the authorities of the community concerned? If there is any truth in the story, and it is not merely a picture of the model jailer, presumably these decrees were sentences passed on particular individuals, or decisions to use torture in their examinations. I do not find in the story evidence of systematic or sustained persecutions of the sort from which the Christians suffered. Furthermore what happened in Khuzistan did not necessarily reflect the will of the central government; for all we know, a local satrap may have tried to collect additional taxes. Rava's reference to a pagan's ordering a Jew to cut grass on the Sabbath could, of course, reflect the conditions of a military occupation, but the context of the discussion, about extreme situations in which a Jew must give his life for the sake of Heaven rather than carry out a desecration of his religion, is mostly theoretical. Levy's interpretation of the accompanying passage, while persuasive, would suggest only that Jews had to give up fire-place tools to the Magi; if so, it would have violated their laws about not cooperating in pagan rites, but reflected no systematic persecution of Judaism as such. So these two accounts contribute little firm evidence about the persecution either of Jews or of Judaism in Shapur's times. Similarly, R. Papa's reference to

---

[1] Trans. J. Rabinowitz (London, 1938), pp. 109-110.

[2] Jacob Levy, *Wörterbuch über die Talmudim und Midraschim*, (Darmstadt, 1963), IV, p. 273. Jastrow's conjecture, that the passage refers to Jews' heating Christian churches on Sunday, in exchange for similar service on the Sabbath (*REJ* 8, 1884, p. 277ff.), has no merit whatsoever. Note the voluntary gift by Rava, below, p. 63.

times of persecution, in his interpretation of Zech. 8:19, does not
specify that in his own lifetime such persecution took place.[1]

According to *Seder 'Olam Zuta*, a persecution of the Jews took place
in 313:

> And the Persians inherited the kingdom, and in the 245th year of
> the destruction of the Temple, the Persians decreed a persecution of
> the Jews.
>
> (*Seder 'Olam Zuta*, Grossman ed., p. 44)

This passage is cited by Bacher (*JE*, II, 409) and others as proof that
in 313, during Shapur II's minority, a persecution of Jews took place.
What the *SOZ* preserves, however, is the memory that *when the Persians
came to power*, they dealt harshly with the Jews, which, as we have seen,[2]
was the case. On the other hand, the context of the sentence clearly is
the third generation of Amoraim, with which we now are concerned,
for in the same passage, the *SOZ* speaks of the sages following R.
Judah b. Ezekiel and R. Sheshet, namely Rava, R. 'Ada', and others,
and the exilarchate of Nathan, Nehemiah, and 'Aqavyah, hence the end
of the third century and the beginning of the fourth. A reference which
immediately follows is made to Shapur's capture of Nisibis in the time
of Rava, who died in 352. The passage is therefore confused as to the
facts. The Persians came to power a century before. If the *SOZ* means
to say—as seems obvious—that when the Persians came to power they
decreed a persecution of the Jews, then it contains no reference whatever to the time of Shapur II. If on the other hand the preservation of
the tradition in the midst of an account of the late third and early
fourth century Amoraim is intentional, as the reference to Shapur's
taking of Nisibis would suggest, then some sort of tradition about a
persecution in this period seems to have been preserved. Had we any
clear Talmudic evidence about persecutions in this time, as we have
about those in the early period, we might be able to cite the above as
corroborative evidence. But we do not, so I suppose that all the *SOZ*
actually preserves is a confused record of what happened when the
Persians came to power. (An earlier reference to a Persian campaign
against the Romans in the 166th year of the destruction of the Temple,
that is to say in 244, appears, but there is no other reference to the

---

[1] b. R.H. 18b. Rava and Abaye also discussed the case of one who engaged in
idolatry through love or fear of men (b. Sanh. 61b), and the possibility of being
forced to worship an idol (b. A.Z. 54a). Neither discussion contains any suggestion
that Jews were at that time being forced to serve "idols."

[2] See vol. II, pp. 27-39 and Funk, *op. cit.*, II, p. 78.

Persians' "inheriting the kingdom.") So the information seems garbled at best, and upon this basis we can hardly conclude that in Shapur's minority anyone maltreated the Jews.

On the other hand, fourth-century Jews did not love the Persians, but felt a deep resentment against their rule. R. Papa interpreted Zeph. 3:15[1] to mean that when haughty people and judges will disappear from the Jewish community, the Magi and *gezirpati*, or chiliarchs, will cease among the Persians.[2] His saying reflects hatred of the Persian priests and administrators who came into frequent contact with the local Jewish community, but it reflects no less a dislike of the Jewish rulers—*not* rabbis—whom he resented. So the saying, which transformed an unconditional messianic promise into a contingent one, stressed that just as the two classes of Iranian authorities would be removed, so too would the similar classes of Jewish ones. It should be interpreted, therefore, as a saying critical as much of local Jewish authorities as of local Persian ones. When all high-handed authorities will be removed, the Messiah will come, R. Papa was saying. Hence he thought that the Persians were disagreeable rulers, but no more so than were Jewish officials.[3] So too did R. Joseph say:

> "I have commanded my sanctified ones" (Is. 13:3). R. Joseph interpreted, "This refers to the Persians who are sanctified and prepared for Gehenna."
>
> (b. Ber. 8b)

> "Behold I shall do a new thing; now it shall spring forth" (Is. 43:19). R. Joseph interpreted, "This refers to the war of Gog and Magog. To what may the matter be compared? To a man who was walking on a road. A wolf met him, and he was saved from it. He went along telling about the incident of the wolf. A lion met him, and he was saved from it. He went along telling about the incident of the lion. A serpent met him, and he was saved from it. He forgot the first two stories, and went along telling about the incident of the serpent. So is Israel—the later troubles make them forget the earlier ones."
>
> (b. Ber. 13a)

R. Joseph's first saying leaves no doubt that he thought the Persians would go straight to hell. Given his perspective on history, in which the empires were even then moving toward a grand cataclysm, the latest troubles would make the Jews forget their earlier ones. I do not

---

[1] See vol. II, p. 54.
[2] b. Shab. 139a.
[3] See below, pp. 114-119.

find much evidence, however, that he thought the current troubles actually approximated the war of Gog and Magog. So we know that R. Joseph and R. Papa interpreted Messianic Scriptures to apply to the Persian regime, and that both rabbis, who were separated by a half-century, disliked the Persians. There is no evidence, however, that the reason for their hatred had anything to do with systematic persecutions. Probably it was the normal resentment of a minority group against the dominant government.

That government, however, was not seen as an unfair one. A century earlier, Samuel had laid down the rule that the law of the Persian government was law, and had to be obeyed.[1] Abaye said that the state would be firm in its decrees, citing Samuel's saying that the state will announce the intention of uprooting mountains and not retract.[2] Rava held that the exercise of the right of eminent domain by the state was quite legitimate, in accordance with Samuel's principle, and therefore it is proper to make use of the bridges built by the state out of confiscated palm-trees.[3] Abaye and R. Joseph, discussing whether Persian courts take bribes, admitted that their decrees were not corruptible:

> R. Joseph taught, "This rule [that a man led out to execution is presumed dead or alive] applies only in an Israelite court [for new evidence may be found], but in a court of star-worshippers, once the decree of capital punishment is issued, he is most certainly killed." Abaye said to him, "A court of star-worshippers may also take bribes." He replied, "If they take (bribes) it is before the Chief Judge *Pursi Shanmag*[4] seals the decree [or, until the court decree is sealed] but afterward, they do not take bribes."
>
> (b. Git. 28b)

What is important here is the admission that the Persian court decrees, once issued, were unalterable.[5]

Rava instructed the people of Maḥoza, "By your leave, hasten to the assistance of one another, so you may be on good terms with the

---

[1] Vol. II, pp. 64-72, and vol. III, pp. 41-48.

[2] b. 'Arakh. 6a.

[3] b. B.Q. 113b. Compare the homily of R. Ḥanina b. Papa or R. Simlai, that the Persians in time to come will claim that they built many bridges and captured many cities and fought many wars for the sake of Israel, so that the Jews may study Torah. God is going to reply that they did it all for their own sake; bridges to extract the toll, cities so as to impose the corvée ('angaria), etc., b. A.Z. 2b.

[4] Levy, *op. cit.*, IV, p. 127, s.v. See also *Arukh* VI, p. 438, and esp. IX, p. 343, Geiger gives the proper Pahlavi form as *puršisn namak* and interprets the word as the detailed court document giving the judgments.

[5] Note b. Sanh. 47a-b, Abaye said that those killed by the state are unjustly slain.

government."[1] In context, one may interpret the teaching to mean that the government would respect a community which supports its own members. *If* so, the implication is that the Persian government was concerned about the welfare of ordinary people and not altogether indifferent toward its subjects.

We have found, therefore, not much evidence that the Persian government in Shapur's time persecuted either the Jews or Judaism. No parallel exists to the Christian records, which tell one story after another of martyrdom, recording an unrelieved and fairly systematic persecution over a period of decades. Shapur's alleged conversations with some rabbis were on the whole neutral, and the rabbinic accounts contain no hint of much hostility. Some rather general references to harsh decrees have come to our attention, but these are in no way similar to the very concrete and specific stories about what happened to Christians, and the references themselves seem on the whole conventional and routine, not based upon particular incidents. It is quite true that the Jews did not have much affection for the Persian government and hated the Magi and local authorities. In Parthian times they had enjoyed almost complete autonomy. In the days of Ardashir and Shapur a different pattern developed, in which a rather strong imperial government made it clear that it would closely supervise Jewish internal affairs, which nonetheless remained wholly in Jewish hands. In the period of Kartir's ascendency, he claimed to have "opposed" the Jews along with other non-Mazdean groups; but his success in driving the Manichaeans out of Babylonia was not in any detail paralleled by his treatment of the Jews, and as we have seen,[2] it is difficult to find in Jewish traditions much verification for Kartir's boast. In any event, whatever the role of Atūrpāt in the creation of a state-church, no similar drive against non-Mazdeans took place in Shapur's time. So matters did not change much from the earlier period of Sasanian rule. Just as R. Shila had trouble about punishing a man who had intercourse with a gentile woman, so too did Rava. The Jews complained against Ardashir's and Shapur's attempts at meticulous collection of taxes, and they did so again in the age of Shapur II. The references to various decrees against Judaism[3] find no close equivalents in the fourth century. When one recalls what the Sasanian government was able to do to the

---

[1] Trans. M. Simon, (London, 1938) p. 41. Perhaps more literally, "So that you may have peace in the kingdom "

[2] Vol. III, pp. 8-10, 17-24.

[3] Vol. II, pp. 35-39.

Christian community, I think it significant that all we can find are rather commonplace and conventional Jewish accounts. The only exceptional stories pertain to the death of Rabbah and the massacre of emigrants from Maḥoza. Both represented specific actions against individuals or small groups which seemed to threaten the welfare of the state. No decrees were issued against the practice of Judaism. No Jew was called upon to confess faith in the sun and stars or to deny the God of Israel.[1] Taxes upon the Jewish community were levied at the same rates as applied to other millet communities. On the whole, therefore, one cannot suppose that Shapur or his government planned and carried out a general persecution either of the Jews or of Judaism.

IX. JUDAISM AND OTHER RELIGIONS

Christianity: Jews continued to convert to Christianity, though the persecutions of Shapur after 337 probably slowed the process considerably. Some converts returned to Judaism. We do not have evidence that the rabbis were so concerned with the Christian problem as they had been in the last third of the third century.[2] Jewish-Christians continued to worship in the synagogues, according to the following:

> A certain man descended [to the reader's place] before Rabbah, and said, "You have had mercy on the bird's nest. Have mercy and compassion on us too."[3] Rabbah said, "How well does this rabbinical student know to please his Master!" Abaye said to him, "But behold we have learned [in Tannaitic tradition] that he is to be silenced [if he says this prayer, for it was a mark of Jewish-Christian leanings]." But Rabbah said so only to sharpen Abaye.
>
> (b. Ber. 33b)[4]

The later comment may have been made only to conform Rabbah's saying to the accepted law. If so, Rabbah actually did approve the prayer. However, the accepted Tannaitic tradition was well-known, and the greater likelihood is that he acted as the later editor said, only to see whether Abaye knew the law. Rava engaged in a dispute with a Jewish-Christian[5]:

---

[1] Though Rava said a rabbinical disciple might do exactly that in order to evade the head-tax.

[2] Vol. III, pp. 12-16.

[3] A prayer believed characteristic of *minut*.

[4] See also b. Meg. 25a.

[5] Following the Munich MS. reading of *min*. On whether most *minim* in Babylonia were Jewish-Christians or not, see vol. III, pp. 13-14.

A certain *min* [current texts: Sadducee] saw Rava at his studies. He
was sitting with his fingers under his feet, and [in intense concen-
tration] he ground them down so blood spurted from his fingers. The
min said, "O rash people! You at first gave precedence to your mouth
over your ears and you still persist in your rashness. In the first instance
you should have listened. If you could do it, you should accept it, and
if not, you should *not* accept it." [The reference is to Ex. 24:7] Rava
replied, "We who have walked walked in wholeness, of us it is written,
'The integrity of the upright shall guide them' (Prov. 11:3). But those
men [you] who walked in perversity—of them Scripture says, 'But the
perverseness of the treacherous shall destroy them' (*ibid.*)."

(b. Shab. 88a-b)

Jews who became Christians were regarded by the rabbis as "treacherous" (*bogdim* in the Scripture in Proverbs). When the *min* saw Rava
studying so intently that he injured himself, he commented on it.
Studying was accompanied by oral repetition, and Rava was likely
to have been reciting his traditions out loud. Hence the *min* remarked
that the Jews were still speaking first but thoughtlessly and un-
consciously and listening only afterward to what they were saying. His
comment was that had they listened to what the Torah contained, they
would not have taken upon themselves so difficult a burden that it
became a source of sin to them. Rava's reply did not deny that the
Torah was a difficult burden. Rather, he said, the Jews who remained
loyal to it had preserved their integrity, which would guide them in the
end, but those who abandoned it would be destroyed because of their
treachery. This was not a new conversation. Neither party did more
than repeat an argument which was now close to three centuries old.
From the time of R. Tarfon,[1] if not before, leading rabbis had argued
that Jews who became Christians thus abandoned the Torah. Jewish-
Christians had replied that the Torah was so difficult to keep that it
became a source of sin. The rabbis regarded Jewish-Christians as
apostates who had known God and denied him.

   Mazdaism: I know of not a single concrete reference to the Mazdean
religion or cult among the sayings of rabbis of the middle fourth
century. R. Joseph explained the *Parvah* of the Temple as the name of
a Persian Magus.[2] Jews and Iranians lived in close contact, and we shall
note below[3] examples of their relationships. But at no point do we find
discussion of anything we might call "religious ideas." The disputes

---

[1] See my *History and Torah*, (New York, 1965), pp. 96-97.
[2] b. Yoma 35a, and see the legend reported by R. Ḥananel in his commentary.
[3] pp. 61-62.

about religious questions between rabbinical Jews and Christian-Jews have no parallel. I should suppose that some sort of religious discussion took place in the *Be'Avidan*:

> Rava was asked, "Why did you not come to the *Be'Avidan*?" He replied, "A certain palm-tree stands in the way, and it is hard for me." They said to him, "Then we shall remove it." "Its place is hard for me."
>
> (b. Shab. 116a)

I do not know what a *Be'Avidan* was.[1] Whether the word is to be compared to odeum (ᾠδεῖον) as Herford suggests I cannot say. He thinks it was a place for philosophical disputations. The rabbis called it 'house of destruction,' Herford asserts (from 'BD). But Herford is wrong in holding that the Babylonian rabbis were not familiar with such an institution. The passage above would suggest the contrary, as would those in which Rav and Samuel discuss the matter. If the passage above is genuine, then Rava would have been asked—we do not know by whom—to attend such a philosophical discussion, and declined on the specious grounds that he could not come near the house on account of its location near an idolatrous place. I think it likely, therefore, that the rabbis quite resolutely refused to discuss religious or theological issues with contemporary Mazdeans, who had government support. It would be dangerous to defeat them in an argument, and any disputation might exasperate them.[2]

"Idolatry": The generic term for pagan, comprehending every possible variation except for the *min*, was "star-worshipper," and for paganism, "star-worship." The rabbis knew about various pagan rites, though we find no evidence that they now distinguished among the various divinities.[3] Their attitude was entirely negative. Rava held that by defacing an idol, a Jew would annul it, that is, render it no longer fit for idolatrous worship.[4]

As earlier, the closest attention was devoted to wine, which was commonly and widely used for libations. From former times[5] the rabbis

---

[1] See vol. II, pp. 72-73, n.1, and vol. III, p. 37, n.1, and R.T. Herford, *Christianity in Talmud and Midrash*, (repr. Clifton, N. J. 1966) pp. 161-169. Compare b. Shab. 152a, A.Z. 17b, 'Eruv, 79b, 80a. The words occur in both Babylonian and Palestinian contexts. See also Funk, *op. cit.*, II, pp. 53-54, n. 5, and Nöldeke, *Tabari*, p. 24, n. 4, p. 349, n. 1.

[2] See Appendix I for the content of later disputations.

[3] See S. Lieberman, *JQR* n.s. 37, 1946, p. 45, "The rabbis, most probably, were not familiar at first hand with the *leges sacrae* of the various divinities, but they knew many of their regulations from personal contact with the Gentiles." Lieberman speaks specifically of Palestine. See also vol. II, pp. 79-92, vol. III, pp. 29-37.

[4] b. A.Z. 42a.

[5] Vol. II, pp. 72-91, vol. III, pp. 29ff.

inherited strict rules that any sort of contact by a non-Jew would render wine unfit for Jewish use. In this generation, these rules were carefully enforced, as is attested by numerous cases. The case reports follow:

> It happened in Maḥoza that a pagan [lit.: star-worshipper] came into a Jewish store. He said, "Do you have wine for sale." They replied, "No." Wine was set there in a bucket. He put his hands in and splashed about and said, "Is this not wine?" Angrily, the shop-keeper took the wine and poured it back into the cask. Rava permitted him to sell the wine to pagans....
>
> (b. A.Z. 57b)

> A certain cask split lengthwise. A pagan jumped forward and clasped it in his arms. Rafram bar Papa—and some say, R. Huna b. R. Joshua permitted it to be sold to pagans...
>
> (b. A.Z. 60b)

> In a certain town there was wine belonging to a Jew. A pagan was found among the jars. Rava said, "If he would be arrested on that account like a thief, the wine is permitted, but if not, it is forbidden."
>
> (b. A.Z. 61b)[1]

> The father of R. 'Aḥa' son of R. 'Ika [a wine-dealer] used to pour the wine for pagans [into their own jars] and carry it across the ford for them. He would be given the jars as a reward. They came and told Abaye. He said to them, "When he worked [by pouring the wine] he did that which was permitted...."
>
> (b. A.Z. 65a-b)

> Wine belonging to a Jew was set in a certain house. A pagan came and locked the door behind him. There was a crack in the door, and the heathen was found standing among the jars. Rava said, "All those which were opposite the crack are permitted, but those on either side are forbidden."
>
> Wine belonging to a Jew was set in a house where a Jew lived on the second floor, and a gentile on the ground floor. Once they heard the sound of an argument. They went out. The pagan came back first and locked the door behind him. Rava said, "The wine is permitted, because he must have thought, 'Just as I came back first, the Jew came back first and he is sitting up stairs and watching me.'"
>
> Wine belonging to a Jew was set in an inn. A heathen was found sitting among the jars. Rava said, "If he would be arrested as a thief, the wine is permitted, otherwise it is prohibited."[2]
>
> Wine was set in a certain house. A pagan was found standing among

---

[1] A second case is found here in which Rava issued a decision. His reasoning in this case is this: If the man were in danger of arrest, he would not touch the casks, for fear that he would be thought a thief.

[2] See b. A.Z. 61b for apparently the same case, as cited above.

the jars. Rava said, "If he has an excuse, the wine is prohibited, otherwise it is permitted."

A Jew and a pagan were sitting and drinking wine together. The Jew heard the sound of prayer in the synagogue. He rose and went. Rava said, "The wine is permitted. The (pagan) would say, 'Now he is going to remember the wine and come back.'"

A Jew and a pagan were seated in a ship. The Jew heard the sound of the ram's horn that the Sabbath was coming. He arose and went away. Rava said, "The wine is permitted. He would say, 'Now he is going to remember the wine and come back...'"

A lion once growled in a wine-press, and a pagan heard it and hid among the casks. Rava said "The wine is permitted, for he would say, 'Just as I am hidden, so a Jew may be hidden here behind me and may be watching me.'"

Some thieves came to Pumbedita and opened many casks. Rava ruled that the wine is permitted because most thieves are Jews.

(b. A.Z. 70a)

A certain pagan girl was found among the casks of wine, holding in her hand some of the froth. Rava said, "The wine is permitted. I should say that she obtained it from outside the cask, and though none was there any longer, we say she happened to find some."

(b. A.Z. 70b)

Rava instructed the wine-dealers, "When you pour wine, do not let a pagan come near to help you..."

(b. A.Z. 72b)

A man was drawing wine through a large and small tube (siphon). A pagan came and put his hand on the large tube, and Rava disqualified all the wine [even that in the full cask]....

(b. A.Z. 72b)

Rava taught, "Scald the vat [of pagans before Jews may use it]." When Rava sent jars to Harpania, he placed them mouth downwards [in bags] the hem of which he sealed. It was his opinion that the rabbis prohibited every utensil into which (wine) is put for keeping (by a pagan) even for a short time...

(b. A.Z. 74b)[1]

We have before us fourteen transcripts and one case cited in a note[2] in which Rava and others issued instructions and, more important, court rulings, on the proper handling of wine. One can hardly come to any conclusions on whether Rava was "lenient" or "strict" in the

---

[1] For further rulings, see b. A.Z. 30a, Rabbah, R. Joseph and Rava on diluted wine which has been left uncovered; on whether boiled wine becomes prohibited in contact with a pagan; 32a, R. Joseph on the vinegar which Aramaeans used to make beer; 33b, Rava on putting beer into a wine vessel of gentiles; etc.

[2] Note p. 59, n. 1 above.

enforcement of the rules prohibiting the contact of pagans with the wine of Jews. Such a judgment would require a study, which would lead us far afield, on the relevant laws and the views held by others about them. What is important is the cases themselves. They indicate that Rava and several others were able to make legal decisions about the permissibility of wine in many doubtful situations. There can be little doubt that the laws prohibiting Jews to consume wine which gentiles have touched in any way, however remote, were carefully and meticulously carried out wherever the rabbinical market-supervisors could enforce them. Many ordinary people must have accepted the rabbinical rulings, for some of the cases cited above involved events which could not have taken place in the actual presence of rabbis. The person would have had to consult a rabbi, and hence would have wanted to, before such a ruling would be issued. I think it clear, therefore, that the taboo concerning the touch of a pagan on any object pertaining to wine was widely believed to be valid. Pagans were supposedly aware of the Jewish taboo. Keeping the taboo, even though it must have led to both inconvenience and financial loss for the wine-dealers—and wine was an expensive commodity in Babylonia—would have reminded ordinary people of the distance that separated them from the pagan and of the strict rules against mingling Judaism with other religions.

x. JEWS AND PAGANS

The rabbis of this generation held that undying hatred exists between Judaism and paganism. They explained it as a consequence of divine revelation to Israel:

> A certain one of the rabbis asked R. Kahana, "Have you heard the meaning of 'Mount Sinai?'" He replied, "The mountain on which miracles (*nissim*) were done for Israel." "Then it should be called 'Mount Nissai.'" "Rather, the mountain on which was made a good sign (*siman tov*) for Israel." "Then it should be called 'Mount Simnai.'" He said to him, "Why are you not found before R. Papa and R. Huna b. R. Joshua, who study *'aggadah*, for R. Ḥisda and Rabbah b. R. Huna both say, 'What is the meaning of Mount Sinai? The mountain on which descended hatred (*sinah*) of the pagans [or, of paganism]'."
>
> (b. Shab. 89a)

Even though the Jewish courts could not adjudicate the affairs of non-Jews and certainly could not punish them for crimes or sins, the rabbis continued to discuss laws which would be applied to them. The

spirit of these discussions was reflected in the saying above.[1] Rava
furthermore proved that a gentile who raped a married woman in an
unnatural manner was not punishable.[2] R. Naḥman b. Isaac explained
a Tannaitic decree that a heathen child defiles by gonorrhea so that a
Jewish child should not associate with him; the danger of sodomy was
believed to be the real reason for the prohibition.[3] R. Naḥman's saying
is in the spirit of that of R. 'Aḥa' b. 'Adda' in the name of R. Isaac:

> "They decreed against their bread on account of their wine, against
> their oil on account of their wine... and against their wine on account
> of their daughters..."
>
> (b. Shab. 17b)[4]

The only formal and not-neutral relationship to gentiles to be encouraged was one in which conversion was at issue. We have one
conversion story dating from this period:

> Rava said, "Issur the convert said to me, 'When we were Aramaeans,
> we used to say that the Jews do not keep the Sabbath, for if they did,
> how many purses would we find in the market, and I did not know...
> [the rule that] ... one may carry a purse found on the Sabbath four
> cubits...'"
>
> (b. A.Z. 70a)

Conversion to Judaism might have been fairly common in some
places because R. Joseph expressed surprise that a certain community,
the Gubaeans, never produced a single convert to Judaism.[5] Discussions on the laws pertaining to conversion included Rava's, that if
a pregnant gentile was converted, the unborn child did not require
baptism.[6] R. Joseph and Abaye spoke about the conversion of the
gentiles in the age to come.[7]

The rabbis made or discussed laws about the proper relationship
between Jews and pagans. Their purpose was invariably to preserve a
high barrier between Jew and pagan, in particular in matters relating
to pagan rite and cult. Rava and Abaye discussed the reason for the
Tannaitic legislation against lending to and borrowing from pagans at

---

[1] See the discussions in b. Sanh. 56b-57a.

[2] b. Sanh. 58b.

[3] b. Shab. 17b. Note also R. Naḥman b. Isaac said that in the same decrees was
included the declaration that a female was unclean in the status of a menstrual
woman from her very cradle, b. Shab. 16b.

[4] Vol. III, p. 32. See b. A.Z. 31b.

[5] b. Ber. 17b. On conversions to Judaism, see Funk, *op. cit.*, II, p. 53.

[6] b. Yev. 78a.

[7] b. A.Z. 24a.

their festival seasons. The prohibition against lending required no discussion, but the reason for that against borrowing did. Abaye held the reason was to safeguard against lending, and Rava thought that even by borrowing, one gave the pagan pleasure by thanking him.[1] Rava further taught, in expounding Ex. 34:15, that one may not in any degree share in the wedding celebration of a pagan, thirty days following a marriage celebration being specified as a period in which social intercourse would be forbidden. R. Papa held it was for a full year thereafter. The reason for this prohibition derived from a Tannaitic teaching in the name of R. Ishmael that even though a Jew eats and drinks of his own food at a pagan celebration, by his very presence, Scripture holds, it is as if he had eaten "the sacrifices of dead idols."[2] R. Joseph explained that a Jewish woman may act as a midwife for a pagan woman only for payment, but not gratuitously. The service in return for payment is permitted to prevent ill feeling, for the Jewish midwife could not then offer an excuse for refusing to do so. R. Joseph considered permitting wet-nursing for payment or the like, but Abaye provided possible excuses for the woman to give, and R. Joseph did not so teach. What is important here is the effort of the rabbis to limit even acts of personal service or kindness of all kinds.[3] By contrast, Rava announced that one may invite a heathen for a meal on the Sabbath, but not on a festival.[4]

Were these laws enforced? The evidence deriving from stories about how rabbis and others actually behaved suggests that they were not. We consider, for example, the following account:

> Rava sent an animal-sacrifice to Bar Shishakh on a pagan festival, saying, "I know concerning him that he does not worship idols." He went and found him sitting up to his neck in a bath of rose-water, and naked whores were standing before him. He said to him, "Do you [Jews] have anything like this in the world to come?" He [Rava] replied, "We have it even better." "Better than this—is there such a thing?" He replied, "You are still afraid of the government, but [in the world to come] we shall no longer be afraid of the government." Bar Shishakh replied, "I am not afraid of the government" While they were sitting, a government agent [parastak] came. He said to him,

---

[1] b. A.Z. 6b.

[2] b. A.Z. 8a.

[3] b. A.Z. 26a. On cooking by gentiles, see R. Joseph, b. A.Z. 38a; on the use of pagans for castrating animals, see Rava and Abaye, b. B.M. 90b. The spirit of Constantine's and Constantius's laws against Jews' owning non-Jewish slaves is reflected here.

[4] b. Beẓ. 21b.

"Come along, for they want you at court." As he was going out, he
said [to Rava], "May the eye that wishes to see evil upon you people
burst." Rava replied, "Amen." And Bar Shishakh's eye burst.

(b. A.Z. 65a)

The importance of this story is not whether Rava "really" sent an
animal-sacrifice to Bar Shishakh or not. We have no way of knowing,
nor does it matter. As the story now stands, the one hard fact is that
someone thought it important to tell a story proving that even the best
of the pagans, a man who, a distinguished rabbi believed, did not
really worship idols—such a man in the end wished ill for the Jews.

The story, however, is patently composite. Its original element was
the report that Rava sent an animal to Bar Shishakh on a pagan festival
and the explanation which Rava either gave, or, it was supposed,
would have given, "Because I know he does not worship idols." Then
comes another story and a different one. In the first story, Rava sent
the animal, in the second, he went himself. The point of the second
story is that the world to come is better than the best of this world
because it also has security from the government. The "original" inter-
locutors may have been Rava and Bar Shishakh, but whether they
were or not, the story is hardly credible. Whether or not Rava had
friends who would receive him in such circumstances, the timely arrival of the summons at the appropriate point in the discussion is
typical of homiletical exempla, not of reports of real life events. As the
complex now stands, the concluding conversation is a third story. It
may have been added entire as such, or it may have grown. The first
stage would be Bar Shishakh's parting remark, meaning "You spoke
well, I now see the superiority of the Jewish hope, admire the Jews,
and wish their enemies evil." And to this, later malice or psychological
interpretation added the present conclusion. At all events the present
form of the story is certainly far later than Rava, and offers no very
firm evidence as to the attitudes of his time or circle. The one fact
concerning his time which it preserves is that he had a gentile friend
to whom he, like Rav Judah earlier, sent a sacrifice on a festival.[1]

Presumably a great many Jews must have thought that their friends
of other religions "did not really worship idols" and did sincerely feel
friendship for the Jews. The details about how a pagan identifies sensual
pleasures with the wonders of the world to come are part of the old,
well-known polemic: "Pagans enjoy this world, we shall enjoy the
next. Their pleasures are coarse. They have no security in their en-

---

[1] I am grateful to Professor Morton Smith for the preceding analysis.

joyment." I should suppose that Bar Shishakh would have been an Aramaean,[1] and that it was with the ordinary, Aramaic-speaking Babylonian gentile, rather than with the Greek-speaking city people, or the Christians, or the Pahlavi-speaking Iranians, that the Jews found closest ties.[2]

Several cases of law came before Rava in which a Jew and a pagan were in partnership with one another and mutually profited from the religion of the other, as the following:

> Certain saffron-growers came before Rava. One was a pagan who watched the field on the Sabbath, the other a Jew who did so on Sunday. Rava declared the partnership permissible ... R. Geviha of Be Katil reported the case of *orlah* plants. The pagan was to eat the produce during the forbidden years, and the Jew during permitted ones. Rava permitted the arrangement...
>
> (b. A. Z. 22a)

Other rabbis did not share Rava's opinion. What is significant is not that the partners worked together to circumvent inconveniences imposed by Judaism, but that they worked together at all. It is striking that in the face of very severe and far-reaching laws about proper relationships with gentiles, Jews and pagans did enter into many kinds of ordinary, day-to-day relationships. Whether or not the rabbis believed that these relationships were proper,[3]—and the stories they told generally emphasized that the gentile felt undying ill-will toward the Jew and was not to be trusted—ordinary people did as they thought best. One story suggests they had good reason to trust their neighbors:

> Abaye lost an ass among the *Kutim*. He sent word to them, "Return him to me." They replied, "Send us evidence of ownership, such as an identifying mark." He sent back, "He has a white belly." They replied, "Were you not Naḥmani, we should not return him to you. How many asses have white bellies!"
>
> (b. Git. 45a)

The "Kutim"[4] clearly respected Abaye, and behaved honestly. The data are not rich, but the evidence all points in the direction of close,

---

[1] Note above, b. A.Z. 70a, Issur said, "When we were Aramaeans."

[2] On the gift of a candelabrum to the synagogue of Rav Judah in Pumbedita by a Tai Arab, see b. 'Arakh. 6b, and vol. III, pp. 30-31.

[3] Note that Rabbah sold an ass to a Jew who was suspected of selling animals to idolaters, b. A.Z. 15b. He explained that there was no reason to suppose he would do so with that particular animal. So some Jews, we do not know how many, ignored the rabbinical laws on this subject.

[4] Generally, Samaritans, but not in Babylonia, and I do not know which group were called "Kutim" by the rabbis.

day-to-day contacts between Jews and pagans. The view of the virtuosi cannot have shaped these contacts, or they would have proved impossible. Even some rabbis thought they could maintain close ties with pagans—Samuel,[1] Rav Judah,[2] Rava—and stories were told in the academies about how unwise they were to trust them. The need to tell such stories reveals more about the actualities of the streets than any contrary sayings about the law on Jewish-pagan relationships.[3]

XI. SUMMARY

Jewry both profited and suffered from the contest for the Middle East which occupied most of the age of Shapur II. On the one hand, both sides were eager to avoid creating new enemies. On the other, they sought to subvert the enemy's population. So in preparation for his Persian campaign, Julian very likely made an effort to win over the Jewish communities of Palestine, Syria and Mesopotamia, first, by freeing them from the onerous and apparently unwanted burden of supporting the Palestinian patriarchate as well as by refraining from demanding discriminatory taxes levied upon Jews alone, and second, by promising to rebuild the Temple. I think, however, that the earlier "anti-Semitic" decrees of Constantine and Constantius, when separated from the nasty language the emperors used when speaking of the Jews, must have been of less consequence than has heretofore been supposed. Following A. H. M. Jones and Saul Lieberman, I suggested that the prohibitions against conversions, against circumcizing slaves and even holding non-Jewish ones, and the like were of no substantial consequence in the life of ordinary Jews. Slave-holding and converting gentiles were of importance mainly to two groups, the former to rich people, the latter to religious virtuosi. I should imagine that the normal life of the Jewish community was not greatly disrupted. It stands to reason, moreover, that the factors which motivated Julian could not have been irrelevant to the Christian emperors. However pious and faithful to the new religion, they had still to consider the effects of their decrees upon the international position of the Roman Empire in the east. The strategic position of the Jews, straddling a contested frontier,

---

[1] Vol. I, pp. 162-163, vol. II, pp. 85-86.

[2] Vol. III, p. 30.

[3] Many of these stories may be considerably later than the period concerned and may reflect a later-developed hostility's trying to explain away evidence of better relations which had prevailed at an earlier time. This matter requires further study in the context of a history of Babylonian rabbinic literature.

numerous in precisely the most endangered areas, namely northern Mesopotamian cities such as Edessa and Nisibis, and throughout the Babylonian countryside, forced the emperors to temper their religious enthusiasm. I think Jones's comment, that whatever their expressed opinions, the Christian emperors' laws were quite moderate, finds explanation in this fact.

In the Sasanian Empire, Jewry enjoyed a no less favorable position. Among the inhabitants of Babylonia, they must have supported Shapur's first efforts to pacify the region and reestablish a strong frontier against the desert tribes. Like others, they found the burden of an efficient collection of taxes to be onerous, but not unbearable, particularly since they sought means of evading them when possible. If, as is alleged in the *SOZ*, there was a persecution of the Jews in 313, then it must have been some local, perhaps private, matter involving a small group, for in the unrest and disorder of the years from 309 to 325, no central administration was sufficiently effective to undertake a large-scale persecution of any minority community. The rabbis in Babylonia enjoyed a reputation as exceptionally sage and powerful wonder-workers. They could make rain, 'Ifra Hormizd believed, and she allegedly warned her son, the emperor, "Whatever they ask of their Master, he gives them." While I think these stories have slight basis in fact, they do preserve a quite accurate picture of the rabbis—among other holy men—as theurges to be cultivated. If so, the Jews would have been seen as a community not to be trifled with, for among them were men who could enlist the favor of heaven. That consideration did not, of course, prevent the government from overseeing the Jewish courts as before or from collecting taxes despite the evasive behavior of the rabbis; but it would have provided a safeguard against gratuitous persecution. Traditions relating to Shapur II do not contain a hint of "anti-Semitism" or of any hostile action whatever. He supposedly respected the religious practices of some rabbis and made inquiries about the biblical foundations of burial, a rite abhorrent to Zoroastrian sensibilities. We have no evidence that a decree against burial of the dead, such as was mentioned in earlier times,[1] was now under consideration, despite the emperor's interest in building a strong state-church. It is true that some generalized references to "harsh decrees" and "persecutions" can be located in the stratum of traditions relating to this period. Nothing comparable to the stories pertaining

---

[1] Vol. II, p. 35.

to Ardashir's time[1] or to the boast of Kartir[2] appeared in traditions on the age of Shapur II.

On the other hand, the Jews preserved hostile attitudes toward the Persians, by contrast, first, to Parthian times, and second to the stories about Shapur I and Samuel. I should suppose that by R. Joseph's time —he died about 330—the long years of unstable government eroded whatever good will had developed within Jewry in the years of Shapur I. R. Papa's comment reveals that the local gendarmes continued to be bitterly resented by the Jews, no more so, however, than "the proud" among their own group. By contrast, both Abaye and Rava remarked about the lawfulness of the government and admitted that the Persian courts did not take bribes once a decree had been issued, a sure sign of a relatively uncorrupted court-system. In the balance, I should judge that Shapur II did establish a system of fair and even-handed administration, but that the Jews, like other communities in Babylonia, nonetheless objected to the high taxes and the petty indignities inflicted by both the wars of the day and the normal, everyday activities of alien local authorities.

Jewry shared not only the cost of the wars but, in 363, the enormous damage to life and property which followed as their consequence. The invasion of that year devastated precisely the lands in which Babylonian Jews were settled. Towns were destroyed by Romans or Persians; the fields ravaged; and as the armies moved across central Babylonia, scorching the crops and flooding the fields, one Jewish village after another must have met the fate of the unnamed town whose burning was described by Ammianus Marcellinus. On the other hand, there is no evidence that large numbers of people died in the invasion, and as soon as it had passed, most people must have been able to return to their villages and fields and undertake the task of reconstruction. We do not have any evidence concerning what the Jews actually did in the invasion. We know that villagers fled out of the line of war. But we do not know whether Jews or others in Babylonia joined in the armies of Shapur or supported those of Julian. Some have supposed that the Jews remained loyal to Shapur, and that in consequence he recognized their loyalty and rewarded it. I think it unlikely that they actually *did* anything at all. The wars were wars of pagan powers—Gog and Magog, so far as anyone knew—and not the affair of Israel. It is a perfect anachronism to speak of the "loyalty" of the "Persian" Jews to "their"

---

[1] Vol. II, pp. 27-39.
[2] Vol. II, pp. 17-19, and III, pp. 17-24.

government. The Jews were not Persians, but Jews. They neither rebelled against the Sasanian government nor went over to the enemy, because they had no reason to do either. But they supported Shapur no more than did the many towns and fortresses along the Euphrates that silently watched the Roman army and armada pass by—unopposed and unaided. If Rome triumphed, they promised their support. For the meanwhile they remained quite neutral. Whether Shapur had given orders to that effect or not we do not know. A very few Persians joined the Roman army, as a few Romans had earlier gone over to Shapur, generally for private reasons. As a group, the Jews did neither; it was only Julian's memories of Trajan's invasion that aroused in his mind a contrary expectation. Shapur's later deportations of Jews from Armenia to Isfahan and Susiana, moreover, are not to be interpreted as hostile to the Jews. Population represented wealth, and just as Shapur I re-settled Roman captives in his empire to enhance its economic life, so his namesake later on both prevented emigration and forced immi-gration when he could. The Jewish population of the Sasanian Empire grew not because of either hatred or love for Jews. Rather the Jews were a useful group who did nothing of a subversive nature in Shapur's reign, and new groups of Jews therefore could be safely moved to developing regions of the empire.

Jewry may have maintained neutrality in international politics but not in religion. The Christians remained in the eyes of Judaism apos-tates, as indeed many must have been. All other forms of religion were called "worship of stars." Distinctions were not made among them. Jews had, the rabbis thought, to be kept quite separate from "pagans." Strict laws about the preservation of wine from contact with gentiles continued to be enforced very widely. We noted fourteen or fifteen examples of such law enforcement. Earlier[1] we found two cases dating to the time of Rav and Samuel, and three instances of law enforcement in the time of Rav Judah and R. Ḥisda. Whether the three-fold increase in the number of instances of law enforcement reflected a vast improve-ment in the rabbis' power to enforce the laws pertaining to wine I cannot say. It may be that the cases, most of which arose in Rava's court, have come down to us because of some peculiarity of literary history. I think that the numerous civil law cases of R. Naḥman reached us because his court records were preserved, and those of other courts were not, and that the reason for their preservation was his high po-sition in the exilarchate and the consequent probative value of his

---

[1] Vol. III, p. 330.

precedents.[1] So we cannot be certain that the laws about wine were kept to a greater degree in the fourth century than in the third; but we may be fairly sure that they were widely enforced where rabbinical courts and market-supervisors were located. The taboo concerning gentile contact with wine would constantly have reminded ordinary Jews of the importance of keeping their distance from other people. The revelation at Sinai had implanted an undying hatred between Israel and the pagan world, so the rabbis believed, and it was the rabbis' task to insure that social separation would preserve the purity of the faith.

That did not mean that ordinary people avoided workaday contact with gentiles, or that they could have had they wanted to. On the contrary, the evidence suggests both close economic and intimate social contacts. Decrees against attending pagans' wedding celebrations, even against coming to their homes within thirty days, or a whole year, of such celebrations, had to be made probably because common people did what they forbade. Stories were told of most distinguished rabbis who believed that exceptional gentiles "do not worship idols" and might therefore be trusted and honored. One might suppose that gifts might even be given to such trustworthy gentiles. But this is not so. Even the best of gentiles are lewd and have evil intent, so the story said. It would suggest that people even in rabbinical circles thought the contrary was the case. The viewpoint of Deuteronomy shaped that of the rabbis of this period, as of earlier times, but it did not necessarily conform to the realities of daily life. Indeed, had the Jews widely observed the strict letter of the law as interpreted by the rabbis and behaved toward "pagans" as the rabbis said they ought, stable community life could not have been sustained for very long. If there is little, if any, evidence of government persecution of the Jews, there is none at all of popular feeling against them in Babylonia (unlike Edessa and other Christian centers). I think one reason for the absence of widespread popular hatred of the Jews is that the Jews probably did little, if anything, to keep the rabbis' laws about how one must behave toward "paganism" and toward "pagans." On the contrary, the Christian hagiographical literature repeatedly preserves stories about how Jews and Magi worked hand in hand in persecuting the Christians, in particular. Whether these stories are true or not, they suggest that the Christians discerned little if any enmity between Jewry and the Iranian political or religious leaders.

[1] Vol. III, pp. 61-75.

For the seven decades of Shapur II's rule, the Middle East thus was in turmoil. First came a period of ineffective government, lasting from ca. 309 to ca. 325, when the conditions of daily life must have proved difficult. Arab tribes seized land and took people captive for ransom; trade must have been disrupted. The government, in the hands of regents, scarcely controlled the powerful local magnates. The empire seemed to be disintegrating, and for the common people of Babylonia, life became dangerous. When Shapur took power, he organized an effective army controlled by the central government. The new army, and the campaigns it fought, first in the south to recover the mouth of the Tigris and Euphrates and to reestablish command of the Persian Gulf, and finally in the west and north, required enormous sums of money. Along with the army, a more effective bureaucracy and a unified state-church were established, and these insured more efficient control of the population and collection of taxes. In place of the ransom paid to marauders by unfortunate people came levies which everyone had to pay. From 337 to 363, moreover, annual campaigns brought the emperor and his army into the field. After the great triumph of 363, Shapur turned to Armenia and made a number of political and military ventures in the north and northwest. Throughout these years, therefore, the farmers and artisans of Babylonia must have found life a succession of trials, some imposed by foreigners, others by the imperial government. One group, the Christians, suffered disaster when the government imposed special taxes which they could not pay, then demanded that Christians worship the sun and the stars and give up monotheism.

Against this background, one must interpret the limited information deriving from mostly Jewish sources concerning the condition of the Jewish community. The data present a mostly negative picture. That is to say, the rabbis did not preserve traditions about persecution. They certainly had to pay no abnormally high taxes on account of their religion. They were not singled out for punishment by the chiliarchs and gendarmes whom they hated. Life was difficult for them, to be sure, but it was far more difficult for the Christians, and it was no easier for others in the Sasanian Empire. It was a time of troubles, but better the troubles coming on account of the campaigns of a strong and eventually victorious empire than those caused by the weak and distracted reigns that separated Shapur I from Shapur II. Many generations would enjoy peace and security on account of the temporary difficulties of the age of Shapur II. His victory settled for centuries the fate of Mesopotamia and insured for as long the stable and placid life of Babylonia.

I do not, therefore, think that the Jews were singled out for special sorrows. If it was a difficult time, everyone shared the difficulties as I said, and some, but not the Jews, had far more than their share. So far as history is the story of politics and wars, emperors and their grand campaigns, the Jews had no history worth much attention. Their surviving records provide remarkably little evidence about what engaged most people in Shapur's day. The records of Sasanian history pay them just as slight heed. The events and movements which constitute Babylonian Jewish history took place upon another stage, and for another audience. Iranian and Babylonian Jewish history scarcely meet in the age of Shapur II.

CHAPTER TWO

EXILARCHATE AND RABBINATE: LOOSENING TIES

I. The Exilarchate at the Turn of the Fourth Century

The exilarch had originally encouraged the growth of the rabbinic movement in Babylonia, supported its academies, and appointed its leaders to high posts in the courts and administration of Babylonian Jewry. In the fourth century, however, he faced a deepening estrangement.[1] In Rav's and Samuel's day, the rabbis had been employees of the exilarch and generally supported his interests in their schools. Now some began to seek greater independence and a freer hand in running Jewry. Traditions pertaining to the early Sasanian period leave no doubt about who earlier had predominated. Rav was imprisoned for failing to enforce the law as the exilarch demanded. Samuel loyally supported the exilarch and was very likely his representative to the new Persian regime in the time of Shapur I. Others of their generation including Shila and Qarna were similarly employed. Whatever actual legal authority rabbis exerted was based upon "authorization," that is to say actual appointment by the exilarch to his administration. Nor did matters greatly change in the last third of the third century. Most, though not all, leading rabbis loyally served and supported the exilarchate. R. Naḥman b. Jacob, Rabbah b. Abbuha his father-in-law, and many others both took a leading place in the rabbinical movement, as law teachers and chiefs of schools, and also served the exilarch as judges and administrators. Before the death of Rav Judah b. Ezekiel in 299, the question was never raised, who appoints the head of the schools? No one doubted that the exilarch, who paid for their support and employed their graduates, had that right. Nor did anyone publicly ask whether the rabbis, who distinguished themselves through variant patterns of behavior, dress, and speech, were liable to pay the poll-tax along with all the other Jews. This latter issue certainly came to the

---

[1] For discussion of the origins and early history of the exilarchate, see vol. I, 2nd printing revised, pp. 50-58, 101-112; the history of the third century exilarchate will be found in vol. II, pp. 92-125, and vol. III, pp. 41-94.

fore in this time, and the former *may* have been raised as well. The central questions of Jewish politics were fought out in them.

Control of the schools meant more than supervision of the curriculum, about which the exilarch cannot have concerned himself. The schools trained the lawyers, administrators, and judges upon whom the exilarch relied for the substance of his day-to-day power over the life of the Jewish community. The loyalty of future graduates as in the past was absolutely essential for control. If the exilarch could not continue to assert his mastery over the rabbis, even in the short run his administration would be compromised. In the long run he would have to accept a figure-head status, as the symbolic head of a community run by others, retaining some importance in dealing with the Persian government, but none at all at home. Having come to rely upon the rabbinical schools in preference to any others which earlier may have flourished,[1] the exilarch could not now afford to lose control of those schools. If the graduates, whose influence was growing, undermined the exilarch or merely ignored him whenever possible, then the exilarch quickly would be reduced to a mere court-Jew, an ambassador to the

---

[1] Since all of our records come from rabbinical schools and were edited in a few of them, we have no knowledge of other, or earlier, centers of legal study in Babylonia. It seems to me likely that before the advent of the first rabbis, in the second century A.D., Babylonian Jewry did enjoy the services of trained lawyers, such as those whose knowledge of the law matched that of the Palestinian messengers in b. Git. 14b (vol. I, 2nd printing revised, pp. 94-96). These Jewish lawyers dressed and spoke like Parthians, so the Palestinians recalled. Whatever they were, they were *not* rabbis. Since we know the names of only a few rabbis in the early Sasanian period, it seems probable that other Jewish authorities from Parthian times enjoyed considerable power, also under the patronage of the exilarch and within his administration. But we hear nothing whatever about them in the Talmudic sources as they come down to us, though R. Papa's reference, cited above, to "the proud" and to the resentment of them felt by himself and those sympathetic to his message, would suggest that powerful Jewish leadership competed even in this period against the rabbis, at least in some places. If, as I suppose, Babylonian Jewry numbered more than 800,000 (see vol. II, pp. 240-250), it stands to reason that the very small number of leading rabbis whose names are known to us (Beer counts 800 over 300 years) were not the sole administrators and legal authorities. The handful of schools could not have produced a sufficiency of learned men. So I may conjecture that the early Babylonian Jewish law-traditions by which Jews lived, married, litigated their affairs, and passed on legacies, long before the first rabbinical school or court was set up among them, continued to be studied in other than rabbinical schools. Indeed, the Talmud was shaped mostly in the schools of Sura and Pumbedita and focuses upon the great rabbis, mainly heads of the schools, whose sayings form the spiritual legacy and authoritative precedents of those two schools. For all we know, other schools and rabbis, who play a relatively minor role in Talmudic discussions, left far more extensive bodies of sayings than were eventually redacted in the Babylonian Talmud as we have it.

Sasanian throne, with no solid foundation even for his role at court.

Whether or not the rabbis paid the head-tax was a similarly pregnant question, for it probably was the exilarch who imposed the taxes, divided them among Jews of various towns and groups, collected, and transmitted them to the state on specified occasions. It would hardly enhance his authority if he could not impose his will upon everyone including the rabbis. Choosing to make the payment of the poll tax the decisive issue, the rabbis asserted that they were not like other Jews, but formed a special class which should not be subjected either to the authority of the exilarch or to the control of the state. Furthermore, if the rabbis did not pay taxes, their share would have to be borne by others. We do not know who the rabbis thought would pay their share other than the rest of Jewry. Whether it was to be divided among everyone else, or whether the exilarch was supposed to make it up from his revenues, in either way the lives of ordinary people would be made more expensive. It was the rabbis who raised the issue for reasons of their own. So both questions now agitated rabbinical circles. For his part, the exilarch saw no reason to change the status quo of two centuries' standing.

Neither did Shapur's government. The Jews had been satisfactorily governed for the century of Sasanian rule. The earlier agreement, that the law of the state is law for Jewish courts, meant that Sasanian officials no longer had to oversee what went on in them. In place of a potentially subversive institution inherited from the Arsacids, the Sasanians thus fostered a loyal and efficient one. The exilarch not only collected taxes, but kept peace within the Jewish community. The Persian state did not intend to force minority groups to conform to Iranian law. The Jewish millet was free to live according to its own laws. When Shapur II came to power, in about 325, he had more pressing worries than the internal affairs of the Jewish community. He spent most of his year on the battlefield. He needed at home a strong, sure, stable government, and it was this that the exilarch and his administration provided among the Jews. So it was very much to the interest of Shapur and his ministers to strengthen the satisfactory arrangement they had inherited. They had no reason to change it, and every reason to be grateful for it. Except on the occasion of major threats to the security of the State, such as Mani's subversion of the state-church, or the pro-Roman attitude of the Babylonian and Adiabenian Christians, Shapur like his predecessors never intervened in minority religions. Such trivial matters as whether some of his subjects believed in the sun, the moon, or some other deity, or whether they married close relatives, or whether they worshipped fire, never interested him. It is not that he recognized so abstract a right as "freedom of religion." Nor would he have been displeased by mass conformity to Mazdean rites. It was simply that he had inherited the government of a varied group of peoples, and was determined to keep the peace with, and a-mong them, while he and his ministers concentrated on more important matters. Nothing suited his purposes for administering Jewry more than the exilarch. Only rabbis now sought change in the old arrangements.

Why did rabbis choose just this time to claim they did not have to pay taxes and possibly[1] also to demand the right to run the rabbinical schools? In part, the reason was that they were convinced they had no other correct course, and in part the time seemed promising. From Shapur I's death, in 273, to the end of the minority of Shapur II, in about 325, the central government was distracted by, among other things, disastrous foreign wars, the suppression of the Manichaeans, dynastic struggles every few years, and finally the centrifugal effects of the weak regency. When Shapur II came to power, his attention was drawn to international and military issues. The Sasanian government in his time simply never paid the Jews much attention, so long as the revenues were forthcoming and nothing subversive happened. Both conditions were met. The rabbis' subversion was not directed at the Sasanian government. Unless the government understood why it was important for the exilarch to appoint the heads of the Jewish schools, it would not intervene. So long as the full quota of head-taxes was paid, it hardly mattered to the state who actually paid them, or who did not.[2] Greater affairs of state must have preoccupied not only Shapur, who was certainly not consulted on trivialities such as these, but also the ministers of Ctesiphon. The Jewish question was a local matter, without much consequence. Had they seen otherwise, the ministers of Shapur would have been perfectly well prepared to investigate anti-government activity and punish those they thought guilty. The same satraps and Mobads who tortured and put to death the Christian monks and nuns, priests, bishops, and laity of Babylonia and Adiabene for not paying taxes were quite capable of "persecuting" the rabbis, if not the Jews as a group, had they thought it useful to the security of the state.

---

[1] See below, pp. 91-100.

[2] I doubt that any rabbis actually had the effrontery to issue such a claim or that the census-takers would have been fooled had they done so. See below, p. 88.

They did nothing of the sort (except, allegedly, in the case of Rabbah)[1] and I suppose they saw no reason to. Once the great persecution against the Christians began, moreover, the exilarch could hardly have called to his aid those whose capacities for bloody mischief now stood fully revealed. Had he asked for state aid in suppressing the rabbinate as a class, he would have embittered the ordinary Jews against himself, and the record of rabbinical martyrdoms, accompanied by the conventional miracles, done by both heavenly messengers and earthly saints, would have rendered him totally distasteful to common folk. Under normal circumstances ordinary people may have supported him, but not in a time of martyrdom of a few particularly holy men. It seems to me therefore that the exilarch at first was unwilling, and then quite unable to enlist the powers of the state. And the state, unknowing and uninterested, paid attention to quite different matters. Still, in such a circumstance, it was a chancy thing. The rabbis took that chance.

They did so because they believed they should. In the years between Samuel's death, ca. 260, and the first major clash, possibly in ca. 279, an anti-exilarchic party had grown up within the rabbinate. Its viewpoint was shaped in theological terms. The rabbis believed that along with the written Torah, God had revealed to Moses at Mount Sinai an oral, unwritten Torah, which had been preserved and handed on from prophets to sages, and finally to rabbis. Israel's life was to be shaped by divine revelation. The rabbis alone knew the full configuration of the will of God.[2] Their claim to rule rested upon that conviction. It clashed with the consequence, phrased in equally theological terms, drawn by the exilarch from the belief that he was qualified to rule because he was descended from the seed of David. Moreover, rabbinic political theology ran counter to the widespread conviction of Jews that anyone holding political power over them had better be able to claim Davidic ancestry. The rabbis, by contrast, authenticated *their* claim not only by their teaching of Torah, but also by their knowledge of the secrets of creation, including the names of God by which miracles may be produced, the mysteries of astrology, medicine, and practical magic, as well as by their day-to-day conduct as a class of religious virtuosi and illuminati.[3] They eagerly recruited students for their schools, who would join with them in the task of studying the

---

[1] See above, pp. 39-44.
[2] The usefulness to the early exilarchs of such convictions is discussed in vol. I, second printing revised.
[3] See vol. III, pp. 95-194, and below, Chapter Five.

"whole Torah," and go forth afterward to exemplify, and, where feasible, enforce its teaching among the ordinary people. They were seeking totally to reform the life of Israel to conform to the Torah as they taught it. They believed that when Israel would live according to the will of "their father in heaven," then no nation or race could rule over them, but the Anointed of God would do so. History as a succession of pagan empires would come to an end. Israel would live in peace in its own land. An endless age of prosperity on account of Israel's reconciliation with God would follow. So the issues were not inconsiderable.

The stories about R. Naḥman b. Jacob, who died, according to Geonic chronology, in ca. 320, make it clear that two tendencies colored the formation and transmission of traditions about the exilarchate and its rabbinical supporters. R. Naḥman believed that the exilarch represented the right and just fulfillment of prophetic hopes for the restoration of a Jewish ruler descended from David. He should therefore be obeyed. Stories were told about R. Naḥman's arrogance and pride and about his modesty, about his great knowledge of civil laws and about his ignorance. Some held that he had defended a rabbinical colleague who had acted contrary to his conviction about a law, and thus renounced claim to superior learning or status. Others said that he had treated the colleague's court document with disdain, saying that "in civil law, everyone is a child compared to me." Some said his only power derived from the exilarch. Others honored his learning. These stories parallel those told in the time of Rav and Samuel about Mar 'Uqba I. Some of these reported that he honored the piety and learning of the great masters of his day, while they deferred to him in all political issues; others, about a nameless exilarch who could only have been Mar 'Uqba I, told that he imprisoned Rav, was ignorant, and did not keep the law as he was supposed to. That conflicting stories were preserved may easily be explained. Schools and masters hostile to the exilarch could not be brought under his control. We saw[1] that people in one place had never even heard of leading rabbinical authorities in towns not far away. So what was taught in one school may not have been known elsewhere. Under such circumstances, it is likely that the exilarch could not suppress unfavorable traditions; he lacked the necessary knowledge about, and effective authority over, what was taught in all the schools everywhere. The favorable traditions may have been preserved in the exilarchic archives or schools

---

[1] Vol. III, pp. 87-94. Moreover, the exilarch R. Isaac, who ruled in Mesene, was not even well-known in Babylonia to the north. See below, p. 184.

from the beginning.[1] Some, both favorable and hostile, may be later inventions. (Though the hostile sayings generally omitted the name of the exilarch, and the favorable ones invariably included it, some neutral sayings were preserved as well.)

The circle of rabbis opposed to the exilarchate—or to its present form—included R. Sheshet, about whom nasty stories were told. R. Sheshet[2] supposedly did not know the law but kept that fact from the exilarchic "servants" whom he had misinformed. He would not honor the exilarch by eating meat at his table. When later on he found out that he had erred, he avoided making apologies to the exilarch. R. Sheshet was thus the butt of unpleasant stories told by the exilarchic rabbinate.

Underlying these accounts is the obvious fact that the rabbinate of the late third century was deeply divided between those rabbis who served the exilarch and others who did not. R. Sheshet, R. Naḥman b. Isaac, and others regarded the former as lackeys of an ignorant, impious

---

[1] That the Babylonian Talmud preserved these favorable sayings suggests that they were formally redacted, in some early form to be sure, before the rabbis of the opposing school had fully won their struggle. Otherwise the antiexilarchic rabbis would have been able to suppress them. A second, less likely, possibility is that by the time the Talmud was completed, the exact implications of the stories favorable to R. Naḥman, and by inference to the exilarch, had been forgotten. A third possibility is that the suppression of the fact that an unnamed "high Jewish authority," such as one of the Mar 'Uqbans, was actually the exilarch was quite deliberately intended to obscure the favorable record of the exilarchate, and to deny that great men of the past had associated in friendly ways with the exilarch of their day. So the hostile tradition, about the exilarch's impiety and ignorance, invariably omitted the name of the exilarch. The favorable ones left out the fact that the man under discussion actually *was* exilarch. Since these are fairly fixed characteristics of the late third-century traditions, I doubt that it was to begin with an accident in the process of transmission. Rather I suppose that conflicting schools shaped the traditions to conform to their opinions, a quite natural and normal procedure. But if that was the case, then some sort of agreement, or unusual accident, must have happened so that the viewpoints of *both* sides were eventually redacted in the final version of the Babylonian Talmud. I suppose, as I said, that the R. Naḥman stories were redacted fairly early, for otherwise they would not have been transmitted at all. An alternative is that a pro-exilarchic school, or circle, may have continued to exist and transmit such stories. On the circle of exilarchic sages, see esp. M. Beer, "The Exilarchate in Talmudic Times," (in Hebrew), *Ẓiyyon* 28, 1963, p. 12.

[2] I simply cannot account for the Geonic traditions that R. Sheshet "guided" the exilarch of his times. Nothing in the Talmudic traditions suggests to me that he actually had any influence over, or even a special relationship with, the exilarch. He seems to me to have been among the most hostile critics. The stories about his relationship to the exilarch, all favorable to the exilarch, record a persistent tradition that R. Sheshet was anything but friendly or close to the Jewish government.

Persian agent. The oppositionist rabbis, no less than the loyalist ones, taught students and directed academies, judged cases and administered the law. "Central" government was too weak to prevent this had the exilarch wanted it to. Both groups looked back upon Rav and Samuel as their teachers, and both claimed to hold superior traditions. The oppositionist group held that its learning, not the Iranian mandate, was the sole basis for authority over the Babylonian Jews. And the oppositionist viewpoint had quite natural appeal to the academies at large. So it was important to the exilarch to oversee the schools and courts through his "own" rabbis. The first significant challenge to his control of the academies came from Geniva, sometime before 279.

Our traditions on Geniva's trial and execution are limited, and derive almost wholly from circles friendly to the exilarch.[1] Geniva was a distinguished rabbi, a student of Rav's who was put to death by the Iranian government, probably at the instigation of the exilarch Mar 'Uqba II. The reason was never made explicit, though Mar 'Uqba did complain to the Palestinian consistery that Geniva was "bothering" him. The only evidence of what that "bother" consisted is Geniva's saying that the rabbis are really called kings, for Torah, personified as Wisdom in Proverbs 8:15, had said, "By me kings rule," so that it was upon the basis of the learning of the rabbis that government was constituted. In so saying, Geniva perhaps implicitly questioned the rabbis' relationship to the exilarch. They should not serve one lesser than themselves. They, not he, were kings. M. Beer suggested mainly upon the basis of circumstantial evidence that Geniva and other sages opposed the involvement of the exilarch in the appointment of the heads of the schools. Beer states, "Geniva opposed the extension of the exilarchic power over the academies, whose influence over Babylonian Jewry was growing as a consequence of the activities of Rav and Samuel." It seems to me that the exilarch was not extending, but possibly defending his authority over the schools. Whether or not the specific issue of who controls the schools was raised I cannot say, though it seems reasonable to suppose that some such practical matter was in dispute.[2]

The rabbis' motive as I said, was salvific: through the reformation of Israel's day-to-day life, redemption would be brought near. The

---

[1] Vol. III, pp. 75-81.

[2] That rabbis admitted the validity of the exilarch's Davidic claim seems beyond doubt, for the stories of both the patriarch's and the exilarch's place in the Davidic lineage are preserved in rabbinic sources.

exilarch thought the Messiah would come, even in their own day if
God willed it, as R. Naḥman had said, in a scion of the exilarchic
family itself. What lay at the heart of the redemptive process?—That
was the theological issue. I suppose that under other circumstances, it
might have been possible to avoid conflict. The exilarch might have
admitted that God *would* will the redemption of Israel when Israel
conformed to the Torah as the rabbis taught it. The rabbis might have
agreed that when he did, he would raise up a scion of David out of the
exilarchic house, which claimed to be David's heir. So both sides might
have continued the partnership of two centuries' standing. But such a
compromise would have left the exilarch no better off than before. He
would now have to subordinate himself to the academies, relinquish
his control of them, and accept their claim to be the real government of
Israel. In return he might expect that his descendant would play a
major role in the eschatological drama. But he already enjoyed that
expectation *and* the practical rule of Israel as well. He did not need the
rabbis' assurance of his, or his heir's, ultimate place in the climax of
history. He did need to exert as much control as possible over the
Jewish community, for it was his task as Iranian agent over Israel to
do just that. He therefore demanded the continued loyalty of the schools
and their graduates, so that his court and local administration might
further enjoy the services of well-trained lawyers. They would win
popular support for themselves and hence for his government because
of their learning and charisma. The exilarch therefore wanted only to
preserve the excellent arrangements of the past, and compromise was
equivalent to surrendering his advantage. Within rabbinical circles,
hostile sentiment had gained new adherents. What had been the dangerous conviction of Geniva, a "man of division" avoided by other leading
rabbis, now became a subject for open debate. The issue was phrased
as follows: First, do the rabbis pay taxes? And second, who appoints
the heads of the schools? If the rabbis paid the poll-tax, they admitted
they were like all ordinary Jews and subject to the jurisdiction of the
exilarch who collected taxes. If the exilarch appointed the heads of the
schools, he could continue to impose his will upon them. Both issues
pointed toward the larger question of the status on earth and in heav n
of the rabbinical estate.[1] After reviewing Geonic traditions, we shall

---

[1] We shall here examine the political issues, and below, in Chapters Three and
Four, explore the religious influence and legal power of the rabbinate, upon which
basis these specific issues were raised to begin with.

consider the issues of taxation and academic politics, and then examine other rabbinic traditions pertaining to the exilarch.

II. GEONIC TRADITIONS

R. Sherira's Letter: The letter of R. Sherira contains no reference whatever to the exilarch in the period from the death of Rav Judah b. Ezekiel to R. Papa (299-376 A.D.) nor does R. Sherira refer to an exilarch until the days of R. Ashi.[1]

Seder 'Olam Zuta: The *SOZ* traditions pertaining to the last third of the third century and the whole of the fourth and fifth centuries are as follows:

> And Nathan his son arose, and the sages guided him. Rav Judah b. Ezekiel and R. Sheshet were his sages. The Persians inherited the kingdom in 245th year [sic!] of the destruction of the Temple [313 A.D.], and the Persians decreed a persecution against the Jews. Nathan died, and his son Nehemiah arose, and the sages guided him. R. Shizbi was his sage. Nehemiah died, and 'Aqaviah his son arose, and the sages guided him. Rava and R. 'Ada' were his sages. In his time, Shapur went up against 'Aramay[2] and conquered it. Mar 'Uqban of Zuzita died and was buried in the land of Israel. There arose after him Huna his nephew, and the sages guided him. Abaye, Rabbah and R. Joseph b. Ḥama were his sages. In his time Shapur went up against Nisibis and took it. Huna Mar died, and after him arose 'Uqba his brother, and the sages guided him. R. Ḥananel was his sage. 'Uqba died and after him arose 'Abba', his nephew, the son of Mar 'Uqban. Rava and Rabina were his sages. In the year 416 of the destruction of the Temple [484 A.D.] the world stood without a king. Abba died and R. Kahana his brother arose. R. Safra was his sage, and R. 'Aḥa' of Difti was his sage. Mar Zutra died and there arose after him Kahana his son. Rabina was his sage. R. Kahana died and after him arose R. Huna Mar his brother. R. 'Aḥa' of Difti son of Ḥanilai was his sage. He died and arose after him R. Huna his uncle the son of R. Kahana. R. Mari and Mar Ḥanina Rava were his sages.[3]

In his definitive monograph,[4] Lazarus discussed the *SOZ* traditions

---

[1] *'Iggeret Rav Sherira Gaon*, ed. B. M. Lewin (Haifa, 1921), pp. 85, 1.9-90 1. 14. As we shall see, Talmudic traditions are similarly sparse, which accounts for R. Sherira's lack of information.

[2] See F. Lazarus, "Die Häupter der Vertriebenen," *JaJGL* X, 1890. p. 35, n. 7. He reads *Armenia*, which is impossible.

[3] Ed. M. Grossberg (London 1910), pp. 43-49. Further traditions pertaining to the fifth century will be discussed in vol. V.

[4] Cited above, n. 2. Lazarus based his exilarchic history and chronology on the *SOZ*, into which he fitted the Talmudic data as best he could.

on the exilarchate in this time.[1] He recognized the difficulty posed by the veritable silence of the Talmudic sources about the exilarchs in the fourth century. Lazarus provided the following list and approximate dates[2]:

Nehemiah I	270-313
'Uqba II (Mar 'Uqban deZuzita,[3] 'Aqaviah, Mar 'Uqba, Rabban 'Uqba, etc.)	313-337
Huna Mar I, Huna III (Brother of 'Uqba II)	337-350
'Abba' (Abba Mari, son of 'Uqba II)	350-370
Nathan II	370-400

So Lazarus identifies 'Uqba II with Nathan of Zuzita, as in the *SOZ*. Rav's grandson, he was the brother of Nehemiah.[4] Lazarus interprets the reference to the invasion by Shapur of *Aramay* to mean Armenia, a campaign he dates in 308-9. It is manifestly impossible for Shapur, an unborn, or new-born, baby to have invaded Armenia. Moreover Shapur's earliest efforts against Armenia were mostly diplomatic, not military. One can hardly say he ever actually conquered Armenia, though of course he did execute a successful invasion after 363. Obviously none of this relates to the *SOZ* reference, which is of no historical consequence. Huna Mar was a third brother of Nehemiah II and 'Uqba II, son of Nehemiah the exilarch from 270 to 313, according to Lazarus.[5] His name is unknown in the Talmud. Lazarus holds,[6] by contrast to his table given above, that Huna Mar I ruled "*at least* from 337 to 363." (Italics supplied). His nephew, 'Abba', is known as a contemporary of Nahman b. Isaac (d. 356), and he was served by Rava (or, Rava "guided" him), who died in 352. Hence Lazarus supposes his rule began about 350, probably for reasons of consistency with the Geonic dating of the rabbis of his time. It seems equally valid to suppose he came to power much earlier than that, since the identification of his whole reign with two rabbis who died very early in it, according to Lazarus's dating, seems far-fetched. The date of 370 is justified, Lazarus says,[7] because of the reference to the taking of Nisibis in 363.[8]

---

[1] *Op. cit.*, pp. 91-107.

[2] *Op. cit.*, p. 130.

[3] See Lazarus, *op. cit.*, p. 53, n. 2, p. 97, n. 4. Lazarus thinks it was originally a place name, which was interpreted to mean, "One who has a holy-glistening visage."

[4] See vol. III, pp. 50-58 for discussion of the traditions relating to both men.

[5] *Op. cit.*, p. 102-3.

[6] *Ibid.*

[7] *Ibid.*, p. 106.

[8] I find remarkable Lazarus's efforts to identify the Geonic dates with fourth-

Lazarus notes that the *SOZ* omits "the sages guided him" when speaking of 'Abba'.

W. Bacher[1] holds that Mar 'Uqban II, contemporary of Rav Judah and R. Sheshet,[2] was succeeded by his *brother*, not son, Nehemiah, advised by R. Shizbi. He held office in 313. In his time "there took place a great religious persecution by the Persians, of which, however, no details are known," Bacher says. His successor was Mar 'Uqban III, advised by Rabbah b. Nahmani and R. 'Adda', and is known also as 'Uqban b. Nehemiah, exilarch (b. Shab. 56b, B.B. 55a). Bacher's Mar 'Uqban III was also known as Nathan deZuzita. Then came Huna III, his brother, who was advised by Abaye and Rava. His son Abba, advised by Rava and Rabina, followed, and was succeeded by his son Nathan II.

A. Krochmal[3] thinks that Nathan deZuzita was the son of the 2nd century Nehunyon/Ahiah[4] and sees no relationship between him and fourth century figures or events. Rabbana 'Uqba, grandson of Rav, became exilarch in 278 A.D., Krochmal supposes, and he was also called Mar 'Uqba (II).[5] He died in 332 or 333,[6] and was succeeded by Abba Mari bar Mar, or Mari bar Mar,[7] who was the son of Rabbana 'Uqba. He was, Krochmal says, succeeded by Mar Zutra.[8]

Y. S. Zuri provides the following chronology[9]:

Huna	240-270
Nathan	270-300
(Rav's son-in-law, and father of the following)	
Rabbana Nehemiah	300-321
Rabbana 'Uqban bar Rabbana Nehemiah (= Nathan deZuzita)	321-337
Huna Mar	337-350
Abba Mari ben Mar 'Uqban deZuzita	350-370
Nathan II ben Abba Mari	370-390

century events of Roman and Iranian history. In fact the *SOZ* traditions are not so credible that such dates require synchronization with known facts.

[1] W. Bacher, "Exilarch," *JE* V, 289.

[2] See vol. III, pp. 81-86.

[3] *Perushim veHe'arot leTalmud Bavli*. German title: *Scholien zum babylonischen Talmud* (Lemberg, 1881), p. 34. Compare p. 55.

[4] See vol. I, 2nd ed., pp. 113-121.

[5] Krochmal, *op. cit.*, p. 47f.

[6] *Ibid.*, p. 55.

[7] *Ibid.*, p. 56ff.

[8] *Ibid.*, p. 58.

[9] Y. S. Zuri, *History of Hebrew Public Law: The Reign of the Exilarchate and the Legislative Academies. Period of Rab Nachman bar Jizchak* (320-355). (in Hebrew, Tel Aviv, 1939) pp. 190-192.

Lazarus relied most heavily upon the *SOZ*, and made few efforts to include a wide range of Talmudic sayings. In general, Bacher follows Lazarus, with little change. Krochmal's long and idiosyncratic discussion includes reference to every possible saying, and while he accuses "historians" of inventing facts for their own purposes, it is difficult to see in his discussion more than a highly private account, of no critical weight whatever. We are left, therefore, to follow the Talmudic evidence as best we can, with Lazarus as chief guide.

III. THE EXILARCH, THE RABBI AND TAXATION

The exilarch was perfectly well prepared to grant unusual favors to the rabbis as an estate. They had special privileges at court. They were given advantages in marketing their produce. The exilarch was quoted as instructing Rava to see whether a certain man, claiming rabbinical status and therefore privilege, was really a scholar. If so, Rava was to reserve a market-privilege for him, so that he might sell his produce before others.[1] Since the rabbis staffed exilarchic courts, it was certainly advantageous to protect them.

The rabbis' claim to be exempt from the poll-tax, or *karga*,[2] was quite another matter. It involved not merely the exilarchate but the Sasanian government. The exilarch could not exempt rabbis from the poll-tax, for it was simply not in his power to do so. On the contrary, one of the principal guarantees of continued peace for the Jewish community was the efficient collection of taxes. The experience of the Christians after 337 shows what could have happened to Jewry on account of tax evasion. All the exilarch actually could do was to shift the burden of taxes to others, so that the rabbis' share would devolve upon ordinary Jews. He naturally was not ready to do so, and I do not think ordinary people would have wanted him to. The tax rates were so high that poor people struggled to find the specie or produce to pay them. References abound to people's selling their property or themselves into slavery to raise the necessary money. The state was not prepared to compromise, for on its part, it simply could not afford to do so. War was necessary to protect its territory, including first and

---

[1] b. B. B. 22a. This detail is included *en passent*, for the point of the story, which is cited in full below, p. 351, is that the curse of a rabbi, or disrespect of a rabbi, brings inexorable punishment, usually death. But it is taken for granted that the exilarch honored the rabbis' right to have special market privileges, and I regard it as a fact. For court privileges, see vol. III, pp. 126-130, and below, pp. 309-315.

[2] See Geo Widengren, *op. cit.*, *IA* 1, 1961, pp. 149-153.

foremost Babylonia itself. Armies cost money. Everyone must help pay, particularly those who lived in so rich and fertile a region. Moreover, those living closest to the capital were least able to evade the taxes. So the exilarch could hardly accede to the rabbis' demand. The Persians would not allow it. The ordinary Jews could not afford it.

The rabbis' claim of tax-exemption was phrased in comments upon Scripture. They were certain that from most ancient times, rabbis were not supposed to pay taxes, and it would be a transgression of Scriptural precedent if they now did so. Rava held that King Asa was punished simply because he imposed forced labor ('NGRY') on the sages of his day, citing the following Scripture, "Then King Asa made a proclamation to all Judah; *none* was exempted" (I Kings 15:22).[1] Rava's comment was merely a warning. A more positive claim was made by R. Naḥman b. Isaac:

> R. Naḥman b. R. Ḥisda applied the head-tax to the sages. R. Naḥman b. Isaac said to him, "You have transgressed against the teachings of the Torah, the Prophets, and the Writings. Against the Torah, as it is written, 'Although he loves the peoples, all his saints are in your hand' (Deut. 33.3). [Moses said before the Holy One blessed be He, 'Lord of the universe, Even when you love the peoples, all his saints will be in your hand.' (The verse continues), 'And they are cut at your feet.' R. Joseph taught, 'These are the students of Torah who cut their feet going from one town to another and one province to another to study the Torah.' 'He shall receive your words' (Deut. 33:3) alludes to their give-and-take in discussing the words of the Omnipresent.] Against the Prophets, as it is written, 'Even when they study (lit.: Give, YTNW) among the nations, now I shall gather them, and a few of them shall be free from the burden of king and princes' (Hosea 8:10). 'Ulla said, this verse is said in the Aramaic language, 'If they all study, now I shall gather them, and if a few of them study, they shall be free from the burden of king and princes.' Against the Writings, as it is written, 'It shall not be lawful to impose upon them [priests and Levites] *minda*, *belo*, and *ḥalakh*' (Ezra 7:24), and Rav Judah explained, *Minda* means the portion of the king, *belo* is the poll-tax, and *ḥalakh* is the *'anona*.'"[2]
>
> (b. B.B. 8a)[3]

The several Scriptures are not of equal weight. The passage in Deuteronomy suggests that "his saints," who, the rabbis thought, were rabbis, were in God's hand. Therefore they do not require the pro-

---

[1] b. Sotah 10a.

[2] Share of the crops, see Widengren, *loc.cit.*

[3] Hyman, *Toledot Tannaim veAmoraim* (London, 1910), II, p. 471, says that R. Naḥman b. Isaac lived in the town of Derokert, which was administered by R. Naḥman b. R. Ḥisda.

tection of walls or armies, and should not have to pay for them. This claim was made quite explicitly by Resh Laqish before R. Judah (the Prince, or R. Judah III) when the former taxed the rabbis for defense. Likewise Rav Judah had said that everyone must contribute to the building of doors for the town gates except rabbis, who do not require protection.[1] So I suppose that R. Naḥman b. Isaac cited only Deut. 33:3. The citations of Moses' conversation with God and R. Joseph's exegetical translation of the Scripture were merely added by the editor of the account as we now have it. The meaning of the passage in Hosea is quite clear: when the Jews study the Torah among the gentiles (i.e. in Babylonia), a few should not have to pay taxes, and these, quite obviously, are the rabbis. 'Ulla's comment changes the eschatological sense of the verse, but the proof-text is clear as it stands. The citation from Ezra explicitly states that priests do not have to pay the "portion of the king" or the poll-tax. What was not made explicit, because everyone in the schools knew it, is that the rabbis believed they had inherited the rights and privileges of the priesthood, since study of Torah was now equivalent to the priestly offerings in Temple times. Therefore, according to Artaxerxes' order reported by Ezra, rabbis do not have to pay the head tax. This was quite explicit in Scripture, and beyond question. So even the Iranian Government should not impose the poll-tax on them, they supposed.

While the exegesis of Deut. 33:3 in Exodus Rabbah contains no hint of R. Naḥman b. Isaac's reading of the verse, that in the Pesiqta de Rav Kahana is quite explicit: those who study Torah will be free of the "yoke of the [earthly] kingdom."[2] R. Huna had earlier taught as an exegesis of this same Scripture that the ingathering of the exiles would take place through the merit of study of the Mishnah.[3] Rav Judah's interpretation of Ezra 7:24 was cited also by Rava in a similar context, as we shall see below.[4] What is interesting, therefore, is that R. Naḥman b. Isaac's citations of Hosea 8:10 and Ezra 7:24 were consistent with the interpretations of Rav Judah and R. Huna, of the preceding generation, as well as of the contemporary, older master, R. Joseph. His

---

[1] Resh Laqish, b. B.B. 7b, Rav Judah, b. B.B. 8a, and see vol. III, pp. 102-126.

[2] See Exodus R. 25:8; *Pesiqta deRav Kahana* ed. B. Mandelbaum, II, p. 450.

[3] Leviticus R. 7:3, R. Huna said, "All the exiles will be gathered in only through the merit of the study of Mishnah." *Pesiqta deRav Kahana*, ed. B. Mandelbaum, I, 118, as in the earlier passage, also in the name of R. Huna. See also Yalkut Shimoʻni I #479, standard printed texts p. 285, in the name of R. Ḥananiah.

[4] A similar interpretation of Ezra 7:24 is given in Gen. R. 64:10, and ascribed to the Samaritans in the days of R. Joshua b. Ḥananiah.

understanding of Deut. 33 : 3 is quite congruent to the opinions of Rav Judah, and Resh Laqish in Palestine, that the rabbis do not require protection and therefore should not have to pay for it. They are students of the Mishnah, and Hosea referred to the fact that those that study should be free of the king's burden. And Ezra says that Artaxerxes (Ardashir)[1] explicitly exempted them from the poll-tax. The point of 'Ulla's remark, therefore, is that study by a Jew—particularly a rabbi—only exempts those few from taxation. Only when all Jews study will the ingathering come. (Hence, most Jews now did not study the Torah.) This idea is not new, for it had been said over and over again in Tannaitic and earlier Amoraic circles that the act of study of Torah was of redemptive and eschatological consequence. Israel would be redeemed through study of Torah (among other holy actions).[2] The teaching that Ezra 7 : 24 refers to the exemption of the priest-rabbi from the poll-tax is not new either, for Rav Judah had so interpreted the verse. The exegesis concerning the implication of Deut. 33 : 3 was not R. Naḥman b. Isaac's invention. What was now new was the practical claim, based upon these Scriptures, of a tax-exemption for the rabbis. To the best of our knowledge, Rav Judah did not publicly demand that the rabbis be free of the poll-tax. R. Huna never openly said that because of the merit of the sages' study, they should actually be free of taxes. The earlier rabbis prepared the way for R. Naḥman b. Isaac's assertion. But it was his, and not their, claim in practice.

And he was not alone. The following extraordinary saying of Rava, alluded to above,[3] is no less explicit:

> Rava said, "It is permitted for a rabbinical disciple to say, 'I will not pay the poll-tax,' as it is written, 'It shall not be lawful to impose *minda belo*, or *ḥalakh*' (Ezra 7 : 24), and Rav Judah said, '*minda* is the king's portion, *belo* is the poll-tax, and *ḥalakh* is the corvée.'" Rava moreover stated, "A rabbinical disciple is permitted to say, 'I am a servant of fire and do not pay the poll tax.'" [What is the reason? It is only said in order to drive away a lion.]

(b. Ned. 62b)

Rava's remarkable saying that a rabbinical disciple may lie to evade the poll-tax, and even deny that he is a Jew, tells us nothing about what would have happened had he done so. The tax-collectors in the Jewish

---

[1] For Artaxerxes as Ardashir, see vol. II, pp. 57-64. So the Persians long ago had exempted the rabbis.

[2] See for example vol. II, pp. 236-240, 282-288.

[3] P. 40.

community were Jews, not Iranians. What Rava has in mind is a Jew's telling the Jewish collector that he is an apostate. There may be an implied threat, that "if you do not leave me alone, I shall become a servant of fire." I doubt that Rava thought a rabbinical disciple would so assert before a Mobad, who knew full well how to assess such a claim. His thought was that it is so wrong to collect the poll-tax from rabbis that the disciples may perjure themselves and even pretend to commit overt apostasy. It is a very strong assertion, so extreme that I can hardly imagine anyone's attributing it to Rava had he not actually said it.

An interpretation of Daniel 10:13, attributed to R. Yoḥanan, Palestinian contemporary of Rav Judah and R. Huna, related a story that Dubiel, the guardian angel of the Persians, had been given power for twenty-one days. He had decreed that Israel should be put down for the poll-tax, and that the sages should likewise be required to pay it. Gabriel intervened, and in the course of discussion, Dubiel swallowed the document decreeing that Israel and the sages would have to pay the poll-tax. Some say it was signed, but he swallowed it. Some say it was written out but not signed. Hence, the account concludes, some people in the Persian empire have to pay the poll-tax and others do not.[1] Whether or not this etiological account of why some pay, and others do not pay, the poll-tax was actually said by R. Yoḥanan or known in Babylonia in this period is not important. It is clear from the evidence cited above, pertaining to R. Naḥman b. Isaac and Rava, that two leading rabbis were perfectly adamant: rabbis do not have to pay the poll-tax. This story would have explained why they thought others did have to pay.

We do not know what the exilarch said or did, for rabbinical sources, which are the only sources we have, do not tell us. If Torah, Prophecy, Writings, and heavenly angels are brought to testify, and public apostasy theoretically was permitted to a rabbinical disciple, one can hardly suppose that rabbis were not under pressure. The greater likelihood is that they paid their tax, but resisted as powerfully as they could through their most effective weapons, namely, ascription of their tax exemption to Gabriel, Moses, Hosea, and Artaxerxes, and publicly announcing permission to evade the taxes even by committing the worst

---

[1] b. Yoma 77a. Urbach, *op. cit.*, *Tarbiẓ* 34, 1965, pp. 158-159, and M. Beer, "On the Tax Exemption of the Babylonian Amoraim," (in Hebrew), *Tarbiẓ* 33, 1964, 252-256. Urbach says that R. Yoḥanan did not in fact tell this story, and that it may not have been in existence in this period at all.

sin they could think of.[1] I can only conclude that the exilarch exerted
such pressure, because he both had and wanted to. The vehemence of
the rabbis' traditions on the subject must be interpreted as evidence of
his success.

We do not know whether R. Naḥman b. Isaac actually managed to
intimidate R. Naḥman b. R. Ḥisda, or, as I said, whether *any* young
rabbinical disciples in fact lied to the tax-collectors. We do know
Shapur's police executed Christian tax-resisters. Since we have absolutely no evidence of "martyrdom" among the rabbinate on account of
non-payment of taxes, I feel sure there was none.[2] The rabbis protested,
but they must have paid. To the exilarch, that would have been all that
really mattered. But the rabbis would have been embittered because
they not only lost money, which would have bothered the poorer ones,
but also were forced to transgress their religious convictions about
their own rights and privileges. Their view of the sanctity of the
rabbinate is clear.[3] They were the "saints" in God's hand. So it was a
sin for them to pay the poll-tax, and it was a greater sin still for the
exilarch, heir of David—and Asa—to force them to do so. Asa had
been punished for imposing the corvée upon the rabbis. What they
hoped would happen to the exilarch in time to come one may only
imagine. So the exilarch's rabbis remained in positions of power and
influence, and all rabbis paid the poll-tax, along with everyone else.[4]

---

[1] Confession of being a "fire-worshipper" would surely have been seen as
public apostasy by ordinary people, who would not have known the rabbinic
excuse that God was described as a 'consuming fire.' The rabbis had long insisted
that a Jew should die rather than commit three sins: murder, sexual crime, and
apostasy in public. So this must have been the worst sin they could think of as
appropriate to the situation.

[2] Except Rabbah, see above p. 41.

[3] See below, pp. 119-124 for further discussion.

[4] See b. Yev. 17a and b. Sanh. 27a-b, cited below, for clear evidence that rabbis
did pay taxes; and M. Beer, *op. cit.*, *Tarbiz* 33, 1964, pp. 254-255 for the same view.
Further discussion of this question will be found in the same article by Beer, pp.
247-259; in Beer's article in *Ziyyon, cited above*, 28, 1963, p. 22; and in his *Maʿamadam*,
p. 67 n. 147; and especially, pp. 81-86, on whether rabbis had to pay other duties
or not. In *Tarbiz* 33, 1964, p. 249, n. 1, 2, and 3, Beer cites other discussions of this
question. He correctly rejects the view of Krauss and others that the rabbis did
not in fact pay taxes. Beer (*Maʿamadam*, p. 84), treats the payment by rabbis as a
new demand on the part of the state, part of the "persecution" of the period. He
does not repeat this idea in *Tarbiz*. I do not believe it was a *new* exaction at all.
The rabbis tried to prove it was, by reference to Artaxerxes. The rabbis now may
have supposed that Ardashir I had renewed it, but we have no evidence to that
effect, and there is no reason to suppose either that he did or even that they thought
so.

Among the loyalist rabbis were men like R. Naḥman b. R. Ḥisda, who collected the tax in the exilarch's behalf.[1]

IV. EXILARCH AND ACADEMY

The most important sources allegedly dealing with the appointment of the head of an academy are as follows:

> Our rabbis taught [in Tannaitic times]: "At first they used to say that a *ḥaver* who became a tax collector would be removed from his status as *ḥaver*. If he separated [from his post as tax collector] they would not again accept him. They later decreed that if he separated, he would be treated [without prejudice] as any other person."

---

[1] On rabbis as tax-collectors, see Beer, *Ma'amadam*, p. 88, who points out that R. Zera's father did so; see on this vol. III, pp. 24-27. On R. Huna b. Ḥiyya, see below, p. 92. On Rava as supervisor of tax collections, see Beer, *Ma'amadam*, p. 136. On the collection of taxes in general, see Christensen, *op. cit.*, p. 124ff., 366ff., and especially, Widengren, *op. cit.*, *IA* 1, 1961, pp. 149-153; and J. Newman. *The Agricultural Life of the Jews in Babylonia between the years* 200 *C.E. and* 500 *C.E.* (London, 1932), pp. 161-186.

Newman points out that the land-tax, or *tasqa*, was also collected by groups or communes, in this case, from a group of fields regarded as a unit. The members paid collectively. It is interesting that we find no rabbinical claim to be exempt from the *tasqa* or land-tax. I should imagine the reason is that the others in the given tax-collection-unit would not stand for it. Since the state simply transferred ownership to the man who actually did pay the *tasqa* on land in a situation of tax deliquency, the rabbi making such a claim would not have occasion to repeat it for very long.

On the *karga*, see Newman, pp. 168-175. Newman supposes (p. 169) that the rabbis were tax-exempt, so Rava's saying that they might pretend to public apostasy merely meant that it would make it easier for them to *gain* their tax exemption if they seemed to be Magi. It is pure fantasy. Beer suggests, rather tentatively, that Rava's gifts (b. Ḥag. 5b, above p. 40) to the court "had something to do with taxes."

Widengren (*IA* 1, 1961, p. 159) supposes that "Some of them [the Jews] as we know possessed a great financial capacity and were capable of lending big sums of money to the King of Kings when they were in need of money... They were therefore protected by the King of Kings but very often had to buy the favour of him or his dignitaries or secretaries by offering them special gifts, all this in accordance with ancient Persian custom." Widengren thereupon refers to b. B.M. 70b and Ḥag. 5b. The passage to which, I imagine, Widengren refers in b. B.M. 70b has to do with Rav's saying, on Prov. 28:8, that King Shapur pities the poor; it further touches on whether or not one may take usury from a heathen. The view of R. Naḥman is that one may not. Rava argues to the contrary. What all this has to do with "lending big sums" to the Iranian government I cannot say. In his note, p. 159, n. 1, Widengren refers to Newman, *op. cit.*, p. 77, n. 2, a passage which consists of the following reference, "B.B. 12a" I find nothing either in Newman or in b. B.B. 12a, relevant to his point, and I imagine it is an erroneous reference or a printer's error. Widengren refers further to Nöldeke, *Tabari*, p. 68, n. 1 where I can find *no* reference whatever to *loans* from Jews to the state, but

The time required R. Huna b. Ḥiyya.[1] Rabbah and R. Joseph and four hundred pairs of rabbis were going to him. He heard they were coming. He wreathed eight hundred chairs.[2] They then heard that he was appointed tax-collecter. They sent to him, "Go to his [your] importance, go to his [your] former status."[3] He sent back to them, "I have withdrawn." [Lit.: I have gone back on myself]. R. Joseph did not go. Rabbah went. R. Joseph said, "We have learned [in a Tannaitic teaching] that if he separated, he is not received back." Rabbah replied, "We have learned [in a Tannaitic teaching] that they later decided if he separated, behold he is like any other person."

(b. Bekh. 31a)

R. Joseph [was] "Sinai" and Rabbah "Uprooter of Mountains." The time required them. [Trans. Maurice Simon: "The time came when they were required (to be head of the academy)."] They sent there [to Palestine], "Sinai and Uprooter of Mountains—which of them takes precedence?" The Palestinians replied, "Sinai takes precedence, for everyone needs the owner of the wheat." Nonetheless, R. Joseph did not accept [the headship] upon himself, for the Chaldeans [astrologers] had said to him, "You will rule two years." Rabbah ruled twenty-two

---

only discussion of 'Ifra Hormiz's gifts to rabbis; the death of Rabbah b. Naḥmani; the Jews and the Magi; and other matters. So far as I can see, Nöldeke makes no reference to Jewish "loans" etc. We do not, as I said, know exactly why Rava sent bribes (*not* loans!) to the court, or why he lost all his money for that matter. The latter point is clearly "illuminated" by b. Ḥag.: "the rabbis set their eyes upon Rava," so naturally he lost all his money. But the former point is nowhere clarified. Moreover, b. B.M. 70b makes *no* reference whatever to loans to the state. At best one can say that Rava believed one may take interest from gentiles. His saying has nothing whatever to do with state-loans, nor of course with any actual loans *he* may have made. The secondary citations are no more persuasive, to say the least. So I cannot conclude otherwise than that Widengren's supposition of "large Jewish loans" to the state, accompanied by the Babylonian Jews' "great financial capacity," is, to say the least, unproven. I do not think it is true. Widengren's contribution in *IA* 1, 1961, nonetheless contains important discussions on the Iranian, Armenian and Syriac texts, especially on philological matters.

[1] This is as literal a translation as I can offer. L. Miller, trans., *Bekorot*, (London, 1938) p. 196 provides, "The scholars required the teaching of R. Huna b. Hiyya," and in his note, *ibid.*, n. 7, he adds, "In order to consult him on some point of Jewish law. Lit., 'the time needed him.' Another explanation is that he fell ill and it was necessary for them [= the rabbis] to visit him." It is reading into the text meaning not there to delete "time/hour" and substitute "the scholars ... teaching..." I do not know whether Š'H (Sha'ah) has astrological significance here.

[2] Following Miller and Jastrow.

[3] Miller and Jastrow read 'ZL for ZYL, hence, "He returned to his former status." Miller translates the passage, "Thereupon they sent him a message that he should adhere to his office. He went back to his former position, and sent back to them, 'I have withdrawn.'" Miller explains, *ibid.*, p. 196, n. 9, "Since he was already a publican let him cling to the position, but as far as they were concerned they would not visit him." He translates the reading followed here, "that he should adhere 'to his (new position) before him,'" which I do not comprehend.

years. R. Joseph ruled two and one-half years. During all those years that Rabbah ruled, [R. Joseph enjoyed such good health that] he did not summon to his house even a cupper.

(b. Ber. 64a)

The former passage contains no hint of the purpose of the rabbinical visitation, but in the latter, "the time required" clearly means, as Dr. Simon said, for one to be head of the school. Neither account contains the slightest hint of exilarchic participation in the decision, but that proves nothing, for such a detail would quickly have been suppressed by a rabbinical redactor or tradent.

Summary of Scholarly Discussion: The first passage above forms the cornerstone of M. Beer's discussion of the relationship between the exilarch and the schools. Beer holds[1] that the Pumbeditan academy was accustomed to choose its own head. The first evidence we have of that fact comes at the death of Rav Judah b. Ezekiel, founder of the academy, conventionally dated in 298-299. Both of his leading students, Rabbah and R. Joseph, declined to accept the succession.[2] R. Joseph allegedly refused because of an astrological prediction that he would hold such a post for only two years. As we saw, the text proceeds, "Rabbah remained head for twenty-two years, and R. Joseph after him for two and a half years."[3] Beer rightly rejects Rashi's interpretation of b. Bekh. 31a, that the sages of the generation were turning with a legal inquiry to R. Huna b. Ḥiyya. He cites the tradition of R. Sherira that R. Huna b. Ḥiyya did in fact head the Pumbeditan academy for a number of years.[4] But Beer finds it quite clear that neither Rabbah nor R. Joseph, nor Abaye afterward, who eventually headed the school, was chosen for that office by the exilarch. He cites the following tradition as evidence:

> Abaye, Rava, R. Zera, and Rabbah b. R. Mattenah were sitting [= in session], and required a head. They agreed that whoever would say something which others could not refute would become the head. The statements of all were refuted except for Abaye's. Rava saw that Abaye held up his head. He said to him, "Naḥmani [Abaye] begin and say something."

(b. Horayot 14b)[5]

---

[1] *op. cit., Ẓiyyon* 28, 1963, pp. 15-20.

[2] Beer cites b. Ber. 64a as evidence of that fact. He says that the reason for their refusal is not given. But in b. Ber. 64a a reason *is* given, as we saw.

[3] b. Ber. 64a.

[4] Beer, *op. cit.*, p. 16, n. 103.

[5] See the translation and note of Israel W. Slotki, *Horayoth* (London, 1938), pp. 105-106, esp. p. 105, n. 12. The reading *Rabbah* is found in current traditions, and Slotki explains that as Abaye's teacher, he could speak to him in such a manner.

Beer's interpretation of the evidence would be more persuasive if some reference to the headship of the school at Pumbedita were included in the above account. But, as the traditional commentaries note, the "head" was, for all we know, to preside over that particular session, or, as Slotki said, "course of studies." Beer continues, "We have seen that the sages found a way to choose from among themselves who would stand as head of the academy without the intervention of the exilarch." He finds it clear, therefore, that from the founding of the Pumbeditan academy in 295 (following Sherira's date) to Abaye's death in 336, there were four heads of the Pumbeditan school, Rav Judah, Rabbah, R. Joseph, and Abaye, "none of whom was selected by the exilarch."

Beer notes the possibility that the exilarch would be required to approve the rabbis' choice—and hence in effect could control it—in exchange for his support of "many students in the school." He rejects this possibility, for, he notes, Rav Judah had in the first place established a fund[1] supported by popular contributions, to support the school. So he did not have to depend upon the exilarchate. This fund was then controlled by Rabbah, R. Joseph, and Abaye in succession, and finally came to Rava, who headed the Pumbeditan school before moving it to Maḥoza. Beer adds, "In Sura such a fund did not exist." He says, "It is reasonable [to suppose] that Rav Judah had to find for his academy a source of financial support *not* through the offices of the exilarchate."

Beer goes further and says that in the Talmud, there is no evidence even of *contact* between the aforenamed sages and the exilarchate; he states, "We find no evidence that they visited the exilarch or appeared with him in public or worked with him in public administration." He recognizes[2] that two sources, b. Shab. 48a[3] and b. B.B. 55a,[4] report that Rabbah visited the exilarch, but, he notes, manuscript evidence provides the reading of Rava. Beer would assign these contacts to the time after Rava headed the Pumbeditan school. If so, the date for 'Uqban b. Nehemiah would be later than anyone supposes, that is to say, after 337. But Beer adds, "One cannot suppose that it is an accident, for we have evidence about both personal and public contact of

He says, "In this case, the head they felt in need of would be not for the school of Pumbedita but for the purpose of taking charge of that particular course."

[1] See b. Git. 60a, cited below p. 97.

[2] *op. cit.*, p. 17, n. 113.

[3] Cited below, the slave and the kettle story, pp. 106-109.

[4] The rules reported in the name of Samuel by 'Uqban, below, p. 113.

the head of the Suran academy with the exilarch." He refers specifically to R. Huna, R. Ḥisda, and R. Hamnuna. When, furthermore, the Pumbeditan school moved to Maḥoza [the exilarch's capital] under Rava's headship, a very different relationship developed between the exilarch and the Maḥozan-Pumbeditan school. Rava now had many sorts of contact with the exilarch and his staff, and joined in administrative work with them. Beer concludes that the Pumbeditan heads in fact did not have anything to do with the exilarchate. Beer explains this by reference to the jealousy existing between the school of the exilarch's "son-in-law," R. Naḥman, at Nehardea and Rav Judah's school at Pumbedita. He supposes that the exilarch favored R. Naḥman's school in order to build it up against the rivalry of Rav Judah's school. A dispute, perhaps financial, must have taken place, if I follow Beer's reasoning, between 295, when Rav Judah founded the school, and 299 when he died. But, Beer says, it was the Suran academy which was the school of the exilarchate. Its founder's daughters married the exilarch's sons. Rav's successor was R. Huna "who was of the family of the exilarchate." So Beer concludes that the exilarch appointed the heads of Sura, but not of Pumbedita.

In his dissertation[1] Beer explicitly states his view that the visit of the rabbis to R. Huna b. Ḥiyya was in connection with the succession of Rav Judah's headship of the Pumbeditan school. He stresses that the language "the hour needed him" was used in b. Ber. 64a (= b. Hor. 14b) with reference to the headship of the academy. He notes[2] that Rava, as head of the school, appointed a tax-collector, and says that he did so with the permission, or at the behest, of the exilarch. He notes, moreover,[3] that while men who eventually became heads of the schools in their youth were frequently poor, when they finally held office they disposed of considerable funds. Abaye earlier worked nights and studied in poverty, but was eventually a rich man.[4]

Ẓuri[5] also discusses the appointment of academic heads after Rava. His account deals mainly with fifth century figures, and is not relevant to our inquiry.[6]

---

[1] *Maʿamadam*, p. 88, n. 252. On support of the students by the exilarch and public contributions, see pp. 99-104.

[2] *loc. cit.*, p. 136.

[3] *loc. cit.*, pp. 47-51.

[4] For earlier examples, see vol. III, pp. 126-130.

[5] Y. S. Ẓuri, *The Reign of the Exilarchate and the Legislative Academies* (Tel Aviv, 1939, in Hebrew), pp. 210-220.

[6] I shall discuss Ẓuri's theses in vol. V.

Halevy[1] discusses the situation after Rav Judah's death. He also interprets the passage in b. Hor. 14b and b. Ber. 64a about the requirement of the hour as a reference to the selection of a new head, "...the matter was difficult before the sages of the academy in Pumbedita to decide, or they did not wish to decide, between Rabbah and R. Joseph, and they asked [about it] in Palestine...." which of the two would be preferable. Halevy cites the passage in R. Sherira's letter, which indicates that because of indecision among the two great masters, R. Huna b. Ḥiyya became head, afterward followed by Rabbah and then R. Joseph. R. Huna b. Ḥiyya, a student of Samuel, could not have held office, Halevy says, for after the death of Rav Judah, Rabbah did hold the office for twenty-two years, and according to R. Sherira's chronology, those years were 298/9 to 320/1. He must therefore have succeeded immediately. So Halevy concludes that R. Huna b. Ḥiyya did not hold the headship at the *famous* school of Pumbedita, but somewhere else in town (Sic!). Halevy venomously criticizes Graetz's view, that R. Huna b. Ḥiyya did head the Pumbeditan school. Graetz had made him head of the school, and said that the school "therefore lost popularity," on account of R. Huna b. Ḥiyya's tax-collections. Huna therefore gave up the tax-collecting business and was now recognized as acceptable by the college. He was succeeded, according to Graetz, by Rabbah and R. Joseph. Rabbah restored the academy to its "extinguished fame."[2]

Comment: I am persuaded by Beer's interpretation of the mission to R. Huna b. Ḥiyya. The headship of the academy following Rav Judah's death surely was at issue. Since R. Joseph and Rabbah were mentioned, R. Sherira's tradition seems quite sensible. The real point of the story was that a tax-collector cannot head an academy. But if R. Huna collected taxes, it was as appointee of the exilarch. So the issue actually was whether the exilarch could appoint a man tax-collector and at the same time head of a school. The rabbis said one cannot hold both offices, so R. Huna b. Ḥiyya declined the former. Rabbah accepted his reversion, and R. Joseph did not. One may speculate that the exilarch's effort to assign both tasks to R. Huna b. Ḥiyya constituted a direct challenge to the rabbinate. Not only must rabbis pay the head tax—they must also collect it! It was a good time for the rabbis to stand firm. Tax-collectors were not very popular, and ordinary folk might well sympathize—as otherwise they would not—with the rabbis' refusal to

---

[1] *Dorot HaRishonim*, II, pp. 216b (= 432)-218a.
[2] H. Graetz, *op. cit.*, II, pp. 576-577.

accept a tax-collector as their chief. Hence R. Huna b. Ḥiyya was told
to choose, and the rabbis rightly expected he would prefer the higher
status as head of a school to the despised one as tax-collector. So they
won an easy victory and established a major precedent.

Beer's reading of b. Hor. 14b seems to me farfetched, for we have
here no hint of an "election" of a successor to Rabbah and R. Joseph.
That particular account would not prove that "the rabbis" selected the
head of the Pumbeditan school.

Beer's supposition that all contacts between Rava and the exilarch
took place in Rava's later years, after the Pumbeditan school had been
moved to Maḥoza, seems to me equally difficult.[1] The absence of much
clearcut evidence on the relationships between exilarch and rabbis
seems susceptible of more than one explanation. Perhaps the rabbis
avoided the exilarch. But perhaps the rabbis did not choose to preserve
accounts of whatever relations existed. We do not know. Beer's explanation of the exilarch's preference for R. Naḥman's school—if that is
what actually took place—is plausible.

Halevy's discussion contributes nothing to our inquiry, but is important only because of his critique of Graetz's view, which seems to
be shared by Beer, about the role of R. Huna b. Ḥiyya.

One piece of evidence seems to me decisive, following Beer's view,
concerning the fund for the support of the schools, described as follows:

> ...then what of that *shofar* which was at first in the house of Rav
> Judah, then of Rabbah, then of R. Joseph, and then of Abaye, and
> finally of Rava....

(b. Git. 60b)

Beer follows the explanation of R. Sherira, that the *shipura*, or *shofar*,
was a fund for the rabbis of the academy, to which people contributed
and which was used for the support of the sages.[2] *If*, as Beer persuasively argues, R. Sherira's explanation is acceptable, then it becomes
clear, as Beer says, that the head of the Pumbeditan academy for more
than half-a-century kept in his possession an independent source of
funds for the support of the school.[3] Beer says that Rav Judah established the fund, and while we do not know exactly how he was able
to secure contributions, we may suppose that he did manage to collect

---

[1] It would be tempting to suppose that the move came as part of an effort to
reassert control of the school, and bring it under closer exilarchic supervision, by
requiring it to meet right near the exilarchic offices. But the whole matter now
seems rather conjectural.

[2] *'Iggeret R. Sherira Gaon*, ed. B. M. Lewin, pp. 87-88.

[3] See *Ma'amadam*, pp. 99-100.

some money for his purpose. Now why should the head of the Pumbeditan school have chosen to search out an independent source of funds? Given his view of the exilarch,[1] whose authority he accepted only on account of R. Huna's advice, according to traditions in our hands, Rav Judah was likely to have sought such financial independence in order to gain another sort of independence as well. His attitude, to be inferred from his views on taxation of rabbis, was that the exilarch was wrong in taxing them. The exilarch's summons to court in Rav Judah's dispute with R. Naḥman[2] may have further exacerbated their relationships. Or, as Beer says, the exilarchic favor shown to R. Naḥman may have produced a hostile reaction in Rav Judah's school. In any event, we have valid grounds to conclude that the Pumbeditan school did seek an independent source of funds to be collected from ordinary people's voluntary contributions and that the reason for that action had to do with the exilarchate. But we shall see that to Rava, R. Joseph and Rabbah, who were said to hold the fund for the school, were attributed both apparently favorable and hostile sayings about the exilarch. The friendly tales must mean that the exilarchic circles were eager to register the "fact" that the Pumbeditan leaders thought the exilarch was a great penitent, the rise of the exilarchate was predicted by the angel to Jacob, and so on. If Beer's interpretation of the meaning of the funds under discussion is sound, and I believe it is, then pro-exilarchic tradents must have wanted to make another point. That point was that whatever some thought the motives of the Pumbeditan leaders to be, they themselves recognized the divine sanction of the exilarchate.

No evidence, however, suggests that the appointment to the headship of the schools of Sura, Maḥoza, and Nehardea and whatever others existed in this time was *not* in the hands of the exilarch. We do not know whether or not that of Pumbedita was in his control. The rabbinical traditions never suggest that he had anything to do with appointing heads of schools, although circumstantial evidence would lead to the supposition that he did, specifically in the cases of Rav, Samuel, R. Naḥman, R. Huna,[3] and Rav Judah.

Summary and Conclusions: The Pumbeditan rabbis' search for funds from Rav Judah's establishment of the school in 295 until the time of

---

[1] See vol. III, pp. 65-67.

[2] Vol. III, p. 66.

[3] R. Huna's relationship to the exilarch is discussed in vol. III, pp. 50-53. I do not think he was exilarch, or that he was related to the exilarch, and have tried to explain why R. Sherira held a contrary view. Nonetheless his advice to Rav Judah, cited above, would suggest he was a loyal supporter of the exilarchate.

Rava was probably motivated by a concern for rabbinical independence from the exilarch. Whether Rav Judah originally founded the school in reaction against the favoritism of the exilarch for R. Naḥman, against the exilarch's collection of the head-tax from rabbis, or for some other reason, I cannot say. But the school's administration did try for fifty years to preserve its freedom. I think Beer is quite correct in supposing that the struggle to remain free of exilarchic interference in the selection of the head of the school was a primary factor in the refusal to accept R. Huna b. Ḥiyya as head. If so, then the purported move of the school to Maḥoza in Rava's times assumes great significance. R. Sherira's text is as follows:

And after Abaye, Rava ruled in Maḥoza which was of Pumbedita...

ולבתר אביי מלך רבא במחוזא דמן פום בדיתא...

And all the years [of Rava],[1] there was only one academy, in Pumbedita

ובכלהו אילין שנין ¹[דרבא] לא הויא אלא חדא בתיבתא בפום בדיתא

(Letter of R. Sherira, ed. B. M. Lewin, p. 88, 1. 6-7, p. 89, 1. 7-8)

The meaning of "Maḥoza which was of Pumbedita" is not clear to me. I take it to mean that there was one school, Maḥoza, inclusive of the Pumbeditan one. Rava was its head. It was located in the exilarchic capital. Upon that basis, I conclude—still most tentatively—that the half-century of Pumbeditan independence thus ended, and that in Rava's time, the exilarch's authority was acknowledged and the school was then moved to Maḥoza.

The exilarch probably appointed the heads of the other schools throughout this period. The heads of schools enjoyed much power.[2] Only the exilarch could confer advantages and provide the political foundation for such power. As I have argued[3] there was only one Jewish government in Babylonia, and the Sasanians wanted it no other

---

[1] Lewin (p. 88, n. 5) says that Rava's father's home was in Maḥoza, citing p. 82 1. 9-17, "R. Joseph b. Ḥama the father of Rava and our rabbis were in Pumbedita at the time Nehardea was destroyed by Papa b. Neẓar." Halevy, *op. cit.*, II, p. 245B, says that for a time, Pumbedita was the only school, in particular during the lifetimes of Rabbah, R. Joseph, Abaye, and Rava.

Lewin (p. 89 n. 2) points out that the French tradition is preferable:

"In all these years, there was only one academy, in Pumbedita."

Omitting the name of Rava, we find no difficulty whatever. The tradition means that there was indeed only the Pumbeditan academy, but in Rava's lifetime, it was located in Maḥoza. Upon that basis, I have come to the conclusion presented here.

[2] See vol. III pp. 126-130, and Beer, *Ma'amadam*, pp. 99 ff.

[3] Vol. II, pp. 119-125, vol. III, pp. 41-48, 87-94.

way. If the exilarch, therefore, continued to grant benefits to the rabbis, particularly to heads of schools, it was because he had no fear of doing so and got something in exchange. So I suppose that the academies remained well within his jurisdiction, except for Pumbedita.

In the period from Shapur I to Shapur II, we saw that the Nehardean and Maḥozan schools were most closely associated with the exilarch; the Suran one, under R. Huna, seemed submissive, yet was surely a center of some subversion, with Geniva as chief provocateur; and the school of Pumbedita. founded by Rav Judah, probably was comparatively independent of the exilarch through most of the period of Shapur II. We cannot however suppose that the difference between pro-exilarch and anti-exilarch sayings, which we now consider, depends upon Pumbeditan or Maḥozan origin. As I said, R. Joseph and Rabbah, who seem to have preserved Pumbeditan independence, were credited with both kinds. Rava, who supposedly ended it, was likewise the source of both favorable and hostile accounts. If the change in the relationship of Pumbedita, both geographical and therefore probably political, to the exilarchate made any difference in the sayings, that difference does not seem obvious. Both R. Joseph and Rava strongly opposed paying the head-tax. If Rava willingly served as the means of reestablishing exilarchic control over Pumbedita, it is simply not reflected in sayings attributed to him. (And he too kept the *shipura*.) Perhaps Beer is right in holding that the more frequent contacts between Rava and the exilarch took place after the reunification of the schools in Maḥoza. But that does not illuminate how the exilarch achieved reunification, what terms of agreement were set, whether the Pumbeditans were reconciled to the change, or, if not, by what means they were coerced to accept it. The only substantial complaint is that rabbis paid taxes and thought they should not have to. On the whole, as we shall now see, the rabbis responded by ominous, angry silence.

v. TALMUDIC EVIDENCE (I): WHO INFORMED AGAINST RABBAH?

The story of Rabbah's flight and subsequent death, which we considered above,[1] has received a novel interpretation at the hands of M. Beer.[2] Beer points out that the Talmudic account does not record who

---

[1] Above, pp. 41-44. On the flight of Rabbah, see also I. Y. Halevy, *op. cit.*, II, pp. 451-455.

[2] Moshe Beer, "Concerning the Deposal of Rabbah bar Naḥmani from the Headship of the Academy. A Chapter in the History of the Relationships between the Sages and the Exilarchs," (in Hebrew), *Tarbiẓ* 33, 1964, pp. 349-357.

46469

informed against Rabbah or relate what were his motives. Beer supposes that a representative of the Palestinian schools, R. Simeon b.
Pazzi, went, or was sent, to Babylonia "to plead with the exilarch
against imposing taxes upon the rabbinate." The exilarch in question
was, he says, Nathan deZuẓita. Beer recalls that Nathan was the exilarch
who turned Geniva over to the government.[1] He supposes that the
exilarch did the same to Rabbah, who was hunted down. The reaction
was so severe, Beer says, that the exilarch repented. Hence the saying of
R. Joseph that ʿUqban b. Nehemiah the exilarch, who was Nathan
deZuẓita, "was the greatest penitent of his generation." Beer states that
he "greatly repented his action against Rabbah." R. Joseph said that
he saw in a dream that ʿUqban-Nathan was received into heaven, so
the exilarch was forgiven. So Beer.

E. E. Urbach[2] rejected Beer's interpretation. He correctly stressed
that no hint of exilarchic involvement can be uncovered in the story
of Rabbah's death. He supposed that Rabbah died in a persecution of
the Jews and found in the language, "there is a certain man among the
Jews" evidence that a non-Jew was the informer. Persecutions, Urbach
said, are attested in the *SOZ* reference to 313. He questioned the evidence upon which Beer's interpretation of the visit of R. Simeon b.
Pazzi is based. He found no grounds whatever to suppose that the visit
of R. Simeon had anything to do with the exilarch to begin with. None
points to a "mission" in connection with taxing the rabbis. He added
that no comparison can be drawn between Geniva and Rabbah, for the
latter did not have poor relations with the exilarch, so far as we know,
and the former did.

I am wholly persuaded by Urbach's criticism. There is simply no
reason to think that the exilarch had anything to do with Rabbah's
death, and no supporting evidence to be derived, except by begging
the question, in interpreting sayings attributed to R. Joseph and R.
Simeon b. Pazzi. It seems to me quite sufficient to note the fact that
Rabbah was highly unpopular in Pumbedita.[3] So we may suppose that
one of Rabbah's many enemies was the informer who called to the
attention of the Persian government Rabbah's alleged complicity in tax
evasion by many Jews. Which enemy we shall never know. I doubt

---

[1] See vol. III, pp. 75-81.

[2] E. E. Urbach, "Concerning Historical Insight into the Account of Rabba bar
Naḥmani's Death," (in Hebrew), *Tarbiẓ* 34, 1965, 156-161.

[3] b. Shab. 153a. See below, pp. 386-390, for further discussion of Rabbah's rule
in Pumbedita.

that Jews were then being persecuted.[1] If Rabbah was punished on account of tax evasion, the government may have had good reason for putting him to death. In any case the Talmudic evidence concerning Rabbah's death provides no clear information whatever about the exilarchate.

VI. TALMUDIC EVIDENCE (II): FAVORABLE TRADITIONS

The division of sayings about the exilarch and his administration into favorable, hostile, and neutral groups is, in a measure, arbitrary. It is my, generally tentative, judgment about the content of a story that must be decisive. Stories about an exilarch, whether named or otherwise, who was kindly, devoted to the welfare of the rabbis, pious by rabbinic standards, interested in the opinions of the rabbis and guided by them —such stories would have emanated from a circle of tradents who wanted to create a favorable impression of the exilarch. Qualities like devotion to rabbis and piety by rabbinic standards were ascribed as praise and hence reflect the values of a rabbinical circle. The same stories told by others might reveal different intentions. Those who disliked the rabbis would have found such qualities to be reprehensible or craven. Our traditions, however, derive entirely from rabbinical academies, and we must assess the intent of a story by reference to the values of those schools alone. It is important, however, to stress that by *favorable*, I mean, favorable from the viewpoint of the rabbis. We shall see that most of the stories revealing a clearly favorable attitude toward the exilarch were reported in the names of R. Joseph, Rabbah, Rava, and R. Papa, all of whom were heads of academies.

R. Joseph: We have the following sayings of R. Joseph:

> Rav said, "There was no greater penitent than Josiah in his generation, and a certain person in ours" ... R. Joseph said, "And there is another in *ours*, and who is it? 'Uqban b. Nehemiah the exilarch, and he is Nathan deZuzita." R. Joseph said, "I was sitting at study and I dozed, and I saw in my dream that a hand went forward and received him."

(b. Shab. 56b)[2]

> R. Joseph said, "Whoever disputes against the rule of the house of David deserves to have a snake bite him. Here it is written, 'And Adonijah slew sheep and oxen and fat cattle by the stone of Zoheleth'

---

[1] See above, pp. 49-56.
[2] See also B. M. Lewin, *Ozar HaGeonim* (Jerusalem, 1930), II, Part B, p. 24.

(I Kings 1:9), while elsewhere Scripture says, 'With the poison of serpents [zoḥale] of the dust' (Deut. 32:24)."

(b. Sanh. 110a)

Rabbah: One saying attributed to Rabbah *may* be interpreted as a friendly comment on the exilarchic line:

"For you have striven [sarita] with God and with men and have prevailed" (Gen. 32:29). Rabbah said, "He hinted to him that two princes [*sarim*] were destined to go forth from him, the exilarch in Babylonia and the patriarch in Palestine...."

(b. Ḥul. 92a)

Rava: In the same passage, Rava refers to the "three men of excellence" who are mentioned by Gen. 40:10, "And in the vine were three branches," as the three princes of the nations, or angels, who plead in Israel's favor in every generation. In the earlier period, the Scripture was interpreted to apply to Rabbana 'Uqba and Rabbana Nehemiah, Rav's grandchildren, who, as we have seen, were the exilarchs of their time.[1] Rava thus revised the former interpretation.

Rava also said that one may depend upon the exilarch to serve abundant fruit to his guests.[2]

R. Papa: In commenting upon the teaching that if a man can forbid his household to commit a sin and fails to do so, he is seized [=punished] for those same sins, and that the same condition pertains to the sins of a whole town, or of the whole world, R. Papa said the following:

"The members of the exilarchic household are seized for the sins of the whole world."

(b. Shab. 54b)

Comment and summary: These few sayings are ambiguous. One finds only a single reference to the name of the exilarch.[3] We can hardly conclude that R. Joseph certainly had a high opinion of the exilarch 'Uqban b. Nehemiah. All we know is that he supposedly believed that he was a great penitent, but, despite Beer's conjecture, we do not know what sin he was accused of having committed. So the extent of R. Joseph's opinion is that the house of David, meaning in Babylonia the exilarchate, was not a safe opponent. Scripture indicated that the opponents of Davidides were bitten by snakes, or should be. And we

---

[1] Rabbana 'Uqba and Rabbana Nehemiah, Rav's grandchildren were designated by the rabbis as among the three "men of excellence that come forth in Israel in every generation," vol. III, p. 48-50.

[2] b. Ber. 42a.

[3] See vol. III, pp. 81-87.

know that he believed the exilarch of his day was a great sinner, had
done penance for his sin, and heaven had accepted his penance. Rabbah's
saying indicates only that Jacob was informed of the eventual rule of
his descendents, a conviction which was rooted in the history of the
exegeses of Gen. 49:10.[1] Rava's saying seems clearest of all: the
exilarch was a good host. On the other hand, he reinterpreted a Scripture earlier applied to the exilarch and said that it referred to heavenly
intercessors. I do not think he confused the exilarch with an angel, and
so his saying would have revised the interpretation of a Scripture
which others earlier had cited in praise of the exilarchs. R. Papa, finally,
believed that the exilarch, who could prevent sin, held a particularly
solemn trust, and therefore would be punished for the "sins of the
whole world." At the very best, these sayings seem not unfavorable.
They contain little outright praise of the exilarch. It is only by contrast
to the hostile sayings and stories that these may be categorized as
"favorable."[2]

A clear-cut illustration, similar to that we have seen earlier,[3] of the
contradictory tendency in reporting traditions relevant to the exilarch
is as follows:

> R. Papa permitted the stewards (BWRDYQY) of the exilarchate to
> mash a dish with parched grains. Rava said, "Is there anyone who
> permits this in a place where slaves are found?" Others report, Rava
> *himself* mashed a dish with parched grains.
>
> (b. Pes. 40b)[4]

The two traditions of Rava's comment upon R. Papa's action *may*
reveal two attitudes toward the exilarchate. On the one hand, he supposedly said that the matter is not permitted where slaves are common,
for their laxity will lead to illegal action. The exilarch, by implication,
employed slaves whose concern for Jewish ritual was slight, and hence
Rava criticized R. Papa's action. R. Papa should have recognized that
in a household as indifferent to the law as the exilarch's such a leniency
would never be advisable. Over and over again the rabbis alleged that
his servants must never be trusted in matters of ritual observance, as in
this case. The second tradition about Rava's comment on R. Papa's
ruling omits all reference to the alleged ritual laxity of the exilarchate

---

[1] See vol. I, 2nd rev. ed., p. 104, 108.
[2] Vol. II, pp. 98-119, III, pp. 61-75, 81-94.
[3] *ibid.*, pp. 62-63.
[4] Trans. H. Freedman (London, 1938). *Diq. Sof.* IV, pp. 114-115 lists no important variants.

and its cooks. It simply said that Rava himself did precisely what R. Papa told the exilarch might be done. No criticism of the exilarch is implied, nor of R. Papa's implicit trust of the exilarch's "slaves." It seems possible that the second tradition constitutes a reply to the first: "While some have criticized the exilarch for following the ritual practice permitted by R. Papa, Rava himself did that same thing." Otherwise a report that Rava himself did it would make no sense in this context, for we should have to read the pericope as follows: "R. Papa permitted...Rava himself mashed..." Without knowing that someone thought R. Papa had erred, and that Rava himself had said so, we should not comprehend the emphatic reference to Rava's *own* action. Hence I should imagine that the two traditions are reported in a logical sequence: "R. Papa permitted. Rava criticized him. No, Rava did not criticize him, but in fact did so himself." If this is the case, then we have before us an example of a tradition which has been edited from two perspectives, first, that of the critics of the exilarchate, second, that of its rabbinic defenders.[1] It is striking that the latter could not remove the reference to Rava's criticism, but could only nullify it. If it was a significant matter, and I do not know that it was, then Rava's criticism was sufficiently well-known so that it could not be convincingly expunged, but only modified. In any event the implications of R. Papa's action remain favorable to the exilarch, for the exilarch listened to his rabbinical advisers, and his servants did what the rabbis said. The comment, "Rava said..." would be intended to turn the story into an attack upon the exilarch. Its presupposition was the same, namely, that if the exilarch did *not* listen to the rabbis, he would be subject to criticism. Hence I should imagine that the story was of concern only to the rabbinical friends of the exilarch, those who held appointment at his will as heads of schools (R. Papa, Rava). What the exilarch thought of the rabbis of his day we simply do not know. What the rabbis thought we can scarcely surmise upon the basis of the evidence cited above.

VII. TALMUDIC EVIDENCE (III): HOSTILE TRADITIONS

The slight, ambiguous evidence interpreted, without much certainty, as praise of the exilarch is outweighed by the unambiguous evidence of rabbinical hostility. The main burden of the stories was that the exilarch was not a pious Jew, but was a sybarite and even ate food which was from the rabbinical viewpoint of doubtful acceptability; did not pray

---

[1] For a second case, see below, pp. 107-109.

like a rabbi; and was not to be relied upon to keep other aspects of the
law. The one fact that emerges is that the exilarch was not a rabbi, and
that rabbis criticized him on that account. We shall here consider the
traditions in the names of major fourth-century teachers.

R. Zera: When R. Simeon b. Pazzi came to spend some time with a
'powerful man' in Babylonia, R. Zera asked him why he did not rebuke
the servants of the exilarch. R. Simeon replied that they would not
accept a rebuke from him.[1]

R. Joseph: The following story may be interpreted as hostile to the
exilarch:

> R. Joseph said, "I once went up after Mar 'Uqba to the baths. When
> I left, I was offered a cup of wine, and I felt [its effect] from the hair
> of my head down to my toe nails. If I had drunk another cup, I should
> have feared lest it be deducted from my merits for the world to come."
> Yet Mar 'Uqba drinks it every day. Mar 'Uqba is different for he is
> used to it.
>
> (b. Shab. 140a)

I doubt that the rabbis' stories about the luxury of the exilarch's way
of living were meant to praise him. They underlined, rather, the differences between his and other Jews' way of living. The implication of
R. Joseph's account was that Mar 'Uqba's enjoyment of this world
actually would diminish his advantages in the world to come. A re-
curring motif in rabbinical discussions is the prayer that God will give
the pagans their reward in this world, so they may suffer for all eternity.
The intention of R. Joseph may not have been dissimilar.

Rabbah: The following story leaves no doubt that Rabbah was alleged
to have criticized the exilarchic servants:

> Rabbah and R. Zera visited the exilarch [on the Sabbath], and saw
> a slave place a pitcher of water on the mouth of a kettle. [The pitcher
> contained cold water, and the kettle was hot]. Rabbah thereupon
> rebuked him [the slave]. Said R. Zera to him, "Wherein does it differ
> from a boiler upon a boiler [which is permitted]." "He preserves the
> heat there," he replied, "while here he creates it." Then he saw him
> spread a turban over the mouth of a cask and place a cup upon it.

---

[1] b. Shab. 55a. See Beer, *Tarbiz* 33, 1964, pp. 351-353. I should suppose that
the late-Midrashic sources cited by Beer are based upon the above Talmudic
source, in particular *Yalqut* Psalms #656, "Rabbi Zeira sent to R. Simai...." But
that R. Simeon b. Pazzi went, or was sent, from Palestine to rebuke the exilarch
seems to me absolutely unsupported by the sources Beer cites, as I said above,
p. 101. Still, R. Zera obviously thought that the exilarch had done something
wrong, and ought to be rebuked. We simply do not know what it was.

Thereupon Rabbah rebuked him. Said R. Zera to him, "Why?." "You will soon see," he replied. Subsequently he saw him [the slave] wringing it out [which is prohibited on the Sabbath]....

(b. Shab. 48a)[1]

Two facts emerge from this account. First of all, Rabbah allegedly criticized the Sabbath ritual practices of the exilarchate. Second, he was able to do so without coming to harm. It seems to me that the story is meant to be hostile to the exilarch, for it conveys the message that his slaves cannot be trusted to keep the Sabbath laws concerning the use of fire and other matters. It is part of a considerable corpus of such stories. It is striking, therefore, that Rabbah was able to instruct the slaves. Perhaps he actually limited his comments to R. Zera. R. Zera was told by R. Simeon that he did not feel he would find similar success, and other traditions of the same incident[2] suggest that R. Simeon did not think he would go unscathed if he rebuked the exilarchate. One may, therefore, derive from this story a quite contrary fact, that the exilarch's servants *would* take seriously the criticism of a leading rabbi. However, whether that was so or not, the intent of the story-teller was quite different; and it cannot be regarded as other than hostile.

Rabbah b. R. Huna: The following story is striking:

'Ulla happened by the exilarchate. He saw Rabbah b. R. Huna sitting in a tub of water and measuring it [on the Sabbath]. He said to him, "I may admit that the rabbis permitted measuring in connection with the fulfilment of a commandment, but not in such a connection." He replied, "I was just keeping myself busy."

(b. Shab. 157b)

So Rabbah b. R. Huna not only spent the Sabbath at the exilarch's, but engaged in a practice which was, at first glance, prohibited by the rabbinical tradition. What is hostile here is the supposition that the exilarch did not care about Sabbath law, but only an outside rabbi would rebuke the apparent breaking of the Sabbath. When Rabbah b. R. Huna visited the exilarch, he acted in accordance with the rabbinical law about how one says the Sanctification of the Sabbath.[3]

The following story relates that the exilarch's ritual standards were low:

Rabbah b. R. Huna happened to visit the exilarchate. He [the exilarch] drank from a *qenishqanim* [a cup with spouts from which several

---

[1] Trans. H. Freedman (London, 1938), pp. 217-218.

[2] Cited by Beer. Compare vol. III, pp. 84-86 on R. Sheshet's experience.

[3] b. Pes. 100b.

could drink at the same time] and [Rabbah] did not rebuke him [lit.:
said nothing to him at all]....

(b. Shab. 62b)

The comment of the Talmudic editor was that there was no rabbinic
prohibition against use of such a luxurious cup on the Sabbath. However, taking the above statement by itself, we note that the presupposition was that the cup should *not* be used, but Rabbah b. R. Huna failed
to say so. Only later on was his "reason" made clear, namely, that using
the cup on the Sabbath really was not prohibited. The person who
preserved the account must have thought it a noteworthy event, and
his reason may have been his supposition that the cup *was* prohibited.
(He may also have wanted proof that it was permitted, since somebody
had disputed that, as he thought, falsely.) The exilarch did not observe
the prohibition. Yet the rabbi said nothing by way of rebuke.

On the other hand, we have the following:

> Rabbah b. R. Huna happened to visit the exilarch, and permitted
> drinking from a *qenishqanim* [by Jews and gentiles together]. Some say
> that he himself did so.
>
> (b. A.Z. 72b-73a)[1]

This story is about drinking from that same vessel with several spouts.
Here, however, the issue was, Does the exilarch keep taboos against
gentile's touch of wine which is to be consumed by a Jew? As we saw
earlier, these laws were extremely strict, and they were not theoretical,
but actually enforced. The rule stated by Mar Zutra b. R. Naḥman was
that the Israelite and the gentile may drink from such a vessel, but only
if the Israelite stops drinking first. If the gentile stopped drinking first,
then the wine left in his tube would flow back into the vessel and dis-
qualify the remaining wine.[2] In the story concerning Rabbah b. R.
Huna, he either permitted doing so without qualification, or actually
did so himself. So according to the story, at the home of the exilarch
the strict laws about rigid protection of wine against the touch of
gentiles were not enforced. A rabbi associated with the exilarch broke

---

[1] See M. Beer, in *Ẓiyyon* 28, 1963, p. 7, whose interpretation of the incident I
have followed. Beer adds that he did so because of his (the exilarch's) "representative function." He cites the description of the vessel in *Oẓar HaGeonim* II,
p. 26.

[2] Even if the exilarch instructed gentile guests that they must *not* stop drinking
before the Jews did, yet the Jews could not thereafter drink from that vessel.
Moreover, rigid laws involved the cleansing of the vessel for future Jewish use,
and as we have seen above, there is some doubt that Jews could again use it for
any purpose whatever.

them as well. It seems possible to suppose that the additional remark, that Rabbah b. R. Huna himself broke the law, may have been intended as a defense of the exilarch. The presupposition would have been that a rabbi would not break the law,[1] and therefore the law was not broken at the exilarch's house either. So the story in its present form contains either a hostile or a friendly attitude toward the exilarchate, hostile in that the exilarch did not keep the law, nor did the rabbi who gave him instruction about it; or, alternatively, friendly in that the rabbi himself acted as did the exilarch, with the possible presumption that the law was actually observed. The former seems much more likely.

In fact the two sayings about the many-spouted vessel, one appearing in connection with Sabbath law, the other with laws about wine, appear to be based on a single anterior tradition, somewhat as follows:

> Rabbah b. R. Huna happened to visit the exilarch. The exilarch [or, someone] drank from a *qenishqanim* and—
>
> a. Rabbah b. R. Huna did not rebuke him
>
> b. Rabbah b. R. Huna permitted him to do so
>
> c. Rabbah b. R. Huna joined him in doing so

on the Sabbath

with Gentiles

Whether the "visit" had to do with Sabbath law or the taboos about gentiles' not touching wine does not matter, except as the story was included in one or another tractate. The story was probably intended as hostile to the exilarch. In the one case, it indicated that the exilarch did not keep the Sabbath. In the other, he did not observe the taboos about wine. Its original form did not affect in the slightest in which discussion it was finally included. It served either purpose equally well. Yet one may suppose that at the root of the matter merely lay the simple fact that an unusual drinking vessel was used by the exilarch.[2] Upon that fact alone, both traditions were based.

Rava: Two apparently hostile stories involve Rava:

> The exilarch had a banquet-hall ['BWWRNQ'] in his orchard. He said to R. Huna b. Ḥinena, "Will the Master make an arrangement so

---

[1] This is *precisely* the understanding of the Tosafists, *ad loc.*

[2] See especially Y. Brand, *Klei HaḤeres beSifrut HaTalmud* (in Hebrew, Jerusalem, 1953), English title: *Ceramics in Talmudic Literature*, pp. 278-279. Brand points out that in b. Shab. 62b, R. Ammi and R. Assi discuss the "bowls of wine" of Amos 6:6, and one regarded Amos's reference to be to *qenishqanim*. Hence the biblical prophet was seen by some rabbis to condemn precisely the luxurious objects used by the exilarch. But I do not know that the fourth-century rabbis knew what had been said earlier in Palestine.

that tomorrow [on the Sabbath] we may eat bread there?"[1] He went and made a reed-fence, fixing each reed less than three handbreadths from the other. Rava came and pulled them out. R. Papa and R. Huna b. R. Joshua followed him and picked them up [to make sure R. Huna b. Ḥinena did not put them back]. On the next day, Rabina objected to Rava ... R. Papa also objected ... R. Huna b. R. Joshua also said to Rava ... The exilarch thereupon quoted concerning them the Scripture (Jer. 4.22), "They are sages to do evil, but they know not how to do good."

(b. ʿEruv. 25b-26a)

Rava and R. Naḥman b. Isaac were once sitting together when R. Aḥa b. Jacob came by sitting in a golden carriage and dressed in a purple cloak. Rava went to him. R. Naḥman b. Isaac did not, saying "Perhaps he is on the staff of the exilarchate. Rava needs them and I do not." When he saw who it was, he went....

(b. Git. 31b)[2]

The latter story simply indicates that R. Naḥman b. Isaac thought some of the rabbis were beholden to the exilarch, but he was not. Those who were, as was Rava when he headed an academy, would naturally humble themselves.

The former story is of greater interest. It indicates that the rabbis as a group were criticized by the exilarch for their expertness in depriving people of their pleasures. Rava apparently disturbed the ritual arrangements made at the exilarch's palace by a court rabbi. His colleagues made certain that the decision of the master would not be ignored. The story is a strange one, for it would suggest that "the next day" the rabbis engaged in a protracted discussion of the law in the presence of the exilarch, who, hearing and understanding the issues, commented as he did upon them. Is the story hostile to the exilarch? I should suppose that among people for whom criticism of the rabbis in such terms would be improper, it would be told as a hostile story. The exilarch emerges in the story as respectful of the rabbis. He was indeed subservient to their legal decisions. So to a rabbinical circle such a story would be both hostile to the exilarch and favorable to themselves. The exilarch's rabbi, R. Huna b. Ḥinena, did not know the law but had to be corrected by others. On the other hand, one could interpret the story as preserving from the rabbinical perspective a favorable view of the exilarch. He patiently allowed rabbis to govern his ritual practices, and faithfully kept the law. When a leading master deprived

---

[1] The legal problems are of no interest here.
[2] Compare vol. III, p. 59, 76.

him of the pleasure of his garden on the Sabbath, he did nothing. Afterward, learning that Rava was in error, he commented that rabbis only
know how to do bad things, not good ones. It may be compared to the
stories about R. Sheshet who acted in a high-handed manner toward the
exilarchate's servants, only to discover that the law was on their side,
not his. He thereupon said that they should not be so informed.[1] These
stories both appear in the same tractate, namely 'Eruvin.[2] They seem
to me generally hostile to the anti-exilarchic rabbis, and the story cited
above may be a part of the same corpus of traditions. Whether or not
it was intended to convey an unfavorable picture depends upon the
viewpoint of the story-teller. If an exilarchic rabbi, he would have
wanted to say that rabbis are clever, but in the end do not concern themselves with the welfare of faithful Jews even though the exilarch himself respects them.[3] If a hostile rabbi, he would have meant to underline that the law was complicated, that even great rabbis may err, but
that the exilarch had no patience with the subtleties of the law and paid
only grudging respect to those who knew it.

Rava supposedly said that when the rabbis ate at the exilarch's
palace, there was a doubt as to whether further wine would be brought
or not.[4] His saying contrasts with the one cited above that fruit was
freely given out at the exilarch's.

The following teaching seems to convey a negative attitude as well:

> Rava said, "When we eat bread at the exilarch's, we bless in groups
> of three." Why not bless in groups of ten? The exilarch may hear and
> be angry. Then let us rely upon the blessing of the exilarch? Since
> everyone will answer loudly, they will not hear the one who says grace.
> (b. Ber. 50a)

Rava's actual saying seems to have been that at the exilarch's table,
rabbis bless quietly, in small groups, rather than relying upon the
exilarch's recitation of grace. Since the rabbis elsewhere discussed saying grace in larger groups, without mentioning the possibility that the
noise would drown out the prayer of the leader, it may be that the
reason given above is not the real one. If so, we are left with the supposition that rabbis do not rely upon the exilarch's recital of grace, but

---

[1] Note the similar motif in the R. Sheshet stories, cited in vol. III, pp. 84-87.
R. Sheshet not only ruled, but enforced the law on the exilarchate *and* against its
desires, but it turned out he was ignorant of the law. He thereupon said that the
exilarch should not be told the truth about the matter.
[2] b. 'Eruv. 11b, 39b.
[3] See the saying of the family of Benjamin the physician, cited below p. 363.
[4] b. Pes. 103a.

must recite it on their own, though surreptitiously. It is highly conjectural to suppose that the rabbis did not want the exilarch to pray in
their behalf, and I mention it only as a possibility.

We see, therefore, that what seems hostile from one perspective from
another appears to be favorable. We cannot be sure of the intention of
the story-tellers. Nonetheless, it is clear that the enemies of the exilarch
repeatedly harped on a few points, touching on his ritual violations and
luxurious living, but contributed little more information than their own
displeasure on these counts. They exhibited contempt for rabbis associated with the exilarch as much as for his slaves or servants. They were
no better than their master, but kept the law in a lax, sometimes even
ignorant, fashion. I am puzzled by the extreme mildness of the polemic
in some of the passages to which I have attributed polemical purpose.
When one has to recognize that a story may be *either* favorable *or* hostile,
there is some reason to consider the possibility of its being neutral. This
literature comes from the schools, in which legal discussion was the
major concern and was frequently enlivened by appeals to the examples
of famous rabbis. It is therefore possible that some examples, even a-
mong those cited here, were remembered simply *qua* examples, without
polemic purpose, and also without intent to praise (as above). When
everybody was arguing about the law, disputed cases must have been
coming up all the time, and everybody must have been found in the
minority at some time, perhaps often. The more important question is,
How often and in what circumstances is the behavior of the exilarch
himself or of his court cited as an authoritative legal precedent? It is
clear that Mar ʿUqba I was so cited. R. Naḥman earlier and Rava now
conducted courts closely affiliated with the exilarch. We cannot conclude, therefore, that the exilarch's *court* ceased to be good precedent
for deciding the law. On the other hand, the stories about Mar ʿUqba
I have no substantial parallels later on. Unless some rabbi (e.g. Naḥman,
Rava) was on hand to make, permit, or approve a decision, it did not
now constitute a good precedent for deciding the law. Since the exilarch
was still the titular head of the Jewish courts and supreme authority to
which cases from them could be appealed, this tacit abandonment of
reference to his practice as authoritative is significant.[1]

---

[1] See below, pp. 114-119, for further comment on the veritable silence of the
rabbinical sources concerning the fourth-century exilarchs. I am grateful to
Professor Morton Smith for his comments on the division of stories into hostile
and friendly categories.

I. TALMUDIC EVIDENCE (IV): NEUTRAL TRADITIONS

A number of stories mention the exilarch quite tangentially, implying no evaluation whatever of his actions. In some, the menu served at the exilarch's was discussed on account of a legal problem, as in the following:

> When Rava was at the exilarch's house, they prepared for him a dish of fish pressed sixty times and he ate it...

> (b. M.Q. 11a)

> At the exilarch's, Rava was served a paste of dough over roasted duck. He said, "Had I not seen it as clear as white glass I would not have eaten it..."

> (b. Pes. 74b)

Of a similarly neutral nature are the occasional references to a rabbis' lectures at the gate of the exilarchic palace.[1] I see no tendency, either hostile or otherwise, in accounts of discussions between the exilarch and noted rabbis, for instance, that of Rabbah b. R. Huna and the exilarch on rescuing sacred writings on the Sabbath.[2] The following seems to me of the same order:

> Rabbah said to those who bind the *hoshanna* at the exilarch's palace, "When you bind *hoshannas* at the exilarch's, leave a handle...."

> (b. Suk. 37a)

The exilarch and his bureaucrats play no role in such accounts. The intent of the story is not to make a judgment upon them, nor even to prove that they were subservient to rabbinical rulings. We may conclude that everyone knew the exilarch did consult with, and was instructed by, rabbis. Rabbah b. R. Huna appeared above as an exilarchic associate. Rabbah and Rava headed the Pumbeditan school. I see no reason to doubt that the exilarch actually did consult the heads of the schools about legal issues. Stories to the contrary must, therefore, have been polemic based upon the exilarch's alleged indifference to the law.

What is important in the following accounts is a similar neutrality in far more important matters:

> Rabbah [or, Rava][3] said, "These three things were told to me by 'Uqban b. Nehemiah the exilarch in the name of Samuel, 'The law of the state is law. The Persians acquire ownership by an occupation of forty years. The sale by rich landlords [grandees] of land bought up in payment of taxes is a valid sale....'"

> (b. B.B. 55a)

---

[1] E.g. b. Ḥul. 84b, b. Shab. 126b.
[2] b. Shab. 115b.
[3] See Rabbinowicz, *Diq. Sof. ad loc.*

Rabbah here expressed no opinion or attitude concerning the exilarchate; he merely repeated an important tradition told to him in Samuel's
name by the exilarch. That the exilarch knew such a tradition is taken
for granted. The matters to which it pertained all had to do with state-
law, in particular the enforcement of Persian rules in Jewish courts. It
was the exilarch's task to oversee such matters, and he was assumed,
therefore, to know what he was talking about. The tradition is entirely
neutral. If so, however, it is most important because it shows the exilarch felt himself capable to lay down the law to the rabbis on such
questions, and the rabbis accepted his rulings. It confirms my supposition that the rabbis owed their authority basically to his appointment
to serve in his courts.

When Rabin and Abaye were sitting before Rabbana Nehemiah
brother of the exilarch, they commented upon his silk garment, but
only by way of reference to a word in the Mishnah.[1] Similarly, in the
context of legal discussion, Abaye's saying about buying a field in the
name of another, "such as the exilarch,"[2] implies no judgment whatever
about the exilarch.[3]

IX. REVIEW AND EVALUATION OF TALMUDIC EVIDENCE

The Talmudic references to the exilarch in the times of Rabbah and
R. Joseph, Abaye and Rava, are hardly unequivocal. Our effort to
distinguish hostile from favorable traditions has not been entirely
successful, for it is not always clear whether a given account was meant
to praise, denigrate, or merely report. I think it clear, nonetheless, that
both hostile and friendly accounts *were* transmitted, often concerning
the attitudes of the same rabbi. We cannot mechanically distinguish
between the intent or spirit of these accounts.

Earlier[4] it seemed that while favorable stories normally mentioned
the exilarch by name, hostile ones spoke of an anonymous figure. Here
no such phenomenon became apparent. R. Joseph referred to 'Uqban

---

[1] b. Shab. 20b. The account is in the context of Mishnah commentary.

[2] b. B.Q. 102b-103a, and the reference to the exilarch is to begin with not
supported by all manuscript evidence.

[3] Further neutral traditions are cited below, the exilarch told Rava to
see whether a certain newcomer was a rabbinical disciple, and if he was, to grant
him special market privileges. The detail, mentioned as matter-of-fact, tells us
that the exilarch continued to favor the rabbis in many ways. The focus of the
story is elsewhere, however, and it was not told either to praise or to criticize the
exilarchate.

[4] vol. III, pp. 61-75, 87-94, vol. II, pp. 92-125.

b. Nehemiah the exilarch, and supposedly[1] identified him with Nathan
de Zuzita, whom he called the greatest penitent of the generation. It
may have been intended as praise to call a man a great penitent, but
it also was hardly a compliment to note that he had a great sin to atone
for. The stories in which the exilarch was mentioned by name, in addition to the above, are as follows: R. Joseph referred to the wonderful
wine consumed by Mar 'Uqba; Nehemiah's citing Samuel as reported
by Rabbah; Rabbana Nehemiah brother of the exilarch wore silk. Two
of the three stories concern the luxurious way of living of the exilarch
and his family. The third merely records in the exilarch's name a saying
of Samuel. Given the exilarch's role in Iranian politics, one can hardly
suppose on this basis that Rabbah thought the exilarch invariably
provided a valid report of all earlier opinions. The subject-matter of
this particular saying of Samuel pertained directly to what the exilarch
was supposed to know. So the four traditions on a *named* exilarch do
not reveal a favorable attitude, but at best, a neutral one. Whatever the
reasons for the fairly general practice, noted in third-century traditions,
of naming an exilarch in favorable stories and leaving him anonymous
in unfavorable ones, they seem no longer to have pertained in the later
period.

The apparently favorable traditions about an anonymous exilarch
included R. Joseph's saying that one should not dispute with the house
of David; Rabbah's equally enigmatic interpretation of Gen. 32:29;
Rava's, that the exilarch is generous with fruit; and possibly R. Papa's,
that the exilarchate will be punished for the sins of the whole world,
from which one may infer that he thought the exilarchate bore weighty
responsibilities and much power. The two traditions concerning Rava's
response to R. Papa's ruling at the exilarchate included a favorable
viewpoint, that Rava did what some felt should not be done, with the
implication that the exilarchic practice was not illegal. One may infer
that the exilarch, accused of laxity in matters of ritual law, was here
defended.

The hostile sayings and stories all contain the implication that the
exilarch deserved rebuke, but that it took courage to deliver it. He lived
luxuriously, and in so doing, used up his store of merit for the coming
world. Rabbah found improper a ritual practice of the exilarch's servant.

---

[1] Urbach says that the words "and he is Nathan deZuzita" were not spoken
by R. Joseph himself. See his critique of Beer, *Tarbiz* 34, 1965, p. 161. I do not
know what to make of such suppositions, or on what basis they are reached,
tested, or evaluated.

(The detail that he delivered a rebuke without coming to harm may indicate that this was rare.) Rabbah b. R. Huna himself violated the Sabbath at the exilarch's house; it is implied that others did likewise. He either refrained from rebuking the exilarch for drinking from a peculiar vessel on the Sabbath, or himself joined in drinking from it in a situation in which the taboos against the gentile's touch of wine were violated. The two strange accounts reveal that the possession of such a luxurious vessel led to the formulation of two separate stories about its use, both intended to reflect a negative judgment upon the exilarch's ritual standards. Rava likewise ruled that the exilarch's rabbi did not keep the law on the Sabbath boundaries—or did not even know it. But the account may be interpreted in a different light: the exilarch put up with rabbinical decisions, even though they turned out to be invalid. Hence he respected rabbis, although complaining against them. Rava supposedly doubted that the exilarch was generous with wine. He *may* have declined to accept the leadership of the exilarch in saying grace.

Neutral traditions report that rabbis ate at the exilarch's house, preached, taught, and judged, at his gate. The latter are doubtless quite factual, for the exilarchate, as the center of Jewish government, was the site of teaching, preaching, and judgment.[1] The stories about Rava's eating at the exilarch's convey both a reliable fact and a polemic purpose. The fact was that the rabbis ate with the exilarch. The polemic purpose was to show that they found it possible to do so, and hence the exilarch *did* observe the dietary rules in a manner that met with rabbinical approval. Since many told stories to the contrary, this was an important matter.[2]

What facts may be derived from these traditions? First, and most certain, there were rabbis who expressed a hostile attitude toward the exilarch. The hostility took several forms, but it is clear that some traditions were deliberately shaped so as to present an unfavorable picture. These rabbis stressed that the exilarch did not keep "the Torah" as he should. He lived luxuriously but was a niggardly host. He did not follow rabbinical instructions, and it was dangerous to give them. Second, some traditions in the rabbinical schools preserved a quite different viewpoint. The exilarch observed the law as did leading rabbinical authorities. He was a generous host. He was a great penitent. He knew rabbinical traditions told in the name of great authorities of the preceding century. These two facts provide some insight into the ways in

---

[1] See for example the stories about R. Naḥman, vol. III, pp. 61-75.

[2] E.g., R. Sheshet, vol. III, pp. 84-87.

which the exilarchate was discussed at this time by rabbis. The issues centered upon whether or not the exilarch was a good Jew by rabbinic lights. Those who supported (or were supported by) him said that he was, and the opposition denied it.

One may discern a shift in the quality of the debate. In the earlier century, the exilarch was accused, to be sure, of not keeping or even knowing the law. The defense, however, alleged not merely that he *did* know and keep it. It added that he was a colleague and friend of the greatest rabbis of the age. Such luminaries as Rav, Samuel, R. Naḥman, and others subjected themselves to his rule. He, no less than they, meticulously observed the law just as the rabbis taught it. Now less seems to have been claimed, and less alleged. The point of the fourth-century opposition was that such a man as the exilarch was not worthy of governing the Jewish people; the defense merely asserted that he was. Little reference was made to the Davidic origin of the exilarch, which had been so widely discussed as fact one hundred years earlier. Perhaps R. Papa referred to that belief—but whether he meant to refer specifically to the exilarch or not we can only guess. No stories were told about how faithfully the exilarch honored rabbis, studied with them, or was honored by them.[1] Now all that was asserted in his behalf was that he was no worse than Rava or Rabbah b. R. Huna for acting just as they did. No leading rabbinical authority appeared in the traditions on the exilarchate to take place of Samuel or R. Naḥman. The pro-exilarchic rabbis played a smaller role in the traditions than earlier, and themselves were portrayed by the opposition as inconsequential. On the other hand, no leading anti-exilarchic rabbi of the stature of R. Sheshet appeared. It is indeed difficult to say whether leading rabbis held favorable or unfavorable views, for to many were ascribed both friendliness and opposition to the exilarchate.

Our earlier consideration of the relationship between the exilarch and the schools suggested that Pumbedita was a focus of hostile attitudes toward the exilarch. Yet we have now seen that one cannot attribute all hostile stories to Pumbeditans, all friendly or neutral ones to Surans or Maḥozans. Beer said Sura was always a center of pro-exilarchic sentiment, having been founded by Rav, whose grandsons held the exilarchic office. Yet I can discern no consequences in the transmission of stories about the exilarch. One should have expected that the heads of Pumbedita, Rabbah, R. Joseph, Abaye, and Rava, all

---

[1] It was still considered a religious action to visit the exilarch on the festivals, however.

of whom held the *shipura*, would have been sources of only negative accounts. Yet my tentative division of stories shows that no such expectation has been realized. I do not know how to account for the transmission of varying attitudes in the name of the same significant rabbis, all heads of the Pumbeditan school. It is of course quite possible that individual rabbis held mixed views of the exilarch. Possibly different exilarchs triggered different sorts of responses. Since we do not know the names of the several exilarchs of this period, we cannot be certain that all of them consistently elicited rabbinical hostility. Perhaps, also, such a rigidly political reading of the data is inappropriate to begin with. By contrast, however, the late third-century sayings seemed to divide according to the schools where they were first redacted. Those attributed to the Nehardean-Maḥozan circle, in particular to Rabbah bar Abbuha and R. Naḥman b. Jacob were invariably friendly; to R. Sheshet, invariably hostile; to the Surans under R. Huna, generally neutral, but in any case rarely hostile. If the Pumbeditans in the brief span of Rav Judah b. Ezekiel's headship were hostile to the exilarch, as we should certainly suppose, we can cite no substantial evidence of that fact, for Rav Judah certainly paid due respect to the exilarch when R. Huna advised that he ought to. So while the earlier traditions seemed relatively clear, those of the fourth-century masters do not. I am unable at this time further to contribute to the study of the problem. Perhaps future research will clarify this puzzling and curious phenomenon.

We may only conclude that the relationship between the rabbinate and the exilarchate was deteriorating. If on the whole the rabbis preserved fewer stories, and hence *seem* less interested in the exilarch than earlier, the reason is neither that they enjoyed a freer hand, nor that his power had diminished. We have no evidence whatever to lead to the supposition that the Iranian government now turned more to the rabbis than to the exilarch who earlier had hired them. I do not for one minute think the Persians would have done so. And their decision mattered most of all. Nor can we suppose that the rabbis modulated their opposition because of the unsettled times, as I think was the case a century earlier.[1] Stories about the exilarch conveyed a bitterer attitude than before, particularly in the time of Rav and Samuel. The rabbis as a group now sought far more power in Jewish community affairs than previously.[2] They asserted claims which were earlier unknown. Yet, whatever they claimed, they no longer told stories of how the exilarch

---

[1] Vol. II, pp. 119-125.
[2] See below, pp. 125ff.

had sat humbly as their student, while they accepted his administrative
or judicial dominance, nor did they preserve accounts of how a few
particularly favored but also learned rabbis represented the interests of
the exilarch and really controlled his administration. I think the silence
of the rabbinic traditions is most ominous, for the rabbis generally preserved few, if any, stories about those they hated. It seems to me a fact
that remarkably few important men in the schools were interested in
contributing stories, or handing on sayings, relevant to the exilarch. A
few critical remarks countered by some outright friendly revisions of
stories are all that we have in hand. Nothing could testify more convincingly to the tension between exilarchate and rabbinate than that
lack of interest.[1]

x. SUMMARY AND CONCLUSIONS

In the schools of the late third century, a small oppositionist group,
led by Geniva, with a larger number of covert sympathizers, had begun
to articulate dissatisfaction with the status quo. Subservience to the
exilarch began to gall some learned rabbis, who supposedly not only
knew the whole of God's revelation to Moses, but also embodied it as
the best exemplification of the "image of God" among men. Rav Judah
and R. Huna evidently taught earlier that Scripture had freed rabbis, as
saints and priests, from poll-taxes .Now a number of distinguished sages
actually claimed to be free of the practical obligation to pay those taxes.

It is striking that despite their veritable silence about the contemporary exilarchs, the fourth-century rabbis pursued extensive studies of

---

[1] Still, we cannot ignore the fact that the earlier stories *were* preserved, pertaining both to Rav and Samuel and to R. Naḥman and Rabbah b. Abbuhah. As
I said (p. 72, n. 1) I think those stories must have entered the process of tradition fairly soon after they were redacted, or they would have been ignored or
suppressed later on. So by the first quarter of the fourth century, most of the
favorable sayings and traditions cited in vols. II and III must have become
"authoritative," or sufficiently well-known so that no one could suppress them.
A second possibility is that the circles around the exilarch were responsible for
their preservation and later inclusion in the Talmud as we have it. If so, however,
in the fourth century such circles proved remarkably unproductive of new
materials of the same sort. One might argue that not much happened which
circles favorable to the exilarch would have wanted to relate, but I think it unlikely. Such circles proved able to "revise" hostile stories in two instances cited
above (p. 97 and p. 106), so I should imagine they could manufacture whatever
they wanted, or could preserve whatever favorable stories they knew about. I
cannot explain why they failed to do so, unless there was simply not much need
for such an apologetic. A manner of living had been established, and perhaps no
further defense or explanation was called for.

the Mishnah of Sanhedrin, making many noteworthy contributions pertaining to that tractate. Ignoring the government at hand, they paid close attention to the forms and requirements of the government which had allegedly existed in temple times and again would be set up when the Messiah came and brought the Jews back to Palestine. The rabbis concentrated their best energies upon their own ideals for the future, as if by so doing they intended to express their displeasure with the reality around them. By contrast, we have almost no Talmudic account of what the exilarch did from day to day, of how his court-system actually operated,[1] of his dealings with Shapur II or lower Persian officials, of any major problems he may have faced in these difficult times, of his studies of the law—even of his name. One might suppose that rabbis normally do not tell about such things, but the third-century traditions suggest the contrary. Furthermore, we do have stories about Shapur II and his mother in relationship to noted rabbis, but none about royal dealings with the one man the Iranian court held responsible, like the Christian Catholicus of Seleucia—Ctesiphon, for the Jewish millet-community. I find it striking that in rabbinic traditions, the exilarch does not even figure in the contacts between Iranian and Jewish officials.

SOZ[2] supplies the names of the exilarchs of this time, which Lazarus arranged in chronological sequence, as Nehemiah I, 'Uqba II, Huna Mar I his brother, and Abba. It is remarkable that the Talmudic traditions on the exilarch derive mostly from stories about Rav's grandchildren, and few, if any, accounts in which the chief sages of this period figure contain any exilarchic names at all. R. Joseph and Rabbah referred by name to Nathan deẒuẓita or 'Uqban b. Nehemiah the exilarch or Mar 'Uqba (II). A story is told about Rabin's and Abaye's sitting before Rabbana Nehemiah the brother of the exilarch. I do not know when, following Lazarus's dates, Rabbana Nehemiah would have become exilarch unless this story refers to Nehemiah I. If so, *all* the few Talmudic references we do have pertain to Rav's grandsons, none at all to Huna Mar I, Abba, and Nathan II. The extant favorable stories about unspecified exilarchs, told by R. Joseph, Rabbah, Abaye, Rava, and their contemporaries, were no more numerous. R. Joseph said it is dangerous to fight with the exilarch. Rabbah held that Jacob was told he was progenitor of two princes. R. Papa said the exilarch was re-

---

[1] See below, p. 187, for the single exceptional account.

[2] See also the Geonic traditions collected and edited by H. Ẓ. Taubes, *Oẓar HaGeonim leMasekhet Sanhedrin* (Jerusalem, 1966), pp. 32-38.

sponsible for everyone's sins. Exhibiting an apparently hostile intent, R. Joseph commented on the luxuriousness of Mar 'Uqba's way of living; Rabbah rebuked the exilarch's house-servants for laxity in Sabbath observance; and Rabbah b. R. Huna noticed a strange drinking vessel, which became the occasion for some nasty stories of ritual looseness. Rava supposedly found similar indifference to, or ignorance of, the law. Neutral traditions generally indicated that rabbis ate at the exilarch's, and lectures were given by rabbis at his palace. The stories in all involved only a few superficial matters, mostly pertaining to the exilarch's way of living.

We must assume that the exilarchate remained strong and influential both at the Iranian court and within the Jewish community. If that assumption is correct, and I see no grounds for any other, then how do we account for it? First, the rabbis' claims and behavior must have provided the exilarch with a powerful appeal among the ordinary people. By demanding tax exemption, the rabbis brought upon themselves the resentment of others who suffered from the heavy burden. People were losing land and even freedom on account of the taxes, and a few rich men were gaining additional property, which rabbinical courts confirmed in their possesion. Poorer people must have resented it. Second, the effort to free Pumbedita of exilarchic domination—a preliminary skirmish in a longer struggle first to achieve independence, then to attain predominance—probably did not win, or even depend upon, popular support. Unless the ordinary people hated the exilarch, they could not have understood, much less sympathized with, the rabbis' move to overcome exilarchic control of the schools. Hence if my conjecture is correct, it was only when the exilarch appointed the same man as both tax-collector and head of a major school that the rabbis were enabled to raise the issue of who runs the schools. His error gave them their chance. Otherwise, it seems unlikely that they publicly could have opposed his choice. We do have some stories told by rabbis about popular dislike of rabbis, but none about popular hostility to the exilarch. Whether that means that the people actually did not hate the exilarch, and therefore produced no stories for the rabbis to tell and preserve in their schools, I do not know. In the rabbis' negative accounts about the exilarch, only rabbis play any role at all. Perhaps that was sufficient, so there was no need to include fables of how the exilarch was also the object of popular derision. The absence of rabbinical stories about mass dislike of the exilarch is hardly probative. My supposition nonetheless is that ordinary folk did accept the exilarchic claim to be a descendent of David, and therefore that acceptance, together with Iranian support, led to submission to the rule of his courts and administration without much objection. The evidence for that supposition is to be found mainly in the stories of the smooth working of the Jewish courts and administration. Effective government depended upon exilarchic sanction, and if the rabbinical courts and administrators did their job, as they certainly did, then not merely the rabbis' personal appeal, but the the political support of the exilarch, made possible by Iranian backing, was the probable cause. And I cannot believe that the Iranians would have backed an unpopular or ineffective agency. So massive, though circumstantial evidence permits us to suppose that the exilarch enjoyed routine popular acceptance. If so, as I said, the rabbis' struggle for academic independence did not elicit much popular concern, let alone sympathy, except in unusual circumstances.

The exilarchate may well have hoped at first, in the second century, to foster the rabbinical movement as a means of counterbalancing the power of local grandees.[1] The growth of bureaus of state in Sasanian times was so intended, and the development within the Jewish community of a parallel administrative structure must have had a similar purpose. The rabbis had a strong claim to influence over ordinary folk. Their manner of living, reputation as wonder-workers and saints, and evident knowledge of the traditions which supposedly emanated from Moses at Mount Sinai—these must have won the attention and the acquiescence of other Jews, especially so when the exilarch placed in the rabbis' hands important judicial powers over property transactions and personal status. The rabbis gave him prestige by propagating the belief in his Davidic ancestry as well as by serving as able administrators and bureaucrats. So the exilarch did everything he could both to win over the rabbis, by educating his own family in their law-schools in Palestine and creating such schools in Babylonia itself, and to make use of their prestige and learning, by placing in their hands the court-system of the Jewish community.

Now, two centuries later, the exilarch had to contend with subversion by part of the rabbinic movement. The rabbis claimed they had the

---

[1] The disappearance of such strong men as Arda, Arta, and Pyl-y Barish (b. Git. 14a, see vol. I, 2nd printing, revised, pp. 94-97) may be accounted for by the close ties of the Jewish nobility to the Arsacid court. While the exilarch managed to make his peace with the Sasanians, the local strong-men did not. The Sasanians, not unconcerned about the cadet branch of the Arsacid dynasty ruling in Armenia, probably felt that they similarly could not trust families closely allied with the Arsacids for many centuries.

right to govern independently, and denied that he was the true source of their authority. Some of them no longer thought they should be subservient to, from their viewpoint, such an ignorant, luxury-loving, high-handed sybarite. His natural response would have been to punish those who publicized such opinions, as he probably did with Geniva earlier, and to encourage his friends within the rabbinate. Most of all he would have wanted to bring under closer supervision the schools which formed the center of subversion. Following Beer, we may specify that Pumbedita was chief among those schools, and therefore under Rava, the Pumbeditan school was moved to Maḥoza. The exilarch had publicly to respond to the criticism and disloyalty of hostile elements in the rabbinate. I should suppose his response would have taken the form of propaganda no less venomous than the rabbis'. He would have stressed, to begin with, the fact that he was descended from the house of David, for that was the foundation of his politics. He would have countered the accusation that he was impious by pointing out that among his sage advisers were distinguished rabbis, and that specific sins of which he was accused had in fact been permitted, or even carried out, by these rabbis. He would moreover have alluded to the cost to others of the rabbinical tax exemptions. The rabbis not only will not pay their fair share of the rising imposts, but some of them even solicited funds, quite separate from those accruing to the Jewish government, for the support of schools which the exilarch in any case paid for. The rabbis wanted to establish a second Jewish government, which the Persians would never allow. 'In these troubled times, when Christians are giving evidence of what happens to minority-communities that fall afoul of the state, it will not pay to solicit Persian hostility.' The condition of the Jews themselves provides the best testimony to the soundness of exilarchic rule. 'Consider the fact that others are persecuted. Jews are secure. Chaos reigns everywhere, but at home, order, or as much order as responsible government can bring when faced with such dissident, provocative elements.' One recalls that hostility must have been directed against the rabbis on account of their indifference to the condition of Jewish slaves.[1] The exilarch could have concluded his message by asking, 'How many wish to enslave themselves to pay heavier taxes so that the rabbis may now enjoy the full benefit of their private, fantastic, and self-serving Scriptural exegesis? Not all rabbis, to be sure, but only a minority of them are guilty of such intended subversion. Most of

---

[1] Vol. III, pp. 24-29.

them,' the exilarch would have concluded, 'remain loyal to the house of David and its living representative.' So the exilarch.

Three centuries earlier, a Pharisaic leader, excluded from the bastions of power and displeased with the Temple's administration of its holy office, had found a suitable polemic in the words of Qohelet 4:18, "Guard your foot when you go to the house of God and be ready to hearken..." He said that it was better to listen to the words of the wise than to offer the sacrifices of fools,[1] meaning the ancient priesthood. Now his words found an echo in the saying attributed to Rava:

> "And be ready to listen." Rava said, "Be ready to listen to the words of the sages, for if they sin, they bring an offering and carry out penance. 'It is better than when fools give.' Do not be like fools who sin and bring an offering, but do not do penance."
>
> (b. Ber. 23a)

Rava stressed that even sages may sin, but if they do, they repent and seek reconciliation with God. We do not know, of course, of any polemic such as I have imagined directed by the exilarch against rabbis. Rava's exegesis is quite outside of a historical context. Yet it would have been an evocative and appropriate response to such an indictment as the exilarch might justly have lodged against his opposition.[2]

---

[1] See my *Life of R. Yoḥanan ben Zakkai* (Leiden, 1962), pp. 44-45.

[2] Since R. Naḥman b. Isaac persistently appears as hostile to the exilarch, perhaps his attainment of the headship of a school after Rava's death and the split of the 'single academy' into two marked the failure of the exilarch to preserve his shaky predominance over the Pumbeditan-Maḥozan academy for the brief period of its unification. We shall return to this matter in subsequent research. As I said, I am not completely satisfied with the results of this inquiry to date.

CHAPTER THREE

BABYLONIAN JEWISH GOVERNMENT (I):
THE RABBI AS ADMINISTRATOR

I. INTRODUCTION

We cannot too often remind ourselves that all we know about Babylonian Jewry consists of what the rabbis chose to transmit in their schools.[1] Nowhere does that fact become more striking than in the study of the life and culture of ordinary Jews. We have limited archaeological data, the magical incantation bowls and the paintings in the synagogue at Dura-Europos. Rabbinic literature provides little persuasive evidence about what the latter may have meant, or what the former were used for.[2] Our consideration of the external structure of the Jewish government of Babylonia quickly came down to study of germane rabbinic sayings and stories. It was the limited usefulness of these data that became in the end the most obvious and convincing result of our inquiry. All we can say with absolute certainty is that there *was* an exilarchate, and that some rabbis disliked the holder of that of-

[1] I have not repeated the extended discussions found in vol. II, pp. 251-260, 281f, and vol. III, pp. 202-213, about the use of Talmudic sources for social history, or the relationship between the rabbis' legal sayings and the actual behavior of the people, nor have I restated the comparisons between the functions in Jewish society of the rabbis and their schools and those in Mazdean, Christian and Manichaean society of Magi, ascetic monks, and elect, respectively, found in vol. II, pp. 147-151, and vol. III, pp. 195-202 and 266-271. I presuppose knowledge of earlier passages, have absolutely nothing to add to what I have already said on these subjects. I can report no significant modifications in my basic theses. My purpose here is to examine the data on fourth-century rabbis by the procedures and criteria offered and employed in the earlier volumes. What is important is the testing of those theses against the data of a later generation and the consideration of evidence, below (pp. 256ff), possibly pointing to broadening and deepening rabbinical influence. It is striking that the rabbis were now willing to say, "Go and see what the people are doing in the streets," and similar expressions. I have not found many such expressions used earlier in Babylonia. Standing by themselves they prove nothing. But as we shall see, some evidence suggests that the rabbis now could control popular behavior more effectively than in earlier times.

[2] I hope in later research to study the meaning for the history of Babylonian Judaism of the incantation bowls and of the synagogue at Dura Europos. See the brief and preliminary comments in vol. II, pp. 57-64, and also my "Judaism at Dura Europos," *History of Religions* 4, 1, 1966, 81-102.

fice. Were we to accept the opinion of rabbis as fact, we should have to suppose the shadowy exilarch to have been a mere figure-head, a marginal Jew whose religious laxity, luxurious manner of living, and indifference to the sentiments of ordinary folk rendered him irrelevant to the "true life" of Israel. Only by extrapolating from the likely choices and facts of Sasanian politics were we able to suggest that the exilarch was more significant and central in Jewish affairs than some rabbis said. References to the exilarch's servants would lead us to suppose that he built a considerable administration, of which the rabbis and their disciples constituted only a part, though perhaps a most important, influential one. But practically all we know about exilarchic government is what the schools reported.

On the other hand, the rabbis' own aspirations render their literature of historical interest. In fact, they make possible the recovery of aspects of Babylonian Jewish history, if not so much as we might have liked. What was most striking about the rabbis as a group was both their intimate involvement in the everyday life of ordinary Jews and their desire to control, direct, and where necessary, reform it. The reason was that they took most seriously the prophetic conviction about the destiny of Israel. The sacred quality of Israel's group life, the morality and ethics of everyday affairs, and the loyalty of the people to the covenant at Sinai and its revealed legislation—these, and not the power of pagan kingdoms or the sword of Israel itself, would finally decide Israel's destiny. Israel would be saved through *Torah*.[1] Regarding themselves as the best exemplars of the divine will for Israel, the rabbis very much wanted all other Jews to become rabbis. Unlike the Manichaeans, who hardly expected that the hearers would eventually be numbered among the elect, and unlike the Christian nuns and monks, who did not suppose ordinary people bore every single obligation which the ascetics carried out, the rabbis demanded that all Jews conform to rabbinical ideals, that is, to the Torah. It was this ethic which brought the rabbis into contact—and conflict—with ordinary people. They could hardly ignore any means of influence or power over the common life.

It was thus that the rabbinical estate hoped to effect a great reformation of the lives of common folk. Israel should conform to the laws of the whole Torah, meaning in particular those of the Mishnah redacted by R. Judah the Prince, studied in the rabbinical schools, and enforced wherever possible in the Babylonian Jewish courts controlled by the

---

[1] See my "Religious Uses of History," *History and Theory* 5, 2, 153-171.

rabbis. The study and application of that law, both the Written and the Oral Revelation supposedly given to Moses and handed on by him to their own day, constituted the rabbis' conception of the holy life. That life was lived in their schools, and only partially outside of the rabbinical group. The rabbis and disciples conformed to the "Torah" in every detail, or regarded their lapses as sin. The masters could thus effect in the schools the fulfillment of the whole Torah. Outside of the schools, they could not, of course, look for equivalent success. The inertia of more than eight centuries of local customs and traditions, which must have taken shape from the first Jewish settlement in Babylonia, at the start of the sixth century B.C., and continued uninterruptedly to develop from that time to the advent of the rabbinical movement in the second century A.D., was not easily diverted. The rabbis nonetheless tried to reshape the accepted patterns of Jewish living and to reform the ideals and values which underlay them. That salvific aspiration brought them, to begin with, to cooperate with the exilarch, by staffing his courts and administrative agencies. It further preserved their patient willingness to cope with a less than satisfactory situation.

The rabbis did not live in monasteries, though their schools have much in common with monasteries and served many of the same functions.[1] They did not regard themselves as divorced from, or not responsible for, the ordinary folk. Therefore their literature contains considerable data upon the relationships between the laws and doctrines of the rabbis, on the one hand, and the life of the people on the other. Both case-reports and some sayings do testify to the condition of that life.[2] The central issue is, What was the relationship between rabbinical law and the sociology and culture of ordinary Jews? I have as yet found no way to illuminate the life of the streets except from that of the academies.[3] The only aspects of religious sociology open to study therefore are those revealed in the interstices between theoretical rabbinical sayings and actual, practical applications of some laws. So far, I have been able to contribute only the beginnings of an account of how the law was applied.

Some have argued that everyday life is of no interest to the historian, including the historian of religion, who should stress the creative achievements of the saints or elite alone. George Foot Moore wrote, for example, as follows:

---

[1] See vol. III, pp. 195-202.
[2] Vol. II, pp. 249-287, vol. III, pp. 202-213.
[3] See below, pp. 256ff.

> It is primarily the religion of intelligent and religious men that is
> [here] described ... Such men are always the minority, but they are the
> true representatives of their religion in any age, teachers and examples
> to their fellows. No religion has ever succeeded in bringing all of its
> adherents to its standards of right living ... and in the highest religions
> the gulf between the intellectual and moral leaders and the superstitious
> and depraved sediment of society is widest. But it is not from ignorance
> and superstition that anything can be learned about a religion; at that
> end, they are all alike.[1]

The supposition that it is the work of only the intelligent and religious men which warrants study seems to me faulty. Morton Smith
comments on Moore's assumption that the true picture of a religion
must be drawn chiefly from those documents which it accepts as au-
thentic. He says:

> This supposes, obviously, that the religion has not changed sub-
> stantially in the course of its history. If what was once a minority party
> has subsequently won control, and if the works of a former majority
> have been lost by neglect or by suppression, then the documents now
> accepted as authentic—the propaganda of the former minority—will
> give a seriously false picture of earlier times. Indeed, even if the
> triumphant party was one of the major parties aforetime, but was then
> matched by equally important competitors, there is a danger that it
> will now represent itself as the one true form of the earlier religion,
> and dismiss the other ancient forms, which, in their day, had equal
> claims to legitimacy, as heretical sects.[2]

Nowhere does it seem more dangerous to ignore the issues of everyday life than in the study of Babylonian Talmudic literature, which
speaks in one and the same language, using quite historical, descriptive
terms, about how things both *were* and *ought* to be. That literature, edited
from the perspective and on the basis of the traditions of the schools of
Sura and Pumbedita, not only contains almost no evidence about traditions and teachings of other than rabbinical authorities, but sup-
presses the whole record of pre-rabbinic Babylonian Judaism as if it
simply had not existed. If we were seeking a true picture of that earlier
period, we simply could not find it in rabbinical literature. But can we
suppose that the period from 200 to 500, about which Talmudic traditions allegedly testify, is any more authentically portrayed? I have
already argued that our records, while useful, are seriously deficient,

---

[1] Cited by Morton Smith, "The Work of George Foot Moore," *Harvard
Library Bulletin* 15, 2, 1967, p. 175.

[2] *Op. cit.*, pp. 177-178.

first of all, in their *interest* in other-than-rabbinical opinions, second, in their willingness to portray at all, or fairly and objectively, other than rabbinical figures, or events pertaining to other-than-rabbinical circles. To assent to Moore's judgment would require, moreover, a theological judgment, including antecedent theological argument, about what is "true religion," and who may be called its "true representatives." It furthermore begs the question to argue that the "leaders" *actually* led, unless we can find evidence to testify to the wide extent of influence and power over the common life.

To assess rabbinic leadership one needs to study those who were led. Obviously we shall have to suppose there were variations between Jews, even among whole communities. Theologically to evaluate these variations requires the kind of judgments that cannot, in the first instance, be offered by historians of religion. The difficulties we faced[1] in finding in the phenomena themselves a valid distinction between "true religion" and "magic" or "superstition," or between "depraved sediments of society" and "moral leaders," and the like—those dificulties are not inconsequential. They must suggest that we had better describe as carefully and critically as we can, rather than evaluate data upon the basis of unexamined principles of theological judgment. I see no better way to obstruct our understanding of the data at hand than to begin by asking about its orthodoxy, heresy, nobility, immorality, or depravity. In studying the life of Babylonian Jewry, we have, therefore, to attempt a description of the way the Jewish government worked. The rabbis described only their own part in political and social life. So we turn immediately to what we are *able* to consider, namely the activities of the rabbinical courts and the work of the rabbis as administrators and judges.

What were the bases of rabbinical power and influence—leadership, in Moore's term—over the ordinary people? We need, first of all, to distinguish between political *power* and religious *influence*. If a rabbi could resort to court punishments, such as the ban, or the lash, or forcibly require a defendant to accept the court judgment in a case of property litigation, or impose fines, then one may say that he had concrete, coercive, political *power* to carry out the law. Another sort of power was that wielded by the rabbi over people who believed he could curse or bless with actual, measurable results, or who thought he was a holy man, able to bring down the favor or wrath of an ever-interested divinity and his legions of angels and demons, or who accepted his

[1] See vol. III, pp. 110-126.

claim to know just what God wanted of Israel in this particular place and time. That power was no less "coercive" in its way than police power in its several forms. I have chosen to refer to it, however, as "religious influence," to distinguish between what the rabbis could do as agents of the Jewish government and what they could do as holy men. As agents of the Jewish government, the rabbi decided according to rabbinical law cases involving personal status and transfers of property. A few other kinds of cases could be adjudicated by their courts as well, but these were the chief categories of law which rabbinical courts enforced with Iranian and exilarchic support.[1] As holy men, they exerted "religious influence" in a most concrete sense. People either were so frightened of the evil the rabbis could bring down upon them, or so eager for blessings they could promise in this world and in the next, or so impressed by their mastery of supposedly ancient teachings which God had revealed at Mount Sinai, that they submitted to the rabbis. Whether it was against their own will or otherwise hardly matters. They therefore were subjected, or subjected themselves, to the "spiritual power" of the rabbis. That spiritual power was not divorced from material matters. On the contrary, it is quite clear that a curse was believed to be practically effective over crops or commerce, a blessing would generate male children or open the gates of heaven.

The only useful distinction between "power" and "influence" must therefore be located in the basis of coercion. When the rabbi could rely on the exilarch to see to it that a court order was obeyed, he exerted political power. When he had to resort to the curse or ban, he used "religious influence." I do not suppose it was charismatic, in the sense that the appeal of individual rabbis' personalities affected or moved ordinary people. Some of the rabbis exhibited striking personalities, but that had little to do with the response of ordinary people to their orders. It was religion or magic and not personal charisma which influenced the workaday world.

Rabbinical *power*, deriving from the authority and ultimate support of Iranian government through the exilarchate, thus effected the widespread enforcement of civil laws,[2] including property exchanges of all kinds. Supernatural *influence* persuaded ordinary folk to pay close at-

---

[1] See vol. III, pp. 317-338. That is to say, precisely the terms of the original agreement between Samuel and Shapur.

[2] The chief handicap was the difficulty of administering widely scattered communities. Poor communications, local strong-men, and other centrifugal forces would have limited the enforcement of law even with great support from the exilarchate and the Sasanian bureaus of administration at Ctesiphon.

tention to rabbinical rules about religious and ritual laws, proper behavior in everyday life, matters of morality and ethics not accessible to
court action, and the like.[1] It would be a mistake, however, to suppose
that these forms of coercion ever were completely distinguished from
one another. The judge in court, able to order lashes or excommunication, could also curse the guilty party or cast an evil eye. The administrator of community affairs, dealing with matters which, by their
nature, could hardly be brought to court, and in general able to achieve
his will through influence rather than political coercion normally was
also the court-judge who might try a civil case involving the same recalcitrant. The sinner was a criminal, and vice versa. And the rabbinical
judge-administrator was always the holy man, who knew the Torah,
whose clothing, speech, and conduct set him apart from other Jews. It
seems most useful, however, separately to consider these two aspects of
the leadership of the rabbinate and to isolate the kinds of law effected
by each. In general we shall see that rabbinical *influence* pertained to ordinary life, to the conduct of normal people in everyday circumstances, as
well as to matters of faith, cult, rite, and taboo beyond court jurisdiction.
Rabbinical *power* applied to extraordinary matters, such as contested
divorces or marriage-contracts, broken contracts, disputed property
and real estate, torts, and similar unusual occurrences. The rabbi as an
extraordinary, holy man achieved his greatest affect in commonplace
and ongoing daily life. The rabbi as lawyer, judge, and administrator,
who carried out fundamentally routine, political tasks, related to exceptional events yielding court cases. We consider first the influence of
the rabbi in the context of his administration of public affairs; second,
in Chapter Four, his power as judge of specific sorts of cases; and finally
in Chapter Five, his appearance as a holy man who exemplified the requirements of revelation.[2]

II. THE COURT

The focal point of rabbinical power and influence over the life of
ordinary people was the court, in which both narrowly judicial and
more broadly administrative functions were combined.[3] To the rabbis,
the academy, not the court, constituted the most important focus of

---

[1] See vol. III, pp. 234-272.

[2] In general, I shall first cite or summarize case-reports, then, where appropriate, present evidence of rabbinical fulfillment of law, and finally, briefly refer
to rabbinical opinions on the law.

[3] See vol. III, pp. 102-110, 130-149.

activities, but it was in court that rabbis normally came together with the common folk.[1] There they were prepared to use all the powers at hand, both political and religious, to enforce the "whole Torah." Nonetheless, matters that came before them as judges and administrators did not, to begin with, encompass the whole of the law. If most people did not keep ritual and moral laws, the rabbis could do little more than issue curses and ominous warnings *and* raise up a generation of disciples to obey it. If most people kept a rite or taboo, they could easily force the deviant person into line. In ligitations of property, on the other hand, their judgment was not disputed.[2]

The rabbis' view of their judicial responsibilities was expressed by Rava:

> When Rava would go to court, he said this: "Of his [my] own free will he [I] goes forth to death, and he [I] does [do] not meet the wishes of his household. He goes [I go] homeward empty-handed, and would that his [my] coming in should be like his [my] going out."
>
> (b. Yoma 86b-87a)[3]

The dangers of misconstruing a case led to Rava's hope that he might be as free of guilt upon his leaving court as upon entering it.

Given their stress of the merits of forefathers, one cannot be surprised that the rabbis insisted upon genealogical "purity," as much as upon ethical righteousness. Rava held that one proselyte may judge the case of another,[4] but not of a native Jew. R. Joseph earlier had taught that the court must be both pure in righteousness and free of all blemish,[5] including all physical defects.[6] Rava explained the prohibition against judges' taking gifts: as soon as a man receives a gift from another, he becomes so favorably disposed toward him that the latter seems like his own person, and the judge can see in him no wrong.[7]

---

[1] I do not mean to suggest that the school and court were invariably conducted in different places. We know that cases were decided in the exilarch's palace, so I should assume that in Maḥoza, the school was not the primary site of court functions. Elsewhere, however, cases may well have been tried where classes met. The distinction is meant as a merely functional one.

[2] Vol. III, pp. 317-338.

[3] The passage that follows in b. Yoma 87a was said by Rav, see b. Sanh. 7b, cited in vol. II, p. 115.

[4] b. Yev. 101b, as an exegesis of Deut. 17:15. Proselytes supposedly could not however judge the cases of home-born Jews.

[5] b. Qid. 76b. In context, his saying applied to the Sanhedrin, not to an ordinary court. But the language is simply "bet din."

[6] b. Yev. 101b. This saying is an exegesis of Song 4:7, and both this saying and that cited above seem originally to have formed a single pericope, which referred to "purity" of righteousness, genealogy, and physical appearance.

[7] b. Ket. 105b.

Sayings attributed to these two generations[1] concerning court procedures included Rava's, on whether a man's or a woman's suit is heard first,[2] on administering court oaths,[3] and on issuing subpoenas.[4] Rules of evidence included Rava's, that a man cannot testify against himself, "A man is his own relative, and therefore cannot declare himself wicked."[5] Abaye held, on the other hand, that the silence of the accused is equivalent to assent. If, for example, a witness testifies that a man ate forbidden food and the accused stands mute, the hostile witness is believed.[6] Other traditions reported the same rule of evidence in cases about the defilement of pure food and bestiality committed against an ox. The administration of court-oaths in Rava's court is illustrated by the following stories:

> A woman was once ordered to take an oath at the court of Rava, but when R. Ḥisda's daughter [his wife] said to him, "I know that she is suspected of [taking false] oaths," Rava transferred the oath to her opponent.
>
> (b. Ket. 85a)[7]

> A man with a monetary claim upon his neighbor once came before Rava, demanding of the debtor, "Come and pay me." "I have repaid you," the latter pleaded. "If so," Rava said to him, "Go and swear to him, that you have repaid." He thereupon went and brought a [hollow] cane, placed the money therein, and came before the Court, walking and leaning on it. He said to the plaintiff, "Hold the cane in your hand." He [the defendant] then took a scroll of the Torah and swore that he had repaid him [the plaintiff] all that he had received [the payment] in his hand. The enraged creditor thereupon broke the cane, and the money poured out on the ground. It was thus seen that he [the borrower] had [deceitfully] sworn to the truth.
>
> (b. Ned. 25a)[8]

Rabbah held that an oath generally will be viable because a man will not normally have the effrontery to deny a whole debt, though he may lie about part of it, a principle he derived from Scripture.[9] R. Joseph

---

[1] See vol. III, pp. 220-234, for the sayings of the earlier generation.
[2] b. Yev. 100a.
[3] b. Shev. 38b.
[4] b. Sanh. 8a, B.Q. 113a. See also b. M.Q. 16a, on the biblical origin of the regulation requiring the sending of a court messenger for a subpoena.
[5] b. Yev. 25b, b. Sanh. 9b. Rava did not, of course, invent the principle.
[6] b. Qid. 65b-66a.
[7] Trans. W. Slotki (London, 1948), p. 537. A second oath-story follows.
[8] Trans. H. Freedman (London, 1948), p. 71. See B. Lewin, *Oẓar HaGeonim, Nedarim*, Ap. p. 25.
[9] b. B.M. 3a.

and Rava discussed the penalties to be paid by witnesses whose testimony was convincingly refuted.[1] Rava and Abaye debated about the testimony of such a witness. Abaye said that the perjurer's testimony was retrospectively disqualified, while Rava held the disqualification was only in future cases.[2] Confirmed liars, Abaye held, could not testify even under oath.[3] Rava said that one who lent on interest was also ineligible to testify in a Jewish court, and the following case report indicates his opinion was put into effect:

> Two witness testified against Bar Bithinus. One said, "He lent money on interest in my presence." The other said, "He lent me money on interest." Rava disqualified Bar Bithinus...
>
> (b. Sanh. 25a)[4]

These and other sayings on court procedures and rules were part of a long development. We have no reason to suppose much, if anything, in them was new. What is important is that these sayings most certainly reflect the actual laws of procedure in rabbinical courts. No obstacle prevented the rabbis from conducting the courts according to rules of procedure and evidence which had been worked out in Tannaitic and earlier Amoraic times.

Punishments available in civil cases included flogging, excommunication, and fines, as well as adjudication of a case in favor of an injured plaintiff.[5] Somewhat irregular punishments involved putting out eyes, cutting off hands,[6] and public defamation of an evil-doer. Rava held that one may call the transgressor of the orders of rabbis "sinner", and no libel suit on that account would be entertained in court.[7] He said that flogging now was a substitute for capital punishment.[8] R. Joseph cited an earlier tradition, that while the four modes of capital punishment were no longer in effect, their equivalents were still commonplace. In place of stoning, one may be accidentally trampled to death by a beast, or may fall from a roof; in place of burning comes accidental injury through fire or snake-bite; in place of decapitation, the government or brigands kill by the sword;[9] in place of strangulation, one suffers

---

[1] b. Sanh. 9b.
[2] b. Sanh. 27a. See also Rava in b. Mak. 5a, b. B.Q. 73b.
[3] b. Sanh. 29b.
[4] Trans. Jacob Schachter (London, 1948), pp. 144-145.
[5] Vol. III, pp. 220-229.
[6] Vol. III, p. 221.
[7] b. Sanh. 40a.
[8] b. Sanh. 10a.
[9] As happened to Christian martyrs, see above, p. 25.

drowning or suffocation.[1] The effectiveness of excommunication depended upon widespread ostracism of the excommunicant. When whole groups, such as the butchers of Huzal, or towns, were excommunicated, it could not have made much difference.[2] On the other hand, Abaye and R. Joseph discussed whether an excommunicant might have sex relations with his wife.[3] If the wife were a faithful Jewess, she could well effectuate the conclusion of their discussion.

A striking story about judicial punishment—in error—is as follows:

> Yemar b. Hashu had a money claim against a certain person who died and left a boat. "Go," he said to his agent, "and seize it." He went and seized it, but R. Papa and R. Huna b. R. Joshua met him and told him, "You are seizing on behalf of a creditor and thereby you are causing loss to others, and R. Yohanan ruled, 'He who seizes on behalf of a creditor and thereby causes loss to others does not legally acquire it.'" Thereupon they [the rabbis] themselves [who were also creditors of the deceased] seized it. R. Papa rowed the boat while R. Huna b. R. Joshua pulled it by the rope. One then declared, "I have acquired all the ship," and the other so claimed as well. They were met by R. Phinehas b. 'Ammi who said to them ... When they appeared before Rava, he said to them, "You white geese [rabbis wore a white cloak] that strip the people of their cloaks [giving a decision in their own favor and robbing the other creditors]! Thus ruled R. Nahman, 'The seizure is valid only if it took place during the lifetime [of the original owner/debtor].'"

> (b. Ket. 84b-85a)[4]

What is interesting for our purpose is the willingness of Yemar b. Hashu's agent to give up his claim upon the boat to the two rabbis, whose citation of a learned master convinced him that he could not go to court and retain possession of the boat for his master. Since the courts could and did adjudicate all sorts of property claims, ordinary people were not prepared to oppose their judgments, even when these were in the rabbis' own interest.[5]

The combination of punishments available to court officials was probably quite sufficient for their ordinary needs. They could not have had great difficulty in effecting more weighty decisions. As I said, whether people paid attention to excommunication probably depended mostly upon the circumstances. If nearby, they would have been sub-

---

[1] b. Sanh. 37b. On capital jurisdiction, see below, pp. 186-190.

[2] Vol. I, p. 148; vol. III, p. 227.

[3] b. M.Q. 15b.

[4] Trans W. Slotki, p. 536. On special distinguishing garments worn by rabbis, see below, p. 295ff.

[5] On rabbinical favoritism of rabbis in court, see below, pp. 309ff.

jected to local court influence. If from distant places, they may have been able to ignore or avoid a summons to court and to escape the most bothersome results of the consequent ban. On the other hand, the court could easily determine the division or possession of disputed property, and had no difficulty in putting the decision into effect. Decisions in land disputes, no less than in litigations over movables, would have produced judicial confirmation of rights of ownership. Documents such as deeds of ownership or possession were drawn up by court scribes. In such circumstances, the bailiff of Bar Ḥashu may well have supposed it futile to contend with the learned rabbis for possession of the boat.[1]

Court errors by an official appointed by the exilarchate would not lead to the judge's having to make restitution. On the other hand, R. Joseph held that while an "unauthorized" judge might have to make restitution in the case of error, his decision was still quite valid:

> Mar Zutra b. R. Naḥman judged a case alone and erred. R. Joseph told him, "If both parties accepted you as judge, you do not have to make restitution. Otherwise, go and pay an indemnity."
>
> (b. Sanh. 5a)[2]

There is no doubt, however, that the decision was a valid one. The reference to an unauthorized judge calls to mind the fact that the exilarch could not supervise what people did everywhere and probably did not try to establish a monopoly on courts. If a learned rabbi was consulted by ordinary people to settle their disputes, the decision he made would not be overturned by other, "recognized" courts. (This is very important for the question of setting up and financing independent schools. It would suggest that a group of rich men could keep their own school of rabbis and might find it worth their while.) I should suppose the reason would have been that he ruled according to the same principles of law followed in the authorized courts, namely the rabbinic traditions. Indeed, Abaye and Rava seem in the following source to suppose the possibility of existence of two competing courts in the same town:

> "You shall not form separate sects" (Deut. 14:1). Abaye said, "The warning against separate sects is applicable in a case where there are two courts in the same town, one ruling according to Bet Shammai, the other according to Bet Hillel." ... Rava said, "The prohibition applies to a court in one town which is divided between Shammaites and Hillelites..."
>
> (b. Yev. 14a)

---

[1] On the Jewish court's unlimited jurisdiction over Jewish property, see Salo W. Baron, *Social and Religious History of the Jews*, II, p. 417, n. 39.

[2] See H. Z. Taubes, *Oẓar HaGeonim, Sanhedrin*, p. 28/15A.

The discussion contains no reference to such a situation in Babylonia, so I very much doubt that two courts actually competed with one another in any significant town, certainly not in any village. So the ruling by Mar Zutra b. R. Naḥman may have been given in a town in which a formally established, exilarchic court, staffed by rabbis, was not to be found; or alternately, if such a court existed, the contending parties preferred for some reason to ask for the decision of Mar Zutra.

In addition to the usual judical functions, the courts oversaw the general welfare of the towns.[1] Among court responsibilities were the suppression of rumors and the annulment of vows. Two cases involving rumors were reported:

> A certain woman was allegedly engaged by the well of Be Shifi [with the gift of] the flesh sticking to date stones. R. 'Idi b. 'Abin asked Abaye what was the rule in such a case. Abaye replied, "Even those authorities who say that as a rule we do not suppress rumors would here suppress them, because people will then say that the rabbis examined the gift of betrothal and found it did not contain the value of a perutah." [Since she was never actually engaged, no harm can result in suppressing the rumor.]
>
> (b. Git. 89a)

> A woman was reported to have been betrothed by one of the sons of a certain person. Rava ruled, "Even those authorities who hold that we should not as a rule suppress a rumor would rule that here we should do so...."
>
> (b. Git. 89a-b)

One recalls that Rava held it was permitted to libel a man who broke rabbinical enactments, so libel in general was actionable, and the courts would probably have suppressed and punished libel. Here we again see that the courts would make the effort to suppress rumors in specified circumstances.[2] How they would have done so we can only surmise. They may have issued a public order that such-and-such a rumor was not true and should not be repeated. Anyone violating their order would have been banned as a transgressor of rabbinical rulings. The effectiveness of such a procedure, however, is unattested by any sources. The rabbis clearly *thought* they could suppress rumors, though it may be that in actuality they could only attempt to do so, going through the routine court procedures, without any certain result.

On the other hand, the courts had no difficulty whatever in annuling

---

[1] We shall consider various other activities of public administration in sections iii-vii, below.

[2] See also b. Yev. 25a = b. M.Q. 18b, Abaye on suppressing rumors.

vows. A faithful Jew who made a vow and later on regretted it could turn to a rabbinical court and seek absolution. The normal ground was that the man had not vowed with such-and-such a situation in mind, and hence the vow was, of itself, invalid. Cases of absolution included the following:

> A man once came before Rabbah b. R. Huna. The rabbi asked, "If ten men had been present to appease you just then, would you have vowed?" The man replied, "No." He thereupon absolved him.
>
> (b. Ned. 21b)

> Abaye's wife had a daughter. He insisted she marry one of his family, and she wanted her to marry one of her relations. He vowed, "Benefit from me is forbidden to you if you disregard my wishes..." She went, ignored his wish, and married the girl off to one of her relations. Abaye came before R. Joseph for absolution. R. Joseph asked, "Had you known she would disregard your wish, would you have vowed?" Abaye said, "No." R. Joseph absolved him.
>
> (b. Ned. 23a)[1]

Rabbah held that in the case of a betrothed maiden, either her father or her fiancé may annul her vows.[2] They may also repeat a prescribed formula of confirmation of a vow.[3] R. Joseph held that absolution on the Sabbath may be granted by a single scholar, but not by three ordinary people, for the latter case would resemble a law-suit, which cannot be tried on the Sabbath.[4] The rabbis discussed the possible interpretations of the language of vows. For instance, Rava said that if a man vowed not to eat but ate dust, he had not transgressed his vow.[5]

Rava's court, like R. Nahman's earlier, seems to have enjoyed appellate status. We have already noted his ruling against two rabbis who had seized property in their own advantage.[6] R. Hiyya 'Arika appealed to Rava when dissatisfied with the ruling of another rabbi. Rava thereupon supported the judgment of the lower court of Rabbah b. Shila.[7] Many of the extant case reports derive from Rava's court, more than from any other court of his time, just as the earlier ones were disproportionately from R. Nahman's. It may be that his close ties with the

---

[1] Note also the case of R. Kahana before R. Joseph, b. Ned. 22b.
[2] b. Ned. 67a.
[3] b. Ned. 69a-b, 70a.
[4] b. Ned. 77a, with Abaye's contrary view.
[5] b. Shev. 22b. On the language of the vows of a Nazir, see Abaye's discussion, b. Nazir 13a, Rava, *ibid.* 17a, etc.
[6] Above, p. 135.
[7] b. Ket. 104b.

exilarch, like those of R. Naḥman, resulted in the preservation of his decisions as binding precedents.[1]

The academies by this time produced few, if any innovations in either the functions or the responsibilities of the court. Long ago, in both Palestine and Babylonia, arrangements for public welfare had been entrusted to the rabbinical judges. The fourth-century rabbis did little more than carry on the tasks first laid down by others, following time-tested rules of procedure, evidence, and punishment. What is important in this time is the steady growth of the effectiveness of the courts, but that did not alter the way they carried on their business.[2]

iii. The Court's Eleemosynary Responsibilities

Chief among the court's responsibilities in maintaining the public welfare were the collection and distribution of funds for the poor. The courts could levy sums to be paid for philanthropic purposes. Rabbah, for example, collected a charity contribution from orphans.[3] The court also kept control of such funds until they were disbursed. In Pumbedita, R. Joseph deposited charity funds with a person who was so negligent that the money was stolen. R. Joseph thereupon required the bailiff to pay an indemnity.[4] He explained that since the poor of Pumbedita receive a fixed allowance, the charity funds were stolen from definite plaintiffs, and hence restitution was legally possible. The chief responsibility involved determining who was eligible for charity and how much he would receive, as in the following miracle-story:

> A certain man came before Rava [asking for charity from public funds]. He said to him, "On what do you usually dine?" The man replied, "On fat chicken and old wine." Rava said, "Do you not take into account the burden of the community?" [That is, can you not live more cheaply?] The pauper rejoined, "Do I eat of theirs? I eat of the substance of the All-Merciful, [as it is taught. 'The eyes of all wait for you, and you give them their food in due season' (Ps. 145:15)." 'In their time' is not said, but 'in his time,' teaching that the Holy One blessed be he provides for everyone in his time.'] Meanwhile Rava's sister, whom he had not seen for thirteen years, came and brought him

---

[1] See vol. III, pp. 61-75, with reference to R. Naḥman. I think it clear that the heads of academies produced a vastly disproportionate number of legal sayings, as well as case reports.

[2] On the growth of rabbinical power, see below, pp. 256ff.

[3] b. B.B. 8a. For his distribution of charity funds, see b. B.B. 8b, Abaye's report.

[4] b. B.Q. 93a.

a fat chicken and old wine. He [the applicant] said, "Just what I was talking about!"[1] Rava replied, "I apologize to you. Come and eat."

(b. Ket. 67b)[2]

Rava was prepared to compel a man to contribute to charity funds against his will, and did so to R. Nathan b. 'Ammi.[3] In dealing with cases of non-support, he would try to force the father to take his children off the charity rolls.[4] Following Beer, I should suppose that the rabbis encouraged the needy to turn at first to private people, and only afterward to the communal funds.[5] Beer says that the poor depended upon the rabbi as such, "because of his uprightness and devotion."[6] Forcible collection and division of funds for charity, however, would have involved more than mere respect for the rabbi as a noble-hearted man. The rabbi possessed the power to collect the funds by government, or exilarchic, fiat, as Beer recognizes.[7] The court in fact was the agent of the government, able to act in its behalf and *legally* to acquire property or funds for philanthropic purposes.[8] So the administration of funds for charity, like the collection of taxes, was among the administrative functions of the court. It was as the *judges* of these courts that the rabbis exerted such legal authority, and not merely as reliable philanthropists. Rava held, as we have noted, that orderly provision for the poor was absolutely necessary for good relations with the Iranian government.[9] Doubtless had large numbers of impoverished Jews been neglected within their own community, the government would have had to step in and establish some sort of responsible party to keep order. Rava urged the townspeople of Maḥoza to help one another, so they might retain the right of self-government. Rava pointed out, moreover, that small as well as large contributions would in the end mount up to meaningful sums.[10] Nonetheless, beggars did go from door to door, and it was difficult for folk to know who really needed

---

[1] Alt.: Rava said, "What a remarkable incident."
[2] For another rule of Rava on distributing charity, see b. R.H. 6a.
[3] b. Ket. 49b.
[4] *ibid.* 49b. See vol. III, p. 284 for a less effective action by Rav Judah.
[5] b. Ned. 65b, see Beer, *Ma'amadam*, p. 139, n. 77.
[6] *op. cit.*, 139-40.
[7] *ibid.* p. 142.
[8] Beer, *op. cit.*, p. 140.
[9] b. B.B. 9a, see above, pp. 54-55. The government may have provided some funds for that purpose, as represented by 'lfra Hormiz's gifts, see above, pp. 35-39. Note also the references to Shapur I as a philanthropist, vol. II, p. 71, *if* Rav's saying was meant as praise, contrary to my earlier interpretation of b. B.M. 70b.
[10] *ibid.* 9a, in the name of R. Sheshet.

help and who did not. So R. Naḥman b. Isaac (in commenting upon Is. 58 : 7) said that if a man was really anxious to give to charity, God would make sure that he found fitting recipients for his money, so that he might gain the merit of having assisted them.[1]

Merit could also be acquired by visiting the sick, Rava, R. Joseph, and Abaye all agreed, and Rava said one must visit even a hundred times a day.[2] Nonetheless, we have no evidence whatever that the courts took responsibility to insure that the sick were visited.

IV. THE COURT AND THE MARKETPLACE

The courts' power to control litigation of cases arising from market transactions resulted in indirect influence over the marketplace.[3] The courts, however, took a quite direct part in economic life. While the Palestinian rabbis had held that market-supervisors must not fix prices, the exilarch, and, one assumes, the antecedent non-rabbinical Babylonian Jewish courts as well, insisted that prices were to be controlled by court officials. Rav was forced to submit to the Babylonian practice,[4] and from that time onward, the rabbis as court-officers followed the exilarchic requirements. In general, the courts were supposed to maintain an orderly market, to prevent great fluctuation in prices, to insure the constant provision of produce and so prevent famine, and to see to it that the ritual requirements of Judaism were met by the merchants and artisans.[5] Ritual law figured in the following rulings:

> A load of turnips came to Maḥoza [on a festival]. Rava saw that they were withered, and permitted the people to buy them, since they had been picked yesterday....
>
> (b. ʿEruv. 40a)

> A boat-load of ẓaḥanta [a fish] came to Sikara. R. Huna b. Ḥinnena went out to inspect it, and since he saw scales [on the boat] he permitted [the fish to be sold]. Rava said to him, "How is it possible to give permission in a place where [scales are] commonly found." He issued an announcement prohibiting the fish, and R. Huna b. Ḥinnena issued one permitting them.
>
> (b. A.Z. 40a)

---

[1] b. B.B. 9b.

[2] b. Ned. 39b.

[3] See vol. III, pp. 295-302, and below, chap. IV sect. IX, pp. 231-233, "Other Commercial Transactions."

[4] Vol. II, p. 112.

[5] On court-supervision of the abbatoir and butcher-shops, see below, pp. 151-156.

In the following inquiry, the concern was for good hygiene:

> The pottery dealer Minyomin once left a pot of honey uncovered. He came to Rava [to ask about it]. Rava said, "What have we to fear [for the law that liquids are prohibited which have been left uncovered applies to water, wine, and milk]?"

(b. Ḥul. 49b)

Rabbah, or Rava, similarly reported a ruling on how clothes-merchants may sell their wares when only gentiles may purchase them.[1] The numerous cases involving sale of or profit from wine touched by a gentile all produced rabbinical rulings about the ritual fitness of marketable wares.[2] There can be no doubt, therefore, that the courts' market-supervision extended, or was extended by the rabbis, to matters of merely ritual concern.

The courts' rulings involved narrowly economic questions as well, so one cannot conclude that the rabbis' were consulted only because of their superior knowledge of the rites and restrictions of Judaism. As court-officers, they had authority over weights, measures, and prices. In general, they used their authority to limit competition and so to protect the rights of the home-born merchants over outside competition. R. Huna b. R. Joshua, for example, said that residents can keep outsiders from setting up in competition, though itinerants cannot prevent other itinerants from coming to town.[3] On this account those who claimed to be rabbis had to prove their rabbinical status, so that they might be exempted from such restrictions and permitted to sell their wares either in direct competition with home-folk or even before the natives were allowed to show their produce.[4] Court supervision of markets assuredly came under the authority of the exilarchate, which had originally required it of the rabbis. Cases illustrating that supervision include the ritual ones cited earlier[5] and above,[6] the special privileges accorded to rabbis, as in the case of R. Dimi,[7] and the litigations involving butchers arising from market-dealings. None of these cases involved supervision of weights, measures, or prices. I see

---

[1] b. Shab. 29b, 46b.

[2] See above, pp. 59-61; for one example, b. A.Z. 57b, a ruling of Rava.

[3] b. B.B. 21b-22a.

[4] See b. B.B. 22a, cited below, and M. Beer, *Ẓiyyon*, 28, 1963, p. 21. Since rabbinical disciples left their native villages to study in the schools, it was important to insure that right.

[5] pp. 59-61.

[6] p. 141.

[7] Below, pp. 151-156.

no reason, however, to think that such supervision had ceased; it was clearly carried on in earlier times.[1] Moreover, one can hardly suppose that officials who could say what wine, fish, and vegetables were suitable for public sale, could not also decide about weights, measures, and prices. As I said earlier[2] when it came to market supervision, the rabbis did not have to wait for litigation to arrive in the courts. They frequented the markets, and were prepared to issue spot-judgments when necessary. The normal, everyday kinds of issues they confronted in the markets allowed them to impose their ethical and moral ideals upon ordinary people. This personal prestige, combined with the power to decide litigations as they chose when in court, would have encouraged most people to conform to their advice and rulings even outside court or the presence of court-officers.

v. The Court and the Farm

Litigations of land disputes produced some court influence over agricultural life, as did the interest of the rabbis[3] in the rights and welfare of laborers and slaves.[4] Agricultural cases, except for property claims, mainly concerned the enforcement of the laws and taboos prescribed by Scripture. The earlier tradition[5] made it explicit that agricultural precepts dependent on "the land," meaning Palestine, were to be practiced only there, while those not dependent on the land, except 'Orlah and Kila'im, apply abroad as well. The Palestinians wrongly thought that Babylonia was "empty of commandments" because of the absence of heave-offerings, tithes, and the like. Rav Judah taught that tithes and other such obligations apply *only* in Palestine and the Pumbeditans held that even 'Orlah-taboos did not apply abroad. So the rabbinical rulings seem quite unequivocal. Nonetheless, there is considerable evidence that some agricultural taboos certainly *were* observed in Babylonia, both earlier and in this period.[6] The biblical understanding of the ordinary people must have been part of the reason. Finding agricultural laws in Scripture, apparently accustomed from

---

[1] Vol. II, pp. 111-119, and vol. III, pp. 295-302.

[2] Vol. III, p. 298.

[3] But I know of no cases before the courts, except in the matter of claims for unpaid wages, see below, pp. 244-247.

[4] On workers and slaves, below, pp. 228ff.

[5] Vol. III, pp. 295-298 for a summary of Mishnaic rulings and the opinions of the preceding generation. See also vol. II, pp. 51-52, n. 3, and pp. 260-262.

[6] Note b. A.Z. 22a, evidence that 'orlah-taboos were really observed. See above, p. 65.

times past to give to the priests their several gifts and to keep such other laws as the Bible seemed to them to demand, the ordinary Jews must have continued to observe the laws. But some Babylonian rabbis for their part said they must do so, and the rabbis yielded to popular opinion (and private interest) and accepted these payments. R. Ḥisda in the preceding generation received priestly gifts. Others now took them.

I can think of no more striking example of the way in which rabbinical authority operated in Babylonia. It was easy for the rabbis to require what the Bible itself clearly demanded, and not much more difficult to convince the people that rabbis knew *how* such laws should be carried out. When, on the other hand, biblical bases for rabbinical teachings and rulings were not obvious or clear, it was difficult for the rabbis to secure widespread conformity to the law as they interpreted it. R. Naḥman b. Isaac taught that the first fruits of the shearing had to be given to the priests in Palestine, but not abroad.[1] We have, however, a number of stories about how leading rabbis of priestly origin actually took priestly parts of slaughtered animals, [MTNT' = gift] including the following:

> Rava once penalized [lit.: fined] a man [for refusing to give priestly dues] by taking away a side of meat, and R. Naḥman b. Isaac did so by taking away his cloak.
>
> (b. Ḥul. 132b)

> Abaye said, "At first I would snatch the priestly dues, thinking, 'I am showing zeal for the commandment,' but when I heard the teaching, 'They shall give (Deut. 18:3)—but he shall not take it himself,' I did not snatch it any more, but would say to all, 'Give them to me.' When I heard [a further teaching, that it was wrong to ask for the gifts] I decided not to accept them at all, except on the day before the Day of Atonement, so as to confirm myself as a priest..."
>
> (b. Ḥul. 133a)[2]

> R. Joseph said, "A priest in whose neighborhood lives a needy rabbinical disciple may [alt.: should] assign his priestly dues to him..."
>
> (b. Ḥul. 133a)

> Rava and R. Safra' once visited the house of Mar Yuḥna' son of R. Ḥana' b. Adda' ... and he prepared for them a third-born calf [or, a calf in its third year]. Rava said to the attendant [a priest who usually received the priestly dues], "Assign to me the [priestly] dues, for I wish to eat the tongue with mustard..."
>
> (b. Ḥul. 133a)

---

[1] b. Ḥul. 136b.
[2] Trans. Eli Cashdan (London, 1948), p. 753, with minor alterations.

The account reports that R. Safra would not eat the meat thinking Rava ought not to take it from the servant. In a dream he heard the Scripture (Prov. 25:20), "As one that taketh off a garment in cold weather, and as vinegar upon nitre, so is he that sings songs to a heavy heart." R. Safra consulted R. Joseph, who approved his conduct and told him not to worry. The Scripture had come to him, and not to Rava, who had disheartened the attendant, the story closes, because Rava was in bad grace with the divinity, either for his conduct here or for some other reason. Gifts of firstlings were further referred to in the following:

> The daughter of R. Ḥisda [Rava's wife] said to him [Rava] "My father once permitted a firstling..."
>
> (b. Ḥul. 44b)
>
> Rafram of Pumbedita had a firstling which he gave to a priest while it had no blemish...
>
> (b. Bekh. 36b)
>
> A certain man brought a firstling before Rava on the eve of a festival towards evening...
>
> (b. Beẓ. 27b)
>
> A woman proselyte was given by 'Aḥa an animal to fatten. She came to Rava [to ask whether the law of firstlings applies to an animal held in partnership with a heathen].
>
> (b. Bekh. 3b)

Rava was asked whether cattle liable to 'arnona, the tax on crops and cattle paid in kind, were subject to the law of firstlings or not.[1]

The stories cited above, like those pertaining to the preceding generation, leave no doubt whatever that some priestly dues and firstlings were collected by rabbis who were also priests. Both Abaye and Rava clearly so indicated. Furthermore courts assisted priests to collect those gifts. We may suppose, of course, that where people could avoid, or did not believe themselves liable to give, priestly taxes, they would not do so. Nonetheless, it is beyond doubt that the rabbis in court did support the claims of the priests to receive their ancient dues. These gifts were originally intended to compensate the priests for their activities in the Temple, government, and schools. Despite the advent of other forms of government, the priests continued to demand their due. The people were thus subjected to the exactions of several groups: the Iranian government, the exilarchate, rabbis seeking support for

---

[1] b. Pes. 6a.

their schools, the poor, priests, and so on. The priestly demand, even
when turned to the advantage of a rabbinical disciple in need—and I
do not suppose it often went to so worthy a recipient—must have
weighed heavily on the folk, who slaughtered animals only seldom,
and then mainly for festival meals. The additional exaction of the
firstlings of the herd, which was surely carried out according to the
above evidence, was of equally sound biblical foundation, and many
people had no doubts about paying it. Since the priests' claim represented a significant property right, it is important to note that Rava
and R. Nahman b. Isaac proved willing to support the priests in court.
Otherwise it would have been difficult indeed for priests to collect
their dues, except when voluntarily handed over. With court backing,
on the other hand, the priests enjoyed a substantial economic benefit.

In addition to firstlings and the priestly gifts of slaughtered cattle,
heave-offering also seems to have been given to the priests of Babylonia
in this time. The following account implicitly suggests that Rabbah
and R. Huna b. R. Joshua accepted heave-offering:

> Rava said, "Heave-offering produced abroad [outside of Palestine]
> is not subject to [a certain ruling]." Rabbah neutralized it in a larger
> quantity [of produce] and used to eat it in the days of his [levitical]
> impurity. When R. Huna b. R. Joshua happened to have heave-offer-
> ing of wine, he used to mix two [measures] of *hullin* [unconsecrated
> wine] with one of heave-offering...
>
> (b. Bekh. 27a)[1]

Abaye ruled that camel-riders were forbidden to eat heave-offering.[2]
His saying presupposed that it was necessary to eat heave-offering in
a state of levitical purity, but whether he intended it as a practical
instruction we cannot say. The laws of heave-offering were studied in
Rabbah's school by Abaye b. Abin and R. Hananiah b. Abin,[3] by Rava[4]
and by R. Nahman b. Isaac,[5] among others. Nothing in the report of
their studies indicates that they intended to apply the laws. Whether or
not ordinary people gave tithes we do not know. Rava held that the
majority of the people of the land do not give tithes.[6] The language

---

[1] Note also the discussion of R. Nahman, R. 'Amram, and Rami b. Hama, who
were asked whether one had to eat heave-offering produced abroad in a state of
levitical purity, b. Bekh. 27b.

[2] b. Nid. 14a.

[3] b. Pes. 34a.

[4] b. Shab. 17b.

[5] b. Ber. 39b.

[6] b. Shab. 13a. Compare b. Shab. 23a, Rava said that the majority of ordinary
people do tithe.

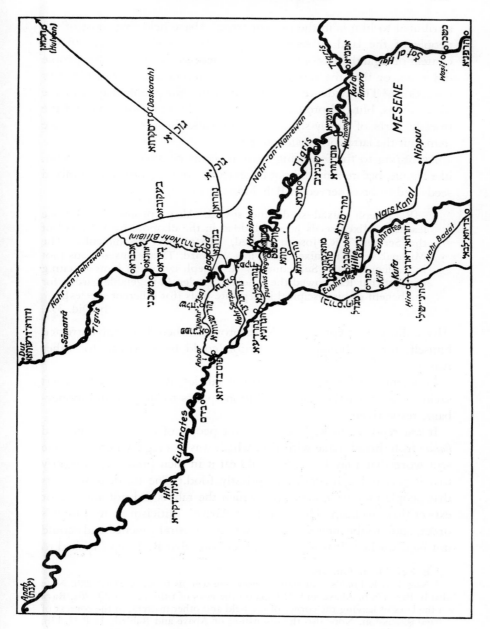

IV. Jacob Obermeyer's Map of Babylonian Jewish Settlements

attributed to him is in the present tense. Abaye held that most of the people of the land *do* separate tithes.[1] Both sayings appear in the context of legal discussions, and do not necessarily indicate that people did tithe, or that the rabbis were even talking about contemporary conditions.[2] The evidence would suggest that the people may not have given tithes, but did present to the priests the heave-offering and the priestly parts of newly-slaughtered animals, the former a negligible item, but the latter of considerable value.

According to the following story it seems possible that R. Joseph, like Samuel before him, did not believe the taboo against sewing mixed seeds had to be observed in Babylonia:

> R. Joseph mixed seeds and sowed. Abaye protested, "But we learned, 'Mixed seeds [are forbidden in the diaspora by a decree] of the Scribes.'" R. Joseph replied, "That poses no difficulty. The Mishnah refers to mixed seeds in a vineyard. This is mixed seeds [not in a vineyard]...." Subsequently R. Joseph corrected himself, citing the fact that Rav sowed the scholars' garden [a vegetable garden for the benefit of his disciples] in separate beds [for different species].
>
> (b. Qid. 39a)

Abaye did not accept the evidence brought when R. Joseph corrected himself, for he thought Rav's action could be explained for other reasons.

Concerning a forbidden mixture of fabrics, R. Papa and Rava left sayings about whether the prohibition applies to slippers and money-bags, respectively.[3]

It was reported to R. Joseph that the people of Khuzistan separated *ḥallah* from bread made with rice, which was not legally necessary. He sent word that a lay Israelite should eat it in their presence, to signify that it was not consecrated as priestly food.[4] The incident suggests that people may have kept laws which the rabbis did not impose or expect them to keep. The context of Abaye's criticism of R. Joseph's orders leads to the inference that it was an ancestral practice and should not be disturbed. It is significant, therefore, that R. Joseph wished to

---

[1] b. Ket. 24a, b. Git. 61a.

[2] Nor does Rabbah's comment on how one weighs tithe, b. Shab. 22b. Note also b. Ber. 47a-b, Abaye and R. Papa on the laws of tithing, b. B.Q. 28a, Rava on the laws of leaving the corner of the field and other matters, in the context of a legal discussion. Note also the discussion of Abaye and Rabbah, b. R.H. 13b, on heave-offering, b. R.H. 15a, on tithing fruit of trees which blossom in the sixth year and ripen in the seventh.

[3] b. Beẓ. 15a.

[4] b. Pes. 50b.

demonstrate publicly the fact that what the rabbis did not regard as holy was *not* to be treated as such. Considerable variation must have characterized local observance.[1]

To summarize: The courts used their power to adjudicate claims against property in order to enforce the donation to the priests of parts of newly-slaughtered animals, and some forms of other priestly dues. The rabbinical judges would penalize those who did not comply. Whether or not the Palestinians thought that the Babylonian Jewish farmers should give tithes and heave-offerings, the Babylonian Jews probably did give heave-offerings, but not tithes, to the priests. The rabbis would have liked to divert that income to their own needy disciples, who, they held, were engaged in work of a sanctity equivalent to making sacrifices in the Temple of old and therefore were entitled to them. The courts did not likely force the priests to make over their dues to rabbinical courts. It also seems that ordinary people did keep agricultural taboos which some rabbis did not believe were required in the diaspora.

VI. THE COURT AND THE SYNAGOGUE

The court had no control over synagogue affairs, nor did the rabbi occupy a higher place than other Jews in the liturgical life of the community. The priestly caste continued to pronounce its blessings, but otherwise, in the synagogue all Jews were equal. The rabbis' arrangements of prayers[2] were certainly followed in the *schools*, and disciples followed in all details the masters' manner of praying.[3] Earlier masters, as well as those of this generation, clearly regarded study of Torah as intrinsically more sacred than prayer.[4] Abaye said that he prayed only where he studied, rather than going to the synagogue for

---

[1] Stories about how rabbis themselves farmed their lands were preserved, e.g. b. Men. 87a, R. Joseph was able to produce a very desirable kind of wine. Since the rabbis were believed to know many kinds of secrets about the natural world, it would have been normal for people to imitate their ways, and so their reputation as holy men would certainly have enhanced their influence over agricultural practices.

[2] See below, pp. 324-330.

[3] On the role of the rabbis earlier, see vol. II, pp. 274-282, and vol. III, pp. 234-238, and my "Rabbis and Community in Third Century Babylonia," in J. Neusner, ed., *Religions in Antiquity: Essays in Memory of Erwin Ramsdell Goodenough* (Leiden, 1968), pp. 438-459.

[4] See below, pp. 290-295.

that purpose. His saying was quite consistent with earlier ones on the same subject.[1] This attitude probably reflects the above-mentioned fact, that the rabbis played no central role in synagogue life, and what they did not control could not have seemed very important.

The only instance of court exercise of rabbinical authority involving synagogues is as follows:

> There was a synagogue of Jews from Rumakan [near Maḥoza] which opened out into a room where a corpse was deposited [before being buried].[2] The priests wanted to go to pray there, and they came to Rava [and asked him what to do]. He replied, "Take the ark and put it down there [to interpose between the room and the synagogue proper]. Since it is a wooden vessel which is meant to be stationary ... it will form a partition to prevent the passage of defilement." The disciples said to Rava, "But sometimes it is moved while a scroll of the Torah is resting on it, and thus becomes a vessel which is moved both when filled and when empty?" "If so," he answered, "there is no remedy."
>
> (b. Meg. 26b)

The priests' problem had nothing to do with the proper conduct of synagogue prayer, but rather with a matter of ritual defilement. Rava did not order that the ark be left in its place, only that the priests see whether they could so arrange things as to prevent corpse-uncleanness. Rava held that a synagogue-building may be sold or exchanged [for secular purposes], but not rented or pledged.[3] He ruled also that one may make a decrepit ark into a smaller one, but not into a reading-stand,[4] and said that one may turn a synagogue into a school-house of the rabbis, but not the reverse.[5] I should imagine that the disposition of synagogue property might well have been adjudicated in local courts. Other rabbinical laws affecting synagogue life, such as specifications of the lections for various occasions, prayers, and proper conduct in the synagogue, would probably have been outside of effective court jurisdiction. As a holy man, the rabbi could, of course, guide and advise the people, but he could certainly do little contrary to public opinion.

---

[1] b. Ber. 8a, see vol. III, p. 235 for other such sayings by earlier masters. And contrast b. Meg. 29a, Abaye studied in the synagogue.

[2] Compare the view of R. Assi, b. Meg. 28b.

[3] b. Meg. 26b.

[4] *ibid*. 26b.

[5] *ibid*. 26b-27a. This was consistent with the view that the school was holier than the synagogue. Note also b. Git. 60a, Rabbah and R. Joseph on the Sabbath lections; b. Meg. 24b, 'Ullah b. Rav asked Abaye whether a child dressed in rags is allowed to read the Torah; b. Ber. 62b, Rava held it was not permitted to spit in the synagogue.

The people would have found in the memory of their forefathers' conduct of synagogue prayers a far more compelling source of guidance than the rabbis' teachings, although buttressed by citations of earlier rabbis or by references to Scripture.

As to art in the synagogue, Abaye held that the Torah absolutely forbade making copies of the four faces of Ezekiel's vision (Ez. 1:10). He exposited Ex. 20:20, "You shall not make *with me*" to mean "*Me* you shall not make," and since man is in God's image, the human face cannot be reproduced.[1] The actual practice in synagogues could not have conformed to the rabbinical rules about art, whether strict or lenient, according to Geonic tradition. R. Ḥiyya b. R. Huna said that he observed Abaye and Rava bending to one side and not completely prostrating themselves at prayer.[2] The Geonic tradition of R. Sherira on this passage explained that they, like his forebears, refrained from falling face-down on the floor of the synagogue "but would keep their faces up, and would not touch their faces to the ground, for *perhaps under the dirt there is a floor of stones and mosaic....*"[3] There can be little doubt therefore that in Geonic times, it was believed that synagogue floors had earlier been decorated by mosaics, now covered up by dirt. It was further believed that Abaye and Rava had refrained from prostrating themselves on the floor precisely because doing so would make it seem that they were bowing down to the mosaic on the floor. Abaye and Rava nonetheless prayed in the synagogue of Shaf veYativ in Nehardea, in which a statue of a man was set up.[4] They believed that the *Shekhinah* lived there and in the synagogue in Huzal, alternatively.[5] They held that the Scripture (Ps. 90:1), "Lord, you have been our dwelling place" referred to both the synagogue and the school house.

VII. THE COURT AND THE ABBATOIR. FOOD TABOOS

Supervision of the slaughter of cattle was entirely within the courts' powers.[6] The rabbis, first of all, inspected the butcher shops and abat-

---

[1] b. R.H. 24a, b. A.Z. 43a.

[2] b. Ber. 34b.

[3] *Ozar HaGeonim* ed. B. M. Lewin I, 83, and note 5.

[4] Note also the Geonic tradition (*Ozar HaGeonim* V, c, p. 43) that the *andarta* mentioned in b. R.H. 24b, which stood in the synagogue of Shaf veYativ in Nehardea and so disturbed the rabbis who prayed there was a statue of the king. "The king decreed to set up against the Jews' wishes a statue such as the Persians themselves worshipped."

[5] b. Meg. 29a.

[6] See vol. II, pp. 274-282, III, pp. 259-266.

toirs, to oversee the butchers in the act of slaughter, and to make certain of the sharpness of their knives. They could moreover prohibit both the participation of a sinning butcher and the sale of improper meat in the Jewish marketplace. It was therefore to the advantage of the Jewish butchers to obey the rabbis' rules to begin with. Quite naturally the butchers consulted the rabbis about doubtful matters, as in the following stories:

> Rava examined an arrow for R. Jonah b. Taḥalifa, who slaughtered with it a bird in flight...
>
> (b. Ḥul. 30b)[1]

> Certain Tai [Arabs] once came to Zikonia [near Pumbedita] and gave the Jewish butchers some rams [to slaughter], saying, "The blood and fat will be for us, and the hide and flesh for you." R. Tobi b. R. Mattena sent the case to R. Joseph and asked what was the law....
>
> (b. Ḥul. 39b)[2]

> The case [of a bird] once came to Rabbah, in which the doubt arose as to whether it was clawed or not, and he was about to examine the gullet from the outside when Abaye said to him....
>
> (b. Ḥul. 43b)

> An ox belonging to the family of R. 'Uqba was slaughtered. The slaughtering started at the pharynx and was completed at the gullet proper. Rava said, "I will impose the restriction..." Meanwhile the case circulated until it came before R. Abba. He said to his disciples, "The ox should have been permitted ... Go tell [Rava] the son of Joseph b. Ḥama to pay the owner the value of the ox."[3]
>
> (b. Ḥul. 43b)

> Rava once declared an animal, which was thought to be a doubtful case of trefah,[4] to be permitted and then bought some of the meat.

---

[1] But the discussion further presupposes that R. Jonah prepared dust in the whole valley where the bird was flying in order to receive its blood as the law required. I therefore suppose that the examination was for theoretical purposes, *or* that the condition of preparing the dust for receiving the blood was not actually met.

[2] It is supposed that the Tai intended to use their share of the animals for their cult.

[3] I do not understand why Rava should have had to repay the ox's owner, unless his decision was not made as a court officer of the exilarchate, for as we have seen above, p. 136, errors made in judgment did not require indemnity unless the judge was "unauthorized." Rava was certainly an authorized judge. It is possible that the incident occurred early in his life ("Go tell the son of R. Joseph b. Ḥama..."), or that R. Abba did not know that Rava was an authorized judge. I should suppose the former to have been the case, since later on Rava's decisions would not have been subjected to the examination of less powerful men than himself. See vol. III, p. 74.

[4] Lit. "torn." Unfit for Jewish use.

[His wife] the daughter of R. Ḥisda said to him, "My father once permitted a firstling but would not buy of its meat."

(b. Ḥul. 44b)

A case of a perforation stopped up by unclean fat came to Rava. He said...

(b. Ḥul. 49b)

A basketful of birds, each with its legs broken, was brought before Rava. He examined each...

(b. Ḥul. 57a)

[The case of a fracture covered with flesh and] tender sinews came before Rava. Rava said, "On what account do we suspect [it to be prohibited]...

(b. Ḥul. 77a)

A case came to Abaye where the bone was broken in a compound fracture, and a fragment had broken off. He held the case over for three festivals. R. Adda b. Mattena said [to the owner], "Go and ask Rava b. R. Joseph b. Ḥama, whose knife is sharp." He took it to him, and Rava said, "Let us see..."

(b. Ḥul. 77a)

There was a certain butcher who was suspected of selling kidney fat for the fat of ileum. [The former is forbidden]. Rava punished [lit.: fined] him [by forbidding him] to sell *even* nuts...

(b. Bekh. 29b-30a)

A certain butcher was insolent to R. Tobi b. Mattenah. Abaye and Rava were appointed to investigate the case, and they banned him. He went and appeased [R. Tobi]...

(b. M.Q. 16a)

Two butchers made an agreement that if either killed on the other's day [for slaughtering and selling meat] the skin of his beast should be torn up. One did violate the other's day, and the other went and tore up the skin. Rava summoned and ordered him to make restitution...

(b. B.B. 9a)

The case-reports cited above provide unequivocal testimony about the nature of the rabbis' authority over the abattoir and butcher-shop. In the instances of R. Jonah's arrow, the clawed bird, the perforation, the birds, and the compound fractures, rabbinic authority was consulted because people or butchers wanted to know whether the meat was fit for Jewish use. The cases of the Tais' rams, the butcher suspected of selling kidney fat, the insolent butcher, and the agreement that was broken, all involved actual rabbinical supervision of the butcher shops themselves. The rabbis' power to enforce both ritual and commercial

law was unopposed. The insolent butcher could be banned. One suspected of selling unkosher parts of the animal actually could be driven
out of business, so far as the Jewish market was concerned. When a
case of contract-violation involving butchers came up, Rava summoned
the miscreant to demand restitution. In both ritual and civil cases,
therefore, the rabbis were quite able to declare the law and to enforce
it.

The rabbis moreover inspected the butchers' implements. Rava
stated several rules with regard to the butchers-knife examination, and
R. Papa ruled:

> "It must be examined with the flesh of the finger and with the finger-
> nail, and the examination must be of three edges."
>
> (b. Ḥul. 17b)

Several reports of earlier and later generations concerned how various
rabbis actually did examine butchers' knives, in either the abattoir,
school, or court. On the whole, therefore, rabbinical authority in these
matters extended far beyond the walls of the schoolhouse.[1] The rabbis'
power over the markets combined with their reputation as masters of
the law to render them effective supervisors.

Food-Taboos: It was probably much more difficult to enforce the food
taboos among the ordinary people. The kitchens of Jewish Babylonia
could hardly be inspected by the rabbis so thoroughly—if at all—as the
abattoirs. Nonetheless, we have some evidence that the rabbis did
enforce the food laws whenever they could. The following stories are
of interest:

> A young pigeon [prepared for cooking] once fell into a jar of milk
> sauce. R. Ḥinena b. Rava of Pashrunia permitted it. Rava remarked,
> "Who except R. Ḥinena ... is so wise as to permit it?"...
>
> (b. Ḥul. 112a)

> The ritually slaughtered meat of R. Mari b. Raḥel was salted to-
> gether with *trefah* meat. He came before Rava who said to him....
>
> (b. Ḥul. 112b)

> Once a vulture seized a piece of meat in the market and dropped it
> among the palm-trees belonging to Bar Marion. When the latter ap-

---

[1] Nonetheless, the inquiry of R. Jonah, cited above, and the decision concerning
Rava's duck, which was found with the neck smeared with blood, b. Ḥul. 28a,
were probably of narrowly academic venue and do not by themselves prove that
the rabbis' authority extended beyond the schoolhouse. The other cases cited
above indicate, however, that it most certainly did.

peared before Abaye, Abaye said to him, "Go and take it for yourself..."

(b. B.M. 24b)

A man once came to Rava and asked, "What is the law [about releasing the bird when taking the young] with regard to the *Temah* [a clean bird]?" Rava said [to himself], "Does not this man know that one has to let a clean bird go?" He said to [the inquirer], "Perhaps there was but one young bird or one egg?" He replied, "That is so." Then said Rava, "This surely should not give rise to doubt...." The other sent it away. Rava then set snares for it and caught it...

(b. Ḥul. 141b)[1]

Abaye, moreover, issued rulings about the permissibility of certain kinds of fish[2] and discussed the punishment for eating an eel,[3] which birds are permitted and which prohibited,[4] and the decision concerning an animal or bird which has been clawed by a dog.[5] These few cases of inquiries to the rabbis are suggestive, though not probative. The inquiry about a pigeon in milk sauce would presuppose the specifically rabbinical interpretation of the commandment not to stew a kid in its mother's milk, for this was long ago extended to prohibit contact between meat and dairy products. The case of the meat dropped by a vulture would suggest that an ordinary Jew observed the rules on proper slaughter of meat. The inquiry to Rava indicates a similar interest in keeping the biblical commandment not to take both the mother and the young. That the rabbi was not so scrupulous as the inquirer leads to the supposition that ordinary people kept that particular law more stringently than the rabbis thought they had to. Since it was a biblical ordinance, promising long life as the reward for obedience, people would have been quite strict about it, and assumed that the rabbis would know precisely how required to keep it.

To summarize: We have considered two different settings for the enforcement of ritual laws relating to food. In the cases of slaughtering and selling meat, we have seen that the rabbis' administrative powers as court officers and market supervisers gave them considerable power over butchers. The slaughterers were, therefore, quite likely to consult with, or to receive inspection visits from, rabbis. The rabbis' authority to enforce the laws would, to begin with, have encouraged widespread

---

[1] On the tendency of rabbis to favor rabbinical interests in making court decisions, see below, pp. 309ff.

[2] b. Suk. 18a.

[3] b. Mak. 17b.

[4] b. Ḥul. 63a.

[5] b. Ḥul. 53a.

compliance. About other food taboos, we have no such certainty. In a few instances, non-academicians asked about the law; of these, one involved a biblical ordinance, one an honest doubt about the rule on ritually-slaughtered meat mixed with non-kosher meat, and the third, an uncooked pigeon in milk. The practices of the people in their homes can hardly be assessed upon the basis of these three cases, nor can we speculate about the extent of rabbinical influence in the domestic enforcement of the food taboos.

viii. Court and Rite (i): Mourning

We turn to consider other areas of law, mostly ritual in nature, where religious influence, and not political or judicial authority, was the chief means of effectuating the law. The evidence is limited.

We have one case of a rabbi's giving public instruction on mourning rites, as follows:

> Rava told the people of Maḥoza, "You who do not follow the bier [to the burial ground] should begin counting [the days of mourning] as soon as you turn your faces from the city gates."
>
> (b. M.Q. 22a)[1]

We do not know whether the Maḥozans followed Rava's rule. The rabbis had numerous principles about proper mourning rites. The funeral cortege, for example, was supposed to halt and sit seven times, to comfort the mourners or express lamentations en route home from the burial place. When, therefore, R. 'Ivya arranged a "halting and sitting" for his wife, the sister of Rami b. Papa, when she died, R. Joseph said he erred in a number of details, and Abaye and Rava noted other errors committed in that connection. Rava referred to the fact that such "haltings and sittings" may be arranged only where they are local practice.[2]

In general the rabbis had to defer to accepted customs, and could do little to force people to change them. Rava, for example, said that a mourner was permitted to bathe in cold water all seven days of his bereavement and may eat meat and drink wine.[3] Another tradition held that he said the mourner may *not* do so. No stories accompany the

---

[1] Trans. H. M. Lazarus (London, 1948), p. 138. On this passage, see B. M. Lewin, ed., *Ozar HaGeonim, Mashqin*, IV, C, p. 34.

[2] b. B.B. 100b.

[3] b. Taʿanit 13a.

discussion, and if Rava's opinion on the law was in doubt, it can hardly be concluded that ordinary people had received, and were following, his instructions. Rava held, further, that on the Sabbath a mourner may walk about in his cloak, although it has been torn as a sign of mourning. On the Sabbath, Abaye found R. Joseph with his head covered with a handkerchief and asked him why he did so, considering that mourning is not conducted on that day.[1] The various sages clearly had different ideas of proper conduct during a period of mourning. Some were based upon the teaching of R. Judah the Prince, others upon Tannaitic tradition. For one thing, R. Judah the Prince urged the people to follow his practice, when he died, of being buried in a cheap shroud. R. Papa said that the people now commonly buried the dead in a shroud worth a few cents.[2] Whether this practice represented a response to rabbinic instruction, or the continuation of earlier Babylonian practices, or mere poverty, we do not know for sure. If, however, Babylonian custom was similar in this respect to the Palestinian, then R. Judah the Prince's instruction would have been quite necessary there. The influence of the rabbis during close to two centuries, we may infer, would have resulted in the modification of former practices.

The court seems, however, to have had little control over how people buried and mourned for their dead. We have no cases to suggest otherwise. I find it hard to suppose that in funerary matters the people turned to the rabbis as court-officials. On the other hand, the rabbis' own practices, exemplified in the schools and in the behavior of the disciples, would have represented an alternative to earlier, established customs, and, given the rabbis' prestige and supposed supernatural powers,[3] the common people would have regarded their instructions with a mixture of respect and awe. Men who were able to communicate with the dead and the divinity would also know how to pay last respects to deceased relatives. So sensitive a matter as burial of the dead must have proved amenable to rabbinical influence, therefore, even though the courts as such seem to have had little to say about it.[4]

---

[1] b. M.Q. 24a.
[2] b. Ket. 8b. But compare below, p. 196.
[3] See below, pp. 353-362 on the rabbis as "holy men."
[4] If so, however, we have remarkably little evidence to suggest how much influence, if any, rabbis actually had over burial rites and customs.

IX. COURT AND RITE (II): PURITY LAWS

The rabbis were believed by 'Ifra Hormizd to be experts in distinguishing various kinds of blood-excretions from one another.[1] Whether or not that story actually reports a historical incident, it is clear that the rabbis themselves told about the expertness of various masters. The biblical injunctions on levitical purity, concerning, specifically, the commandment to refrain from sexual relations during a woman's menstrual period, were generally obeyed by the people, so far as we can tell. The reason was that the Mosaic law prescribed menstrual taboos. The rabbis praised the Jews for their loyalty to the taboos:

> Rava exposited the Scripture, "And at our doors are all manner of precious fruits" (Song 7:14) as an allusion to the daughters of Israel who tell their husbands about their doors.
>
> (b. 'Eruv. 21b)

In earlier periods, numerous cases were reported of ordinary people, mostly women, who brought samples of blood for rabbinical inspection.[2] For this period, apart from the story about 'Ifra Hormiz(d), no similar accounts were recorded.

On the other hand, we have the following sayings which concern purity laws:

> R. Joseph said, "It once happened in Pumbedita that the infant was made to undergo ritual immersion [to protect heave-offering which may come in contact with her] before her mother...
>
> (b. Nid. 32a)[3]

> Rabbah acted similarly [permitted immersion on the eighth day, instead of the night preceding] at Maḥoza on account of the guards at the city gates [who could not be trusted to refrain from molesting the women at night]....
>
> (b. Nid. 67b)

R. Joseph's report suggests that people were careful to avoid rendering heave-offering unclean. Rabbah's ruling in Maḥoza indicates two facts. First, the women did take a ritual bath when they were supposed to, and second, some people in Maḥoza asked for, and probably accepted, his ruling about the matter. (It cannot be taken for granted that his ruling was considered valid by everybody in the town.) Rava explained that a menstrual woman may perform the normal household

---

[1] Above, p. 35.
[2] Vol. II, pp. 276-277, vol. III, pp. 240-243.
[3] Trans. W. Slotki (London, 1948), p. 222.

tasks for her husband, except making his bed in his presence.[1] Following R. Huna's dictum, that she also may not fill his cup, the wives of the several rabbis did so in a manner different from ordinary days.[2] Other forms of levitical uncleanness were discussed by the rabbis, whether or not practical cases arose, or were likely to arise, for decision.[3] Rava ruled that the lizards of Maḥoza are unclean if their shapes are retained.[4] I do not know the practical implications, if any, of this ruling, or under what circumstances, and for what purpose, it was issued. In fact, the laws of ritual cleanness had been suspended for Babylonian Jewry, and few, if any practical applications of such rulings existed.[5]

To summarize: If, as I suppose, the people continued to observe the taboos concerning menstrual separation, then it seems that the rabbis were consulted on how to do so. Whether the consultation came to them as court officers or as learned and holy men, I cannot say, though I imagine it was, at least in the case of 'Ifra Hormizd, on the latter account.

---

[1] b. Ket. 61a.

[2] Specifically, Abaye's, Rava's and R. Papa's, b. Ket. 61a.

[3] E.g., b. Shab. 28a, Rava on the uncleanness of the skin of an unclean animal; b. B.Q. 25b, Rava on the length of time which the uncleanness arising from a corpse may last; b. 'Eruv. 4b, Rabbah b. R. Huna on whether or not knotted hair constitutes an interposition in a ritual bath; b. Shab. 95b, Rava on five principles in the uncleanness of an earthen vessel; b. Shab. 84b, Rava on the same subject; b. Shab. 58b, Rava vs. Abaye on the uncleanness of a bell and its clapper; b. Ber. 19b, Rava on interposition before uncleanness, etc.; b. Shab. 14a, Rava and Abaye on waters of purification.

[4] b. Nid. 56a.

[5] Clearly, some priests ate their sacred food in a state of ritual purity. Perhaps some who adhered to the old way of the *ḥavurah* did likewise, but I find little grounds to suppose that rabbis ordinarily ate secular food (*ḥullin*) in a state of ritual purity. See my *Fellowship in Judaism* (London, 1963), pp. 22-30.

In fact, the purity laws were originally intended, as later understood by the Sadducees and Temple priesthood, for observance in the Temple alone. It was the Pharisees who made keeping the ritual purity laws (apart from those concerning menstrual purity, to be kept by everyone) a mark of membership in the Pharisaic party, and hence the Pharisees held that one must keep those laws even outside of the Temple, in particular at meal-time. There was no earlier basis in Babylonian Jewry for keeping ritual purity laws, and I suppose most of them would have died away of disuse long before the first rabbis made their way to Babylonia. Hence whether or not the Pharisees and later rabbis thought that one ought to keep ritual purity taboos when eating even ordinary meals, to the ordinary folk such taboos could have seemed wholly unreal, and such a teaching far beyond their expectations of Sinaitic revelation. It is especially noteworthy that priests did eat their consecrated offerings in a state of ritual purity, according to the little evidence we have considered.

x. Court and Rite (iii): Holy Objects

Numerous sayings pertain to *tefillin*, *mezuzot*, and other holy objects, but we have no evidence either that the courts were able to enforce the laws about their sanctity, or that the rabbis greatly affected the conduct of ordinary people in their regard.[1] The following account is suggestive:

> Our [Tannaitic] Rabbis taught, "A linen garment—Bet Shammai say it is exempt from [the requirement of] fringes, and Bet Hillel declare it liable. The law follows Bet Hillel." R. Eliezar b. R. Zadoq said, "Is it not a fact that anyone in Jerusalem who attaches blue threads [to linen] causes amazement?" Rabbi said, "If that is so, why did they forbid it? Because people are not well versed in the law."
>
> Rava son of R. Ḥanan said to Rava, "Then let ten people insert [fringes into linen garments] and let them go about in the market place, and so the law will be made known to all." "People will wonder at it all the more." "Then let it be announced at the public lecture." "It is to be feared that people will use imitation blue." "But it is no worse than if it were white?" ... "But it can be announced on public notices?" "And are we to rely upon public notices?" Rava then said, "If in respect of leaven on the Passover or in respect of the Day of Atonement ... we rely on public notices, how much more so may we rely upon them here where only the transgression of a positive precept can be involved..."
>
> (b. Men. 40a)[2]
>
> Rabbah b. R. Huna once visited the house of Rava b. R. Naḥman and saw that the latter was wearing a garment that was folded over, with the fringes inserted in the folded corners. [It became clear that these were improperly inserted, and Rava b. R. Naḥman took off the garment. Rabbah b. R. Huna then said to him,] "Do you think [fringes] are an obligation upon the person? They pertain to the garment. Go and insert the fringes properly."
>
> (b. Men. 41a)

What is interesting in the second account is the fact that the son of the greatest authority of the preceding generation not only did *not* carry out the law properly but did not even know it. The possibility that ordinary people would have known and followed rabbinic injunctions seems all the more remote, especially in the light of the first story. Rava seemed reluctant to announce the law in public, apparently because of the good chance of popular misunderstanding.[3] Whatever

---

[1] Compare vol. III, pp. 238-240.

[2] Trans. Eli Cashdan (London, 1948), p. 246.

[3] See vol. III, pp. 252-259, for astonishing instances of such misunderstanding of rabbinical instruction on ritual matters.

reliance Rava was prepared to place in public notices, in the end, the story does *not* say that such notices were posted or issued.

While a number of sayings pertain to the *mezuzah* and its proper placement, the only stories concern how rabbis placed the *mezuzah* in their own houses.[1]

Abaye explained circumstances affecting the rule prohibiting sexual intercourse in a place where a scroll of the Torah was located.[2] Rava taught some rules for scribes of sacred books.[3] The latter rules could have been enforced if the rabbis had declared that improperly written scrolls could not be used for public lection. We have no evidence that such cases arose, certainly nothing equivalent to the cases indicating rabbinical rule over the abattoir. The former rule also produced no practical results so far as we can tell.

One recalls that an Arab woman brought *tefillin* to Abaye for ransom.[4] The reason was that she thought he would pay well for them, and one may infer that rabbis had the reputation of being especially concerned for the sanctity of *tefillin*. Even if that was the case, it does not prove that they also had any authority, through the courts or otherwise, over how the people handled, used, or manufactured them. On the other hand, as holy men, they would have been believed to know how to make powerful charms, and so their instructions would not usually—when known—have been ignored. Abaye explained how to make *tefillin*, and said that the parchment had to be flawless.[5] We have the following story as well:

> Abaye was once sitting before R. Joseph when the strap of his *tefillin* snapped. He asked R. Joseph, "May one tie it together?..." R. Aḥa b. R. Joseph asked R. Ashi, "May one sew it together, turning the seam on the inside?" He answered, "Go and see what the people do."[6]
>
> (b. Men. 35b)

The latter saying, from the fifth century, indicates that the rabbi did not know the answer but was willing to depend upon popular custom.

---

[1] Sayings: b. Men. 33b, Rava, the *mezuzah* should be affixed in the handbreadth nearest the street. R. Ḥanina of Sura said the reason was that it should thus protect the entire house. Note also Rava's saying in the same place that faulty doors are exempt from the requirement of a *mezuzah*. Stories: b. Men. 33b, Abaye about the *mezuzot* in Rabbah's house; b. Men. 34a, R. Papa about the *mezuzot* in Mar Samuel's house.

[2] b. Ber. 25b-26a.

[3] b. Men. 29b.

[4] b. Git. 45b, cited above.

[5] b. Men. 35a.

[6] Hebrew: DBR.

In the former case, a disciple inquired of his master, who supplied an answer. Either R. Ashi later on did not know what R. Joseph had said, or the ordinary people eventually learned the proper rabbinic practice so it was necessary only to refer to what they were actually doing. But the latter supposition is unlikely, since it is easier and safer to give a direct answer than to refer to popular custom, chance observation of which is always in danger of yielding an erroneous result. Explaining R. Yannai's opinion, that *tefillin* demand a pure body, Abaye said that he meant one should not pass wind while wearing them, and Rava that one should not sleep in them.[1] Mar. b. Rabina asked R. Naḥman b. Isaac whether *tefillin* may be written on the skin of a clean fish. R. Naḥman b. Isaac replied that Elijah will some day come and answer his question.[2] R. Naḥman thus did not know the answer to the question. Now let us suppose that ordinary people were engaged in the manufacture of *tefillin*, and thought to make use of the skin of a clean fish. Had they asked a rabbi, he would not have known. Had they not done so, but gone ahead and made the *tefillin* in such a fashion, then later on, it would hardly have been easy to instruct them that they were wrong. It would have become rooted in their traditions, and in time to come, the best a rabbi could do when faced with the same question in the school would have been to say, "Go, see what the people are doing." Saying so would not necessarily have meant approval, but rather implied a confession that no tradition existed on the subject, so it would be just as well to do what ordinary folk now did. Not all instances in which the custom of the people was found normative or acceptable are of the same weight, to be sure. Many recent scholars have thought, however, that such a saying would invariably indicate widespread conformity to the law. In some instances it may rather have meant simply that the rabbis had no traditions on a question, or were unwilling to run contrary to folk practice in some minor matter, or were unable to overcome customs of many years' standing.

The evidence that the rabbis as court officers supervised the preparation and use of holy objects is very slight. I see no reason to suppose that their instructions were sought out by ordinary people, or that they made much effort to impose their laws outside of the schools. We simply do not know what ordinary people were doing. We know that *tefillin* were thought to be worn characteristically by disciples of the

---

[1] b. Shab. 49a, 130a.
[2] b. Shab. 108a.

rabbis,[1] and therefore probably not by non-academicians. Laws about *mezuzot* have yielded no probative evidence one way or the other. In Nippur, the equivalents to *mezuzot* were magical bowls. The Jews clearly used them. If so, perhaps common people were following the practices of their non-Jewish neighbors in preparing a prophylactic against demons for their homes, rather than using the rabbinical amulet intended for the same purpose. (But it is also possible that Jews used these bowls first, and that the usage spread to Mandaean and Christian neighbors. Neither Montgomery nor Yamauchi is clear on this point.) It is most striking that the instructions about preparing a Torah-scroll are unaccompanied by evidence as to how they were carried out. Since the Torah-scroll was prepared mostly for synagogues, it may be that the rabbis' lack of control of synagogue life[2] extended even to the preparation of sacred objects used there.

XI. COURT AND RITE (IV): HOLY DAYS

The rabbinical courts exerted only limited influence over the celebration of the holy days. Whether or not the rabbis preached in the synagogues, outside of them they could direct festival behavior only in a few, highly visible details. Their discussions ranged over all legal technicalities, to be sure, but I seriously doubt outsiders listened to them.[3]

The Days of Awe: Rava said that one who sounds the *shofar* for the sake of making musical noises has fulfilled his obligation in that regard.[4] He also instructed a disciple about the obligation to hear the *shofar* during prayers.[5] Rabbah explained that the requirement to recite kingship, remembrance, and *shofar*, or revelation, Scriptures, was so "that the remembrance of you may come before me for good, through the *shofar*."[6] The obligation to fast on the Day of Atonement, which the Scriptures had imposed, was probably enforced so far as possible by the rabbis. The following story indicates that the rabbis had *some* public authority:

> Rava permitted [ŠR'] the people of Southside [Maḥozan suburb] on
> the Day of Atonement to walk [pass] through water for the purpose of

---

[1] See vol. III, p. 130-149.
[2] See above, p. 149.
[3] See vol. II, pp. 279-280, vol. III, pp. 252-259.
[4] b. R.H. 33b.
[5] b. R.H. 34b.
[6] b. R.H. 34b.

guarding the crop [even though it appeared to be forbidden as act of washing]...R. Joseph permitted the people of Be Tarbu to walk through the water to go hear the lecture [on the Day of Atonement] but did not allow them to return...

(b. Yoma 77b)

Both instances pertained to villagers outside of the towns. In order to encourage their attendance at the rabbis' Atonement lecture, crossing water was permitted. It stands to reason that they had actually asked about the law in at least the latter case, for the subsequent discussion indicates that had permission not been granted, the people would not have come, certainly not in future years, and the rabbis were eager to encourage just such attendance.

Other stories about practices concern the rabbis' own behavior on the Day of Atonement. Rabbah fasted for two days, because of doubt about the right date.[1] Rava would cool off through sitting on fresh twigs, Rabbah through a silver cup.[2] Rabbah's household scraped pumpkins on the Day of Atonement.[3] Sayings on what constituted a culpable act of eating, such as Rava's that chewing pepper or ginger is not punishable, could not have meant much outside of the schools.[4]

Tabernacles: The laws on proper construction of the *sukkah*, on the festival prayers and rites, on preparation of the *lulav* and the like produced numerous legal discussions.[5] Only two stories about actual practice are extant, and both involve rabbis and disciples. Abaye asked R. Joseph why he was sleeping on a certain kind of bed in the *Sukkah*; Rava permitted a disciple, R. Aḥa b. Adda, to sleep outside of the *Sukkah* because of an odor.[6] That people kept the festival is beyond question. But we do not know how they did so.

---

[1] b. R.H. 21a.

[2] b. Yoma 78a.

[3] b. Shab. 115a.

[4] b. Yoma 81b.

[5] E.g. b. 'Eruv. 3a, = b. Suk. 2a, Rabbah on Lev. 23:43 to prove that the *Sukkah* must be less than 20 handbreadths high; b. Suk. 4a, Abaye vs. Rava on the laws pertaining to roof of the *Sukkah*; b. Suk. 7a, Abaye vs. Rava on the walls; b. Suk. 12b, Abaye on whether one may use licorice wood for the roofing; b. Suk. 29a, Rava on what can be kept in the *Sukkah*; b. Suk. 32b, Abaye and Rava on using myrtle for the roofing; b. Suk. 36b, Rava on how to make a *lulav*; b. Suk. 37a-b, Rabbah and Rava on the four species and the *lulav*; b. Suk. 41b, Rava on lending an *etrog*; b. Suk. 44a, Abaye asked Rava about the *lulav* ceremony; b. Suk. 55a, Abaye and Rava on the lections; see also b. Qid. 34a-b, Abaye and Rava; b. A.Z. 3b, Rava, One who is bothered by heat is not obligated to remain in the *Sukkah*.

[6] Abaye, b. Suk. 19b, Rava, b. Suk. 26a.

Passover: The rabbis gave public lectures[1] about proper observance of Passover, in particular on how to observe the strict taboos against using, or even possessing, leaven during the festival. Rava's public lecture is reported as follows:

> Rava lectured, "A woman may not knead in the sun nor with water heated by the sun, nor with water collected from the caldron, and she must not remove her hand from the oven until she has finished all the bread [she must continue working it until baked], and she requires two vessels, one with which she moistens, the other in which she cools her hands."
>
> (b. Pes. 42a)[2]

The lecture was on preparing unleavened bread. Women normally must have had traditions based upon what they had seen their mothers do. Presumably Rava's lecture was intended to teach the ordinary people to conform to the standards of the rabbis. R. Mattena, who had earlier given a public lecture, found that the people simply did not comprehend his instructions, and we do not know what people understood of Rava's, or how they responded. A likely guess is that the women went on doing as their mothers had taught them. On the other hand, because of his supervision of the marketplace, Rava was able to control the sale of wheat:

> A ship of grain foundered in Hishta [before Passover]. Rava permitted selling [the wet grain, which had become leaven] to gentiles... and subsequently allowed it to be sold to Jews in small quantities, so that it might be consumed before the festival.
>
> (b. Pes. 40b)

As market-commissioners, rabbis had no difficulty in supervising the sale of products in connection with Passover. No similar circumstance provided them with a basis for controlling home-celebrations. We do not know the origin of such a question as the following:

> R. Naḥman b. Isaac was asked, "If one rents a house to his neighbor from the fourteenth [of Nisan], who is obligated to search out [the leaven]?..." He said to them, "We have learned [in Tannaitic tradition]...."
>
> (b. Pes. 4a)

The question was a technical one, and had nothing to do with such simple, annual tasks as the baking of unleavened bread. The reply, phrased in legal terms, presupposed knowledge and comprehension of

---

[1] See vol. III, p. 255.

[2] = b. Yoma 28b. Note also Rava's comment on the kneading basins used in Maḥoza, b. Pes. 30b.

the Tannaitic traditions (= "we have learned"). The obligation for searching leaven was probably not assigned to purchasers by the courts.

We see, therefore, three kinds of Passover law. The first involved the sale of produce in the marketplace, the second, the preparation of unleavened bread and other home duties, and the third, other, non-ritual legal issues arising from the technicalities of Passover observance. The rabbis could easily enforce the law in the market. They could encourage observance at home. If consulted on a legal technicality, they could offer an opinion. The first type of law was easily effected through control of the markets. The second and third kinds of law were not litigable and produced no cases for court action. While they were not enforced, observance could be encouraged through rabbinical influence.

The Passover *seder* produced no cases or questions arising from the circumstances of the common life. While numerous stories told what the rabbis said and did in their schools or homes, none at all pertained to people outside of rabbinical circles. The following illustrate the nature of the stories:

> Rava used to drink wine the whole of the day preceding the first evening of Passover, in order to whet his appetite to eat more unleavened bread in the evening...
>
> (b. Pes. 107b)

> Abaye said, "When we were at the Master's [Rabbah's] house, we used to recline on each other's knees. When we came to R. Joseph's house, he remarked to us..."
>
> (b. Pes. 108a)

> Rava counted the beams, while Abaye's mother, when he had drunk one cup, would offer him two cups with her hands. The attendant of R. Naḥman b. Isaac, when he (the rabbi) had drunk two cups, would offer him one cup...
>
> (b. Pes. 110a) [1]

> Meremar asked, "Who recites the *Haggadah* at R. Joseph's?" They told me, "R. Joseph."
>
> (b. Pes. 116b)

> Abaye was sitting [at the Passover meal] before Rabbah. Seeing him dozing, he said to him, "You are dozing, Sir!"....
>
> (b. Pes. 120b)

Stories about how the rabbis conducted themselves at the *seder* were important for the study of the law and were therefore carefully pre-

---

[1] Preventive magic, see below, p. 335-336.

served in the schools. They do not indicate what ordinary people did in their homes, nor were they intended to. One recalls that the laws of Grace and other blessings for foods and material pleasures produced many accounts of what rabbis said and did, but practically none about life outside of the schools. What happened within rabbinical circles could not have influenced outsiders unless the rabbis made the effort to shape the lives of the common folk *and* had the power to do so. Conduct at meals, including the Passover *Seder*, was far beyond their direct powers of persuasion or influence.

Academic discussions about Passover focussed upon the laws of searching out and removing the leaven.[1] These discussions were technical and frequently involved far-fetched examples, such as Rava's, "If a mouse enters the house with a loaf, is a new search for leaven required?" which evoked a long discussion on the mouse and the loaf.[2] Other issues involved the Scriptural basis for contemporary practice[3] and the interpretation of Scriptures relevant to Passover.[4]

The Intermediate Days of Festivals: It is a paradox that while the rabbis had little power over the actual celebration of festivals, they had a great deal of authority to enforce their beliefs about proper conduct on the intervening, semi-festival days. The reason was that these beliefs pertained mostly to what work on those days was prohibited and what was permitted. Activities which were publicly performed could easily come under their surveillance, and their supervision of the markets placed within their control the artisans and small merchants as well as the farmers who sought to sell their produce. In consequence, while the laws about building the *Sukkah* or searching out leaven or celebrating the Passover meal seem to have affected rabbinical or academic circles alone, with ordinary people hearing lectures about the most basic questions of preparing unleavened bread and similar matters, the laws

---

[1] Rava provided the liturgy of a blessing for the act of searching out the leaven, b. Pes. 7a; on the laws of the search and removal of leaven, see also b. Pes. 4b, Abaye; b. Pes. 6a, Rava, if one turns the house into a granary before thirty days before Passover, he is not obligated to remove the leaven; b. Pes. 8a, Rava said the courtyard does not require a search; b. Pes. 8a, Rabbah b. R. Huna said salt sheds and wax sheds must be searched, etc.

[2] b. Pes. 10b-11a.

[3] b. Pes. 40a, on Ex. 12:17; b. Pes. 39a, R. Reḥumi to Abaye, how do you know that *maror* in Ex. 12:8 refers to a kind of herb? b. Pes. 5a, Rava deduced the prohibition of leaven from noon of the day preceding the Passover seder from Ex. 34:25, see also b. Pes. 120a, Rava on the Scriptural and rabbinical origins of the commandments to consume unleavened bread and bitter herbs.

[4] e.g. R. Naḥman b. Isaac, b. Pes. 6b.

about observing the intermediate days of Tabernacles and Passover produced a number of enforcement-sayings, including the following:

> Rava enacted ['YTQYN] at Maḥoza, "Whatever one carries with great effort must on a festival be carried on a carrying pole. Whatever is normally carried on such a pole must be carried by a yoke..."
>
> (b. Beẓ. 30a)

Rava's principle was that one should deviate from his normal way of carrying a load, so as to recognize the obligation not to work on the intervening days. We do not know what the people did in response to Rava's enactment. The following is suggestive:

> Rava b. R. Ḥanin said to Abaye, "We have learned... yet we see that people do this and we do not take them to task!" He replied, "...but let Israel [go their way]. *It is better that they should err in ignorance than presumptuously...*"
>
> (b. Beẓ. 30a)[1]

This is a striking reply, for Abaye apparently thought it hopeless to seek to impose conformity to rabbinical rulings. It was better not to raise some issues to begin with. That does not mean that the rabbis refrained from issuing rulings about the observance of the intermediate festival days, but it does suggest that widespread obedience to the law could *not* be taken for granted. Among other rulings are the following:

> Abaye allowed [ŠR'] the people of Harmekh to clear away [during the festival week growths obstructing]the canal.
>
> (b. M.Q. 4b)

> Rava allowed [ŠR'] bleeding of cattle during the festival week... Rava allowed fulled clothes to be rubbed. Rava said, "With regard to one who clears his field [of chips of wood] if it is for gathering fire wood, it is allowed, but if for clearing the ground, it is forbidden. How can we tell? If he picks up the larger pieces and leaves the smaller, it is to gather fire wood... Rava said also, "With regard to one who opens sluices to let water run off into his fields, if to get the fish, it is permitted; to water the soil, forbidden. How can we tell?..." Rava further said, "With regard to one who trims his palm tree, if it is for [food for] the beasts, it is allowed, but for the palm's sake, it is forbidden. How can we tell?..."
>
> (b. M.Q. 10b)[2]

---

[1] = b. Shab. 148b. Italics supplied.
[2] Note also Rava's lecture, b. Beẓ. 33a.

According to the interpretation of R. Ḥananel, the following took place on the festival:

> Some rams once came to [were brought for sale] Mabrakta [near Maḥoza] and Rava permitted the people of Maḥoza to buy them [and take the purchases back to town...] (After some discussion, Rava changed his ruling and said), "Let them be sold to the people of Mabrakta...."
>
> (b. ʿEruv. 47b)

The ruling of Abaye seems unequivocal. At his say-so, the people cleared out the water-channel serving their village. The several rulings of Rava cited in the second source are in varying forms; the first two state that Rava allowed (ŠRʾ) certain actions, in the latter ones, he merely *said* (ʾMR) they might be done. Whether the difference in language implies a difference between a case and a merely theoretical ruling I cannot say. The third case clearly refers to Rava's administration of the markets. By contrast, in the several examples given earlier, the activities of private persons were at issue, and the rabbis may not have had equivalent control of what people did at home and on their farms. The question, "How do we know what a person's intent is," is important. It leads to the inference that rabbis, who might observe a man's work in the fields, wanted to know whether they should intervene or not. If so, one may suppose that had they observed illegal action, they might declare a ban, as happened in earlier times.[1] Upon that basis, I suppose that the Rabbi's several rulings were actually enforced.

The rabbis' hosts, that is to say, inn-keepers, brought them a number of questions concerning the rules about work on the intermediate festival days, including the following:

> The host of Rav b. R. Ḥanan had bundles of mustard stalks and asked him, "Is it permissible to crush it on the festival and eat of it." He could not answer, so he turned to Rava, who ruled...
>
> (b. Beẓ. 12b)

> The host of R. Papa—some say it was another who came before R. Papa—had some eggs from a Sabbath [which he wished to prepare] on the following day [Sunday, a festival]. He came and asked him, "Is it permitted to eat them tomorrow?"...
>
> (b. Beẓ. 4a)

The inquiry to a rabbi would have been natural. The innkeeper certainly did not want to serve foods or act in a manner prohibited

---

[1] Vol. II, p. 253 and vol. III, pp. 220-229.

by the law, and with rabbis at hand, it was normal to inquire about
doubtful matters. Such inquiries would suggest that the rabbis had
influence over the people among whom they lived, indeed whose
patrons they were, as is to be expected, but they lead to no further
inference. We have stories, moreover, about how the rabbis themselves
acted on the festival-week, including the following:

> R. Joseph had beams of timber brought in in daylight...
>
> > (b. M.Q. 12b)
>
> Rain trickled into Abaye's mill-room, and he asked Rabbah...
>
> > (b. Beẓ. 36b)
>
> The wife of R. Joseph sifted flour...
>
> > (b. Beẓ. 29b)
>
> R. Ḥama had a folding bed which was put up on festivals. Rava was
> asked whether it was permitted....
>
> > (b. Shab. 47b)
>
> [R. Joseph said] "...it once happened that at Dura deReʿuta an alley
> ended in a backyard, and when I came to ask Rav Judah [or, when the
> case came to...] he ruled..."
>
> > (b. ʿEruv. 7b)

Academic discussions touched upon many practical matters, such as
sharpening a knife on the festival-week,[1] putting out a fire,[2] burial,[3]
and the like.[4]

Purim and Ḥanukkah: The rules about reading the *Megillah* (Scroll of
Esther) were extensively discussed. Rava held that reading it was more
important than the service in the Jerusalem Temple,[5] that one was
duty-bound to get drunk on Purim,[6] and that one must not recite the
Megillah from memory but from a proper scroll. Rava[7] and R. Papa
discussed the blessing to be recited before reading the *Megillah* and the
division of the lections.[8] Rabbah and R. Joseph explained why the

---

[1] b. Beẓ. 28a-b, R. Nehemiah b. R. Joseph before Rava, etc.

[2] b. Beẓ. 22a, Abaye asked Rabbah.

[3] b. M.Q. 19b, Abaye asked Rabbah; b. Beẓ. 6a, Rava says gentiles take charge
of the corpse on the first day of a festival.

[4] b. Beẓ. 8b, Rava on preparing dirt before the Sabbath or festival to cover
excrement; b. Beẓ. 8b-9a, Rabbah on covering blood on the festival; b. Beẓ. 18b,
R. Naḥman b. Isaac on bathing on the festival; b. Beẓ. 23a, Rabbah and R.
Joseph on using perfume on the festival; b. A.Z. 6b, the general principles of
laws of work on the festival, explicated by R. Naḥman b. Isaac.

[5] b. Meg. 3b.

[6] b. Meg. 7b.

[7] b. Meg. 18a.

[8] b. Meg. 21b.

Megillah was not to be read on the Sabbath.[1] Rava said that the *Hallel* was not recited on Purim.[2] Among numerous sayings and stories, none pertains to what ordinary people did or did not do. Since the *Megillah* was read in the synagogues, the rabbis' rulings were theoretically relevant, but I have found no evidence that they were actually carried out.

Two stories, both involving sages, were told about the observance of Ḥanukkah, first, Rabbah's practice in regard to the oil used in the Ḥanukkah light,[3] second, R. Huna b. Judah's confusion about when to say the Ḥanukkah prayer in the Grace after Meals, during his visit to Rava's school.[4] Other sayings relate to the blessing over the Ḥanukkah lights,[5] where they should be placed for public display at home,[6] the reason for the (earlier) prohibition of counting money by the Ḥanukkah lights,[7] prohibited and permitted uses of the Ḥanukkah lights[8] and other matters.[9] While the Ḥanukkah lights involved legal issues, no other aspect of the festival celebration was discussed. The issues pertained therefore to the Grace after Meals, of importance in the academy, and to the preparation and placement of the Ḥanukkah lights, done at home. Nothing tells us what ordinary people did.

XII. COURT AND RITE (v): THE SABBATH

Certain aspects of Sabbath observance were well within the power of the courts, and others quite beyond it. Two kinds of laws were publicly enforced by the rabbis, concerning, first, "working" on the Sabbath, and second, the establishment of Sabbath limits.[10] In the former case, the rabbis' police power, combined with the weight of public opinion, gave them considerable ability to discourage outright Sabbath-breaking. In the latter, because they themselves could control the establishment of the Sabbath boundary, they had no difficulty whatever in doing as they thought proper. Where others established it, they increasingly did so under rabbinical supervision. Numerous other

---

[1] b. Meg. 4b.
[2] b. Meg. 14a.
[3] b. Shab. 23a, Abaye reports Rabbah's action.
[4] b. Shab. 24a.
[5] b. Suk. 46a, R. Naḥman b. Isaac.
[6] b. Shab. 22a, Rabbah.
[7] b. Shab. 22a, R. Joseph gives the reason for a ruling by R. Assi.
[8] b. Shab. 21b, Rava.
[9] b. R.H. 18b, Abaye and R. Joseph; b. Shab. 23b, Rava; b. Shab. 23a, R. Huna and Rava; b. Shab. 22b, Rava.
[10] See vol. I, pp. 148-149, vol. II, pp. 277-278, vol. III, pp. 243-252.

Sabbath laws, however, were by no means enforced among common people, so far as we know.

The Sabbath boundary: We have many instances in which rabbis supervised the preparation and placement of the Sabbath boundary:

> Rava b. R. Ḥanan said to Abaye, "What is the law [about the thickness of the sideposts]?" He replied, "Go and see what the people do [DBR]."
>
> (b. 'Eruv. 14b)[1]

> There was at Pum Nahara an open area. One side opened into an alley in the town, and the other into a path between vineyards that terminated at the river bank. Abaye said, "How are we to proceed? Should we put up for it a fence..." Rava said to him, "Would not people infer [from Abaye's ruling] that a sidepost is effective..."
>
> (b. 'Eruv. 24b)

> R. Safra said to Rava, "Behold the people of Ctesiphon for whom we measure the Sabbath limits from the further side of Ardashir, and the people of Ardashir for whom we measure the Sabbath limits from the further side of Ctesiphon..."
>
> (b. 'Eruv. 57b)

> Once the warm water [for a child's circumcision, prepared the day before the Sabbath]was spilled. "Let some warm water be brought for him from my house," Rabbah said...
>
> (b. 'Eruv. 67b)

> Once the warm water of a certain child was spilled out. Rava said, "Let us ask his mother. If she needs any, a gentile may warm some for him indirectly...
> [A similar incident.] Rava said, "Remove my things from the men's quarters to the women's and I will go and sit there, so that I may renounce in favour of the tenants of the child's courtyard the rights I have in this one..."
>
> (b. 'Eruv. 68a)

> Some men from Qorqonai [Circesium]once came to R. Joseph, and said to him, "Send us a man to prepare an *'eruv* for our town'" He said to Abaye, "Go and prepare the *'eruv* for them, but see there is no outcry against it at the school house." He went, and observed that certain houses opened on the river...
>
> (b. 'Eruv. 60a)

> Mar Judah saw the people of Mabrakta depositing their *'eruv* in the synagogue of Be'Agobar, and said to them, "Go deeper into the interior so that you may be allowed to walk a greater distance..."
>
> (b. 'Eruv. 61b)

---

[1] Compare the saying of R. Ashi, above, p. 161.

There was a certain alley in which Laḥman b. Ristak [a gentile] lived. The other residents [who were Jews]asked him, "Will you let us your domain" [for the Sabbath, so they may prepare an *'eruv*]? He refused. They went to Abaye and reported it to him. [Abaye told them how legally to get around the difficulty.]

(b. 'Eruv. 63b)

R. Tavla, visiting Maḥoza, saw a bolt suspended from the side of a doorway, and made no remark whatsoever about it...

(b. 'Eruv. 102a)

On the rabbis' own practices, we have the following stories:

A number of skin bottles were once lying in the manor of Maḥoza. While Rava was coming from his discourse, his attendant carried them in...

(b. 'Eruv. 44b)[1]

Rabbah and R. Joseph were once under way [on the eve of Sabbath before dusk], when Rabbah said to R. Joseph, "Let our Sabbath base be under the palm-tree that is supporting another tree...."

(b. 'Eruv. 51a)

The above stories are not of the same probative significance. The first indicates only that R. Joseph asked about the law in a certain situation, but does not say whether R. Joseph thereupon went and enforced it or not. As to Abaye's advice to see what the popular practice is, it may indicate that he thought the people were bound to be doing the right thing, or he may have felt that the question was of no importance, and so the peoples' practice should be relied upon and not disturbed. In either case, however, it does indicate that Abaye thought the ordinary people *were* keeping the laws on *'eruvin* so that they would exhibit *some* practice in a particular detail. It seems to me probative evidence that some laws of *'eruvin* were, in fact, widely observed. Since these laws represented a Pharisaic-rabbinic tradition, it is important to note that by the middle of the fourth century, they were probably observed among the masses.[2] The same inference is to be drawn from Rava's comment to Abaye in the case in Pum Nahara. There Rava was afraid that the ordinary people might draw the wrong conclusions from Abaye's teaching and practice. What is clear, therefore, is that the people were interested in these laws and apparently were prepared to observe them. The measurement for the people of

---

[1] Trans. and interpretation of W. Slotki (London, 1948), p. 306.

[2] For discussion of the evidence pointing to the expansion of rabbinic Judaism *by* this time, see below, pp. 256ff.

Ctesiphon and Ardashir again leads to the supposition that some Jews in these major cities were concerned about the laws of 'eruvin and expected that the rabbis would explain how they were to be fulfilled.

The three cases on the spilled water are less decisive, for they indicate only the behavior of people who dwelt in close proximity to a rabbi.

The request to R. Joseph, by contrast, is striking. The later commentaries try to explain why at just this time the people of Circesium asked for a rabbi to prepare an 'eruv for the town. The obvious implication was that formerly, no 'eruv, or no rabbinical 'eruv, was available. Upon this basis alone we can hardly conclude that some mass conversion to keeping the 'eruv-laws had taken place. It seems likely, however, that the request indicated greater rabbinical supervision than formerly existed. The advice contributed by Mar Judah and requested from Abaye strikingly reveals once again the concern of ordinary people to keep these particular rules.

The case reported to Abaye is of special interest, for one may suppose that the Jews and gentile had lived for a long time without such arrangements. In that case, the question was a new one, and the need for Abaye's advice leads to the inference that these Jews too now wanted to keep laws they had formerly ignored. If we knew when Laḥman b. Ristak moved into the alley, we would have a clearer idea when Jews began to keep these laws. The story about R. Tavla, like those cited from the preceding generation,[1] suggests that had R. Tavla said anything about the matter, he would probably have been able to correct the situation.

The stories about the rabbis' own practices, on the other hand, simply illustrate that they continued strictly to observe the laws. Rava's instructions to his attendant not to repeat the action reported above were intended to prevent the people who accompanied him from gaining a false impression about the law. By contrast to the limited evidence of popular obedience to, and rabbinic enforcement of, other laws, we can only regard the above stories as an impressive indication of widespread conformity to the laws of 'eruvin.

Academic discussions such as the following would therefore have reflected practical problems:

> There was a certain piazza at the house of Bar Ḥabu [one of whose supporting poles was situated at the entrance to an alley] and Abaye and Rava were forever disputing about it...
>
> (b. 'Eruv. 15a)

---

[1] Vol. III, p. 245.

Rabbah was asked, "What is the ruling where a man [beyond the Sabbath limit] had to attend to his needs?" He replied, "Human dignity supersedes a negative commandment..."

(b. 'Eruv. 41b)

Abaye asked Rabbah, "What is the ruling according to R. Meir, where one extended the corner piece..." He replied, "You have learned [in the Mishnah]..."

Abaye asked Rabbah, "What is the ruling according to R. Judah..." He replied, "You have learned [in Tannaitic tradition]...."

Abaye asked Rabbah, "Is a mound that rises to a height of ten [handbreadths] within an area of four cubits treated as a corner-piece or not?" He replied, "You have learned, 'R. Simeon b. Eleazar ruled...'"

(b. 'Eruv. 19b)[1]

The academic study of the law is illustrated in the above citations. The rabbis would argue about practical cases, respond to what must have been theoretical inquiries (for in the case brought to Rabbah, one can hardly suppose a man was then awaiting his comment or authorization), and inquire of the masters about various issues of legal theory. None of these cases, however, would have been remote from daily life, and doubtless rabbinical studies would eventually have resulted in practical application of the law in specific circumstances. Other issues under discussion included the following: How much food is required for the 'eruv?[2] What is the law for an alley in the shape of a centipede?[3] Under what circumstances does the presence of the property of a gentile result in restrictions upon Jews?[4] How does one measure distances?[5] and the like.[6]

Other Sabbath Laws: The observance of the Sabbath formed a central theme in the rabbis' theology. Abaye taught that Jerusalem was destroyed only because of profanation of the Sabbath[7] and R. Naḥman b. Isaac said, conversely, that one who delights in the Sabbath is saved

---

[1] Further such inquiries by Abaye of Rabbah follow in the same place.

[2] b. 'Eruv. 29a, R. Joseph, Rabbah, and Rava.

[3] b. 'Eruv. 8b, Rava and Abaye.

[4] b. 'Eruv. 67b, Rabbah and R. Joseph.

[5] b. 'Eruv, 57a, Rava re Num. 35:4; Rava and Abaye; 58a, R. Joseph on rope used for measuring; b. 'Eruv. 56b, the surveyor bar Adda explained to Rava and Abaye about surveying; b. 'Eruv. 48a, R. Papa on rabbinical measurements.

[6] E.g. b. 'Eruv. 5a, Abaye and R. Joseph; 12a, R. Joseph and Abaye on a decision by Rav Judah; 16a, Abaye; 21b. R. Papa; 22b, Abaye on Babylonia as surrounded by rivers and therefore theoretically a single domain; 24a, Mar Judah visited R. Huna b. Judah; 31a = 82a, R. Joseph on the 'eruv as a religious duty only; 45b, Abaye; 52b, Rabbah b. R. Ḥanan corrected by Abaye.

[7] b. Shab. 119b.

from the subjugation of exile.[1] The rabbinic discussions of Sabbath law were extensive, detailed, and searching. It is quite striking, therefore, that among all the traditions, we find only the following stories about enforcement of Sabbath laws or popular Sabbath observance:

> A certain person once came before Rava and asked whether it was permissible to perform a circumcision on the Sabbath. He replied that it was. After the person left, Rava thought, "Is it likely that he did not know it was permissible to perform a circumcision on the Sabbath?" He followed him and asked, "Tell me the circumstances of the case." The man replied, "I heard the child cry late on the Sabbath eve but it was not born until the Sabbath...."
>
> (b. Nid. 42b)

> A corpse was lying in Derokeret. R. Naḥman b. Isaac permitted it [over the objections of R. Naḥman brother of Mar son of Rabbana...] to be carried out into an area which was neither public nor private domain.
>
> (b. Shab. 94b)

> A person came before Rava, and he gave a ruling in accordance with his view [on bathing a new-born infant on the Sabbath in the usual way]. Rava fell ill. [He ascribed the illness to his erroneous ruling.]
>
> (b. Shab. 134b)

One also recalls that Rava told the Maḥozans how to carry soldiers' garments on the Sabbath.[2] These stories hardly constitute a rich body of case-reports. In the first, Rava assumed it was commonly known that circumcision may be performed on the Sabbath, and that ordinary people kept that law. In the third, he was asked about a parallel situation. The second involved what to do with a corpse on the Sabbath, a problem which must have arisen many times before R. Naḥman b. Isaac finally gave his ruling. On the basis of these three cases, one can hardly reach any firm conclusions about the extent of rabbinical influence over popular Sabbath observance. The only significant evidence is that ordinary folk were thought by the rabbis to know a simple, basic law regarding circumcision on the Sabbath. When one considers the enormous range of rabbinical laws pertaining to the Sabbath, the above evidence seems impoverished and limited. No one asked, so far as we know, about the numerous laws of work, carrying, clothing, cooking on the Sabbath, or of the various rites and rituals connected with the holy day.[3] The extensive reports of rabbinic enforcement of

---

[1] b. Shab. 118b.
[2] b. Shab. 147b, see above, p. 46.
[3] See below, pp. 324-330, on liturgy.

the laws in connection with the Sabbath boundary hence present a noteworthy contrast.

It should not be supposed that no one kept stories or traditions on how the Sabbath laws were actually carried out. We have a considerable number of such accounts, and *all* of them deal with what one or another rabbi did, refrained from doing, or inquired about. So there is no doubt that when stories about fulfilling the Sabbath laws were available, they were preserved and discussed in the schools. Among such stories about rabbis and their families are the following:

[Regarding killing vermin on the Sabbath]: Rabbah killed them. R. Sheshet killed them. Rava threw them into a basin of water...

(b. Shab. 12a)

R. Joseph's wife used to kindle [the Sabbath lamp] late. R. Joseph [corrected her].

(b. Shab. 23b)

R. Joseph said, "I saw the calves of R. Huna's house go forth with their cords round about them on the Sabbath..."

(b. Shab. 52a)

R. Huna b. R. Joshua said, "I saw that my sisters were not particular about [openwork bands on the Sabbath...]"

(b. Shab. 57a)

R. Judah brother of R. Salla the Pious had a pair of sandals...He went to Abaye and asked him [about tying them on the Sabbath]

(b. Shab. 112a)

R. Mari b. Raḥel had some pillows lying in the sun. He went to Rava and asked whether they may be moved... Rava was walking in the manor of Maḥoza, when his shoes became soiled with clay. His attendant took a shard and wiped it off. The rabbinical disciples rebuked him...

(b. Shab. 124b)

Abaye's [foster-] mother prepared [a certain food on the Sabbath] for him and he would not eat it....

(b. Shab. 140a)

R. Aḥa b. Joseph was walking along, leaning on the shoulder of R. Naḥman b. Isaac, his sister's son.... He asked him, "How about rubbing linen..."

(b. Shab. 140a)

[In preparing for the Sabbath] Rabbah and R. Joseph chopped wood.

(b. Shab. 119a)

Abaye placed a ladle on a pile of sheaves. Rava placed a knife on a young dove and handled it [R. Joseph ridiculed their actions...]

(b. Shab. 142b)

Abaye was standing before R. Joseph. He (R. Joseph) said to him, "Give me my hat." Abaye saw some dew on it, and hesitated to give it to him. "Shake it and throw it off," R. Joseph ordered, "we are not concerned at all about it."

(b. Shab. 147a)

R. 'Avia was sitting before R. Joseph, when his hand became dislocated. He asked him [whether it was permitted to reset it. Meanwhile] the hand slipped back...

(b. Shab. 148a)

Abaye found Rabbah letting his son slide down the back of an ass [on the Sabbath]. He said, "You are making use of animals?"...

(b. Shab. 154b)

The stories cited above should indicate that the rabbis recorded how various authorities behaved, criticized one another, consulted one another, instructed disciples properly to keep the Sabbath, and in all, carried out the law according to their own traditions or opinions. There can be no doubt that such stories were preserved to illustrate the way the law was to be kept. In no instance have we seen a non-academician's turning to a rabbi for advice. Numerous questions on Sabbath laws came to the rabbis, but few, if any, from ordinary people. I should therefore suppose that the rabbis' behavior on the Sabbath was one of the distinctive marks of their estate, and like their manner of saying Grace after Meals and other ritual actions, it indicated that a man was a rabbi or disciple. On the other hand, one cannot conclude that ordinary people did not keep the Sabbath. It is simply inconceivable to suppose that the masses of Jews did other than refrain from work on that day. I doubt that they refrained from work in just the manner the rabbis said they should or paid close attention to rabbinical laws about other details of Sabbath observance.[1]

---

[1] Among the numerous teachings about Sabbath laws and observances were the following: b. Shab. 12a, R. Joseph, an important law on Sabbath observance is that one must examine his garments before darkness on the eve of the Sabbath; b. Shab. 7b, Abaye vs. Rava on whether cavities of a private domain are regarded

XIII. SUMMARY AND CONCLUSIONS

The rabbinical courts administered laws pertaining to the marketplace, including the abattoir, and supervised the collection and division of funds for the poor.[1] Clearly the courts had no difficulty in overseeing commercial life, ascertaining that butchers slaughtered and sold meat which conformed to Jewish ritual requirements, and exercising other functions relevant to public welfare. The courts manifestly took full responsibility for the establishment of the Sabbath limits, entirely within their control as communal administrative agencies. Certain other kinds of law which ordinary people intended to keep were probably carried out according to rabbinical rules, because rabbis were presumed to know what Scriptures required. These pertained to a few agricultural offerings and gifts to priests, taboos against sexual relations with a menstruating woman, and the like. I assume that the rabbis' reputation as men of great learning, rather than their position in the courts, accounts for success in guiding popular observance of those particular laws. Yet that same reputation seems to have had little or no affect upon other rites. The rabbinical rules about mourning, the ob-

---

as private or public; b. Shab. 3b, Abaye on whether a man's hand is like public or private domain; b. Shab. 8a, Abaye vs. Rava on the law about throwing a large round vessel into the street; b. Shab. 20b, R. Joseph on fires kept burning on the Sabbath; b. Shab. 49b, R. Joseph and Abaye on forms of labor which are prohibited and permitted; b. Shab. 60a, Rava, R. Joseph, and Abaye on what a woman may wear in the streets; b. Shab. 69b, Rava on how a man in the wilderness will observe the Sabbath; b. Shab. 70b, Rava and Abaye on reaping and grinding corn the size of a fig on the Sabbath; b. Shab. 73b, Rava on the punishment for filling up a hole on the Sabbath, see also b. Shab. 81b, Rabbah on the same subject; b. Shab. 74b, Rava and Abaye on the number of different counts for which a person would incur guilt by making an earthenware barrel on the Sabbath, or a wickerwork barrel; b. Shab. 74b, Rava vs. Abaye on untying on the Sabbath; b. Shab. 72b, Abaye vs. Rava on whether one is guilty who intended to lift up something detached from, but instead cut off something attached, to the ground; b. Shab. 91a, Rava asked, What if one carries out as much as a dried fig for food and then decides to use it for sowing; b. Shab. 92a, Rava and Abaye on carrying; b. Shab. 99b-100a, Rava and Abaye on throwing, and on covering a pit in the road with a mat; b. Shab. 102a, Rava and Rabbah on throwing; b. Shab. 107b-108a, Rava and Abaye on picking fungus; b. Shab. 117b, Rava on saving objects from a fire on the Sabbath; b. Shab. 123a, Rabbah and Abaye on forbidden labors; b. Men. 64a-b, Rabbah and Rava on desecrating the Sabbath in order to save lives; b. Ber. 31b, R. Naḥman b. Isaac on fasting on the Sabbath; b. Ḥag. 5a, Rava on sending on the evening of the Sabbath to one's wife meat which has not been porged; b. Shab. 50b, R. Joseph and Rava on what may be used to clean one's face on the Sabbath; b. Shab. 35a, Abaye asked Rabbah the law about removing honey from a honeycomb on the Sabbath; b. Shab. 141a, Abaye and Rava on cleaning clay from one's foot.

[1] See vol. III, pp. 266-271.

servance of holy days, festivals, and the Sabbath (except for the laws of ʿeruvin), the preparation and use of amulets, charms, and holy objects —these seem to have produced little or no impact upon popular behavior. People buried their dead, kept the Jewish festivals, resorted to amulets to guard their houses from demons, prepared and read sacred Scrolls, and the like. Yet the role rabbis played in these matters, if any, is simply not revealed by the evidence in our hands. Had we no stories about what *anyone*, rabbi or common folk, actually did, and no case reports or records of inquiries to the rabbis from ordinary people, then we could offer no hypothesis whatever. We do, however, have a considerable body of evidence about how some laws were enforced, and none at all about others. I can see no reason why, if cases on the others had arisen, stories about them should not have been preserved. Therefore since none is preserved, I suppose the reason was that people outside of the schools hardly could have kept, or cared about, these particular rabbinical laws.

The rabbinical courts, therefore, served mainly to administer public affairs and had slight direct impact upon the homes and synagogues of common people. Since the rabbis carefully defined laws pertaining to ordinary life, and not merely to the specific matters under their control, the reason for their failure to effect common practice was not that they did not aspire to direct it, but rather that they were unable to do so. Presumably either the exilarch or the Persian government did not let them. The original agreement between the exilarch, through Samuel, and the Sasanians in the time of Shapur I had specified that the Jewish courts would not transgress Persian law.[1] The cases cited in connection with Samuel's saying that government-law is law involved the payment of taxes, the adjudication of property rights, including the status of heathen property, and the means by which property is acquired. In ritual matters, the Jewish courts were probably left free to decide as they liked—if they could. It is hard to see how the Persian government would have cared whether or not rabbis told ordinary Jews what to do on the Sabbath. So if the rabbis' power over ritual life seems to have been narrowly restricted to public, administrative roles, the exilarch, and not the Persians, would have set that restriction. For him, the rabbis served as useful court officials. Their knowledge of law purported to have been given by Moses was considerable. They formed a disciplined, dependable party, or estate.

---

[1] Vol. II, pp. 64-72.

People must have looked up to them on account of their theurgical abilities.[1] The exilarch, however, was probably opposed to their making unrestricted use of the courts to control people's behavior. It was one thing to care for the poor, collect taxes, preserve an orderly, and ritually acceptable market. It was quite another to intervene in the lives of private people.

The contrast in Sabbath laws is suggestive. If ordinary folk liked, they could ask the rabbis about keeping the Sabbath, and occasionally, some people did so. But if not, the rabbis apparently had little power to punish people who from their viewpoint had sinned. Sabbath limits meant nothing to people who did not want to be guided by them. The rabbis, however, could do as they liked, for their public position as community administrators left them free to set up the boundaries. Had ordinary people simply ignored the Sabbath, and gone about their daily business, the rabbis would surely have punished them—and would have been expected to. But I feel certain very few people actually did so. Where rabbinical power was *both* necessary *and* lacking was in the middle ground between uncommon public violation of the biblical rules against work, and unopposed public administration of rabbinical rules about the Sabbath limit. What people wore or carried on the Sabbath or how they prepared food at home—these kinds of matters were essentially private, so far as the exilarch was concerned, and beyond rabbinical regulation.

Yet I do not mean to suggest that an individual's religious observance would greatly have varied from that of the community in which he lived. Such a supposition would be an anachronism. What was from the court's perspective "private," that is, beyond court authority, was, from the exilarch's and the peoples' viewpoint alike, most probably the accustomed way of doing things. As I have said, the pre-rabbinic patterns of Babylonian Judaism must have been deeply rooted. These were doubtless shaped by biblical laws and local customs, *ad hoc* decisions, and ancient, accepted exegeses of Scripture. For many centuries Babylonian Jews had kept the Sabbath and festivals, offered synagogue prayers and read the Torah, buried the dead, and observed other rites, laws, and taboos. The exilarch was hardly prepared to allow the disruption of popular and accepted practices or to provoke a revolution. So if, as seems clear, the rabbis' control over many rites was slight, except in such ways as the people invited their rulings, the reason was

---

[1] On which more below, Chapter Five.

that the exilarch did not find it in the public interest to allow rabbinical intervention.[1]

The people seem not to have asked the rabbis about Sabbath observance, festivals, holy objects, and the like, but they wanted their advice about some of the purity laws and food taboos. In either circumstance, the rabbis' powers were circumscribed. The rabbis did control other, equally ancient practices, such as the manner of slaughtering animals. Here, however, the rabbis' administrative duties produced considerably greater power. The courts' administrative functions were, on the whole, minor and tangential. The chief power of the courts, revealed above only with reference to the marketplace and abattoir, derived from the power to decide issues or cases of personal status and to litigate conflicting property claims. People did not have to come to court for advice about synagogue prayers or burial rites, although many may have respected the views of the holy men of the schools on these matters as well. Ordinary folk assuredly did have to bring property adjudications to rabbinical courts or to obtain their authorization, confirmation, or recognition for changes in personal status, as we shall now see.

---

[1] Perhaps the exilarch's failure to support the rabbis' effort to control Sabbath observance accounts for their harping on how he himself did not properly keep the Sabbath and on how his house-servants were thoroughly unreliable.

CHAPTER FOUR

BABYLONIAN JEWISH GOVERNMENT (II):
THE RABBI AS JUDGE

I. INTRODUCTION

We turn to study the judicial functions of the Babylonian Jewish government. As earlier, we shall review the case reports indicating that in a specific litigation, a court decision was issued in accordance with a given law. I have already argued at length[1] that case reports constitute probative evidence, while academic discussions on legal issues at best provide equivocal testimony about practical law enforcement. One cannot readily rely upon "common sense" to distinguish between theoretical and practical law, for, as I have demonstrated,[2] statutes pertaining to dedications of property and personal value to the Temple of Jerusalem, in ruins for two centuries and more, most certainly were obeyed at the end of the third century A.D. in Babylonia. Without case reports, no one guided by "common sense" could have supposed that people would devote valuable property to a sanctuary which was no longer in existence. Nor can we rely upon legal theory to indicate that laws which were not supposed to apply in the diaspora, including Babylonia, were not obeyed. The evidence of rabbinical and popular practice has already suggested a confused state.[3] Some believed agricultural offerings and taboos did not pertain, at all or in part, to Babylonia. Others, by contrast, gave some of the offerings and observed the taboos.

It is important, however, to delimit the probative value even of case reports. I have argued that laws on civil litigations and personal status[4] were probably enforced by the Jewish judiciary. The *extent* of enforcement of these laws, however, cannot be easily estimated. The case reports derive mostly from courts associated with the schools and the exilarchate. On the other hand, we do not know much, if anything, about

---

[1] Vol. II, pp. 251-260, vol. III, pp. 202-213.
[2] Vol. III, pp. 207ff.
[3] Vol. II, pp. 260-261, vol. III, pp. 295-302, and above, pp. 143-149.
[4] Vol. III, pp. 317-338.

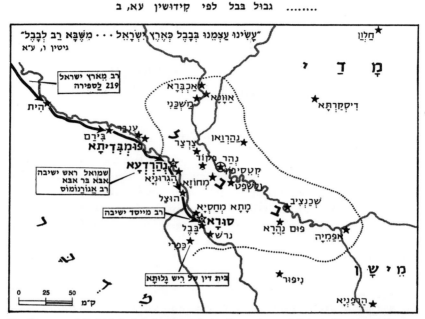

V. Centers of Rabbinical Schools and the Boundary of Babylonia according to
b. Qid. 71b.

Source: Michael Avi-Yonah, *Carta's Atlas of the Period of the Second Temple, the
Mishnah, and the Talmud.* (Jerusalem, 1966: Carta, Jerusalem), p. 98, Map#153.

towns outside of exilarchic, and therefore, academic, jurisdiction. M.
Beer persuasively argued[1] that the exilarch about whom we have information in the Babylonian Talmud governed the Jews in Babylonia
only. In second-century Nisibis, an exilarch or *archisynagogus* is mentioned.[2] An exilarch ruled in Apamea in this period, and Abaye and Rava
supposed that his name would not be commonly known in Babylonia,
as in the following:

> *Resh Galuta* Isaac, son of R. Bebai's sister, once went from Kurdafad
> [near Ctesiphon] to A[s]pamea and died there. A message was sent
> from there, "*Resh Galuta* Isaac, son of R. Bebai's sister, went from
> Kurdafad to Apamea and died there." The question arose whether [the
> possibility of] two [men by the name of] Isaac is taken into account or
> not. Abaye said that it was, Rava said that it was not.
>
> (b. Yev. 115b)[3]

---

[1] *Ẓiyyon,* 28, 1963, 1-33, see vol. III, pp. 87-95.

[2] Vol. I, p. 124, n. 2.

[3] On the place names, see Obermeyer, *op. cit.,* p. 183, n. **1.**

So an exilarch lived at Apamea at the southern limit of Babylonia on the Tigris, and was apparently not well known in Babylonia. We have very little evidence about the situation in Mesene, Elam, Persia Proper (Fars), Hycrania, Khorrasan, or Khuzistan, not to mention more distant satrapies. We have an apparent reference to Seistan, and a number of stories about Jews from nearby Khuzistan in Babylonia. The Babylonian schools preserved no data whatever about Armenian Jewry, though we know full well that Jews lived there, and that thousands of families were deported from Armenia to Fars during Shapur's campaigns of ca. 365-375.[1] No reason whatever exists to suppose that the Babylonian exilarch controlled courts or schools outside of Babylonia itself, or that the Babylonian schools issued decrees concerning, or even discussed the affairs of, Jews outside of that satrapy. The situation within Babylonia itself is somewhat clearer. There, rabbinical courts did exert substantial authority in the towns where they were located. We may be reasonably certain that in Maḥoza, Nehardea, Sura, Pumbedita, Nersh, and the other larger towns, the courts proved effective instruments of administration and justice. Nearby villages, along the same canal or in the hinterland, could not have been quite so easily controlled. On the other hand, when the villagers brought their produce to market they would have come into contact with rabbinical administrators. These authorities certainly did whatever they could to guide, and where possible, to control life in the outlying villages.[2]

Even though numerous case reports were attached to discussions of specific Mishnaic laws, on that account we cannot conclude that all of the laws in a specific tractate were everywhere enforced in Babylonia. As we have seen,[3] case reports generally are grouped in discussions about a few specific laws. Those of Rava's decisions about wine taboos, for example, suggest that he had considerable power.[4] Yet that power pertained to the marketing of wine alone. Upon the basis of these case-reports, one can hardly conclude that he could effect all laws pertaining to relationships between Judaism and idolatry. Only where we can offer an explanation of why courts were able to issue effective decisions are we able finally to conclude that a specific body of laws was normally carried out. I have tried to offer such an explanation, based upon a

---

[1] See above, p. 16.
[2] But see b. B.B. 133b, a reference to uninformed judges by Rava, below, pp. 218, 222. Note by contrast the instructions to villagers who came to the towns on the Day of Atonement, above, p. 163.
[3] Above, p. 59, and vol. III, pp. 317ff.
[4] See above, p. 59.

comprehensive view of the evidence. I do not propose to utilize the individual case reports as proof-texts.[1] We must attempt as comprehensive and cogent an account as seems possible. My purpose here is only to describe the workings of Babylonian Jewish government, not to exposit specific laws, and hence the citations of case reports will be accompanied by as brief an explanation of their content as seems absolutely necessary.[2]

II. CAPITAL JURISDICTION

When a miscreant died while being flogged at the order of Rava's court, the Iranian government made immediate inquiries into the matter.[3] From the advent of Sasanian rule, it was clear that the Jewish

---

[1] Therefore the narrow issue of "historicity" seems irrelevant here. It is of course interesting to know that a given rabbi at a given time and place "really" made such-and-such a decision. What is beyond doubt, however, is that in the schools, such a decision was believed to have been made. The report of various decisions is given *en passent* and in no way suggests that the tradent hoped to prove such-and-such a law was "really" enforced by the rabbi. It was self-evident to him that the case came to judgment and provided illustration of some principle of law. Even though theoretical statements about the law may not have been made by one or another authority to whom they were attributed, as in vol. II, p. 267, and below, pp. 193 and 196, case reports were generally tested, and all kinds of evidence were preserved about them, from whatever eyewitnesses or traditions of the event were available. So whether Rava "really" decided about wine-taboos in the marketplace I cannot say. Perhaps his school, or an agent of the school made such decisions, and not Rava himself. But there seems no valid reason to doubt such decisions were actually made and enforced as described in the traditions. I distinguish, therefore, between the historicity of an attribution to a given authority in a specific place or time, on the one hand, and of the narration of a given court action on the other. The former may be tendentious, the latter probably was not. At the very least, we have a perfectly factual account of the scholastic traditions about the enforcement of various laws through the courts. I can think of no reason to doubt the accuracy of the schools' information on the subject. I find no evidence to suggest academic traditions were intended to establish the claim of a wider range of court power than actually existed.

[2] Below, pp. 253-254, I shall discuss the issue of when does a case-report or story report an actual court case, and when is it merely a fictional narration of a point of law in the guise of a case. Clearly the language "If so-and-so does such-and-such, Rabbah says the law is so-and-so" does not preserve an actual case-report. On the other hand, in many instances of civil law, such language may well be the form in which actual court actions were preserved. We have a few such instances, as in vol. II, p. 267, and below, pp. 193, 196 and 217, in which we can show that the casuistic form did conceal an actual event. On the other hand, the language "A certain man did so-and-so. Abaye said...Rava said..." may just as well have constituted the way theoretical law was preserved, and sometimes may not report an actual court action.

[3] See above, p. 36, b. Ta'anit 24b.

courts could not impose capital punishment,[1] so the case in the time of Shapur II indicates that Sasanian policy had not changed. Jewish courts were not deprived of the right to try cases of theft, murder, and other serious offenses. The following indicates the punishment they might inflict:

> Bar Ḥama killed a man. The exilarch said to R. Abba b. Jacob, "Go, examine the matter. If he certainly killed, put out his eyes." Two witnesses came and testified against him that he had certainly killed [a man]. The accused came and brought two witnesses. They testified against one of the hostile witnesses. One said, "Before me he stole a *kav* of barley," and one said, "Before me he stole the handle of a *burtya* [spear, javelin]." [R. Abba] said to him, "What is your view? [To disqualify this man in accordance] with the view of R. Meir? But wherever there is disagreement between R. Yosi and R. Meir, the law follows R. Yosi, and R. Yosi said, 'A witness who is refuted in matters of money is acceptable to testify in capital cases.'" R. Papi said to him, "But that ruling [concerning legal disputes between R. Meir and R. Yosi] applies only where the Tanna has not stated R. Meir's view anonymously. Here however he has... [R. Papi proved his point.]" Thereupon Bar Ḥama arose and kissed his knees, and took upon himself his [R. Papi's] poll-tax for the rest of his life.
>
> (b. Sanh. 27a-b)

Bar Ḥama was certainly tried for murder, and had he been convicted, he would have received corporal, but *not* capital punishment. Blinding one's eyes was an exceptional punishment, not provided for in rabbinical law.[2] The traditional commentaries were troubled by that fact, and interpreted "blinding" to mean that the murderer's property would be confiscated, and hence the indemnity would have entered the category of a fine. (Of course, fines were supposedly not imposed in Babylonian courts.) The language seems satisfactorily clear, however, and quite unambiguous. The exilarch, not following rabbinical rules in such a matter as this, was prepared to blind a convicted murderer. He obviously could not put him to death.

Whether the accused enjoyed the services of a defense attorney or not is not specified. R. Papi's defense manifestly could not have been offered by an ordinary person, for it required detailed knowledge of Tannaitic traditions and Amoraic principles on how to resolve moot points. He gave it, by all accounts, because he "happened" to be present at the examination of the case. Bar Ḥama's joy was quite well justified. Whether Bar Ḥama himself otherwise would have had to know the

---

[1] Vol. II, pp. 30-35. But compare below, p. 188.

[2] Nor is it referred to in the Pahlavi law code, so far as I can see.

laws of refuting hostile testimony we cannot say. The account simply said that he brought two witnesses to discredit the accusing parties, so I suppose he knew enough law to be prepared on that account.

What is most important here is the fact that the exilarch took responsibility for murder trials. We have no earlier capital case. Whether the exilarch succeeded at this time—I should estimate about 350 A.D.—in regaining jurisdiction of murder cases in the Jewish community after the long lapse of nearly two centuries, or whether he had had it all along, I cannot guess. In any event, it is clear from the aftermath of Rava's case, and from the above, that capital penalties could not be imposed by the Jewish government. It is striking that the exilarch, and not a rabbinical court, judged the only murder case known to us to have been tried in the fourth-century. It may be that the exilarch was supposed to judge such cases, and did not leave them for the normal, town-courts to decide. On so slight evidence as a single case, however, we cannot come to a firm conclusion.

Other evidence relating to the death penalty includes the following sayings and stories:

> He who is born under Mars will be a shedder of blood. [R. Ashi observed, "Either a surgeon, a thief, a slaughterer, or a circumciser."] Rabbah said, "I was under Mars." Abaye replied, "You too punish and kill."
>
> (b. Shab. 156a)

> R. Joseph said, "Once...a Jewish court condemns to death, the condemned man is executed." Abaye replied, "Even in a Jewish court it is possible that something may be found to mitigate the sentence..."
>
> (b. Git. 28b-29a)

> Rava said, "If a man bound his neighbor and he died of starvation, he is not subject to execution... If he tied him up in the sun, or in a cold place, and he died, he is liable... If he tied him before a lion, he is not liable; before mosquitoes, he is."
>
> (b. Sanh. 77a)[1]

> A man came before Rava. He said to him, "The master of my village said to me, 'Kill so-and-so, and if not, I shall kill you.'" Rava replied, "Be killed, but do not kill. How do you know that your blood is redder? Perhaps that man's blood is redder."
>
> (b. Yoma 82b)[2]

---

[1] Further such examples of culpable negligence are cited, b. Sanh. 77a-78a.
[2] See also b. Sanh. 15a, Abaye and Rava on the death penalty applied to an ox.

Birth under the sign of Mars had not, Rabbah claimed, made him into a shedder of blood. Abaye's reply was that he did kill. We have no examples whatever of Rabbah's decreeing the death penalty, and I do not believe he did inflict it. The story is part of the tradition about Abaye's pointing out to Rabbah how unpopular he was in his town and cannot be interpreted to show that Rabbah actually put people to death. R. Joseph's and Abaye's comments on a decree of execution in a Jewish court, and Rava's about possible situations of manslaughter, culpable negligence, and the like, are quite theoretical. None of the numerous examples discussed by Rava is accompanied by the slightest hint that such events ever took place or came before Rava's court. We cannot suppose that they were too far-fetched. But we do not know that they ever actually happened, and I doubt that they did.

The inquiry to Rava was a strange one; if the master of a man's village was powerful enough to order a man to kill another, then he might well have had the power to force him to do so immediately. Consulting the rabbi does not, in any case, permit the inference that Rava would have been able to punish the man had he not followed rabbinical advice.[1] We do not know whether the master of the village was a Jew or not; he certainly was not a rabbi.

The Jewish court was quite able, on the other hand, to punish petty crimes such as theft, and to adjudicate the disposition of property which had been stolen. The following cases exemplified that power:

> A man of Nersh stole a book and sold it to a man of Papunia for eighty *zuz*. The latter went and sold it to a Maḥozan for hundred and twenty *zuz*. The thief was caught. Abaye said the owner of the book could come and pay the man of Maḥoza eighty *zuz*, and get his book back, and the Maḥozan could get the other forty *zuz* from the man of Papunia. Rava disagreed... Rava said...
>
> (b. B.Q. 115a)

> Rava was robbed of some rams when a thief broke in. The thieves subsequently returned them, but he refused to accept them...
>
> (b. Sanh. 72a)

One can only suppose that the thieves returned the rams because they were caught, as in the earlier case, and so it seems likely that there *was* someone who was supposed to catch and punish them, and also to return stolen property to the original master. That person must have restored Rava's rams, and Rava's refusal to accept them, based upon

---

[1] See also b. Sanh. 74a, and David Daube, *Collaboration with Tyranny in Rabbinic Law* (London, 1965), p. 27.

rabbinical theories about changes in the ownership of property, could not have been anticipated by the Jewish policeman. Had he known and accepted the rabbinical viewpoint, he would not have returned the rams to begin with. So the courts controlled by rabbis would have refrained, in certain circumstances, from making restitution of property recovered by police or agents of the exilarch, who would have naturally assumed it right and proper to recover and restore stolen goods. This is the only instance where a victim refused restitution. I should imagine ordinary folk would not have followed the rabbinical law, but would have expected that whatever could be recovered would return to their possession. What the courts controlled by rabbis would have been willing to do in such a circumstance is not clear. If the law prohibited the restoration of stolen property in specific circumstances, then the rabbinical courts would hardly have mandated restitution. On the other hand, if the people expected to get their property back, they would have demanded that the police who had caught the thief give them back what was theirs. In such a case, the police (or, the persons who recovered the property) would not have had to repair to the court for a decision, unless some contrary claim existed. In the absence of a contrary claim, the police would have given the property back to the original owner, thus bypassing the court. In any case, there can be no doubt that the Jewish courts did adjudicate cases of theft, and we may assume that thieves were punished when apprehended, though it is difficult to say just what that punishment was in this period. We have already noted earlier cases in which the courts tried and punished thieves.[1] It is clear, therefore, that the judiciary was responsible for crimes against persons and property, but that the penalties which might be imposed were limited. The court could inflict bodily punishment, not only in the rabbinically approved form of flogging, but also in the quite irregular form of corporal punishment through blinding, cutting off hands, and the like. The Sasanian government relied upon the Jewish administration to maintain peace and order within the Jewish community, but set limits to the means that might be employed to achieve it.[2] The courts nonetheless possessed very substantial power over the property of ordinary Jews.[3]

---

[1] See vol. III, pp. 302-305.

[2] I cannot, however, explain why courts which could inflict extreme corporal punishment could not also impose the death penalty. It is perfectly evident that the Sasanians never allowed the latter, and I suppose that their policy was based upon clearcut reasons. But I do not know what they were.

[3] For enslavement as a judicial penalty, see vol. III pp. 26-29.

III. Betrothals and Marriage Contracts

Two factors led to court supervision of the institution of marriage, first, the need for court action, either immediately or in case of later litigation over the marriage contract, and second, the occasional resort to the courts for a decision upon whether a betrothal had been properly carried out.[1] Court powers to certify that a betrothal was valid, or to require, through appropriate legal procedures, clarification or dissolution of a doubtful or improper betrothal, were considerable. It was not necessary for the court officials to cajole or persuade, for their power over the property cases which easily might emerge and over determinations of personal status was not limited. In some cases it was necessary for the rabbi as court official to make and effect an uninvited decision, but in most, conflicting parties came before him for decision. We shall here review cases of betrothal, dowry and marriage-contract, and below (section iv), contrast these with the good advice and counsel offered by rabbis upon marriage and family life. Wise counsel was rarely, if ever, accompanied by court action, but by promises or threats; property litigations and investigations of the validity of betrothals and marriages by contrast were rarely accompanied by moral maxims. The two sorts of sayings reflect entirely different circumstances and were based upon differing bases of public influence and leadership.

Betrothals: In the following cases, the courts' power over marriage derived from their right to determine whether or not the gift of betrothal was worth the stipulated amount, a few *zuz*, or not:

> A certain man betrothed with silk. Rabbah ruled, "No valuation is necessary [to ascertain whether it is worth the minimal sum for a betrothal]. R. Joseph held, "It must be valued [= evaluated]."
>
> (b. Qid. 7b)[2]

> A certain man betrothed with a mat of myrtle twigs. It was said to him, "But it is not worth a *perutah*." "Then let her be betrothed for the four *zuz* it contains," he replied. Having taken it, she remained silent. Rava said, "It is silence after receipt of the money, and such silence has no significance." [She knew the matting was not worth a *perutah*, and it was unnecessary for her to reject the proposal. Subsequent silence meant nothing.]
>
> (b. Qid. 12b)[3]

---

[1] Vol. II, pp. 268-274, and vol. III, pp. 274-283.
[2] Trans. H. Freedman (London, 1948), p. 27. Further discussion follows.
[3] *ibid.* p. 50.

A certain man betrothed with a myrtle branch in the marketplace. R. Aḥa b. Huna sent to R. Joseph, "What is the rule in such a case?" He replied, "Have him flogged ... and demand a divorce..."

(b. Qid. 12b)

A woman was washing her feet in a bowl of water. A man came, grabbed a *zuz* from his neighbor, threw it to her, and said, "You are betrothed to me." Then he went before Rava [to confirm the betrothal]...

(b. Qid. 52b)

A certain sharecropper betrothed with a handful of onions. When he came before Rava, Rava said to him, "Who renounced it in your favor [for the onions belong in part to the landlord]?" [Hence it was not wholly his property to begin with.]

(b. Qid. 52b)

A certain brewer [who brewed beer from dates provided by farmers, and received a fixed proportion of the returns] betrothed with a measure of beer. The owner of the beer came and found him. He said to him, "Why did you not give this beer, which is stronger?" When the matter came before Rava, Rava said...

(b. Qid. 52b)

In the above instances, the issue was clear, namely, did the gift of betrothal constitute a sufficiently valuable item, and was it the property of the giver? On the other hand, what is *not* clear to me is how the courts came to rule on the issue in the first place. If both parties were satisfied with the betrothal, then no court decision would have been solicited, and consequently, none given. In this instance, the groom claimed the woman was married to him, and she claimed she was still a free-agent. Her status was thus called into question. Both parties would therefore want to come to the rabbinical court, the one to protect his alleged marriage, the other to establish her alleged unmarried status.

In such a case, the rabbis' power would have come to bear. By contrast, in the following instance, no litigation came to court, and the rabbis could do little except "remain aloof." What that means is simple: the rabbis would do everything in their power to discourage their followers from marrying into that particular family.

Some of the family [which had descended from a marriage disapproved by Abaye and Rava on account of a legal principle] remained in Sura, and the rabbis held aloof from them (not because they agreed with Samuel but because they agreed with Abaye and Rava).

(b. Qid. 12b)

The courts had to decide other issues of betrothal concerning, specifically, the intent of one who gives his word to betrothe his daughter
to a certain person, the rules of when one might effect betrothal, and
finally, the conditions of a donation in connection with betrothal. In
these instances, the courts' role was clear. In the first case, the conflicting claims for the daughter had to be settled. In the second, information was requested from a rabbi. In the third, property had to be
equitably divided according to law. The cases were as follows:

> [A couple disputed on whom their daughter should marry.] She
> nagged him until he told her that the daughter could be married to her
> relative. While they were eating and drinking [at the betrothal fes-
> tivities], the father's relative went up to a loft and betrothed her. Abaye
> said, "It is written, 'The remnant of Israel shall not do iniquity, nor
> speak lies' (Zeph. 3:13)." [The father gave his word, and could not
> therefore have consented to the betrothal which actually took place.]
> Rava said, "It is assumed that one does not trouble to prepare a
> banquet (for betrothal) and then destroy it."
>
> (b. Qid. 45b)

> Abaye's sharecropper once came to him and asked, "Is it permitted
> to betrothe [a nursing woman] fifteen months after [her child's
> birth]?" He replied...
>
> (b. Ket. 60b)

> Rava said, "Such a deed (of gift) can serve as a *moda'ah* (notification
> of gift) in respect of another." R. Papa said, "*This statement attributed
> to Rava was not explicitly made by him, but was inferred* [incorrectly] from
> the following case: A certain man wanted to betroth a woman. She
> said, 'If you assign to me all your property, I shall become engaged to
> you, but otherwise I shall not.' He did so. Meanwhile, his oldest son
> came and said, 'What is to become of me?' He took witnesses and said,
> 'Go hide yourselves in the Southside ['Ever Yemina, a suburb of
> Mahoza] and write out [an assignment of my property] to him.' The
> case came before Rava who ruled..."
>
> (b. B.B. 40b)[1]

Actions on the validity of betrothals thus could have come to court
if one of the parties sought an annulment and return of all property, or,
less likely, if both parties sought court confirmation of what they had
already done. In the cases of betrothal with silk and with a mat of
myrtle twigs, the difficulty was whether sufficient property had changed
hands. The betrothal with silk ought not to have produced a court case.
Perhaps it did not, for the issue may have been a *post facto* rabbinical
discussion of what *might* have been required in a litigation, had a case

---

[1] Trans. M. Simon (London, 1948), p. 175. Italics supplied.

arisen. Rabbah's and R. Joseph's rulings do not hint that the case had actually come before them, and the matter may just as well have been phrased in theoretical, casuistic language. The betrothal with a *zuz* hidden in a mat of myrtle twigs, by contrast, does seem to have involved a litigation, for the woman's silence is at issue. I suppose that she had subsequently become disaffected with the original arrangement. The cases of betrothal with a myrtle branch in a marketplace, the latter setting certainly contrary to the rabbis' rules, and of the family in Sura, indicate two means of rabbinical, or court, enforcement of the law. In the instance of the family at Sura, the rabbis could do little but discourage their followers from marrying into a family whose ancestry was of dubious legal standing. In the matter of an open, flagrant, and one-time violation of rabbinical laws, the court could also order a flogging. It would be meaningless to do so to descendants of the family of Sura.

The rabbis' presuppositions on the intentions of ordinary people were revealed in the suit of the secret betrothal that ended in Abaye's court. Abaye and Rava both assumed that people were of upright character, did not give their word and intend to break it,[1] and did not arrange a festive banquet only to hoodwink the other party. The reference to how the "remnant of Israel" will conduct itself is important. For the rabbis, honest behavior must always characterize that remnant. Those who did not act uprightly thereby testified they were not part of the "remnant of Israel" which would be saved.

The three cases of betrothal by means of disputed property, or of property not wholly belonging to the man, reveal little about why courts had to intervene. In the first, it is clear that the man sought confirmation of a contested betrothal, but we may only suppose it was the woman who was contesting it. The second and third cases seem even less clear. What is important in the final case is R. Papa's report of an actual court action before Rava. It is evident that the action involved a clearcut property dispute. We know in this instance who initiated action and why. R. Papa's criticism and correction of the saying attributed to Rava, like similar, false attributions to Rav and Samuel, upon the basis of a misinterpretation of court action, occurred

---

[1] But contrast Abaye's vow, cited above, p. 138, in a similar case. I suppose the difference is that in the case involving Abaye himself, he took a vow and meant to keep it, and hence had to come to court to annul it, but intended no dishonest or surreptitious action. Here on the other hand, the intention of the father in agreeing to a betrothal was at issue, and the presupposition of the rabbis seems clear.

specifically in matters of property litigation.[1] What happened is obvious. Rava made a ruling in a case. That ruling was preserved in the
form of an abstract opinion, "Rava said, 'Such a deed of gift can
serve...'" Had R. Papa not criticized the tradition, we should not know
that Rava had actually so ruled in a practical case. But R. Papa did
criticize the abstract tradition upon the basis of his own observation
and interpretation of an event. This case, standing by itself, indicates
only that some rabbinical sayings were carefully evaluated by the succeeding generation. One cannot conclude that all such sayings were
critically studied. It is, however, significant that all the abstract sayings
which were corrected by the subsequent generation upon the basis of
the recollection of court action pertain to matters of property or cases
of personal status also involving property transactions. Where court
action was not taken, as in the teachings of Rava about culpable negligence in homicide,[2] no such criticism was possible. I should suppose
that a great many other sayings about betrothals would have been
effectuated through the courts, though it is difficult to know which
ones actually came to trial.[3]

Marriage-Contracts: Court rulings on dowries and marriage-contracts
obviously effected property exchanges or judgments between conflicting claims. Generally the marriage-contract would produce litigation
after the death of the husband, when the widow sought payment of the
sums of money and property specified in her marriage-contract. The
rabbis held that a woman could not remain with her husband without
the protection of such a contract. The wife of a rabbi inquired about
whether that rule applied in practice. A third kind of litigation involved
the disposition of property covered by the marriage contract during the
life of the marriage, as in instances of the husband's misappropriation
or misuse of such property. Cases of court adjudication of issues pertaining to dowries and marriage contracts included the following:

> The sister of Rami b. Ḥama was married to R. 'Ivya' and her
> marriage-contract was lost. When they came before R. Joseph [to

---

[1] See below, p. 196, for a second such case involving property litigation. See
vol. II, p. 267 for R. Ḥisda's criticism of sayings attributed to Rav and Samuel,
based in fact upon court actions and not scholastic lectures.

[2] Cited above, p. 188.

[3] See for example b. Qid. 7a-b, Rava said that partial betrothal was permitted;
b. Qid. 6b, Abaye said one cannot betroth with a debt; Rava added, or with a
gift which is to be returned. Rava held that the rabbinical rules were supported by
Scriptures, b. Qid. 9a; R. Naḥman b. Isaac on Ex. 22:15, b. Qid. 46a. Note also
b. Ket. 8a, Rava on saying a certain prayer included in the Grace in a home where
a marriage takes place.

ask whether she may continue to live with her husband without it],
he ruled...

(b. Ket. 56b-57a)

Rava said, "At first I thought, a woman is entitled to seize money-
bags of Maḥoza for her marriage-contract [payable from the deceased
husband's estate]...When I observed, however, that they took them
and went out with them [to the market], and as soon as a plot of land
came their way they purchased it with this money, I decided that they
only rely upon land [and hence should not be allowed to seize money]."

(b. Ket. 67a)

The question was raised, "What is the ruling where a husband sold
property for usufruct?"...Judah Mar b. Meremar replied in Rava's
name, "Whatever he has done is done." R. Papa in the name of Rava
said, "His act has no validity." R. Papa said, "*The ruling reported by
Judah Mar b. Meremar was not explicitly stated, but arrived at by inference.*
A woman once brought her husband two bondwomen [in her dowry.]
The man went and married another wife and assigned one of them to
her. She [the first wife] came to Rava and cried, but he disregarded her.
One who observed it formed the opinion that Rava's view was, whatever the husband did is valid, but in fact it is not so..."

(b. Ket. 80a-80b)[1]

A certain widow once seized a silver cup on account of her marriage-
contract, and then claimed maintenance. She appeared before Rava,
who told the orphans, "Provide maintenance for her...."

(b. Ket. 98a)

A woman once brought into her marriage a robe of fine wool as
part of her marriage-contract. When the man died, the orphans took it
and spread it over the corpse. Rava ruled the corpse had acquired it
[as a shroud].

(b. Yev. 66b)[2]

The first case does not indicate that ordinary people would have
made such an inquiry, and we do not know whether others beside
rabbis were so scrupulous about the required document. The saying of
Rava is probative, for it indicates that women ordinarily did have

---

[1] Italics supplied.

[2] See also b. Ket. 104b, cited below. If so, the sumptuary laws concerning
modest burial rites could not have been observed by the family or enforced by
the court. No criticism of the use of such an expensive cloth for a shroud was
recorded by the rabbinical judge. He did not enforce the recommendation against
it, and I should therefore assume he could not do so. The court (perhaps after the
fact) could not tell the people how to bury their dead, but it could determine to
whom property used in connection with burial actually belonged. Compare above,
p. 157.

marriage-contracts and usually collected them. So the law was both enforced and obeyed. The suits that came for trial must have represented only a small and hardly significant proportion of the instances in which the law was properly carried out without court action. R. Papa criticized Judah Mar b. Meremar's saying in Rava's name. He based his view upon actual observation of a court litigation over property covered by a marriage-contract. This suggests that other sayings would have been based upon inference from observed actions, rather than upon teachings handed on in school. The fourth and fifth cases record court actions of Rava in litigations over property involved in a marriage-contract. We have no reason to wonder how such cases came to court, for it is clear that the conflicting parties brought them, specifically because they wanted the court to rule on who should receive disputed property, or who must pay a contested claim. It seems reasonable to suppose that numerous other relevant sayings would have guided court decisions.[1]

To summarize: The courts therefore exerted considerable influence over certain aspects of the marriage-relationship, in particular, the disposition of property exchanged in effecting betrothals, the supervision of documents drawn up for dowries and marriage-contracts, and the adjudication of property claims resulting from conflicts over such documents. The cases mostly devolve upon narrow property claims and generally inconsequential sums. The rabbis' views of proper conduct in effecting betrothal, right motivation in choosing a spouse, the importance of finding a wife who would bring up one's children according to the Torah as the rabbis exposited it, and similar religious matters—these played no role whatever in court actions. When an ordinary person such as Abaye's sharecropper came for advice, the rabbi gave it, but not in his capacity as judge of a local court. By contrast, the case before Rava concerning a suitable legacy to one's eldest son involved fair division of an estate. On the whole, one gains the impression that the courts could not have significantly affected most normal marriages. Where the betrothal was beyond legal doubt, the marriage perfectly regular, the necessary documents in order, and the marriage-contract legally paid out, the courts had no role whatever. If, however, when these things were not correctly done, the court could act, then the possibility of court action must have encouraged normal people to obey the law to begin with.

---

[1] E.g., b. Ket. 52b, Abaye and Rava on how great a dowry may be given to a daughter; b. Ket. 53a, Rava on the sale of a marriage-contract.

IV. FAMILY LIFE IN PRACTICE AND THEORY

While scholastic discussions on family affairs included attention to matters which could not have posed much practical difficulty, for instance the laws pertaining to the Temple rite of trial for a woman accused of adultery[1] and to the suitable candidates for marriage to the High Priest in the Temple of Jerusalem,[2] one can not so easily distinguish among more practical sayings. We shall first review the case reports, and then examine some rabbinic sayings about marriage and family life.

Adultery and Illegitimacy: The following relate to instances of adultery and other forms of illicit sexual relations:

> Rabbah said, "If [a woman's] husband is in town, we do not suspect [the results of] privacy [of a woman and another man]." R. Joseph said, "If the door opens to the street, we have no fear on that account." R. Bibi visited R. Joseph. After [eating] he [R. Joseph, who was going to a lower room with his wife, leaving R. Bibi above, and then planned to leave the house] said to the servants, "Remove the ladder from under Bibi."
>
> (b. Qid. 81a)

> A certain man was alone in a house with a [married] woman. Hearing her husband come in, the [supposed] adulterer broke through a hedge and fled. Rava ruled, "The wife is permitted [to remain with her husband]. If he had committed wrong, he would have hidden himself [in the house]."
>
> (b. Ned. 91b)

> A certain adulterer visited a woman. Her husband came, and the adulterer went and hid behind a curtain before the door. Some cress was lying there, and a snake (ate of it). The husband was about to eat the cress without his wife's knowledge. The [supposed] adulterer warned, "Do not eat it, for a snake has tasted it." Rava ruled. "The wife is permitted. Had he committed wrong, he would have wanted the husband to eat and die..."
>
> (b. Ned. 91b)

The first story reported that R. Joseph was extreme in his observance of the laws prohibiting a married woman from remaining by herself

---

[1] E.g., b. Sotah 6a, R. Joseph, on whether the "water of cursing" actually affects the accused woman or not; b. Sotah 17a, Rava on why dust is put into the water, with reference to Gen. 18:27; and 17a-b, on writing the scroll; b. Sotah 26b, Abaye and Rava on Num. 5:13, what did the husband actually warn against; b. Sotah 5b, R. Joseph says a suspected adulteress performs *ḥaliẓah*.

[2] E.g., b. Qid. 78a, Rava and Abaye on the marriage of a high priest; b. Sotah 44a, Rabbah on Lev. 21:15; b. Yev. 22b, Rava on Lev. 18:10 and 18:17.

with a man other than her husband. It was characteristic of the rabbis, like other holy men, to observe very strictly such laws of separation.[1] But no legal action could have come of it. The cases that came to Rava devolved upon the principle of whether a woman who had seemingly been compromised may remain with her husband. A property issue emerging in such cases was, Would the woman retain a right to her marriage-contract? If convicted, she would lose it. Upon that issue, litigation would have to take place. Nonetheless, the rabbis' administrative authority may have been sufficient so that had Rava only ruled upon the narrower issue of adultery, as the case reports indicate, he may have been able to decree that the woman must leave her husband in disgrace. He followed R. Naḥman's principles in deciding these cases.[2] (A story was also told of how 'Imarta daughter of Tali, a priest, committed adultery, and R. Ḥama b. Tobiah ordered her to be burned at the stake.[3] R. Joseph criticized his decree. However, Funk holds that this particular R. Joseph was the first Saboraic authority, in the time of the Jewish independent state under Mazdak. He points out that only in a situation of independence could a Jewish court have issued a death sentence. In vol. V, we shall return to the situation of the Jews in the time of Mazdak.)

Two cases in which rabbis decided questions of legitimacy were as follows:

> A betrothed couple once came before R. Joseph. She said [concerning her premarital pregnancy], "He is from him," and he admitted it. R. Joseph ruled...
>
> (b. Ket. 13b-14a)

> A woman came to R. Joseph and said to him, "Sir, I was unmarried after my husband [died] for ten years, and now I gave birth to a child." He said to her, "My daughter, do not discredit the word of the sages!" She confessed, "I had intercourse with a non-Jew."
>
> (b. Yev. 34b)

In these cases no property claim was at issue. They indicate that the courts were able to judge cases of personal status, in particular the

---

[1] See vol. III, pp. 195-202, 142-145. See Rava's action in enforcing such a strict separation in his court, b. Ket. 28a.

[2] Vol. III, pp. 275-276. Rava's opinion in b. Ket. 51b, on the right of a woman who has been raped to remain with her husband, is consistent.

[3] b. Sanh. 52b. A. Hyman, *Toledot Tanna'im ve'Amora'im* (London, 1910), II, p. 461, reports of R. Ḥama b. Tuviah only this pericope, and says, "From here we see that he was the head in his town." However, no firmer date on when he lived is given. S. Funk, *Juden in Babylonien*, II, 123 comments on the peculiarity of the case and its punishment.

legitimacy of the child, and to punish presumptive adultery or illicit sexual relations. The punishment would have been flogging or excommunication. Rava also ruled that R. Mari b. Raḥel, Samuel's grandson born of the relationship between Samuel's daughter and a non-Jew, was legitimate and even allowed him to hold office.[1] So the future status of a child born of a questionable relationship could also be determined. The courts could also see to it that fathers supported their families,[2] and order that maintenance be paid from estates for daughters as well as sons.[3]

Pure Lineage and Other Non-Litigable Matters: The rabbinical discussions about the boundaries of Babylonia[4] were intended to specify the towns or districts from which rabbinical Jews might take wives. Babylonia was believed to be the only "pure" country. That is to say, only in parts of Babylonia were the rabbis certain that Jews had observed the rabbinical laws about proper selection of mates. Hence the inherited "merit" of Babylonian Jews was undiminished by illegal or improper ancestral relationships. R. Joseph said that a person who spoke with a Babylonian accent might take a wife of superior birth.[5] So when Abaye asked him about the limits of Babylonia on the west side of the Euphrates, R. Joseph replied.

> "What is your motive? On account of Biram? The most distinguished [people] of Pumbedita took [wives] from Biram."
>
> (b. Qid. 72a)

Naturally, people who were stigmatized by the rabbis became outraged. They would, after all, have difficulty in finding suitable wives for their sons, and husbands for their daughters, if the word of the rabbi about their unsuitability was widely accepted. The following story suggests what might happen:

> R. Zera lectured in Maḥoza, "A proselyte may marry a bastard." [Since there were many proselytes in Maḥoza], everyone threw *etrogs* at him. Rava commented, "Is there anyone who lectures thus in a place where proselytes abound?" Rava lectured in Maḥoza, "A proselyte may marry the daughter of a priest," so they loaded him with silks. Then he lectured, "A proselyte may marry a bastard." They said to him,

---

[1] b. Yev. 45b.

[2] b. Ket. 49b, Rava compelled fathers to support their children, see above, p. 140.

[3] Below, pp. 213f.

[4] See vol. II, pp. 240-250. For this generation, note also R. Joseph, b. Git. 6a, and b. Ber. 59b.

[5] b. Qid. 71b.

"You have destroyed your first. [That is, you took away what you gave.]"
He replied, "I have done the best for you. If one wishes, he can may
here [priests], if he wishes, he can marry there [bastards]."

(b. Qid. 73a)

It is clear that the people of Mahoza took quite seriously the rabbis'
traditions about genealogy.[1] The Mahozans were concerned about R.
Zera's and Rava's rulings. On the other hand, while the rabbis could
keep their distance from a family of whose marriage they disapproved,
as we noted above,[2] they could not impose a divorce upon a happily
married couple. Hence their teachings were important, but hardly litigable, and so the rabbis buttressed the law with fanciful warnings
about the poor quality of the off-spring of such a marriage or about
the bad luck destined to afflict one who married unwisely, as in the case
of Abaye:

> Rava said, "...a man should not take a wife either from a family of
> epileptics or from a family of lepers...This applies, however, only when
> it has happened in three cases..." Abaye...married Homa daughter of
> 'Isi b. R. Isaac son of Rav Judah, although Rehava of Pumbedita and
> R. Isaac b. Rabbah b. Bar Hana had both married her and died. After
> he married her, he also died..."

(b. Yev. 64b)

Rava taught that before one marries, he should find out about the
woman's brothers.[3] He also recommended that a woman be similarly
concerned. Commenting on R. 'Aqiva's saying, that when a husband
and wife are unworthy, fire consumes them, Rava said that the fire of
the wife was worse.[4] There were many rules about prohibited relationships, and such sayings would have encouraged some people to learn
what the rabbis had to say about them.[5] One inquiry was recorded,
from the "men of Be Miqse" to Rabbah about the status of the child of
a man who was half-slave and half-free and a Jewish woman.[6] Rava
taught that a foundling was fit for Jewish marriage.[7] R. Nahman asked
him whether a person who has "lifted up his hands" in priestly blessing
of the congregation was thereupon elevated to full status as a priest.[8]

---

[1] See vol. III, p. 66, for Rav Judah's similar lecture.
[2] Above, p. 192.
[3] b. B.B. 110a, with reference to Ex. 8:23.
[4] b. Sotah 17a.
[5] E.g. b. Yev. 21a, Rava on the biblical origins of the prohibition of relations
in the second degree; b. Yev. 21b, Abaye gives examples of prohibited connections.
[6] b. Yev. 45a. But such inquiries generally came from the local school-house.
[7] b. Qid. 73b.
[8] b. Ket. 24b. I assume it was R. Nahman b. Isaac.

Such questions would quite naturally come to the rabbis as teachers, but whether court action resulted is not clear. If the courts could certify that a man was truly a priest, he hence might receive and consume priestly gifts. They could allow a foundling to benefit from community philanthropy, enter into a Jewish marriage, and declare his children to be Jewish. They could certify the child of a mixed marriage whose mother was Jewish to be similarly acceptable. We have no examples of such court action.

Sayings about normal married life were of another order entirely, for they constituted merely a corpus of good advice and wise counsel. The rabbis hardly expected to enforce these teachings through court action, which was either irrelevant to begin with or unthinkable. Such sayings convey the values of the schools. How much or how little they shaped the values of the streets we can hardly estimate. It was not through the courts that the rabbis could act in the following:

> Rava said…"Until the age of twenty, the Holy One blessed be He sits and waits [wondering], 'When will (a man) take a wife?' As soon as he reaches twenty, and has not married, he exclaims, 'Blasted be his bones!'"
>
> (b. Qid. 29b)

> Abaye said, "With a husband (the size of an) ant, her seat is placed among the great."
>
> (b. Yev. 118b)[1]

> Rava said, "Whoever has intercourse with a whore in the end will go begging a loaf of bread."
>
> (b. Sotah 4b)[2]

> Rava said to the people of Maḥoza, "Honor your wives, that you may be enriched."
>
> (b. B.M. 59a)

> Rava said, "It is meritorious to divorce a bad wife[3]… A bad wife who owns a large marriage-contract should be given a rival at her side[4] …A bad wife is as troublesome as a very rainy day[5]… Come and see how precious is a good wife and how baneful is a bad wife[6]…."
>
> (b. Yev. 63b)

---

[1] See *Oẓar HaGeonim*, ed. B. M. Lewin, VII, p. 233.
[2] With reference to Prov. 6:26.
[3] With reference to Prov. 22:10.
[4] See also b. Yev. 12b, Rava on permission to marry the "rival" of a woman incapable of bearing children.
[5] See also Prov. 27:15.
[6] See also Prov. 18:22 and Qoh. 7:22.

> Rava said, "A man may marry wives in addition to his first wife, if he can support them."
>
> (b. Yev. 65a)

R. Joseph taught that Gen. 35:11 indicates that a woman may use contraceptives, though a man may not.[1] Rava explained why in some situations, one had to wait as long as ten years between one marriage and the next.[2] R. Naḥman b. Isaac said that a barren woman ('YLW-NYT) was a "ram-like man."[3] Rabbah and R. Joseph discussed compensation for rape.[4] Rabbah held that if the wife of a priest was raped, her husband might be flogged if he had sexual relations with her thereafter.[5] Most of these sayings could hardly lead to court action. If a man did not marry before twenty, God might curse him, but the rabbis could do little to force him to marry. A woman might be proud to have any sort of a man, rather than none at all, but the rabbis could hardly find a husband for everyone. Whatever the disastrous results of intercourse with prostitutes, the rabbis could only admonish. People had better honor their wives; riches would result. If they did not honor wives, however, rabbinical intervention would hardly follow in most circumstances. Rabbis could not punish men's use of contraceptives; indeed it would be difficult to see how evidence could come to court on such a matter.

To summarize: The authority of the courts extended to abnormal situations, such as cases of adultery, pre- and extra-marital pregnancies, and the like. The rabbinical court could determine that adultery had been committed or that a child was not the true heir of his supposed father. While the rabbis would merely instruct the people about whether proselytes might marry illegitimate women or the daughters of priests, proselytes certainly cared what they said. Whether they would then do what the rabbis taught is not revealed in the sources. For all we know, they were angry at the insult to their honor, but would continue to marry as they pleased. Finally, the rabbis could impress upon ordinary people their ideas about entering into early marriage, refraining from intercourse with prostitutes, divorcing bad wives, honoring spouses, and the like. One cannot suppose that the courts could ever make judgments about violations of such good

---

[1] b. Yev. 65b.

[2] b. Yev. 42a. He himself waited ten years before marrying his wife, R. Ḥisda's daughter, b. Yev. 34b. See also b. Yoma 18b, If one has proposed marriage, the couple wait seven "clean" days, that is, days without a sign of menstrual blood.

[3] b. Ket. 11a.

[4] b. Ket. 42b, re. Deut. 22:29.

[5] b. Yev. 56b.

counsel. No litigation would conceivably result. Yet it was the good counsel of the rabbis that pertained most widely and directly to the everyday lives of common people, who did not normally commit adultery, dishonor their wives, father or bear extra-marital progeny. The rabbis' ideals for the normal marriage were accompanied by promises of heavenly favor or threats of heavenly disfavor precisely because no earthly power could effect such ideals. The reputation and influence of the rabbis rather than their court powers affected the normal and regular circumstances of life, while decisions made by rabbinical judges usually came to bear upon abnormal and irregular events alone.

v. DISSOLUTION OF MARRIAGES

While the rabbis had no role in the ritual of marriage, they had considerable power over the formalities of its dissolution. Marriages were dissolved through either death or divorce.[1] If through death, the biblical provisions, where applicable, concerning levirate marriage were carried out in the courts. Divorce documents had to conform to court rules, or they would not be confirmed. Lack of judicial recognition meant that the parties could not remarry. Lack of confirmation meant that the woman could not collect her marriage settlement.[2] So under practically no circumstance, except the normal one of the death of a man whose wife had borne children, could a marriage come to an end without provoking some sort of rabbinical involvement.

Levirate Ceremonies: When a man died childless, his widow was supposed either to contract a levirate connection or to carry out a ceremony of *ḥaliẓah*, as the Bible prescribed, with the surviving brother. Since biblical rules were quite explicit, the people expected the courts to oversee, and where necessary to enforce, the law. The courts assuredly did so. The following cases were reported of fourth-century masters:

> Abaye once stood before R. Joseph, when a sister-in-law came to him to perform *ḥaliẓah*. He said to Abaye, "Give him your sandal," and Abaye gave his left sandal...
>
> (b. Yev. 103b)

> A daughter of R. Papa's father-in-law fell to the lot of a levir who was unworthy of her [but insisted upon contracting the levirate marriage]. When he came before Abaye, Abaye said, "Submit to her *ḥaliẓah*

[1] See vol. III, pp. 274-283.
[2] We shall consider the administration of estates below, pp. 212-220.

and you will thereby marry her." [R. Papa suggested to Abaye a better way out, that Abaye order him to submit to *ḥaliẓah* in exchange for a large sum of money. Abaye so ordered.][1] After the levir had submitted to *ḥaliẓah*, Abaye said to her, "Go and give him." R. Papa replied, "She was merely fooling him."..."Where is your father," Abaye asked [the levir].[2] "In town," he replied. "And your mother?" "In town." He (Abaye) set his eyes upon them and they died.

(b. Yev. 106a)

A couple both of whom admitted [after the levir haa declared that consummation of marriage had taken place] that they had lied [and no levirate marriage had taken place]: Rava ordered the disciples to arrange for *ḥaliẓah* and to dismiss the case......

(b. Yev. 112a)

A certain man was known to have no brothers [or sons], and at the time of his death he so declared. R. Joseph said, "What is there to apprehend [in permitting the widow to remarry]?"...

(b. B.B. 135a)

The above accounts make it quite clear that *ḥaliẓah* ceremonies were conducted by rabbinical courts. The story of Abaye's decision about the levirate claim of an "unworthy" man who chose to marry into a rabbinical family presents a strange contrast. On the one hand, the court could not legally forbid the man from entering a levirate marriage. On the other, it was quite determined to prevent it. So the court tricked the man into a *ḥaliẓah* ceremony. The imprecision of the distinction between what the rabbi could do as judge and what he could only do as holy man here is most clearly revealed. He could not legally prevent the levirate marriage—but he could try to stop it in any other possible fashion, including casting an evil eye on the man's parents.

Other sayings on the laws of levirate marriage included the following: R. Naḥman b. Isaac held that it was better to arrange a ceremony of *ḥaliẓah* than to permit levirate marriage;[3] Abaye asked Rabbah about the divorce of a levirate wife;[4] Rabbah and Rava discussed accidental intercourse between a levir and his sister-in-law;[5] Rava taught a tradition on the place of a *ḥaliẓah* ceremony, how it should be read, the certificate of *ḥaliẓah* and its wording.[6] The certificate was as follows:

---

[1] I shall discuss the tendency of rabbis to favor one another in court, below, pp. 309f.

[2] Rashi: He asked R. Papa, for they must have sharpened his mind to think of such deceit.

[3] b. Yev. 39b.

[4] b. Yev. 52a.

[5] b. Yev. 54a.

[6] b. Yev. 101b.

> "We have read for her from 'My husband's brother refuses' (Deut.
> 25:7) to 'will perform the duty of a husband's brother unto me,' and
> we have read for him from 'not' to 'take her,' and we have read for her
> from 'So' to 'him that had his shoe drawn off' (Deut. 25:9)."
>
> (b. Yev. 106b)

The laws regarding levirate marriages and *ḥaliẓah* ceremonies were
wholly in the hands of the courts. I have no doubt whatever that in
practically all relevant details, whatever legal discussions and theories
were transmitted in the schools represented law which was actually
enforced. The laws of levirate marriage and *ḥaliẓah* did not entail an
exchange of property. In the latter instance they were quite simply
ritualistic. Nonetheless the people kept these laws and supported all
rabbinical court rules necessary to do so properly. The reason was, as
I said, that the Scriptures clearly imposed the requirement, and the
people fully intended to live by the revelation of Moses.

Divorces: The rabbis determined the exact language and form of
divorce-documents, the means by which they were to be delivered from
the husband into the possession of the wife, and the consequences of
such a divorce-action. Few, if any, laws pertaining to divorce can be
thought to have been of mere theoretical consequence. Most of them
were actually enforced through the courts, and the rest through the
influence or intimidation represented by the potentiality of court action.
The following divorce-cases pertained to this period:

> A man went to the synagogue, took a scroll of the Torah, and gave
> it to his wife, saying, "Here is your divorce." R. Joseph ruled, "Why
> should we take any notice of it...."
>
> (b. Git. 19b)

> In the case of a bill of divorce which was found among the flax in
> Pumbedita, Rabbah acted according to the rule just laid down [that the
> divorce is to be delivered as written unless two factors mitigate against
> it].
>
> (b. Git. 27a=b. B.M. 18b)

> A certain man sent a divorce to his wife, telling the agent not to give
> it to her until thirty days had passed. Before then, the man found he
> could not carry out the commission, and therefore consulted Rava....
> He said to the man, "Transmit your commission to us, so after thirty
> days we can appoint a bearer who will give the divorce to the wife..."
>
> (b. Git. 29b)

A certain man said to the court, "If I do not make up with her in thirty days, it will be a [bill of] divorce." He went and tried, but she was not reconciled. R. Joseph said, "Has he offered her a bag of gold coins and still been unable to appease her?" According to another version, he said, "Must he offer her a bag of gold coins? He has done his best to make it up with her, but she would not be reconciled..."

(b. Git. 30a)

Giddal b. Re'il'ai sent a divorce to his wife. The bearer went and found her weaving. He said to her, "Here is your divorce." She said to him, "Go away now and come back tomorrow." The agent returned [to Giddal] and told him, and he [Giddal] exclaimed, "Blessed be he who is good and does good." Abaye said, "Blessed is he who is good and does good, and the divorce is not cancelled," and Rava ruled, "Blessed...but the divorce is cancelled."

(b. Git. 34a)[1]

A certain man who was dying wrote a divorce for his wife[2] on the eve of the Sabbath, but had no time to give it to her [before the Sabbath]. The next day he was critically ill. Rava was consulted, and ruled, "Go and tell him to make over to her the place where the divorce is, and [let her acquire that place] and take [the formal] possession...."

(b. Git. 77b)

A certain man threw a divorce to his wife as she was standing in a courtyard, and it fell on a block of wood. R. Joseph said, "We have to see..."

(b. Git. 77b)

A certain divorce was dated by the term of office of the *astandara*[3] of the town of Bashkar. R. Naḥman b. R. Ḥisda sent to Rabbah to ask how to deal with it. He replied....

(b. Git. 80b)

Abaye once found R. Joseph at court, compelling [certain men[4]] to give a bill of divorce....

(b. Git. 88b)

A certain priest married a proselyte who was under the age of three years and one day. R. Naḥman b. Isaac said to him, "What is this?"

---

[1] Two further such cases are cited, in which the disagreement of Rava and Abaye is noted, but we have no evidence of court action on account of their respective comments.

[2] So that she would be free of the obligation of levirate marriage.

[3] *Astandara*=istandara, Levy, *Wörterbuch*, s.v., I, p. 120, der Depeschenüberbringer.

[4] Following Rashi's interpretation.

[That is, on whose authority do you contract such a marriage?] The
other replied [quoting a rabbi's view of the law]. "Go and arrange for
her release, or else I will pull R. Jacob b. 'Idi out of your ear," R.
Naḥman b. Isaac replied.

                                                                (b. Yev. 61a)

A divorce was once found in Sura, and in it appeared the following,
"In the town of Sura, I, 'Anan son of Ḥiyya of Nehardea, released and
divorced my wife so-and-so." When the rabbis searched from Sura to
Nehardea, there was no other 'Anan b. Ḥiyya except one, of Hagra,
who was then in Nehardea, and witnesses came and declared that on
the day on which the bill of divorce was written, 'Anan b. Ḥiyya of
Hagra was with them. Abaye said.... Rava said....

                                                                (b. Yev. 116a)

Once a certain man was dying. He was asked to whom his wife
might be married, and replied, "She is suitable for a high priest." Rava
said, "What is there to apprehend [for if a man says he divorced his
wife, he is believed]...."

                                                                (b. B.B. 135a)

Moses b. ' Azri was guarantor for his daughter-in-law's [marriage
contract]. His son, R. Huna, was a rabbinical disciple and in need of
money. Abaye said, "Is there no one to advise R. Huna to divorce his
wife so she may claim her marriage-contract from her father-in-law and
he may then take her back." Rava said to him, "But we have learned,
'He must vow that he will not derive further benefit from her'?"
Abaye's reply was, "Does every one who divorces his wife do so before
a court?" [Only in a court would such a vow be enforced, but a divorce
can be given outside of court.]....

                                                                (b. 'Arakh. 23a)

A man once bought a boat-load of wine, but had nowhere to store
it. He asked a woman, "Do you have a place for rent?" She said no. He
married her, and she gave him a place for storage. He went home, wrote
a divorce, and sent it to her. She went out and hired carriers (to pay
them of that wine) and had it put out in the road. R. Huna b. R. Joshua
ruled....

                                                                (b. B.M. 101b)

In general the cases cited above all pertained to court recognition of
the validity of a bill of divorce. Special cases were before the courts,
for ordinary ones would not require court action. In the first two
instances, the issue was whether a valid bill of divorce had actually been
handed over. In the third, fourth, and fifth, the question was whether

the interposition of an agent had resulted in complications either on account of delivery or on account of postponement of delivery. In the sixth and seventh, the question was whether a woman was legally able to acquire the divorce under special circumstances. In the eighth, the dating of the divorce document was in doubt. The ninth and tenth cases show that as earlier, the courts were able to force a man to prepare, or approve the preparation of, a bill of divorce for his wife. The eleventh case indicates how carefully the rabbis investigated the status of divorce documents which had been discovered in unusual circumstances, and the twelfth, similarly, shows that the courts meticulously investigated the intent of the husband. The thirteenth and fourteenth cases indicate that in extraneous matters, in which a divorce was used for some ulterior purpose, the rabbis were still able to rule on the validity of the document.

Divorces were not prepared by the courts. But all who hoped to have court backing for their documents had to conform to court rules. Only a few cases seem to have come for direct litigation. In most, as I said, the rabbis were asked to comment upon exceptional problems. R. Joseph's ruling in the first case represented such a court decree, for by saying that he would take no notice of the man's action, he ruled that the couple was still married and required a proper bill of divorce to be written. The consultation of Rava in the third case was probably more representative of what generally took place. The conflicting traditions attributed to R. Joseph pose a problem, for if the divorce were regarded as invalid, there is no reason why another could not have been issued. The only practical consequence of the divorce of the dying man and of R. Joseph's comment could have come because of some extenuating circumstance. Had the man in the meantime died without issue, his wife would have been subject to the law of levirate marriage. Hence the length of time in R. Joseph's case might have created a practical issue where none, in fact, would ordinarily have existed. The divorce of Giddal b. Re'il'ai reveals no such practical outcome, and I suppose there was none. In such an instance, the report of a "case" does not prove there was actual court action but may represent mere scholastic discussion. On the other hand, the inquiry of R. Naḥman b. R. Ḥisda was important, for it involved how a divorce should be properly dated.

The enforcement of divorce-documents found in the street raised a number of practical problems. Had the woman denied receiving the document, the validity of the divorce would depend upon the testimony of those who had witnessed and delivered it. The final two cases show that divorces were relatively common and lightly given. The opinion attributed to (though not necessarily said by) Abaye was that most people did not in fact divorce their wives before a court. What is especially interesting is that R. Naḥman b. Isaac and R. Joseph were able to force men to divorce their wives, on grounds specified in the law, and so had the power to disrupt a marriage. This was a most irregular procedure, and Abaye specifically commented on R. Joseph's exceptional act. Nonetheless, R. Joseph defended himself, and since we have earlier evidence of similar powers, we need not doubt that the courts could do what R. Joseph was said to have done. So the rabbis' extended discussion of points of divorce law reflected the exact procedures and practical requirements of their courts.[1]

Three further cases illustrate other powers of the courts:

> A man once drowned in the Tigris and after five days was hauled up at the Shebistana bridge, and on the evidence of the groomsmen, Rava permitted the wife to marry again.
>
> (b. Yev. 121a)

> A man once went around saying, "Alas for the valiant rider who was at Pumbedita, for he is dead." R. Joseph [or Rava] allowed his wife to remarry.
>
> (b. Yev, 121b)

> A certain pagan once said to a Jew, "Cut some grass and throw it to my cattle on the Sabbath or I will kill you as I killed so-and-so, that Jew, to whom I said, 'Cook me a dish on the Sabbath' and whom I killed when he refused." The wife [of the man who had refused to cook on the Sabbath] heard, and she came to Abaye. He kept her waiting for three festivals. R. 'Adda' b. 'Ahavah said to her, "Apply to R. Joseph whose knife is sharp." She turned to him, and he ruled...
>
> (b. Yev. 121b-122a)

It is clear from these instances that the courts could rule upon the validity of a claim that a man had died, and so in still a third way could control the dissolution of a marriage. Such a ruling was particularly important. If a woman did not obtain it, she could be prevented from

---

[1] Note for example the long opening discussion, b. Git. 2aff., on how the bearers of a bill of divorce must testify concerning the preparation of the document; b. Git. 21a, Rava, if a man writes a divorce for his wife and gives it to the slave for delivery; b. Git. 67b, Rava on the orders of the bearers of a bill of divorce; b. Git. 72b, 83b-84a, Rava on a conditional bill of divorce; b. Git. 75b, Rava on the language of a conditional bill of divorce; b. Ket. 2b, on a plea in regard to divorce; b. A.Z. 37a, Abaye on a bill of divorce after death; b. Qid. 5a, Rava on a divorce through a written document and not through a money-payment, etc.

remarrying. If she did remarry, her future children could be stigmatized as illegitimate, of impure or tainted genealogy, being the children of adultery.

To summarize: A combination of circumstances therefore endowed the rabbinical courts with substantial power over dissolution of marriages. First, the people believed that the Scriptural requirements about levirate marriages and *halizah* ceremonies must be fulfilled. They came to the courts for execution of the latter and for rulings about the former, as the occasion required. Second, the Scriptural requirement that a bill of divorce be issued made it necessary to provide such a document. Because of the ramifications of an improper document, it was necessary to draw it up according to rabbinical rules so the courts would enforce it. The bill of divorce had, moreover, to be conveyed, or handed over, to the wife according to rabbinical law. Whatever conditions the husband set had to be carried out, or the document was invalidated. While ordinary divorces obviously would not provoke intervention, extraordinary circumstances would lead directly to court. Common people therefore tried to do things to begin with to conform to rabbinical regulations. Third, in both levirate connections and bills of divorce, the most practical issue concerned the status of future progeny of the respective parties. If a woman was not satisfactorily freed of her obligations to her levir or to her former husband, then her children out of a later marriage would be illegitimate. Nothing mattered more to Babylonian Jewry than purity of lineage. The people would do everything to make certain their descendants would not be stigmatized. Besides the requirements of Scripture and the possibility of court action, the most important impulse to keep the law therefore lay in the fear of tainting one's descendants. Fourth, since the courts could compel the payment of sums pledged in marriage contracts, and now due on account of divorce or death, it was necessary not only to consult rabbinical judges, but also to apply to them for court orders when payment was not satisfactorily forthcoming. Fifth, the right of the courts to declare that a man was legally dead gave them further power over women who claimed they had lost their husbands, and hence required no bill of divorce before remarrying. So the courts' power over the dissolution of marriages was practically unlimited. I doubt that in enforcing any other part of the law they possessed practical power to a greater degree than here.

VI. WILLS AND ESTATES

The predominant issues in the above cases concerned the personal status of individuals, for example whether a woman was betrothed or not, married or properly divorced, indisputably widowed, free of levirate obligations, and the like. In actions of personal status, the exchange of property, while important, was secondary to, and dependent upon, the determination of an individual's legal circumstance. We turn now to the wide variety of cases in which the disposition of property was the primary and central issue. In all commercial, business, real estate, and other property matters, the courts could transfer possession from one man to another, confirm rights of ownership, and settle every sort of conflict. From the viewpoint of the exilarch, the adjudication of property disputes represented the courts' chief task, and the rabbis' laws about such issues therefore were easily effected.

The point at which the courts entered into a case now is no longer in doubt. Earlier we found occasion to wonder why the rabbis offered an opinion in matters which seemed to be phrased as cases, "A certain man did so-and-so." In property litigations we need no longer speculate on how a given issue came before the courts, for in most instances it is clear that either the possessor of a property requested court confirmation of his rights, or a plaintiff challenged them, or property in the hands of neither had to be properly adjudicated, or an alleged malefactor damaged the rights or property of another.

Most closely associated with family life, the settlement of wills and division of estates constituted an important source of litigation.[1] Nonetheless it was only when such matters were disputed that the courts' power came to bear. A person could ordinarily give instructions about the disposition of his property to three men, who might thereupon draw up and witness a will or actually execute it on the spot. The desired division did not require the supervision or intervention of the courts. Earlier the largest single group of cases dealt with the issues of gifts in contemplation of death, mainly because of R. Naḥman's innovations in the law covering that circumstance.[2] In this period, no single principle similarly predominated in litigations.

Wills and estates produced three kinds of court cases, first, the final disposition of contested wills, second, applications for maintenance

---

[1] Vol. II, pp. 263-264, and vol. III, pp. 286-295.
[2] Vol. III, pp. 288-290. See also b. B.B. 149a, and Rabbah, b. B.B. 175a.

from legacies for widows and orphans, and third, the sale of estates under various conditions. The third kind of case was by far the most frequent. Our brief review of the case-reports will indicate that the rabbinical courts had no difficulty in making and executing judgments, because in all instances, property was at issue. Litigations of wills yielded the following case reports:

> A certain man declared (in his will), "Give four hundred *zuz* to so-and-so and let him marry my daughter." R. Papa said, "He receives the four hundred *zuz*, but as for the daughter, if he wishes, he may marry, but he need not..."
>
> (b. Beẓ. 20a)

> A man once declared (in his will), "Give four hundred *zuz* [of the value] of this wine to [my] daughter." The price of wine rose. R. Joseph ruled that the profit goes to the orphans [that is, to the residuary estate].
>
> (b. Ket. 54a-54b)

In both of the above cases, the task of the court was to interpret the language and intent of the will. Both involved substantial sums of money. Hence we may suppose that the cases were actually brought to court for litigation, in the first instance by the daughter, whom the man refused to marry, or by the man, whom the daughter refused to pay; in the second, by either party seeking to gain the excess value of the original quantity of wine.[1]

The rights of the widow to be supported by her deceased husband's estate conflicted with the interest of the orphans, in many cases born of a different, perhaps earlier marriage. The rights of both parties were carefully protected by the courts. In general litigations devolved upon two issues, first, by what procedures and from what possessions the widow receives her marriage settlement, and second, what are the obligations of the estate to support her and other female legatees. The following cases were recorded:

> A similar case [of a daughter claiming maintenance out of her deceased father's estate] came before R. Joseph, "Give her of the dates that are spread on the reed-mat" [that is, movable property]. Abaye said to him....
>
> (b. Ket. 50b)

> A male and a female orphan came before Rava, who said, "Raise [a larger maintenance] for the male, for the sake of the girl [that is, an allowance sufficient for both]." The rabbis said to Rava....
>
> (b. Ket. 51a)

---

[1] On inheritances, see also Abaye and Rava, b. B.B. 111b.

Ḥoma, Abaye's widow, came to Rava and asked him to grant her an allowance of board, and he did so. She asked for an allowance for wine, but he said, "I know that Naḥmani did not drink wine." [She swore that he gave her wine]. "By the life of the Master, he gave me to drink from horns [ŠWPRZY] like this." As she was showing to him, her arm was uncovered and light shone upon the court. Rava rose, went home, and solicited [his wife] R. Ḥisda's daughter. "Who has been today at the court?" she asked. "Ḥoma, the widow of Abaye," he replied. Thereupon she followed her, striking her with the straps of a chest until she chased her out of Maḥoza. "You have already killed three men, and now you come to kill another?"

(b. Ket. 65a)

The wife of R. Joseph b. Rava came before R. Neḥemiah the son of Joseph and said to him, "Grant me an allowance of board," which he did. "And of wine!" He granted it to her, saying, "I know the people of Maḥoza drink wine."

(b. Ket. 65a)

The wife of R. Joseph son of R. Menashia of Devil came before R. Joseph and asked for an allowance of board and wine, which he granted. "Grant me an allowance of silk." "Why of silks?" he asked. "For your sake and for the sake of your friend and for the sake of your colleagues."[1]

(b. Ket. 65a)

The mother-in-law of R. Ḥiyya 'Arika was wife of his brother, and when widowed, she lived in her father's house. R. Ḥiyya maintained her for twenty-five years at her maternal home. At the end, she said, "Supply me with maintenance." He denied she had a further claim. "Pay me my marriage-contract," and he denied her right to it. She summoned him to court before Rabbah b. Shila [who ruled in her favor]. R. Ḥiyya disregarded the ruling, so the judge wrote out for her an 'adrakhta' (a document). He came and appealed to Rava....

(b. Ket. 104b)[2]

In these cases, the issue was whether and how a wife was to be supported from her late husband's estate. The first case was cited to show what an orphaned daughter was given, namely, movables, but not real property. In the second, the son's portion was increased so he might support his sister. Three of the four cases of widows, apparently all of rabbis, claiming that the court should provide for them out of their deceased husbands' estates, involved the appropriate extent of

---

[1] To keep up her social standing.
[2] See below, p. 243, for further discussion of this case.

that support. The claim to wine was thought to be excessive unless the woman and her husband usually made use of it. The same issue pertained to the provision of silk garments. In the final case, the issue was whether a woman, having been maintained for many years outside of her late husband's household, still would be able to demand the settlement of her marriage contract. Having sustained her claim, the court then issued an appropriate document so that she might collect her dues. Among other sayings about maintenance of a widow and orphans were those of R. Joseph, that daughters must be maintained until they are married, and that if the widow painted her eyes or dyed her hair, she lost her claim to maintenance, and the like.[1]

The courts exercised guardianship over the estates of widows, orphans, the deaf, and others who were not wholly able to manage their own affairs. An example of control of the property of a deaf man is as follows:

> A deaf man once lived in the neighborhood of R. Malkio, who arranged for him to take a wife to whom he [R. Malkio] assigned in writing the sum of four hundred *zuz* out of his estate. Rava remarked, "Who is so wise as R. Malkio...."
>
> (b. Yev. 113a)

The rabbinical court sought the ablest guardians:

> Abaye said [after deciding a case involving orphans' land], "Anyone who appoints a guardian should appoint one like this man, who understands how to turn the scales in favor of orphans."
>
> (b. Ket. 109b)

A more difficult case in which the courts ruled on the settlement of estates follows:

> A certain old woman had three daughters. She and one of them were taken captive. Of the remaining two daughters, one died, leaving a child. Abaye said, "What shall we do? Shall we (temporarily) assign the estates to the (third) sister? But perhaps the old woman is dead, and a relative is not permitted to enter upon a minor's estate. Shall we assign the estates to the child? But perhaps the woman is not dead, and a minor cannot enter a captive's estate." Abaye ruled, "Therefore half is given to the (last) sister, and a guardian is appointed over the other half in the child's behalf." Rava commented...
>
> (b. B.M. 39b)

---

[1] b. Ket. 53b-54a; see also b. Qid. 17b, Rava said that by biblical law, a pagan is entitled to receive an inheritance from his father, based upon Lev. 25:50.

The case would have come to court when the settlement of the deceased daughter's estate was demanded. The court appointed a guardian to administer the child's property. The power of the court over the disposition of orphans' property, illustrated in the several claims for widows' maintenance from estates and in the above cases, extended also to marketing or sale of land and other holdings, as in the following:

> Reḥavah was in charge of an orphan's capital. He went before R. Joseph to ask permission to use it. He replied...
>
> (b. B.M. 29b)

> A certain man once made a field a boundary mark for another person. When one of the witnesses who contested the ownership died, a guardian was appointed over the estate, who came before Abaye...
>
> (b. Ket. 109b)

In these two cases, the court's approval had to be obtained for the disposition of the funds and property of an orphan. The guardians appointed by the court came under supervision later on, and could be removed or even fined for misappropriation of funds. In the following, more direct court action was involved, because of conflicting claims:

> It was rumored that Rava b. Sharshom [a guardian of orphans' property] was using for his own benefit land that belonged to orphans. Abaye summoned him and said, "Tell me the facts." He said, "I took over this land from the father of the orphans as a mortgage and he owed me other funds in addition...." [Abaye ruled against him].
>
> (b. B.B. 32b-33a)

> Did not Rava order some orphans to return a pair of shears for clipping wool and a book of 'Aggadah which were claimed from them, though the claimants adduced no proof [that they had loaned them to the father]....
>
> (b. B.B. 52a)

The two cases reflect the difficulties of settling an estate. It was not always clear what the deceased had done. The courts had therefore both to protect orphans' rights and to see that debts were paid and loans returned, so that legitimate property relationships would be not disrupted by the possibility of sudden death. Hence in the first instance, the court had to protect the orphans' rights, and in the second, Rava ordered the return of property the deceased had borrowed and the heirs retained as their own. The sale of property by minor-orphans was carefully regulated, as in the following instances:

Rava in R. Naḥman's name said that the intervening period [the eighteenth year] was regarded as being under age.... *That view of Rava was not stated explicitly but through inference.*[1] [Italics supplied] A certain youth during his intervening period sold the estate [of his deceased father]. He came before Rava who decided the sale was illegal...

(b. B.B. 155b)

A certain youth under twenty sold his inherited estate. When he was to appear before Rava [desiring to withdraw from the sale, on the plea of being a minor] the relatives told him, "Go, eat dates and throw the pits at Rava" [to show the boy was irresponsible]. He did so, and Rava said, "The sale is no sale." When the deed was written out the buyers said, "Go tell Rava, the scroll of Esther may be obtained at a *zuz*, and the court deed may be obtained at a *zuz*!" He went and delivered the message. Rava then changed his mind and ruled that the sale was legal [as the boy was knowledgeable.] When the relatives said that the purchasers had so instructed the lad, he replied, "But he understands what is explained to him, and if so, he possesses intelligence, so his earlier act was due to exceptional gall."

(b. B.B. 155b)

In the above instances, the right of under-age orphans to dispose of their inheritances was at issue, and the principle was that if the minor knew what he was doing, he could not retract his action. The second case is of great interest, for it shows that the relatives and the aggrieved

---

[1] It is particularly curious that what was incorrectly attributed to Rava was not a simple saying, but an alleged attribution *by* Rava *to* R. Naḥman. The passage begins with a legal question, followed by "Rava said in the name of R. Naḥman..." and then, "Rava b. R. Shila said in the name of R. Naḥman...", each supplying a tradition of R. Naḥman's supposed opinion. The account proceeds as given here. Hence it was "originally" supposed that Rava merely transmitted an opinion of the earlier master. If so, the person who witnessed Rava's court-decision thereupon presumed that he had acted in accordance with R. Naḥman's teaching. Why the supposition was not simply concerning Rava's *own* opinion I cannot say.

Perhaps the apparent existence of a tradition on the subject in R. Naḥman's name led the tradent to assume as follows: "Rava could not have acted contrary to R. Naḥman's tradition, as cited by Rava b. R. Shila, unless he actually held a contrary teaching from the master, for Rava would otherwise hardly act contrary to the acknowledged and known dictum of R. Naḥman." So four separate thought-processes had to intervene between event and the false tradition. The witness to Rava's court decision had first to take note of it, and, second, to compare it with an existing tradition of R. Naḥman. He, thirdly, had to reflect that since Rava could not "possibly" contradict R. Naḥman, he therefore must have followed another tradition in R. Naḥman's name. Finally, the tradent(s) would have rendered the tradition as we have it, "Rava in the name of R. Naḥman said ... Rava b. R. Shila in the name of R. Naḥman said...." Later on, it was added, "Rava did not really *say* anything of the sort, but in court he *ruled* as follows. By false inference his principle was supposed to be such-and-so; yet that was not the principle by which he acted at all."

purchasers both knew full well upon what basis the court would make its decision, and tried to conform to the conditions necessary to achieve, in the one case, confirmation, in the other, retraction, of the sale. The following instance shows that the courts could oversee how the orphans carried out the instructions of a will:

> A dying man gave orders to give a palm tree to his daughter. The orphans divided the estate and did not do so. R. Joseph intended to rule ... But Abaye said to him...
>
> (b. Ket. 109b)

Other rulings about the disposition of estates[1] included the following:

> A certain man bought a field adjacent to his father-in-law's estate. When they came to divide the latter's estate, the man said, "Give me my share next to my own field." Rabbah said, "This is a case where a man can be compelled [to act generously, and] not to act after the manner of Sodom." R. Joseph objected, "The brothers can claim the field to be especially valuable..."
>
> (b. B.B. 12b)

> Rava b. Ḥinnena and R. Dimi b. Ḥinnena were willed by their father two female-slaves, one of whom knew how to cook and bake, the other to spin and weave. They came before Rava [to decide whether one could force the other to divide them, the one who received the more valuable to compensate the other]. He said to them...
>
> (b. B.B. 13b)

> A certain man once said to his fellow, "My estate will be yours, and after you, it will go to so-and-so." The first was entitled to be his heir. When [both the testator and] the first man died, the second came to claim the estate. R. 'Ilish proposed in Rava's presence to decide that the second was also entitled to receive the bequest. Rava said, "Such decisions are given by arbitration judges..."[2]
>
> (b. B.B. 133b)

> A certain man said to his wife, "My estate will belong to you and your children." R. Joseph said, "She acquires the ownership of half of it."
>
> (b. B.B. 143a)

---

[1] See also b. Ket. 98a, Rabbah b. Rava asked R. Joseph whether a woman is required to take a court-oath who sells an estate without court supervision or authorization; b. Ket. 100b, R. Joseph on the sale of an estate without public bidding; b. Shev. 46b, Rava on orphans' property.

[2] Rashi: Arbitration judges are not experts in the law, and divided property in half, as in the case of money whose ownership was disputed.

A certain person once said, "My estate is to go to my sons." He had a son and a daughter. Do people call a son "sons" or perhaps he meant to include his daughter in the gift. Abaye said ... and Rava said ... and R. Joseph said....

(b. B.B. 143b)[1]

A certain man died and left a brother. [The case involved a loan. The lender died childless and left a brother as heir. The borrower had died and left children. The lender's brother now claims the debt from the borrower's children.] Rami b. Ḥama thought of ruling ... Rava corrected him...

(b. Shev. 48b)

The above cases involved several different issues. The first and second centered upon the fair assessment of one's share in an estate. If a man signified that he desired his share of land in a particular place, in this case near his own property, that land would have therefore become more valuable to him than otherwise, and that added value had to be taken into account in settling the estate. In the second case the issue was whether the special skills of slaves had to be compensated for. In the third, fourth, and fifth cases, the language and intent of the testator were at issue. In the final case, settlement of the deceased's loan was arranged by the court.

The wide range of cases concerning the disposition of estates and the interpretation of wills leaves no doubt that the court had full power to decide such matters. Litigations involved rather specialized questions, for instance, the fulfillment of a condition set by the testator, as "Give him money and let him marry my daughter," or the unusual situation in which the interpretation of the testator's language would affect considerable property (as in the case of the rise in the price of wine). Several widows' claims were reported. In general the courts had to rule on the fairness of those claims, for the rights of others, particularly orphans, had to be protected. Excessive claims would be denied. Further, the courts were supposed to see that minor-orphans' property, as well as that of incompetents, was protected. They therefore appointed and supervised guardians, who had to apply to the court for permission to use the orphans' funds, and who had also to explain their actions to the court when called upon. When orphans acted in their own account, the courts could also examine their competence, and decide whether their action was legal or not. In the final group of cases, other aspects of the settlement of estates by the courts were illustrated.

---

[1] Quoting biblical language, Gen. 46:23, Num. 26:8, and I Chron. 2:8.

The courts exercised no monopoly on the settlement of estates, for arbitrators[1] might give decisions, and the relatives of orphans might also take a hand in protecting their rights and property. Nonetheless the fact that the courts were ready to intervene and preserve the rights of all concerned would have set high standards for the whole community. In the end, one could always appeal for justice to the rabbinical authority, so the law might as well be kept to begin with. The Iranian government clearly expected that orderly community life would be maintained by all sub-groups in its empire. One of the characteristics of an orderly community was that the rights of widows and orphans were carefully protected. From prophetic times onward, Jews also believed that, being weak and without protection, widows and orphans were the objects of special heavenly concern. So both social and religious policy required the courts to take an active interest in the fair settlement of estates and related issues. With sufficient political power and religious warrant, the courts were well able to do so.

VII. MORTGAGES, DEBTS, AND BONDS

Normal commercial relationships did not provoke the courts to intervene.[2] People usually paid their debts, did not cheat or defraud one another, did not enter disputes about ownership of goods or property, and did not, therefore, have to resort to the courts for judgment. The fact that the courts were prepared to act and had the power to do so, however, provided ordinary folk with security. If the law could be enforced, then most people would keep it even when no political authority was actually present to make them do so. The few cases cited below merely adumbrate the many instances in which life went on uneventfully and correctly. Three sorts of cases involving mortgages, bonds, and debts, now came before the courts, first, collection of debts, second, disposition of pledges and security given for loans, and third, the prohibition of interest. In all three, court action proved quite sufficient to settle litigations.

Debt collections came to court generally because of a claim of fraud. The debtor claimed that he had paid the debt, and the creditor denied it. Rava held[3] that if one lends money in the presence of witnesses, he must

---

[1] On the significance of Rava's reference to arbitrators, see above, p. 185.
[2] See Vol. III, pp. 295-302.
[3] b. Shev. 41b.

also collect it before witnesses to prevent cases of fraud, such as the following:

> There was a certain person who said to his neighbor, "When you repay me, repay me before Reuben and Simeon."[1] He went and repaid before two others. Abaye said, "He told him to repay before two witnesses, and he repaid before two." Rava said to him, "For this reason he said, 'before Reuben and Simeon,' so he should not be able to put him off [by saying he had repaid before two others who were not available. It is no excuse, and he must pay.]"
>
> (b. Shev. 41b)

> A certain man said to his neighbor, "Give me the hundred *zuz* I lent you." [The other denied the loan.] The lender went and brought witnesses that he had lent, [but they also said] that the debtor had already paid the money. Abaye said, "What shall we do? They say he lent, but they themselves say he was also repaid." Rava said, "If the borrower said, 'I did not borrow,' it is as if he said, 'I did not repay.'"
>
> (b. Shev. 41b)

> There was a certain man who said to his neighbor, "Give me the hundred *zuz* I claim from you." The man replied, "Did I not repay before so-and-so and so-and-so?" The two alleged witnesses came and denied the event ever happened. R. Sheshet thought of ruling that the man was proved a liar. Rava said to him, "Anything which does not rest upon a man [= for which he is not obligated] he will do unconsciously [lit.: is not in his mind.]"
>
> (b. Shev. 41b)

> A certain man claimed, "Give me the six hundred *zuz* that I claim from you." The other replied, "Did I not repay you a hundred *kavs* of gallnuts which were worth six per *kav*?" He replied, "No, they were worth four per *kav*." Two witnesses came and said they were indeed worth four. Rava said, "He is proved a liar" [and must pay the difference.] Rami b. Ḥama said, "But you said that anything which does not rest upon a man he will do unconsciously?" Rava replied, "But people remember the market price."
>
> (b. Shev. 41b-42a)

> A certain man said, "You are believed by me whenever you say to me that I have not paid you." He went and paid before witnesses. Abaye and Rava both said, "Behold he believes him."
>
> (b. Shev. 42a)

---

[1] These would be conventional names, like Smith and Jones, but an actual case could well be reported according to such fixed conventions, and this is not necessarily a theoretical account. Another such convention must be "four hundred"-*zuz*, barrels of wine, etc., which would mean, "a great quantity."

Twelve thousand *zuz* were owed to R. Papa by people in Khuzistan. He transferred ownership of them to Samuel b. 'Abba' [or, 'Aḥa'] by means of the threshold of his house....

(b. B.Q. 104b)[1]

A certain judge once allowed a creditor to take possession of the property of the debtor before he had sued the debtor. R. Ḥanin b. R. Yeva' removed him [= gave the property back to the debtor]. Rava said, "Who would have been so wise as to do such a thing if not R. Ḥanin...."

(b. B.B. 174a)

The central issue in the above cases was whether and how a debt had actually been paid. In the first, the lender had set a condition that certain witnesses must attest to the repayment of the debt. When the man al- ledgedly repaid before others, the court had to rule on whether the borrower had fully conformed to the conditions originally agreed upon. In the second suit, witnesses attested to the loan, but went on to say that the borrower had already repaid it. The court had to evaluate their testimony. In the third, the witnesses simply denied that they had seen the transaction to begin with. In the fourth, the issue was whether a loan had been repaid in kind and devolved upon the value of what had been handed over in payment. In the fifth case the original stipulation was tested in court. In the sixth, the conditions of repayment of a loan of a considerable sum were described, in particular the means by which ownership of property in settlement of the debt was transferred. In the seventh case, the right of the lender to seize property of a delinquent debtor without appropriate court action was at issue, and Rava set aside the judgment of what was apparently a lower court. Two further debt cases, both involving rabbis, were those of Abba b. Martha's debt to Rabbah, in which the law of the Seventh Year remission of debts was observed,[2] and the action of R. Papa and R. Huna b. R. Joshua in seizing a ship from the estate of Yemar b. Ḥashu, as cited above.[3] R. Joseph said that the law of *'anparut* (a debt payable by installments with forfeiture if a payment is missed) does not apply in Babylonia.[4] Rava held that creditors might repossess lands sold by a debtor to others and resold by them, while Abaye held that the creditor could not repossess land already resold.[5] Rava held that it was permitted to repay a large

---

[1] Also b. B.B. 77b, 150b.
[2] b. Git. 37b, See *Oẓar HaGeonim*, X, p. 73.
[3] b. Ket. 84b-85a, see above, p. 135.
[4] b. Git. 58b. See also *Oẓar HaGeonim*, ed. B. Lewin, X, p. 124.
[5] b. B.Q. 8b.

debt in very small parts. Though the lender might bear resentment against the borrower for dissipating his capital, he could not repair to the court for any reason.[1] Abaye and Rava judged a case involving commercial paper:

> A certain deed of [debt] acknowledgement did not contain the phrase, "He said to us, Write it, attest and give it to him [to the creditor]." Abaye and Rava both said...
>
> (b. Sanh. 29b)

The clerks of their courts knew the law, and hence they usually drafted such documents correctly. It is likely that the courts prevented the need to litigate a larger number of cases by seeing to it that loans were properly documented.

Biblical laws about holding and returning security for a debt were naturally enforced in the courts, as in the following cases:

> A certain heathen gave a house in pledge to R. Mari b. Raḥel and then sold it to Rava. R. Mari waited a full year and collected the rent, and then offered it to Rava [for the coming year]. He explained to Rava, "The reason I did not offer you rent before this is that an unspecified pledge is a year. Had the heathen wished to make me quit [within the year], he would have been unable, but now you may take rent for the house." He replied, "Had I known it was pledged to you, I should not have bought it. Now I will treat you according to their law. Until they redeem the pledge they receive no rent. So I will take no rent from you until you are paid out."
>
> (b. B.M. 73b)

> A man once pledged an orchard to his neighbor for ten years. After the creditor had taken the usufruct for three years, he proposed to the debtor, "If you will sell it to me it is well. If not, I will hide the mortgage deed, and claim I have bought it." Thereupon the debtor transferred the property to his son (a minor), and sold it to him. The sale is certainly no sale, but the purchase money—is it accounted as a written debt and collectable from mortgaged property, or perhaps it is only a verbal debt, which cannot be collected from mortgaged property? Abaye said ... Rava said...
>
> (b. B.M. 72a)

> A certain man pledged an orchard for ten years, but it aged after five. Abaye said, "The [aged trunks] rank as produce." Rava said, "As principal. Therefore land must be bought therewith, and the mortgagee enjoys the usufruct."
>
> (b. B.M. 109b)

---

[1] b. B.M. 77b.

> A certain man took a butcher's knife in pledge. On coming before Abaye, Abaye ordered, "Go return it, because it is a utensil for preparing food, and then come to stand at judgment for the debt." Rava said, "He need not stand at judgment for it, but can [now] claim the debt up to the value of the pledge"....
>
> (b. B.M. 116a)

In the first case, Rava purchased a property from a non-Jew after it had been pledged as security for a loan. R. Mari b. Raḥel held the land and enjoyed the usufruct, as was his right, and then transferred ownership to Rava. Rava responded by saying that the land held as security should be retained by the original lender until the debt was paid out, and then he would accept ownership. This was, he said, according to "their" law. In the second instance, the creditor attempted to force the debtor to sell him the land which he had held for three years. Since in Jewish law, three years of usufruct unimpeded by protest constituted the *prima facie* establishment of ownership through squatter's rights, the lender would, he supposed, have a strong case in court. The debtor protected himself against fraud as best he could. The issue before the court did not devolve upon the fraud, but rather upon the disposition of money transferred by the debtor in the act of self-protection. The fourth case involved a change in the condition of the security. The fifth was closest to the original biblical requirement about returning the pledge if it was used for the maintenance of life. R. Joseph held that a court officer must recover the pledge, but that the creditor ought not to do so, should he have a claim on it according to the biblical law (Deut. 24:6).[1] Rava said with reference to Deut. 24:13 that a man may take as a pledge an item of clothing worn by day and hold it through the night, but he must return it in the morning.[2] He also said that if one declares his slave to be security for a debt and then sells the slave, the creditor can seize the slave, but if he so declares of an ox or an ass and sells them, the creditor cannot seize them.[3]

Whether bonds had been paid was at issue in the following case:

> Once R. Papa and R. Adda b. Mattena sat in [Rava's] presence when a bond was brought to him. R. Papa said to him, "I know that this bond has been paid." Rava asked, "Is there anyone with the Master to confirm the statement"....
>
> (b. Ket. 85a)

---

[1] b. B.M. 113a.

[2] b. B.M. 114b.

[3] b. B.B. 44b. For another opinion of Rabbah, see b. B.Q. 49b.

We shall see (below, p. 227) the discussion of the case of a bond issued against the children of R. 'Ilish, in which the possibility of usury was discussed. Rava held that a man possessing a bond of one hundred *zuz* cannot have it converted into two bonds each worth fifty *zuz*, nor can two bonds of fifty be converted into one for one hundred.[1] Such bonds of indebtedness would have to be drawn up, if not by court-appointed scribes, then according to the rules which would render them negotiable in the courts; contested bonds would have to come to courts. Hence there was no practical limit upon the enforcement of the rabbinical laws covering bonds.

Biblical prohibitions against taking interest on loans were clear and unequivocal. Legal fictions intended to circumvent the prohibitions were strongly disapproved, and documents to effect such fictions would not be enforced by the courts. Usury was regarded by Rava as equivalent to robbery whether the victim willingly paid it or not.[2] He also said that the exodus from Egypt was mentioned along with laws of interest, fringes, and weights (Lev. 25:36-38; Num. 15:38, 41, Lev. 19:38) because God thereby wished to say, "It is I who distinguished in Egypt between the firstborn and others. Even so, it is I who will exact vengeance from him who ascribes his money to a gentile and [directly] lends it to a Jew on interest, or who steeps his weights in salt, or who uses fringes dyed with vegetable blue and maintains that it is real blue."[3] Such a saying would suggest that the courts were unable to act against a man who surreptitiously made use of a gentile as a front for usurious practices within the Jewish community. Hence the divine curse was invoked, there probably being no satisfactory, this-worldly alternative means to prevent the practice. On the other hand, Rabbah and R. Joseph ruled that dealings in futures were legitimate. A man may therefore contract to supply provisions at the current market price, even though the price may change later on.[4] One who lends money at the early market price must personally appear at the granary.[5] Abaye and Rava both held that the courts would reclaim funds paid in usury, and in compelling repayment of a debt, would check on the possibility of usury.[6] A mortgage, on the other hand, was understood as a temporary sale, so that the lender's right of usufruct did not constitute usury.

[1] b. B.B. 172a.
[2] b. B.M. 61a.
[3] b. B.M. 61b.
[4] b. B.M. 63b.
[5] b. B.M. 63b.
[6] b. B.M. 65a.

Nonetheless, Rava strictly required the creditor to allow a fixed deduction of the debt annually, even though the usufruct was less than that amount.[1] Rava said,

> "The law permits neither the credit interests of R. Papa, nor the bonds of the Maḥozans, nor the tenancies of the people of Nersh."

> (b. B.M. 68a)

The first reference was to R. Papa's view that beer sold for credit might be priced higher than when paid for in cash. R. Papa held that the beer would not deteriorate. Since the brewer did not need the money, he merely conferred a benefit on the purchaser by giving it to him earlier than otherwise.[2] The purchaser paid a higher price. The Maḥozan bonds would add the (estimated) profit to the principal and record the whole in a bond, so that the lender's share of the profits of a commercial loan was guaranteed at the outset. Since there was no certainty that profit would accrue and also no sharing of risk, it was in fact a usurious clause. In the tenancies of Nersh, they wrote the following clause, "*A* mortgaged his field to *B*, and then the debtor rented it from him." The rental was fixed and paid in produce. Since the creditor had not in fact acquired the land which he has allegedly rented to the debtor, and therefore the land has not been formally transferred to the debtor, it is a thinly disguised form of direct interest. Rava provided for a "proper" kind of interest:

> Rava said, "One may say to his neighbor, 'Take these four *zuz* and lend money to so-and-so' [on interest] for the Torah prohibited only usury which comes directly from the borrower to the lender ... One may say to his neighbor, 'Here are four *zuz*, and persuade so-and-so to lend me money.' The neighbor merely receives a fee as advocate [and is not guilty of usury]."

> (b. B.M. 69b)

With so simple an alternative at hand, it is easy to see why the rabbis' rules could otherwise be strict. Both the laws of Moses and the needs of a highly developed commercial life could be easily satisfied. Three practical cases were recorded:

> A woman once told a man, "Go and buy me land from my relatives," and he went and did so. The seller said to the agent, "If I have money, will she return it to me?" "You and Navla," he replied, "are relatives [so she will certainly permit you to repurchase the land when you are

---

[1] b. B.M. 67b.
[2] b. B.M. 65a.

able to do so]." Rabbah b. R. Huna said, "Whenever one says 'You ... are relatives,' the seller relies upon it, and does not completely transfer [the object of sale]. The land is returnable, but what of the crops? Is it direct usury, which can be legally reclaimed, or indirect usury, and not reclaimable? Rabbah b. R. Huna said it must be considered indirect usury and cannot be reclaimed in court. Rava similarly ruled, "It is considered indirect usury and cannot be reclaimed in court."

(b. B.M. 67a)

A bond was issued against the children of R. 'Ilish, stipulating half profits and half loss [that is to say, a bond whereby R. 'Ilish undertook to trade on these terms, and this is regarded as usury]. Rava said, "R. 'Ilish was a great man[1] and would not have fed another person with forbidden food [resulting from profits such as these]. It must be taken to mean, either half profit and two-thirds loss, or half loss and two-thirds profit. [That is, the borrower must have agreed to receive half the profits but to bear two-thirds of the loss, or if R. 'Ilish were to stand half the potential loss, he must receive two-thirds of the profit]."

(b. B.M. 68b-69a)

Rava advised those who watch over the fields, "Go and find some work in the barn so that your wages may not be payable until [that work is done], since wages are not payable until the end, it is only then that they remit in your favor" [what they pay over and above the stipulated wage].

(b. B.M. 73a)

The watchers were not paid until the wheat was winnowed, though wages were due immediately after the harvest. In consideration, they were given something above their due, which appeared to be usurious interest. Rava advised them to keep busy, so their wages would not actually be payable until they received their pay, in which case the additional payment would not come on account of their having waited, hence as interest on their salary, but rather as a gift.

In the first case, therefore, the issue was whether land was intended to be given over for acquisition by the lender, and what was the status of the usufruct in reference to the prohibition of usury. In the second, the issue was whether a contract had actually stipulated an arrangement of profits and loss which the rabbis regarded as usurious. Rava said that it was unthinkable for so great an authority as R. 'Ilish to have stipulated a usurious agreement, and he therefore interpreted the language of the bond to conform to the law. In the third instance, Rava advised workers how to avoid violating the law against usury.

---

[1] See vol. III, p. 134.

The courts' supervision of collections of mortgages and debts generally came in consequence of violation of the law. Otherwise there was no need to intervene. The cases of alleged fraud in repayment of debts would have been brought to court by the borrower, from whom excessive payment was demanded, or by the lender, who found himself unable to recover his funds, or by both, when the two issued conflicting claims. By contrast, cases of alleged usury would not necessarily have come before the courts at all if both parties had mutually agreed to the arrangement, unless some extraneous factor led to court action and thus revealed an illegal agreement. Rava could only advise the workers how to avoid breaking the law of usury, but no actual case could arise. In other cases, the basic agreement was regarded as sound and enforceable, but the issue of what to do about subsidiary or tangential returns had to be settled. It is striking to note the limited range of cases. We have no instance where the court simply had to force a recalcitrant debtor to pay his debt or to issue a decree against him. Doubtless such cases did arise, and we can only assume that they were not of sufficient legal or scholarly interest to warrant inclusion in a legal commentary upon the Mishnah. The only cases actually set down involved unusual circumstances or exemplified exceptionally interesting principles of law. We must therefore suppose that many more cases involving the collection of mortgages and debts, the transfer of ownership of pledges or securities for debts which had been defaulted, and the like, came to the courts. And, as I said, still more transactions would have been legally carried through without eliciting court action of any sort.

VIII. CONTRACTS

Contracts of various kinds, involving the exchange of property or services, would naturally come to the courts if not properly carried out, or if the original conditions required the judges' interpretation. Cases included these:

> R. Papa and R. Huna b. R. Joshua bought some sesame on the bank of the Royal Canal and hired some boatmen to bring it across, with a guarantee against any accident that might happen to it. After a time the canal was stopped up. The rabbis said to the boatmen, "Hire asses and deliver the material to us, since you guaranteed against any accident that might happen." The rabbis then appealed to Rava, who said to them, "White ducks who want to strip men of their cloaks![1] It is an

---

[1] Compare above, p. 135.

exceptional kind of accident [for which no one is responsible]."

(b. Git. 73a)

A certain man said to his sharecropper, "The general rule is that one irrigates the land three times annually, and takes a fourth of the produce. You irrigate four times, and take a third of the crop." Before he finished, the rain came. R. Joseph said, "He has not actually irrigated [the fourth time]." Rabbah said, "There was no need [for the fourth]...."

(b. Git. 74b)

A certain person sold a field to his neighbor, with a guarantee against any accident that might happen to it. They turned a canal through the land. The seller consulted Rabina, who said that he must go and clear the land, since he had guaranteed it against accidents. R. Aḥa b. Taḥalifa remarked to Rabina that it was an unusual accident ... The matter at last came before Rava, who ruled that it was an exceptional accident [and not covered by the agreement of sale].

(b. Git. 73a)

A certain man once leased a field from his neighbor and said, "If I do not cultivate it, I shall give you a thousand *zuz* [as a percentage of the lease]." He left a third of the field uncultivated. The Nehardeans said, "It is just that he should pay him 333 1/3rd *zuz*." Rava ruled, "It is an *'asmakhta* [an assurance that one will pay in case of non-fulfilment of a condition which a man is confident he will fulfill] which is not enforceable...."

(b. B.M. 104b)

A person once hired out an ass, and said to the hirer, "Do not go by way of Nehar Peqod, where there is water, but by way of Nersh, where there is none." He went by way of Nehar Peqod, and the ass died. He came before Rava, and made the plea, "I went by way of Nehar Peqod, but there was no water." Rava ruled....

(b. Bekh. 36a)

A certain man gave money for poppy seed. The price went up, and the vendor retracted, and said, "I have no poppy seed, take back your money." He would not take his money, and it was stolen. When they came before Rava, he ruled, "Since he told you to take back your money and you refused, he is not accounted as a paid bailee, and is not even an unpaid one...."

(b. B.M. 49a)

A certain man leased a field by the bank of the Old Royal Canal [near Maḥoza] on a money rental for sowing garlic. The Old Royal Canal was dammed up. When the man came to Rava, he said to him, "It is unusual for the Old Royal Canal to be dammed. It is a widespread blow. Go and deduct..."

(b. B.M. 106b)

Rava also commented on the *'isqa*, or business-partnership contract, whereby a man invested money with a trader who traded on their joint behalf. The investor took a greater share of the risk than of the profit (as in the case of R. 'Ilish above), receiving either half the profit and two-thirds of the loss, or a third of the profit and half the loss. The arrangement prevented the possibility of usury. The Nehardeans held that such an agreement was part-loan, part-bailment. If the partner dies, the funds cannot be held to be movable property in the heirs' hands, Rava held. He said also that if a man accepted an *'isqa* and suffered a loss, but then made it good, and had not yet informed the investor, he cannot then say to him, "Deduct the loss." The latter can reply, "You took the trouble of making it good to avoid being called a poor trader." Similarly, Rava said, "If two men accept an *'isqa* and profit, and one wants to divide before the agreed schedule to wind up the agreement, and the other objects and wishes to earn more profits, he can legally restrain him from closing the transaction."[1]

In the first three cases as well as the last cited above, the issue was whether a catastrophe constituted a foreseeable event which the contract would have covered, or so extraordinary a happening that no contract could have conceivably taken it into account. The decision of the courts rested upon their assessment of the possible intent of the contract, and this depended upon the nature of a disaster. The courts were therefore able to decide what private parties had intended by their original accord in ordinary times. In the fourth instance, similarly, the intent of the lessor had to be determined by the court. If he had merely promised something in full certainty that he would be able to carry it out, then it was not his intention to give over to the owner such a substantial claim. Rava's view was that it was a mere encouragement to complete the contract, but no enforceable stipulation. In the fifth case, the issue was whether the condition set forth in a contract was to be narrowly or broadly interpreted. If the owner said not to take a certain route because of the water, and no water in fact impeded the road, then the hirer could not be held responsible, the original clause having been irrelevant to the facts of the case. In the sixth story default on a contract caused an impasse, at which the injured party tried to force the vendor to keep his agreement. Rava ruled in favor of the vendor, and the injured party's error in failing to resort to court action, rather than attempting to force the issue on his own, became evident. (One recalls that the canals were dammed up, and then cleared out, in the course of

[1] b. B.M. 104b-105a.

the Romans' campaign in central Babylonia. It took place, however, after the death of Rava, and the normal management of the canals, not the exceptional situation brought on by the tactics of war, produced the cases cited here.) Rava's comments on the *'isqa* contract seem quite practical. There was no reason why the courts could not easily enforce rabbinical rules, and in fact the case of R. 'Ilish, cited earlier, must be interpreted in the light of Rava's comments on the business-partnership agreements permitted by the courts.

We once again note that the chief issues in fourth-century cases were exceptional. Normally the occurrence of an unusual event preventing fulfillment of a guaranteed contract would not have forced litigation over that contract. The language of contracts was usually sufficiently clear so that court interpretation was unnecessary. We have no cases in which the sole issue was, What do you do if one party simply fails to keep his part of a contractual agreement? The reason was surely *not* that no such cases came to court, but rather that they were not of sufficient interest for preservation.

We may reasonably assume that the courts enforced the provisions of a great many unremarkable agreements of all kinds, but that the bulk of their decisions therefore were not preserved, being of no special legal interest.

IX. OTHER COMMERCIAL TRANSACTIONS

One cannot readily distinguish between commercial transactions and the various issues of debts, contracts, mortgages, bonds, and other loans, already considered above.[1] Here we shall review cases which do not readily fall into the earlier categories, but indicate more general supervision of market litigations. Such cases included the following rulings on transactions in wine, an expensive and perishable commodity:

> Rava once brought wine from a shop. After diluting it, he tasted it, found it was sour, and returned it to the shop. Abaye protested....
>
> (b. B.M. 60a)
>
> R. Joseph decided a case [in which wine went sour]....
>
> (b. B.B. 96b)
>
> A man was once moving a barrel of wine in the market [RYSTQ']²

---

[1] See pp. 220ff. Note also the decisions on the suitability of wine for sale, cited above, pp. 59-60, and see also b. B.B. 24b, 98a-b, for a similar case.

[2] Ristaqa = market-place outside of town, cf. Jastrow, s.v., II, 1475b.

of Maḥoza, and broke it on a projection, so he came before Rava, who
ruled...

(b. B.M. 83a)

A man told his neighbor to buy four hundred barrels of wine. He
did so. [He then claimed they had soured.] ... The case came before
Rava, who said, "When four hundred barrels of wine turn sour, the
facts should be widely known. Go and bring proof that the wine was
originally sound..."

(b. B.M. 83a)

Rava said that if a man sold wine to a shopkeeper intending to retail
it, with the shopkeeper keeping a percentage of the proceeds, and when
about half had been sold, the wine soured, then the vendor must take
the wine back from him. If a man accepted wine intending to sell it in
the market of Vologasia, and the price fell by the time he got there, the
original owner must bear the loss in value.[1]

Other kinds of commercial judgments involved renunciation of sale,
when the seller wanted to cancel an agreed and completed transaction,
or sale of movables or land on some contingency, as follows:

A man had silk beads [WRŠKY] for sale. He demanded six [zuz]
while they were worth five. If five and a half were offered, he would
have accepted it. A man came and said, "If I pay him five and a half,
it is renunciation [since the overcharge was less than a sixth, it was not
actionable]. Therefore I will pay six and sue him." When he went to
Rava, he ruled [that he had no claim of fraud].

(b. B.M. 51a)

A certain man sold property intending to emigrate to Palestine, but
when in the act of selling, he said nothing. Rava ruled, "It is a mental
stipulation and not recognized."

(b. Qid. 49b)

A certain man sold his property with the intention of emigrating.
He migrated but could not settle down. Rava ruled, "When one goes
there, it is with the intention of settling, but this man has not done so.
[The sale is cancelled]." Others state that he ruled, "He sold it intending
to emigrate, and has done so. [The sale is valid.]"

(b. Qid. 50a)

On the laws of overcharge, Rava held that one may legally withdraw
from a sale on account of any fraud in measure, weight or number,
even if less than the standard of overreaching.

Still another kind of case centered upon what was included in an
agreement of sale, as follows:

---

[1] b. B.M. 56b.

A certain man said to another, "I sell you this olive press and all its accessories." There were shops abutting on to it on [the roofs of] which they used to spread out sesame seeds. R. Joseph was asked [whether they were included in the sale]. He said....

(b. B.B. 68a)

The law long ago had provided numerous rules for such a situation as this, and the court had no difficulty in settling the case according to rabbinic traditions.

These cases all arose in normal market transactions. In the first two, the tendency of wine to sour or to fluctuate in price raised a number of issues, mainly to do with who must bear the loss. In the third, the willingness of the courts to set aside transactions in which fraud or overcharge had taken place was tested by a shrewd buyer. In the next two cases, the intent of a stipulation was at issue. It was made clear that a stipulation had to be stated expressly, but the more difficult matter of whether it had been met or not resulted in an ambiguous tradition in Rava's name. In the final case the issue was simply what had been comprehended in a sale-agreement.

Commercial transactions, contracts, various kinds of documents and deeds, debts, bonds, and mortgages—all of these matters could easily be settled by the Jewish courts. The Iranian government would certainly not trouble itself with such petty matters. Appeal of court rulings in such inconsequential cases, small sums or minor issues was hardly practical. One might, therefore, suppose that the Jewish courts were effective mainly in matters of commerce and disputes over movables, contracts, and the like, but not in far more important suits, such as real estate cases or litigations over immovables, for such cases could never have been finally decided without Persian confirmation.

x. Litigation over Immovable Property and Real Estate

The right of Jewish courts to decide cases about property rights obviously depended upon Iranian approval. In cases of immovables, there was always time to appeal to Iranian courts, which might have produced a different decision if appeal were possible. In such a situation, the Jewish courts could have done little to support their decisions. Commercial or contract cases, by contrast, produced a very quick result. Whether or not appeal was theoretically possible, the Jewish courts could so rapidly have effected their decisions as to present a *fait accompli*. In immovable property cases, on the other hand,

Iranian courts could always intervene. They probably never did, for an appeal, successful or otherwise, was never recorded or referred to. Litigations over immovables by Jewish courts therefore prove beyond any doubt that the Iranian government supported the Jewish court-system, validated its decisions when necessary, and refused to consider appeals from its courts, even in real estate cases, so long as decisions were congruent to Persian law.[1]

Reports of actual real estate cases include the following:

> A man against whom was a claim of a thousand *zuz* had two houses ['PDNY], each of which he sold (to a single person) for five hundred. The creditor thereupon came and seized one of them, and was going to seize the other. The purchaser took one thousand *zuz*, and went to the creditor and said, "If the one is worth one thousand *zuz*, well and good, but if not, take your thousand *zuz* and go [give up both houses]." Rami b. Ḥama proposed ... but Rava said to him...
>
> (b. Ket. 91b)

> A certain man against whom was a claim for a hundred *zuz* had two [small] plots of land each of which he sold for fifty [to the same purchaser]. The creditor came and seized one of them, and them came to seize the other. The purchaser took a hundred *zuz* and went to him and said, "If one is worth a hundred *zuz*, well and good, but if not, take the hundred *zuz* and go." R. Joseph proposed to say ... But Abaye said to him...
>
> (b. Ket. 91b)

Two further cases, one to Abaye, the other to Rami b. Ḥama, involved the same principle. In both, the borrower had not guaranteed the sale against further claims, so the purchaser had to make good on legitimate claims against his property. The courts commented upon, but do not seem to have intervened in, the matter. The discussions presupposed the possibility of intervention if necessary. Further land disputes coming before the courts included the following:

> R. Papa bought a field from a certain person who claimed it contained an area of twenty *griva*, but it contained only fifteen. He came before Abaye, who said to him, "You surely realized the size and accepted..."
>
> (b. B.B. 106a-b)

> A man once said to a neighbor, "If I sell this land, I will sell it to you," but he went and sold it to another person. R. Joseph said that the first one had acquired it. Abaye said to him, "But he had not settled the price..."
>
> (b. A.Z. 72a)

---

[1] See vol. III, pp. 334-335. Note the contrast in criminal matters, in which excessive punishment provoked state inquiries.

In the above cases, the courts were able to decide whether fraud had been committed in the sale of land, and whether a man had acquired an option to buy land, thus preventing others from purchasing it. More commonplace issues pertained to the settlement of disputed boundaries, as in the following:

> A certain man once made a boundary mark for another, [and one of the witnesses to whom he sold a nearby field] contested its owner-ship. The man died, and a guardian was appointed over his estate. The guardian came to Abaye...
>
> (b. Ket. 109b)

Many other sayings were handed on concerning the sale of houses and land, and what was included in such sales.[1] Rabbah said that if a man who owns half a field sells it and says, "I sell you the half which I have in the land," he sells half of the whole. If he says, "I sell half of the land that I have," he sells a quarter of the whole. If a man writes in the deed, "The boundary of the land is the land from which half has been cut off," he sells half.[2] Rava said, "If the seller says, 'I sell you a residence,' it means that he refers to apartments."[3] He also ruled about riparian sales, and held that if a man sells the shore of a river and its bed, the purchaser takes possession of the shore and the bed separately.[4] Other riparian cases included the following:

> Certain [farmers]in Be Ḥarmakh [near Pumbedita] went and dug a trench from the upper [waters of the] Shanvata [SNWWT'] canal and brought it around via their fields to the lower waters. Those higher up came and complained to Abaye, saying, "They are spoiling our canal [by slowing the current]." He said to them, "Deepen the bed a little." They said to him, "If we do so, the trenches will be dry." He replied [to the first group], "Then leave the canal alone."
>
> (b. Git. 60b)

The state made a continuing investment in the management and repair of the canals, which fructified Babylonia. Without the canals, nothing would grow. The right of the rabbinical court to decide a case in which water rights were at issue testifies to state authorization to do so, for without it, Abaye could have issued no such decree, nor, indeed, could he have heard the case at all. By contrast, the rabbinical courts had no authority whatever over non-Jewish property rights, including

---

[1] For comments of R. Joseph and Rava, b. B.B. 61a-62b.
[2] b. B.B. 62b.
[3] b. B.B. 67a.
[4] b. B.B. 67a.

rights to use of the canal-water, and could not order outsiders to obey Jewish law, as the following indicates:

> Rabbah b. R. Huna had a forest by the canal bank. He was asked to make a clearing [by the water's edge] and replied, "Let the owners above and below me first clear theirs, then I will clear mine." ... The neighboring forests belonged to the Chief Gendarme.[1] Therefore Rabbah b. R. Huna said, "If they cut down theirs, I will do so also, but if not, why should I? For if the ropes can be still hauled, they have room for walking. If not, they cannot walk there no matter what I do." Rabbah b. R. Nahman was traveling in a boat and saw a forest on the canal bank. He said, "To whom does it belong?" "To Rabbah b. R. Huna," he was told. He cited the Scripture (Ezra 9:2), "Yea, the hand of the princes and rulers has been chief in this trespass." He ordered, "Cut it down, cut it down." Rabbah b. R. Huna came and found it cut down. "Whoever cut it down, may his branches be cut down." They say that during Rabbah b. R. Huna's lifetime, none of the children of Rabbah b. R. Nahman remained alive.
>
> (b. B.M. 107b-108a)

First, Rabbah b. R. Huna clearly had no recourse, nor could he sue the rabbi who ordered his trees cut down. Hence he resorted only to a curse. On the other hand, the Jewish court manifestly had no power to order the Iranian official to cut down his trees and clear the passage. Rabbah b. R. Huna originally relied upon that fact. So the Jewish court *could* make rulings over Jewish property, but not over that of others, certainly not over state lands, in matters of riparian rights. No case more clearly illustrates the nature of Jewish courts' authority. Where they had power, it was complete, and appeal for restitution was not possible. Where they had no power, it was possible to do absolutely nothing.

Many cases arose from disputes about squatters' rights. Such disputes, in which the right of possession was disputed by owners unable to evict squatters, depended upon the rule that three years' actual possession conferred presumptive right [hazaqah]. R. Joseph found biblical evidence for the rule in Jer. 32:44. Rava held that the reason was that a man may forgo his rights of usufruct for a year or two, but not for three years.[2] The following litigations were recorded:

> A certain man said to another, "What right have you [lit: What do you want] in this house?" The other replied, "I bought it from you, and have used it for the period of [three years of] hazaqah." The other said, "I was in foreign markets [and could not protest]." "But I have

---

[1] *Bozorg Rufila*, see vol. III, p. 20, n. 1.

[2] b. B.B. 29a, Abaye and Rava discuss the matter further.

witnesses to prove you used to come here for thirty days every year."
"Those thirty days," he replied, "I was occupied with my business."
Rava ruled, "It is quite possible for a man to be fully occupied with his
business for thirty days."

(b. B.B. 30a)

A certain man said to another, "What right have you on this land?"
He replied, "I bought it from so-and-so, who told me he had bought it
from you." The first said, "You admit that this land was once mine and
that you did not buy it from me. Clear out then, you have no case with
me." Rava ruled, "He was quite within his rights in what he said" [for
the squatter had no proof that the man from whom he bought it had
bought it from the original owner].

(b. B.B. 30a-30b)

A certain man said to his neighbor, "What right have you on this
land?" He replied, "I bought it from so-and-so and have used it for
[three years]." The other said, "So-and-so is a robber." The first replied, "I have witnesses to prove that I came and consulted you and
you advised me to buy the property." The plaintiff replied, "The reason
is that I preferred to go to law with you than with him." Rava ruled,
"He replied quite legally...."

(b. B.B. 30b)

A certain man said to another, "What right have you on this land?"
"I bought it from so-and-so, and I have had the use of it for [three
years]." The first one said, "So-and-so is a robber." The other said,
"But I have witnesses to prove that you came the evening [before] and
said to me, 'Sell it to me.'" "My idea was to buy [what I was already]
legally entitled to," the plaintiff answered. Rava ruled, "It is not unusual
for a man to buy what he is already legally entitled to."

(b. B.B. 30b)

A certain man said to his neighbor, "What right have you on this
land?" He replied, "I bought it from so-and-so and have had use of it
for the period of the *ḥazaqah*." The other said, "But I have a title deed
to prove I bought it from him four years ago." The other replied, "Do
you think when I say the period of *ḥazaqah*, I mean only three years?
I mean a lot of years." Rava said, "It is not unusual to refer to a long
period of years as 'the period of *ḥazaqah*'...."

(b. B.B. 30b)

This man claims, "This land belonged to my father" and the other,
"To my father." One brought witnesses to prove it belonged to his
father, and the other did so to prove he had used it for the period of
ḥazaqah. Rabbah said, "What motive did [the occupier] have to lie?
He could [merely] have pleaded that he had purchased it and used it
for the period of *ḥazaqah*...."

(b. B.B. 31a)

None of these cases contested the principle that *ḥazaqah*, or squatters' rights, might be attained through sufficient use of property. The issues were narrower and concerned various claims which came, or might have come (as in the final instance), before the court. Rava ruled that a man might claim he had no occasion or opportunity to inspect his property, and consequently to enter a protest against illegal occupation of his land; that a weak claim could be thrown out of court; that the owner might arrange by subterfuge for the recovery of his property, either by permitting a weaker party to purchase the land from a stronger one, or by promising to repurchase what was legally his own land. The conflicting claims before Rava, in which one party attempted to weaken the plea of another to have completed the period of the *ḥazaqah*, required the court to interpret the language of the first litigant. In the final suit, the court of Rabbah confirmed [or, was willing to confirm, in case litigation should arise] possession in the hands of the party who already possessed the land. Rava's rulings seem generally to have favored the plaintiff against the alleged squatter, but only a thorough survey of all such traditions could show whether in fact he consistantly *intended* to do so on principle. Other real estate cases involved the plea before Rabbah that a deed to land was forged,[1] a plea before Abaye in which the litigant brought only one witness in support of his claim,[2] and the decision of R. Naḥman b. R. Ḥisda about the inquiry of the people of Pum Nahara on whether ploughing a fallow helps to confer *ḥazaqah* or not.[3] In the case of the seizure by Tai tribesmen of land around Pumbedita, one recalls, Abaye was asked to register duplicate deeds, in case one was forcibly seized from them, and Abaye said it would be illegal to do so.[4] We have two further cases of eviction,[5] and one concerning the assignment of the cost of building a fence between land.[6] Other rulings concerned the following issues: making parapets for the roof of a house;[7] digging a pit near one's neighbor's boundary;[8] and setting up the bounds of a property.[9]

To summarize: The Jewish courts clearly had full control of cases involving real estate litigations among Jews. Normal issues of contested

[1] b. B.B. 32a-b.
[2] b. B.B. 33b-34a.
[3] b. B.B. 36b.
[4] b. B.B. 168b.
[5] See below, pp. 244-245.
[6] b. B.B. 5a, to Rava.
[7] Abaye, b. B.B. 6b.
[8] Abaye vs. Rava, b. B.B. 17b.
[9] R. Joseph, b. B.M. 103b.

ownership as well as boundary questions came to trial, along with cases on rights to the use of irrigation water, and on the duties of riparian owners to clear their banks. The courts could transfer owner- ship from one party to another, and settle other cases in whatever manner they thought legal. Actions in such matters testify, as I said, to the perfectly regular status of Jewish court decisions. If Jews did not voluntarily acquiesce in such decisions, they could have had no recourse to other authorities. I can think of no more striking evidence of the normality of Jewish community life, for were a serious persecution intended by the Sasanian administration, the first act would have been to strip the Jewish courts of all powers and subject the Jews to Sa- sanian court jurisdiction.[1]

XI. BAILMENTS

Disputes arising from bailments were well within the courts' juris- diction in earlier times.[2] In this period, the following litigations were reported:

> There was a shepherd to whom people daily entrusted cattle in the presence of witnesses. One day they did so without witnesses. Subse- quently he completely denied [receipt of the cattle]. Witnesses testified he had eaten two of them. R. Zera ruled ... Abaye answered him...
>
> (b. B.M. 5a)

The discussion had to do with court procedures, specifically whether or not the bailee had to take an oath in connection with his claim. In the following cases, the dispute was over restitution for loss of the bailment:

> A certain man deposited money with his neighbor, who placed it in a cot of bulrushes. It was stolen. R. Joseph said, "Though it was proper care in respect to thieves, it was negligence in respect to fire. Hence the beginning [of the incident] was with negligence though its end was through an accident, and he is liable..."
>
> (b. B.M. 42a)

> A certain man deposited money with his neighbor. When he de- manded the return of the money, the bailee claimed, "I do not know

---

[1] Just as the Catholicus was the first target of persecution, so the exilarch would have been. The Iranian State could simply have removed the legal foundations for the exercise of exilarchic functions and thereby suspended the operations of the Jewish courts. I think it is obvious that the State did no such thing, and had not the slightest intention of upsetting the old arrangements with the Jewish community.

[2] Vol. III, pp. 316-317.

where I put it." Rava ruled, "Every plea of 'I do not know' constitutes negligence, so go and pay."

(b. B.M. 42a)

A certain man deposited money with his neighbor, who gave it over to his mother. She put it in her workbasket and it was stolen. Rava said, "What ruling shall judges give in this case? Shall we say to him, 'Go and repay?' He can reply, 'All who deposit do so with the understanding that the wife and children [may be entrusted with the bailment].' Shall we say to the mother, 'Go and pay?' She can plead, 'He did not tell me the money was not his own, that I should bury it.' Shall we say to him 'Why did you not tell her?' He can argue, 'I told her it was mine, so she was more likely to guard it well.' But he must swear that he entrusted that money to his mother and she must swear she had placed that money in her workbasket and it was stolen. Then the bailee goes free."

(b. B.M. 42a-b)

A certain steward for orphans bought an ox on their behalf and entrusted it to a herdsman. Having no [proper] teeth to eat with, it died. Rami b. Ḥama said, "What verdict shall judges give in this case? Shall we say to the steward, 'Go and pay?' He can reply, 'I entrusted it to the herdsman.' Shall we say to the herdsman, 'Go and pay?' He can plead, 'I put it together with other oxen and gave it food. I could not know it was not eating'...."

(b. B.M. 42b)

A shepherd was once pasturing his sheep by the Papa canal, and one slipped, fell into the water, [and drowned] ... Rabbah exempted him, with the remark, "What could he have done? He guarded them in the usual way." Abaye protested...

(b. B.M. 93a-b)

When a man did not accept responsibility for a bailment, Rava held that he is completely free from responsibility, and so ruled in an actual claim.[1] In the case of bailee's negligence, if the bailee afterward died a natural death, Abaye in Rabbah's name held that his estate was liable, and Rava in Rabbah's name held that the estate was not liable.[2] Rava ruled that a paid bailee who hands over his charge to another retains liability for all consequences.[3] Rabbah said that a person who took charge of a lost article which he has found and has to return to the owner is in the position of an unpaid bailee, and R. Joseph thought he

---

[1] b. B.M. 49b, see above, the case of the sesame sale, pp. 228-229.
[2] b. B.M. 36b.
[3] b. B.Q. 11b.

was a paid bailee.[1] In the following, Abaye as finder became such an unpaid bailee:

> Abaye was sitting before Rabbah when he saw some lost goats standing, and he took a clod and threw it at them. Rabbah said to him, "You are now liable for them, so get up and return them [to their owner]."
>
> (b. B.M. 30b)

Other possible cases were discussed, and there is no doubt that practical situations would have arisen in which the conclusions would have been put into effect.[2]

XII. DOCUMENTS AND DEEDS

Proper documents could produce court action, and those improperly drawn up resulted in considerable loss, not only in relationships of marriage and divorce, but in all business, commercial, and property transactions. The court scribes drew up such documents, and others who did so had to conform to the court rules. In consequence, the courts exercised substantial authority over all kinds of legal documents and deeds, as illustrated by the following cases of deeds of gift:

> A certain woman came before Rava [to ask for a ruling on a deed of gift in which she wrote, 'From life'. She now wished to withdraw the gift.] Rava decided in accordance with his tradition [that she was not entitled to withdraw]. She nagged him. He said to R. Papa b. R. Ḥanan, his scribe, "Go, write for her..."
>
> (b. B.B. 153a)

> A certain deed of gift was witnessed by two robbers. R. Papa b. Samuel wished to validate it on the grounds that their ineligibility as witnesses had not been made public. Rava said to him...
>
> (b. Sanh. 26b)

> A certain deed of gift was attested by two brothers-in-law. R. Joseph thought to validate it...
>
> (b. Sanh. 28b)

Forgery of a deed was discovered in court, as in the following:

> In a certain [deed] it was entered, "a third of an orchard", and subsequently the buyer [forged the document to read] "and an or-

---

[1] b. B.Q. 56b.
[2] b. B.Q. 108b.

chard". He appeared before Abaye, who said to him, "Why has the *vav* so much space around it?" Having been bound, the man confessed.

(b. B.B. 167a)

In a certain deed was entered, "The portion of Reuben and Simeon, brothers". They had a brother whose name was "Brother", ['ḥy] and the buyer added to it a *vav*, and converted [the word into] 'and Brother'. [w'ḥ'y] When the case came before Abaye [the purchaser claimed the third share], Abaye said to him, "Why is there so little space around the *vav*." The man was bound and confessed.

(b. B.B. 167a)

A certain deed bore the signatures of Rava and R. Aḥa b. Adda. The holder of the deed came before Rava, who said, "This signature is mine. However I never signed before R. Aḥa b. Adda." The man was bound and confessed. Rava asked him, "I can understand how you forged mine, but how could you manage R. Aḥa b. Adda's, whose hand trembles." The man replied, "I put my hand on a rope bridge..."

(b. B.B. 167a)

The courts therefore were quite able to detect, and punish forgeries of commercial documents. In the following cases, we see that they were empowered to determine the disposition of other issues involving forged legal documents:

A certain man said to another, "What are you doing on this land?" He replied, "I bought it from you, and here is the deed of sale." "It is forged," said the first. The other party whispered to Rabbah, "It is true that it is a forged document. I had a proper deed but I lost it, so I thought it best to come to court with some sort of document." Rabbah ruled [in his favor].

(b. B.B. 32a-b)

A certain man said to another, "Pay me the hundred *zuz* that I claim from you, and here is the bond." The other claimed it was forged. Leaning over to Rabbah, the first admitted it, but claimed he had lost the genuine document. Rabbah ruled [in his favor].

(b. B.B. 32b)

Abaye ruled in a case in which a man paid a lender in behalf of another man and reclaimed his bond, which he presented to the court.[1] R. Joseph adjudicated a case in which two deeds of sale relating to the same field came before R. Joseph. One was dated "On the fifth of Nisan" and the other "In Nisan." R. Joseph confirmed the property in the hands of the person whose document read "Fifth of Nisan." The

---

[1] b. B.B. 32b.

other then requested that the court write a *tirpa*, a document author-
izing seizure of property sold to a third party, so that he might seize
and recover his money.[1] Rava similarly examined a court document,
found it improperly drawn up, and refused to enforce it.[2] Abaye interpreted the language of a deed:

> In a certain deed it was written, "Six hundred and a *zuz*". R. Shera-
> vya' asked Abaye, "['Does it mean] six hundred *'istira* and a *zuz*, or
> six hundred *perutot* and a *zuz*?" He replied, "Dismiss the question of
> *perutot*, which could not have been written in the deed, since they would
> have been added up and converted into *zuzim*...."
>
> (b. B.B. 166b-167a)

Abaye also held that one who had to present his signature at court (for
example, to help the court determine that his signature is the same as one
appearing to attest a court document) must not present it at the end of a
scroll, for a stranger might find it and write in that he had a claim of
money upon him.[3] Rava held that a document in Persian which has
been handed over in the presence of Jewish witnesses was sufficient
warrant for recovering property on which there was no previous lien.[4]
When R. Papa had to deal with a Persian document drawn up in a
Persian archive, he would have two Persians read it separately, without
telling them his purpose. If their readings agreed, he would permit
recovery, on the strength of such a document, even of mortgaged
property.[5] Rava would give his scribes careful instructions on how to
draw up a bill of divorce[6] as did Abaye.[7] Rava laid down the formula
as follows,

> "We are witnesses how so-and-so son of so-and-so dismissed and
> divorced his wife from this day and for all time...."
>
> (b. Git. 85b)

These cases and stories of court actions show that the Jewish judges
were fully able to require proper preparation of such papers, knew how
to detect forgeries, displayed great care in the choice of language for
deeds and documents, and were able to interpret that language in court-
actions. In the first instance, Rava decided on the basis of the legal

---

[1] b. Ket. 94b. See *Ozar HaGeonim*, vol. VIII, p. 329.
[2] b. Ket. 104b.
[3] b. B.B. 167a.
[4] b. Git. 11a.
[5] b. Git. 19b.
[6] b. Git. 84b.
[7] b. Git. 85b.

formula whether a deed of gift was revocable; in the second, R. Papa
b. Samuel evaluated attestation of a document by people whose testimony would normally not be accepted in court, and in the third, a
similar issue, for other reasons, came before R. Joseph. Abaye's and
Rava's rulings on forged documents suggest that the courts would not
hesitate to force a suspect to testify against himself. Claims of forgery
were not however always decisive, for a man could admit a forgery and
by so doing, establish the truthfulness of a more important claim. In
the two cases above, Rabbah thought that the man could simply have
denied the forgery and so establish his claim upon the basis of the
document he actually held in his hand. Admitting the forgery when he
did not have to, the man was able to secure greater credibility than
otherwise. Bonds and two deeds of sale for the same field were likewise
adjudicated. The language of deeds was not always clear, and Abaye's
ruling was based upon common sense. The rabbis could understand
spoken Pahlavi, but could not read it (which is not surprising, given its
defective alphabet). They nonetheless managed with the help of
Persians to judge cases based on Pahlavi documents. They could
scarcely hope to reject out of hand all documents written in Persian,
especially if they expected the Persian government to respect bills
issued in their courts. A court system had to have the power to issue
legal documents, to control their enforcement, and to judge cases upon
their basis. It is clear that the Jewish courts had all the necessary power
to do so.

XIII. WORKERS AND SLAVES

The courts judged cases involving payment of workers' salaries and
the rights of sharecroppers. Slaves were regarded as property pure and
simple, and so numerous decisions concerning their disposition came
to court. The fourth-century rabbis never condemned the institution
of slavery. It was an accepted part of economic life. Because of their
jurisdiction over property, the rabbis had considerable authority over
slaves, never used to mitigate the conditions in which slaves lived out
their lives.

Two cases of eviction of sharecroppers were recorded in this period:

> R. Joseph had a gardener, who worked for one-half the profits. He
> died and left five sons-in-law. R. Joseph said, "Beforehand, there was
> one, now there are five. Beforehand they did not rely on each other [to
> do the work] and so caused no loss, while now they will." He said to

them, "If you accept the improvements due to you and quit, it is well.
If not, I will evict you without [even] giving you the improvements..."

(b. B.M. 109a)

Ronia was Rabina's gardener. He spoiled the garden, and was dis-
missed. He then went to Rava and [complained about how he was
treated]. Rava ruled, "He has acted within his rights." "But he gave
me no warning," the gardener claimed. "No warning was necessary,"
Rava answered. Rava held that elementary teachers, gardeners, cuppers,
butchers' and the town scribe were all regarded as on permanent
notice...

(b. B.M. 109a-b)

These cases both involved rabbis who knew their rights and exercised them. Rabbah b. R. Huna held that the market traders of Sura
are not guilty of transgressing the commandment not to hold back
wages when they do not pay them promptly, because they pay on the
market-day. All tacitly understand that under that stipulation the
workers are employed.[1] There can be little doubt that the contrary
view would have led to action on the part of Rabbah b. R. Huna to see
to it that the workers were paid day by day. As a result, the workers
must have had to wait for their wages, perhaps to borrow to obtain
immediate necessities until that time.

Rava held that if one engaged laborers to cut dikes, and rain fell so
that the work was impossible, if the employer inspected the situation
in the previous evening, the loss is the workers'; otherwise the loss is
the employer's. He said that if one hired workers for irrigation and it
rained, the workers lose; if the river overflowed, the employer must
bear the loss, but he pays them at the reduced rate of unemployed
laborers.[2] Rava ruled that if one engaged workers for work, and they
finished it in the middle of the day, he can give them easier work, or
work of the same difficulty, but not of more difficulty; he must pay
them for the full day of work.[3] These rulings reveal an effort to come
to a just appraisal of the rights of both parties.

Slaves had few, if any rights. The rabbis did not favor the emancipation of non-Jewish slaves, and did little to secure the emancipation
of Jewish ones, beyond the biblical requirements. The following reveals the contemporary view:

---

[1] b. B.M. 111a.
[2] b. B.M. 76b-77a.
[3] b. B.M. 77a.

There was a certain female slave in Pumbedita who was immorally used by men. Abaye said, "Were it not for the opinion of Rav Judah in Samuel's name, that whoever emancipates his heathen slave breaks a positive commandment, I would compel her master to make out a deed of emancipation for her ...."

(b. Git. 38a)

Rabbah similarly said that men become impoverished for emancipating slaves, inspecting property on the Sabbath, and taking their main Sabbath meal when the sermon was given in the school.[1] *Refraining* from freeing slaves was thus equated with observance of the Sabbath and hearing the Sabbath lesson, as an act of very great religious consequence. We do not know whether ordinary people frequently emancipated their slaves, so necessitating a rabbinic pronouncement against it. In any case, we know full well that Rabbah thought it a sin equivalent to violating the Sabbath. These views were quite consistent with those of the earlier generation.[2]

Contested title to a slave was litigated in the following case:

Rami b. Ḥama and R. 'Uqba b. Ḥama bought a female slave in partnership. The arrangement was that one should have her services during the first, third, and fifth years, the other during the second, fourth, and sixth. The title was contested, and the case came before Rava. He said to the brothers, "Why did you make this arrangement? So that neither of you should obtain the presumptive right [ḥazaqah] against the other? Just as you have no presumptive right against each other, so you have no presumptive right against outsiders...."

(b. B.B. 29b)

In general, Jews were enslaved because they had to sell themselves to obtain funds, either to feed their families, or to pay debts or taxes, as in the following cases:

Some of the servants of R. Joseph b. Ḥama used to seize slaves of people who owed them money, and made them perform work. Rava (his son) said to him, "Why do you allow this to be done?"...

(b. B.Q. 97a)

R. Papa said to Rava, "The master must have observed the men of Papa b. Abba's house, who advance sums of money on people's accounts to pay their head taxes, and then force them into their service. Do they, when set free, required a deed of emancipation or not?" He replied, "... thus said R. Sheshet, The surety of these people is deposited

---

[1] b. Git. 38b.
[2] Vol. III, pp. 24-29.

in the king's archives, and the government has ordained that whoso-
ever does not pay his tax must become the slave of him who pays it
for him .... ."

(b. Yev. 46a=b. B.M. 73b)

In the former instance, the slave was treated as property, to be seized
in payment of debts just like land or movable goods. In the latter, the
rabbis found themselves in the position of having to approve the
practices of the Iranian government. In no instance did they collect
funds to pay such a tax and so prevent people from being enslaved.
They apparently did not use charity funds for that purpose.[1] Hence
poor people must have found that the Jewish government did little, if
anything, to prevent their enslavement.

Other opinions on slavery include that of R. Naḥman b. Isaac, If a
man bought a slave on condition that he would set him free, he would
give him a written declaration, "Your person shall become yours as
from now as soon as I have bought you."[2] He held with reference to
Ex. 21:3, that if a slave has a wife and children when entering service,
his master may give him a heathen slave to beget further slaves; but
if not, his master may not do so.[3] Abaye tended to interpret Scriptures
applying to slaves in a lenient manner, and held that God had favored
slaves.[4] Rava held that the Jewish slave belongs bodily to his master.[5]
Rava also said that if a master emancipated his slave, a creditor could
not reenslave him.[6]

XIV. DAMAGES

In the exceptional situations created by damages and torts, the rabbis'
task was to maintain public order. Their main concern was to assure
that people did not have to take the law into their own hands but

---

[1] Yet such funds *were* collected to ransom captives.

[2] b. Yev. 93b.

[3] b. Git. 8b, 45a, b. B.Q. 20a.

[4] b. ʿArakh. 30b, b. B.Q. 20a.

[5] b. Qid. 28a.

[6] b. B.Q. 90a, Ket. 59b, Git. 40b, etc. See also *Ozar HaGeonim*, ed. B. M. Lewin,
X, p. 81. For a brief account of Christian attitudes toward slavery, see Marvin
R. Vincent, *A Critical and Exegetical Commentary on the Epistles to the Philippians
and to Philemon* (N.Y. 1897) pp. 162-169. Note also the remarks of Vladimir G.
Lukonin, *Persia II*, trans. from Russian by James Hogarth (N.Y.-Cleveland, 1967),
passim. I regret I do not now have access to the scholarship of Soviet Iranists, in
particular on the question of slavery and other social-economic relationships,
except for the relevant passages of N. Pigulevskaja, *Les Villes de l'État Iranien*
(Paris, 1963), pp. 79-92, 141-150, etc.

could resort to the courts for quick and effective justice. R. Naḥman b. Isaac and Rava both were firm in holding that one may not execute his own justice.[1]

Evidence that the fourth-century masters judged cases of damages in the law courts derives from the following cases:

> In a case where a goat noticed turnips on top of a cask and climbed up and consumed them and broke the jar, Rava ordered full payment....
>
> (b. B.Q. 20a)

> The goats of Be Tarbu used to damage R. Joseph's [fields]. He said to Abaye, "Go tell their owners to keep them indoors." Abaye said, "What is the use? Even if I go, they will say to me, 'Let the master build a fence....'" It was announced by R. Joseph, or, some say, by Rabbah, "[that...] in the case of goats kept for the market but meanwhile guilty of causing damage, a warning is given to their owners. If they comply, well and good, but if not, we tell them, 'Slaughter the animals immediately, and sit at the butcher's stall to get whatever money you can.'"
>
> (b. B.Q. 23b)[2]

> Such a case occurred [in which a utensil was broken] in Pumbedita and Rava ordered compensation to be paid.
>
> (b. B.Q. 27b)

> A certain woman once entered the house of another to bake bread, and the goat of the owner came, ate up the dough, became sick and died. Rava ordered the woman to pay damages...
>
> (b. B.Q. 48a)

> An ass once bit off the hand of a child. R. Papa b. Samuel ruled in the case, "Go forth and assess the value...." Rava said to him, "Have we not learned..." Abaye replied... The father of the child said, "I do not want [this method of valuation] as it is degrading." They said, "What right have you to deprive the child of his payment?" He replied, "When he comes of age, I shall reimburse him..."
>
> (b. B.Q. 84a)

> An ox once chewed the hand of a child. The case came before Rava, who said, "Go and assess the child as if it were a slave..."
>
> (b. B.Q. 84a)

What is most important in these cases is the fact that the courts decided them. In the first and third, the court determined that the owner was liable, and ordered payment for damages. In the second, Abaye

---

[1] b. B.Q. 28a. But rabbis could do so, see below, p. 314.
[2] See B. M. Lewin, ed., *Ozar HaGeonim* XII, p. 26.

was unable to protect R. Joseph's property, because the neighbors had a perfectly legitimate response. R. Joseph, or Rabbah, was able to announce a public ruling which would protect the entire community from similar inconvenience. On the other hand, we do not know whether the ruling was carried out, or whether it constituted a mere threat. In the fourth case, the task of the court was to determine whether the woman was liable for the death of the goat. In the fifth and sixth, the issue was how to determine the exact amount of compensation. There was no doubt however that compensation would be ordered, assessed by court procedures, and duly paid. In the following, the issue was the extent of secondary liability for damages:

> R. Huna b. Judah happened to be at Be 'Evyone and visited Rava, who asked him, "Have any cases recently been decided by you?" He replied, "I had to decide the case of a Jew whom pagans forced to show them another's property, and I ordered him to pay." Rava said, "Go and reverse the judgment in favor of the defendant...."
>
> (b. B.Q. 117a)

> Two men were quarreling about a net. Both claimed it. One went and surrendered it to the royal *frahanga*[1] [who confiscated it, for by Sasanian law, all ownerless objects belong to the state]. Abaye ruled... Rava said... Rava therefore said, "We would have to impose an excommunication upon him until he brings back [the net] and appears before the court."
>
> (b. B.Q. 117a)

> A certain man had a silver cup which had been deposited with him, and when attacked by thieves, he took and handed it over to them. He was summoned before Rava [current printed text: Rabbah], who declared he was exempt. Abaye said, "Was he not rescuing himself by means of another man's property?"...
>
> (b. B.Q. 177b)

> A certain man had a purse of money for redemption of captives deposited with him. When attacked by thieves, he handed it over. Rava ruled he was exempt...
>
> (b. B.Q. 117b)

> A certain man managed to get his ass on a ferry boat before the people in the boat had disembarked. The boat was in danger of sinking, so a man came along and pushed the ass into the river, where it drowned. When the case came to Rava, he declared him exempt...
>
> (b. B.Q. 117b)

---

[1] On *parangaria*. See *'Arukh* VI, 415A, and I, s.v. 'PRHNG. The meaning here is *judge*.

In the above cases, the courts had to determine whether a man could be held liable for causing loss to another through no ultimate act of his own. In the first, the man was forced to reveal property for tax purposes; the property was confiscated, and the court had to decide whether the informer was liable. In the second, a man had in anger destroyed property which might actually belong to another, by giving it over to the state. In the third, fourth, and fifth cases, a man saved himself by giving up another's property to thieves or other misfortune. In all cases, the liabilities were determined by the court, which enjoyed full authority.

Other litigations of damages included the following:

> Two men were traveling together, one tall, the other short. The tall one was riding on an ass, and had a [linen] sheet, while the short one was wearing a cloak, and walked on foot. On coming to a river, he took his cloak and placed it on the ass, and took the linen and covered himself with it [since linen could stand the water better than wool]. Then the water swept the sheet away. They came before Rava, who ruled...
>
> (b. B.M. 81b)

> Some porters broke a barrel of wine belonging to Rabbah b. R. Huna. He seized their garments, and they complained to Rava, who ordered their return....
>
> (b. B.M. 83a)

> A man borrowed an axe from his neighbor, and it broke. Rava said to him, "Go and bring witnesses that you did not put it to unusual use, and you are free from liability..."
>
> (b. B.M. 96b)

> Meremar b. Ḥanina hired a mule to the people of Khuzistan, and went out and helped them to load it. Through their negligence, it died. Rava held them liable...
>
> (b. B.M. 97a)

> Rava b. R. Ḥanan had some date trees adjoining a vineyard of R. Joseph, and birds used to roost in the trees and fly down and damage the vines. Rava b. R. Ḥanan told R. Joseph to cut down his trees. The latter said, "But I have kept them [the proper distance] away..."
>
> (b. B.B. 26a)

These cases pertained to negligence, and the rabbinical courts had no problem in determining liabilities and inflicting penalties. The claim of Rabbah b. R. Huna against the workers was not evaluated; he simply could not seize their garments to compensate the damage he had suffered. In the case of the borrowed axe, the issue was whether the man had done anything out of the ordinary; if not, he incurred no special liability. The same rule pertained to the case of the hired mule. In the final case, the issue was whether the owner had done all he was required to do to prevent damages. Other sayings included many which must have guided court decisions in practical cases.[1] Court rulings in cases of torts and damages generally resulted in exchanges of property, either as a penalty or in compensation for damages. Control of the courts over the possessions of the Jewish community made it easy to enforce all such rulings. In consequence, people could normally look to the courts for quick and fair actions and did not have to undertake vigilante justice.

xv. Summary and Conclusions

Babylonian Jewish government consisted of more than what rabbis said and did, but the bulk of our information tells us little more than that. I have stressed the circumstances which produced cases, as earlier,[2] since my interest is not in the history of Jewish law, but in the substance of Jewish politics and of religious-historical sociology. It is perfectly clear that the political structure, constituted by a Jewish millet-regime headed by the exilarchate, supported and legitimized by the Sasanian authorities, actually was made up of local courts and related authorities responsible for maintaining an orderly and peaceful community life. These courts were staffed by the graduates of rabbinical law-schools. By the fourth century, the schools had produced a considerable number of well-trained lawyers, and these graduates served as the chief, though probably not the only,[3] means by which the exilarchate carried out its political responsibilities.

What, exactly, did the Sasanians expect the Jewish courts to adjudicate? I think it clear that determinations of personal status and litigations over property of all kinds were the sole state-recognized functions. When, moreover, we review the kinds of examples, we cannot suppose the Jewish courts were particularly important. On the whole, the size of litigations corresponded to those likely to come before a small-claims

---

[1] E.g., b. Git. 50a, Rava on land payments for damages, also b. B.Q. 7a, Abaye and Rava, b. B.Q. 85b, Rava, etc.

[2] See Vol. II, pp. 251-260, and Vol. III, pp. 319-334.

[3] Note above the reference to uninformed "arbitrators," who not knowing the law simply divided disputed property among the several claimants, rather than coming to a decision based upon a true assessment of what Jewish law required.

court in modern society. Thefts involved a book, or a few rams. Betrothal cases concerned a few *zuz*, a willow-branch, some onions, or a piece of silk. Settlements of marriage-contracts required litigation of a robe of fine wool, a silver cup. A few cases of alleged adultery were recorded, all of sufficient innocence for the court to rule that no adultery had taken place. Ceremonies of *ḥaliẓah* and the preparation and delivery of proper divorce documents hardly amounted to weighty matters of state. The exilarchate itself could not have paid much attention to the technicalities of the dissolution of a marriage. Divorce litigations in any event were provoked by peculiar and exceptional circumstances; normally a man could divorce his wife without court intervention. The settlement of estates entailed somewhat larger sums of money. "Four hundred *zuz*," a round number, represented approximately enough capital for two years' maintenance of a woman, it is generally supposed. The provision by the court for widows—of food, wine, clothing—represented humble and more typical matters. Even most estate-cases pertained to rather small claims, such as a few trees, a slave, the choice plot of ground. Settlement of debts, collections of mortgages and bonds, and the like required rulings on somewhat more substantial sums, but the real issues were still relatively inconsequential, a hundred *zuz*, or whether a pledged spoon or knife had to be returned. Broken contracts likewise were entered into by a few ferrymen and sharecroppers, or devolved upon a hired ass, the purchase of some wine or poppy-seed, a flooded field. Other commercial litigations demanded that the courts decide about a few *zuz* worth of silk beads, some sour wine, the sale of a wine press or of a field. Property cases similarly involved alleged fraud in a relatively small plot, the supposed existence of an option to purchase a field, the use of some canal water, and very frequently, squatter's rights over a house or a field the owner had not seen for some time and the eviction of tenant farmers. Damages were done to a jar or utensil, a dead goat, a silver cup, a purse of money stolen in part through negligence, a broken ax and a broken wine-barrel. I have continually stressed the circumstances and facts of cases because it seems to me these clearly reveal the real substance of issues left in the rabbis' hands. With a few exceptions, strikingly petty sums of money or barely consequential amounts of property were all that the courts actually adjudicated. So in general the affairs of mainly the lower classes of society were subject to rulings by the rabbinical courts. Large commercial transactions, for many thousands of *zuz* worth of silk or pearls, wine, or beer, enormous property transactions involving a whole village or town, claims of a considerable number of workers against a single employer, or vice versa, the affairs of large estates, rich landowners, big businessmen, important officials—none of these occur with any frequency, if at all, in the reports available to us. The reason only in part was that not many Jews seem to have been located in the higher strata of society. In part, it must have been that the rabbinical courts' jurisdiction was limited. The absence of significant criminal actions, apart from the single murder case before the exilarch, moreover is suggestive. It would indicate that some other authority than the rabbinical courts was responsible for criminal prosecutions. I therefore suppose that the exilarch must have held the chief responsibility—if the Sasanian courts did not retain it for themselves—for anything that really mattered.

The rabbis could not have agreed, however, that the humble and petty issues before them were of no consequence. It was their view, a very old one in Judaism, that the least and humblest affairs, as much as the largest and most weighty ones, testified to Heaven about the moral state of society. If Amos had condemned Israel of old because a poor man was cheated of his shoes, then one can hardly be surprised that a later rabbi insisted upon the return of a cooking utensil given in pledge. What was important to the rabbis was that justice should prevail. They knew that if justice did not characterize the streets, petty trading market, small farms and shops, then great affairs of commerce and the state would not likely prove to be morally superior. We have already stressed that the ethics of daily life—and that meant the life of exchanges of onions and the use of water in a small canal—determined the destiny of Israel according to rabbinic theology.[1] So the petty cases settled by courts controlled by the rabbis mattered very much to them.

As I said, it may be that some of the instances we have cited above do not always necessarily report actual court cases. The fixed language of so many reports, beginning "A certain man...," the conventional sums of money, such as a hundred or four hundred *zuz*, and the fairly fixed and limited forms in which the cases were written down—these characteristics raise some doubt in my mind that every report actually recorded a real case. Moreover, we have already wondered about the circumstances which led to some court decisions, for occasionally, the reason a case came to court is not at all obvious. We can readily assume that in litigations of property, one or both parties brought the case to court. In other matters, however, one can only assume that if a rabbi gave a decision or an opinion, and if that decision or opinion is recorded

[1] Vol. II, pp. 52-57, 180-187, 236-240.

in the context of a specific circumstance, then some actual event underlay it. Even in such "cases" as did not really come to court, however,
the story of a theoretical event does provide helpful information about
what the schools and the tradents thought was taking place in court—
and what was not coming to rabbinical courts at all. Hence at the very
least, we have an accurate picture of the mind of the schools about the
raw material of the courts. On the other hand, some theoretical dicta
may in fact conceal actual court action, as in the false ascription of an
opinion to Rava.

We need not dwell too long on the curious contrast between reports
about observance of the laws on ritual matters and those dealing with
personal status and property transactions. The former clearly revealed
that the rabbis could do little if anything through their political position
to enforce, or even to guide, the observance of many laws related to the
Sabbath and festivals, holy objects and taboos about sex, food, and
clothing, and the like. The exceptions to the rule were mostly explicable in terms of the rabbis' public position. They supervised the market-
places, and so could determine what kind of meat and wine was suitable
for sale and what was not. They could thus instruct the butchers and
supervise the abattoirs. As communal officials, they could also see to it
that the Sabbath-limits were properly established. They did not have to
wait to be consulted, but simply went and carried out the law as they
saw fit. On the other hand, having no special place in the synagogue,
they had more influence over the disposition of synagogue property
than over the rites and prayers normally carried on there. They could
preach, as we shall see, and so acquired some further influence over
the ordinary people through public instruction in the synagogue. But
that influence cannot be confused with power exerted by public officials
and judges. On the other hand, the extensive legal discussions about
Grace after Meals, prayers to be said on various special occasions,
Sabbath and festival rites and taboos, the preparation of the home for
Passover, the conduct of the Passover *Seder*, building the *Sukkah*, observance of the New Year and the Day of Atonement, special fast days,
reading the Scroll of Esther on Purim, conduct on the intermediate
days of festivals, not to mention the whole range of laws dealing with
other aspects of ritual life—few if any of these discussions produced
such significant exemplifications of popular obedience in this or any
earlier period as to persuade us that ordinary people were much affected.
It is similarly curious, as I said, that while the courts could easily determine proper judicial procedure, decide on how documents were to be

drawn up, determine the rules of evidence and oath-taking, by contrast the Talmudic discussions on the laws of the Sanhedrin and the structure of Jewish judiciary do not indicate that Babylonian courts were even set up according to rabbinic tradition. I should suppose that the exilarch organized the courts and administration without reference to rabbinical traditions on the subject. Once set up, however, they were run as the rabbis wanted.

It is therefore clear that for the rabbis, the limited control they now enjoyed could not have been wholly satisfactory. They did not regard the Mishnaic laws about civil damages and torts as holier than those about prayers or the Sabbath. It was simply that their circumstances permitted them to enforce the former in court, but only to teach about the latter in school. The reason they acquiesced in an only partially acceptable situation was that they hoped in time to improve it. They could not have aspired to less than complete, public, communal conformity to the "whole Torah," both the written part all the people seemed to know about, and the oral traditions only the rabbis now possessed. They chose to cooperate with the exilarchate to enforce as much of the law as they could—and dared. But in time, they intended to reconstruct Jewish community life so that the whole Torah would pertain, so far as relevant. And, as I said, when they succeeded, they fully expected that all of it *would* be relevant, for on that day, the Messiah would come, the Temple would be rebuilt, and the Jewish people would be restored to its own land and to its own government. In Meanwhile, they wanted to construct as full a replica of that ideal situation as was possible before redemption, so as to effect that redemption. The school, like the monastery of the Christian community nearby,[1] would provide the opportunity. There the Torah was studied and carried out in all possible detail by the masters and disciples. In the school, man in the image of God and society in the paradigm of the heavenly academy were to be embodied. And from the school students and masters would go forth to exemplify the will of God, eventually to reshape the life of the streets, homes, farms, and marketplace to conform to it.

The remarkable fact is that the rabbis were able to see themselves as lawyers and politicians at all. They exercised no sovereignty. The state was alien. Outside pressure laid stress upon keeping a peaceful and orderly community, but certainly not upon keeping to the laws of Moses just exactly as the rabbis in particular exposited them. Thus the

---

[1] Vol. III, pp. 195-202.

cohesion of the Jewish community produced by that external pressure did not in any way depend upon, or result in faith in, the supremacy of *rabbinic* law.[1] The state lent a measure of sovereignty to an exilarch from whom the rabbis were increasingly alienated. To the rabbis, the State gave no sovereignty whatever, nor in effect did the exilarch. The schools were their nation and constituted their real sovereignty. If their laws were academic laws, for their part, rabbis made no distinction between theoretical and practical law nor recognized as final or acceptable a disjuncture between sacred law and the reality of actual practice. When Pharisaic-Tannaitic-Rabbinic Judaism determined to conquer a nation through the steady extension of its concept of the school to all of national life, I cannot say. But it was when the last Jewish state before the present one lost all semblance of sovereignty, with the fall of Jerusalem in 70 A.D., that R. Yoḥanan ben Zakkai actually made the schoolhouse into the sole legitimate instrumentality of Jewish sovereignty. From that time onward, sovereignty as others knew it began to pass out of the hands of other powers in Jewry and into the houses of study, so far as the rabbis were concerned. In time, they proved in practice to be quite correct.

One must ask, To what degree did the rabbis now approach the realization of this ideal? The following tables survey the reports of cases and other evidence suggesting that the rabbis were able either to enforce the law or to influence people to keep it. The tables are not meant to provide more than suggestive evidence. Some items which have been excluded would lead to the supposition of rather widespread law enforcement or obedience. For example, while I have not counted as a "case" Abaye's saying that one should see how "the people" say a blessing over water, that dictum may be significant. It may mean that he was willing to rely upon popular practice and therefore approved it. Or it may mean that he meant by "people" *the common practice of the schools*. Similarly, though more conclusively, the saying that one posts public notices to inform people of the dates of holidays has not been counted. Nonetheless, that saying presupposed that people did keep Passover and the Day of Atonement, and provides important evidence that the rabbis decided when these festivals took place. Other bracketed examples are included to indicate the range and quality of evidence testifying to rabbinical authority and influence.

---

[1] Compare Joseph Schacht, *An Introduction to Islamic Law* (Oxford, 1964), pp. 2-3.

I. *b. Berakhot*

	Ca. 310-330 [*Rabbah, R. Joseph*]	Ca. 330-350 [*Rava, Abaye*]
Court Cases		
Questions from Outside of the Academy		1. b. Ber., 54a. Man saved by miracle told by Rava what blessing to say.
Stories and Sayings about Enforcement of, or Obedience to, Law Outside of the Academy	**1. [b. Ber. 31a (= b. Nid. 66a), R. Zera, Israelite women are strict about menstrual taboos.] 2. b. Ber. 33b, Rabbah comments on error in disciple's prayer, in synagogue.	*[1. b. Ber. 45a, *Re* blessing for water, Abaye (or R. Joseph), "Go see what the people do."] 2. b. Ber. 50a, Rava comments on disciple's error in synagogue prayer at Abi Gobar.

* General statement, not counted as a case.
** Duplicate. Duplicates are signified by [—] and are counted only once.

II. *b. Shabbat*

	Ca. 310-330 [*Rabbah, R. Joseph*]	Ca. 330-350 [*Rava, Abaye*]
Court Cases		
Questions from Outside of the Academy		
Stories and Sayings about Enforcement of, or Obedience to, Law Outside of the Academy		1. b. Shab. 94b, R. Naḥman b. Isaac permitted carrying a corpse out of the house on the Sabbath. 2. b. Shab. 134b, Rava ruled a man might bathe an infant on the Sabbath in the usual way. 3. b. Shab. 147b, Rava told Maḥozans how to carry soldiers' cloaks on Sabbath.

III. b. ʿEruvin

	Ca. 310-330 [Rabbah, R. Joseph]	Ca. 330-350 [Rava, Abaye]
Court Cases		
Questions from Outside of the Academy		
Stories and Sayings about Enforcement of, or Obedi- ence to, Law Outside of the Academy	1. b. ʿEruv. 60a, Men of Qa gonai asked R. Joseph to send a man to prepare ʿeruv for their town. 2. b. ʿEruv. 67b, Rabbah advised on getting hot water for circum- cision on Sabbath	*[1. b. ʿEruv. 14b = b. Ber. 45a Abaye said to see what blessing people said for water]. 2. b. ʿEruv. 15a, Abaye and Rava disagreed about sidepost of house of Bar Ḥabu. 3. b. ʿEruv. 24b, Abaye ruled on ʿeruv for open area at Pum Nahara. 4. b. ʿEruv. 40a, Rava permitted people to buy turnips which came to Maḥoza on festival. 5. b. ʿEruv. 47b, Rava permitted Maḥozans to purchase rams though Gentiles had brought them from beyond Sabbath limit. 6. b. ʿEruv. 57b, R. Safra told Rava how one measures Sabbath limits for people of Ctesiphon and Ardashir. 7. b. ʿEruv. 61b, Mar Judah told people of Mabrakta where to place their ʿeruv. 8. b. ʿEruv. 63b, Abaye advised neighbors of Gentile on preparing ʿeruv. 9. b. ʿEruv. 68a, Rava advised on getting hot water for circum- cision on Sabbath. 10. b. ʿEruv. 68a, Rava.

* Duplicate.

III. *b.* *'Eruvin*

	Ca. 310-330 [Rabbah, R. Joseph]	Ca. 330-350 [Rava, Abaye]
		*[11. b. 'Eruv. 102a, R. Tavla did not object to Maḥozan practice.] *[12. 'Eruv. 102a, R. 'Ivya did not object to Nehardean practice.]

* — Inconclusive. Not counted.

IV. *b.* *Pesaḥim*

	Ca. 310-330 [Rabbah, R. Joseph]	Ca. 330-350 [Rava, Abaye]
Court Cases		
Questions from Outside of the Academy		
Stories and Sayings about Enforcement of, or Obedience to, Law Outside of the Academy	1. b. Pes. 50b, R. Joseph told Jews of Khuzistan they do not have to separate *ḥallah* on rice.	1. b. Pes. 5b, Rava told Maḥozans to remove the leaven left by troops in their houses before Passover. **[2. b. Pes. 25b, Rava told man not to kill, even if it meant being killed.] 3. b. Pes. 40b, Rava permitted wet grain to be sold to Gentiles before Passover. *[4. b. Pes. 76a=b. Ḥul. 112a, R. Ḥinena b. Rava of Pashronia permitted a pigeon which fell in dairy-relish].

* Duplicate. Not counted.
** Not counted. Inconclusive.

V. *b. Yoma, Sukkah, Beẓah* [= Y., S., B.]

	Ca. 310-330 [*Rabbah, R. Joseph*]	Ca. 330-350 [*Rava, Abaye*]
Court Cases		
Questions from Outside of the Academy		1. b. B. 12b, Host of Rav b. R. Ḥanan asked about crushing mustard stalks on Festival.
Stories and Sayings about Enforcement of, or Obedi- ence to, Law Outside of the Academy	1. b. Y. 77b, R. Joseph permitted people of Be Tarbu to walk through water to hear the lecture on the Day of Atonement.	1. b. Y. 56b, Rava corrected prayer of synagogue prayer- leader on Day of Atonement. 2. b. Y. 77b, Rava per- mitted people of 'Ever Yemina to walk through water to guard crop on Day of Atonement. *[3. b. Y. 82b (= b. Pes. 25b) Rava tells man not to kill.] 4. b. B. 27b, Rava ruled on firstling. **[5. b. B. 30a, Rava en- acted in Maḥoza *re* carrying on festival.]

    * Duplicate.
    ** General rule, not a case. Not counted in summary table.

VI. *b. Rosh HaShanah, Ta'anit* [= R.H., T.]

	Ca. 310-330 [*Rabbah, R. Joseph*]	Ca. 330-350 [*Rava, Abaye*]
Court Cases		
Questions from Outside of the Academy		
Stories and Sayings about Enforcement of, or Obedi- ence to, Law Outside of the Academy	1. b. T. 24a, Rabbah decreed a fast.	1. b. T. 24b, Rava decreed a fast. 2. b. T. 24b, Rava ordered corporal punishment for intercourse with Gentile woman.

VII. *b. Megillah, Moʿed Qatan, Ḥagigah*

	Ca. 310-330 [Rabbah, R. Joseph]	Ca. 330-350 [Rava, Abaye]
Court Cases		
Questions from Outside of the Academy		
Stories and Sayings about Enforcement of, or Obe- dience to, Law Outside of the Academy	1. b.Meg. 25a, Rabbah corrected synagogue prayer of prayer- leader.	1. b. Meg. 26b, Rava told priests what to do about corpse in synagogue. 2. b. M.Q. 4b, Abaye al- lowed people of Ḥarmekh to clean canal during festival week. 3. b. M.Q. 10b, Rava al- lowed bleeding. 4. b. M.Q. 16a, Abaye and Rava excommunicated butcher who was insolent to rabbis. 5. b.M.Q. 22a, Rava told Maḥozans *re* mourning.

VIII. *b. Yevamot*

	Ca. 310-330 [Rabbah, R. Joseph]	Ca. 330-350 [Rava, Abaye]
Court Cases	1. b. Yev. 34b, Paternity case to R. Joseph. 2. b. Yev. 103b, R. Joseph officiated at *ḥalizah*. 3. b. Yev. 121b, R. Joseph permitted woman to remarry. 4. b. Yev. 122a, R. Joseph permitted woman to remarry.	1. b. Yev. 45b, Rava de- clared man legitimate and gave him public office. 2. b. Yev. 66b, Rava ruled corpse acquired cloak [*re Ketuvah*.] 3. b. Yev. 97a, Rava instructed how to ascertain impotency. *[4. b. Yev. 100a, Rava *re* court procedure] 5. b. Yev. 106a, Abaye officiated at *ḥalizah*. *[6. b. Yev. 106b, Abaye

* Not counted. Example of court procedure.

VIII *b. Yevamot*

	Ca 310-330 [*Rabbah, R. Joseph*]	Ca 330-350 [*Rava, Abaye*]
		on text of *ḥaliẓah* certificate.] 7. b. Yev. 112a, Rava officiated at *ḥaliẓah*. 8. b. Yev. 114b, Rava permitted woman to remarry. 9. b. Yev. 115b, Abaye permitted woman to remarry. 10. b. Yev. 116a, Abaye on bill of divorce. 11. b. Yev. 121a, Rava permitted woman to remarry.
Questions from Outside of the Academy	1. b. Yev. 45a, Men of Be Mikse to Rabbah.	
Stories and Sayings about Enforcement of, or Obedience to, Law Outside of the Academy		

IX. *b. Ketuvot*

	Ca. 310-330 [*Rabbah, R. Joseph*]	Ca. 330-350 [*Rava, Abaye*]
Court Cases	1. b. Ket. 13b-14a, R. Joseph ruled on legitimacy of child. 2. b. Ket. 50b, R. Joseph ruled on maintenance for daughter from estate. 3. b. Ket. 54b, R. Joseph ruled on legacy to daughter. 4. b. Ket. 57a, R. Joseph ruled on lost *ketuvah*. 5. b. Ket. 65a, R. Joseph ruled on maintenance for widow.	*[1. b. Ket. 27b (=b. Bekh. 36a), Rava ruled on case of hired ass.] 2. b. Ket. 28a, Rava ruled in case of betrothed and former fiancé. 3. b. Ket. 49b, Rava ruled *re* non-support. 4. b. Ket. 49b, Rava in case of R. Nathan b. Ammi, forced gift for charity. 5. b. Ket. 51a, Rava ruled on maintenance of orphans from estate.

* Duplicate.

IX. *b. Ketuvot*

	Ca. 310-330 [*Rabbah, R. Joseph*]	Ca. 330-350 [*Rava, Abaye*]
	6. b. Ket. 61b, R. Joseph ruled *re* settlement of estate. 7. b. Ket. 91b, R. Joseph ruled *re* collection of debt. 8. b. Ket. 94b, R. Joseph ruled *re* dispute of sale of land. 9. b. Ket. 109b, R. Joseph ruled *re* legacy to daughter. 10. b. Ket. 111a, R. Joseph banned man for moving from Pumbedita.	6. b. Ket. 65a, Rava ruled on maintenance for widow. **[7. b. Ket. 76a, Rava observed women's preference for land.] 8. b. Ket. 67b, Rava provided charity for applicant. 9. b. Ket. 80b, Rava ruled *re ketuvah*. 10. b. Ket. 84b-85a, Rava ruled *re* collection of debt. 11. b. Ket. 85a, Rava ruled *re* collection of debt. 12. b. Ket. 85a, Rava ruled *re* bond of indebtedness. 13. b. Ket. 86a, R. Papa and R. Hama discussed case decided by Rava *re* debt. 14. b. Ket. 91b, Abaye ruled *re* debt. 15. b. Ket. 91b, Rava ruled *re* sale of *ketuvah*. 16. b. Ket. 98a, Rava ruled *re* collection of *ketuvah*. 17. b. Ket. 104b, Rava ruled in appeal *re* collection of *ketuvah*. 18. b. Ket. 109b, Abaye ruled *re* contested land.
Questions from Outside of the Academy		
Stories and Sayings about Enforcement of, or Obedience to, Law Outside of the Academy		

** Not counted as a case.

X. *b. Nedarim, Nazir, Sotah* [= *Ned., Naz., S.*]

	Ca. 310-330 [*Rabbah, R. Joseph*]	Ca. 330-350 [*Rava, Abaye*]
Court Cases	*[1. b. Ned. 23a, R. Joseph absolved Abaye of oath.]	1. b. Ned. 21b, Rabbah b. R. Huna absolved oath. 2. b. Ned. 25a, Rava judg- ed case of debt collection. 3. b. Ned. 91b, Rava ruled in case of suspect- ed adultery. 4. b. Ned. 91b, Rava ruled in case of suspect- ed adultery.
Questions from Outside of the Academy		
Stories and Sayings about Enforcement of, or Obedience to, Law Outside of the Academy		

* Not counted. Pertinent to law-enforcement in schools only.

XI. *b. Gittin*

	Ca. 310-330 [*Rabbah, R. Joseph*]	Ca. 330-350 [*Rava, Abaye*]
Court Cases	1. b. Git. 19b, R. Joseph ruled on *get*. 2. b. Git. 30a, R. Joseph ruled on conditional *get*. 3. b. Git. 74b, R. Joseph ruled in contract dispute. 4. b. Git. 77b, R. Joseph ruled on acquiring *get*. 5. b. Git. 88b, R. Joseph forced men to to give divorce.	*[1. b. Git. 6a, Rava generally required de- claration of witnesses *re get* in Maḥoza.] 2. b. Git. 29b, Rava ruled on delivery of *get*. 3. b. Git. 34a, Abaye and Rava ruled on validity of *get*. 4. b. Git. 60b, Abaye ruled in case of riparian rights. *[5. b. Git. 67b, Rava in- instructed how to pre- pare *get*.] 6. b. Git. 73a, Rava ruled in contract dispute.

* Not counted. Description of court procedure, not a case.

XI. *b. Gittin*

	Ca. 310-330 [*Rabbah, R. Joseph*]	*Ca. 330-350* [*Rava, Abaye*]
		7. b. Git. 77b, Rava advised on how to acquire *get* on Sabbath. *[8. b. Git. 84b, Rava instructed scribes who wrote *get*.] *[9. b. Git. 85b, Rava laid down text of *get*.] 10. b. Git. 89b, Rava suppressed a rumor.
Questions from Outside of the Academy		
Stories and Sayings about Enforcement of, or Obedience to, Law Outside of the Academy		

* Not counted. Description of court procedure, not a case.

XII. *b. Qiddushin*

	Ca. 310-330 [*Rabbah, R. Joseph*]	*Ca. 330-350* [*Rava, Abaye*]
Court Cases	1. b. Qid. 7b, Rabbah ruled on validity of betrothal with silk. 2. b. Qid. 12b, R. Aḥa b. Huna ruled on betrothal with myrtle branch in market.	1. b. Qid. 12b, Rava ruled on validity of betrothal with myrtle twigs. 2. b. Qid. 45b, Abaye and Rava commented on disputed betrothal. 3. b. Qid. 49b, Rava ruled on retraction of sale of property. 4. b. Qid. 50a, Rava ruled on sale of property. 5. b. Qid. 52b, Rava ruled on disputed betrothal. 6. b. Qid. 52b, Rava ruled on disputed betrothal. 7. b. Qid. 52b, Rava ruled on disputed betrothal.

XII. *b. Qiddushin*

	Ca. 310-330 [*Rabbah, R. Joseph*]	*Ca. 330-350* [*Rava, Abaye*]
Questions from Outside of the Academy		
Stories and Sayings about Enforcement of, or Obedience to, Law Outside of the Academy		1. b. Qid. 73a, Rava lectured about whom proselytes may marry, and was alternately honored and threatened.

XIII. *b. Bava' Qamma'*

	Ca. 310-330 [*Rabbah, R. Joseph*]	*Ca. 330-350* [*Rava, Abaye*]
Court Cases	1. b. B.Q. 93a, R. Joseph ruled on liability for charity purse. 2. b. B.Q. 117b, Rabbah ruled on misappropriation of bailment. 3. b. B.Q. 117b, Rabbah ruled on drowning of ass to save boat.	1. b. B.Q. 20a, Rava judged case of damages by goat. 2. b. B.Q. 48a, Rava judged case of damages by dough to goat. 3. b. B.Q. 84a, R. Papa b. Samuel assessed damages done by ass to child. 4. b. B.Q. 84a, Rava assessed damages done by ox to child. 5. b. B.Q. 115a, Abaye ruled on sale of stolen book. 6. b. B.Q. 117a, R. Huna b. Judah ruled about liability of Jew who was forced by Gentiles to show another's property [for confiscation]. 7. b. B.Q. 117b, Abaye ruled on misappropriation of bailment.
Questions from Outside of the Academy		

XIII. *b. Bava' Qamma'*

	Ca. 310-330 [Rabbah, R. Joseph]	Ca. 330-350 [Rava, Abaye]
Stories and Sayings about Enforcement of, or Obedience to, Law Outside of the Academy	*[1. b. B.Q. 23b, R. Joseph and Abaye despaired of ending damage from goats.]	

* Not counted. Inconclusive.

XIV. *b. Bava' Mezi'a'*

	Ca. 310-330 [Rabbah, R. Joseph]	Ca. 330-350 [Rava, Abaye]
Court Cases	1. b. B.M. 18b, Rabbah decided on validity of *get* discovered among flax. 2. b. B.M. 42a, R. Joseph ruled on bailment. *[3. b. B.M. 81b (=b. Ket. 27b, etc.), Rabbah (N.B.) ruled on case of hired ass.] 4. b. B.M. 93a, Rabbah ruled on liability for drowned sheep. 5. b. B.M. 101b, R. Huna b. R. Joshua ruled on dispute over rental of warehouse.	1. b. B.M. 5a, R. Zera ruled in case of bailment. 2. b. B.M. 23b, Abaye ruled on possession of wine. 3. b. B.M. 24b, Abaye ruled on ownership of meat dropped by vulture. 4. b. B.M. 28b, Rabbah b. R. Huna ruled on restoration of lost ass. 5. b. B.M. 31b, Rabbah b. R. Huna ruled on business litigation. 6. b. B.M. 39b, Abaye ruled on estate of captives. 7. b. B.M. 42a, Rava ruled on bailment. 8. b. B.M. 42a-b, Rava ruled on bailment. 9. b. B.M. 49a, Rava ruled in case of futures. 10. b. B.M. 49b, Rava ruled in case of bailment. 11. b. B.M. 51a, Rava ruled on fraud through renunciation of sale. 12. b. B.M. 67a, Rabbah b. R. Huna ruled on land purchase.

* Duplicate. Not counted.

XIV. *b. Bava' Mezi'a'*

	Ca. 310-330 [Rabbah, R. Joseph]	Ca. 330-350 [Rava, Abaye]
		13. b. B.M. 68a, Rava ruled on bond in which interest seemed stipulated. 14. b B.M. 69a, Abaye ruled on division of herd. 15. b. B.M. 72a, Abaye ruled on disposition of pledged field. 16. b. B.M. 81b, Rava ruled on liability for lost cloak. 17. b. B.M. 83a, Rava ruled on liability for broken wine barrel. 18. b. B.M. 83a, Rava ruled on liability for sour wine. 19. b. B.M. 96b, Rava ruled on liability for broken ax. 20. b. B.M. 97a, Rava ruled on liability for ass. 21. b. B.M. 104b, Rava ruled on contract dispute. 22. b. B.M. 106b, Rava ruled on dispute over lease. 23. b. B.M. 109b, R. Papa b. Samuel ruled on whether tenant farmer may receive value of improvements. 24. b. B.M. 109b, Rava ruled on litigation over pledge. 25. b. B.M. 116a, Abaye ruled on disposition of pledge. 26. b. B.M. 116a, Rava ordered orphans to return borrowed implements.
Questions from Outside of the Academy		

XIV. *b. Bava' Mezi'a'*

	Ca. 310-330 [Rabbah, R. Joseph]	Ca. 330-350 [Rava, Abaye]
Stories and Sayings about Enforcement of, or Obedience to, Law Outside of the Academy		

XV. *b. Bava' Batra'*

	Ca. 310-330 [Rabbah, R. Joseph]	Ca. 330-350 [Rava, Abaye]
Court Cases	1. b. B.B. 8a, Rabbah levied charity tax on orphans. 2. b. B.B. 12b, Rabbah ruled on division of estate. 3. b. B.B. 31a, Rabbah ruled *re ḥazaqah*. 4. b. B.B. 32a-b, Rabbah ruled on forged deed of sale. 5. b. B.B. 32b, Rabbah ruled on forged deed of sale. 6. b. B.B. 68a, R. Joseph ruled on disputed sale. 7. b. B.B. 96b, R. Joseph decided case *re* sour beer. 8. b. B.B. 135a, R. Joseph ruled on need of *ḥaliẓah*. 9. b. B.B. 143a, R. Joseph ruled on disposition of estate.	1. b. B.B. 9a, Rava ruled on contract of butchers. 2. b. B.B. 13b, Rava ruled on division of estate. 3. b. B.B. 24a, Rava permitted use of wine discovered between tree trunks. 4. b. B.B. 29b, Rava ruled on title to female slave. 5. b. B.B. 30a, Rava ruled *re ḥazaqah*. 6. b. B.B. 30a-b, Rava ruled *re ḥazaqah*. 7. b. B.B. 30b, Rava ruled *re ḥazaqah*. 8. b. B.B. 30b, Rava ruled *re ḥazaqah*. 9. b. B.B. 30b, Rava ruled *re ḥazaqah*. 10. b. B.B. 32b, R. Idi b. Abin ruled *re* bond of indebtedness. 11. b. B.B. 33a, Abaye ruled *re* trusteeship of orphans' estate. 12. b B.B. 33b, Abaye's disciples ruled *re ḥazaqah*. 13. b. B.B. 40b, Rava ruled *re ḥazaqah*. 14. b. B.B. 106b, Abaye judged case of misrepresentation of real estate for sale.

XV. *b. Bava> Batra>*

	Ca. 310-330 [*Rabbah, R. Joseph*]	*Ca. 330-350* [*Rava, Abaye*]
		15. b. B.B. 126a-b, Rava ruled on disposition of estate.
		*[16. b. B.B. 130b, Rava instructed R. Papa and R. Huna b. R. Joshua not to tear up his decisions, nor to infer after death laws from them.]
		17. b. B.B. 133b, R. 'Ilish before Rava ruled on division of estate.
		18. b. B.B. 135a, Rava ruled on alleged divorce of wife of dying man (*re ḥaliẓah.*)
		19. b. B.B. 143b, Abaye ruled on language of will.
		20. b. B.B. 153a, Rava ruled on deed of gift.
		21. b. B.B. 155b, Rava ruled on disposition by minor of estate.
		22. b. B.B. 155b, Rava ruled on disposition by minor of estate.
		23. b. B.B. 167a, Abaye ruled on forged deed.
		24. b. B.B. 167a, Abaye ruled on forged deed.
		25. b. B.B. 167a, Rava ruled on forged deed.
		26. b. B.B. 167b, Abaye ruled on forged receipt.
		27. b. B.B. 168a, Abaye ruled on forged receipt.
		28. b. B.B. 168b, Abaye ruled on making duplicate deeds.
		29. b. B.B. 174a, R. Ḥanin removed creditor from property of debtor.

* Court procedure.

XV. *b. Bava² Batra²*

	Ca. 310-330 [Rabbah, R. Joseph]	Ca. 330-350 [Rava, Abaye]
Questions from Outside of the Academy		
Stories and Sayings about Enforcement of, or Obedience to, Law Outside of the Academy		

XVI. *b. Sanhedrin*

	Ca. 310-330 [Rabbah, R. Joseph]	Ca. 330-350 [Rava, Abaye]
Court Cases	*[1. b. Sanh. 5a, R. Joseph told Mar Zutra b. R. Naḥman what to do when he erred in a case.] 2. b. Sanh. 28b, R. Joseph ruled on deed of gift.	*[1. b. Sanh. 25a, Rava ruled on eligibility to give testimony.] 2. b. Sanh. 26b, R. Papa b. Samuel ruled on deed of gift witnessed by robbers. 3. b. Sanh. 27a, R. Aḥa b. Jacob tried murder case. 4. b. Sanh. 29b, Abaye and Rava ruled on deed of debt acknowledgement. **[5. b. Sanh. 74a, Rava told man not to kill.] 6. b. Sanh. 100a, Rava judged suspected *trefa*.
Questions from Outside of the Academy		
Stories and Sayings about Enforcement of, or Obedience to, Law Outside of the Academy		

* Not counted. Court procedure.
** Not counted. Inconclusive.

XVII. b. ʿAvodah Zarah

	Ca. 310-330 [Rabbah, R. Joseph]	Ca. 330-350 [Rava, Abaye]
Court Cases	1. b. A.Z. 39a, R. Joseph was asked to rule on possible fraud. 2. b. A.Z. 49a, R. Joseph ruled on use of manure from. idolatrous source. 3. b. A.Z. 72a, R. Joseph ruled on disputed land sale.	1. b. A.Z. 22a, Rava ruled on partnership of Jewish and Gentile farmer. 2. b. A.Z. 22a, Rava permitted partnership of Jewish and Gentile farmer. 3. b. A.Z. 40a, Rava prohibited purchase of fish. 4. b. A.Z. 57b, Rava ruled on ritual fitness of wine. 5. b. A.Z. 61b, Rava ruled on ritual fitness of wine. 6. b. A.Z. 61b, Rava ruled on ritual fitness of wine. 7. b. A.Z. 65b, Rava permitted wheat into which unfit wine had fallen to be sold to Gentiles. 8. b. A.Z. 70a, Rava ruled on fitness of wine. 9. b. A.Z. 70a, Rava ruled on fitness of wine. 10. b. A.Z. 70a, Rava ruled on fitness of wine. 11. b. A.Z. 70a, Rava ruled on fitness of wine. 12. b. A.Z. 70a, Rava ruled on fitness of wine. 13. b. A.Z. 70a, Rava ruled on fitness of wine. 14. b. A.Z. 70a, Rava ruled on fitness of wine. 15. b. A.Z. 70a, Rava ruled on fitness of wine. 16. b. A.Z. 70b, Rava ruled on fitness of wine. 17. b. A.Z. 72b, Rava ruled on fitness of wine.
Questions from Outside of the Academy		

XVII. *b. ʿAvodah Zarah*

	Ca. 310-330 [Rabbah, R. Joseph]	Ca. 330-350 [Rava, Abaye]
Stories and Sayings about Enforcement of, or Obedience to, Law Outside of the Academy		

XVIII. *b. Horayot, Shevuʿot, Makkot* [= H., Sh., M.]

	Ca. 310-330 [Rabbah, R. Joseph]	Ca. 330-350 [Rava, Abaye]
Court Cases		1. b. Sh. 41b, Abaye ruled in case of debt repayment. 2. b. Sh. 42a, Rava ruled in case of debt repayment. 3. b. Sh. 42a, Abaye and Rava ruled in case of debt repayment. [4. b. Sh. 46b, Rava ruled orphans must return objects borrowed by father.] 5. b. Sh. 48b, Rami b. Ḥama ruled in debt collection.
Questions from Outside of the Academy		
Stories and Sayings about Enforcement of, or Obedience to, Law Outside of the Academy		

XIX. b. Zevaḥim, Menaḥot, Ḥullin

	Ca. 310-330 [Rabbah, R. Joseph]	Ca. 330-350 [Rava, Aabaye]
Court Cases		
Questions from Outside of the Academy		
Stories and Sayings about Enforcement of, or Obedience to, Law Outside of the Academy	1. b. Ḥul. 39b, Inquiry to R. Joseph on deal with Arabs to share animal. 2. b. Ḥul. 43b, Case to Rabbah about bird that may have been clawed.	*[1. b. Zev. 116b, Rava ordered offering of sacrifice of Ifra Hormiz.] **[2. b. Men. 40a-b, Rava said we rely on public notices to inform people of the dates of Passover and the Day of Atonement.] 3. b. Ḥul. 31a, Rava examined arrow for R. Jonah b. Taḥalifa. 4. b. Ḥul. 43b, Rava ruled on improperly slaughtered ox. 5. b. Ḥul. 44b, Rava declared animal permitted and bought the meat. 6. b. Ḥul. 49b, Rava ruled on case of perforation. 7. b. Ḥul. 49b, Rava ruled on uncovered pot of honey. 8. b. Ḥul. 50a, Rava ruled on perforated intestines. 9. b. Ḥul. 57a, Rava ruled on birds with broken legs. 10. b. Ḥul. 77a, Abaye ruled on animal with broken leg. 11. b. Ḥul. 112a, R. Ḥinena b. Rava of Pashrunia permitted pigeon which fell into milk. 12. b. Ḥul. 133a, Abaye used to receive priestly dues.

XIX. *b. Zevaḥim, Menaḥot, Ḥullin*

	Ca. 310-330 [*Rabbah, R. Joseph*]	Ca. 330-350 [*Rava, Abaye*]
		13. b. Ḥul. 133a, Rava used to receive priestly dues. 14. b. Ḥul. 141b, Rava was asked about trapping a certain bird.

* Inconclusive and irrelevant.   ** Not counted. General rule, not a case.

XX. *b. Bekhorot, ʿArakhin, Temurah, Keritot, Meʿilah, Tamid*

	Ca. 310-330 [*Rabbah, R. Joseph*]	Ca. 330-350 [*Rava, Abaye*]
Court Cases		1. b. Bekh. 36a, Rava ruled in case of hired ass.
Questions from Outside of the Academy		
Stories and Sayings about Enforcement of, or Obedience to, Law Outside of the Academy	1. b. Bekh. 27a, Rabbah ate heave-offering.	1. b. Bekh. 3b, Rava told woman proselyte about partnership in animal with heathen.

XXI. *b. Niddah*

	Ca. 310-330 [*Rabbah, R. Joseph*]	Ca. 330-350 [*Rava, Abaye*]
Court Cases		
Questions from Outside of the Academy		*[1. b. Nid. 20b, Ifra Hormiz to Rava *re* meaning of blood.]
Stories and Sayings about Enforcement of, or Obedience to, Law Outside of the Academy	**[1. b. Nid. 66a, R. Zera said Israelite women were strict about menstrual taboos.] 2. b. Nid. 32a, R. Joseph said infant was to be immersed to protect heave-offering from uncleanness. 3. b. Nid. 67b, Rabbah permitted immersion on eighth day.	

* Inconclusive and irrelevant. Not counted.   ** General rule, not a case.

XXII. *Summary*

	Ca. 310-330	Ca. 330-350	Total	Approximate Percentage of Total
Civil Law (including commercial and real estate, settlement of estates, gifts to charity, maintenance of widows and orphans, collection of debts, marriage contracts, damages and liabilities).	26	90	116	51.1%
Personal Status (including marriage, divorce, *ḥaliẓah*, etc., excommunication for moving from place to place, adultery).	13	22	35	15.0%
Food and Sex Taboos (including slaughter and ritual fitness of wine).	3	28	31	13.7%
Fasts, Holidays, Sabbath.	3	13	16	7.1%
Sabbath Limits.	1	5	6	2.6%
Synagogue Liturgy (including blessings).	2	4	6	2.6%
Punishment of Common People for Disrespect to Scholars; Suppression of Rumors.	2	2	4	1.7%
Mourning.	—	1	1	0.4%
Vows.	1	1	2	0.8%
Agricultural Rules.	3	3	6	2.6%
Capital Crimes.	—	2	2	0.8%
Total	54	171	225	98.4%

XXIII. *Comparisons*

	Ca. 220-265		Ca. 265-310		Ca. 310-350	
	Number	Per Centage	Number	Per Centage	Number	Per Centage
Civil Law (including commercial and real estate, settlement of estates, gifts to charity, maintenance of widows and orphans, collection of debts, marriage contracts, damages and liabilities).	23	33.8%	85	52.1%	116	51.1%
Personal Status (including marriage, divorce, *ḥaliẓah*, etc., excommunication for moving from place to place, adultery).	16	23.5%	24	14.1%	35	15.0%
Food and Sex Taboos (including slaughter and ritual fitness of wine).	15	22.0%	21	12.9%	31	13.7%
Fasts, Holidays, Sabbath.	10	14.7%	19	11.6%	16	7.1%
[Sabbath Limits.	7	—	7]	—	6	2.6%
Synagogue Liturgy and Blessings	3	4%	2	1.2%	6	2.6%
Punishment for Disrespect to Scholars.	—	—	2	1.2%	4	1.7%
Vows and Dedications.	—	—	7	4.2%	2	0.8%
Agricultural Rules.	1	1%	3	1.8%	6	2.6%
Capital Crimes.	—	—	—	—	2	0.8%
Total by periods	68	99.0%	163	99.1%	224	98.0%

The table of comparisons (XXIII) shows general consistencies between the periods ca. 220-310 and 310-350 both in the absolute number of case reports, and in the proportions of cases pertaining to various categories of law. Approximately 60% of all instances pertained to matters of civil law and personal status; approximately 15% to food and sex taboos; approximately 20% to Sabbath and festival observances, of which approximately half involved the 'eruv. The scattering of cases and other exemplifications of law-enforcement among other categories of law proved consistently inconsequential. It is difficult to see any striking increase in the number of stories. The preservation of these accounts was certainly the result of literary and academic, not historical or sociological factors. (Almost all cases in third and fourth-century strata derive from, or were attributed to, the courts conducted by heads of schools, Samuel, Rav, Rav Judah, R. Naḥman, R. Huna, R. Ḥisda, Rabbah, R. Joseph, Abaye, and Rava.) Had there been noteworthy increases in the number of cases from one period to the next—as indeed there seems to be from 220-265 to 265-310, and from 310-330 to 330-350— one still could not persuasively argue that such an increase by itself proves there was an increment in the rabbis' influence or power over Jewry. The phenomenon remains at best suggestive, but hardly probative.

It is nonetheless clear that almost all instances of law enforcement derived from the rabbis' narrow judicial and administrative role in the Jewish community or from their supervisory functions in the marketplace. In addition to court adjudication of civil law and determinations of personal status, most, though not all, decisions on religious taboos (food, Sabbath law, menstrual separation) were made possible by the rabbis' communal position. Of the thirty-one instances of the enforcement of food-taboos listed on Table XXII, approximately twenty-six related to ritually-contaminated wine or the slaughter of animals, both being aspects of market-supervision. Of the twenty-two exempla of enforcement of Sabbath and festival law, six in this period, and a much greater proportion earlier, pertained to the Sabbath limits. On the other hand, a number of cases, sayings, and stories, either not counted here at all, or counted as merely a single exemplification of law enforcement, permit the inference of fairly widespread popular observance of certain laws, all of biblical, not rabbinic, origin. It is hardly necessary to recapitulate our earlier conclusions.[1] As I said, whatever rabbinical law-enforcement actually took place generally depended upon the rabbis' position in the Jewish government headed by the exilarch and recognized and legitimated by the Iranian government.

---

[1] Vol. III, pp. 334-336.

CHAPTER FIVE

THE LIFE OF THE SCHOOLS

I. INTRODUCTION. THE RABBI AND THE IMAGE OF GOD

The rabbis' traditions represent the rabbis as that group in Babylonian Jewry which decided what was normative in all social and cultural affairs. The results of our inquiry into the effective influence and power of the rabbinate suggest, to the contrary, that the rabbis formed an important, but not dominant element. They may have constituted the sole well-organized creative force in cultural life, and they did try to control Babylonian Jewry. They succeeded in taking over the courts and in using them for their own purposes. But they did not wield the only effective power, whether political or cultural, within the Jewish community. The exilarchate held most political power, which it parcelled out to the rabbis for specific purposes. The masses of the people, inchoate and inert, could not easily be moved, and in some crucial ways certainly did not conform to the rabbis' demands. The schools were far from coextensive with Babylonian Jewry, let alone with the Jewries of the other Sasanian satrapies. Because of the nature of our sources, however, the two themes upon which Babylonian Jewish history centers are, first, the relationship between the rabbis and the ordinary people, and second, the configuration of the rabbi as a religious figure, of the schools as a cultural phenomenon, and of the rabbinical movement as a historical force.

Had later history worked out otherwise, we might have a wholly different picture of Babylonian Jewry. To take two hypothetical cases: If in post-Sasanian times, the exilarchate had vanquished the rabbinate in its struggle for the control of Babylonian Jewry, the exilarch and not the rabbis would have shaped the consequent legal and theological literature. That literature would surely not have consisted of a great commentary upon the Mishnah, but, one may guess, of a collection of legal rules and precedents as preserved in the exilarchic court archives, and stories about various exilarchs.[1] In a word, it would have been not

---

[1] The contrast between Babylonian stories about the exilarch in relationship to the Parthians and Sasanians, and Palestinian ones about the Patriarch and the Romans, is noteworthy. Since the exilarch lost control of the transmission of legal

a Gemara, but a Mishnah, the Mishnah of the legal head of Judaism in the Sasanian territories, or Babylonian satrapy at any rate, just as the preserved Palestinian Mishnah is that of the legal head of Judaism in the Roman territories. When the influence of Babylonian Jewry began to be felt in other parts of the world, for reasons largely irrelevant to the rightness or wrongness of anyone's theology or law, the exilarch would have loomed not only as the dominant figure in earlier times, but more important, as the single most significant source of right doctrine and law in the present age. It is possible that the great theme of Judaism might not have been "the Torah" and how to effect its laws in everyday life, but rather, the Messiah, and how to extend his power through the rule of his earthly surrogate, the heir of David and holder of the sceptre of Judah (Gen. 49:10). The exilarchic view of Jewish history might have preserved an account of a useful but dangerous group of heretics and fanatics, known in olden times for their abilities to work wonders and for their loyalty to a law-code now forgotten, superseded, or ignored, the Palestinian Mishnah. In writing the story of "normative Judaism" of "Mar 'Uqba's age"—and no longer,

---

and other traditions, he was unable to secure the inclusion of accounts of his dealings, successful or otherwise, with Iranian governments. Therefore all we have are the rabbis' traditions about *their* dealings with the Persians, Samuel and Shapur, R. Ḥama and Shapur II, and so forth. I earlier supposed that Samuel had in fact represented the exilarch before the Persian government, and hence to him was attributed the saying that "the law of the kingdom is law." However, it is equally plausible to suppose that later tradents deliberately excluded the participation of Mar'Uqba I or some other exilarch of the day in those dealings. Similarly, the Jewish representative to Ardavan V was supposedly Rav, and not Huna I, about whom we know a bit more than other exilarchs. In Palestine, by contrast, we have a rich corpus of "Rabbi Judah and Antoninus" stories, revealing the patriarch in a quite honorable and influential position at the Roman "court." Since the patriarch had considerable control over the formation of Palestinian traditions, he was able to provide for himself a far more favorable press than the exilarch received. We may conclude that had the exilarch preserved his power over the schools in the decisive centuries in which the Babylonian Talmud was formed, he would have been able to include stories similar to those told in Palestine about his counterpart. The fact that such stories were not included does not prove that the exilarch was a mere figurehead, only that he failed to retain control of those who later on decided who earlier had counted, and who had not. So literary and political factors help us understand why the patriarch appears as a pious, learned, noble figure, while the exilarch was "not a religious figure at all", or was "a mere tool of the Persians," or was "not pious," etc. Modern historians generally swallow these characterizations without bothering to chew on them. But the contrast between the patriarch and the exilarch is a striking instance of how different history would seem to us if we had either some additional Jewish data, or only data from other than rabbinical circles. Hence the mental experiment here attempted.

"Talmudic times"—the historian would pay approximately as much attention to the rabbinate as he now pays to the exilarch. He would stress the rabbinate's submission to the exilarch, who decided all important questions. The result would be an appendix and oblivion. It would carry us far afield to speculate on the consequent shape of Judaism, its theology, law, and history, which would have resulted from exilarchic revision and transmission of the sources.

If, to consider a second possibility, neither the exilarchate nor the rabbinate had flourished, if the Sasanians had refused to deal with *any* recognized Jewish authorities whatever, another kind of history might have emerged. It would be the history of a mass of Jews, living according to ancient customs and traditions, without particular impact upon Judaism in other times or other parts of the world. Like the Jews of Afghanistan, Bokhara, or Samarkand, Babylonian Jewry would have represented an ethnological curiosity. Its customs would have been interesting, along with its magic, astrological beliefs, sorcery, and laws. Its surviving ancient legends would have been written down by anthropologists, but neglected by historians. Such was the historiographical fate of Kurdish (Adiabenian) Jewry, which did survive to this century.[1] Its customs constitute mere relics, not the basis of "the law" for all "good Jews." With neither politics, law, nor theology to attract the attention of later historians, lawyers, and theologians, Babylonian Jewry would similarly have survived, much like its ancestors of Achemenid, Seleucid, and Arsacid times, mostly as a blank page in history, sometimes as the object of rather hesitant speculation. In either case, the rabbis would have been no more clearly remembered than were the preliterary prophets of ancient Israel. Their deeds might have been recorded, but their doctrines would surely have been forgotten.

In fact, however, the rabbis won out. The literature which issued from their schools became normative for all European Judaism. It has therefore shaped our picture of their times. For this reason we have to stress what other kinds of sources might have taught us, and how they

---

[1] Perhaps Moses Xorenaẓi's account of pre-Christian Armenian history might approximate the historiographical traditions we should have, had the Jews produced such a figure at about the same time. A still more striking comparison would be to the Mandaean writings, "an extraordinary farrago of theology, myth, fairytale, ethical instruction, ritual ordinances, and what purports to be history. There is no unity or consistency, and it is not possible to give a succinct summary of their teaching," so C. H. Dodd, *The Interpretation of the Fourth Gospel* (Cambridge, 1953), p. 115.

might have shaped our picture of historical reality. This we must do especially because the schools provide a strangely impoverished view of history. Heirs of Scriptures which found in historical politics a partial revelation of divine judgment or intentions, the rabbis might have derived chastisement, reasons for hope, and theological information, from worldly happenings. Yet they paid remarkably little attention to contemporary events. Shapur II is barely mentioned, and Julian not at all, in the literature of the schools. The exilarch appears only when he said or did something of interest to the lawyers. The fate of the Jewish people was timeless, never specific or concrete. Even the academic politics involved in selecting the head of an academy was barely recorded, except in terms so veiled that only searching interpretation enables us to guess what may have taken place. Petty day-to-day "events" such as the meeting of one master with another, an occurrence in the school-house, a contretemps in the marketplace—these are reported, but only incidentally. Mishnaic and Biblical exegesis, legal and theological speculation based upon such exegesis, predominated in the literature to the near-exclusion of everything else. What we can say about the schools therefore concerns less what happened in or to them, than the broad, static phenomena they seem to reveal.[1] We can, therefore, barely describe what took place in Abaye's school, who came or went, what was said on a given occasion, and why. But we know a good deal about the opinions held in that school and in others and about the roles the rabbis seem to have played in the larger society of Jewry.

One important body of opinions is preserved in the stories told about various rabbis, especially the wonders of learning and magic ascribed to them. These stories contain clear, incontrovertible, and factual testimony not as to what the rabbis did, but as to what disciples believed, and thought it important to say, about them. This is what matters when we are told that Rabbah was taken up to heaven because the heavenly academicians required his advice, and the rabbis received letters from heaven informing them when to start and when to cease their mourning for Rabbah. I see no value in speculating about naturalistic explanations for such fabulous tales. Even if we could plausibly argue that the storyteller actually was talking about some earthly phenomenon or meant to convey a "rationalistic" idea in folkloristic terms, we should not as

---

[1] While I have made a number of suggestions about the phenomenon of the rabbi as a religious figure, as in Vol. III, pp. 95-194, I hope eventually to treat that topic more comprehensively within the context of the history of Judaism in this period.

historians have gained much. The account is all we have as fact, and no interpretation or philology can add very much to the historical information it contains. The historical question, second, is for us relatively unimportant. We are reasonably sure that the stories are false, and we cannot discover just how they originated. What is both important and reliable is the picture they give of the religious life of the schools.

That picture is strangely unchanging. We have now studied four generations in succession, counting the present ones, of Babylonian masters, those of Rav and Samuel, of Ravs Judah, Huna, Sheshet, and Nahman b. Jacob and finally, of Rabbah and R. Joseph, Abaye and Rava. I find it difficult to think of a type of miracle-story unique to any single generation. I cannot point to a genre of story introduced in a later period and not found earlier, as the summary-tables make clear. The literature exhibits stability not only when legal issues but also when most other kinds of data are presented. (The magical powers characteristic of the Babylonians were usually attributed to the Palestinians as well.) It seems a priori likely that academic ideas and values broadly and generally changed over a period of two hundred years, but no considerable changes are reflected in the preserved material. It therefore seems likely that evidence of changes has been eliminated by the editors, and that our pictures of the life of the schools, drawn from this material, will picture the life of *the editors'* schools, not the original rabbis'.[1] Be that as it may, what we have before us, therefore, is a mass of uniform data about the rabbi, his life, legal and theological traditions. We must now examine the picture of "the rabbi" which emerges from these data.

The Rabbi and the Image of God. What is most striking about the schools is the conception that in them lived holy men, who more accurately than anyone else conformed to the image of God conveyed by divine revelation through the Torah of Moses "our rabbi." The schools were not holy places in the sense that pious people made pilgrimages to them, though they did,[2] or that miracles were supposed to take place there, though many miracle-stories were told in a scholastic setting. The schools were holy because there men became saints. They became saints by learning the lessons and imitating the conduct of the masters. In doing so, they conformed to the heavenly paradigm, the Torah, believed to have been created by God "in his image," revealed at Sinai, and handed on from prophets to sages, to their own teachers. In the

---

[1] See above, pp. 114-119.
[2] On the institution of the *Kallah*, see below, pp. 384-386.

schools, sainthood was achieved through study of Torah and imitation of the master. What sainthood consisted of, how Torah was studied and what were its consequences—these are the issues of our present inquiry.

Obedience to teachings of the rabbis surely led not merely to ethical or moral goodness, but to holiness or sainthood:

> Abaye said, "Whoever carries out the teachings of the sages is called a saint (*qadosh*)."
>
> (b. Yev. 20a)

That disciples were called saints is also seen in the following:

> "Even though he loves the peoples, all his saints are in your hand, and they are cut at thy feet. He shall receive of your words" (Deut. 33:3)....R. Joseph learned, "These [saints] are the students of the Torah who cut their feet going from town to town and country to country to study Torah. 'He shall receive of your words' alludes to their give-and-take in [discussing] the words of the Omnipresent."
>
> (b. B.B. 8a)[1]

So discussion of legal traditions, rather than ascetic disciplines or long periods of fasting and prayer, was the way to holiness.[2] If the masters and disciples obeyed the divine teaching of Moses "our rabbi," as they surely supposed they did, then their society, the school, would replicate on earth the heavenly academy, just as the disciple would incarnate the heavenly model of Moses "our rabbi."[3] We must take

---

[1] Cited above, p. 86.

[2] b. Meg. 16b. R. Joseph held that study of Torah was superior to the saving of human life.

[3] See especially Wayne A. Meeks, *The Prophet King. Moses Traditions and the Johannine Christology* (Leiden, 1967, Supplements to Novum Testamentum XIV), pp. 176-215. Meeks's excellent discussion of "Moses-piety" provides the background for these remarks. See also Moses Hadas and Morton Smith, *Heroes and Gods. Spiritual Biographies in Antiquity* (N.Y., 1965), for an account of the aretalogical literature on the "divine-man," a figure of pagan antiquity contemporary with the rabbis, and both as miracle worker and "living law", analogous to them. In this regard, the numerous insights of Mircea Eliade greatly help us to understand our data, which simply constitute a further illustration of Eliade's analyses.

Of greatest interest is Ludwig Bieler, ΘΕΙΟΣ ANHP, *Das Bild des "göttlichen Menschen" in Spätantike und Frühchristentum* (I, Vienna, 1935, II, Vienna, 1936). In suggesting that the rabbi may be analogous to the *theîos anḗr*, I do not mean to imply that any specific rabbi known to us conformed in all respects to the ideal-type described by Bieler. On the contrary, the characteristic birth-legends, name-magic, personality-traits, and life-style may not be located in stories about any single rabbi. Nonetheless, the rabbis as a group seem to me to exhibit most of the important and relevant characteristics. If we had a richer hagiographical literature produced in the rabbinical schools, we might well have a fuller account

very seriously indeed the facts that the rabbis believed Moses was a rabbi, God donned phylacteries, and the heavenly court studied Torah precisely as did the earthly one. We may see these beliefs as projections of rabbinical values onto heaven, but the rabbis believed that they themselves were "projections" of heavenly "values" onto earth. That

---

of individuals according to the canons and conventions of divine-man literature. The rabbi certainly functioned in the Jewish context much as did the "divine-man" in other settings. On the other hand, when one compares the story of R. Yoḥanan ben Zakkai, as it might have been compiled, he finds many of the expected qualities and characteristics, though not all of them; see my *Life of R. Yoḥanan ben Zakkai* (Leiden, 1962).

See also the excellent discussion of Jesus as divine-man in Rudolf Bultmann, *The History of the Synoptic Tradition*, trans. John Marsh (Oxford, 1963), pp. 209-244, and in the supplementary section, pp. 419-424. I am less persuaded by Bultmann's conclusions, pp. 368-374, than by his analysis, especially in the light of Smith and Hadas, cited earlier.

On rabbinic and Christian miracle-stories, see also Martin Dibelius, *From Tradition to Gospel*, trans. B. L. Woolf (N.Y., 1935), pp. 133-151. Of special interest is Dibelius's discussion of when a "case" is actually a case-story, and when it is merely a narration in *case-form* of a legal doctrine. Dibelius discusses (p. 138) the story of the goat who ate the dough, and consequently died, judged by Rava (b. B.Q. 48a, cited above, p. 248). He says that the story might be true, but correctly points out that it is not told *because* it is true, but "because Rava had to decide this case just the same whether it was true or only possible." But, Dibelius adds, we have many hypothetical examples which have not developed into story-form, and so he concludes that this case was handed down as a happening "and thus probably was originally a happening." On b. Ned. 91b, cited above p. 198, see p. 139. Dibelius comments also on b. Sanh. 65b, Rava made a man and sent him to R. Zera, cited below, p. 358. He points out that it is a strikingly short account, standing without introduction, and very briefly told. He supposes "that an old, vivid report has been artificially shortened and put into the Talmud." On the miracle stories, Dibelius points out that such tales generally sought to prove that God exercises providence; but some were told simply to glorify certain rabbis or holy places. Dibelius says (p. 148) that miracle-working rabbis generally were puissant at praying. While I think he is not entirely wrong, what is more striking, as we shall see, is the intrinsic relationship between great learning, *not* prayer, and magic. He also states, "Miracles are not recorded of the great teachers of the law amongst the rabbis, but of others whose fame in the school is smaller." While he is certainly right of the early Tannaim, he is most certainly wrong concerning the third- and fourth-century Amoraim. See Table XXIII, below, p. 398-9, for a review of the evidence.

A further discussion of the historicity of case reports in ancient legal texts, germane both to the legal material studied above, and to the magical stories under consideration here, is John Crook, *Law and Life of Rome* (Ithaca, 1967), pp. 15-18. Crook points out that while we do not know whether legal situations are real or imaginary, we may circumscribe the range of uncertainty. First, references to specific dates or events are important. Second, even if imaginary, with the use of stock names showing that a case was invented for purposes of discussion, the relevance to practical situations is undeniable. Specific names or situations are more often than not patently real, and these do not differ in character from those discussed under stock names.

is not to suggest that the rabbis thought of themselves as consubstantial with the divinity.[1] They carefully preserved the distinction between the master of Torah and the giver of the Torah.

But they did believe that those whose lives conformed to the image of God, the Torah, participated in God's holiness and also in his power, and this was attested by their ability to create men and resurrect the dead, to control angels and demons, and to perform other spectacular miracles, as we shall see.

II. THE MASTERS IN THE TIME OF SHAPUR II

Talmudic historians have provided rich accounts of the lives and teachings of various rabbis.[2] Our purpose here is simply to allude very briefly to the chief results of their studies. Since the focus of this account vastly differs from that of "Talmudic history," little will be achieved by rehearsals of earlier inquiries or by reopening issues debated by Talmudic historians, on which I find nothing to contribute.

R. Sherira's Traditions: In the *Letter of R. Sherira Gaon*, we find the following information, beginning before the death of R. Ḥisda in 309 [610]:

> And Rabbah and R. Joseph had been in Pumbedita together with Rav Judah [who had died in 299]. Each one said to the other, "You rule", but neither would accept upon himself the mastership as [academic] head...[3] Rabbah [finally] accepted the headship [of the Pumbeditan academy] and ruled twenty-two years, and died in 320 [631]...[4] And in these years, when Rabbah b. Naḥmani was in Pumbedita, Rabbah b. Ḥiyya was teaching Torah in Sura. And after Rabbah b. Naḥmani, R. Joseph ruled in Pumbedita two and a half years, and died in 323 [634]. And after him, Abaye ruled for thirteen years, and died in 338 [649]....[5] And after Abaye, Rava ruled in Maḥoza which was near [or,

---

[1] On the "ancient passion to 'be like God'", see Shalom Spiegel, *The Last Trial. On the Legends and Lore of the Command to Abraham to Offer Isaac as a Sacrifice: The Akedah*, translated by Judah Goldin (N.Y., 1967), pp. 83-4, and p. 83., n. 25.

[2] They have not, however, produced an adequate history of the Babylonian rabbinical academies. See vol. III, p. 213, n. 1, for reference to existing works.

[3] R. Sherira here refers to the passages in b. Hor. and b. Ber., cited above, pp. 91ff, and on the astrological prediction which moved R. Joseph to decline see below, pp. 330ff.

[4] R. Sherira summarizes the story of Rabbah's death, cited above, p. 41f.

[5] R. Sherira here refers to the fund which was kept by the several heads of the Pumbeditan school.

thought of as a single academy with] Pumbedita¹...And the years of Rava's rule were fourteen, and he died in 352 [663]. And in all the years of Rava, there was only one academy, in Pumbedita, and after Rava, they were divided into two schools. R. Naḥman b. Isaac [headed that] in Pumbedita for four years, and he died in 356 [667], and R. Papa, in Nersh, near Sura. He ruled there for twelve years, and died in 376 [687].² And after R. Naḥman b. Isaac there ruled in Pumbedita a number of *geonim* [including] R. Ḥama [who] died in 377 [688]...And after him, R. Zevid ruled in Pumbedita, and he died in 385 [696].³

R. Sherira thus concentrated upon naming the heads of the several schools. It is clear that some sort of reorganization of the schools took place, for there seems to have been an interruption in the succession of the Suran academy between Rabbah b. Ḥiyya and R. Papa's assumption of the headship at Nersh, which was identified with Sura as Maḥoza was with Pumbedita. Moreover the identification of Nersh with Sura and Maḥoza with Pumbedita is unexplained. Why the head of one school was regarded as head of another nearby I cannot say. In any case, the schools known earlier, Nehardea, Sura, Maḥoza, and Pumbedita, along with Nersh, were the only Babylonian schools extensively represented in the traditions in our hands. What others existed and what happened in them we do not know. Moreover, since almost all of the preserved material concerns the heads of these few schools, we know very little about ordinary rabbis or disciples in these schools, except in relationship to the heads as sons or major disciples.

Rabbah b. R. Huna, son of the distinguished head of the Suran academy, was educated by his father and by R. Ḥisda. He taught at Sura, where he was also communal judge. Weiss holds that the Suran academy was then in a period of decline.⁴ Other sons of leading masters of the earlier generation included R. Isaac son of Rav Judah, and the sons of R. Naḥman and R. Naḥman b. R. Ḥisda.⁵

---

¹ See I. Y. Halevy, *Dorot Harishonim* II, p. 248a=495. Halevy says that the Pumbeditan and Maḥozan schools were thought of as a single academy. He discusses this passage at some length, and holds that only after the death of Rava were the schools divided and under separate masters. See also Z. Yavetz, *Sefer Toledot Yisrael* VIII, pp. 69-70.

² I suppose that his independent rule of Nersh began, therefore, in 364.

³ *'Iggeret R. Sherira Gaon*, ed. B. M. Lewin, Sephardic tradition, pp. 84-90. I found no significant variations in the French tradition.

⁴ On Rabbah b. R. Huna, see Yavetz, *op. cit.* VIII, pp. 2-4; J. H. Weiss, *Dor Dor veDorshav* (Vilna, 1904), pp. 172-173; A. Hyman, *Sefer Toldot Tannaim veAmoraim* (London, 1910), III, pp. 1071-1074; Graetz, *op. cit.*, II, pp. 583-584. On Rabbah in Palestine, see Funk, *op. cit.*, II, p. 97.

⁵ Yavetz, *op. cit.*, p. 4. Hyman, *op. cit.*, on R. Isaac b. Rav Judah, II, pp. 792-793, on R. Naḥman b. R. Ḥisda, III, p. 941.

Rabbah b. Nahmani, a priest, studied at Sura with R. Huna. He and his colleague, *R. Joseph b. Hiyya*, studied with R. Nahman, Rav Judah, and R. Sheshet as well. Yavetz holds that R. Joseph's chief master was Rav Judah, and Rabbah's, R. Huna. Rabbah allegedly went to Palestine and studied with R. Yohanan, though only for a short time. We have already discussed the succession of Rav Judah at Pumbedita, and noted that Rabbah did succeed almost immediately upon Rav Judah's death, and held the post until his death in 320. Until R. Hisda's death in 309, Rabbah subjected himself and Pumbedita's school to the higher authority of Sura. Afterward, however, Pumbedita "took precedence," Yavetz states. R. Joseph was a wealthy man, with large landholdings. We shall note below his translation of Scriptures. His sons R. Nehemiah and Mar studied with Rava, their father's disciple.[1]

Interchange with Palestinian schools: Two leading students of Rav Judah, Rabbi Abba and Rabbi Zera, settled in Palestine in this period. Like ʿUlla in the time of R. Huna and Rav Judah, others went back and forth between Babylonian and Palestinian schools, and brought with them the traditions of each center to the other. R. Dimi, Rabin, R. Isaac b. R. Joseph, and R. Samuel b. Judah were among this group. (R. Dimi's first trip took place while R. Yohanan was still alive, that is, before 279.) All were born in Babylonia and educated there. They were consequently able to transmit Babylonian traditions to the Palestinian schools, as well as the converse. Their influence in Babylonian studies was substantial, for they made possible the inclusion of Palestinian Amoraic traditions of the third century in the later Babylonian corpus. Yavetz holds that the phenomenon ceased after the conversion of Constantine.[2]

Abaye and Rava: Abaye, also a priest, was raised by his uncle Rabbah b. Nahmani, and regarded Rabbah's wife as his mother. He cited many of her medical traditions. His studies were mainly with Rabbah and R. Joseph, although he had some traditions from Rav Judah and other masters of the preceding generation. He became rich later in life, probably because of his appointment as head of the school of Pumbedita. Rava b. R. Joseph b. Hama, by contrast, was born to considerable wealth. His father also was a rabbi. Rava studied with R. Joseph, and

---

[1] Yavetz, *op. cit.*, pp. 4-18; H. Graetz, *op. cit.*, II, pp. 575-583; Weiss, *op. cit.*, pp. 167-172; Funk, *op. cit.*, II, pp. 28-34; Halevy, *op. cit.*, II, pp. 432-447; on Rabbah, Hyman, *op. cit.*, III, pp. 1062-1071, on R. Joseph, II, 742-750.

[2] Yavetz, *op. cit.*, pp. 34-39; Weiss, *op. cit.*, p. 173; Funk, *op. cit.*, pp. 25-27; Halevy, *op. cit.*, II, pp. 455-473. For Rava's complaint about the treatment of Babylonians in the Palestinian schools, b. Men. 52a.

married the daughter of R. Ḥisda. Abaye and Rava also studied with R. Isaac b. 'Avdimi (Eudymos) and Rabbah b. Mari.[1]

Other Contemporaries of Abaye and Rava: We have already mentioned R. Zera, who studied with R. Joseph, migrated to Palestine, and returned in the time of Rava and Abaye. Another returnee was R. Abba b. R. Mattenah. Palestinian-born rabbis who came to Babylonia included R. Ḥezekiah and R. Huna, students of R. Jeremiah, as well as R. Yosi b. Abin, R. Yosi b. Zevida, R. Ḥana, R. Ammi and R. Abba. R. Papa b. Samuel lived in Pumbedita and held court there. Other Babylonians of the period were Rava b. R. Ḥanan who was brought up by Rabbah with Abaye, and later lived in Artabana, near Pumbedita; R. Manasiah b. Taḥalifa; and Rami b. Ḥama. R. Adda b. Abba was Rava's student. R. 'Idi and R. Ḥiyya, sons of R. Abin of Sura studied with R. Ḥisda, and remained in Sura.[2]

R. Naḥman b. Isaac: His father was apparently not of the sages' estate, but his mother was the sister of R. Aḥa. Rabbinic stories of his youth suggest that she was particularly pious and eager to influence him to study in the rabbinical schools. Like Rava, he studied with R. Naḥman b. Jacob. He may have lived for a time in Derokert, but spent much of his life in Pumbedita, whose school he headed from 352 to 356.[3]

A Decline in the Schools? J. H. Weiss and Z. Yavetz both comment upon the obvious phenomenon that, apart from heads of academies, remarkably few rabbis and disciples were mentioned by name or cited very often in the traditions produced in this period. Weiss holds that in the time of Abaye and Rava, because of "Persian persecution" and the "decline of the generations," fewer students came to study, and achieved less than in former times. By contrast, Yavetz says that on account of "the brilliance [of the achievements] of Abaye and Rava,"

---

[1] Yavetz, *op. cit.*, pp. 39-64; Weiss, *op. cit.*, pp. 174-178; Graetz, *op. cit.*, pp. 583-593; Funk, *op. cit.*, on Rava, pp. 66-77; on Abaye, pp. 34-40; Y. L. Maimon, *Abaye ve Rava* (Jerusalem, 1965), in particular, on Abaye's life, pp. 15-22, on Rava's, pp. 236-244; Halevy, *op. cit.*, II, 473-480; Hyman, *op. cit.*, on Rava, III, pp. 1039-1057, Abaye, I, pp. 74-87.

[2] Yavetz, *op. cit.*, pp. 64-70; on R. Adda b. Abba, pp. 77-78; on R. 'Idi and R. Ḥiyya b. Abin, pp. 78-80. See also Hyman, *op. cit.*, R. Zera, I, pp. 386-398; R. Papa b. Samuel, III, 1029; R.' Idi b. Abin, I, 140-141, R. Ḥiyya b. Abin, II, 437-441.

[3] Yavetz, *op. cit.*, pp. 71-77; Weiss, *op. cit.*, pp. 179-180; Graetz, *op. cit.*, p. 593; Funk, *op. cit.*, II, pp. 86-88; Hyman, *op. cit.*, III, 941-945. We shall consider R. Naḥman b. Isaac as head of the school more fully in Vol. V. See especially Y. S. Ẓuri, *The Reign of the Exilarchate and the Legislative Academies* (in Hebrew, Tel Aviv, 1939).

all others of their time paled by comparison. Rabbah and R. Joseph had more students than we know about. Indeed, it seems to me that only those who headed academies were able to leave significant bodies of sayings, so no judgment is possible about either the decline or the extraordinarily splendid accomplishments of the other rabbis of the age.[1]

It is striking that many of the leading rabbis were related to one another or were children of distinguished teachers and heads of schools of the earlier generation. Rabbah b. R. Huna falls into the latter category. Rabbah b. Naḥmani was Abaye's uncle. Rava was married to R. Hisda's daughter, who had previously wed two other rabbis. The chief figures not only studied with the same masters, but knew one another in their childhood. While the rabbinic movement seems to have achieved very wide influence, if the literature is at all representative, its leadership seems to have remained in the circles of a small number of schools, and within these schools, in the hands of relatively few families, often of priestly origin. On the other hand, R. Joseph explained that it was not the rule for sages to raise their sons as sages so that people should not be able to say that the Torah is merely their inheritance.[2] So it may be that the heads of the schools, about whom our information is abundant, more regularly succeeded in raising their sons as masters of rabbinical traditions than did others.

III. THE WAY OF TORAH (I): LEARNING

At the center of the academy activities was the enterprise of learning. The rabbis regarded their studies as the most consequential and sacred element in the life of Israel. Rava said that when a man died and was brought to judgment, he would be asked six questions, as follows: "Did you deal with other people in good faith? Did you set aside times for Torah? Did you beget children? Did you look forward to salvation? Did you engage in the dialectics of wisdom?[3] Did you penetrate into the heart of things?"[4] Of the six 'cardinal rules,' therefore, three involved academic matters. In the rabbinic tradition it thus was as important to study the Torah as it was to contribute to the mainte-

---

[1] On the schools in this period, see Funk, *op. cit.*, II, pp. 22-41; Weiss, *op. cit.*, III, pp. 179-180; Yavetz, *op. cit.*, VIII, 68-69.

[2] b. Ned. 81a.

[3] So H. Freedman for PLPLT BḤKHMH.

[4] b. Shab. 31a.

nance of civilization and to obey the ethical laws about proper conduct in business. We cannot regard these words as mere platitudes. If the rabbis regarded study of Torah as intrinsically important, the reason must be that that study had immediate consequences. As we saw, these consequences included the creation of saints and the formation of a holy community. Why study, and not some other, equally sacred action, was seen as leading to saintliness is clear: the holy man was a replica of the "image of God," as I said, or of Moses "our rabbi," and the community of the saints was an earthly copy of the the academy on high.[1] God and the angels studied Torah. Study, as the memorization, repetition, and discussion of legal and other traditions, was, in effect, a peculiar form of incantation. As repeating the words of an incantation formula, so repeating words of Torah gave a man access to supernatural power and the ability to work wonders on earth. It was therefore important to describe precisely the manner in which one studied Torah, for the ritual actions used in that study, as well as the mastery of the content of Torah, were of no small consequence.

Praise of the act of study was repeated from one generation of masters and disciples to the next. So Rava said in an exegesis of Song 7:12:

"What is the meaning of the Scripture (Song 7:12f.), 'Come, my beloved, let us lodge in the villages, let us get up early to the vineyards, let us see whether the vine has budded, whether the vineblossom is opened, and the pomegranates are in flower. There will I give you my love.' 'Come my beloved'—The congregation of Israel says before the Holy One, blessed be he, 'Lord of the World, Do not judge me like those that dwell in cities, who are masters of thieving, lewdness, vain and lying oaths.' 'Let us go to the field'—'Come and I shall show you the disciples of the sages who occupy themselves in the Torah in the midst of poverty.' 'Let us lodge in the villages'—Read not 'villages' (KFRYM) but infidels (KWFRYM). Come and I shall show them to you. You bestowed upon them goodness, and they denied you. 'Let us get up early to the vineyard'—These are the synagogues and schools. 'Let us see whether the vine has budded'—These are the masters of Scripture. 'Whether the vine-blossom is opened'—These are the masters of *Mishnah*. 'Whether the pomegranates are in flower'—These are the

---

[1] Yet I see here a certain circularity. Study because Moses was "our rabbi," and we must be like him. Yet that begs the question. What made the rabbis suppose that what was important about Moses was his mastery of Torah? The greater likelihood is that the myth of Moses "our rabbi" came into being to explain the everyday certainty of rabbis that Moses had to be like them. In other words, the myth came to explain, or account for, the highly ritualistic behavior of the rabbis themselves. See below, p. 309, n. 2, for further comment.

masters of *gemara*. 'There will I give you my love'—I shall show you my glory and my greatness, the praise of my sons and daughters."

(b. 'Eruv. 21b)

Further exegeses in praise of Torah as Israel's chief ornament included the following:

Rava said [with reference to Song 8:10], "'I am a wall' refers to the congregation of Israel. 'My breasts are like towers' refers to synagogues and houses of study."

(b. B.B. 8a)

Referring to Qoh. 10:9, "Who quarries stones shall be hurt therewith, and who cuts wood is warmed thereby"], Rava said, "'He who quarries stones....' refers to masters of Mishnah, and 'he who cuts wood...' refers to masters of *gemara*."

(b. B.B. 145b)

This was therefore the rabbis' vision of the true Israel, a community wholly devoted to study of Torah, embodying and exemplifying its lessons. It was, indeed, study which separated Israel from the nations and constituted its chief glory.

The sages thought that study weakened a man and diminished his strength. Rava said that by "the sick," rabbis are meant.[1] Many disciples, moreover, spent long periods of time away from their wives and children, suffered poverty and even starvation in order to continue their learning. Rabbah's and Rava's exegesis recognized these facts:

'And black as a raven' (Song 5:11)—Rabbah explained [the Scripture to refer to] "him who for their sake [for Torah] blackens his face like a raven [suffers hunger for the sake of learning]." Rava explained it to refer "to him who can be as cruel to his children and family as a raven [by abandoning them for the academy]."

(b. 'Eruv. 22a)

The following stories present contrasting viewpoints. On the one hand, a rabbi who neglected to come home once a year and so caused his wife to weep was therefore miraculously killed as punishment for her tears. On the other, Rava implacably refused to permit his son to return home after a three-year absence, bitterly saying that he returned for an improper motive and should continue to devote himself wholly to the school:

R. Reḥumi frequented the school of Rava in Maḥoza. He used to come home annually on the eve of the Day of Atonement. Once his

---

[1] b. Ned. 59b.

tradition engrossed him. His wife waited expectantly, "He is coming soon, he is coming soon." He did not come. Her heart was broken and she began to weep. He was then sitting on a roof, which collapsed under him so he was killed.

(b. Ket. 62b)

R. Joseph son of Rava was sent by his father to school before R. Joseph. He arranged for him to study six years. When three had passed, he came home at the eve of the Day of Atonement, saying "I shall go and see the people of my house." His father heard, took a weapon and went out to meet him, saying "You have remembered your whore!" ... They were so perturbed that neither ate a meal before the fast.

(b. Ket. 63a)

Since students were thus supposed regularly to stay away for extensive periods of time,[1] the school took the place of home and family, constituting a new locus of existence, and providing a new father and a new bride, the master and the Torah, respectively. So becoming disciples radically transformed the students' way of living. They were expected not merely to acquire knowledge, but rather to devote their whole being to a singular mode of life. The school therefore represented a new society superimposed upon the conventional one, requiring total devotion even at the most extreme sacrifice. Since Jewish tradition had characteristically affirmed sexual and family life, it was hardly possible for the rabbinical schools to demand celibacy. Expecting the student to separate himself from wife and family for most of the year, however, came to much the same thing. So long as he returned home to procreate from time to time, it was sufficient. Otherwise, his life was lived in a world quite separate from that of women and ordinary folk. Through such separation, the rabbinical movement effectively created a new personality, not merely a learned man.

The rabbinical traditions preserved many sayings about how one should go about his studies, how to memorize rapidly and retain what was learned, and how to concentrate closely, as in the following:

R. Naḥman b. Isaac said, "Legal study requires as much clarity as a north wind day." Abaye said, "If my mother told me, 'Bring me the kutḥa', I would not have been able to repeat [Tannaitic traditions]." Rava said, "If a louse bit me, I could not repeat."

(b. 'Eruv. 65a)

---

[1] R. Reḥumi's sin was merely his failure to return for a single, annual visit. He was not punished for being away the whole year, only for failing to return home once during it.

Abaye said, "...a disciple should not begin his session in the evening of the thirteenth breaking into the fourteenth [of Nisan] lest his studies draw [absorb] him away and he neglect his religious duty..."

(b. Pes. 4a)

R. Naḥman b. Isaac said that because he learned little by little, he was able to retain his learning.

(b. 'Eruv. 54b)

Rava said, "One can only study that part [of Torah] which is his heart's desire....Let one by all means learn even though he may forget or does not fully understand all the words which he studies..."

(b. A.Z. 19a)

Rava said, "A man should always learn Torah and then meditate on it."

(b. Ber. 63b)

That is to say, a person should first listen to the teacher, and then discuss what he has taught. Rava said that one should appoint fixed times for the study of the Torah (as an exposition of Prov. 7:4). He also observed that the Torah will not be found with the proud, and therefore warned against taking pride or showing expansive self-esteem on account of knowledge of Torah.[1] Rava derived from Ps. 21:3 that one should study out loud.[2] So the techniques of study of Torah were highly developed. One had to concentrate upon repeating traditions, and the slightest interruption would prevent it. The disciple's powers of concentration were such that he might even forget to do other religious duties, just as R. Reḥumi had forgotten about his wife at home. It was best to repeat one's tradition out loud, to learn little by little, and to choose materials one found interesting. But what was most important was *that* one study, and whatever he actually learned was of secondary interest. Thus Rava said one did not have to understand everything he memorized. Rabbis nonetheless made great efforts to understand and retain what they had learned. R. Joseph fasted forty times to ensure that "the Torah" should stay with him.[3] When R. Joseph fell ill and forgot his traditions, Abaye his disciple restored them to him.[4] Why fasting should have been thought to be mnemonically significant I cannot say, since it was a ritual, rather than an intellectual, action.[5] R. Joseph may have felt that he would receive heavenly

---

[1] b. 'Eruv. 54b, 55a.

[2] b. 'Eruv. 54a.

[3] b. B.M. 85a.

[4] b. Ned. 41a. For an example, see b. Nid. 39a.

[5] We shall see, below p. 359, how Abaye made use of magic to increase his mastery of Torah.

assistance in retaining his learning if he were by fasting to show himself sufficiently pious.

It is reasonable to suppose that where the rabbinical schools were located, the resident masters possibly supervised local primary education as well. Abaye and Rava discussed the training of children before they came to the advanced schools:

> Abaye said, "Mother told me, 'At six to Scripture, and ten to Mishnah, and thirteen to a full fast, and for girls, at twelve...'"
>
> (b. Ket. 50a)

> Rava [discussing the ordinance for universal education ascribed to Joshua b. Gamala] said that each teacher was to have twenty-five students; if there are fifty, then two teachers are to be appointed; if forty, then an assistant is appointed at communal expense. He also recommended that if one has a choice between two teachers, one of whom moves quickly but makes mistakes, and the other of whom moves slowly but without mistakes, one appoints the faster one, for mistakes correct themselves in time.
>
> (b. B.B. 21a)

Doubtless sensible advice such as this would have guided educational practices wherever rabbinical influence was effective.

IV. THE WAY OF TORAH (II): CONDUCT

The rabbis held that study of the Torah must lead to a reformation of the disciple's entire way of living. Ordinary folk should be able readily to recognize that a man was a disciple. Deportment testified to the status of a disciple at least as authoritatively as his ability to quote rabbinic traditions. As a group, the rabbis and disciples constituted an estate[1] within the Jewish community, enjoying special privileges and bearing special responsibilities. Entry into that estate was attained not through birth, although some rabbis were the children of masters of the early generations. It was not reached through social or economic status, for most of the disciples came from the poor classes,[2] and only the heads of schools consistently achieved great wealth. Political preference did not help, for the exilarch could not appoint ordinary people to the rabbinate, but probably had to accept the qualifications first achieved and recognized in the schools. One entered the rabbinical estate not only by learning, but by imitation of the rabbis, resulting in

---

[1] See vol. III, pp. 95-102.
[2] Compare pp. 390-391, below.

the acquisition of clearcut patterns of behavior and personal bearing, which thus became signs of membership. To be a disciple thus represented a highly ritualistic and formal way of living, in which one's manner of speaking, eating, walking, and of greatest consequence, conduct with certain other similarly designated figures, took on religious consequence.[1]

We may discern two reasons for the rabbis' stress upon the significance of rabbinical deportment-rituals, one political and sociological, the other religious. If the ordinary folk were expected to obey the rabbi and copy his patterns of behavior, people must immediately recognize that he was a holy man, not like themselves but obedient to supernatural disciplines. Just as the Christian monks and nuns achieved such a holy status by their exceptional asceticism, often leading to sacred vagrancy, so the rabbis did by their constant repetition of words of Torah, by their extraordinary deference to their masters, as well as by their speech, clothing, way of walking, behavior with women, and the like. An important source of the rabbi's influence over ordinary people thus was the strange and awesome behavior which both set him apart and attested to his singular character and was thought holy. Second, the ritualistic pattern of behavior was meant to conform to the heavenly archetype, as we have noted. If the rabbi was not an ordinary man, his way of living as much as his intellectual resources and his theurgical capacities testified to that fact.

Three kinds of advice are found, given by the rabbis first to ordinary people, second to their own children, and third to their disciples. One cannot, therefore, interpret all sayings indiscriminately as pertaining only to the life of the schools. The rabbis themselves recognized the limits of their effective counsel. Not all of their sayings revealed values and ideals unique to the schools. Advice to children included the following:

> Rava said to his children, "When you are cutting meat, do not cut it upon your hand. Do not sit upon the bed of an Aramaean woman. Do not pass behind a synagogue when the congregation is praying."
>
> (b. Ber. 8b)

Such advice would have been equally useful to disciples or ordinary folk. The following saying of Abaye, on the other hand, was directed toward the common society, and meant to shape ordinary conduct:

---

[1] See vol. III, pp. 102-110, 130-149.

> A pearl in the mouth of Abaye [was], "A man should always be subtle in reverence [quoting Prov. 15:1], and increase peace with his brothers and relatives and with everybody, even with a stranger in the market place, so that he may be beloved above and cherished below and acceptable to everyone."
>
> (b. Ber. 17a)

Abaye thought that if a man pleased people on earth, the heavenly court would be pleased with him as well. Hence if one wanted to do the things which would win heavenly favor, he would be wise to start with man, made in the image of God and therefore a useful source of information about the responses and desires of heaven. By contrast, the third sort of advice pertained most directly to the life of masters and disciples:

> A pearl in the mouth of Rava was, "The purpose of wisdom is repentence and good deeds, that a man should not study [Scripture] and repeat [his Mishnaic learning] and then rebel against his father, mother, master, and someone greater than himself in wisdom and in years, as it is said, (Ps. 111:10), 'The beginning of wisdom is the fear of the Lord, and good understanding have all they that do thereafter.' It does not say, 'that do,' but 'that do *thereafter*', implying that one should do them for their own sake and not for ulterior motives. If one does them for ulterior motives, it would be better for him had he not been created."
>
> (b. Ber. 17a)

The excessive pride engendered by study was a problem for the schools, not primarily for the streets or for family life.

While the rabbis surely wanted the whole community to conform to their values, it was mainly to the schools that they directed their attention. There they tried as best they could—and that was very well indeed—to enforce conformity to the ideals of their movement. They recognized, as in Rava's saying above, that mastery of rabbinic traditions could lead to arrogance and pride, and more broadly, to hypocritical behavior, for learning alone did not qualify a disciple, but only learning joined with "deeds," that is, the total configuration of his daily conduct. So Rava warned:

> 'And this is the law which Moses set [SM] before the children of Israel', (Deut. 4:44) ... Rava said, "If he uses it properly, it is a life-giving drug [SM ḤYYM] to him, but if not, it is a [SM MWT] deadly drug."
>
> (b. Yoma 72b = b. Shab. 88b)

> Rava said [with reference to Ex. 25:11], "Any disciple of the sages whose inside is not like his outside is no disciple of the sages." Abaye ... said, "He is called an abomination..."
>
> (b. Yoma 72b)

Abaye also found occasion to warn against hypocrisy. A way of living which stressed mastery of holy books and performance of ceremonial actions could easily be made a facade behind which various vices could flourish. The content of Torah consisted of more than legal prescriptions about property damages and divorces, for it included a great many rules of moral conduct. The disciples therefore had to be warned repeatedly against failing to live up to the "whole Torah." Part of that warning consisted of threats of the bad consequence of failure. Even more germane to the student's deepest concern, Rava interpreted Ps. 1:3-4 to mean that a student's deeds must be consistent with the Torah, so that his study will be of lasting benefit.[1] Improper behavior could lead to one's forgetting what he had learned, surely a disaster for the disciple. Further:

> Rava said (as an exegesis of Ps. 21:3) that a worthy student is rewarded by being granted without even asking what he desires, but an unworthy student has to ask [in prayer] for what he wanted.
>
> (b. ʿEruv. 54a)

> Rava contrasted these verses, "My doctrine shall drop as the rain" and "My speech shall distil as dew" (Deut. 32:2), [and said], "If a disciple of the sages is worthy, he is like dew, and if not, drop him like rain."
>
> (b. Taʿanit 7a)

So it is clear that Rava and other masters ascribed great importance to proper conduct and motivation.

Discipline within the schools themselves was easily maintained, first of all by the powerful personalities of the masters, second by the coercive influence of the environment, and third, in the case of most recalcitrant disciples, by means of flogging and excommunication, as in the following:

> R. Nathan b. ʾAsyaʾ went from school to Pumbedita on the second day of the Festival of Pentecost. R. Joseph put him under the ban. Abaye said to him, "Why not punish him with flogging?"...
>
> (b. Pes. 52a)

(A second tradition holds that R. Joseph had him flogged, and Abaye asked why he had not banned him instead.) For a disciple excommunication was a serious matter. He was thereby excluded, or ostracized, from all social relationships. Normal life in school was impossible. Ordinary people, such as the butchers of Huẓal,[2] might ignore a rabbi-

---

[1] b. A.Z. 19b.
[2] Vol. III, p. 225.

nic decree of excommunication. One whose life was bound up with the community of the school could not. R Papa said that he should be rewarded because he had never excommunicated a rabbinical disciple.[1] Others made no such claim. If ordinary people failed to honor the teachings of the sages, and these teachings had no reference to court litigations, the rabbis could at best threaten or curse them:

> "And much study is a weariness of flesh" (Qoh. 12.12). R. Papa b. R. Aḥa b. Adda in the name of R. Aḥa b. 'Ulla said, "This teaches that one who ridicules the words of the sages will be condemned to boiling excrement." Rava demurred...
>
> (b. 'Eruv. 21b)

Excommunication of ordinary folk was less effective than in the scholastic community. On the other hand, however unworthy a disciple might be, one should still pay attention to the traditions he has acquired, as Rava said:

> Rava expounded, "What is the meaning of the Scripture, 'I went down to the garden of nuts, to look at the green plants of the valley...' (Song 6:11). Just as the nut, though caked with mud and dirt,—still its contents are not discarded, so a disciple of the sages, though he may have sinned,—still his Torah is not discarded."
>
> (b. Ḥag. 15b)

The traditions were not measured by the personality of the one who repeated them, but had their own integrity.

Rabbinical attitudes toward sex revealed extraordinary stress upon chastity and modesty.[2] The assumption was that under almost any circumstance, any man, unless prevented by powerful self-control, would engage in sexual relations with any woman. It was a primary requirement for rabbinical status, therefore, that a man should avoid even looking at a woman, as Abaye's saying revealed:

> Abaye said that a disciple of the sages is not in the habit of taking note of a woman's appearance. Therefore when he goes to betroth stet a woman, he should take an ordinary person [ignorant—lit. 'am ha'arez] with him so that another [woman] will not be substituted [at marriage] for the one [with whom arrangements had been made].
>
> (b. B.B. 168a)

Abaye also instructed the rabbis that when they go through the streets of Maḥoza to reach the fields, they should not look to either side,

---

[1] b. M.Q. 17a.

[2] See vol. III, pp. 276ff.

lest women may be sitting on the sides of the road, for it is not proper
to gaze at them.[1] The reason for Abaye's warning was that he believed
disciples, being away from their homes, had a much greater desire for
promiscuous sexual relations than ordinary people, as in the following
story:

> Abaye said that the evil inclination acts against disciples of the sages
> most of all. Abaye heard a certain man say to a certain woman, "Let us
> arise and go on the road." He said, "I shall go and keep them away
> from a forbidden [sexual] action." He followed after them three para-
> sangs in a swamp. When they separated from one another, he heard
> them saying, "Our company is pleasant, but the way is long." Abaye
> said, "If it were I [lit.: if it were the one who hates me], I should not
> have been able to restrain myself." He went and leaned against a post
> and was troubled. A certain old man came and taught him, "Whoever
> is greater than his fellow, his desire [impulse, *yiẓro*] is also greater."
>   (b. Suk. 52a)

Abaye had intended to prevent the couple from engaging in sexual
relations, thinking that as soon as they got into the fields, they would
take the opportunity, regardless of the danger of being caught. So he
marveled that they were able to keep away from one another till they
had gone the long distance into the swamp, where they were (they
thought) safe from observation.

Strict rules, moreover, governed sexual relations between a disciple
and his wife. They must take place in darkness and complete privacy,
which could not be taken for granted in the relatively crowded housing
of Babylonia. Rabbah b. R. Huna would even drive away wasps from
his curtained bed, Abaye, flies, and Rabbah, or R. Papa, would chase
away mosquitoes.[2] The reason for the prohibition of sexual relations
in the day-time or in a lighted room was that the demons might be
attracted and cause trouble.[3] What is interesting is that the rabbis taught
their disciples how to avoid demons and made it a specific mark of
rabbinical status that various anti-demonic prophylaxes be taken. We
shall note below that the people of Maḥoza were condemned by the
rabbis for having sexual relations in day-light.[4] From the rabbinical
perspective, they not only behaved lewdly, but also foolishly ignored

---

[1] b. Ber. 62b.

[2] b. Nid. 17a.

[3] The prohibition against sexual relations in the light or in day-time, Trachtenberg says, "goes back to the Talmudic apprehension that the demons who are
driven off by light may also perversely be attracted by it." See Joshua Trachtenberg, *Jewish Magic and Superstition* (Repr. N.Y., 1961), p. 86.

[4] p. 388.

rabbinical counsel on avoiding demons. Some sayings, such as Abaye's, that a woman is made joyful by her husband with fine clothes[1] and Rava's, that a man is required to have intercourse with his wife,[2] were directed at ordinary people, not merely at disciples. On the other hand, carefully avoiding a glance at a woman obviously was expected only of sages, and marked them as such.

Torah was supposed to produce circumspection not only in sexual matters, but in other aspects of conduct as well. It was expected to help a man to overcome his natural impulses to anger, pride, arrogance, bad temper, and cruelty, and to produce excellent self-control, shaping a self-contained person.[3] That is not to suggest that only disciples of sages were supposed to exhibit such qualities. Rava said that a person who was merciful, bashful, and benevolent may be sure that he was of the seed of Abraham the patriarch.[4] To be sure one was of the seed of Abraham meant certainty that the merit of the forefathers would protect one against evil, so it was a significant and practical promise. Everyone should be kindly, modest, and quiet, but it was the disciple, above all, who had better exhibit these qualities.

The disciple should kindly treat younger novices in the school house:

> R. Naḥman b. Isaac said, "Why are words of Torah likened to a tree [Prov. 3:18, 'It is a tree of life']? To teach that just as a small tree may kindle a larger one, so with disciples of the sages, the younger ones sharpen the minds of the older ones."
>
> (b. Ta'anit 7a)

He should also give himself and his learning freely to all men:

> Rava b. R. Joseph b. Ḥama explained (Num. 21:19), 'And from the wilderness...' to mean, "When one makes himself like the wilderness, which is free to all, Torah is presented to him as a gift ... And once he has it as a gift, God gives it to him as an inheritance ... and if so, he ascends to greatness. But if he exalts himself, the Holy One blessed be he casts him down ... And should he repent, the Holy One ... will raise him again..."
>
> (b. Ned. 55a)

Rava warned that a disciple must be careful to respect himself as a master of Torah, but not too much so:

---

[1] b. R.H. 6b, see b. Qid. 34b.
[2] b. Pes. 72b.
[3] On personality-traits of the "divine-man," see Bieler, op. cit., I, pp. 49ff.
[4] Kallah Rabbati 55a, see also b. Yev. 79a, Beẓ. 32b.

> Rava said, "[A disciple] who is haughty deserves excommunication, and if not, he also deserves excommunication…"
>
> (b. Sot. 5a)

Like R. Naḥman, with the same dubious humility, R. Joseph said he himself was humble:

> [Mishnah: When Rabbi (Judah the Prince) died, humility and fear of sin ceased.] R. Joseph told the Tanna, "Do not include the word humility, because there is I."
>
> (b. Sot. 49b)

Bad temper was a disgrace, and signified that a disciple was a sinner. On the other hand, bad temper might be explained away as the result of the 'inflammation' of Torah:

> Rabbah b. R. Huna said, "He who is temperamental, even the Divine Presence is unimportant in his eyes." … R. Naḥman b. Isaac said, "It is certain that his sins outnumber his merits…"
>
> (b. Ned. 22b)

> Rava said, "This disciple of the rabbis is like seeds under a hard clod. Once he sprouts, he soon shoots up. A disciple of the rabbis who rages does so because Torah inflames him, as it is said, 'Is not my word like fire, said the Lord' (Jer. 23:29)."
>
> (b. Taʿanit 4a)

One must not show excessive merriness, Rabbah told Abaye.[1] Above all, the disciple of the sages must refrain from publicly shaming or embarrassing anyone. So David replied to those who tormented him, saying that while he was guilty of a sin [with Bath Sheba] which would put him out of *this* world, those who ridiculed him for it would lose their portion in the world to come:

> Rava expounded, "What is meant by the verse, 'But in my adversity they rejoiced and gathered themselves together … they did tear me and ceased not' (Ps. 35:15). David said before the Holy One, blessed be he, 'Lord of the Universe, It is fully revealed before you that if they had torn my flesh, my blood would not have poured out on the ground [he had blanched white at their insults]. Not only so, but even when they study the laws of leprosy and tents they say to me, 'David, What is the punishment of one who has intercourse with another man's wife,' and I say to them, 'His death is by strangulation and he has a portion in the world to come, but one who shames his fellow in public has no portion in the world to come.'"
>
> (b. B.M. 59a)

---

[1] b. Ber. 30b.

Not only social ethics and personality but also matters of etiquette signified that a man was a disciple of the sages. For example, a disciple must not take advantage of peoples' hospitality, and must drink wine in the proper manner:

> It was taught in a Tannaitic tradition, "Every disciple of the sages who feasts much in every place ... brings an evil name upon himself..." What is that name? Abaye said, "He is called a heater of ovens." Rava said, "A tavern dancer." R. Papa said, "A plate licker."
>
> (b. Pes. 49a)

> Rava said, "Wine and fragrant spices made me wise..."
>
> (b. Yoma 76b)

> Rava said, "A disciple of the rabbis who has not much wine should swallow it in quaffs." Rava used to gulp down the cup of blessing.
>
> (b. Suk. 49b)[1]

A striking example of the rigid, ritualistic etiquette expected of rabbis is provided by the following conversation, which took place between R. Huna b. R. Nathan and R. Naḥman b. Isaac, when the former visited the latter:

> [R. Naḥman b. Isaac] asked him, "What is your name?" He replied, "*Rav* Huna." He said, "Will the master sit upon the couch?" He [forthwith] sat down. They gave him a cup of wine. He took it at the first [invitation] but drank it in two [gulps], and he did not turn his face away. He [R. Naḥman b. Isaac] asked him, "Why did you call yourself *Rav* Huna?" He replied, "Because that is my name." "Why, when you were asked to sit on the couch, did you sit down?" "Because whatever the householder invites one to do, he should do." "And why, when they gave you a cup, did you take it on the first invitation?" He replied, "Because one may show reluctance to an unimportant man, but not to an important one." "Why did you drink it in two gulps"? R. Huna replied, "As it has been taught [in Tannaitic tradition], 'He who drinks his cup in one gulp is a gourmand, in two shows good breeding, in three is arrogant.'" "Why did you not avert your face?" "Because we have learned [in a Tannaitic tradition], 'A bride turns her face away' [but other people do not]."
>
> (b. Pes. 86b)

R. Huna had sufficiently mastered traditions both to act correctly and to explain his actions *according to rabbinic rules*. Hence he was truly a disciple of the sages. The rabbinic movement held many traditions on humble actions such as drinking wine, on titles, or on modes of ad-

---

[1] Note also b. Ber. 35b, Rava's custom of drinking much wine to improve his appetite.

dressing other people. These traditions, as much as general teachings about humility, compassion, and shyness or circumspection, were to be obeyed as signs of a person's mastery of Torah.

The important rabbis, heads of schools and teachers of great reputation, naturally were thought to exemplify the etiquette of Torah, and so their actions in humble situations were carefully observed and reported later on. The rabbis' deeds were no less authoritative than Tannaitic teachings, for it was presumed that a rabbi would know what he was doing in all circumstances, and so could be relied upon. While R. Huna could cite Tannaitic warrant for what he had done, he might as well have said that he had seen such-and-such a master do the same thing so he had adequate precedent for his behavior. We find reports of how the great masters engaged in sex relations,[1] how long they slept and hence thought it proper to sleep by day,[2] how they observed the rites of fasting,[3] and mourning,[4] how they made their market purchases of vegetables and meat,[5] where they kept *tefillin*,[6] how they dealt with fullers,[7] and how they relieved themselves:

> Rava used to go as far as a *mil* to relieve himself in the day-time, but at night he said to his attendant, "Clear me a spot in the street of the town."
>
> (b. Ber. 62a)

> Rabbah had the bricks [of the privy] placed for him east and west, and Abaye changed them to face north and south [so the back would not face the Temple in Jerusalem]. Rava explained [that one should wipe oneself with the left hand] because the Torah was given with the right hand [with reference to Deut. 33:2].
>
> (b. Ber. 61b, 62a)

> Rava said, "More numerous are those slain by delayed calls of nature than as victims of starvation..."
>
> (b. Shab. 33a)

Thus every aspect of daily life was to be subjected to Torah. Indeed, Torah transformed quite natural functions into formalized, ritual actions.

---

[1] Above, p. 300.

[2] b. Suk. 26b, Abaye and R. Joseph.

[3] b. Ta'anit 12b, Abaye and Rava.

[4] b. M.Q. 23a, Abaye and Rava.

[5] Rava's instructions to his attendant, b. Ber. 44b.

[6] R. Hamnuna son of R. Joseph concerning Rava, b. Ber. 24a.

[7] b. Shab. 19a, Abaye's dealings with the fuller.

Relations between disciple and master, and among the disciples as a community, naturally produced the most specialized forms of Torah. Ordinary people might be expected to observe and imitate the rabbis' etiquette, and take to heart their teachings about how to preserve good health.[1] On the other hand, only disciples were responsible to honor their particular teacher in the extreme forms of humility and perfect submission demanded by the protocol of the schools. To outsiders, Jewish and non-Jewish alike, the rites of discipleship must have seemed alien. Indeed, they heightened the sense of participating in a special, sacred community, which must have set the rabbinical estate apart from the ordinary society of Jews. This was made quite implicit:

> Rava was serving the drinks at his son's wedding. When he offered a cup to R. Papa and R. Huna b. R. Joshua, they stood up before him. When he offered it to R. Mari and R. Phineas b. R. Ḥisda, they did not stand up. He was offended, and exclaimed, "Are these rabbis and the others not rabbis?"
>
> (b. Qid. 32b)

The implied argument is that the others are rabbis no less than these, yet the others stood before me, therefore these, in spite of their rabbinical rank, should have stood also. It was a mark of the rabbinical estate to pay great deference to the master. At the heart of their sense of exclusiveness was that very deference shown to the teacher, as in the following instances:

> Abaye used to rise as soon as he saw the ear of R. Joseph's ass approaching.... [But a sage should not trouble the people]. Abaye said, "We have a tradition that if [the sage] takes a roundabout route [to avoid bothering people and causing them to rise in his honor] he will live a long time." Abaye took a roundabout route.
>
> (b. Qid. 33a)

> Mar Zutra b. R. Naḥman was once going from Sikara to Maḥoza, while Rava and R. Safra were going to Sikara, and they met on the way. Thinking they had come to meet him, Mar Zutra said, "Why did the rabbis trouble themselves to come so far?" R. Safra replied, "We did not know our master was coming. Had we known, we should have put ourselves to more trouble than this." Rava said to him, "Why did you say so? You have upset him." He replied, "Otherwise we would be deceiving him..."
>
> (b. Ḥul. 94b)

> When Rava would take his leave of R. Joseph, he would go backward so that his feet were bruised and the threshhold of R. Joseph's

---

[1] See below, pp. 363ff.

house was stained with blood. R. Joseph was told what Rava had done, and he said to him, "May it be the will (of Heaven) that you raise your head above the whole city."

(b. Yoma 53a-b)

Abaye and Rabin were once going along the road. The ass of Rabin took precedence over that of Abaye and he did not say to him, "Let the master go ahead." Abaye said, "Since this one of the rabbis came up from the west, he has grown proud." When they came to the door of the synagogue, Rabin said to him, "Will the master enter?" He replied, "Until *now* I was not a master?" He replied...

(b. Ber. 47a)

A master must not only rebuke his erring disciple, Rava held, but he must also accept correction when given in the proper form and spirit.[1] R. Huna instructed his son Rabbah that he must not spit before his teacher.[2] Rava did not hesitate to punish a disrespectful disciple:

R. 'Avya' visited Rava. His boots were muddy with clay, but he sat down on a bed before Rava. Rava was annoyed and wished to try him [so he asked various difficult questions, which R. 'Avya' was able to answer.] R. Naḥman b. Isaac commented, "Blessed be the All-Merciful that Rava did not put R. 'Avya' to shame."

(b. Shab. 46a-b)

Punishment was not always so mild. When R. Papa felt himself denigrated by the students of Rava, he cursed them. Rava insulted a disrespectful disciple:

When Rava suffered a loss, Abba b. Martha ... went to the house. Rava sat on an upright couch, while Abba sat on an overturned one. Rava said, "How lacking in sense is this disciple of the rabbis."

(b. M.Q. 26b)

R. Huna b. Manoaḥ, R. Samuel b. 'Idi, and R. Ḥiyya of Vestania used to frequent Rava['s classes]. When Rava died, they came before R. Papa. Whenever he told them a tradition which did not seem reasonable to them, they would hint [make gestures] together. He was saddened [lit.: his mind weakened]. In a dream this Scripture was read to him, "And I shall cut off three shepherds" (Zech. 11:8). The next day when they took leave of him he said to them, "May the rabbis go *in* peace" [a greeting addressed to the dead].

(b. Ta'anit 9a-b)

R. 'Avya' was once ill and did not go to hear R. Joseph's lecture. On the next day when he came Abaye tried to appease R. Joseph. He

---

[1] b. B.M. 31a, as an exegesis of Lev. 19:17.
[2] b. Ned. 49b.

asked R. 'Avya', "Why did the master not come to the lecture yester-
day?" R. 'Avya' gave the excuse, "I felt weak and was not able." He
said, "Why did you not take some food and come?..."

(b. Ber. 28b)

R. 'Avya"'s excuses made it clear that there were sound legal grounds
for his refraining from eating and thus not attending the lecture.

Great respect was paid to a master when he died.[1] Funeral orations
were preserved, including the following, which was recited at the death
of Rabbah b. R. Huna by "a certain child" (in the translation of H. M.
Lazarus [London, 1948, p. 159]):

> A scion of ancient stock from Babylon came
> With records of prowess in combat and fame
> Twice numerous pelican and bittern from far
> Came for the ravage and ruin in Shinear.
> When [God] views his world with displeasure
> He seizes souls in exacting measure.
> Awaiting their coming as new brides, with delight
> And, riding on Araboth in empyrean height,
> He welcomes the souls of the pure and right.

(b. M.Q. 25b)

At the death of R. Zera, the following was recited (in Lazarus's
translation, p. 163):

> The land of Shinear was his home of birth
> The land of glory reared her darling to fame
> "Woe is me," said Rakath in lament
> For she has lost her choicest ornament.

(b. M.Q. 25b)

When great rabbis died, it was believed that the natural world
marked the loss. So when Rabbah and R. Joseph died, "the rocks of
the Euphrates kissed each other, and when Abaye and Rava died, the
rocks of the Tigris did the same" (b. M.Q. 25b).

It was no less important for disciples to treat one another respect-
fully and to avoid bitter personal animosities on account of disa-
greements over matters of law or tradition:

> Rava said, "Two disciples who live in the same city and are not
> forebearing to one another in legal matters provoke [heavenly] anger
> and bring it [upon themselves]..."

(b. Ta'anit 8a)

---

[1] On miracle-stories in connection with the death of the θεῖος ἀνήρ, see Bieler,
op. cit., I, pp. 45ff.

Where a master was present, a disciple should not give practical
decisions of any kind, for that would imply he held his own judgment
superior to that of his master, or regarded consulting the master as
superfluous. Such a sign of pride could not be endured, except in
special circumstances, as in the following:

> Rava said, "When it is a question of preventing a person from com-
> mitting a transgression, it is quite proper [for a disciple to give a legal
> decision] even in his master's presence ... Rava ruled, "In the presence
> of one's master, it is forbidden [to give a legal decision] on penalty of
> death. In his absence, it is forbidden also, but no penalty of death is
> incurred..."
>
> (b. 'Eruv. 63a)[1]

The master, on the other hand, bore equally grave responsibilities to
his disciples. Rava held that if a student did not progress, it was his
teacher's fault. Rabbah tried to put his students at their ease before he
taught them:

> Rava said, "If you have seen a student whose studies are as hard to
> him as iron, it is on account of his master who does not show him a
> pleasant face..."
>
> (b. Ta'anit 8a)

> Before Rabbah would begin [his discourse] for the rabbis, he used
> to say something humorous, and they were cheered, Then he sat in
> awe and began reciting his tradition.
>
> (b. Shab. 30b = b. Pes. 117a)

Abaye likewise said:

> "May I be rewarded, for when I saw a disciple complete his tractate,
> I made a holiday for the rabbis."
>
> (b. Shab. 119a)

When taking leave of one another, the rabbis of Pumbedita would
say the following blessing, according to Rabbah:

> "May he who gives life to the living give you a long, good, and
> sweet life."
>
> (b. Yoma 71a)

How shall we account for the profound, ritualistic deference to be
paid to the rabbi? First, the rabbi stood in the same relationship to the
student as did the father, to whom great respect was due. But second,
while the father brought his son into this world, "his rabbi brings him
into the world to come." That is to say, the rabbi provides the disciple

---

[1] For Abaye's view of the same matter, see b. 'Eruv. 62b.

with the key to eternal life, preparing him to gain entry into, and to participate in the studies of, the heavenly academy. Most important, however, the Pharisaic-rabbinic tradition held that the Oral Torah was exemplified, not merely taught, by the rabbi. The teacher was the living Torah, a form or vehicle of divine revelation. To sit in his presence, hear his words, accompany him, all the while observing his actions, was to receive a revelation no less authoritative or sacred than that given to Moses at Sinai.[1] Hence no reverence was too great, no deference too profound. If gentiles paid honor and reverence to their kings and emperors, how much the more so should Jews, but especially the disciples, revere and honor their rabbis, the worldly exemplifications of revelation, therefore of the will and the image of the King of Kings. The forms of that respect, no less than prayers or festival observances or other pious practices, therefore represented a religious ritual. It was a ritual based upon, or expressive of,[2] the rabbinical myths about Moses "our rabbi", the heavenly academy and its study of Torah, and God's image as conveyed in oral and written revelation at Mt. Sinai and handed on thenceforward to prophets, sages, and now, to the rabbis.[3]

v. The Rewards of Torah

The reward of studying and living up to the lessons of Torah was both this-worldly and other-worldly. First of all, study was its own reward, a joy:

[1] See b. Mak. 22b, Rava said it is stupid to stand up before a Scroll of the Torah but not before a rabbi, who had authority to alter its content by his interpretation. The passage is cited below, p. 388.

[2] I do not mean to imply the opinion that the myth of the rabbi preceded the various rituals of *being a rabbi* or of signifying that one is a member of the rabbinical estate. It is more probable that the rabbinical rites preceded the formation of the myth of Moses "our rabbi," which would have come only afterward as a way of explaining the religious signification of the earthly phenomena already quite well known and widely established. But if so, that development must have been completed substantially before the arrival of the first rabbis in Babylonia, in the first and second centuries A.D. An inquiry into the transformation of the wise man, philosopher, or sage of Proverbs or Ben Sira into the rabbinical lawyer and holy man of the first century A.D., and of the myths and stories told to explain him, would be interesting for historians of religion.

[3] Bieler, *op. cit.*, I, pp. 36ff., stresses that miracle-stories pertained not only to the divine-man, but also to his master. In this connection, we have no important variation in the case of leading rabbis, concerning whose masters many unusual fables were told. But the reason was not to single out any particular rabbi. Rather, it was characteristic of the rabbinical movement as a whole that all major authorities were accredited with exceptional and often supernatural talents.

> Rava said, "All human beings are carriers.[1] Happy are they who are worthy of being carriers of the Torah [lit.: our light]."
>
> (b. Sanh. 99b)

As in Abaye's case, the completion of studying a tractate of the law was the occasion of special joy:

> R. Papa and R. Huna b. R. Joshua once came before Rava. He asked them, "Have you mastered a certain tractate?" They replied, "Yes." "And are you a little richer?" "Yes," they replied, "For we have bought a small piece of land." He exclaimed, "Happy are the righteous to whom things happen in this world according to the work of the wicked of this world!"
>
> (b. Hor. 10b)

Rava said that the righteous who enjoy this world in the way the wicked do are happy, but the wicked who enjoy this world according to the way of the righteous are unhappy. The reason was that the wicked enjoy this world, but the righteous suffer in it. Hence his question, "Are you a little better off?" When the disciples said that they had gotten richer in real estate, he commented that they had enjoyed this world the way the wicked do, so they were particularly fortunate. The presupposition of the question was therefore that the rewards of Torah are mostly other-worldly, and so will come later on. The sages however, also believed themselves the recipients even in this world of heavenly favor, concern, and special love:

> R. Naḥman b. R. Ḥisda held that even the angel of death loves the disciple of the sages.
>
> (b. A.Z. 35b)

When they went to the heavenly world, yet more awaited them:

> R. Naḥman b. Isaac said [expositing Jer. 23:19] that the disciples of the sages wrinkle themselves over the words of Torah in this world, but the Holy One blessed be he will reveal a secret to them in the world to come...
>
> (b. Ḥag. 14a)

Moreover, Rava said that the rabbis are descended from Levi or Issachar.[2] So they enjoyed not only the reward of learning, but also special merit derived from the patriarchs. It was quite natural, there-

---

[1] DRPTQY: Jastrow, I, 322, "mail bags." See also ʿArukh, III, p. 161. Neither provides a satisfactory explanation.

[2] b. Yoma 26a, as an exegesis of Deut. 33:10, 11.

fore, for them to believe that their traditions brought supernatural blessings of many kinds.[1]

The rewards of Torah proved to be quite practical and material as well. First of all, the sage enjoyed a special status within society. Whether or not people obeyed the laws as he exposited them, they certainly paid him respect as a holy man. R. Joseph stated explicitly, as had R. Naḥman before him[2] that it was knowledge of the Torah that made him different from ordinary men:

> R. Joseph would order that a third-born calf be prepared for him on *Shavuʿot* [Pentecost, which commemorates the revelation of the Torah]. He said, "But for this day, how many Josephs are there in the market-place?"
>
> (b. Pes. 68b)

Among the many honors paid to the sage were unusual mourning rites,[3] exceptional regard at public celebrations,[4] as well as widespread reputation:

> Rava said, "If one studies Torah indoors, Torah proclaims his merit abroad."
>
> (b. M.Q. 16b)

> R. Joseph said, "We have a tradition that a rabbinical disciple does not suffer poverty." But lo, we see that he does? Even so, he does not go begging.
>
> (b. Shab. 151b)

Since people believed rabbis were holy men, they tried to win their favor by entertaining them in their homes, giving them gifts of considerable value, and making them partners, with little or no investment of capital, in business ventures. The rabbis did everything they could to encourage people to lavish hospitality on rabbis. Abaye said that a blessing follows immediately upon entertaining scholars.[5] Rava stated quite explicitly:

> "He who is kind to rabbis has rabbis for sons. He who cherishes rabbis will have rabbis for sons-in-law. He who reveres rabbis will himself become a rabbinical disciple. And if he is not fit for this, his words will be listened to like those of a rabbinical disciple."
>
> (b. Shab. 23b)

---

[1] b. Zev. 45a, Abaye said to Rava that expositing even a useless law was worthwhile because one would receive a reward for doing so.

[2] Vol. III, p. 61.

[3] As in the case of R. Joseph, b. Ber. 19a, and see above, pp. 41f., 307.

[4] B. Ket. 17b, Abaye noted that at the wedding of a disciple, the mother of the groom poured oil on the heads of the disciples attending the wedding feast.

[5] b. Ber. 42a, with reference to Gen. 39:27 and Gen. 39:5.

While the masters did not normally receive salaries for teaching, they could nonetheless attain material benefit on that account, as in the following story:

> R. Shimi b. Ashi asked Abaye to allow him to sit before him [as a student]. Abaye replied, "I need my time for my own studies." "Then," R. Shimi asked, "Let your honor teach me at night." Abaye replied, "I have to take care of irrigating my field then." Said the other, "I will irrigate for your honor by day, and you teach me by night." Abaye agreed...
>
> (b. Git. 60b)

What is important here is that in exchange for teaching, Abaye received services of a field-worker. Rava, moreover, received free labor without teaching:

> Rava's brother, R. Se'orim used to seize people of poor reputation and make them draw Rava's litter [GWHRQ']. Rava approved what he had done, for it has been taught, 'If you see a man who does not behave in a proper fashion, how do we know that you may make him your slave?...'
>
> (b. B.M. 73b)

R. Se'orim's action had nothing to do with a court penalty. It was in fact quite outside normal legal procedures.

The fourth-century rabbis moreover made use of their position as masters in the schools and as judges in the courts both to achieve personal gain and to discriminate in favor of others of the rabbinical estate. The following story is the most striking instance:

> The proselyte 'Issur had twelve thousand *zuz* [on deposit] with Rava. The conception of his son R. Mari was not in holiness [it took place before his conversion to Judaism] though his birth was. He was at school. Rava said, "How could Mari gain possession of this money? If as an inheritance, he is not entitled to inherit anything. If as a gift, the gift of a dying man has been given the same legal force as that of an inheritance, and whoever is entitled to an inheritance is entitled to a gift but otherwise he is not ... " R. 'Ika son of R. 'Ammi objected, "Why? Let 'Issur acknowledge that that money belongs to R. Mari, who would then acquire it by virtue of such an admission." Meanwhile such an acknowledgement [actually] came from the house of 'Issur. Rava was annoyed, and said, "They teach people what claims [to make] and so cause loss to me."
>
> (b. B.B. 149a)

Rava's intent was apparently to seize the inheritance of a disciple through a legal technicality. The disciple was the child of a convert to

Judaism, and because he was conceived before his parents' conversion, he was not entitled to inherit his father's wealth. We know that Jews were generally aware of that rule, and certainly took advantage of it when they could.[1] They did so with judicial support and approval. Rava hoped, therefore, to hold on to R. Mari's father's money—a huge sum—but was prevented when the convert found a way around the law. Israel W. Slotki[2] argues that the whole discussion was merely "for instructional purposes." It was Rava's method "of impressing these subtle laws upon his students' minds. No one at the academy suspected for one moment that the master would in all earnestness desire to retain the money he held as a deposit from one who obviously confided in him. Had Rava been in earnest, he would not have spoken publicly about such a matter when he well knew that Issur was still alive...." I am not persuaded by Slotki's argument or by his interpretation of Rava's saying, "They teach people what to claim," as an ironical statement.[3] As we shall see, there is considerable evidence of the attitude of the schools about benefiting from rabbinical status. There are numerous other examples of Jews' defrauding proselytes. We have no reason whatever to suppose that it then was even regarded as reprehensible behavior.[4] The plain sense of the story is that Rava hoped to hold on to twelve thousand *zuz* which had been deposited with him by an unsuspecting proselyte, and that he would have done so had the proselyte not found out how to prevent it. Whoever told him, it was not Rava.

Other examples of court favoritism of rabbis over ordinary folk included the following:

> Rava stated, "May I be rewarded for whenever I saw a disciple come to me with a lawsuit, I did not lay my head on the pillow before I saw points in his favor."
>
> (b. Shab. 119a)

> Rabbah b. R. Huna said, "If a disciple of the sages and an illiterate person have a litigation, we persuade the disciple to sit, but to the illiterate we say, 'Sit', and if he stands, it does not matter ... If a disciple of the sages and an ignorant person have a litigation, the disciple should

---

[1] See for example vol. II, pp. 264-265.

[2] Trans., (London, 1948), pp. 645-646, n. 14.

[3] In fact, 'Issur did not depend upon R. 'Ika's saying, for the story makes it clear that it was a quite independent action which did not depend upon what was said in the school house. Someone, not in Rava's school, must have told 'Issur what to do, according to the story as we now have it.

[4] See vol. II, p. 264, and III, p. 306, for cases in which the courts sustained such actions against proselytes' estates.

not come first and sit down, because it will look as if he is setting forth
his case ... If he knows some testimony and it is undignified to him
to go to the judge who is his inferior to give testimony before him,
he need not go..."

(b. Shev. 30b)

R. Joseph interpreted, "In righteousness shall you judge your
neighbor" (Lev. 19:15) to mean, "He who is *with you in Torah and
commandments*—try to judge him favorably."

(b. Shev. 30a)

It was the disciple or rabbi who was "with the judge in Torah and
commandments," and R. Joseph's meaning is quite clear. In the light
of the sayings of Rava and Rabbah b. R. Huna, one need not doubt
that wherever possible, the rabbinical litigant was given an advantage
in court. Moreover, rabbis were not required to come to court at all,
if they could get away with enforcing their "rights" outside of litigation:

R. Joseph said that a disciple of the rabbis may enforce his own
rights in a matter where he is quite certain [on the law]...

(b. M.Q. 17a)

(Rabbinical disciples did not have to ask masters to examine their
slaughtering knives, but were permitted to examine their own.[1] In this
matter, the reason was not "favoritism" but merely sufficient knowledge.)

Two concrete economic privileges were enjoyed by the rabbis, in
addition to their unsuccessful claim to be free of the poll tax.[2] First,
according to the following, they did not have to pay certain other tolls:

A collector of bridge tolls [bazbana][3] once came before Abaye, and
said, "Let the master give me his signature so that when rabbis come
and present to me an authorisation [from you] I will allow them to
pass without paying the toll..."

(b. B.B. 167a)

Abaye was apparently able to certify disciples so that they did not
have to pay a bridge toll, at least here. Of far greater economic consequence was the rabbis' privilege of selling their produce in the market
before other people:

Rava said, "A disciple of the sages may assert, 'I am a disciple of the
sages. Let my business receive attention first [deal with my case first

---

[1] b. 'Eruv. 63a.
[2] Above, pp. 39-44, 85-91.
[3] Bazbina = bazbana, Jastrow, I, 152, "collector of bridge tolls." *'Arukh* II, p.
32.

in a shop or marketplace],' as it iswritten, 'And David's sons were priests' (II Sam. 8:18). Just as a priest receives first, so does a scholar."

(b. Ned. 62a)

We have already noted examples[1] in which rabbis demonstrated their knowledge of Torah and so received the right to sell their produce at advantageous prices.[2] The exilarch supported that privilege.[3] Moreover, the rabbis were not slow to make that claim, and did so by announcing their status:

> Rava said that a man may reveal his identity [as a rabbi] where he is unknown, [as an exegesis of I Kings 18:12.]
>
> (b. Ned. 62a)

I think it is beyond question that revealing one's identity as a rabbi could result in considerable economic advantage.

The rabbis were not wholly unjustified in claiming economic privileges. They served the public interest and generally did so without regular compensation. They had to devote valuable time to teaching disciples, judging cases, and supervising public life. The exilarch clearly supported their right to special market-privileges, for one thing, and he doubtless regarded those privileges as a means of compensating rabbis for their services. Otherwise he would have had to tax the ordinary people to pay salaries. By contrast, honor in this world, and heavenly rewards in the next, the enjoyment of public respect and hospitality, the indirect economic advantages derived from the public's belief that rabbis were charmed or could bring blessing (it was the same thing)—these benefits could not be so easily rationalized.

VI. THEOLOGY

The study of Torah in rabbinical schools followed highly rationalistic lines. Its method was based upon strict logic, and made extensive use of practical reason. The rabbis however lived in a world in which supernatural beliefs and phenomena were everywhere taken seriously. They believed in God. They believed in prayer as an effective action, so words could affect the physical world. They believed in angels, demons, astrology, and heavenly revelations. These constituted the supernatural environment, and produced an expectation that miracles

---

[1] Vol. III, p. 65.

[2] On the social position of the rabbis, see especially Beer, *Ma'amadam*, pp. 150-185; on market privileges, p. 80, and also his "Rashut HaGolah," *Ziyyon* 33, 1963, p. 21.

[3] b. B.B. 22a.

could and would be done through divine favor. Consequently, the essentially rational structure of the Babylonian Talmud, a legal commentary, is filled with teachings on supernatural subjects and stories of miracles. These teachings and stories we have now to examine, and we begin with the general world-view from which they derived, with what may be called, loosely, "rabbinic theology."

We have no evidence that an individual sage ever prepared a systematic, abstract treatise on theological issues, for example in the manner of Aphrahat. Whether or not various individual sages conceived an orderly, consistent view of God, sin and atonement, eschatology, and divine judgment, we simply do not know.[1] The reason is that most sayings germane to theological issues were transmitted in the conventional form of discrete comments, or in the context of arguments or dialectical discussions, or, most generally, as exegeses of various Scriptures. We know therefore what opinions some people held, but we do not know how they put together these opinions into a systematic account of fundamental issues. Most of the comments available to us were transmitted because they were regarded by later tradents as authoritative, and hence we may suppose they represented general opinion held in one or another school.

A part of that opinion was surely shared outside of the circles of the rabbis and their disciples. But an important part was held to be the secret doctrine of the schools, and not all men, not even all disciples, were permitted to know what it said. In the secret theological doctrines of the schools were four elements: first, the secret name of God himself, second, traditions concerning creation and the divine 'chariot' as envisioned by Ezekiel, third, the configuration of heaven and of God, and finally, the mystery of the coming of the Messiah. These elements were to be confided only to the worthy few, never to ordinary folk. They were handed on from one generation of schoolmen to the next, and the traditions on creation and the chariot in particular were by now at least three centuries old, if not older.[2] Knowledge of the pronunciation of the Tetragrammaton was illustrated in the following:

---

[1] This is not to say that one cannot show a few individuals to have held self-consistent positions. Heschel's discussions of R. Akiba and R. Ishmael have already been cited (vol. II, pp. 232-236). Until further detailed and analytical accounts of other major rabbinical masters have appeared, however, we can hardly come to a general conclusion.

[2] See my *Life of R. Yoḥanan b. Zakkai*, pp. 96-104, and the literature cited there. For Babylonian evidences of these traditions, see vol. II, pp. 180-188, and vol. III, pp. 149ff.

Rabbah b. Bar Ḥanah said in the name of R. Yoḥanan, "[The pronunciation of] the Four-lettered Divine Name is confided by sages to their disciples once in seven years." ... Rava thought to lecture upon it at the [public] session. A certain old man said to him, "It is written (Ex. 3:15), *'le'allem'* [to be kept secret]."

(b. Pes. 50a)

It is clear that only rarely were even the most worthy disciples to be told about the four-lettered name. Why Rava thought of lecturing about it publicly I cannot say. The accounts of the chariot and of creation were traditions which individuals received from masters only in exceptional circumstances. Not all the masters knew the whole tradition, and they would not share even with one another what they knew:

R. Joseph was studying the 'Work of the Chariot', while the Elders of Pumbedita [= Rav Judah and R. 'Ana'] were studying the 'Works of Creation'. The latter said to him, "Let the master teach us the 'Works of the Chariot.'" He replied, "Teach me the 'Works of Creation.'" After they had done so, they asked him to keep his word. He replied to them, "We have learned concerning it, 'Honey and milk are under your tongue' (Songs 4:11). The things that are sweeter than honey and milk should be *under* your tongue'" ... They replied to him, "We have already studied as far as 'And he said to me, Son of man' (Ezek. 2:1)." He replied to them, "These are the very 'Works of the chariot' . ."...

(b. Ḥag. 13a)

R. Joseph thus indicated that they had, in fact, a more substantial knowledge of the Works of the Chariot than they realized. But he apparently did not contribute to their knowledge beyond what they already knew. Rava seemed to know something of the *Shi'ur Qomah* tradition, which contained the measurements of the heavenly firmament and of God. The following statement is handed on in the context of *Shi'ur Qomah* sayings:

Rava said, "The world is six thousand parasangs (in diameter) and the thickness of [the second] heaven (*raqi'a*) is one thousand parasangs..."

(b. Pes. 94a)

The heavens were divided into seven parts. The lowest was *Vilon*, and the next, much brighter still, was *Raqi'a*. Certain meteorological splendors were explained as taking place when *Vilon*, the lowest, was torn asunder so the next firmament appeared, R. Huna b. R. Joshua said.[1] Above all sat God enthroned on high, the brightest of all phe-

---

[1] b. Ber. 58b.

nomena. So although the righteous were arrayed in front of him, each
with a glow of his own, God outshown them all:

> Rava said, "What is the meaning of the Scripture, 'And his brightness
> was as the light. He had rays coming forth from his hand, and there
> was the hiding of his power' (Hab. 3:4)? To what are the righteous
> compared when in the presence of the Shekhinah? To a lamp in the
> presence of a torch."
>
> (b. Pes. 8a)

Among the righteous, thirty-six were permitted to see the face of the
Shekhinah, or Presence of God, but many others were also able to
perceive it:

> Abaye said, "The world must contain not less than thirty-six
> righteous men in each generation who receive the face of the
> *Shekhinah,* for it is written, 'Blessed are all they that wait *lo* [for him]'
> (Is. 30:18), and the numerical value of *lo* is thirty-six." But Rava said,
> "The row [of the righteous] immediately before the Holy One ...
> consists of eighteen thousand, for it is written (Ezek. 48:35), 'There
> shall be eighteen thousand round about.'" There is no difficulty.
> Thirty-six see him through a bright speculum [= mirror, 'YSPQL-
> RY'], but eighteen thousand see him through a dim one...
>
> (b. Sanh. 97b = b. Suk. 45b)

No disciple could have doubted that the righteous were those who
conformed to the rabbinical rules and mastered rabbinical teachings and
traditions.

Since God was conceived of in the image of rabbinical man, it was a
natural supposition that God wore *tefillin.* So R. Naḥman b. Isaac and
R. Ḥiyya b. Abin discussed what was written in the parchment of those
divine *tefillin.* The reply was, "And who is like your people Israel, a
singular nation on earth" (I Chron. 17:21).[1] Rabbah b. R. Huna held
that men are obliged to touch their *tefillin* every hour, as a reminder of
God.[2] God for his part would thus have been constantly reminded of
the singularity of Israel. We have already noted that Abaye thought
that the *Shekhinah* was present in Babylonia in certain ancient synagogues.[3]

The following story indicates a more philosophical view of theology:

---

[1] b. Ber. 6a.

[2] b. Yoma 7b.

[3] b. Meg. 29a, see also *Oẓar HaGeonim* V, part i, p. 53. See above, p. 151. Note
also b. Zev. 119a, R. Joseph said there were three divine residences, at Shiloh,
Nob-Gibeon, and Jerusalem.

Abaye and Rava were sitting before Rabbah. He said to them, "To whom do we say a blessing?" They replied, "To the All-merciful." "And where does the All-Merciful dwell?" Rava pointed to the roof. Abaye went outside and pointed to heaven. He said to them, "You are both going to be rabbis."

(b. Ber. 48a)

So the principles of immanence and transcendence were ascribed to the two disciples in their youth, with the comment that both were correct.

Eschatological issues were similarly discussed mostly in the privacy of the school. Great historical events would naturally arouse popular unrest, as people looked forward to a heavenly resolution of earthly tensions in the coming of the Messiah.[1] We have noted the report that a Messianic pretender won widespread popular attention when he revealed himself and assembled the people for a return to Zion.[2] The rabbis' discussions supposed that some knew the solutions of the mysteries—When the Messiah would come, how long the world would last, and what would be the pattern of redemption. They therefore paid attention to whatever information they could get:

R. Ḥanan b. Taḥalifa sent to R. Joseph, saying, "I once met a man who had a scroll written in Hebrew in Assyrian [square] characters. I said to him, 'How did you get this'? He replied, 'I hired myself as a mercenary in the Roman army and found it in the Roman archives. In it is written that 4291[3] years after the creation the world will be orphaned. Afterward, some of the years will be spent in the war of the great sea monsters [TNYNYM], some in the war of Gog and Magog, and the remaining will be the Messianic era, while the Holy One ... will renew his world only after seven thousand years.'"

(b. Sanh. 97b)

The supposition was that among the holy books taken by the Romans when they conquered Jerusalem and put away in their archives was a text which reported the secret of when the world would come to an end. The rabbis believed that great cataclysms would precede his coming. R. Joseph, however, doubted that the cataclysms were accurately described:

Abaye said, "We hold [a tradition that] Babylonia will not see the travails of the Messiah..."

(b. Ket. 111a)

---

[1] See vol. II, pp. 52-57, and vol. III, pp. 23-24, 176-179.
[2] Above, pp. 32-3.
[3] 531 A.D.

[Our rabbis taught, "In the seven year cycle at the end of which the son of David will come—in the course of these years there will be various calamities, including dearth of rain, famine, death of saints, forgetfulness of Torah, and wars."] R. Joseph objected, "But so many septennates have passed and he has not yet come!" Abaye replied, "Were there the heavenly sounds in the sixth and wars in the seventh? Have the troubles come in the proper order?"

(b. Sanh. 97a)

In any case, the suffering of the Messiah's coming was much feared.[1] Since the rabbis were thought to be saints, some supposed they would not have to undergo these sufferings, being protected by their study and good deeds:

Rabbah said, "Let him [the Messiah] come, but let me not see him." R. Joseph said, "Let him come, and may I be worthy of sitting in the shadow of the saddle [or, dung] of his ass." Abaye asked Rabbah, "Why do you not wish to see him? [You will be spared because of your study and good deeds from the pangs of the Messiah]." He replied, "I fear lest sin [neutralize these advantages, so I may suffer]."

(b. Sanh. 98b)

None of these eschatological sayings reveals anything about world history in that day. No specific historical event elicited comment on its meaning in terms of an anticipated eschatological pattern. No equivalent to Aphrahat's Fifth Discourse, which is an effort to explain the Byzantine-Iranian wars of the age, appeared in the sayings attributed to contemporary rabbis.

The public side of rabbinic theology concerned sin, suffering, atonement, and divine mercy. Sin was caused by the 'evil impulse,' which God had formed:

R. Naḥman b. R. Ḥisda said that the word *vayyiẓer* ('And the Lord God *formed* man,' Gen. 2:7) is written with two *yods* to show that God created both inclinations, the good one and the evil one.

(b. Ber. 61a)

Nonetheless the wicked are guilty, not merely fated to do evil by their star. Though he said all things depend on the stars, Rava held:

---

[1] Note also b. Nid. 61b, R. Joseph held that the commandments would be abolished in the hereafter, presumably since people would no longer need to pile up merits. See the excellent article by Professor Judah Rosenthal, "Ra'yon Bitul HaMiẓvot b'Eskatologya HaYehudit," *Meyer Waxman Jubilee Volume*, (Chicago, Jerusalem, and Tel Aviv, 1967), pp. 217-233.

"This their way is their confidence [kesel]" (Ps. 49:14). Rava said, "The wicked know that their way is to death, but they have fat on their loins [kislam]."

(b. Shab. 31b)

That is to say, their loins, the seat of understanding, are closed, and that is why they sin. Abaye held a deterministic view:

"We have learned that a good man does not become evil."

(b. Ber. 29a)

Most people are neither wholly wicked nor wholly righteous:

[Ordinary people are swayed by both inclinations, as proved by Ps. 109:31]. Rava said, "People such as we are ordinary." Abaye replied, "The master leaves no creature a chance to live." Rava further stated, "The world was created only for the wholly wicked and for the wholly righteous [—this world for the wicked, the next for the righteous]."

(b. Ber. 61b)

It was Abaye's view that the rabbis were not ordinary, but able to free themselves of the snares of the evil impulse. Rava described the progress of the evil impulse. He showed from II Sam. 12:4 that first the evil impulse is called a passer-by, then a guest, and finally a man [an occupier of the house].[1] The worst sins were those of speech:

"Life and death are in the hand of the tongue" (Prov. 18:21). Rava said, "He who wants life [can find it] through the tongue, and he who wants death [can find it] through the tongue."

(b. 'Arakh. 15b)

The rabbis were certain that if a person suffered, it was in consequence of some sin or other. No suffering could escape explanation as punishment for sin. The presupposition of the following story was that premature death as well as suffering came on account of sin:

Rava said, "I used to think there is no truth [QWŠT'][2] in the world, but one of the rabbis, ... who would not lie for all the money in the world, told me he once came to a place called Truth, where no one lies [lit.: alters his word] and no one dies before his time. He married and had two sons with her. One day his wife was sitting and washing her hair. A neighbor came and knocked at the door. Thinking it would not be polite [to say what she was doing] he called out, 'She is not here.' His two sons died. People came and questioned him. He told what had happened. They said, 'We ask you to leave this town and do not incite death against us.'"

(b. Sanh. 97a)

---

[1] b. Suk. 52b.

[2] On *kušta* in Mandaean texts, see Edwin Yamauchi, *Mandaic Incantation Texts* (New Haven, 1967) p. 38, and n. 86.

Premature death meant death below the age of sixty, in the view of
Rabbah and R. Joseph.[1] Sickness was similarly presumed to be a sign
of heavenly displeasure. R. Isaac b. Rav Judah said that one should
beseech mercy that he not become sick, for if he becomes sick, he would
be asked to "show his merit" that he be restored to health.[2] Rava held
that if one suffers, he should accept it in joy, as a sign of his submission
to heaven.[3] Suffering was, after all, an occasion for overcoming sin.
Nonetheless, no one really hoped that he would have to atone through
suffering. So after Rava prayed, he recited the following:

> "My God, before I was created I was unworthy, and now though
> I have been created it is as if I were not created. I am dust in my life,
> all the more so after death. Behold I stand before you like a vessel full
> of shame and humiliation. May it be your will, O Lord my God, that
> I shall no more sin, and as to sins I have already committed before you,
> wipe them away in your mercy, but not by means of suffering or
> illness."
>
> (b. Ber. 17a)

(This was also the Confession of R. Hamnuna on the Day of Atonement, and may have been a prayer existing from earlier times.) God's
wrath was seen to pass quickly. Abaye said that God was angry during
one of the first three hours of the day, when the comb of the cock is
white and when the cock stands on one foot.[4] When he exacts payment
of Israel, God exacts it only a little at a time, Rava said in commenting
on Job 30:24 and Ezek. 21:32.[5] Above all, he was merciful to those
who submit to his will:

> Rava expounded, "'Go now and let us reason together, the Lord
> shall say' (Is. 1:18). It should say 'Come now,' not 'Go now,' and 'says'
> rather than 'shall say.' In time to come, the Holy One, blessed be he,
> will say to Israel, 'Go now to your forefathers and they will convince
> you.' And they shall say before him, 'Lord of the world, to whom
> shall we go? To Abraham ... who did not seek mercy for us?' 'To
> Isaac? ... To Jacob who also did not seek mercy for us. To whom then
> shall we go now? Let the Lord state it.' The Holy One shall answer
> them, 'Since you have made yourselves utterly dependent [lit. sus-
> pended] upon me, 'Though your sins be as scarlet, they shall be white
> as snow' (Is. 1:19)."
>
> (b. Shab. 89b)

---

[1] b. M.Q. 28a, When R. Joseph became sixty, he was very happy.
[2] b. Shab. 32a. Note also b. B.Q. 91a, Rava said that recovery from an illness
was likewise the result of heavenly favor.
[3] b. Ber. 60b.
[4] b. Ber. 7a.
[5] b. A.Z. 4a.

In criticizing the doctrine of the merits of the forefathers and patri-archs, Rava stressed that they were not sufficiently concerned or ef-fectual; so only God could truly grant mercy. One could encourage him to do so through several means. First of all, one could show him-self worthy of mercy:

> Rava said, "How do we know that if one solicits mercy for his fellow man while he himself needs mercy, he will be answered first?..."
>
> (b. B.Q. 92a)

Similarly, compassionate action would follow from waiving one's rights:

> Rava said, "One who fails to exact punishment [of his neighbor] has all his sins forgiven."
>
> (b. Meg. 28a)[1]

The third, and most effective means, was to demonstrate one's perfect submission to God, by keeping the commandments not as an act of favor toward heaven, but because one sees himself as obligated by Heaven to do so. R. Joseph, who was blind and therefore not obligated to keep many of the commandments, said that one who kept the commandments because he was commanded to do so was better off than one like himself who did so merely because he wanted to, without such heavenly-imposed obligation.[2] Best of all was to keep the com-mandments "for their own sake," as in the following:

> Rava contrasted the scriptures, "'For your mercy is great *to* the heavens' (Ps. 57:11) and 'For your mercy is great *above* the heavens' (Ps. 108:5). It is to be explained thus: Those who perform command-ments for their own sake find God's mercy great above the heavens, but those who do the commandments with an ulterior motive find God's mercy great [merely] to [but not above] the heavens."
>
> (b. Pes. 50b)

Nonetheless, many pious actions did supposedly produce rewards for specified sacrifices:

> R. Zera said, "The reward of attending a lecture is given on account of the running." Abaye said, "The reward of attending a *Kallah* is given on account of the crowding." Rava said, "The reward of re-peating a tradition is given on account of the understanding of it."
>
> (b. Ber. 6b)

---

[1] b. R.H. 17a, Yoma 23a, Yoma 87b, and here, as an exegesis of Micah 7:18.
[2] b. B.Q. 87a, Qid. 31a.

Rabbinic theology thus consisted of two main elements, first, mostly secret doctrines pertaining to the being and essence of God, the mysteries of history and redemption, and the like. These doctrines were studied in the schools, and rarely if ever taught, or even alluded to, outside of them. Second, the rabbis publicly offered a self-consistent and comprehensive view of man's relationship to God. Man must submit to God's will and demonstrate his submission through observing the commandments. If he sins by not doing so, he will be held responsible. Punishment will follow in this world through suffering, but suffering must be gladly accepted, for it insures that one has at least begun atonement here, and hence need worry less about the world to come. If people sin and nonetheless prosper, or if they do not sin and yet suffer, an easy explanation was available. The wicked enjoy this world, but in time to come will pay a terrible penalty. The righteous suffer now, but in time to come will enjoy a great reward. This neat account sufficed for the orderly conceptions of the schools, but probably not for the disorderly life of the streets.

We cannot ignore other equally important elements of rabbinic theology. Demons, witchcraft, incantations, revelations through omens, dreams, and astrology, the efficacy of prayers and magical formulae, rabbinical blessings and curses, the merit acquired through study of the Torah and obedience to both the commandments and the sages—all of these constitute important components of the rabbinic world-view. A comprehensive account of the rabbis' view of this world and those above and below and of the invisible beings that populate space and carry out divine orders would yield a considerably more complicated theology than that briefly given here. Its main outlines, however, would not be much modified, for magic, angels, demons, and the rest mostly represented the way the rabbis thought matters worked themselves out; that is, they constituted the technology of the rabbis' theological world-view.[1]

VII. THE LIFE OF PRAYER

Over the seen and unseen worlds alike, God presided, and he was to be approached through prayer. The rabbis believed that God sat enthroned above the seventh heaven, surrounded by his heavenly court.

---

[1] It seems to me a useful way of relating the two kinds of data, but I offer the distinction only tentatively, for I cannot prove that the rabbis saw different functions for different sorts of metaphysical and supernatural information. Abaye, for example, did not distinguish between his incantation and his prayer, p. 325.

One recalls that the court above was busy studying Torah (and therefore, required the opinion of Rabbah b. Naḥmani). It also attended to man's wants, when asked or otherwise, according to his merits and its compassion. It was just as important properly to phrase a prayer to heaven as it was properly to inscribe a court document on earth. Hence much discussion focused upon the laws of praying, how properly to enunciate various prayers,[1] the appropriate time, place, circumstance, gesture, and spirit.[2]

Abaye's incantation-like prayer before entering the privy, against the demons of the place, contrasts with his benediction of Heaven afterward:

> [Before entering he should say:] "Guard me, guard me, help me, help me, support me, support me, wait for me, wait for me until I go in and come out, for that is the way of mankind." When he goes out, he should say, "Blessed is he who formed man in wisdom and created in him various orifices...."
>
> (b. Ber. 60b)

The prayer before entering the privy therefore was a formula to secure angelic protection and to drive away demons. The blessing upon leaving was addressed to God. Satan was believed to listen to prayers, just as God did, and therefore Abaye prohibited a certain prayer, because one had to be careful not to say a prayer to heaven which might be heard and answered by Satan in a malevolent manner.[3]

Since prayer went up to heaven, Rava did not order a fast on a cloudy day, citing Lam. 3:44, "Thou hast covered thyself with a cloud so that no prayer can pass through."[4] R. Naḥman b. Isaac said one should take special care properly to say the morning prayers, citing Ps. 5:4, "Lord, in the morning hear my voice...."[5] A good prayer was as effective in propitiating heaven as a sacrifice in the Temple:

> Rava said to R. Ḥiyya b. Abba in the name of R. Yoḥanan, "If one satisfies nature and washes his hands, puts on *tefillen* and says the *Shemaʿ* and the Prayer [Eighteen Benedictions],[6] Scripture accounts it to him as if he had built an altar and offered a sacrifice...."
>
> (b. Ber. 15a)

---

[1] See for example R. 'Ovadyah before Rava, b. Ber. 15b; Rava, b. Suk. 39a, on how to say various prayers.

[2] On saying the *Shemaʿ* nude, Abaye v. Rava, b. Ber. 25b; on the text, b. Ber. 14b, Abaye; on other issues with reference to the Shema, b. Ber. 25a.

[3] b. Ber. 60a.

[4] b. Ber. 32b.

[5] b. Ber. 6b.

[6] Reference to *Prayer* henceforward denotes the Eighteen Benedictions.

The reward of prayer was to come in this world. Rava criticized R. Hamnuna for prolonging his Prayer, and said that he was forsaking study of Torah, which promised eternal life, to occupy himself with merely temporal affairs.[1] Divine response to prayer was regarded as a sign of heavenly love or approval:

> Rava expounded, "What is the meaning of the Scripture, 'I love that the Lord should hear my voice and my supplications (Ps. 116:1)?' The congregation of Israel said, 'Lord of the World, when am I loved before you? When you hear the voice of my supplications.' 'I was brought low and he saved me (Ps. 116:6).' The congregation of Israel said to the Holy One blessed be he, 'Lord of the Universe, though I am poor in religious deeds [miẓvot] yet I am yours and it is fitting [N'H] that I should be saved.'"
>
> (b. Pes. 118b)

Not only were congregational prayers answered, but also those of individuals. Hence individuals were expected to take account of their own circumstance when praying:

> A man was once traveling through the South Side [of Maḥoza = 'BR YMYN'] when a lion attacked him. He was miraculously saved. He came before Rava. Rava told him, "Whenever you pass that place, say 'Blessed is he who did a miracle for me in this place.'"
>
> (b. Ber. 54a)

Similarly, Rabbah and R. Joseph said that one should say something new in his prayers each day and not merely repeat the required liturgy.[2] Private prayer was best when rabbis guided it:

> Rava heard a certain person praying, "May that girl be destined to be mine!" Rava said to him, "Do not pray thus, for if she is appropriate for you, you will not lose her, and if not, you will have challenged Providence..."
>
> (b. M.Q. 18b)

One had better know what to request of heaven.
    Best of all was prayer in a group:

> R. Joseph said, "One should not recite in private the Additional Service on the first day of the New Year during the first three hours of the day, for judgment is then going on, so his deeds may be scrutinized and the prayer rejected." But if so, the same rule should apply to the congregation as a whole. In that case, the merits of the congregation [are collectively greater] so the congregation will not be rejected.
>
> (b. A.Z. 4b)

---

[1] b. Shab. 10a.
[2] b. Ber. 29b.

Prayer was a risky thing, for it drew the attention of heaven to the praying person and his merits, and hence the community as a whole rather than the individual had best pray together on the day on which men were summoned to judgment. That judgment was for the coming year, and each individual was then assessed.[1] The less the private person was scrutinized the better. If a person prayed improperly, his prayer was regarded as an abomination and could arouse heavenly wrath instead of the desired result.[2]

Of greatest importance was the constant recognition that when praying, a person really faced God. One therefore should not move his feet, and if he does, he returns to the beginning of the prayer.[3] The following reveals how Abaye and Rava envisioned praying:

> "A thousand may fall at thy side, and ten thousand at thy right hand (Ps. 91:7)." Seeing Abaye say 'peace' first to the right, Rava said, 'Do you mean *your* right hand is meant? It is *your* left hand, which is the right of the Holy One...."
>
> (b. Yoma 53b)[4]

In all, when one prays, he must pray fearfully, for which R. Naḥman b. Isaac found Scriptural warrant in Ps. 2:11, "Serve the Lord with fear, and rejoice with trembling."[5]

In the synagogues, old traditions endured, and some of these were not approved by the rabbis.[6] The rabbis however prayed in them, and naturally where great authorities were found, people consulted them. We have a few stories about synagogue prayer under rabbinical supervision, including the following:

> Rafram b. Papa happened to be at the synagogue of 'Abi Gobar [near Maḥoza]. He arose, read in the scroll [of the Torah], saying "Blessed be the Lord", and was silent, [not saying "Who is to be blessed."] The whole congregation cried out, "Blessed be the Lord who is to be blessed." Rava said to him, "Black pot...."
>
> (b. Ber. 50a)

A certain person went down to lead prayers in the presence of

---

[1] I do not know how faith in astrology was harmonized with faith in annual divine judgment. It is clear that R. Joseph did believe what astrologers said.

[2] b. Ber. 22b.

[3] b. Ber. 29b.

[4] On bowing, see Rava, b. Ber. 28b.

[5] b. Ber. 29b, R. Naḥman b. Isaac discussed the rules about what happens if one moves his feet while saying the Prayer.

[6] Vol. II, pp. 274ff, vol. III, pp. 234-238.

Rabbah. Rabbah heard him say "Truth, truth" twice. Rabbah said, "All truth truly has seized him!"

(b. Ber. 14b)[1]

Abaye cursed anyone who said [an abbreviated form of the Prayer, instead of the full text].

(b. Ber. 29a)

The first two stories indicate that Rava criticized a student for following a custom not accepted in 'Abi Gobar, and Rabbah criticized a person for changing the liturgy. They do not provide substantial evidence that rabbis could determine the rites of the synagogue, only that they could criticize what was wrongly done, in one instance by a disciple. Abaye's curse must have discouraged some people from saying a prayer of which he did not approve. Other rabbis, however, did accept the abbreviated version, which Samuel had permitted a century earlier, and all Abaye could do was curse those who acted contrary to his own opinion. Whether or not ordinary folk knew Abaye's view we cannot say. The schools, nonetheless, discussed various aspects of public, synagogue worship. Since such worship would have taken place in the schools as well, we cannot readily distinguish between sayings pertinent to the folk-synagogues and those which would have been effective only in the synagogues of the academies.[2]

Characteristic of the academy was stress upon the benediction for various benefits, foods, miracles, and the like. We saw that when a man was saved from a lion, he went to Rava who told him that he must say an appropriate blessing. That the rabbis regarded the art of benedictions as peculiarly their own[3] is seen in the following:

[Tannaitic tradition teaches, It is forbidden for a man to enjoy anything in this world without a benediction ... What is his remedy? He should go to a sage.] What good is that? He has already committed a sin. Rava said, "*Let him go to a sage in the first place, so that the sage may*

---

[1] See also b. Ber. 33b, Abaye said if one says a prayer in the manner of the *minim*, by inadvertently repeating a word, you call his attention back to what he is doing by hitting him with the hammer of a smith. On repeating words in prayer, see Blau, *op. cit.*, p. 147, *re* b. Meg. 25a.

[2] For example, b. Shab. 24b, Rava on whether the precentor must say a certain prayer; b. Git. 59b, Abaye on the priestly benediction; b. Ber. 14a, Rabbah on how an individual says the Hallel. Note also b. Ber. 33a, R. Joseph explaining the structure of the Prayer, and why certain supplementary blessings are included as they are. I am by no means certain that the academicians did not attend the communal services in towns were schools were located.

[3] See vol. II, pp. 177-180.

teach him the blessings, so that he may not commit sacrilege [by enjoying something in this world without a benediction]." (Italics supplied.)

(b. Ber. 35a)

It was therefore the sage who knew the proper benedictions, and if a person wanted to learn them, he had to go to the school.

The extensive discussions of blessings for various kinds of food mostly had been completed by this time, and few significant contributions came from the fourth-century schools.[1] Most of the stories about liturgical practices of rabbis concerned how they said benedictions, the Grace after Meals, the Sanctification of the Sabbath Wine, and the *Havdalah* prayer:

Rabbah b. Mari happened to the house of Rava on a weekday. He saw that he blessed [wine] before the meal and afterward as well....

(b. Ber. 42b)

R. Isaac b. R. Joseph happened to come to the house of Abaye on a festival. He saw that he blessed each cup of wine....

(b. Ber. 42b)

R. Papa and R. Huna b. R. Joshua and Rava b. Samuel were eating together. R. Papa said, "Let me say grace, because nine pails of water have been thrown on me [so I am ritually pure]...."

(b. Ber. 22b)

Rava said the blessing over the light in [a neighboring house] in the *Havdalah* ceremony.

(b. Ber. 53b)

R. Huna b. Judah was once at the house of Rava and saw him say the *Havdalah* blessing over spices first...

(b. Ber. 52b)[2]

Abaye said, "When I was at Rabbah's house and he recited the Sanctification, he would say to us, 'Eat a little here, lest by the time you reach your lodgings your lamps be upset and you do not recite the Sanctification in the house where you eat....'"

(b. Pes. 101a)

---

[1] b. Men. 75b, R. Joseph on the blessing for *havizah*; b. Ber. 36a, Rava on the blessing over wheat flour; b. Ber. 36b, Rava on the blessing over pepper; b. Ber. 38b, Abaye on the blessing for boiled vegetables, see also b. Ber. 38b, R. Naḥman b. Isaac; b. Ber. 38a, Abaye asked R. Joseph on the blessing over dough baked in a hole in the ground; b. Ber. 37b, Rava on the bread of field workers. On the laws of Grace after Meals, see b. Ber. 48a, Rava, b. Ber. 45b, Abaye. Compare vol. III, pp. 164ff.

[2] See also b. Pes. 103a-b, on *havdalah* at the home of Rava.

Some stories pertained to how various rabbis said their prayers:

> R. Ḥiyya b. R. Huna said, "I observed Abaye and Rava bending to
> one side [rather than fully prostrating themselves in saying the Prayer]
> ... Rava kneeled, and was asked why. He said, "Because I saw R.
> Naḥman and R. Sheshet do so."
>
> (b. Ber. 34b)[1]

> [When Abaye heard the blessing 'Who builds Jerusalem'] he
> answered in so loud a voice that the workers could hear him and
> arise...."
>
> (b. Ber. 45b)

It was natural for the students to observe the masters' behavior and
to record their actions in matters about which there was some dispute.
Grace after Meals, benedictions, the Sanctification of the Sabbath Wine,
and similar matters pertained most directly to the schools and the
homes of the rabbis. We have no stories whatever about how people
who were not academicians or associated with rabbis observed or
copied the rabbinical procedures.

VIII. ASTROLOGY

The world had been created by the Holy One, blessed be He, and He
might alter it at any moment in answer to prayer, but He left its ordinary administration in the hands of his ministers, as the emperor did
thus of the empire, and His ministers, though more powerful than the
emperor's, were not necessarily better. In general charge of the world
were the angels of the stars and planets, whose influence varied according to their characters, and whose power, according to the positions of their stars or planets. Hence, the guide to this cosmic administration was the science of astrology.

While a few rabbis, mostly Palestinian by birth or education, doubted
that the Jews were subject to planetary influences, all were quite certain
that astrology was a valid science.[2] Most, moreover, believed that its
findings pertained to Israel as much as to the gentiles. Some qualified

---

[1] But see above, p. 151, for another reason.

[2] On the rabbis and astrology, see especially S. Lieberman, *Greek in Jewish
Palestine* (N.Y., 1942), pp. 97-100. Lieberman stresses that astrology was regarded
as an accurate science: "To deny at that time the efficacy of Astrology would mean
to deny a well established fact." Lieberman affirms that the rabbis thought astrology a science "but only for the gentiles, not for the pious Jews. The opinion
of the Rabbis finally prevailed even on the Gentile Astrologers." Perhaps, but not
in this period—and astrology now applied to the most "pious" Jews of all!

that conviction, for they thought that astrological fate could be modified by study of Torah, practice of the commandments, or merits acquired by good deeds. The larger number did not even make that qualification. In this time, not a single master in Babylonia known to us doubted the inexorability of astrological influence.[1]

What is striking, however, is the fourth-century rabbis' failure to leave sayings which indicate their own mastery of astrological sciences. In the stories cited below, we shall see numerous references to Chaldeans and many instances of rabbinical faith in their predictions. Apart from some rather generalized traditions, however, we find no astrological sayings of much consequence, and not a single example in which a rabbi or another Jew prepared a horoscope or otherwise predicted the future upon the basis of the stars. It was a science of the Chaldeans, one which the fourth-century rabbis believed valid, but, in contrast to so many other wonderful capabilities, now did not apparently claim to have mastered.

The Palestinian schools believed that the day and hour of one's birth would affect his fate. In R. Joshua b. Levi's notebook it was recorded that one who was born on the Sabbath would be a seeker, on which R. Naḥman b. Isaac commented,

> "A seeker after good deeds."
>
> (b. Shab. 156a)

R. Ḥanina said concerning R. Joshua's traditions that it was not the constellation of the day, but that of the hour, which was determinative. If born under the constellation of the sun, a man would be distinguished; under Venus, he would be wealthy and unchaste; under Mercury, he would have a retentive memory, because Mercury was the scribe of the sun. He who was born under Mars would shed blood, on which we have the following exchange:

> Rabbah said, "I was born under Mars." Abaye said to him, "You too inflict punishment and kill."
>
> (b. Shab. 156a)

R. Ḥanina flatly stated that planetary influence gives wisdom and wealth, and Israel is subject to it. Some distinguished masters supposedly opposed this view, in particular, R. Yoḥanan, Rav, Samuel, and R. 'Aqiva. In the traditions on alleged opposition to astrology, we find the following:

---

[1] See below, pp. 332-334.

From R. Naḥman b. Isaac [we learn] Israel is not subjected to the
stars. For R. Naḥman b. Isaac's mother was told by Chaldeans, "Your
son will be a thief." She did not let him go bareheaded, saying, "Cover
your head so the fear of heaven may be upon you, and pray for mercy."
He did not know why she said so. One day he was sitting and studying
under a palm. His covering fell off his head, and his desire overcame
him, so he climbed up, bit off a cluster of dates with his teeth [and thus
was a thief.]

(b. Shab. 156b)

Thus R. Naḥman b. Isaac's alleged "rejection" of astrology was based
upon the belief that the predictions it made possible might be satisfied
in trivial fashions, and thus be insignificant for the individual's life.
When, furthermore, one reexamines the stories told to prove that
earlier masters had rejected the belief in astrology, we find similarly
equivocal evidence. R. Yoḥanan actually did leave a saying that Israel
is not subject to the stars, and he cited Jer. 10:2 as evidence. However,
the story told in Rav's name was about Abraham's disbelief in the
prediction of God that he would have a son. God then replied, "If it is
on account of your constellation, go forth from astrology, for Israel is
free from astrological influence." God then corrected Abraham's calcu-
lation, and, the story concludes, "I will turn Jupiter back and place it
in the east" so as to correct your fate.[1] The story about Samuel and
'Ablat proves only that Samuel believed one's merits might overcome
his astrological destiny. It was an effort to harmonize astrology with
belief in merits, which were achieved in this instance through compassionate action.[2] The story about R. 'Aqiva specifically says that he
was worried about a prediction of Chaldeans concerning his daughter;
indeed, what they predicted would have come about, had not R. 'Aqiva
taken action against it, and had not the girl's own merits protected her.
So the pericope about how leading masters did not accept astrology
proves only that Yoḥanan was firmly opposed to it. The other materials show quite to the contrary that leading rabbis did believe astrological predictions had to be taken seriously, but in some cases,
knew how to overcome the stars, or believed merit would do so. Whoever compiled these stories clearly believed that the ancient rabbis had
rejected astrology, and it is clear that one or two of them had left traditions to support his conviction. But most of the materials he tried to
include in the passage proved the contrary.

Had a later editor chosen to prepare a pericope to prove that the

---

[1] Vol. II, pp. 84-85.
[2] Vol. I, pp. 162-163.

leading fourth-century masters had faith in astrology or thought that Israel was subjected to planetary influence, he would have included the following:

> R. Papa said, "A Jew who has a case with gentiles should avoid them in 'Av, because his luck [star=MZLYH] is bad, and make himself available in 'Adar when his luck is good."
>
> (b. Ta'anit 29b)

> Rava said, "[Length of] *years, children, and a good living depend not on merit* [ZKWT'] *but on one's star* [MZL'] (Italics supplied) for Rabbah and R. Ḥisda were both righteous rabbis. One prayed for rain and it came, and so did the other, [which proves they were both righteous]. R. Ḥisda lived to ninety-two, and Rabbah to forty. R. Ḥisda held sixty marriages, Rabbah, sixty bereavements. [R. Ḥisda was rich, Rabbah ate poorly...]."
>
> R. Seʿorim, brother of Rava, was sitting at Rava's deathbed. He saw Rava nodding. Rava said to him, "Do tell him [the angel of death] not to torment me." R. Seʿorim said, "Are you not his intimate friend?" Rava replied, "Since my star [MZL'] has been delivered [to him], he takes no heed of me." R. Seʿorim said, "Show yourself to me in a dream [after death]." He did so, and was asked, "Did you suffer?" He replied, "No more than the prick of the cupping instrument."
>
> (b. M.Q. 28a)

Abaye offered proof that prophecy continued to be given to the sages, for when a great man makes a statement, the same statement is then reported in the name of another great man. Such a "coincidence" would supposedly indicate that each had received divine revelation. Rava replied,

> "What is so strange? Perhaps both were born under one star."
>
> (b. B.B. 12a)

So the stars, in Rava's explicit view, might even determine a *legal* opinion. One recalls, moreover, that R. Joseph had been told by Chaldeans that he would "reign" for two and a half years, so he declined to accept the headship of the school in fear of abbreviating his life. When he finally did become head, it was for two and a half years.[1]

Not all astronomical observations and comments pertained to astrology. On the Tannaitic teaching, that one who sees "the sun at its turning point, the moon in its power, the planets in their orbits, and the signs of the zodiac in their orderly progress" should say a certain blessing, Abaye explained when these all coincide:

---

[1] b. Ber. 64a, cited above, p. 93.

"Every twenty eight years, when the [solar] cycle begins again, and the spring equinox falls in Saturn on the evening of Tuesday going into Wednesday."

(b. Ber. 59b)

Abaye similarly possessed traditions on various meteorological phenomena. He said:

"We have a tradition that a hurricane never comes at night."

(b. Ber. 59a)

The editorial comment was,

"But behold, we see that it does!"

It is clear that some traditions were tested against actual experience. If so, it stands to reason that the rabbis and ordinary people as well did not doubt that astrological predictions would similarly stand up against the test of experience.

IX. DEMONS AND ANGELS

Belief in demons was ancient and widespread in Babylonia.[1] What set the rabbis apart from ordinary people was not their conviction that they could see demons, but their claim to be able to master them by Torah or divine assistance elicited on account of merit. Demons were believed the cause of a great many natural inconveniences. Abaye said that demons are more numerous than people, and stand around each person like a ridge around a field. Rava said that the crowding at the kallah-assemblies, fatigue in the knees, wearing out of clothing, bruising of the feet—all are caused by demons.[2] Many everyday actions were believed subject to the rule of demons, and hence prohibited by rabbinic tradition:

---

[1] Joshua Trachtenberg, *Jewish Magic and Superstition* (repr. N.Y., 1961), p. 25, "Talmudic Jewry owned a highly elaborated demonology, distinguishing between classes and even individuals.... This lore served a dual need: it conveyed the power of control and at the same time of self-protection. But the rabbis were generally opposed to demon-magic, and though they were not so severe with it as with sympathetic magic (some of the most distinguished Talmudic authorities themselves had recourse to it at times), they frequently expressed their strong disapproval." The stories we shall consider here contain no hint whatever of such allegedly strong disapproval. I know of no stories from this time which make explicit any disapproval, strong or otherwise.

[2] b. Ber. 6a.

Abaye said, "At first I thought the reason why the last washing [after a meal] may not be performed over the ground was that it made a mess, but now my master [Rabbah] told me that it is because an evil spirit rests on it."

(b. Ḥul. 105b)

Abaye said, "At first I thought one collects crumbs because of tidiness. but now my master [Rabbah] has told me it might lead to poverty. Once the angel [prince] of poverty was following a certain man, but could not prevail over him because the man was careful about crumbs. One day he ate bread on the grass. [The angel] said, "Now he will surely fall into my hand." After eating, he [the man] took a spade, dug up the grass, and threw it [all] into the river. He heard the angel exclaiming, "Alas, he has driven me [lit.: that man] out of his house."

(b. Ḥul. 105b)

Rava thought that some plagues are due to ghosts. R. Papa said some are due to witchcraft.

(b. Hor. 10a)

Abaye said one does not sit under a drain pipe because demons are found there.

(b. Ḥul. 105b)

Similarly, one pours off water from the mouth of the jug because demons sip from the top of the jug. As we saw, demons were believed to afflict people especially at the privy, and were driven away by *tefillin*, by the presence of more than one person, or by noise. So Abaye's mother trained a lamb to go with him into the privy, and Rava's wife would rattle a nut in a brass dish. After he became head of the school, she made a window and put her hand on his head to protect him. Apparently rattling a nut was no longer thought sufficiently dignified.[1]

Demons supposedly punished people who drank two, or any multiple of two, cups of wine at the same sitting. R. Joseph was specifically told by the demon Joseph that Ashmedai, king of demons, was in charge of the matter:

The second cup of wine at a meal was believed by R. Naḥman b. Isaac to be unlucky.

(b. Ber. 51b)

R. Joseph was told by the demon Joseph that Ashmedai, king of demons, is appointed over all "pairs"...R. Papa said that Joseph the demon told him, "we kill for two's, but not for four's. For four's, we harm...."

(b. Pes. 110a)[2]

---

[1] b. Ber. 62a.

[2] See b. Pes. 110a, R. Ḥisda and Rabbah b. R. Huna on the seventh cup. Also b. Pes. 110b-111a, wine and beer do not combine for bad luck.

One should therefore be careful not to drink two cups and then go outside. Rabbis, however, knew what to do. They would make some mental or physical effort to avoid "drinking in multiples of two," as in the following stories:

> When he drank a cup of wine, Rava [mentally] counted the beams, so as to avoid drinking "in pairs." When Abaye drank one cup, his [foster-] mother would give him two more.
>
> (b. Pes. 110a)

Rabbis did not have to resort to the magic on which ordinary people depended, for, because of their piety, Torah, and genealogical merits, they were supposed to be able to overcome the influence of demons. Abaye was specifically informed that in heaven, the queen of demons was told to leave him alone:

> ['Igrat daughter of Maḥalat, queen of demons] once met Abaye. She said to him, "Had they not proclaimed concerning you in heaven, 'Take heed of Naḥmani and his Torah', I should have endangered you." He replied, "If I am important in heaven, I order you never to pass through inhabited areas."
>
> (b. Pes. 112b)

We do not know the result. The same discussion continues, "But we see that she *does* pass through [inhabited regions]?" The reply was that demons frequent narrow paths and their horses bolt from there and thus bring them into settled places. What is important is that people believed, or were expected to believe, that because of Abaye's merits, specifically his learning, he and other people were protected from demons, as from other dangers.[1]

A rabbi's prayer was also believed potent against demons:

> ... A certain demon haunted Abaye's schoolhouse, so that when two [disciples] entered even by day they were harmed. [Abaye ordered that R. Aḥa b. Jacob spend the night in the school.] The demon appeared to him in the guise of a seven-headed dragon. Every time [R. Aḥa] fell on his knees, one head fell off. The next day he reproached [the school-men], "Had not a miracle occurred, you would have endangered my life."
>
> (b. Qid. 29b)

Abaye had believed that R. Aḥa's merits would be sufficient to exorcize the demon, and the reply, like R. Zera's to Rabbah when the latter

---

[1] Above, p. 325, below, p. 357.

cut the former's throat and resurrected him, was that in any case one should not rely upon miracles.[1]

Not only merit but also knowledge of astrological laws was believed to operate to protect the rabbis:

> Abaye was walking along with R. Papa on the right and R. Huna b. R. Joshua on his left. Seeing a [certain kind of demon, named] Bitter Destruction [QTB MRYRY, see Deut. 32:24] approaching on the left, he moved R. Papa to the left and R. Huna b. R. Joshua to the right. R. Papa asked, "Why do I differ that you are not afraid on my behalf?" He replied, "For you, the hour [Š'T'] is favorable."
>
> (b. Pes. 111b)

So along with reliance upon Torah, piety, and other merits, the rabbis regarded knowledge of astrological circumstances as consequential in protecting themselves from demons.[2]

Rava explained that if one wanted to see demons, he should take sifted ashes and sprinkle them about his bed. In the morning he will see something like the footprints of a cock. Further, he said,

> "If one wishes to see them, let him take the afterbirth of a black cat, the offspring of a black she cat, the first-born of a first-born, and roast it in fire and grind it up, and fill his eyes with it. Let him pour the rest into an iron tube and seal it with an iron signet, that it should not be stolen from him [by demons]. Let him close his mouth, lest he come to harm." R. Bibi b. Abaye did so and saw them, but came to harm. The rabbis prayed for mercy for him and he recovered.
>
> (b. Ber. 6a)

Obviously if one rubbed ashes into his eyes, he would see something, and his eyes would probably be damaged, at least for a time. One would naturally ascribe what he saw and suffered to the effects of demons.

We have seen, therefore, that the rabbis believed demons were both real and particularly active in the schools. Rabbis knew how to cope with them. They avoided drinking two cups at a time and attracting demons by pouring water or crumbs on the ground. They were able to counteract the demons of the privy by making noise, so frightening them away. Leading rabbis, particularly Abaye and R. Joseph, supposedly had conversations with important demons, who conveyed

---

[1] See b. B.B. 73a-b, Rabbah said he saw Hormin the son of Lilith running on a parapet. However immediately following are stories about Rabbah b.b. Ḥanah's miraculous visions, and it may be that this account belongs to the latter traditions. See Blau, *op. cit.*, p. 12.

[2] On communication with angels, see below, p. 338. For further astrological beliefs, see above, pp. 330ff.

information concerning what orders were given in heaven. Rabbis who were particularly meritorious were able to overcome demons by praying. Others were safe, at least sometimes, on account of their horoscope or their Torah. In the stories considered here we have found neither the slightest trace of disbelief in demonology, nor a single expression of disapproval of such belief *or* of the magic used against them. What is more to the point is that "divine-men" in antiquity were expected to be able to master not only natural phenomena, illness, and death, but also demons.[1] If one supposes that the rabbis were attempting here or elsewhere to purify, ennoble, or elevate the "superstitions" of the ordinary people, and so transform them into "true religion," he simply misses the point of these stories. The point is that *no* "divine-man" could be taken as such who could *not* manipulate or otherwise dominate the world of demons. A rabbi was a rabbi in part because he could do so. It was just as integral to his character to use Torah against demons as it was to learn legal sayings for court-action. The reason the data contain no evidence of rabbinical disapproval of belief in demons is that such disapproval would have been anachronistic and incredible. Just as astrology was an exact science, so were the devices to avert or subjugate demons; these devices required prayer, or incantation, or repeating words of Torah, or astrological good fortune.[2]

The angel of death held seances with some of the rabbis. One recalls that Rabbah was able to keep the angel away because he engaged in study of Torah so fervently that he did not cease even for a moment. In the following story, we see that the angel of death was said to have communicated frequently with R. Bibi b. Abaye, and to have reported that when a man's star "was impaired," he might have power over him:

> R. Bibi b. Abaye was frequently visited by the angel of death. Once the angel told his messenger, "Go, bring me Miriam, the women's hairdresser." He brought Miriam, the children's nurse. He said, "I told you Miriam the hairdresser." "If so," he answered, "I will take her back." He said, "Since you brought her, let her be added [to the

---

[1] Bieler, *op. cit.*, I, pp. 94ff.

[2] It is deplorable that pious scholars have tried to explain away magical, demonological, astrological, and other supernatural rabbinical exempla in various ways. They are motivated by quite sincere theological convictions. What I regret is their inability to discern where historical scholarship ends, and theological apologetic begins. As I have repeatedly stressed, whatever we find in the Babylonian Talmud is there because the schools and authorities approved of it and wished to preserve it. We assuredly err by imposing our judgment of what is "elevated," or "noble," or "true" religion upon theirs. For a different view of anti-demonic talents, see Josephus's description of Solomon, cited p. 362.

number of the dead]." "How were you able to get her [before her time]?" The messenger replied, "She was holding a shovel in her hand, heating and raking it over. She took it, and put it on her foot, and burned herself. Her luck [star] was impaired, so I brought her." R. Bibi b. Abaye said to the angel of death, "Do you have the right to act in such a way?" He replied, "Is it not written, 'There is that is swept away without judgment' (Prov. 13:23)." He replied, "But it is written, 'One generation passes away, and another comes' [in due time, not before]? (Qoh. 1:4)" He replied, "I have charge of them until they have completed the generation, and then I hand them over to Dumah [Silence, the angel in charge of the dead]." He asked, "But what do you do with her years [which she should have lived]?" He replied, "If there is a disciple of the rabbis who overlooks his own hurt, I add them to *his* years in her stead."

(b. Hag. 4b-5a)[1]

The following story provided corroborative evidence concerning rabbinic belief in what the angel of death had said:

Rava said, "One who forgoes his rights is forgiven all his iniquities..." R. Huna b. R. Joshua fell ill. R. Papa went to ask about him, and seeing that he was very ill, said to those present, "Ready provisions for his journey." R. Huna recovered, and R. Papa was ashamed to see him. He asked, "What did you see?" He replied, "It was indeed as you thought [I was really dying] but the Holy One blessed be he said to them [the angels], 'Because he does not insist on his rights, do not be particular about him...'"

(b. R.H. 17a)

Furthermore, rabbis were able to communicate easily with the dead:

There was a certain Magus ['MGWŠ'] who used to rummage among the graves [to exhume the bodies and expose them to the birds]. When he came to that of R. Tovi b. Mattenah, R. Tovi took hold of his beard. Abaye came and said to [the deceased rabbi], "Pray, leave him." A year later he again came and the same thing happened, but the deceased would not leave the Magus alone until Abaye brought scissors and cut off his beard.

(b. B.B. 58a)[2]

The purpose of telling this story is quite obvious. The Magi desecrate Jewish graves, but that does not mean that they do so with impunity. Dead rabbis can punish them for their actions. Living rabbis can sometimes control dead rabbis and tell them what to do. In any event, rabbis are able to communicate with, and instruct, the dead, and Magi

[1] See B. Lewin, *Ozar HaGeonim*, IV, part ii, p. 6.
[2] See above, Rava appeared to his brother in a dream, b. M.Q. 28a, cited p. 333. See vol. III, pp. 108-109 for other examples.

cannot. This story, like the long account of Bar Sheshakh cited above, is part of the polemical tradition shaped in the schools. That tradition held that pagan magicians were powerful but dangerous; rabbinical magicians were more powerful but benevolent.[1]

Receiving heavenly greetings and other messages was regarded as a sign of heavenly favor, and was not at all uncommon, as we have seen. In the following account, the receipt of heavenly greetings was regarded as recognition of one's ethical or moral merits:

> Abba was a cupper. He daily would receive greetings from the Heavenly Academy. Abaye received greetings every Sabbath eve. Rava annually received them on the eve of the Day of Atonement. Abaye was dejected [lit. "his mind weakened"] because of Abba the cupper. People said to him, "You cannot do what he does ... When he performed operations, he would separate men from women, [and otherwise was fastidious in keeping patients from unchastity.] He had a hidden place where patients deposited their fees ... Those that could afford it put their fees there, and those that could not pay were not put to shame. Whenever a rabbinical disciple consulted him he would accept no fee, but would give him some money..." One day Abaye sent to him two disciples to test him. He received them, gave them food and drink, and in the evening prepared woolen mattresses for them. In the morning they rolled them up and took them to the market [to sell them]. There they met Abba and asked him how much they are worth. He said so-and-so-much. "Perhaps more?" He replied, "That is what I paid for them." They said to him, "They are yours and we took them. By your leave, of what did you suspect us?" He replied, "I thought the rabbis needed money for the redemption of captives and were ashamed to tell me." They said, "Sir, take them back." He answered, "From the moment I missed them I put them out of mind and gave them to charity." Rava was dejected because of Abaye. He was told, "Be content that [through you] the whole city is protected."
>
> (b. Ta'anit 21b-22a)

The purport of the first story is to show that even an ignorant money-maker may by generosity excell great rabbis in merit and consequent reward. But such a man will respect and think only good of the rabbis (as they indeed deserve). This has several cutting edges, against popular pietists who are critical of the rabbis, against rabbinical students who are unscrupulous, and against the avaricious. For our present purpose the important thing is that it shows a reward dangled before the ava-

---

[1] Bieler (*op. cit.*, I, pp. 24ff) points out that normally the birth of the Θεῖος ἀνήρ was announced in a dream. I know of no rabbinical account of a prediction of the birth of a rabbi by means of a dream or other revelation. Nor are miracle-stories told in connection with the birth of rabbis, compare Bieler, I, 28ff.

ricious was that of daily communion with heaven by means of special messengers or messages. Rava was told that he possesses sufficient merits to protect a whole city. The rabbis certainly believed their presence itself contributed to the protection of the city, and made this an excuse to refuse to pay for the cost of building walls or defending them. So the heavenly message was both believed and put into effect.

x. Dreams and Other Revelations

Conceiving of the world as populated by demons and angels, and presided over by God, with his heavenly court and school, the rabbis thought that the spiritual and heavenly beings communicated with men in various ways, both directly and through signs, wonders, and omens. Direct communication between supernatural beings and men has just been considered. Even the Holy One, blessed be He, might speak to men directly in prophecy—but this prophecy was practically ruled out. One recalls the discussion between Abaye and Rava about whether prophecy had truly ceased. Abaye maintained that prophecy remained in the hands of the sages, but he would probably have given a frigid welcome to any scholar who actually professed himself a prophet. Earlier Pharisaism had denied that prophecy lasted beyond the time of Malachi, Haggai, and Zechariah. Next to prophecy, and terminologically sometimes confused with it, came the utterance of "ominous" sayings, i.e. sayings rarely more than a single sentence, and often only a word or two, which indicated, independently of the speaker's intention, what was to happen. The rabbis shared with non-rabbinic Jews and their pagan neighbors the belief that such sentences might be uttered by anyone. A nice example considered as prophecy and with the high-priest as speaker, occurs in John 11:49, while Augustine's conversion by such an utterance was later to be famous (Confessions VIII, 12, 29). In Augustine's case, the speaker was a child, and the rabbis too shared the common belief that such utterances were particularly likely to come through children and imbeciles, as the following story indicates:

> The daughter of R. Ḥisda was sitting on her father's lap. In front of him were Rava and Rami b. Ḥama. He said to her, "Which of them would you like?" She replied, "Both." Rava said, "And let me be the second."
>
> (b. B.B. 12b).

Quotation by a child of the Scriptural lesson he had just learned might produce a revelation, Rava believed.[1] Omens to be interpreted included any sort of change in the normal routine of daily life, and Rava[2] and Abaye both held that omens were meaningful, should be interpreted and heeded.[3]

After omens, as recognized revelations of the future came dreams. Rava took a rationalistic view of dreaming, saying that if one goes to sleep in good spirits, he will have a good dream.[4] He also held that one dreams only what is suggested by his own thoughts; therefore one does not see in a dream [lit.: they do not show a man]

> a golden palm-tree or an elephant going through the eye of a needle.
> (b. Ber. 55b)

Since such things do not exist, one supposedly will not dream about them. Rava along with all other rabbis of the generation paid attention to the interpretation of dreams, a subject on which the rabbis claimed, and were believed, to speak with authority. Dreams were not only revelations from heaven, but even signs that Israel was not wholly rejected by God. So Rava explained Deut. 31:17, "And I will hide my face in that day,"

> Rava said, "Although I hide my face from them, I shall speak to them in a dream."
> (b. Ḥag. 5b)

Such revelations through dreams were illustrated as follows:

> Two disciples were once sitting before Rava. One reported that in a dream, the following Scripture was read to him, "O how great is your goodness which you have laid up for them that fear you?" (Ps. 31:20), and the other said in his dream he heard the following Scripture, "But let those that ... love your name be joyful in you" (Ps. 5:12). He replied, "You are both completely righteous rabbis, but one is motivated by love and the other by fear."
> (b. Sot. 31a)

To the corpus of the rabbinic traditions about the interpretation of omens and dreams, this generation of authorities added the following sayings:

---

[1] b. Yoma 75b.

[2] b. Yoma 75b. One day his field-hand did not bring him quail, as he ordinarily did.

[3] b. Ker. 6a, Hor. 12a, Abaye said that omens are meaningful, so therefore on the New Year one should eat pumpkin.

[4] b. Shab. 30b.

[In the school of R. Ishmael it was taught that one who experienced a nocturnal emission on the Day of Atonement should be anxious through the coming year, but if he survives the year, he may be sure he will enter the world to come.] R. Naḥman b. Isaac said, "You may know it for all the world is hungry and he is satisfied..."

(b. Yoma 88a)

R. Zera said, "A pumpkin, a palm-heart, wax, and a reed are all good omens in a dream."

(b. Ber. 56b)

[If one sees a camel in a dream, death has been decreed from heaven, but the man has been delivered from it.] R. Naḥman b. Isaac said that this was proved by II Sam. 12:13.

(b. Ber. 56b)

R. Joseph said, "If one sees a goat in a dream, he will have a blessed year. If he sees several goats, he will have several good years. [The proof-text was Prov. 27:27]. If one sees myrtle, he will have good luck with his property; if he has no property, he will inherit some ... If one sees a citron, he is honored in the sight of his Maker [a play on the words *hadar* and *hadur*, with Lev. 23:40 as proof-text]. If one sees a palm branch in a dream, he is single-hearted in devotion to his father in heaven. If he sees a goose, he may hope for wisdom ... and if he dreams of being with one, he will become head of an academy...."

(b. Ber. 57a)

If one dreams that he goes up to the roof, he will attain high position. If he dreams he goes down, he will lose it. Abaye and Rava both say that once he has attained a high position [and dreams he goes down] he will remain there...

(b. Ber. 57a)

The following story[1] indicates that the rabbis, though in this field they claimed to speak authoritatively, believed in the dream-interpretation of others outside of their schools, just as they were prepared to depend upon the predictions of astrologers [= Chaldeans]. It is clear that while it was theoretically the dream which determined matters, and not the intervening interpretation of the dream-interpreter, nonetheless the interpretation here seemed decisive:

Bar Hedya was an interpreter of dreams. To one who paid him he used to give a favorable interpretation and to one who did not pay him he gave an unfavorable interpretation. Abaye and Rava each had a dream. Abaye gave him a *zuz*, and Rava did not give him anything. They said to him, "In our dream we read the verse, 'Thine ox shall be slain before thine eyes' (Deut. 28:31)." To Rava he said, "Your

---

[1] Trans. Maurice Simon, (London, 1948) pp. 342-347, with minor changes.

business will be a failure, and you will be so grieved that you will have no appetite to eat." To Abaye he said, "Your business will prosper, and you will not be able to eat from sheer joy." They then said to him, "We read in our dream the verse, 'Thou shalt beget sons and daughters but they shall not be thine,' (Deut. 28:41)." To Rava, he interpreted it in its [literal] unfavorable [sense]. To Abaye he said, "You have numerous sons and daughters, and your daughters will be married and go away, and it will seem to you as if they have gone into captivity." [They said to him] "We read the verse, 'Thy sons and thy daughters shall be given unto another people,' (Deut. 28:32)." To Abaye he said, "You have numerous sons and daughters; you will want your daughters to marry your relatives, and your wife will want them to marry her relatives, and she will force you to marry them to her relatives, which will be like giving them to another people." To Rava he said, "Your wife will die, and her sons and daughters will come under the sway of another wife." [They further said]: "We read in our dream the verse, 'Go thy way, eat thy bread with joy,' (Qoh. 9:7)." To Abaye he said, "Your business will prosper, and you will eat and drink, and recite this verse out of the joy of your heart." To Rava he said, "Your business will fail, you will slaughter [cattle] and not eat or drink and you will read Scripture to allay your anxiety." [They said to him]: "We read the verse, 'Thou shalt carry much seed out into the field [and shall gather little in, for the locusts will consume it]' (Deut. 28:38)." To Abaye he interpreted the first half of the verse; to Rava the second half. [They said to him:] "We read the verse, 'Thou shalt have olive trees throughout all thy borders, [but thou shalt not anoint thyself,']' (Deut. 28:40)." To Abaye he interpreted the first half of the verse; to Rava the second half. [They said to him:] "We read the verse: 'And all the peoples of the earth shall see that the name of the Lord is called upon thee' (Deut. 28:10.)" To Abaye he said: "Your name will become famous as head of the college, and you will be generally feared." To Rava he said, "The King's treasury [BDYYN'] will be broken into, and you will be arrested as a thief, and everyone will draw an inference from you." (The next day the King's treasury was broken into and they came and arrested Rava.) They said to him, "We saw a lettuce on the mouth of a jar." To Abaye he said, "Your business will be doubled like a lettuce." To Rava he said, "Your business will be bitter like a lettuce." They said to him, "We saw some meat on the mouth of a jar." To Abaye he said, "Your wine will be sweet, and everyone will come to buy meat and wine from you." To Rava he said, "Your wine will turn sharp, and everyone will come to buy meat to eat with it." They said, "We saw a cask hanging on a palm tree." To Abaye he said, "Your business will spring up like a palm tree." To Rava he said, "Your goods will be sweet like dates." They said to him, "We saw a pomegranate sprouting on the mouth of a jar." To Abaye he said, "Your goods will be high-priced like a pomegranate." To Rava he said, "Your goods will be stale like a [dry] pomegranate." They said to him, "We saw a cask fall into a pit." To Abaye he said, "Your goods

will be in demand." ... To Rava he said, "Your goods will spoil and
they will be thrown into a pit." They said to him, "We saw a young
ass standing by our pillow and braying." To Abaye he said, "You will
become a king, and an *Amora* will stand by you." To Rava he said,
"The words 'The first-born of an ass' have been erased from your
tefillin." Rava said to him: "I have looked at them and they are there."
He replied to him, "Certainly the *vav* of the word *ḥamor* [ass] has been
erased from your *tefillin*."

Rava finally went to him by himself and said to him, "I dreamt that
the outer door fell." He said to him, "Your wife will die." He said to
him, "I dreamt that my front and back teeth fell out." He said to him,
"Your sons and your daughters will die." He said, "I saw two pigeons
flying." He replied, "You will divorce two wives." He said to him, "I
saw two turnip-tops." He replied, "You will receive two blows with
a cudgel." On that day Rava went and sat all day in the school. He
found two blind men quarrelling with one another. Rava went to
separate them, and they gave him two blows. They wanted to give him
another blow but he said, "Enough! I saw in my dream only two."

Rava finally went and gave him a fee. He said to him, "I saw a wall
fall down." He replied, "You will acquire wealth without end." He
said, "I dreamed that Abaye's villa ['PDN'] fell in and the dust of it
covered me." He replied to him, "Abaye will die and [the presidency
of] his school will be come to you." He said to him, "I saw my own
villa fall in, and everyone came and took a brick." He said to him,
"Your teachings will be disseminated in the world." He said to him,
"I dreamt that my head was split open and my brains fell out." He
replied, "The stuffing will fall out of your pillow." He said to him, "In
my dream I read the *Hallel* of Egypt." He replied, "A miracle will happen
to you."

Bar Hedya was once travelling with Rava in a boat. He said to
himself: "Why should I accompany a man to whom a miracle will
happen?" As he was disembarking, he let a book fall. Rava found it,
and saw written in it, "All dreams follow the mouth." He exclaimed,
"Evil man! It all depended on you and you gave me all this pain! I
forgive you everything except [what you said about] the daughter of
R. Ḥisda. May it be God's will that this man be delivered up to the
government, and that they have no mercy on him." Bar Hedya said to
himself, "What am I to do? We have been taught that a curse uttered
by a sage, even when undeserved, comes to pass; how much more this
of Rava, for justly did he curse." He said, "I will rise up and go into
exile." ... He rose and fled to the Romans. He went and sat at the door
of the keeper of the King's wardrobe. The keeper of the wardrobe had
a dream, and said to him, "I dreamed that a needle pierced my finger."
He said to him, "Give me a *zuz*!" He refused to give him one, and he
would not say a word to him. He again said to him, "I dreamed that a
worm fell between two of my fingers." He said to him, "Give me a
zuz." He refused to give him one, and he would not say a word to
him. "I dreamed that a worm filled the whole of my hand." He said

to him, "Worms have been spoiling all the silk garments." This became
known in the palace, and they brought the keeper of the wardrobe in
order to put him to death. He said to them, "Why execute me? Bring
the man who knew and would not tell." So they brought Bar Hedya,
and they said to him, "Because of your *zuz*, the king's silken garments
have been ruined." They tied two cedars together with a rope, tied one
leg to one cedar and the other to the other, and released the rope, so
that even his head was split. Each tree rebounded to its place and he
was decapitated and his body fell in two.

(b. Ber. 56a-b)

The purport of this long account seems at first glance to be that
dream-interpreters are charlatans. They will give you a good interpretation if you pay them and a bad one if you do not. Their interpretations, however, are not doubted. They may not only predict what
would happen, but they can also make it happen by their prediction.
Nevertheless, even this story ridiculing dream-interpreters indicated
that the interpretations of a charlatan were heeded by distinguished
masters and came true. Conversely, it took for granted that Hedya
recognized miracles would be done for the rabbis. Moreover, Rava's
curse proved far more powerful than anything Bar Hedya could do, and
brought him to a bad end. It seems, likely, therefore, that the story was
meant to warn people against dealing with dream-interpreters who
demanded money. If Bar Hedya had not been a Jew, then the people
would thus have been told to be careful about having others than
qualified Jews, presumably rabbis, interpret their dreams. As in other
instances,[1] the rabbis did not doubt that gentile or Jewish non-rabbinical astrologers, magicians, and dream-interpreters knew what they
were doing. But they did not want ordinary people to consult with
non-rabbinical interpreters of dreams, who used their power only to
obtain money. The rabbi, by contrast, could be trusted.

The rabbis not only believed in the interpretation of dreams, but also
acted upon that interpretation. Dreams were an accurate vehicle of
heavenly revelations. The conflicting Scriptural evaluation of dreams,
in Num. 12:6, "In a dream I shall speak concerning him," and Zech.
10:2, "All dreams speak falsely," were harmonized by Rava, who said
that when through a dream an angel speaks, it is an accurate revelation,
but when a demon does, it is false.[2] Dreams even carried some legal
weight, as in the following story:

> R. Joseph said, "If one dreamed he has been excommunicated, ten
> men are necessary for annulling the decree. They must have studied

---

[1] See for example vol. III, pp. 108-109.
[2] b. Ber. 55b.

law, but if they have only repeated [Tannaitic traditions] they cannot
lift the decree..."

(b. Ned. 8a)[1]

Similarly, in the administration of community affairs:

> Rava came to Hagronia and ordained a fast, but no rain came. He
> told the people to fast overnight. The next morning he asked whether
> anyone had had a dream. R. Eleazar of Hagronia said, "I had a dream,
> and the following was said to me, 'Good greetings to the good teacher
> from the good Master who from his goodness gives good to his
> people.'" Rava exclaimed, "This is a favorable time to pray." He
> prayed and it rained.

(b. Ta'anit 24b)

Since heaven had been displeased by Rava's actions, its message was
conveyed in a dream to R. Safra.[2] Hence a dream might be withheld
as a sign of disapproval.

Heavenly communications might come by other means as well. One
recalls that the heavenly academy dropped a letter to the earthly one,
with reference to Rabbah b. Nahmani,[3] to tell the rabbis to begin
lamenting the death of Rabbah. The letter stated, "He who now holds
aloof from lamentation shall be excommunicated." Excommunication
was a serious, legal penalty.[4] Nonetheless, R. Joseph held people do not
normally go up to heaven and get a legal decision for the earthly
academy:

> [In expressing his rejection of a view that the law regarded a man
> as immune from heavenly prosecution if the earthly court did not try
> him], R. Joseph [sarcastically] said, "Who has gone up [to heaven]
> and come back [to bring such information]."

(b. Mak. 23b)

XI. WITCHCRAFT, INCANTATIONS, AND AMULETS

Belief in the existence of angels, demons, and spirits of the dead,
with whom men could communicate in various ways, provided a
"justification" for age-old magical practices, most of them, perhaps,
originally impersonal, but many reinterpreted as means of persuading

---

[1] See B. Lewin, *Ozar HaGeonim*, XI, part i, p. 4.

[2] b. Hul. 133a.

[3] b. B.M. 86a, see above, p. 41ff.

[4] Rabbah was unpopular in his town, as we shall see, and some may not have
wanted to lament when he was killed.

or compelling supernatural beings to act in the magician's behalf. Such belief in witchcraft seems greatly to have grown in the fourth century.[1] The following account suggests that between the time of Abaye (d. 338) and that of R. Papa (d. 376), fears of witchcraft had so increased that academic discussions were affected:

> [If one gives a loaf to a child, he must tell the mother. What should he do so the mother may know?] Abaye said, "He must rub him with oil and paint him with kohl." But nowadays that we fear witchcraft, what [is to be done]? R. Papa said, "He must rub him with whatever he has given him."
>
> (b. Shab. 10b)

The rabbis certainly shared the convictions of ordinary people that witchcraft was effective. They transmitted traditions about how to prevent or control it, including the following:

> Abaye said that Rabbah told him the reason one should not eat vegetables from the bunch was that one thereby lays himself open to witchcraft.
>
> (b. Ḥul. 105b)

> Abaye said that his mother told him that seven garlands [of a certain vegetable] work against witchcraft.
>
> (b. Shab. 66b)

What is striking is that Abaye's traditions about witchcraft came from two different sources: first, the teaching of his master, Rabbah, second, the tradition of his foster-mother [Rabbah's wife]. No distinction was made between the two, since both women and rabbis were commonly supposed to be authorities on magic. Women were notorious for their practice of it—they had been the first to learn it from the fallen angels. As for the rabbis, their reputation for knowledge, and especially secret and traditional knowledge, led to their being credited with magical knowledge, especially of amulets and healing-incantations, and many of them spoke as authorities on these subjects.

On the other hand, witchcraft or sorcery performed by shady supernatural beings was feared as much as magic performed by ordinary mortals. R. Mari the son of the daughter of Samuel witnessed a miracle performed by angels and warned people against benefitting from it:

> R. Mari son of the daughter of Samuel told, "Once I was standing on the bank of the Papa canal, and saw angels appearing [in the guise of] sailors who brought sand and loaded ships with it, and it turned into

---

[1] As is clear in the summary table, below, p. 399.

[fine] flour. When the people came to buy it, I warned, 'Do not buy it because it resulted from a miracle.' The next day shiploads of wheat came from Perezina."

(b. Ta'anit 24b)

Traditions about incantations were most commonly repeated in connection with medical remedies.[1] Few remedies were performed without the recitation of some sort of incantation. For example, Abaye reported:

"Mother told me, 'For a daily fever one must take a white (new) *zuz*, go to a salt deposit, take its weight in salt, and tie it up in the nape of the neck with a white twisted cord. But if this is not possible, let one sit at acrossroads. When he sees a large ant carrying something, let him take it and throw it into a brass tube, and close it with lead and seal it with sixty seals. Let him then shake it, lift it up, and say to it, 'Your burden on me and mine on you.'"...

(b. Shab. 66b)[2]

Abaye said, "Mother told me, 'All incantations which are repeated several times must contain the name of the patient's mother. All knots [tied for magical purposes of healing] must be tied on the left ... All incantations are to be repeated the number of times as required in the prescription. Where the number is not prescribed, they should be repeated forty-one times.'"

(b. Shab. 66b)

The source of incantation-magic was not only old-wives tales. Rabbah[3] reported that he had heard an effective incantation to prevent a ship from sinking, as follows:

Rabbah said, "Those who go down to the sea told me, 'The wave that sinks a ship appears with a fringe of white fire at its crest. When hit by clubs on which is engraven, *I am that I am, Yah, the Lord of Hosts, Amen Amen Selah*, it will subside.'"

(b. B.B. 73a)

---

[1] On incantation, Trachtenberg says, "The magic of the Talmud depended largely upon the potency inherent in the form of the incantation, that is, in the word, and upon the magical action, for its most striking effects, and in consequence we find the barbaric word coming to occupy an important place." Trachtenberg, *op. cit.*, p. 88. See also Blau, *op. cit.*, pp. 61-86, on incantations; pp. 86-96 on amulets; pp. 152-156 on the evil eye. On charms, see S. Lieberman, *Greek in Jewish Palestine* (New York, 1942), pp. 100-110.

[2] For other examples of incantations for the purpose of healing, see below, pp. 365-366.

[3] Since the subsequent stories concern Rabbah b. B. Ḥana, this saying may likewise be his, and not Rabbah b. Naḥmani's.

The use of the divine names on these clubs is similar to their use in other magical ways, evidenced both in Palestine and in Babylonia. What is striking is that the *rabbis* preserved stories of how a magical incantation including the divine name was used, and themselves made use of incantations, not only for healing, but also as in the following saying of Abaye:

> Abaye said that it is forbidden to cast a spell over a wasp and a scorpion, though if they are following a man, he may do so.
>
> (b. Ker. 3b)

Whether or not fringes and phylacteries were regarded as charms or amulets—and I am sure they were—the rabbis certainly believed that other charms and amulets could effectively prevent demons or other evil forces from harming a person. Not all amulets were acceptable. The test was a practical one:

> R. Papa said, "It is obvious to me that if three amulets [QMY'] work for three people three times each, both the practitioner [man] and the amulets are approved. If three amulets work for three people once each, the practitioner is approved but not the amulets. If one works for three men, the amulet is approved but not the practitioner. But what if three amulets work for one person? The amulets are not approved, but does the practitioner win approval or not?"...
>
> (b. Shab. 61b)

If the man was approved, R. Papa said, then one would be permitted to go out on the Sabbath wearing an amulet he had prepared.[1] Rava held that no one bothers to make an amulet in the shape of *tefillin*, so he assumed that *tefillin* were not regarded as amulets. But *tefillin* were generally believed to protect against demons, as we have seen.

Like the Magi,[2] some rabbis learned the arts, which were regarded as a form of magic, of juggling:

> Abaye used to juggle before Rabbah with eight eggs or some say four eggs.
>
> (b. Suk. 53a)

Rabbis, however, regarded themselves as greater masters of magic than Magi.[3]

---

[1] b. Shab. 61a.
[2] See Vol. II, pp. 149-151.
[3] Above, p. 339.

XII. THE RABBI'S CURSE

The rabbis were believed to be able to curse, and so call down evil and even death upon the accursed. The acceptable curse might take the form of words, as when R. Dimi of Nehardea was treated in a manner he thought disrespectful by R. Adda, and complained to R. Joseph. R. Joseph then said the classic imprecation:

> "He who did not delay to avenge the wrong done to the king of Edom will not delay to avenge the wrong done to you..." Shortly afterward, R. Adda b. Abba died. R. Joseph said, "On my account he was punished, because I cursed him." R. Dimi said, "It was on my account, because he made me lose my figs..."
>
> (b. B.B. 22a)

Similarly, one recalls, Rabbah b. R. Huna cursed "whoever cut down" his trees, saying that "his branches should be cut down," and in consequence, during his lifetime the children of Rabbah b. R. Naḥman did not survive.[1]

A rabbi might employ his knowledge of magic to bring down misfortune and even death upon the head of one who displeased him, as in the following case:

> A certain bully was bothering a certain disciple of the rabbis. He came before R. Joseph, who told him, "Go and excommunicate him." The student replied that he was afraid of him. He said, "Then take out a subpoena [PTYHʾ] against him [That is, write out the decree of excommunication]." "I am all the more afraid of him." "Then take it [the decree] and put it in a jar, take it to a cemetery, and blast into it a thousand horn-blasts on forty days." He went and did so. The jar broke, and the bully died.
>
> (b. M.Q. 17a-b)

Another curse was the laying on of the 'evil eye.' One recalls that Abaye cursed the parents of a man of whom he disapproved. He asked where they were, looked in that direction, and the parents died.[2]

If a rabbi was treated dishonorably, heaven itself might automatically avenge the insult. For example, Rava said that Rami b. Ḥama died only because he would not count R. Menashiah b. Taḥalifa for a quorum in reciting the Grace after Meals, despite the fact that R. Menashiah was learned in various Tannaitic traditions. Rami b. Ḥama had thought that he was merely a good memorizer, and did not treat him like a true disciple of the sages. Since R. Menashiah used to hear the rabbis'

---

[1] b. B.M. 108a, above, p. 236.
[2] b. Yev. 106a, cited above pp. 204-205.

discussions and memorize them, he was regarded as of the same status, and hence Rami erred—and died. No explicit curse was issued.[1] One who disobeyed a rabbinical decree might suffer misfortune whether the rabbi cursed him or not. When a certain Pumbeditan was bitten by a snake, it was impossible to prepare the proper antidote. Several apparent accidents prevented it. One antidote was to tear open the embryo of a white ass and sit on it:

> There were thirteen white asses in Pumbedita and they were all torn open and found to be *trefah* [and therefore unusable or ineffective]. On the other side of town was another, but before they could go and get it, a lion ate it. Abaye observed, "Perhaps he was bitten by a snake of the rabbis, for which there is no cure, as it is written, 'And who breaks through a fence, a serpent shall bite him' (Qoh. 10:8) ..."
>
> (b. Shab. 110a)

If people widely believed that dishonoring or disobeying a rabbi would lead to inexorable doom, they would naturally take pains to honor and obey him.

It should be stressed that the rabbis, and other holy men, enjoyed no monopoly over magical arts. Ordinary people might learn the proper incantations and rituals to cast spells, curses, and the like.[2] One such instance is as follows:

> [A woman cursed Rava for making a decision which displeased her.] "May your ship sink," she called out, "Are you trying to fool me?" Rava's clothes were soaked in water [to carry out the curse symbolically, and so prevent its realization] and yet he did not escape the drowning.
>
> (b. B.B. 153a)

It was quite natural for the rabbis to take seriously the curse of an ordinary woman. On the other hand, if magic was real, then the rabbis were surely going to be greater masters of it than anyone else so far as the schools were concerned. Hence their curses would have been regarded as especially potent. While some curses depended upon heavenly assistance, others were not dependent upon angels' or demons' responding to prayer, but rather upon rabbis' knowledge of the proper way to compose and effect the curse. Clearly rabbinic tradition contained uncontingent magical formulae, believed to be useful and in no way reprehensible.

---

[1] b. Ber. 47b.
[2] See vol. III, p. 108.

XIII. TORAH AS A SOURCE OF SUPERNATURAL AND MAGICAL POWER

If we now review the role of the rabbi in the supernatural world he believed in, we discover a remarkable set of facts. The rabbi was the authority on theology, that is, among other things, on the structure and order of the supernatural world. He knew the secret names of God and the secrets of the divine 'chariot'—the heavens—and of creation. If extraordinarily pious, he might even see the face of the Shekhinah; in any event, the Shekhinah was present in the rabbinical schools. The rabbi was therefore a holy man, overcame the evil impulse which dominated ordinary men, was consequently less liable to suffering, misfortune, and sickness. He knew the proper times and forms of prayer, and could therefore pray effectively. Moreover, the efficacy of his prayers was heightened by his purity, holiness, and merits, which in turn derived from his knowledge of the secrets of Torah, and consequently, his peculiar observances. Therefore not only his prayers in general, but also his prayers for particular purposes, were effective. He could bring rain or cause drought. His blessings brought fertility, and his curses, death. He was apt to be visited by angels and to receive communications from them. He could see demons and talk with them and could also communicate with the dead. He was an authority on the interpretation of omens and of dreams, and on means to avert witchcraft, on incantations for cures, knot-tying (for phylacteries), and the manufacture and use of amulets. He was, in anthropological terms, a medicine man. Could a modern anthropologist spend a few years in ancient Pumbedita, Sura, or Nehardea, to study the social role of the rabbi, his resultant book would certainly be called something like "The Lawyer-Magicians of Babylonia."

Here, however, we must offer an important distinction.[1] The fact that the rabbis performed the functions and claimed the powers characteristic, in primitive societies, of magicians might justify a modern anthropologist in applying to them that term, but it does not prove that they applied the term to themselves or would have approved its application. In fact the rabbis would not have regarded their power

---

[1] Note also the comment of W. L. Knox, "The boundary between magic and religion on the one hand and medicine on the other is not too easy to fix in the first century A.D. 'He that casteth out devils by Beelzebub' suggests that 'magic' was a term of abuse, implying that you disagreed with your opponent, but could not deny that he produced remarkable results." See his "Pharisaism and Hellenism," in H. Loewe, ed., *Judaism and Christianity, II. The Contact of Pharisaism with Other Cultures* (London, 1937), pp. 61-114. Quotation on p. 106.

as magical or the Torah as a source of magic. The dividing line between true religion and magic was clearly drawn, widely recognized,
and by virtue of that recognition, became a social reality. What was
approved by society—in this case, the schools—required by custom,
and unquestionably seen to be part of the established religion was
usually thought to be in no way magical. Abaye said:

> "The sorcerer [who insists upon exact paraphernalia noting different
> properties of different kinds of magic] works through demons. He who
> does not, works by [pure] enchantment ... The laws of sorcery are like
> those of the Sabbath. Certain actions are punished by stoning, some
> are not punished but forbidden, and others are entirely permitted. If
> one actually performs [magic], he is stoned. If he merely creates an
> illusion, he is exempt, but the act is prohibited." What is entirely
> permitted? Such as [the magic performed by] R. Ḥanina and R.
> ʾOshaiʿaʾ, who spent every Sabbath eve studying the Laws of Creation,
> by means of which they made a third-grown calf and ate it.
>
> (b. Sanh. 67b)

One may only suppose that "magic" was permitted if the rabbis did
it. Working through demons and enchantment may be to modern eyes
no different from studying the "Laws of Creation" and applying them.
But the distinction was important to Abaye.[1]

Jewish society, including the rabbis', was not primitive. It had long
since sharply distinguished, by its own standards, between what *it*
considered magic, and what *it* considered religion—neither identical
with what we should class under those terms—and by *its* standards, the
rabbis were not magicians, as I just said. Some of them did practice
magic on the side, but this is a different matter. The distinction has
been best illustrated by Professor Morton Smith, in an unpublished
lecture:

> In antiquity, the practice of magic was a criminal offense and the
> term 'magician' was a term of abuse. It still is, but the connotation has
> changed. It now primarily connotes fraud. Then the notion was that
> of social subversion. The efficacy of magic was almost universally be-
> lieved and the magician was conceived of as a man who, by acquiring
> supernatural powers, had become a potential danger to the established
> authority and to the order that they sought to maintain. Consequently
> magic was widely practiced but rarely admitted.
>
> For Judaism there was a further limiting factor in the dogma that
> there was no god save the Lord. This did not lead to a denial of the

---

[1] Lieberman stresses, "Magic is effective in the case of the ordinary man only,
but not in that of the really righteous, whose merit is great ... it is powerless in
the face of the virtuous man," *Greek in Jewish Palestine*, (N.Y. 1942), p. 113.

efficacy of pagan magic nor did it prevent Jews from using the same magical practices as pagans. On the contrary, the Jews were famous as magicians, as Josephus says. And new discoveries by Professor M. Margalioth show that as late as the fourth and fifth centuries Jews, steeped in the Old Testament and thoroughly at home in the Synagogue, were composing a magician's handbook which listed pagan deities and prescribed prayers and sacrifices to be offered to them in magical ceremonies. Among the prayers there is an invocation of Helios in transliterated Greek; and the conclusion comes upon reaching the Seventh Heaven with a celebration of Yahweh as the supreme God.

At least the more scrupulous of the Jews distinguished their marvels as performed by the power of the supreme God from those of the pagans whose gods were demons and impure spirits. Rabbi 'Aqiva, complaining of his own ill success in magic, said, "When a man fasts in order that an unclean spirit should rest on him, the unclean spirit does so. It should happen, therefore, that when a man fasts in order that a pure spirit should rest on him, the pure spirit should do so. But what can I do since our iniquities are the cause of our difficulties? For it is said that your iniquities are dividing you from your God." The context leaves no doubt of the magical reference. But 'Aqiva is not, of course, represented in the Talmud as a magician, because that term was a term of abuse. The fact that a man was represented as a supernatural being is in itself a suspicious item, for this was a common claim of magicians and a regular result of magical operation.

Smith's reference, in successive paragraphs, to the handbook discovered by Margalioth [M. Margalioth, *Sefer HaRazim, Hu Sefer Keshafim Mitequfat HaTalmud* (Jerusalem, 1967)], points to the necessity of further distinction, for the two are certainly not in the same class, yet both of them reflect attitudes different from the one common in stories of rabbis whose merits enabled them to pray with good hope that their prayers would be answered. At the pagan end of the scale, we may suppose, was the Jew who simply learned and practiced pagan magic as such, throwing in, perhaps, for good measure a few extra conjurations by the sacred name, Yahweh, or some prayers for him or to the Jewish angels. Of such men we have plentiful evidence in the magical papyri. Next to them come men like the author of *Sefer Ha-Razim* who took over pagan magic, but made it part of a picture of the cosmos in which Yahweh was the supreme God, to whom all the pagan deities were subordinate. Then there was the position familiar as that of "normative Judaism": the rabbi does not practice "magic" at all, but his "acts of piety and religious observances" so increase his "merits" that he can pray, bless or curse, with the hope that his prayers would be answered and his blessings and curses be made effective by divine or angelic action. Finally there were those who, by study of the Torah, sought to master it so as to be able to use directly, for their own purposes, its creative and miraculous powers; in 'Aqiva's words (which, however, reflect slightly different notions), they "fasted that a pure spirit should rest upon them." Such men could do miracles for and by themselves, not just ask to have them done for them. And this mastery and use of the Torah made Torah a source of magical, not merely supernatural, power. Since these beliefs were preserved within the schools themselves, but were consistently overshadowed, especially in exoteric presentation, by stories and teaching presenting the "normative theory," it is not unlikely that many of the other magical functions of the rabbis, which our texts represent as answers to prayer or acts of divine grace in response to human merit—or do not explain at all—were seen by many contemporaries, and probably by many of the rabbis themselves, as exercises of this supernatural power conferred by study of the Torah. It follows that the rabbis never called themselves magicians. On the contrary, they consistently and explicitly disapproved of "magic," as I have just shown in Abaye's case. But many of the things they did, especially the supernatural character alleged to have been imparted to them by their knowledge of Torah, must be seen in the context of antiquity as appropriate to divine-men or magicians. Unique to the rabbis is the claim that their miracles, supernatural graces, and magical actions derived from the Torah, rather than from some other source of supernatural power. To them this was sufficient justification.

The rabbis were believed to be able to pray more effectively than other people, heads of schools most effectively of all. So we are told that "in the time of R. Joseph," meaning, when he was the head of the school:

> ... there was a famine. The rabbis asked him to offer prayers for mercy. He replied, "If Elisha with whom, when the rabbis departed, there still remained two thousand two hundred disciples, did not offer up prayers for mercy in a time of famine, should I...?"
>
> (b. Ket. 106a)

Further, only when R. Joseph became head of a school was he able to solve a certain legal problem.[1] Rava said that Ahasuerus believed that the rabbis would protect Israel because they were careful to keep

---

[1] b. B.Q. 66b.

the commandments.[1] One recalls that the Jewish marketman in Be Lapat informed the rabbis when harsh decrees were made against the Jews, "so they would pray and have the decree annuled."[2] There can be no doubt that the basis of the belief that the rabbis enjoyed exceptional powers lay in the anterior conviction that study of Torah and performance of the commandments produced heavenly favor. Rava and Abaye said that sin can be expiated not through sacrifice, but through study of the Torah and good deeds. Rabbah and Abaye were supposedly descended from the house of Eli, but were able to overcome the ancient curse against that house through devotion to Torah and, in Abaye's case, good deeds as well. Hence though descendents of Eli were not supposed to live past the age of twenty, Rabbah was rewarded by a life of forty years, and Abaye, sixty years.[3] It was stated quite explicitly that study of Torah and performance of the commandments were supposed to produce heavenly favor, resulting in protection against evil and also special blessings:

> R. Joseph said that a commandment protects [from suffering] and rescues [from evil inclination] when one is doing it, but afterwards, while it protects, it does not rescue. Rava said that while one is engaged in study of Torah, the act of study protects and rescues, but otherwise, study of Torah protects but does not rescue. As to a commandment, under all circumstances it protects but does not rescue.
>
> (b. Sot. 21a)

The "protection" was from demons and Satan. (R. Aḥa b. Jacob, when swinging the *lulav*, for example, said, "An arrow in the eyes of Satan.")[4]

Obviously study of Torah was supposed to yield exceptional prowess, for when it did not, that was the subject of comment:

> Rava said, "Is there any greatness in propounding problems? In the years of Rav Judah, their whole studies were confined to the laws of *Neziqin*, while we study [much more...], yet Rav Judah [merely] took off his shoes and the rain came, while we cry out but are not heard [lit. "no one pays attention to us"]. But [it is because] the Holy One blessed be he requires the heart...."
>
> (b. Sanh. 106b)

---

[1] b. Meg. 13b. For rabbis as protectors of the community, see vol. III, pp. 102ff., and above, pp. 340-341.

[2] b. Taʿanit 22a, see above, p. 50.

[3] b. R.H. 18a, b. Yev. 5a. See my *Life of R. Yoḥanan ben Zakkai*, p. 64, for an earlier example.

[4] b. Men. 62a.

R. Papa said to Abaye, "What is the difference between us and the ancients? For them, miracles were done, and for us, no miracles are done. If it is on account of learning, in the years of Rav Judah, they studied only *Neziqin*, and we study all six orders of the Mishnah, and when Rav Judah reached [a certain passage, he was perplexed by it, while we achieve much more in studying that same passage but he could produce rain, ... as above]." Abaye replied to him, "The ancients gave their lives for the sanctification of God's name, but we do not do so..."

(b. Ber. 20a)

Rabbah once decreed a fast. He prayed, but no rain came. People thereupon remarked to him, "When Rav Judah ordained a fast, rain did fall." He replied, "What can I do? Is it because of studies? We are superior to him, because in the time of Rav Judah ... [as above]. Yet when Rav Judah removed one shoe ... But when we cry out the whole day, no one hears us. Is it because of some deed? If so, let anyone who knows of it tell it. What can the great men of the generation do, however, when their generation does not seem good [warrant miracles]."

(b. Ta'anit 24a-b)

So study of Torah and practice of the commandments would be rewarded by rain as well as protection. Moreover, the disciples of Rava, Abaye, and Rabbah preserved three fundamentally different stories of how the several masters had uttered the same saying on the disparity of learning and miraculous power between their generation and the former one. The saying must therefore be prior to the stories both in time and in importance, and it clearly presupposes some intrinsic relationship between mastery of Torah and the ability to make rain. The masters did not deny it. It was a disappointment to them that they could not do what the ancients, whose achievements in learning were less impressive than theirs, could easily accomplish. The articulated sense of disparity between intellectual achievement and theurgical power leaves no doubt that the former was naturally expected to yield the latter.

The view that the righteous even have the creative power of God is strikingly manifested in the following:

Rava said, "If a righteous man desires it, he can be a creator of a world for it is written, 'But your iniquities have distinguished...' (Is. 59:2). [That is, but for sin, a man's power would equal that of God, and he could create a world.]

Rabbah created a man [GBR'], and sent him to R. Zera. R. Zera spoke to him, but he did not answer. He said to him, "You are a creature of the magicians [ḤBRY' = Magi]. Return to your dust."

(b. Sanh. 65b)

Learning and piety reshape a man in the likeness of God, and therefore endow him with God's powers of creation. God had made the world through Torah, and masters of Torah could similarly do wonderful acts of creation. Rava said that only sin prevented man from performing miracles, like both Rabbah, who was able to make a man, and R. Zera, who was able to destroy him. The following contains another story of a rabbi's extraordinary power:

> Rabbah and R. Zera feasted together on Purim. They became drunk and Rabbah arose and cut R. Zera's [throat]. The next day he prayed on his behalf and resurrected him. Next year he asked, "Will your honor come and feast with me?" He replied, "A miracle does not always happen."
>
> (b. Meg. 7b)

The rabbi was able to persuade God to resurrect the dead. That does not mean he was "like God." Had Rabbah been able to do it like God, R. Zera would have had no reason to refuse a second invitation, unless he did not want to repeat the experience. The refusal as given indicates that the miracle was not strictly by magic but by prayer and rather uncertain reward for merits. God does miracles without praying to anybody, and the rabbi generally relies upon prayer or merits. That is the difference between this story, which is an ordinary one of prayer and its reward, and the former ones in which the rabbis' own extraordinary powers, probably acquired by prayer, study, or other merits, *now are usable directly and uncontingently.*

Furthermore, if Torah yielded magic, magic could also be used to produce greater Torah. Abaye believed that a certain bird, properly eaten, would help one increase in wisdom. One eats half the right side and half the left, and places the remainder in a brass tube, to be sealed with sixty sealings. This is to be suspended on his arm. One then studies to his heart's content, and finally consumes the other half.[1] That seals in the new learning. If he fails to do so, he will forget what he has learned.

This view of the worldly benefits of studying the Torah, keeping the commandments, and acting virtuously was not the invention of the rabbis. From biblical times, it had been believed that if the Israelites faithfully kept the covenant and did the commandments, they would enjoy rain and other forms of prosperity. Such was the theory of Deuteronomy. The rabbis simply arrogated to themselves and their

---

[1] b. Shab. 90b.

activities promises earlier believed to depend upon the good works of
priests, prophets, and other holy men, and upon popular adherence to
their teachings.

   To summarize: After noting that leading rabbis were said to be able
to create men, cows, and rain, one can hardly conclude that the rabbis
were not seen as magicians. That people commented upon the disparity
between learning and one's capacity to produce rain, furthermore,
manifests their sense of an intrinsic relationship between them. Theurgical skills were regarded as an authentication, though not the only one,
of the fact that rabbis were holy men, or saints, or righteous. The saying
that only sin prevented men from doing the things God could do,
followed by the story about how Rabbah created a man, may simply
be reversed. If Rabbah could create a man, then he was sinless, a master
of great learning and merits. Theurgical ability thus testified to his pure,
sinless condition as a master of Torah. That is not to suggest that
repeating words of Torah was invariably an incantation, of the same
substance as saying an anti-demonic formula. But if, as we have seen,
repeating words of Torah could prevent the angel of death from approaching Rabbah and others, or not repeating them in the privy laid
one open to demonic mischief so that other anti-demonic measures had
to be taken, then repeating words of Torah served on occasion as an
incantation. Similarly, great learning in Torah did not lead *only* or
invariably to ability to do such wonders as making men, cows, or rain.
   The ascription of supernatural power must nonetheless be seen as
one frequent attribute of leading masters in the schools.[1] It is the attribute which most closely parallels those of the "divine-man," for, as
Bieler stresses,[2] the unity of faith, wisdom, and unusual ability, was
everywhere taken for granted. Knowing and "doing" were in no way
separable. Bieler states, "Σοφία hat die ganz allgemeine Bedeutung von
Wissen und Können." The rabbi's "wisdom" derived from Torah, and
so did his supernatural, or magical, skills. To no one in antiquity could
such a conception have been alien. The only issue was whose σοφία
was really true. Bieler asks, Was the "divine-man" a Magus? Certainly

---

   [1] See the excellent notes of Salo W. Baron, *Social and Religious History*, II, pp.
335-337, ns. 23-27 for a bibliographical survey of Jewish magic in antiquity. My
purpose is not to survey that literature, but only to stress that magic, like super-
naturalism, was an intrinsic part of the life of the schools, and to call attention to
some of the stories which indicate the genres of magic found there. On the
sources of Jewish magical science, see Blau, *op. cit.*, pp. 37-49.
   [2] *Op. cit.*, I, pp. 73ff.

many "divine-man" of antiquity were so considered, and among them assuredly Jews, who were famed for the excellence of their magic, as in Acts 19:11-20. So far as magicians were disreputable, no faithful community would regard its holy men as magicians. But so far as magic was an expected and normal trait of religious virtuosi, everyone supposed his community's holy men could produce magic. What was "Torah" or perhaps "white magic" to Jews may have been witchcraft or black magic to gentile meighbors, and vice versa. It was, as Bieler says, a subjective distinction at best.[1] Bieler offers a more striking and fruitful distinction, that between "Θεῖος ἀνήρ in den Augen seiner... Zeitgenossen, Θεῖος ἐπιφανής im Glauben seiner Bekenner."[2] It would be foolish to suggest that that distinction applies without modification to the Jewish circumstance. For Jews, the rabbi as living Torah was surely as close as one could possibly come to the Θεῖος ἐπιφανής of Bieler's distinction. It does not, however, seem very remote.[3] We note the striking portrait of the wisdom of Solomon drawn by a first-

---

[1] Even though the rabbi does not conform to the pattern of the "divine-man" in every detail, the important point in common noted here is striking. Indeed, I wish Bieler had had access to the rich corpus of Talmudic rabbinic hagiography, which would have enhanced his discussion of the "divine-man" as an ideal-type.

[2] *Op. cit.*, I, p. 150.

[3] I note considerable change from Palestine in Tannaitic times. Then miracle-stories were rarely, if ever, told concerning leading Tannaitic authorities, though, to be sure, theurges of various kinds were active within the Jewish community. Morton Smith points out, [*Tannaitic Parallels to the Gospels* (Philadelphia, 1951), p. 81], "For as a matter of fact Tannaitic literature contains almost no stories of miracles performed by Tannaim, and this not because the authorities behind the literature did not believe in miracles, nor yet because they did not like to talk of them, for when they commented on the stories of the Old Testament—which already contain enough miracles for the average man—they added to their accounts many more miracles of the most miraculous sort, but when they came to tell of the doings of the Tannaim they ceased almost altogether to tell miracle stories, and this fact is strikingly obvious from the collection of stories made by Fiebig in his book." Here Smith refers to P. Fiebig, *Jüdische Wundergeschichten des neutestamentlichen Zeitalters* (Tübingen, 1911). Smith then surveys the thirteen passages cited by Fiebig, and shows that most of them do not pertain to Tannaitic authorities, or do not contain what can be called "miracles." Smith's general conclusion (p. 84) is as follows: "As for stories of miracles done by men of that period ... the parallels between the Gospels and Tannaitic Literature are not so important as the difference between them, and that difference is, that stories like these are very frequent in the Gospels, and almost totally lacking in Tannaitic literature." The tables below (pp. 392-399) reenforce Smith's point, for in general, we have only a few miracle-stories from each generation of Babylonian Amoraim. That does not change the fact, which I have stressed here, that the Babylonian Amoraim did suppose there was an intrinsic relationship between Torah and wonderful power (δύναμις = גבורה). Whether that notion characterized Tannaitic masters I cannot say, nor am I certain how it would have been expressed.

century Pharisaic disciple who went on to a career outside of the schools:

> There was no form of nature with which he [Solomon] was not acquainted or which he passed over without examining, but he studied them all philosophically and revealed the most complete knowledge of their several properties. And God granted him knowledge of the art used against demons for the benefit and healing of men. He also composed incantations by which illnesses are relieved, and left behind forms of exorcisms with which those possessed by demons drive them out, never to return. And this kind of cure is of very great power among us to this day....
>
> (Josephus, Jewish Antiquities, VIII, 44-45, trans. H. Thackeray, V, 595).

Healing arts, exorcisms, incantations—these testified to the grace of God, no less than mastery of Torah or other forms of saintliness. Far from disapproving of "magic," the rabbis took pride in their theurgical attainments, which, they said, Torah enabled them to do.[1]

To conclude: Contingent rewards for merit are different from reliably effective magic. We have in the preceding sections noted examples of both kinds of miracles. Rainmaking shows a general expectation that learning produces merit, which produces a claim on the diety for performance of services requested. Rabbah could not raise the dead like God, but only with God's help. We have been careful to examine first the supernatural environment, second some examples of actual uncontingent magical power attributed to rabbis. Miracles therefore must be divided into two kinds, according to the distinction herein inferred, first, those produced by divine grace elicited through right action; second, those produced by rabbinical power attained through Torah. The rabbi's own mastery of Torah produced power he could exert independent of heaven, in the form of witchcraft, amulets, blessings, curses, and the like. Rabbinic tradition often makes the point that these were not powers but merits; even the efficacy of prayer depended on additional moral conditions. In function, however, it is clear that these theoretical distinctions were less conclusive, for the ability to do miracles on one's own, not merely to ask to have them done for him, is evident in some of the stories we have considered.

---

[1] For non-rabbinic, Jewish magicians of the age, see Marcel Simon, *Recherches d'Histoire Judéo-Crétienne* (Paris and The Hague, 1962), pp. 142ff.

xiv. Medicine

Although the rabbis were not physicians, they possessed many kinds of traditions pertaining to hygiene, medicine, and healing. These they acquired from several sources. First, their own schools preserved important medical traditions on account of their relevance to legal issues. Second, they learned whatever they could from folk-medicine. Third, they solicited medical information from other groups in Babylonia, in this period in particular from Tai tribesmen. M. Beer persuasively argues[1] that the rabbis were not professional physicians, never received fees for medical advice, and did not regularly practice medicine. Physicians did exist within the Jewish community but among them were no sages. The physicians of Maḥoza regarded rabbinical medicine as a form of competition with their own practice, especially when the rabbis publicly taught people how to heal themselves, as in the following instance:

> Abaye said, "Mother told me that a salve ['YSPLNYT'] for all pains is seven parts of fat and one of wax." Rava said, "Wax and resin." Rava taught this publicly at Maḥoza. The family of Benjamin the doctor tore up their bandages. He said to them, "I have left you one [unrevealed trade secret] for Samuel said, 'He who washes his face but does not dry it well will have scabs....'"
>
> (b. Shab. 133b)

Rava reported a tradition of Minyomi, which would have been a form of Benjamin:

> Abaye said, "My mother told me that kidneys were made to heal [a pain in] the ear..." Rava said, "Minyomi the physician told me that any kind of fluid is bad for the ear except the juice from kidneys. One should take the kidney of a bald buck, cut it cross-wise, and place it on glowing coals.... [etc.]"
>
> (b. A.Z. 28b)

This same family criticized the rabbis:

> [Who is an epikoros('PYQWRWS)?] R. Joseph said, "Those who ridicule [rabbis, saying], 'Of what use are the rabbis to us? For their own sake they study [Scriptures], for their own sake they repeat [Mishnaic traditions].'" Abaye said, "But this denotes acting impudently against the Torah...." Rava said, "For instance the family of Benjamin the physician, who say, 'Of what use are the rabbis to us? They never permitted us the raven not forbade the dove.'" When a suspected trefa of the

---

[1] Beer, Ma'amadam, pp. 114-116.

family of Benjamin was brought before Rava, if he saw reason to permit it, he would remark to them, "'See, I permit you the raven." If there were grounds to prohibit it, he would say, "See, I forbid you the dove..."

(b. Sanh. 99b-100a)

Rava cursed the family of Benjamin as rank disbelievers, saying they were hostile to the rabbis and ridiculed legal decisions.[1] Nonetheless, the physicians subjected themselves to rabbinical rulings on the suitability of food, specifically of slaughtered animals. Rava gave them such rulings, which they presumably obeyed. His sarcastic remark tells us that their criticism stung.

The rabbis' medical traditions focused in part upon matters they were likely to have to know for legal reasons or would have observed as part of a legal inquisition. Rava said, for example, that pregnant and nursing mothers must fast on the 9th of Av.[2] To give such a ruling, he would have had to know whether such a fast would endanger life or not, for if it would, no fasting was allowed. A second issue of forensic medicine concerned whether a youth had passed his minority, which was signified by the appearance of two pubic hairs. Rava had to know how to tell whether a young man was potent or not:

> Whenever people came to Rava [to ask about a young man who reached the age of twenty without showing signs of puberty] he would instruct them as follows: "If the youth was thin, he should be fattened. If fat, he should reduce. [For sometimes the signs do not appear on account of emaciation, and sometimes on account of fatness.]"
>
> (b. Yev. 97a)

Similarly, it was necessary for rabbis to know whether to order a circumcision to be delayed past the eighth day, on account of the potential danger to a child's life. As a result, the lessons of midwives were repeated in the schools, even though these did not pertain directly to the narrow and practical legal issue:

> Abaye said, "Mother told me an infant whose anus is not visible should be rubbed with oil and stood in the sun, and where it shows transparent, it should be torn crosswise with a barley grain, but not with a metal instrument, which will cause inflammation...If an infant

---

[1] Beer, *Ma'amadam*, pp. 178-180. Beer regards the criticism as a sign of social tension between a non-rabbinical elite and the rabbinical estate. However, it seems plausible that the particular tension was caused in this instance by professional jealousy. Compare Beer's view, p. 116.

[2] b. Pes. 54b. See b. Yoma 78b, Abaye on washing a child on the Day of Atonement.

cannot suck, his lips are cold. Bring a vessel of burning cloths and hold it near his nostrils so as to heat his lips. He will suck...If an infant does not breathe, he should be fanned...If an infant cannot breathe easily, his mother's after-birth should be brought and rubbed over him. He will breathe easily...If an infant is too thin, do the same with the afterbirth from the narrow to the wide end; if too fat, in the opposite direction.... If an infant is too red, so that the blood is not yet absorbed in him, we must wait until his blood is absorbed and then circumcise him. If he is green and anemic, we must wait until he is full-blooded..."

(b. Shab. 134a)[1]

R. Papa said that circumcision should not be performed on a cloudy day.[2] Much of the above data has no direct bearing upon the legal question of whether a circumcision may take place. On the other hand, knowing how to revive a new-born infant would have been important if ordinary people came to rabbis for advice in such a crisis. Because rabbis had to judge paternity cases, it was important for them to know about sexual potency, the healing of perforations in the male membrum, and the like.[3] Other information about sex had no legal bearing. For example, Rava said that if one wants male children, he should cohabit twice in succession.[4] Abaye said that eating a residue of fish hash, as well as vermin in the linen, sleeping on a tanner's hide, pouring hot water over oneself, and treading on egg shells are all debilitating for sexual relations.[5] Other sayings included the following:

> Rabbah b. R. Huna said, "If a man who comes home from a journey has sexual intercourse, his children will be weaklings."
>
> (b. Git. 70a)

> Abaye said that an aphrodisiac was made by taking three small measures of safflower and grinding and boiling them in wine. One drinks the potion.
>
> (b. Git. 70a)

Cures for various illnesses constituted a mixture of theology, magic, Scriptural exegesis, and practical medicine. Trachtenberg points out that three causes of disease were generally supposed: human, supernatural, or natural. Human agency included the sorcerer; supernatural

---

[1] Trans. H. Freedman (London, 1938), p. 675.

[2] b. Yev. 72a. For other opinions of Abaye and Rava on circumcision, see b. Shab. 135a-b.

[3] See b. Yev. 76a, Rava b. Rabbah asked R. Joseph how to find out whether semen will reopen a closed perforation; Abaye on healing a perforated membrum; b. Yev. 75b, Rava on Deut. 23:2-3.

[4] b. 'Eruv. 100b, b. Nid. 31b.

[5] b. Pes. 112b.

agency, the demon; and natural causes, diet, accident, or old age.[1] The rabbis believed that when a man's star fated him to die, the angel of death had power over him, and no medicine would avail.[2] Rava in the name of Rabin said that the Holy One sustains the sick, which is proved by Ps. 41:4, "The Lord supports him on the couch of languishing."[3] Tannaitic tradition had taught that the Divine Presence was above the pillow of an invalid, so one should not sit on the bed or a seat, but must sit on the ground.[4] Abaye and Rava said one may borrow the medical teachings of other peoples, and did not prohibit them although they were part of the rituals of paganism.[5] Prayer was believed to be an effective medicine. When Rava was ill, after the first day of his sickness he told his attendant to make a public announcement of that fact, so that those who loved him may pray for him.[6] From Jer. 9:20, Rava learned that in time of epidemic, one should close his windows. It was advisable to publicize one's ailments, so that others would pray in one's behalf. The Tannaitic tradition had so taught concerning Lev. 13:45. R. Joseph reported that an incident occurred at Pumbedita in which people prayed for a woman who thus was healed.[7] Abaye said that Mal. 3:20 proved that the motes dancing in the rays of the sun have healing power.[8]

Among many remedies using magic was the following:

> A mad dog rubbed itself against R. Huna b. R. Joshua in the market. He stripped off his garments and ran [quoting Qoh. 7:12].
>
> What is the remedy of a rabid dog bite? Abaye said, "Let him take the skin of a male hyena and write on it, 'I, so-and-so-, the son of such-and-such a woman, write upon the skin of a male hyena, *Kanti* [=*KNTY*] *Kanti, qliros* [*QLYRWS*]—some say *Qandy Qandy Qloros*—God, God, Lord of Hosts, Amen, Amen, Sela.*' Then let him strip off his clothes and bury them in a grave, leaving them for twelve months. Then he should take them out and burn them in an oven, and scatter the ashes at the crossroads. During these twelve months he should drink water only out of a copper tube, lest he see the shadow of a demon and be endangered...."

(b. Yoma 84a)

---

[1] Trachtenberg, *op. cit.*, pp. 197-199.
[2] Above, p. 333.
[3] b. Shab. 12b.
[4] *Ibid.*, and b. Ned. 40a.
[5] b. Ḥul. 77b.
[6] b. Ber. 55b, with reference to Prov. 24:17.
[7] b. Nid. 66a.
[8] b. Ned. 8b.

Other, more naturalistic remedies included these:

> Abaye said, "I tried every remedy [for scurvy] until a Tai recommended, 'Take the pits of olives ... burn them in a fire upon a new rake, and stick them inside of the gums.' I did so and was cured."
>
> (b. Yoma 84a=b. A.Z. 28a)

> Abaye said, "Mother told me that roasted ears are good for the heart and banish morbid thoughts ... . If a man suffers from weakness of the heart, let him take the flesh of the right flank of a male beast and excrements of cattle of the month of Nisan, and if not available, then willow twigs, and let him roast it, eat it, and after that, drink some diluted wine ..."
>
> (b. 'Eruv. 29b)[1]

> Abaye said, "Mother told me that a child of six whom a scorpion has bitten on his seventh birthday normally does not survive. What is the remedy? The gall of white stork in beer. This should be rubbed into the wound, and then drunk. A child of the age of one year whom a bee has stung on his first birthday does not survive. What is the remedy? The creepers of a palm tree in water should be rubbed in and then drunk."
>
> (b. Ket. 50a)[2]

> "The cure for ra'atan [a disease which causes the eye to tear, the nostrils to run, spittle to flow from the mouth, and flies to swarm about the victim]," Abaye said, "is pila, ladanum, the rind of a nut tree, the shavings of a dressed hide, *melilot*, and the calyx of a red date. These are boiled together and carried into a house of marble, or, if unavailable, a house with walls thick as seven and a half bricks. Three hundred cups are then poured on his head until the cranium is softened, and then the brain is cut open. Four leaves of myrtle must be brought, and each foot [of the insect causing the disease] should be lifted up, and one leaf placed beneath. The insect is then grasped with a pair of tweezers and burned. Otherwise it would return."
>
> (b. Ket. 77b)

> Abaye said, "Mother told me that for sun-stroke, the remedy is to take a jug of water on the first day. On the second, let blood. On the third, take red meat broiled on the coals and highly diluted wine. For a chronic heat stroke, bring a black hen and tear it lengthwise and crosswise and shave the middle of his head and put the bird on it and leave it there until it sticks. He should then stand in the water up to his neck until he is faint. Then he should swim out and sit down. If that is not possible, he should eat leeks .... For a chill one should eat fat meat broiled on the coals and undiluted wine ..."
>
> (b. Git. 67b)[3]

---

[1] Trans. W. Slotki (London, 1948), p. 204.
[2] Trans. W. Slotki (London, 1948), p. 287ff.
[3] Trans. M. Simon (London, 1948), pp. 320ff. The following two passages are in M. Simon's translation as well.

"For a toothache," Rabbah b. R. Huna said, "One should take the top of garlic with one stalk only, and grind it with oil, and salt, and put it on his thumb nail on the side where the tooth aches, and put a rim of dough around it, making sure it does not touch his flesh, as it may cause leprosy..."

(b. Git. 69a)

As to a burning in the bones, Abaye said the remedy, told to him by his foster-mother, was this: "All medicines are taken either for three, seven, or twelve days, but he [afflicted with burning in the bones] must go on until cured. All other medicines are taken on an empty stomach. This one is different. After he has eaten and drunk and relieved himself and washed his hands, they must bring a handful of a flour-and-honey mixture, with lentils, a handful of old wine, and mix them together. He must eat it and then cover himself and sleep, and must not be disturbed until he wakes up. When he wakes up, he must remain covered."

(b. Git. 70a)

We have already noted[1] the cures for snakebite and fever.

In addition to cures, the rabbis studied how to prevent diseases. Such "preventive medicine" included warnings about how to avoid arousing demons against oneself.[2] Abaye also was told by Rabbah that the reason one does not drink froth is that it may cause catarrh; but, as we noted, the reason one does not sit under a drainpipe was not because of the waste water, but because demons are found there.[3] Advice on diet included Rava's, that wine and spices have made him wise,[4] and R. Joseph's, that a person should not overeat:

R. Joseph said, "One who eats sixteen eggs, forty nuts, and seven caperberries and drinks a quarter of a *log* of honey on an empty stomach in the summer snaps his heart-strings asunder."

(b. Ḥul. 58b)

Abaye said that a well-boiled broth of beet is good for the heart, eyes, and bowels.[5] Other comments on diet pertained to beer[6] and mustard grain.[7] R. Joseph said that poor eyes were caused by combing one's hair when it is dry, drinking the lees of wine, and putting on

---

[1] Above, p. 364, b. Shab. 110a.
[2] E.g. b. Ḥul. 105b, one collects crumbs from the floor to avoid the angel of poverty, and above, pp. 334ff.
[3] *Ibid.*
[4] b. Hor. 13b.
[5] b. Ber. 39a.
[6] R. Joseph on Egyptian beer, b. Shab. 110a; on vows against drinking beer, R. Joseph and Rava, b. Pes. 107a.
[7] Abaye would not eat mustard grain, b. Shab. 140a.

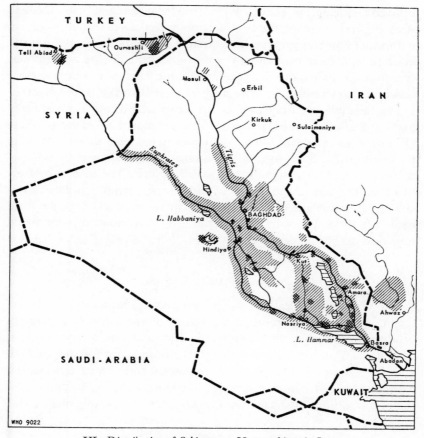

VI: *Distribution of Schistosoma Haematobium in Iraq.*

Source: *Schistosomiasis.* Departments of the Army, Navy and Air Force,
Washington, D.C. 20 June 1962, p. 24 figure 7.

shoes when the feet are damp.[1] Rava observed that an abscess is a forerunner of fever[2] and fever, of the angel of death, but it can be a healthy sign as well.[3] As earlier[4] it was believed important to warm oneself after letting blood,[5] as well as to eat a great deal.[6]

A disease endemic in present-day Iraq, *schistosomiasis haematobium*, or Bilharzia disease, is prevalent in irrigation ditches, canals, small streams, and stagnant pools. Infection is acquired through contact with water contaminated with cercariae. Contaminated drinking water infected with feces containing eggs produces the disease as well. The symptoms include nocturnal fever, chills, muscle aches, cough, and the onset is characterized by dysentery and fever, an enlarged liver or spleen, and bloody discharge in the urine and feces. The confused medical traditions cited above include references to many of these symptoms, as in *ra'atan*, but we do not know whether they appeared in the combination likely to yield a diagnosis of schistosomiasis; those of schistosomiasis are easily confused with malaria. The disease is likely to have been one of the causes of some of the symptoms referred to above. Since the larger part of Babylonian Jewry worked the land and made extensive use of irrigation canals, the likelihood of widespread infection cannot be denied.[7]

XV. SCRIPTURAL EXEGESIS

The Written and Oral Torah, and not prayer, incantation, medicine, magic, or astrology, stood in the center of the rabbis' curriculum. Study of Torah made them into rabbis, and so qualified them as saints. Mastery of Torah therefore provided the foundation for supernatural and political power alike. Study of the content and history of Scriptural exegesis in the Babylonian schools, like study of the development of the oral tradition, Mishnah commentary, and law, is tangential to our

---

[1] b. Pes. 111b.
[2] b. A.Z. 28a.
[3] b. Ned. 41a.
[4] Vol. II, pp. 138-139, vol. III, p. 112.
[5] Rabbah, b. Shab. 129a.
[6] R. Naḥman b. Isaac, b. Shab. 129a.
[7] Dr. Elihu D. Richter, M.D., M. P. H., provided the above information, as well as the pamphlet, *Schistosomiasis* (Washington, 1962: Departments of the Navy, Army, and Air Force, TB MEd 167, Nav MEd P-5052-6A, AFP 161-1-7). The best comprehensive account of rabbinic traditions about medicine and hygiene remains Julius Preuss, *Biblisch-talmudische Medizin. Beiträge zur Geschichte der Heilkunde und der Kultur überhaupt* (Berlin, 1923).

present inquiry.[1] Scriptural exegesis is here surveyed as one phenomenon of the life of the schools. We shall merely review the exegetical
teachings attributed to various masters in this period.[2] Our purpose
now is not to characterize the exegetical tendencies of various individual
masters, to investigate their respective legacies, or to search out the
sources of exegetical traditions.[3]

Pentateuch: R. Joseph taught (TNY) that the reference to Ashur
(Gen. 2:14) meant Seleucia, which, he said, proves that the Bible
speaks of things which will come into existence in future times.[4] Rava
said that the reward of Abraham for having said, "I am but dust and
ashes" (Gen. 18:27) and "I will not take a thread or a shoe latchet"
(Gen. 14:23) was that his descendants would receive commandments
using ashes and dust, threads, and straps, namely, the ritual of the

---

[1] For earlier data, see vol. I, pp. 157-164, II, pp. 188-240, and III, pp. 179-192.
Two questions of particular interest have been discussed, first, the alleged translation of the prophets and Writings by R. Joseph; second, the exegetical innovation
of Abaye.
    Y. L. Zunz, *HaDerashot beYisra'el*, ed. H. Albeck (Jerusalem, 1954), p. 37 and
p. 253 n. 21, roundly denies that R. Joseph prepared any such translation. See also
Wilhelm Bacher, *Die Agada der Babylonischen Amoräer* (Frankfort a/M, 1913), pp.
101-107, in particular, p. 103 n. 11. The so-called "translation" of R. Joseph is
frequently introduced by TNY. Bacher holds that R. Joseph was transmitting
Tannaitic traditions. We shall specify those passages. Zuri would like to change
such a reading to 'MR, "R. Joseph *said*." See also Graetz, *op. cit.*, II, pp. 581-582,
and Yavetz, *op. cit.*, VIII, p. 1ff. See also W. Bacher, "Targum," *JE* 12, p. 61.
    As to the alleged distinction by Abaye between the PŠT, plain-meaning of
Scripture, and MDRŠ, more fanciful exegesis in terms of later values, ideas, or
issues, see Bacher, *Agada*, p. 113, but especially Raphael Loewe, "The 'Plain'
Meaning of Scripture in Early Jewish Exegesis," *Annual of Jewish Studies*, (London,
1964), pp. 140-185, esp. pp. 160-162. Loewe states (p. 162), "According to Bacher,
it was Abaye who first distinguished PŠT from DRŠ as separate exegetical ap-
proaches; but the substance of Abaye's distinction cannot be established. It is true
that in one of the instances ... discussed above, Abaye preferred an explanation
which ... takes the context into account; but in another, he was apparently content
to acknowledge as PŠT an explanation that merely made explicit the entirely
arbitrary application of a verse of Proverbs ... Yet in Abaye's time there was current
the principle, formulated in Pumbeditha, that a text cannot be distorted from the
meaning of its *peshat* ... This formulation seems to have been employed to counter
exorbitant deductions from identity or close analogy of expression ...." Loewe
also discusses Rava's attention to the plain meaning of Scriptures.
    [2] I intend simply to summarize some of the exegetical traditions. It may be
useful to specify the part of the *content* of "Torah" revealed by Scriptural commentary and exegesis and that is my sole purpose here.
    [3] The best available account of individual rabbis' exegetical legacies remains
Bacher, *op. cit.*, for Rabbah b. Naḥmani, pp. 97-101; for R. Joseph, as cited above;
for Abaye, pp. 107-113, for Rava, pp. 114-133; for Rava's successors, pp. 133-143.
    [4] b. Ket. 10b.

Sotah, the thread of blue in the fringes, and the thong of the *tefillin*.[1] Rabbah exposited Prov. 18:19, "A brother transgressed against a strong city, and their contentions are like bars of a castle," with reference to Gen. 13:11; the brother was Lot, and the contentions were those between Israel and Ammon (Deut. 23:4).[2] Commenting on Ex. 1:13, Rava said that at first the service was in mortar and brick, but afterward in all manner of field work.[3] R. Joseph said that God revealed himself in a bush (Ex. 3:2) because he prefers humility.[4] R. Joseph taught (TNY) concerning Ex. 18:20, "And you will show them the way wherein they must walk and the work which they must do," that the *showing* referred to the source of their livelihood, the *way* referred to deeds of lovingkindness, *they must walk*, to visiting the sick; *wherein*, to burial; *and the work*, to the law; *which they must do*, to the margin of judgment.[5] Rabbah explained the contradiction between Lev. 20:21, "They shall *be* childless" and Lev. 20:20, "They shall *die* childless" by saying that if the sinner has children he will bury them, but if not, he will not have any in the future.[6] On Num. 13:22, "And they went up by the South and he came to Hebron," Rava explained that Caleb went away from the spies, and prayed at the graves of the patriarchs in Hebron that he might be delivered up from the plan of the spies.[7] Rabbah explained how Caleb won the people over with words to the cause of Moses. In the manner of a rhetorician, Caleb first stilled them by pretending to criticize Moses, and then praised Moses.[8] Rava explained the spies' report, that the land consumes its inhabitants (Num. 13:32). God had meant it for the advantage of the spies. Wherever they came, the chief of the city died, so the people were busy with funerals and had no time to bother the spies.[9] Abaye said that the Tammuz of the year of the spies was full, so that the weeping of the people would coincide with the full moon.[10] Rabbah interpreted Deut. 8:26, "Thou shalt cast them away," to mean, "Thou shalt alienate

---

[1] b. Ḥul. 88b, Sot. 17b.

[2] b. Hor. 10b.

[3] b. Sot. 11a.

[4] b. Sot. 5a.

[5] b. B.Q. 100a.

[6] b. Yev. 55a. Other exegeses of Leviticus pertained to legal matters, e.g. b. Yev. 97a, Rava on Lev. 18:10, to prove that a rapist can marry the daughter of the woman he raped; b. Yev. 83b, Lev. 18:22, Rava says, refers to a hermaphrodite, etc.

[7] b. Sot. 34b.

[8] b. Sot. 35a.

[9] *ibid.*

[10] b. Pes. 77a. For a translation of R. Joseph for Num. 31:50, see b. Shab. 64a.

them from thee as a stranger."[1] R. Joseph taught (TNY) concerning Deut. 10:2 that both the whole tablets and the fragments were deposited in the ark of the covenant.[2] He taught (TNY) concerning Deut. 11:17 that the "shutting up of heaven" was in respect to clouds and winds.[3] Rava explained Deut. 32:39, "I kill and resurrect, have wounded and heal." He pointed out that if God resurrects, how much the more so does he heal! But the Scripture proves that the Torah so taught the doctrine of divine resurrection of the dead, "What I put to death I revive, just as I have wounded and heal."[4] As a general exegetical principle, R. Joseph said that even those who do not derive lessons from the juxtaposition of texts in all the rest of the Pentateuch do so in interpreting the book of Deuteronomy.[5]

Former Prophets: Abaye said that Delilah knew that Samson was a righteous man, and would not utter the divine name in vain. When he said "I have been a Nazirite to God" (Judges 16:17), she therefore believed that he told the truth.[6] Rava (or, R. Zevid or R. Oshaia) said that I Sam. 17:12, "And the man was an old man in the days of Saul" referred to Jesse.[7] He also said, with reference to I Sam. 16:12, "Arise, anoint him, for this is he," that only he required anointing, but no king not of the Davidic dynasty required anointing.[8] Rava explained I Sam. 19:22, "Where are Samuel and David? One said, Behold they are at Naiot in Ramah," as follows: What was the connection between Naiot and Ramah? It means that they sat at Ramah and were "engaged with the glory of the world". They were discussing, Rava held, the place where the Temple should be built.[9] Rava taught that II Sam. 3:37 originally read, "And all the people came to pierce David" but that it reads "to make him eat bread" [the change of a single letter, KH to B] because at first they wanted to destroy him on account of Abner's death, but that he appeased them with words, so they comforted him

---

[1] b. Shab. 82b.

[2] b. B.B. 14b.

[3] b. Ta'anit 3b.

[4] b. Pes. 68a, b. Sanh. 91b. Note also b. Sanh. 92a, Rava derived the same dogma from Deut. 33:6, "'Let Reuben live and not die,' 'live'--in this world, and 'not die'—in the world to come."

[5] b. Ber. 21b, Yev. 4a. In the same context, R. Abbahu, arguing with a *min*, says that he does not derive lessons from juxtapositions of texts. Hence R. Joseph may be referring to the Babylonian Jewish-Christians, who, he would infer, do derive such lessons from the Book of Deuteronomy.

[6] b. Sot. 9b.

[7] b. Ber. 58a.

[8] b. Hor. 11b.

[9] b. Zev. 54b.

instead.[1] R. Joseph expounded I Chron. 27:23 and II Sam. 16:23. These scriptures show David took counsel with Aḥitofel and consulted the *Urim* and *Tumim* before he went to war.[2] R. Joseph said that the daughter of Pharaoh (I Kings 3:1) had converted to Judaism.[3] Rava said, with reference to I Kings 22:38, that Ahab was frigid, so Jezebel painted the pictures of two harlots on his chariot.[4] R. Joseph translated II Kings 2:12, "And Elisha saw it and cried, My father, my father, the chariots of Israel and the horsemen thereof," as follows: "My master, my master, who was better [protection] for Israel with his prayer than chariots and horsemen."[5]

Latter Prophets: R. Joseph said that Is. 1:9-10, "We should have been like unto Gomorrah... Hear the word of the Lord, you rulers of Sodom," proves that one should never "open his mouth to Satan," that is to say, utter ominous words.[6] Rava interpreted Is. 1:19, "You shall be fed with the sword" to mean, with coarse salt, hard baked barley bread, and onions.[7] Rava said that the Messiah will be able to smell a man and judge him, in explaining Is. 11:3, "He shall not judge after the sight of his eyes... or the hearing of his ears."[8] R. Joseph exposited Is. 12:1, "I will give thanks to you, O Lord, for though you were angry with me, your anger is turned away and you comfort me," as an allusion to two men who set out on a trading expedition. One got a thorn in his foot, could not go along, so he began to curse. Then he heard that his friend's ship had sunk into the sea, and was gratified that he could not join him, so he began to give praise instead.[9] R. Joseph taught (TNY) that Is. 13:3, "I have commanded my sanctified ones" referred to the Persians, who were "sanctified and appointed for Gehenna."[10] He translated Is. 19:18, "One shall be called the city of Ḥeres," as follows: "The city of Beth Shemesh, which is destined to destruction." He pointed out that Job 9:7 uses the word Ḥeres to mean sun.[11] R. Joseph taught (TNY) that "It shall not be stored nor treasured" (Is. 23:18)

---

[1] b. Sanh. 20a.
[2] b. Ber. 3b-4a.
[3] b. Yev. 76a.
[4] b. Sanh. 39b.
[5] b. M.Q. 26a. For the rabbis as protectors of Israel, see above, pp. 340-341, and vol. III, pp. 118ff.
[6] b. Ket. 8b.
[7] b. Qid. 62b.
[8] b. Sanh. 93b.
[9] b. Nid. 31a.
[10] b. Ber. 8b.
[11] b. Men. 110a.

refers to storehouses or treasurehouses of gold and silver.[1] He translated "Thou shalt fan them, and the wind shall carry them away" (Is. 41:16) as follows:"Thou shall winnow them, and a wind shall disperse them."[2] He taught that the "new thing" referred to in Is. 43:19, was the war of Gog and Magog. The later tribulations will cause the people to forget the earlier ones.[3] R. Nahman b. R. Hisda explained that Cyrus was not really referred to as the Messiah in Is. 45:1. What the verse means is that God said to the Messiah, "I have a complaint against Cyrus on your behalf, for I said 'He shall build my house and gather my exiles' (Is. 45:13) and he merely said that whoever wanted to might go back to Jerusalem."[4] R. Joseph explained to Abaye that despite the virtue of the Jerusalemites of the Second Temple, they were punished because they did not mourn for Jerusalem, citing Is. 66:10, "Rejoice with Jerusalem and be glad for her. All you that love her rejoice for joy with her all you that mourn for her."[5] Rava held that Manasseh tried Isaiah and put him to death, claiming that he was guilty of blasphemy, for Moses had said one could not see God and live (Ex. 33:20) and Isaiah had seen God (Is. 6:1). Isaiah knew that he would not be able to make a convincing defense, so he pronounced the divine name and was magically swallowed up by a cedar. This log was sawn apart. Isaiah died when the saw reached his mouth, as punishment for saying that the Jews had unclean lips.[6] Rava proved from Jer. 5:1 that Jerusalem was destroyed when faithful men ceased to exist in the city.[7] Rava asked Rabbah b. Mari to explain the alleged contradiction between Jer 8:2 and 8:3 as follows: "They shall not be buried... and death shall be chosen rather than life." How could such a death be preferable? Rabbah b. Mari replied that "Death shall be chosen" for the wicked, so they may not live in this world; they thus sin and fall into Gehenna.[8] Rava expounded Jer. 18:23, "But let them be overthrown before you. Deal with them in the time of your anger." He said, "Jeremiah spoke to the Holy One, blessed be he, 'Lord of the world, even when they are ready to do charity, cause them to be frustrated by people unworthy of consideration so they may have no reward for that

---

[1] b. Pes. 118b.
[2] b. A.Z. 44a.
[3] b. Ber. 13a.
[4] b. Meg. 12a.
[5] b. Git. 57a.
[6] b. Yev. 49b.
[7] b. Hag. 14a, Shab. 119b.
[8] b. Yev. 63b.

charity.'"[1] R. Joseph proved that the Davidic kings both judge and are judged, from Jer. 21:12.[2] He paraphrased [translated] Jer. 46:20, "Egypt is a very fair heifer, but the *kerez* [gadfly] out of the north is come...," as follows: "A fair kingdom is Egypt, but murderous nations from the north will come upon it."[3] Rava explained that Jer. 52:6-7 referred to the destructions of the First and Second Temples respectively, so there was no contradiction in the dates of the two verses. Rava saw no conflict between Isaiah's and Ezekiel's visions of God. All that Ezekiel saw, Isaiah also saw. "However," he said, "Ezekiel was like a villager who saw a king, and Isaiah like an urbanite." The one less accustomed than the other to the glory of the throne related more details.[4] R. Joseph taught (TNY) that Ezek. 9:6, "Begin the slaughter with my sanctuary" should be read "My sanctified ones," namely, "those who fulfilled the Torah from first to last."[5] Rava proved from Ezek. 16:14 that Jewish women are not hairy.[6] He showed from Ezek. 18:13 and 18:10 that lenders on interest are like shedders of blood.[7] R. Joseph taught (TNY) that Ex. 12:22, "And none of you shall go out-of-doors until the morning" shows that once the Destroyer has the right to do his work, he does not distinguish between righteous and wicked; and Ezek. 21:8, "I will cut off righteous and wicked," indicates that he begins with the righteous.[8] R. Joseph translated Hos. 4:2, "By swearing, lying, killing, stealing, committing adultery, they spread forth, and blood touches blood" as follows: "They beget children by their neighbors' wives, piling evil upon evil."[9] Rava explained Hos. 7:15, "Though I have trained [yissarti] and strengthened their arms, yet they imagine mischief against me," as follows: "The Holy One, blessed be he, said, 'I thought I would chastise them [YSR] with suffering in this world, so that their arm might be strengthened in the next, yet they..."[10] Rava explained Hos. 13:2 to mean that if one sacrificed his son to the idol, the priest would then praise him, "You have offered a precious gift to it, now come and

---

[1] b. B.Q. 16b.
[2] b. Sanh. 19a.
[3] b. Yoma 32b.
[4] b. Ḥag. 13b.
[5] b. A.Z. 4a.
[6] b. Sanh. 21a.
[7] b. Tem. 6b.
[8] b. B.Q. 60a.
[9] b. Qid. 13a.
[10] b. A.Z. 4a.

kiss it."[1] R. Joseph translated Amos 7:14, "I am no prophet nor a son of a prophet but a herdsman and gatherer of sycamore fruit" as follows: "Behold I am the owner of flocks and possess sycamore trees in the valley."[2] He translated Obadiah 1:6, "How is Esau searched out? How are his hidden places sought out?" as follows, "How was Esau ransacked? How were his hidden treasures exposed?"[3] R. Joseph explained the vision of Habakkuk 3:2, "He stood and measured the earth, he beheld..." "What did he see? He saw the seven commandments accepted by the descendents of Noah, and since some rejected them, he rose up and granted them exemptions."[4] R. Joseph similarly taught (TNY) with reference to Hab. 3:6, "He stands and shakes the earth, he sees and makes the nations tremble," as follows: "He saw the nations did not observe the seven commandments of the sons of Noah, so he released them from those commandments."[5] Rava explained Hab. 3:11, "The sun and moon stood still in their *zevul*, and at the light of your arrows they went" as follows: "The sun and moon ascended from the firmament (*raqi'a*) to the *zevul* above." He explained that "if God would not punish Koraḥ (Num. 16) they would not go forth. So God shot arrows at them because they were more zealous for the honor of Moses than for his own honor. Therefore they now do not go forth until they are driven to it."[6] R. Joseph translated Zeph. 3:18, "I will gather them that are destroyed because of the appointed season who are of you," as follows: "Destruction comes upon [the enemies of] Israel because they put off until late the times of the appointed seasons in Jerusalem."[7] Rava explained Zeph. 2:14, "Their voice shall sing in the windows, desolation shall be in the thresholds" to mean that "when there is song in a house, destruction lurks on the threshhold."[8] R. Joseph translated Zech. 9:6, "And the bastard shall dwell in Ashdod," as follows: "The house of Israel shall dwell securely in their land, where they were as strangers."[9] He explained Zech. 12:11, "In that day there shall be a great mourning in Jerusalem as the mourning of Hadadrimmon in the valley of Megiddon," saying, "Were it not for the *Targum* of this verse, we should not know what it means: 'On that day there shall be a great

---

[1] b. Sanh. 63b.
[2] b. Ned. 38a.
[3] b. B.Q. 3b.
[4] b. B.Q. 38a.
[5] b. A.Z. 2b.
[6] b. Sanh. 110a, b. Ned. 39b, Num. R. 18:20.
[7] b. Ber. 28a.
[8] b. Sot. 48a.
[9] b. Qid. 72b.

mourning in Jerusalem like the mourning of Ahab son of Omri who was killed by Hadadrimmon son of Rimmon in Ramoth Gilead and like the mourning of Josiah son of Ammon who was killed by Pharaoh the Lame in the plain of Megiddo."[1]

The Writings: Rava expounded a number of passages in Psalms, like Rav before him, as if they applied to the life of King David. So he explained Ps. 11:1: "What is meant by the verse, 'To the chief Musician, a psalm of David. In the Lord I put my trust. How do you say to my soul, Flee as a bird to the mountain.' Here David was seen as pleading to God, Lord of the Universe, Forgive me that sin [with Bathsheba] so that men may not say, 'Your mountain [the king] has been put to flight by a bird.'" Several other passages in Psalms, particularly Ps. 51:6, 38:18 and 35:15, were seen as referring to the same sin.[2] Rava expounded Ps. 11:7, "For the Lord is righteous. He loves righteousness; the upright shall behold his face" to mean, "Abraham comes and brings redemption to the wicked."[3] He expounded Ps. 25:9, "Good and upright is the Lord. Therefore he instructs sinners in the way," as follows: "Come and see the righteousness of the Holy One... Whoever has the intent of performing a commandment but under duress fails to do so is credited by Scripture as if he had done it, but if he intends to sin, he is not regarded as guilty unless he actually does it."[4] He expounded Ps. 40:6, "Many things have you done, O Lord, my God, even your wonderful works and thoughts toward us," as follows: "Not toward me, but toward us, is this passage written, to teach that Rehoboam sat on David's lap, and David said to him, 'Those two verses [Gen. 18:9 and Ps. 45:14, showing that an Ammonite and a Moabite woman might enter the congregation of Israel] were said concerning you and me [for as descendants of Ammonites and Moabites, we are thereby admitted into the congregation of Israel.]" Concerning Ps. 40:8, "Lo, I am come with the roll of a book which is prescribed for me," Rava explained that David came with a roll but did not know that it was already written about himself [with reference to Gen. 19:15 and Ps. 89:21].[5] Rava interpreted Ps. 62:4, "How long will you imagine mischief against a man? You shall be slain... You are as a bowing wall and a tottering fence." He held that the verse referred to the way of the men of Sodom, who used to cast envious eyes at wealthy men, so

---

[1] b. Meg. 3a.
[2] b. Sanh. 107a. On Ps. 35:15, see also b. B.M. 59a.
[3] Kallah Rabbati 55a.
[4] Kallah Rabbati 51b.
[5] b. Yev. 77a.

would put them by a wall and push it over on them.[1] R. Joseph taught
(TNY) concerning Ps. 104:20, as follows: "'You make darkness and
it is night'—refers to this world, which is comparable to night. 'Wherein all the beasts of the forest creep forth'—refers to the wicked of the
world, who are like beasts of the forest. 'The sun rises'—for the
righteous. 'The wicked are gathered in'—for Gehenna. 'And lay them
down in their habitations'—not a single righteous man lacks a habi-
tation appropriate for his honor. 'Man goeth forth to his work'—the
righteous go forth to receive their reward. 'And to his labor until the
evening'—as one who has worked fully until the very evening."[2] Rava
said that the first part of Ps. 112:7 should be explained in terms of the
second, or vice versa. "He shall not be afraid of evil tidings, his heart is
steadfast, trusting in the Lord." "Either he will not fear evil tidings
because his heart is steadfast, or his heart is steadfast and therefore he
will not fear evil tidings."[3] The following was in the same mode:

> "It is time to work for the Lord. They have voided your Law." (Ps.
> 119:126) Rava said the first clause can be taken as explaining the second,
> or vice versa. Thus, "It is time to work for the Lord because they have
> made void your law," or "They have made void your law *because* it is
> time to work for the Lord."
>
> (b. Ber. 63a)

Rava exposited Prov. 18:1, "He that separateth himself seeks his own
desire and snarls against all sound wisdom" as a reference to Lot, who
separated himself from Abraham.[4] Rava said that Prov. 23:31 proves
that only red wine may be used for drink-offerings, including wine for
Sanctification.[5] He held that Job lived in the time of the spies (Num.
13), on the basis of an exegesis of 'land of Uz' (Job 1:1) and 'whether
there be wood [*'ez*] therein' (Num. 13:20), as follows: "Moses said to
Israel, 'See if that man is there whose years are as the years of a tree and
who shelters his generation like a tree.'"[6] Rava also said that while "In
all this, Job did not sin with his lips" (Job 2:10), he did sin with his
heart, saying (Job 9:24), "The earth has been given into the hand of
the wicked..." Rava expounded Job 10:7, "Although you know that I
am not wicked, and there is none that can deliver out of your hand."
He said, "Job sought to exculpate the whole world. Job thus said,

[1] b. Sanh. 109a.
[2] b. B.M. 83b.
[3] b. Ber. 60a.
[4] b. Hor. 10b.
[5] b. B.B. 97b.
[6] b. B.B. 15a.

'Lord of the world, you have made the ox with cloven hoofs, and the ass with whole ones; Paradise and Gehenna; righteous and wicked men—and who stands in your way?'" That is to say, God does as he likes, but man has no free will. The companions answered, (Job 15:4), "Yea, you do away with fear and restrain devotion before God"— meaning, "If God created the evil inclination, he also created the Torah as its antidote."[1] Rava held that Job 7:9, "As the cloud that... vanished, so he that goes down to Sheol shall come up no more" proves that Job denied the resurrection of the dead.[2] He taught that Job 12:5 teaches that when Noah rebuked his contemporaries, they made fun of him.[3] He said that Job 37:6 proves that snow is beneficial for the mountains as fivefold rain for the earth.[4]

Of the five Scrolls, the Scroll of Esther elicited the most extensive comments, because the rabbis probably preached in the synagogues at Purim.[5] Rava said, with reference to Esther 1:2, "In those days, when the king sat [on his throne], that "when he sat" means, 'When he began to feel secure.' The king reasoned that sufficient time had passed so that he might now make use of the vessels of the Temple, for the years when redemption had to come, he thought, had gone by with no result.[6] Rava explained "Also Vashti the queen made a feast for the women in the royal house" (Est. 1:9), saying, "It should have said 'the women's house,' but both Ahasuerus and Vashti had no immoral purpose."[7] "The king was very angry" (Est. 1:12) because Vashti accused him of being unable to hold his wine.[8] Rava said that "After these things" (Est. 3:1) referred to God's having created a healing before the blow which was about to fall.[9] Rava's discourse on Esther began with Prov. 29:2, "When the righteous are increased the people rejoice, but when the wicked rule, the people sigh." He said, "'When the righteous are increased' is illustrated by Mordecai and Esther, as it says, 'And the city of Shushan shouted and was glad' (Est. 8:15). 'But when the wicked rules' is illustrated by Haman, as it says, 'But the city of

---

[1] b. B.B. 16a.
[2] b. B.B. 16a.
[3] b. Sanh. 108b.
[4] b. Ta'anit 3b.
[5] See vol. II, pp. 57-64, for an explanation of why the Scroll of Esther attracted disproportionate interest in the Babylonian schools. Sermons would have been preached on all five Scrolls, not only Esther.
[6] b. Meg. 11b. See also Rava an Est. 1:7, b. Meg. 12a.
[7] b. Meg. 12b.
[8] b. Meg. 12b.
[9] b. Meg. 13b.

Shushan was perplexed' (Esther 3:15)."[1] Rava interpreted Est. 9:27, "They confirmed and took upon them" to mean that the Jews reaccepted the Torah in the days of Ahasuerus.[2] R. Joseph held that Est. 9:28 proves that the Scroll of Esther was composed under the inspiration of the Holy Spirit.[3]

Rava said that as a reward for the four tears which Orpah shed upon her mother-in-law, she merited that four mighty wariors should issue from her. The four tears are indicated in Ruth 1:14, "And they lifted up their voice and wept again"; one weeping produced two tears (one from each eye), and the second, two more.[4] We have already noted that Rava interpreted many of the Scriptures in the Song of Songs to refer to study of the Torah,[5] or, in the more common exegetical tradition, to the relationship between God and Israel. His exposition of Song 7:2, "how beautiful are thy steps in sandals, O prince's daughter," was as follows: "How beautiful are the steps of Israel when they go up to celebrate a festival [in Jerusalem]." "O prince's daughter" refers to the daughter of Abraham our father, who is called a prince (Ps. 47:10).[6] The reference was to proselytes, who are regarded as children of Abraham. R. Joseph explained that the book of Ezra, which was narrated by Nehemiah, was not called by Nehemiah's name because he spoke disparagingly of his predecessors, evidence of which is Neh. 5:15.[7]

R. Joseph said that one should not read the book of Ben Sirah, yet he held that one may expound "the good things it contains."[8] Despite his numerous Aramaic paraphrases of Scripture, he said that one should speak either Hebrew or Persian, but not Syriac.[9]

Another kind of exegesis involved the derivation from Scriptures of popular or rabbinical proverbs. Rabbah b. Mari apparently specialized in research on such matters. The following passage recorded some of these traditions:

---

[1] b. Meg. 11a.

[2] b. Shab. 88a. The implication *may* have been that in times of trouble, the Jews should rededicate themselves to the Torah, and would find salvation, as they had in the times of Ahasuerus.

[3] b. Meg. 7a.

[4] b. Sot. 42b.

[5] Above, p. 291f. on Song 7.14, see b. 'Eruv. 21 b; and above, 1 p. 292 on Song 8:10, b. Pes. 87a.

[6] b. Suk. 49b, b. Ḥag. 3a.

[7] b. Sanh. 93b.

[8] b. Sanh. 100b.

[9] b. Sot. 49b.

Rava said to Rabbah b. Mari, "Whence can be derived the lesson taught by our rabbis that one who solicits mercy for his fellow while he himself is in need of the same thing [will be answered first]?" He replied, "As it is written: 'And the Lord changed the fortune of Job when he prayed for his friends' (Job. 42:10)."

Rava [again] said to Rabbah b. Mari, "Whence can be derived the proverbial saying that together with the thorn the cabbage is smitten?" He replied, "As it is written, 'Wherefore will you contend with Me, ye all have transgressed against Me, says the Lord' (Jer. 2:29)."

Rava [again] said to Rabbah b. Mari, "Whence can be derived the popular saying that poverty follows the poor?" He replied: "We have learned: 'The rich used to bring the first fruits in baskets of gold and silver, but the poor brought it in wicker baskets made out of the bark of willow, and thus gave the baskets as well as the first-fruits to the priest.'" He said to him: "You derive it from there, but I derive it from this: 'And shall cry unclean, unclean' (Lev. 13:45)."

He [again] said to Rabbah b. Mari, "Whence can be derived the advice given by our rabbis, Have early breakfast in the summer because of the heat, and in the winter because of the cold, and people even say that sixty men may pursue him who has early meals in the mornings and will not overtake him?" He replied, "As it is written, 'They shall not hunger nor thirst, neither shall the heat nor sun smite them' (Is. 49:10)...."

Rava [again] said to Rabbah b. Mari, "Whence can be derived the saying of the rabbis, 'If thy neighbor calls thee an ass put a saddle on thy back?'" He replied: "As it is written: 'And he said: Hagar, Sarai's handmaid, Whence comest thou and whither goest thou? And she said: I flee from the face of my mistress Sarai' (Gen. 16:8)."

Rava [again] said to Rabbah b. Mari, "Whence can be derived the popular saying: 'If there is any matter of reproach in thee be the first to tell it?'" He replied, "As it is written: 'And when the Lord shall have dealt well with my lord then remember thy handmaid' (I Sam. 25:31)."

Rava [again] said to Rabbah b. Mari, "Whence can be derived the popular saying, 'Sixty pains reach the teeth of him who hears the noise made by another man eating while he himself does not eat'?" He replied: "As it is written, 'But me, even me thy servant and Zadok the priest, and Benaiah the son of Jehoiada, and thy servant Solomon, hath he not called' (I Kings 1:26)."

Rava [again] said to Rabbah b. Mari, "Whence can be derived the popular saying, 'Though the wine belongs to the owner, the thanks are given to the butler?'" He replied, "As it is written, 'And thou shalt put of thy honor upon him, that all the congregation of the children of Israel may hearken' (Num. 27:18-20), and it is also written, 'And Joshua the son of Nun was full of the spirit of wisdom, for Moses had laid his hands upon him; and the children of Israel hearkened unto him' (Deut. 24:9)."

Rava [again] said to Rabbah b. Mari, "Whence can be derived the popular saying, 'A dog when hungry is ready to swallow even his [own] excrements'?" He replied, "As it is written, 'The full soul loatheth an honeycomb, but to the hungry soul every bitter thing is sweet' (Prov. 27:7)."

Rava [again] said to Rabbah b. Mari, "Whence can be derived the popular saying: 'Into the well from which you have once drunk water do not throw clods?'" He replied, "As it is written, 'Thou shalt not abhor an Edomite, for he is thy brother, thou shalt not abhor an Egyptian because thou wast a stranger in his land' (Deut. 23:8)."

Rava [again] said to Rabbah b. Mari, "Whence can be derived the popular saying: 'Behind an owner of wealth chips are dragged along'? He replied: "As it is written: 'And Lot also who went with Abram had flocks and herds and tents' (Gen. 13:5)."

(b. B.Q. 92a-93a)[1]

In summary: The various modes and methods of Scriptural exegesis inherited from earlier generations all were represented in the traditions attributed to the fourth-century masters. R. Joseph's many citations of Tannaitic traditions as well as his paraphrastic translations leave no doubt that in a history of Jewish Bible exegesis, he would play a considerable role. Nonetheless, our brief survey has revealed little fundamental innovation. If the distinction between 'plain-meaning' and more fanciful exegesis of Scriptures was widely recognized, we can hardly cite much evidence of that fact in these traditions. The past tendency to read into Scriptures the ideas, concerns, and issues of the current generation continued without significant modification. Indeed, the long citation of Rabbah b. Mari indicates how much interest was now attached to showing the Scriptures to be the ultimate source of all wisdom, just as in earlier times. Various ethical and theological ideas appeared in the context of exegesis. God preferred humility. The right way of living involved deeds of lovingkindness, visiting the sick, burying the dead, keeping the commandments, and showing mercy in judgment. God's ways were forever justified, even when men did not fully comprehend them. Scripture contained many proofs of the coming resurrection of the dead. Pagan monarchs were not to be trusted. Cyrus was not the Messiah. The Persians were destined to Gehenna. Historical events were determined by the moral character of the participants, just as the prophets had said. People must be willing to accept heavenly chastisement in this world, so they may enjoy the

---

[1] Trans. E. W. Kirzner (London, 1948), pp. 533-538. For other popular sayings, see b. Pes. 28a, Abaye, Rava, and R. Joseph; b. Suk. 22b, R. Papa; b. B.M. 107b, Rabbah asked Rava b. Mari about the Scriptural source of a rabbinical proverb.

world to come. The merits of one's ancestors produce blessings for generations to come. Job was a blasphemer, who sinned in his heart and denied the resurrection of the dead. The conventional repertoire of rabbinical exegesis uncovered here could be duplicated in studies of any other generation of rabbinical masters.[1]

XVI. THE KALLAH

In addition to students regularly resident in the vicinity of the schools, many others would come for two months in the year, 'Elul (August-September) and 'Adar (February-March) to hear the lectures and discussion. We noted above[2] that Rabbah supposedly attracted as many as twelve thousand students. Being absent from their homes when the census for the head-tax was taken, the students were able to evade their taxes. If that is the case, then we may suppose that among this vast number were some whose interest in not being at home when the tax-collector came exceeded their interest in what they learned at the school.[3] In any event, the *kallah*[4] was one effective means by which the schools retained their influence over students who had completed full-time studies. Large numbers came, as evidenced by Abaye's and Rava's references to great crowding at the sessions.[5]

We noted above[6] stories about younger students' remaining away from home as long as six years at a time. At some point, however, one normally would have to take up a gainful occupation. R. Ishmael and R. Simeon b. Yoḥai had earlier discussed whether one should engage in anything other than study of the Torah, the former holding that one

---

[1] From the time of Zunz, it has been the assumption of all scholars that the *sitz im leben* of academic exegesis was synagogue preaching. It is difficult to locate in the data considered here, or in vols. II, 188-240, and III, pp. 179-192, examples of actual public sermons. The few clear-cut public speeches referred to in vol. III, pp. 253 and 255, pertained not to Scripture but to the laws of Passover, the Day of Atonement, and the Sabbath; these were introduced by "So-and-so lectured in such-and-such a town....." It seems to me that rabbinic Scriptural exegesis may just as well have been presented in the schools, and mainly for the edification of disciples, as in the synagogues.

[2] b. B.M. 86a, cited above, p. 41.

[3] For imposters at the *kallah*, see R. Naḥman, b. B.Q. 113a.

[4] For the meaning of the term, see the brief but excellent summary of previous suggestions provided by S. K. Mirsky, "Types of Lectures in the Babylonian Academies," in J. L. Blau and others, ed., *Essays on Jewish Life and Thought Presented in Honor of Salo Wittmaye⁻ Baron* (New York, 1959), p. 395, ns. 102-104. See also Tannenblatt. *op. cit.*, pp. 229-230.

[5] See b. Ber. 6a-b.

[6] Above, p. 293.

should combine Torah with a wordly occupation, the latter, that one should study Torah only, and have faith that God will provide. On this discussion Abaye said,

> "Many followed the advice of R. Ishmael and succeeded, and many followed that of R. Simeon b. Yoḥai and did not succeed."
>
> (b. Ber. 35b)

Rava, moreover, advised his students not to come to the school during *Nisan* and *Tishre* (April-May, September-October), after the *kallah* ended,

> "So that you do not have to worry about your sustenance for the entire year."
>
> (b. Ber. 35b

These were the months of planting, before the start of summer, in May, and toward its conclusion, in October. Frost may occur any time from November to March. In modern times half the land is left fallow in the summer, and half in the winter. Hence, if the same system was followed then, the farmers would have to plant twice annually, on different parts of their land. The ploughing takes place between January and April, and between August and October. Barley was a winter crop; wheat was also grown generally in the winter. Rice was a summer crop, sown between February and April, and harvested from July to September.[1] While we do not know Rava's specific intentions, they do conform to the pattern of contemporary agriculture and climate. It seems likely that the students, who were mostly either farmers or farm-workers, would have to be home at that time, probably for both harvesting and planting, as conditions required. There was, therefore, a biennial exchange of populations. Former students would come to the schools, and present students would go home. Under the circumstance, the influence of the schools must have radiated throughout the Jewish communities in Babylonia.

Mirsky holds that following the *kallah*, others who had not been educated in the schools would come for a month at a time: "The general public flocked to the academy during the months of *Nisan* and *Tishri* to hear lectures on the laws of holidays."[2] I know of no evidence that such gatherings took place in this time. We know that rabbis did

---

[1] See K. Mason, ed., *Iraq and the Persian Gulf* (London, 1944: Royal Navy Intelligence Division, B.R. 524), pp. 166ff., 447-457. Compare Beer, *Ma'amadam*, pp. 52-53.

[2] *Op. cit.*, p. 401.

lecture about the holiday observance before Passover, but it is not clear whether these lectures took place in the schools or in the synagogues, or whether people really "flocked" to them.[1]

XVII. THE SCHOOLS AND THE STREETS

The rabbis and their disciples emerged from the masses, distinguished by their carriage, dress, manner of speech, alleged theurgical capacities, and, mainly, learning. Ordinary people thus confronted a kind of man claiming to be something quite different from themselves, namely, the incarnation or realization of the revelation of Sinai, to be honored as much as the Torah of Sinai was honored. Rava so stated explicitly:

> Rava said, "How stupid are those other people who stand up before the Scroll of the Torah but do not stand up before a *great man*...."[2]

> (b. Mak. 22b)

Rava explained that the rabbis were able by their interpretation actually to alter the content of the Torah. He pointed out that the Torah prescribed forty lashes, but the rabbis interpreted the passage so as to reduce the figure to thirty-nine. What Rava claimed was not merely that people should respect rabbis, but that they should revere them as masters of oral Torah *just* as they revere the Written Torah itself. Ordinary people certainly honored rabbis in many ways, deferring to them in the synagogue, paying respect to them in the streets, and treating them as holy men in other ways.[3] Rava, however, demanded much more than such natural, ordinary respect. He asked for religious reverence such as was paid to holy objects, even the Torah-scrolls.

The response of ordinary folk is difficult to assess. We noted the critical view of the family of Benjamin the physician, who may have seen rabbis as competition when they gave out medical advice. In regarding as blasphemous infidelity the perfectly normal question of the family of Benjamin, "What good are the rabbis?" the rabbinical advocates transformed mere social criticism into heresy. Not all who opposed the rabbis or disobeyed them, or merely refrained from

---

[1] For two examples, see vol. III, pp. 253, 255. Y. S. Zuri, *History of Hebrew Public Law. The Reign of the Exilarchate and the Legislative Academies, Period of Rab Nachman bar Jizchak* (320-355) (In Hebrew, Tel Aviv. 1939) discusses data pertaining mostly to the next generation.

[2] On "great man" as a technical term for a rabbi able to reason, see vol. III, p. 83, n. 3.

[3] See the excellent discussion of Beer, *Ma'amadam*, pp. 178-184.

obeying them, were seen as heretics or blasphemers on account of their "disrespect" of rabbis. Some were scoffers to be sure. R. Aḥa b. ʿUlla said those who scoff at the 'words of the sages' will be condemned to boiling excrement.[1] We recall that Rava likewise contrasted the city-dwellers, who rob, swear falsely, and commit adultery, with the students of Torah who live in poverty among disbelievers.[2] That people kept important parts of the law seems beyond doubt. How they responded to the rabbis' political power and religious and cultural leadership may be gauged from the following saying:

> Abaye said, "If a disciple of the rabbis is loved by the townspeople, it is not because of his superiority but because he does not rebuke them for matters of Heaven."
>
> (b. Ket. 105b)

Abaye regarded it as normal for the disciple of the rabbis to be hated, and ascribed the hatred to his rebuke of the ordinary folk for neglect of religious matters.

More concrete evidence of the relationship between local rabbinic authorities and the townspeople derives from the rule of Rava in Maḥoza and of Rabbah at Pumbedita:

> Rava said, "At first I thought all the people of Maḥoza loved me. When I was appointed judge, I thought some would hate me and others would love me. Having seen that the one who loses [in court] today wins tomorrow, I concluded that if I am loved they all love me, and if I am hated they all must hate me."
>
> (b. Ket. 105b)

Rava was referring to the reactions of people who came to him at court. His comments on the Maḥozans in general leave no doubt that *he* hated them:

> "They that strive with the Lord shall be broken to pieces" (I Sam 2:10)...Rava said, "Among them are the best of the people of Maḥoza, and they are called 'sons of Gehenna'."
>
> (b. R.H. 17a)[3]

> "Woe to you, cows of Bashan that...oppress the poor and crush the needy" (Amos 4:1). Rava said, "These are the women of Maḥoza, who eat without working."
>
> (b. Shab. 32b)[4]

---

[1] Above, p. 299, b. ʿEruv. 21a.

[2] Above, p. 292, b. ʿEruv. 21b.

[3] Whatever the variant readings, the "best of Maḥoza [who shall be called] sons of Gehenna" seems a firm one.

[4] Note also Rava's saying, b. Pes. 50b, that the women of Maḥoza are lazy and never work.

> Rava said, "The reason why the people of Maḥoza...have red spots
> is that they indulge in sexual intercourse in the daytime..."
>
> (b. Ber. 59b)[1]

Maḥoza was a great commercial center, suburb of the capital at Seleucia-Ctesiphon and the center of urban Jewish life. Rava's references to
living among infidels and the licentious and immoral people of great
cities suggest a preference on the part of the schoolmen for the simpler
way of living of the country-folk. The people of Maḥoza were always
on the move, Rava said, so it was hard to confirm their signatures.[2]
They were delicate, so wine heated them up.[3] They were regarded as
sharp "because they drink the waters of the Tigris," Rava said.[4] (The
Maḥozan working people felt faint if they were idle.[5]) The women
were spoiled, and unlike the farm wives, did not work. Such idleness
could hardly win rabbinical approval. But Rava saw the women as the
cause of their husband's sharp business practices. In such a setting, it
must have been difficult to force or much encourage people to conform
to rabbinical standards of life. There was no law against idle women.
The rabbis could scarcely prevent people from engaging in sexual relations in the daytime, much as they disapproved because it attracted
demons. No wonder, then, that Rava said the best of Maḥozans would
end up in hell. It should not be supposed, moreover, that Rava was
alone in feeling tension between himself and the city which he served
as rabbinical authority. Rabbah at Pumbedita earlier found matters no
easier:

> Abaye asked Rabbah, "You whom all the Pumbeditans hate [SNW]
> —who will mourn for you?" He replied,"You and Rabbah b. R. Ḥanan
> are enough."
>
> (b. Shab. 153a)[6]

If the man who informed against Rabbah was a Pumbeditan, Abaye's
question cannot have exaggerated matters. Heaven itself supposedly
had to force people to mourn for Rabbah. Abaye later on told Rava
about the sharp tricks of Pumbeditans, who would cleverly defraud
the public if they could.[7] Nor were other places regarded more favorably. Rava said that Harpania was deeper than hell:

---

[1] See above, p. 300.
[2] b. Git. 6a.
[3] b. Shab. 109a.
[4] b. Ber. 59b.
[5] b. B.M. 77a.
[6] Note also Abaye said Rabbah inflicted murderous punishments on the Pumbeditans, above, p. 331.
[7] b. B.B. 46a, see also b. Ḥul. 127a.

Rava said, "It [Harpania] was deeper than Sheol, for in Scriptures it says, 'I shall ransom them from the power of Sheol, I shall redeem them from death' (Hos. 13:14)—But for the unfitness of these there is no remedy at all. The unfit of Harpania [are forbidden to marry rabbinical Jews] on account of those of Mesene, of Mesene on account of those of Palmyra..."

(b. Yev. 17a)[1]

Harpania was thus seen to be a place of the deepest immorality. The people there had so long ignored rabbinical rules about suitable marriage partners that "good Jews" could not marry them. In earlier times, Rav and Samuel had roundly condemned the Jews of Mesene and other outlying regions.[2] Now, a century or more afterward, Rava repeated that condemnation, which would suggest that matters had improved not at all. Students from such places were not likely to achieve much mastery of Torah. R. Joseph said that coming from Babylon (?) or Borsippa was a bad omen for "Torah."[3] That is to say, one who settles there will quickly forget his learning. Nonetheless, the bitter hatred between sage and 'am ha'arez earlier expressed by the Palestinian schools[4] cannot be said to have characterized the Babylonian academicians. Rabbah b. R. Huna merely said that it was permissible to call an insolent person "wicked,"[5] which is a far cry from the violent language and hostile attitudes of the Palestinians. Nonetheless, the rabbis did try to force people to remain in towns of which they approved:

Rav Judah in the name of Samuel said, "As it is forbidden to leave the land of Israel for Babylonia, so it is forbidden to leave Babylonia for other countries." Both Rabbah and R. Joseph said, "Even from Pumbedita to Be Kubi." A man once moved from Pumbedita to Be Kubi. R. Joseph excommunicated him. A man once left Pumbedita for Astunia [nearby, Piruz Shapur, according to Obermeyer] and died. Abaye said, "If this young rabbinical disciple wanted it, he could still have been alive."

(b. Ket. 111a)

It therefore seems that rabbinical influence was more effective in some places than in others. Where schools were located, or rabbis adminis-

---

[1] But in the same passage, R. Zera explains "Harpania" as "the mountain [HR] to which all turn [PWNYM]."

[2] Vol. II, pp. 240-249, 268-275.

[3] b. Sanh. 109a. I do not know what town he meant by "Babylon." I do not see how he could have referred to all of Babylonia.

[4] Note that most of the bitter statements against the ordinary folk in b. Pes. 48a-50b derive from Palestinian, *not* Babylonian masters.

[5] b. Ta'anit 7b.

tered the courts and civil affairs, there the rabbis' influence and power were probably substantial. They encouraged ordinary folk to remain in such places and tried to prevent them from going to Jewish communities of which they disapproved.

It is difficult to say whether the rabbis formed a separate economic class or manipulated the people for their own economic benefit. We have already noted that rabbis as a class enjoyed considerable economic benefits. Some of these came in consequence of their public service, for the exilarch's support of the rabbis' market-privilege must be interpreted as a means of compensating them for time spent in study and in court. Others naturally followed upon popular reverence for the rabbis as holy men, whom it would be profitable to include as partners in economic ventures to bring good fortune, to whom it would be wise to marry off one's daughters, whom one ought to entertain and otherwise favor. The complex combination of political and legal power with religious and magical reputation certainly resulted in greater economic advantage than the rabbis would otherwise have enjoyed. I see however no basis whatever to suppose that the rabbis, or any individual rabbi, ever consciously and knowingly fostered belief in rabbinical magic for personal benefit. And yet, the rabbis' economic ideas, examined in connection with slavery, for example, reveal a bias in favor of the proprietary classes against the working classes. While communal funds administered by rabbis were used to ransom people taken captive, they were not available to pay the head-taxes of those who could not do so. Hence impoverished people had to sell themselves into slavery. The rabbis' comments on slaves are typical of people who were not slaves, but owned them. Slaves were lazy, untrustworthy, licentious, and did not deserve the normal dignities afforded to ordinary people. Little if any evidence suggests that in practice rabbis favored improving the lot of slaves; no evidence whatever shows how they attempted to remove the causes of slavery to begin with. Similarly, all the cases of squatters' rights examined earlier revealed the rabbinical judge's ruling in favor of the putative owner and against the squatter. Whether Rava's rulings revealed a consistent policy was not clear. And yet, those rulings remain a fact to be reckoned with. At no point do we find rabbis' decisions in this period on the side of the defendant in a case of land-seizure, and that would suggest, once again, a tendency to favor the proprietary classes, whose property was endangered by the rules of ḥazaqah, against the landless classes, for whom the right of squatting constituted the sole realistic hope of gaining a piece of land.

If we had a wider variety of cases and examples, we might conclude that the rabbis as a class did indeed favor mainly the landholding groups within Jewry. In the absence of such evidence, we may only note that most of what we do know points in one direction only. The criticisms of the rich, with their lazy wives and their strange sexual license, do not much change the pattern. It is one thing to fulminate against immorality, but quite another to legislate against the economic interests of those who were supposedly immoral, and this, I think, the rabbis did not do. The rabbis' unabashed use of their position in the courts and schools to favor their own interests, including favoritism of their own estate when trying cases, their asserted claim of tax exemption and their undeniable enjoyment of substantial economic benefits—these, combined with their apparent identification with the interests of the land-holding classes, must help to account for the tension they referred to between themselves and the ordinary people.

XVIII. SUMMARY AND CONCLUSIONS

The following tables summarize the data concerning various supernatural feats, events, heavenly or demonic visitations, and magical exampla of the first four generations of Babylonian masters. They are intended not only to recapitulate, but also to place into more accurate perspective the magical materials stressed in the preceding pages. It quickly becomes clear that however limited the number of case-reports and other exemplifications of the enforcement of law (above, pp. 256-277), the number of magical accounts is far less still in proportion to the total literature. We actually have relatively few stories about rabbinical magic. I have omitted reference to sayings and stories not associated with a particular rabbi. Even if we were to add the entire corpus of supernatural passages pertaining to Babylonian schools, however, it would not greatly augment the data before us. The first, obvious conclusion is that the editors of the Babylonian Talmud were not concerned to preserve magical sayings and stories. But it is equally clear—and this must be reemphasized—that they did *not* attempt to suppress such data. As I said, the ascription of supernatural powers to various authorities was not only normal and natural but also important. It was taken for granted that rabbis could combat demons and communicate with angels. If the Babylonian Talmudic editors were concerned with systematically providing a hagiographical, instead of legal literature, many more such stories assuredly would have reached us than we now have in hand. It is the nature of the literature, not the attitude or character of the academies, which accounts for the *relative* sparseness of supernatural materials. As in the earlier tables, we must recognize that the specification of an "exemplification of supernatural ability" is somewhat arbitrary. I have not included astrological accounts or stories about how prayers were answered, or would surely be answered, if one did a certain rite, or, more commonly, exhibited a certain moral virtue. The tables are not offered as "proof" of a particular proposition, but rather, as I said, merely as a review of scattered material.

I. *b. Berakhot*

Ca. 220-265	Ca. 265-310	Ca. 310-350
1. b. Ber. 18b. Samuel talks with deceased father. 2. b. Ber. 58a. Elijah rescued R. Shila.	*[1. b. Ber. 23b. R. Nahman says *tefillin* keep away demons]. 2. b. Ber. 54b. Rav Judah —guard sick, bridegroom and bride from demons. 3. b. Ber. 58a. Curse of R. Sheshet.	1. b. Ber. 6a. Rava—how to detect demons. 2. b. Ber. 19a. Derogatory remarks about Mar Samuel produced death. 3. b. Ber. 20a. Abaye *re* Rav Judah's ability to make rain. 4. b. Ber. 56a. Abaye's and Rava's dreams, interpreted by Bar Hedya, are realized. 5. b. Ber. 60b. Abaye's privy incantation against demons. 6. b. Ber. 62a. Rava's wife protected him in privy against demons.

* Not counted. General principle.

II. *b. Shabbat*

Ca. 220-265	Ca. 265-310	Ca. 310-350
*[1. b. Shab. 11a. Rav— fasting is potent against dreams.]	1. b. Shab. 81b-82a. R. Hisda and Rabbah b. R. Huna overcome pagan's charms and free boat.	1. b. Shab. 66b. Abaye's mother on correct incantations (2 sayings).

* Not counted. General principle.

II. *b. Shabbat*

Ca. 220-265	Ca. 265-310	Ca. 310-350
*[2. b. Shab. 32a. Rav and Samuel feared power of Satan over bridge.] 3. b. Shab. 108a. Rav cursed Qarna. 4. b. Shab. 153a. Rav warns he will attend his own funeral. 5. b. Shab. 156b. Samuel predicts miracle.	2. b. Shab. 152b. Rav Judah receives visit from deceased in dream.	2. b. Shab. 66b. Abaye's mother on incantantion over ant to cure fever. *[3. b. Shab. 110a. Abaye said, Snake of the rabbis gives incurable bite.] 4. b. Shab. 134b. Rava fell ill for giving wrong ruling. 5. b. Shab. 156b. R. Naḥman b. Isaac fulfills astrologers' prediction.

*Not counted. General principle.

III. *b. ʿEruvin*

Ca. 220-265	Ca. 265-310	Ca. 310-350
	1. b. ʿEruv. 43a. Did not Elijah teach in R. Hisda's school at Sura and Rabbah's at Pumbedita on same Sabbath?	

IV. *b. Pesaḥim*

Ca. 220-265	Ca. 265-310	Ca. 310-350
		1. b. Pes. 110a. Abaye, Rava, and others avoided drinking wine in two-cup sequences, to avoid demons. 2. b. Pes. 110a. R. Joseph talked with demon. 3. b. Pes. 111b. Abaye saw demon. 4. b. Pes. 112b. Abaye saw demon.

V. *b. Yoma, Sukkah, Bezah*

Ca. 220-265	Ca. 265-310	Ca. 310-350
		1. b. Yoma 22b. R. Naḥman b. Isaac saw vision of Saul in dream. 2. b. Yoma 84a. Abaye gives formula for amulet to cure dog-bite.

VI. *b. Rosh HaShanah, Ta'anit*

Ca. 220-265	Ca. 265-310	Ca. 310-350
1. b. Ta'anit 20b. R. Adda b. Ahava holds up wall through merit. 2. b. Ta'anit 20b. R. Adda b. Ahava holds up house through his study of Torah. 3. b. Ta'anit 21b. People thought Rav's merit stopped plague.	1. b. Ta'anit 21b. People thought R. Huna's merit stopped fire. 2. b. Ta'anit 24a. R. Naḥman ordained fast, and it finally rained. 3. b. Ta'anit 24b. Rav Judah casts evil eye.	1. b. R.H. 17a. R. Huna b. R. Joshua had vision during illness. 2. b. R.H. 18a [= b. Yev. 105a]. Abaye and Rava averted curse by study of Torah and good deeds. 3. b. Ta'anit 21b. Abaye, Rava regularly received greetings from the heavenly academy. 4. b. Ta'anit 24b. Rabbah *re* Rav Judah rain-making. 5. b. Ta'anit 24b. R. Mari saw angels. 6. b. Ta'anit 24b. Rava makes rain after dream reveals time is propitious.

VII. *b. Megillah, Mo'ed Qatan, Ḥagigah*

Ca. 220-265	Ca. 265-310	Ca. 310-350
1. b. Meg. 5b. Rav cursed flax. 2. b. Meg. 27b. Rav blessed R. Huna.	1. b. Meg. 29a. R. Sheshet argued with Shekhinah. 2. b. M.Q. 27b. R. Huna cursed woman for excessive mourning, and all her sons died.	1. b. Meg. 7b. Rabbah cut R. Zera's throat and resurrected him. 2. b. M.Q. 17a-b. R. Joseph advises how to put bully to death through magic. 3. b. M.Q. 25b. When Rabbah and R. Joseph died, Euphrates rocks kissed.

VII. *b. Megillah, Mo'ed Qatan, Ḥagigah.*

Ca. 220-265	Ca. 265-310	Ca. 310-350
		4. b. M.Q. 25b. When Abaye and Rava died, Tigris rocks kissed. 5. b. M.Q. 28a. Rava saw his brother in dream after death. 6. b. M.Q. 28a. Rava communicated with R. Naḥman after latter's death. 7. b. Hag. 4b-5a, R. Bibi b. Abaye visited by angel of death.

VIII. *b. Yevamot*

Ca. 220-265	Ca. 265-310	Ca. 310-350
		1. b. Yev. 106a. Abaye killed man's parents by evil eye.

IX. *b. Ketuvot*

Ca. 220-265	Ca. 265-310	Ca. 310-350
1. b. Ket. 67b. Mar 'Uqba's wife immune to fire because of charity.	1. b. Ket. 106a. R. 'Anan received regular visits from Elijah.	1. b. Ket. 61a. Elijah conversed with son of R. Ḥisda. 2. b. Ket. 62b. Roof collapsed on student of Rava.

X. *b. Nedarim, Naẓir, Sotah*

Ca. 220-265	Ca. 265-310	Ca. 310-350
1. b. Ned. 50b. Woman burst for insulting Samuel.		1. b. Sot. 31a. Rava's students dream of Scriptures.

XI. *b. Gittin*

Ca. 220-265	Ca. 265-310	Ca. 310-350
	1. b. Git. 45a. Birds communicated with R. 'Ilish. 2. b. Git. 45a. Daughters of R. Naḥman were sorceresses.	

XII. *b. Qiddushin*

Ca. 220-265	Ca. 265-310	Ca. 310-350
		1. b. Qid. 29b. Abaye has R. Aḥa b. Jacob miraculously slay demon.

XIII. *b. Bava' Qamma'*

Ca. 220-265	Ca. 265-310	Ca. 310-350

XIV. *b. Bava' Meẓi'a'*

Ca. 220-265	Ca. 265-310	Ca. 310-350
		1. b. B.M. 85a. R. Joseph received message in dream. 2. b. B.M. 86a. Rabbah called up to heaven to settle dispute. 3. b. B.M. 86a. Abaye received letter from heaven. 4. b. B.M. 108a. Rabbah b. R. Huna cursed Rabbah b. R. Naḥman's children, who died.

XV. *b. Bava' Batra'*

Ca. 220-265	Ca. 265-310	Ca. 310-350
	*[1. b. B.B. 8a. Rav Judah said rabbis do not require protection of walls.] 2. b. B.B. 9b. R. Sheshet cursed colleague, who lost learning and power of speech.	1. b. B.B. 22a. R. Dimi cursed R. Adda b. Abba, who died. 2. b. B.B. 58a. Abaye helped magician free self from corpse. 3. b. B.B. 73a. Rabbah on incantation. 4. b. B.B. 153a. Woman cursed Rava, who suffered on that account.

* Not counted.   General rule.

XVI. *b. Sanhedrin*

Ca. 220-265	Ca. 265-310	Ca. 310-350
1. b. Sanh. 47b. People took dirt from Rav's grave for a medicine.		1. b. Sanh. 65b, 67b. Rava created a man and sent him to R. Zera. [2. b. Sanh. 106b. Rava on Rav Judah's skill at making rain.]

XVII. *b. 'Avodah Zarah*

Ca. 220-265	Ca. 265-310	Ca. 310-350
		1. b. A.Z. 65a. Bar Shishakh's eye burst for cursing Rava.

XVIII. *b. Horayot, Shevu'ot, Makkot*

Ca. 220-265	Ca. 265-310	Ca. 310-350

XIX. *b. Zevaḥim, Menaḥot, Ḥullin*

Ca. 220-265	Ca. 265-310	Ca. 310-350
		1. b. Men. 41a. Angel argued with R. Qattina about fringes. 2. b. Hul. 105b. Abaye said demons sit under drain pipe.

XX. *b. Bekhorot, ʿArakhin, Temurah*
 Keritot, Meʿilah, Tamid

Ca. 220-265	Ca. 265-310	Ca. 310-350
		1. b. Ker. 3b. Abaye on casting a spell over wasps or scorpions.

XXI. *b. Niddah*

Ca. 220-265	Ca. 265-310	Ca. 310-350
1. b. Nid. 37a. Miracle at grave of Rav and Shila.		

XXII. *Summary*

	Ca. 220-265	Ca. 265-310	Ca. 310-350	Totals by Category

Heavenly Visitations (Dreams, Angels, Elijah)		Rav Judah - 1
		R. Sheshet - 1
		R. ʿAnan - 1
		R. ʾIlish - 1
		      —
		      4
			Abaye - 3
			R. Joseph - 2
			R. Naḥman b. Isaac - 2
			R. Huna b. R. Joshua - 1
			Rava - 5
			   —
			  13 17
				22.3%

XXII. *Summary* (continued)

	Ca. 220-265	Ca. 265-310	Ca. 310-350	Totals by Category
Demons -encounters with -magic against	Samuel - 1 Rav - 1 — 2	Rav Judah - 1 Elijah at Sura, etc. - 1 — 2	Rava - 3 Abaye - 5 R. Joseph - 1 R. Mari - 1 — 10	14 18.4%
Rain-making		R. Naḥman - 1 Rav Judah - 1 — 2	[Abaye, Rabbah Rava with reference to Rav Judah]	2 2.6%
Witchcraft, sorcery, magic (except against demons)		R. Ḥisda - 1 Rabbah b. R. Huna - 1 Daughters of R. Naḥman - 1 — 3	Abaye - 3 Rabbah - 2 R. Joseph - 1 Rava - 1 — 7	10 13.1%
Curses and the Evil Eye (Rabbinical)	R. Shila - 1 Rav - 2 Samuel - 1 — 4	R. Sheshet - 1 Rav Judah - 1 R. Huna - 1 — 3	Mar Samuel - 1 Rava - 3 Abaye - 2 Rabbah b. R. Huna - 1 R. Dimi in Babylonia - 1 — 8	15 19.7%
Other Supernatural Stories told about Rabbis	Samuel - 1 Adda b. Ahava - 2 Rav - 4 Mar Uqba - 1 Shila - 1 — 9	R. Huna - 1 — 1	Rabbah - 2 R. Joseph - 1 Abaye - 2 Rava - 3 — 8	18 23.6%
Totals	15	15	46	76 99.7%
Percentages	19.7%	19.7%	60.5%	

We clearly see a fairly random distribution of supernatural stories and sayings of various kinds. Given the content of Tractates *Berakhot*, *Ta'anit*, and the funerary passages of *Mo'ed Qatan*, one can hardly be surprised to find a greater number of magical passages there than elsewhere. While tractates which contained numerous cases of law-enforcement apparently included a disproportionately small number of miracle stories, e.g. '*Eruvin*, *Yevamot*, *Qiddushin*, and *Bava' Qamma*', it is difficult to regard that fact as significant, since other tractates containing mainly theoretical laws, such as *Horayot*, *Makkot*, *Bekhorot*, '*Arakhin*, and *Temurah*, likewise contain few, if any, such passages. What is more interesting is the obvious increase in the number of supernatural stories and sayings told about, or attributed to, fourth-century rabbis. No single category showed much variation, with the exception of rain-making, so we have an approximately even division. We find by contrast that about three times more stories and sayings pertained to the fourth-century masters than to either preceding group, and twice the two earlier groups put together. In the individual categories, the proportions are equally interesting:

	220-265:310-350	265-310:310-350
Heavenly visitations	—	1:3
Demons	1:5	1:5
Witchcraft	—	1:2
Curses	1:2	1:2
Miscellany	1:1	1:8

Viewed by categories and *in toto*, the corpus of stories quite clearly shows a predominance of fourth-century figures. If, however, we analyze the 310-350 attributions, we find the following:

Rabbah - 4	R. Naḥman b. Isaac - 2	Abaye - 15
R. Joseph - 5	Scattered - 5	Rava - 15

So the preponderance of fourth-century exempla merely shows that more supernatural stories were told about Abaye and Rava, and more magical sayings were attributed to them, than any other Babylonian masters. If we eliminate their exempla, we find that the three periods are represented in approximately equal measure, 15, 15, and 16. We cannot conclude from this evidence that there now was an increase in public or academic credulity, all the more so an increase in actual supernatural events and sayings. However there is so much evidence for a general increase of credulity and particularly an increase of magic in the Roman Empire during the fourth century, that to suppose a similar change in Mesopotamia at that time is not unlikely. Why did Abaye and Rava become the foci of more such stories and sayings? I do not know. Their disciples obviously preserved more fabulous stories than did the disciples of earlier or contemporary masters. Whether or not they did so because Abaye and Rava were more interested in occult matters, and therefore claimed to have done more miracles than others, I cannot say.

To conclude: The rabbis conceived, first, that on earth they studied Torah just as in heaven God, the angels, and Moses "our rabbi" did. The heavenly schoolmen were even aware of Babylonian scholastic discussions, requiring Rabbah's information about an aspect of purity-taboos, acknowledging Abaye's Torah as a prophylactic against demons.

This conception, second, must be interpreted by reference to the belief that the man truly in the divine image was the rabbi, who embodied revelation, both oral and written, and all of whose actions constituted paradigms of not merely correct, but heavenly norms. Rabbis could create and destroy men because they were righteous, free of sin, or otherwise holy, and so enjoyed exceptional grace from heaven.

Third, it follows that Torah was held to be a source of supernatural power. The rabbis enjoyed protection without knowing it; they indeed controlled the power of Torah because of their mastery of its contents. They furthermore used their own mastery of Torah quite independent of heavenly action. They could issue blessings and curses, create men and animals. They were masters of witchcraft, incantations, and amulets. They could communicate with heaven. Their Torah was sufficiently effective to thwart the action of demons. However they disapproved of magic they were expected to do the things magicians do.

A fourth central conception was that all Jews were expected to become rabbis. This belief set rabbinic Judaism apart from Manichaeism, Mazdaism, Oriental Christianity and other contemporary cults, for no one expected that everyone would assume the obligations or attain to the supernatural skills of Manichaean Elect, Mazdean Magi, Christian nuns and monks, or the religious virtuosi and cultic specialists of other groups. The rabbis by contrast wanted to transform the entire Jewish community into an academy where the whole Torah was studied and kept.[1]

These four beliefs enable us to understand the rabbis' view that Israel would be redeemed through Torah. Because Israel had sinned, she was punished by being given over into the hands of earthly empires. When she atones, she will be removed from their power. The means of atonement or reconciliation were study of Torah, practice of commandments, and doing good deeds.[2] These would transform each Jew into a rabbi, hence a saint. When all the Jews had become rabbis, they then would no longer lie within the power of history. The Messiah would come. So redemption depended upon the "rabbinization" of all Israel, that is to say, upon the attainment by all Jewry of a full and complete embodiment of revelation or Torah. The reason was that precisely when Jewry did so, it would achieve a perfect replication of heaven. When Israel on earth became, or attained to, such a replica of heaven, as a righteous, holy, saintly community, it would, like some rabbis even now, be able to exercise the supernatural power of Torah. With access to the consequent theurgical capacities, redemption would naturally follow.

---

[1] See vol. III, pp. 192-194.
[2] See vol. II, pp. 52-64, 180-188, 236-240, and 282-288, and vol. III, pp. 87-94.

APPENDIX ONE

ŠKAND GUMANIK VIČAR CHAPTERS XIII AND XIV
TRANSLATION AND EXPOSITION

I. INTRODUCTION

Geo Widengren notes that the chapters of the Škand Gumanik Vičar relevant to Judaism, though written in post-Sasanian times, may well contain elements of the earlier Mazdean polemic against Judaism. He states, "We know that in general post-Sasanian Pahlavi works are based on Sasanian or even older material. For this reason it is quite possible that there existed in Sasanian times a Pahlavi polemical literature directed against the religious minorities, accordingly also against the Jews." (See *IA* 1, 1961, p. 160). P.-J. de Menasce, whose text and translation I have closely followed in preparing the following, also holds that such a polemical literature antedated Moslem times. Widengren adds, "It is conceivable that when religious matters were brought into court the proceedings when Jews were prosecuted because of their religion had to be accompanied by polemical attacks on Judaism, as was the case with Christians in corresponding situations. The polemical passages may thus echo the arguments used by the Mobads as prosecutors." In light of the views of Widengren and de Menasce, I think it useful to present here the most important post-Sasanian Mazdean text dealing with Judaism.

Martan Farrux, son of Ohrmazddat, who traveled the world to investigate the varieties of religion, provided for the young Zoroastrian of the ninth century a critique of the competing faiths of the day, and a defense of his own.[1]

---

[1] The Pazend text was published by Hoshang Dastur Jamasphi Jamasp-Arana and E. W. West, *Shikand Gumanik Vijar, The Pazand-Sanskrit Text together with a Fragment of the Pahlavi* (Bombay, 1887). A transcription and translation were provided by P.-J. de Menasce, *Une Apologétique Mazdéenne du IXe Siècle: Škand Gumanik Vičar, La Solution Décisive des Doutes* (Fribourg in Switzerland, 1945). West's translation appeared in *Sacred Books of the East*, American edition, Vol. XII (New York, 1901), pp. 115-252. One other translation of chapters XIII and XIV appeared, by James Darmesteter, "Textes Pehlvis Rélatifs au Judaisme," *REJ* XVIII (1889), pp. 1-15, and XIX (1890), pp. 41-56. Further discussion is in Lewis H. Gray, "The Jews in Pahlavi Literature," *Actes du XIV Congrès International des Orientalistes* (Paris, 1906), pp. 161-192, reprinted in *JE* s.v. Further literature includes the following: J. C. Tavadia, *Die Mittelpersische Sprache und Literatur der Zarathustrier* (Leipzig, 1956), pp. 92-7; Otakar Klíma, "Das Mittelpersische Schrifttum," in J. Rypka, ed., *Iranische Literaturgeschichte* (Leipzig, 1959), pp. 41-2; E. W. West, "Pahlavi Literature," in W. Geiger and E. Kuhn, ed., *Grundriss der Iranischen Philologie* (Strasburg, 1896), II, pp. 106-7.

Here are presented a translation[1] of the chapters relevant to Judaism and an exposition of the arguments in them.[2]

It is difficult to ascertain whether a Pahlavi translation of the Hebrew Scriptures existed from which the citations in the following text were drawn.[3] The importance of this question transcends the problem of the use of Hebrew Scriptures by Martan Farrux son of Ohrmazddat. Professors Frank Cross and William Brownlee both speculate on whether Babylonian Jews possessed textual traditions different from those of Palestine. We know that Alexandrian Jewry did, for we have their translation of Scripture, indicating numerous textual traditions different from those in Palestine. Brownlee states:

> ...the ancestry of the Massoretic edition of Samuel must derive from some other quarter [than Egypt or Palestine], most probably from Babylonia. This is a reasonable suggestion, for in Babylonia there was a large Jewish population which was sufficiently remote as to have its own special editions of Biblical books.[4]

---

[1] I am greatly indebted to Professor Richard N. Frye of Harvard University for detailed discussion of the text, assistance with numerous difficult passages, references to Sanskrit, and many suggestions for more accurate translation. The text and translation of de Menasce were very closely followed, and his notes utilized with profit. The translations of West and Darmesteter proved useful. I have reconsidered each problem, and with Professor Frye's help, have offered new translations for many lines, always aiming at greater literalness.

[2] Davidson holds that there is little doubt that Ḥiwi al-Balḥi knew the critique of Martan Farrux, and utilized some of the arguments in these chapters. See Israel Davidson, *Saadia's Polemic against Ḥiwi al-Balḥi* (New York, 1915), pp. 17-18, 29-31, 80-82. Davidson says, "We find not only a similarity of tone, but an actual identity of topics in at least three instances." The three parallels cited by Davidson are to XIII, 122, 132-4; 135-7; XIV, 32-3. One may add the following: XIII, 102-3, parallel to Ḥiwi, line 21 (Davidson, p. 49); XIV, 52 parallel to Ḥiwi, line 52-3, and 55; and XIV, 36-8, 75-9, parallel to Ḥiwi, line 71-2. It should be pointed out, however, that these criticisms of Judaism and its Scriptures were by no means original with Martan Farrux, but are frequently prefigured in *midrashic* literature and elsewhere, and answered there. Professor Moshe Zucker of the Jewish Theological Seminary of America points out, moreover, that Ḥiwi's source of rationalistic-skeptical criticism could have been other than the Škand. See also DeMenasce, *op. cit.*, pp. 179-181.

[3] On Martan Farrux's biblical knowledge and quotations, see Gray, *op. cit.*, pp. 183-4, and de Menasce, *op. cit.*, pp. 176-8. It should be noted that some divergences from the Hebrew text may be explained by reference to the author's polemical purposes. One cannot conclude that the author has reference to a Pahlavi translation of Hebrew Scriptures. The difficulty in identifying his citations with specific verses renders that possibility remote. On the other hand, many instances of awkward, or simply bad, Persian suggest than an Aramaic or Syriac version is being literally translated. For a specific example, see XIV, 19-20. This is a problem for further study.

[4] Frank Cross, Jr., "New Light on Early Recensions of the Hebrew Bible," *BASOR* 140, Dec. 1955, pp. 27-33, and W. H. Brownlee, *The Meaning of the Qumran Scrolls for the Bible* (N.Y., 1964), p. 18, p. 29.

Likewise Cross says:

> It is not impossible that the ancestral proto-Masoretic tradition [of Samuel]
> developed independently in Babylonia (after return of the exiles), and was
> reintroduced into Palestine in the Hellenistic period or later.[1]

One may reasonably infer that if Babylonian Jewry possessed academies,
and if it was necessary for these academies to produce translations or ren-
ditions of Scripture into languages spoken by Jews in the Iranian Empire,
then, as in Alexandria, specific textual traditions *may* have been preserved
likewise by such Babylonian Jewish academies.

We may be quite certain that such academies did flourish by the first
century A.D. and afterward, for we know that Hillel and Nahum the Mede,
both of Babylonian origin, came to Palestine with substantial knowledge of
traditional sciences. We also know that in Babylonian academies, specific
textual interpretations (*midrashim*) were handed down, as the *midrashic* tradition on Deut. 15.10 suggests. On that verse, the same interpretations
were preserved at the academy at Huẓal, in the 2nd century, handed down
by the disciples of R. Ishmael, who had settled there about 135 A.D., to
R. Aḥa and R. Ḥiyya of the next generation (ca. 180 A.D.), to R. Naḥman
a century later.[2] We know likewise that the Babylonian teacher, Rav,
taught to his uncle R. Ḥiyya "the laws of the Babylonians." R. Nathan
possessed a collection of *mishnayot* from Babylonia. R. Ḥiyya gave an
interpretation of the expression *wayehi* [ויהי] which, he said, had been
handed down from the Exilic period. A Babylonian exegete, R. Ḥanina b.
Ḥama, corrected a scriptural reading by R. Judah the Prince of Ezek. 7.16,
a correction based upon the tradition of R. Hamnuna the Scribe of Babylonia.[3] All of this points to the probability of Babylonian Jewish traditions
of exegesis and possibly of text, different from those of the Palestinians.
Furthermore, the following tradition may refer to translations or transcriptions of Scripture into Egyptian (Coptic), Median, and Elamite, among
other languages or scripts:

> If written in Coptic, Median, 'YBRYT [Hebrew?], Elamite, or Greek,
> even though one may not read in them, they should be saved from burning.
>
> (b. Shab. 115a)

This *beraita* refers to a period much later than that with which Professors
Brownlee and Cross are concerned. It does not *prove* the existence of
translations of Scripture into Iranian languages in the absence of other
evidence. It may well suggest, however, that Palestinian Tannaim *thought*
that there were such translations, if KTWBYN means "translated." If not,
transcriptions into such alphabets were believed to exist.

We know that Babylonian Jewry had academies which preserved independent legal and exegetical material. That fact conforms to the hypothesis
of Brownlee and Cross. By analogy to the situation of Alexandrian Jewry,

---

[1] Frank Cross, Jr., *Ancient Library of Qumran* (N.Y., 1961), pp. 191-2.

[2] Compare Lamentations Rabbati I, 10-11, 39; Shemot Rabbah 31.14; b. Shab.
151b; Vayiqra Rabbah 34.9.

[3] Further discussion will be found in Vol. I, pp. 148-63.

their hypothesis is plausible. It is surely congruent to other facts available about Babylonian Jewry. If so, such textual traditions could well have reached Palestine at the time Brownlee and Cross say they did, for political and economic relationships were substantial.[1] I must stress, however, that the hypothesis of an early Jewish-Babylonian textual tradition must be proved on its own merits, and derives only slight support from the analogy offered here.

ii. Translation

XIII

1. Again, regarding the contradictory and harmful[2] statements of the First Book [Genesis],[3]
2. which is called by them AWAT [the Fathers],[4]
3. and about which all of them are of one mind, that God wrote it by his own hand and gave it to Moses.
4. Since it is full of error, I shall here reveal for your information some of its foolishness and many secrets.
5. It is said at the beginning of the Scripture:

---

[1] On political and commercial relations, *ibid.* pp. 23-30, 58-67, 68-97.

[2] *zewa-gawešni*: zewa, Pahl. *ziyan* = harmful, hence, harmful sayings.

[3] *naxustin niwe* = first scripture, first writing, meaning not Old Testament but Genesis, as all discussion in chapter XIII is on Genesis.

[4] AWAT: de Menasce reads, AZAT, free or noble. Professor Saul Lieberman of the Jewish Theological Seminary of America has kindly offered the following:

Since the word AWAT, according to the context, must refer to the Book of Genesis only, and to a Hebrew or an Aramaic name ("called by them"), perhaps the Jews of Babylonia called the Book of Genesis 'BHT' [אבהתא], Hebrew H'BWT [האבות] on the basis of Babylonian Talmud 'Avodah Zarah 25a.

The passage to which Professor Lieberman refers is as follows:

What is the "Book of Yashar"? R. Ḥiyya b. Abba said in the name of R. Yoḥanan, "It is the book of Abraham, Isaac, and Jacob, who were called 'the upright,' as it is said, 'Let me die the death of the upright' (Num. 23.10)."

Rashi (*ad loc.*): The Book of Abraham means the Book of Genesis, for the acts of the fathers are written in it.

Thus the Jews would have called Genesis "the Fathers." Compare "fathers" as AWBAT, in the Pahlavi translation of Psalm 95.10, "Pat han AWBAT," meaning "generation," F. C. Andreas and Kaj Barr, *Bruchstücke einer Pehlevi-Übersetzung der Psalmen* (Berlin 1933), *Sitz. Preuss. Ak. Phil.-Hist. Kl.*, 1933, I p. 9. See also H. F. J. Junker, *Das Frahang-i Pahlavik* (Leipzig 1955), p. 15, where the heterogram for pit, pitar, is 'B and 'BYTR, respectively.

If so, however, I am unable to offer other examples of the same kind of correspondence. It is, moreover, conceivable that if a Semitic, and not an Iranian, word is involved, other etymologies are possible. Nor can I explain how 'BHT' yields AWAT. Hence the etymological and linguistic basis for this suggestion requires investigation by those competent to do so.

6. At the beginning were earth, which was dark water; and unformed substance,[1] darkness, and dark water,[2]

7. and the spirit of God (Yazat) was passing over the body of water, which was that black water.[3]

8. Then God said, "Let there be light,"[4]

9. and there was light.

10. And the light seemed very good to him.[5]

11. And by him was the light placed for the day, and darkness for the night.[6]

12. And in six days he created this world, and the heaven and the earth.

13. For on the seventh day he was sleeping and at ease.[7]

14. On account of this mystery, nowadays the Jews are at ease on the day of Šumbat.[8]

15. This also: Adam and his woman Hava he created,[9]

16. and he placed [lit. made] them in the garden of Vahešt

17. so that Adam might do work in this garden and guard it.[10]

18. Adonu, which is this self-same God, commanded to Adam:

19. "Eat from all the trees which are in this garden, excepting that tree of knowledge,

20. for when you eat from that, you die."[11]

21. Then he placed a snake in the garden.

22. That snake spoke deviously to Hava: "From this tree will I eat the fruit, and give to Adam."

23. And she did likewise.

24. Adam also ate.

25. And his knowledge was such that by him good was distinguished from evil, and he did not die.[12]

26. And he saw and knew that he was naked.

27. And he was hidden under a tree.

---

[1] *tan* = unformed substance. I believe the word is not, contrary to de Menasce to be compared to NP tān, but is the good Pahlavi word *tan*. See H. S. Nyberg, *Hilfsbuch des Pehlevi* (Uppsala 1928), s.v. tan, Glossary, 222, "Tan als kosmologischer Terminus bezeichnet die der Formung (Gestaltung) unterworfene Substanz, auf der die irdische Schöpfung beruht..." See also lines 49, 64. The Pazand vocalization a can stand for 'a' as well as 'ā,' Professor Frye points out.

[2] Gen. 1:1-2. Frye notes that dark-water (blood), in the phrase "earth, which was dark-water" corresponds to ὕλη = raw matter. The Platonic distinction between matter and form implies that both were, before creation, unorganized.

[3] Gen. 1:2.

[4] Gen. 1:3.

[5] Gen. 1:4.

[6] Gen. 1:4-5.

[7] Gen. 2:1-2.

[8] Ex. 20:11.

[9] Gen. 2:8.

[10] Gen. 2:15.

[11] Gen. 2:15-17.

[12] Gen. 3:1-6.

28. And he put the leaves of the tree on his body, on account of shame of his nakedness.[1]

29. Then Adonu went out to the garden, and called Adam by name, saying: "Where are you?"

30. Adam gave an answer: "Here I am under the tree, for I am naked."[2]

31. Adonu became angry

32. and said: "Who told you that you are naked?"

33. "Have you not eaten from the tree of knowledge, concerning which I said: 'Do not eat from it?'"

34. Adam said: "By this woman whom you gave to me I was fooled, and I ate."

35. And Adonu asked Hava: "Why did you do this?"

36. Hava said: "This snake fooled me."[3]

37. And Adam and Hava and the snake, all three, under curses he expelled from the garden of Vahešt.[4]

38. Then he said to Adam: "Your eating will be by the outpouring of your sweat and the heaving of your nostrils

39. until the end of your life.

40. And for you the earth will produce manure and thorns."[5]

41. Then he spoke to Hava: "Your pregnancy will be in pain and suffering and your giving birth in great oppression."[6]

42. And to the snake he spoke: "From among the four-legged beasts, and the creatures of the steppe and mountains, you will be cursed,

43. and you will not have feet.

44. Your movement will be on your belly, and your food will be dirt.

45. And between your descendants and those of woman there will be such hatred and enmity that their children will harm [your] head."[7]

46. Thus they say, that he made and created this world and all that is in this world for mankind,

47. and that he made man head over all creatures and creation and over sea and land.

48. Now let us say something about their stories, what is in them of foolishness and erroneous opinions,

49. namely: Earth, which is dark water, and unformed matter, and darkness, and God and his spirit, and the black water—where and how were they defined?

50. And God himself—what was his essence?[8]

---

[1] Gen. 3:7.

[2] Gen. 3:8-10.

[3] Gen. 3:11-13.

[4] Gen. 3:23.

[5] Gen. 3:17-19. *Hustarasni*: de Menasce translates from *ostartan*, from the ideogram KPR, hence, rejection, here 'outpouring.' The parallel, *damašni*, is not breathlessness (West), so much as 'heaving,' labored breathing, parallel to outpouring.

[6] Gen. 3:16a.

[7] Gen. 3:14-15.

[8] *ainaa* = mirror, essence.

51. Certainly he was not light,

52. for when he saw the light,

53. it was because he had not [previously] seen it that it seemed good [to him].

54. If they say that he was darkness, the reason is that darkness is the basis of the emanation of light.[1]

55. If they say that he was not dark, but light,

56. then if he himself were light, why when he saw the light did it appear surprising [to him]?

57. And if they say he was neither light nor dark,

58. then they have to demonstrate a third [state of being] which is neither light nor dark.

59. Essentially, he whose place and dwelling is in darkness and black water, and who had never seen the light, how was he able to see light?

60. And from what [source] was his divinity?

61. For now whatever [being] lives in darkness cannot see light.

62. Furthermore, if his foundation and dwelling were darkness, then how could he face up to light?

63. For one knows this, that darkness cannot face up to light, for it [light] drives away and overwhelms it [darkness].

64. Furthermore, were earth, which is dark water, and unformed matter, limited or unlimited?

65. If they were limited, then what was outside of them?

66. If they were unlimited, then his infinity—where did it reach?

67. And how is it that this land and world which we are seeing are not as they were at the beginning?

68. Concerning Adonu's saying:

69. "Let there be light!" and it was,

70. Hence it is appropriate to know that Adonu existed before light.

71. Then wanting to make the light, he ordered that it come into being; then in thought, he wondered, this light, of what essence might it be, good or evil seed?

72. And if the light by its own nature came into the knowledge and thought of Adonu, then it is clear that light always existed in the knowledge and contemplation of Adonu

73. and outside of it also,

74. for one cannot know or hear except about that whose existence is [already] manifest.

75. But if the light always existed, then it could not have been the creation of Adonu.

76. And if they say [to the contrary] that light did not exist in and of itself in the knowledge [of Adonu], then he besought it without knowing it, for he was wholly ignorant of its essence.

77. And how is it possible ever to consider in thought something about which one has never thought or known?

---

[1] *bun* = root, foundation; *vaz-afra* = give forth, cause to emanate.

78. And further, that command that there should be light, did he give it to something, or to nothing?

79. For this is certain, that a command must be given to someone who is commanded.

80. If he gave it to an existing light, that light itself already existed;

81. and if he gave the commandment to nothingness, how does nothingness hear the command of Adonu?

82. And how did he know that Adonu thus wanted, that I should become light?

83. For nothingness does not even hear the command of Adonu, since it has not been created.

84. For that which has no essence cannot be thought.

85. That which is nothing produces nothing, but that which is, is known, having previously been perceived by the knower. Thus [the knowledge that] Adonu wants me to be such-and-so [implies the existence of a knower]. Then will he not be the essence which he [Adonu] wants [him to be]?

86. If they say that the light was from the word of Adonu, then he said: "Be," and it was,

87. while Adonu and his essence were darkness. Hence he had never seen light, and in what manner was it possible that that light should come from his word?

88. And this is known, that the word which comes into being is in his [God's] mind.

89. If they say that the word was the light [itself], this is very surprising, for it would signify that the light [will then be] fruit of the darkness, and darkness of the family of light; or [alternately] this, that the light was hidden in the darkness.

90. Wherefore I said that the command can only be given to one who is commanded,

91. and this is necessary, that light existed before the commandment could [possibly] have been given!

92. Furthermore, this: He has arranged and created this creation, and the world and heavens and earth in six days;

93. the seventh he rested from it.

94. Then if he created this world not from something, but uniquely from his command, which was, namely: "Be," and it was—

95. then this length of six days, where does it come from?

96. For if his only labor was so much as to say: "Be,"—then was the six-day measure [of creation] a very difficult thought [for him, that it should have exhausted him]?

97. So much toil could not have come to him from it!

98. If one can make something from nothing, and if it is possible to create a world which lasts,

99. and if he could not create in a day's time [i.e. rather than in six], one cannot say that *he* could create something out of nothing!

100. And furthermore, this: If the order of the days is known from the sun, then before the creation of the sun, how did he know the number of the days, and their names?

101. For they say that the sun was created on the fourth day, that is, the fourth of the Sabbath [week].

102. Further, this: On the seventh day, why did he have to rest and take his leisure?

103. For in creating and making the world, the toil and pain were only so much as this, namely, saying: "Be."

104. And how did he count the days that he had to rest and take his leisure when he had finished the toil?

105. For if he said: "Be," instantaneously, then the toil and rest should also have taken place instantaneously!

106. Furthermore, this: Adam and Hava, for what purpose and end did he create them?

107. If it was to do his will, then why did he not so make them that they would not turn from keeping his will?

108. For if before making them, he knew that they would not be obedient to [his] command, and nonetheless he made them, then it was unreasonable for him nonetheless to be angry and furious with them.

109. Thus it is clear that Adonu himself was not fully consistent to his own will, and he was obviously his own adversary and antagonist!

110. If he did not think before making them, and did not know that they would not obey his word, then he is ignorant and bad-thinking.

111. If they say that his will itself was that they *not* do [it], then why did he give the order that they *do* it?

112. Then why was not doing it a sin? And how does a horse move

113. who is harnessed to a chariot and then hurried with a whip?

114. From this kind of talk are revealed the signs and insignia of deceivers

115. among whom will and command are contradictory and incompatible to one another.

116. And if his will and requirement were that [they] should not turn aside from his will,

117. then nonetheless *their* power and desire not to do his will were more powerful and predominating over *his* that they not turn aside.

118. And if the will that they not turn away and knowledge of the result of it were his, and [nonetheless] he gave them the commandment not to turn away, then the wretched Adam, how could he *not* transgress?

119. Then the original will could not actually have come into existence [at all].

120. For by turning away from his command, the command [prophecy] is made into a lie [i.e. Adam did not die], but [his] not turning away makes both will and omniscience into a lie.

121. Again this: This garden which he prepared, why and for what result did he create it?

122. And the self-same tree of knowledge, concerning which he commanded: Do not eat, and as to the advice not to eat from it, what need was there to make it?

123. This injunction and command make it obvious that little knowledge and ignorance are more desirable

124. and preferable [to him] than knowledge and understanding,

125. and that his advantage was greater from ignorance.

126. For while he [Adam] had not eaten from the tree of knowledge, he was ignorant, and applying to him were neither disobedience nor evil.

127. As soon as they [Adam and Eve] became knowledgeable, they became disobedient.

128. Of their ignorance he [God] was not afraid, but as soon as they became knowledgeable,

129. then he became petulant and choleric,

130. and he drove them from Vahešt with great ill-will and antipathy, and threw them out onto the earth.

131. Briefly this: Man's inherent knowledge in this world is on account of the evil of the deceitful snake.

132. They say this, that all things were created for man, thus it is clear that the tree was created for man,

133. and that he made man ruler over all creation and creatures [Gen. 1: 28].

134. If so, then why was his wish to injure [him] by this tree which was [actually] his?

135. From this saying it is clear that he [God] was not the source of knowledge,

136. for, if when he went back to the garden, and raised his voice, and called Adam by name, [saying]: "Where are you,"—it is as if he was unknowing of where he was!

137. And if there had been no answer, then he would have been ignorant of where Adam was.

138. And if he had not raised his voice before he saw him, he would have been unaware whether or not he had eaten from the tree, whether and what and how much he had eaten, and by whom they had been deceived!

139. If he had known, then why thus: "Why did you eat from the tree about which I commanded: 'Do not eat?'" Why did he have to ask?

140. And at first, when he went out, he was not petulant, but after he knew that he had eaten, he then became petulant and angry.

141. And his slight knowledge is seen from this, the snake which he himself created as an enemy and placed in the garden.

142. Why did he not make a wall for the garden, so that the snake and other enemies might not set foot in it?

143. And his lying is clear from his [God's] saying: "If you eat from this tree, you will die," but he [Adam] ate and did not die, but became knowledgeable,

144. and he knew the difference between good and evil.

145. And this shows how inconsistent and competing is his knowledge with his will and command:

146. If he [God] wanted him [Adam] to eat from the tree, then he gave the commandment not to eat from it, knowing [nonetheless] that he would eat.

147. Now it is clear that among all three—desire, knowledge, and command —there is a contradiction.

148. This: that when Adam sinned, the curse which he made applies unlawfully to all kinds of men age after age.

149. By whatever way in which I deliberate, they are senseless, ignorant, and stupid statements.

150. Concerning this theme, because of length, this seems sufficiently well-founded.

XIV

1. My desire is that I write some of the mysteries of the mutual contradictions and abundant fallaciousness of this same Scripture,

2. which is full of every kind of iniquity and devilishness, and I shall expose briefly one thousandth of it.

3. Therein one is commanded to examine it.

4. First this, which he says about his own essence

5. that: "I am Adonu seeking vengeance

6. and repaying vengeance,[1]

7. and I will repay vengeance seven fold upon the children,[2]

8. and by me original vengeance is not forgotten."[3]

9. And that also is said there, that he has acquired anger and harsh thought,

10. and his lips are full of poison,

11. and his tongue is like a burning fire,

12. and his breath is like a river of swift water,[4]

13. and his voice, like the voice of weeping, is even more like the voice of the demon,[5]

14. and he is enthroned among gloom, dew, and cloud,[6]

15. and his steed is the parching wind,[7]

16. and from the movement of his feet arises the dusty whirlwind[8] [Lit.: the earth is stirred into dust].

17. When he walks, behind him arises the fire.[9]

18. And this he said about his own wrathfulness:

---

[1] Compare Deut. 32:35 and the citation of the verse in Romans 12:19. On lines 5-7, see also Nahum 1:2.

[2] Exodus 20:5, compare Genesis 4:5. "Seven-fold" is the Sanskrit reading. De Menasce emends *OBADAA* to *APATAK*, descendents.

[3] Compare the Targum of Pseudo-Jonathan, "jealous God" becomes "jealous and avenging God, and avenging myself with jealousy." The phrase "by me original vengeance is not forgotten" recalls Ex. 34:7.

[4] Isaiah 30:27-8.

[5] Darmesteter says that the identification is doubtful, while de Menasce refers to Ps. 77:19 and 104:7, and West to Isaiah 30:30; but none of these verses is congruent. Professor Shalom Spiegel, however, notes that the reference is probably to II Sam. 5:24 = I Chr. 14:15. It [הבכאים] is associated with weeping, both in rabbinic and patristic tradition. He refers to Midrash Tehillim c. 27 (ed. Buber p. 223) and Pseudo-Jerome on II Sam. 5:24, and to L. Ginzberg, *Legends* VI, p. 255 n. 54. On the demon, Professor Spiegel refers to Ex. 23:22 f., and comp. Is. 42:13, Ruth 1:13, I Chr. 21:16. I am grateful to him for this comment.

[6] Deut. 4:11, 5:22, compare also Ps. 97:2.

[7] Ps. 104:3, but compare Nahum 1:3.

[8] Nahum 1:3.

[9] Is. 66:15, Ps. 50:3.

19. "Forty years I was angry with [that] generation,"
20. And he said: "The generation is defiled at heart."[1]
21. He says: "Who is blind if not my servant?
22. Who is deaf, if not the messenger whom I am sending?
23. Who is blind like the Lord?"[2]—and it is obvious that their "Lord" is Adonu himself![3]
24. Here also it is said that the messengers of his fire are defiled,[4]
25. and this: His deeds produce blinding smoke,[5]
26. and his combat is full of blood,[6]
27. and this: "I pour forth men one upon the other;[7]
28. I am sitting in heaven and laughing at you."[8]
29. This: That in one night, six hundred thousand of the seasoned army of Mazandarigan he slew with an unpleasant death,[9]
30. and another time, he slew six hundred thousand men, not counting women and suckling-children, out of the generation of the wilderness
31. except for two men who were true.[10]
32. Furthermore, he indicates that his final outcome is utter regret,
33. just as this which he stated: He became so despondent that he said, "I regret making man on the earth."[11]
34. Here it says that he is seated on a throne which four angels are carrying on their wings; from each one of whom, on account of the heavy burden, a river of fire flows out.[12]

---

[1] Ps. 95:10-11. '*Asarasaran*' would seem to signify 'generation' as in the Hebrew. It ought not in any case to be emended to read '*Asrayilan*,' *contra* West and de Menasce. This is supported by the Pahlavi translation of Psalms, which preserves the precise Hebrew, see F. C. Andreas and Kaj Barr, *Bruchstücke einer Pehlevi-Übersetzung der Psalmen* (Berlin, 1933), in *Sitz. Preuss. Ak.*, *Phil.-Hist.*, 1933, I p. 9. Ps. 95:10, *pat han AWBAT*, generation, see also Glossary, p. 29 s.v.

[2] Is. 42:19.

[3] Is. 33:22.

[4] Darmesteter refers to Job 4:18 and Ps. 104:4, but the meaning is certainly *not* that the messengers are defiled, but only that they err, as in Job 4:18, "and his angels he charges with error." West refers to Ez. 18:16-17, which is simply impossible. A closer approximation is in Isaiah 6:4-9, in which case this is an epitome, rather than an exact quotation.

[5] Ps. 18:8.

[6] Compare Ex. 15:1f.

[7] If the meaning of "pour forth" is "to stir up trouble" then see Is. 19:2.

[8] Ps. 2:4.

[9] Compare Is. 37:36. The army of Sennacherib, 185,000 men, was wiped out in one night. Darmesteter explains that "devs of Mazandaran" means merely "barbarians" or savages. The reference may be, however, to a tradition that Sennacherib was to have been Gog and Magog, see Louis Ginzberg, *Legends of the Jews* (Philadelphia, 1946), IV, p. 272.

[10] Ex. 12:37 and Num. 14:30-32.

[11] Gen. 6:6, compare XIII, 108f.

[12] Ezekiel chapter 1, Daniel 7:10. Compare Genesis Rabbah 78:1, "the perspiration of the *ḥayyot* was caused by their bearing God's throne." See below, p. 415 n. 1.

35. Now if he is spiritual and not material, then these four wretched and contemptible creatures, why does this grievous burden so trouble them?
36. Furthermore, this: Every day with his own hand he makes nine thousand angels, and they worship him until night-time, and then he lures them by a river of fire to hell.[1]
37. When one sees the violence and injustice which are [done] in this manner, how is it possible to exist in this world by duty, good works, and good deeds,
38. when the wretched angels who are respectful, obedient, and doers of good deeds are cast together with others, the doers of evil deeds, to eternal hell?

---

[1] Genesis Rabbah 77:1, Lamentations Rabbati on 3:23. In Genesis Rabbah 78.1, a "River of Fire" was described by R. Joshua b. Ḥananiah as issuing forth from the *ḥayyot* referred to in Ezekiel 1, caused by the exertion of bearing the divine throne. Still another relevant passage is as follows:

> And R. Jeremiah b. Abba said, "A thousand thousands served the river of fire, as it is said, 'A stream of fire issued and came forth from before him, a thousand thousands served it, and ten thousand times ten thousand stood before it [RSV: served him ... stood before him].' Whence are they? From the perspiration of the *ḥayyot*." And whither do they pour forth? R. Zutra son of R. Tobia said in the name of Rav, "Upon the head of the sinners in Gehenna, as it is said, 'Behold the storm of God! Wrath has gone forth, a whirling tempest. It will burst upon the head of the wicked' (Jeremiah 23.19)."
>
> (b. Ḥag. 13b)

With reference to Škand XIV 36, we take note also of the following passage:

> Samuel said to Ḥiyya son of Rav, "Your father said, 'Every single day ministering angels are created from the river of fire, and they proclaim a song, and are extinguished, as it is said, 'They are new every morning' (Lamentations 3.23).'"
>
> (b. Ḥag. 14a)

In Lamentations Rabbati on 3.23 the same passage is given in the name of R. Joshua b. Ḥananiah, and includes *both* the teaching about the fiery sweat of the angels *and* that about creating and destroying them. In that passage, R. Joshua b. Ḥananiah states, "Every day, the Holy One blessed be He creates a new band of angels who utter a new song and then pass away, and they go to the river of fire which originates from the sweat of the *ḥayyot* caused by their carrying the divine throne."

Interestingly, both passages are ascribed to the early third century Babylonian Amora, Rav, the former by his student R. Zutra b. R. Tobia, the latter by his colleague Samuel. How then did these traditions reach Rav in Babylonia? Since both apparently originated with R. Joshua b. Ḥananiah, to whom they are ascribed in the above passage, it seems reasonable to suppose that R. Joshua's nephew, R. Ḥananiah, brought them to Babylonia, as he did other mystical sayings of his uncle, when he settled there some time after 100 A.D. Rav would have learned these sayings from R. Ḥananiah's disciples. The traditions were separated, one being taught by Rav to R. Zutra, the other by Rav to Samuel. From the form in which they appear in Škand XIV 34 and 36, they would seem to have continued as separate sayings. In any case, it is clear that the *Merkavah* tradition, at least as represented in this fragment, was transmitted in Babylonia from the first century A.D. onward, and became known to non-Jews as well, perhaps in only partial form.

39. It is like that which another sect says, that God on the judgment day casts the sun and moon together with evildoers to hell, because there are men who were worshippers of them![1]

40. Further it is said that the aged Abraham, the friend of Adonu, was afflicted in the eyes, and Adonu himself came to visit him

41. and sat on a pillow and inquired after his health.

42. And Abraham secretly summoned his dearest son, Isaac, saying,

43. "Go out to Vahešt, and bring tasty and pure wine."

44. He went and brought it.

45. And Abraham made many entreaties to Adonu:

46. "In my house, drink wine and [eat] bread."

47. Adonu said: "I shall not eat, because it is neither from Vahešt, nor pure."

48. Then Abraham gave word: "Pure is that wine, from Vahešt, and Isaac, my son, brought it."

49. Then Adonu, convinced by Isaac, and because of Abraham's testimony, drank some wine.

50. Then, when he wanted to go, he would not let him until he took [lit. ate] a solemn oath, one to the other.[2]

51. See this singular silliness, full of foolishness, is not congruent to God.

52. Coming corporeally to the house of Abraham, and eating bread and drinking wine—none of these actions is congruent to him!

53. This is obvious, that the ailment of Abraham was not from Adonu, but from another creator.

54. He was so deluded of knowledge and insensitive that about the purity and origin of the wine he knew nothing.

55. His lying is seen in this, that he said he would not drink the wine, but in the end, drank it.

56. Then he admitted that the wine was pure.

57. Now one such as this, how would it be fitting to worship him as all-knowing and omnipotent divinity?

58. And there they speak of one who was among the sick, with his wife and children suffering greatly, poor and without resources.[3]

59. At all times he was efficient and active in prayer, fasting, and the services of God.

60. One day in prayer, he made one request: "Give me pleasure in my daily lot.

---

[1] Compare the conversation of Hadrian and Rabbi Joshua ben Ḥananiah in Tosefta A.Z. 6:7, and see also Sifré Deut. paragraph 84.

[2] This is a combination of two midrashim, one on Abraham after the circumcision, the other on Jacob and Isaac. See Genesis Rabbah 48, b. B.M. 86b, Gen. 27:35, and compare also Yalkut to Genesis par. 115, and the Targum on Gen. 27:35. See also L. Ginsberg, *op. cit.*, I, p. 240 on God's visit to Abraham; in reality the angels did not eat, V, p. 235; and compare Genesis Rabbah 48:12, Avot de Rabbi Natan 13, 56; on Isaac and the wine of Paradise, Ginzberg, *op. cit.*, I, p. 334, V, p. 284 n. 93, and Midrash Tanḥuma [ed. Buber], Genesis I, p. 135.

[3] The story of Ḥanina b. Dosa and his wife is in b. Taʿanit 24b. For further such stories about Ḥanina, see my *Life of Rabban Yoḥanan ben Zakkai*, pp. 29-32.

61. that my life may be more comfortable."

62. Then one angel, descending, said: "God has not allowed to you by the stars a daily measure[1] greater than this.

63. A new distribution is impossible.

64. But I have created for you in Vahešt a jeweled throne with four legs, on account of your service, worship, and prayer.

65. If you want, I shall give you one leg of this throne."

66. This prophet asked advice of his wife.

67. The wife said: "It is more desirable to be satisfied with the little daily-portion and bad-living in this world

68. than that our throne in Vahešt among our companions be three-legged.

69. But if you can, ask for us our daily portion from that court."

70. Secondly, the angel who had come said: "But if I destroy this sphere, and make anew the heaven and earth, and arrange and set the movement of the stars anew, still it is not clear whether your destiny will fall out good or bad."

71. Thus it is clear from this answer that he himself is not the dispenser of daily portion and lot,

72. and the division is not by his will, and he cannot change fate,

73. and the movements of the sphere, and the sun, moon, and stars are not under his agency or knowledge or will or command.

74. And this, that the throne concerning which he announced, "I will give it in Vahešt," is not of his making or knowing.

75. And in another place he speaks about his own foolishness thus:

76. "I have struck the flock of sinners just as much as the innocents."

77. And when the angels protested this unreasonable action, thus he replied: "I am Adonu, self-willed

78. and supreme, without rival, doing as I will, no one dares to speak complainingly about me."[2]

79. That is most of the multitudinous foolish nonsense, and it seems to me that I have written tediously.

80. To contest and reject this teaching, one needs to call a dastur who is familiar with that AWAT [XIII, 2].

81. So far as I know, that which I have written is true as I said it.

82. Now if there is a God to whom these signs and characteristics apply, then truth is far from him.

83. Forgiveness is a stranger to him.

84. Knowledge has not been bestowed upon him.

85. Then he is himself the Hellish Lie, the prince of the lair of the gloomy race,

86. whom those defiled by the devil glorify by the name of Adonu, and worship.

87. This subject is here completed.

---

[1] *baxt* = daily measure, portion, hence, one's lot, which cannot be changed even by God. See J. Duchesne-Guillemin, *La Religion de l'Iran Ancien* (Paris, 1962), p. 132, and R. C. Zaehner, *Zurvan, A Zoroastrian Dilemma* (Oxford, 1955), p. 254.

[2] Compare b. Sanh. 38b, and see also Ezekiel 21:3-5, Daniel 4:35, Job 9:12, 22. Compare Ginzberg, *op. cit.*, I, pp. 52-3, III, p. 110, and a remote parallel in Genesis Rabbah 8:5.

III. Exposition

After his brief preface (XIII, 1-4), the author turns to an epitome of the stories of creation and the fall of Adam (XIII, 5-45). It is noteworthy that he recounts only the creation of light (Gen. 1:3-5), and then skips to the end of the seven days. He argues (below) that the creation ought not to have taken six days, since it required merely the divine fiat "Be," and it was. Omitting the second through sixth days makes for a more effective argument. Likewise, for the purposes of argument, he later emphasizes that God *placed* the snake in the garden. Additionally, the Hebrew text says nothing about God's becoming angry (XIII, 31; compare Gen. 3:11), but the author subsequently emphasizes God's anger, and hence in his summary, includes it. Three obvious divergences from the sense of the Genesis account thus are explicable by reference to later argument.

Criticism of the Genesis account begins with the argument (XIII, 49-63) that God's essence, whether it be light or dark, is not clarified in the Genesis story. For the Zoroastrian, this was the central theological issue. Failure of the Jewish Scriptures to give a clear statement about it would make them seem not only foolish but irrelevant. God was not light, for he recognized light as something other than himself. He was not, on the other hand, darkness, for the only reason to maintain such a proposition was to explain the origin of light as something other than darkness. Yet to maintain that light emerged from darkness is manifestly absurd. Adonu could not, if he were darkness, have been able to see or face up to light, which would have overwhelmed him. Thus the argument is as follows:

Was God's essence light or darkness?
A. Not light
    1. It was not light, for light was not known to Adonu, and when he saw it, it seemed good (hence, formerly strange) (XIII, 51-53; 55-56).
B. Not darkness
    1. The only reason the Jews would say his essence was darkness is to maintain that light emanated from his darkness (XIII, 54).
    2. Yet if he were darkness, and had never seen light, how could he have faced up to [=look at] light? For we know that light overwhelms darkness (XIII, 59; 61-63).
C. Nor a third state of being
    1. The Jews have to demonstrate the existence of a third state of being and have not done so (XIII, 57-58).

The author turns briefly to the question of whether God was finite or infinite. The Genesis account refers to the existence of dark water, unformed matter and earth (XIII, 64). Were these finite? If so, he asks, what was beyond them (XIII, 65)? If they were infinite, on the other hand, he is *not* infinite (XIII, 66), but rendered finite by these preexistent realities. He does not develop this issue, but turns directly to the problem of preexistent matter, which is inherent in the question raised in XIII, 64. He leaves off with an enigmatic question (XIII, 67): Why has nature exhibited signs of change after creation? The author seems to imply the criticism that creation was not final or perfect, because if it were, then the world as we see it would be identical to that which he made at the outset.

The author argues against the conception of *creatio e nihilo* (XIII, 68-91) and for the proposition that matter, specifically (because of the character of both Zoroastrianism and the Genesis account itself) *light*, pre-existed creation. His presupposition (XIII, 74) is that the mind can only conceive already manifest realities. Yet in the case of light, Adonu seems to have had an unclear notion. Thus he wondered whether light was of good or evil origin, for he found that it was, in fact, good (see XIII, 10), implying an earlier doubt. This would imply that he did not quite know what he was making, but (XIII, 72) that light naturally entered his mind, and hence pre-existed in his mind and (XIII, 73) outside of it also, implying, as earlier, that he was not infinite. In that case, however, light was not his creation (XIII, 75). On the other hand, if he had no clear idea about what light was, then he was ignorant of its essence. This is (XIII, 76-77) manifestly absurd, for how could Adonu seek without knowing what he was seeking. A further issue is raised concerning the act of creation by commandment (XIII, 78-90). Commandment implies that there is one who can be commanded (XIII, 78-79). But in this case, again, light must have been pre-existent (XIII, 80). On the other hand, if he gave the commandment to a non-being (XIII, 81-83), a further absurdity emerges, for non-being could not possibly know what God was asking, could not even receive the commandment (XIII, 82-83). Nothing produces nothing; therefore, the command that "light should be" implies that light already was (XIII, 85). The source of light was not, moreover, the word of God (XIII, 86), for his essence must have formerly been darkness (light not having been created), and hence his word could not produce light. Finally, the Jews might say that the word itself was light, but this returns us to our earlier argument: Since he and his essence were darkness, light having been uncreated, how could he have produced light? Light, therefore, necessarily pre-existed creation, and *creatio e nihilo* is absurd.

The course of the argument is as follows:
Five arguments against *Creatio e Nihilo* from the origin of light
  A. Light always existed in the knowledge and contemplation of God,
      1. and came by its own nature into his mind (XIII, 70-73),
      2. for one can only know about what is, not about what is not (XIII, 74):
Therefore: if Adonu thought about making light, then light must already have existed, for the contrary is absurd, that he could have contemplated something non-existent (XIII, 75), and thus light was pre-existent.
  B. If light did not exist by its own nature in his mind, then he besought it without knowing its essence (XIII, 76).
      1. but this is manifestly absurd, for how can one think about or desire something one has never known in essence (XIII, 77)?
Therefore: Adonu's desire to create light indicates the pre-existence of light.
  C. If he commanded that light come into being, then light must already have existed in order to be the object of the commandment (XIII, 78-79),

1. for a commandment must be received by something;
2. that something could not have been non-existence, for non-existence could neither hear nor understand *nor carry out* the commandment (XIII, 81-83; 85).
3. Nor could the commander himself have conceived of it (XIII, 84).

Therefore: Adonu gave it to an existing, and thus pre-existing light (XIII, 80; repeated in XIII, 90).

    D. If the Jews say that the source of the light was Adonu's word, this is (as A, 1-2) either a sign of pre-existence, or absurd,
        1. for before the creation of light, he was in darkness, and had never seen light (XIII, 86-87).
        2. Therefore, the word coming from his mind must have carried with it the conception of light (XIII, 88).

Therefore: light pre-existed creation in the word which came from his mind.

    E. If the Jews say the word itself was light, then light pre-existed God, or the proposition is absurd (XIII, 89),
        1. for if the word itself was light, then light would have to have been produced by darkness—manifestly absurd—
        2. or must have been hidden, pre-existent, in the darkness (XIII, 90).

Q. E. D. Light existed before Adonu gave the commandment to come into existence (XIII, 91).

The author proceeds to a more polemical critique of the Genesis account, exaggerating the formidable difficulties of the biblical account, and employing a measure of irony. He deliberately ignores the account of the second through sixth days' activities (which he cites below [XIII, 100-101]) to ask why God was tired if all he had to do was to say "Be," for the world to come into being. One hears here an echo of a Jewish heteronym for God, "He who spoke and the world came into being." For the author, extravagant claims have been made in behalf of Adonu—that he can create something from nothing. If this is the case, then the six-days' labor of creation is indeed incongruous (XIII, 98-99).

A series of brief criticisms follows:

First (XIII, 100-101), the biblical account presents an absurdity in enumerating the first four days of creation, before the existence of the sun.

Second, it presents an absurdity (XIII, 102-105)—that God had to rest after speaking the word "Be" (as above, lines 94-97). Why was he tired?

Third, how did he know the number of days? For if creation happened instantaneously upon the pronouncement of the word, then all the work and the necessarily consequent rest should likewise have been instantaneous (XIII, 103-104).

The above criticisms obviously repeat the argument in lines 94-97. The author is anxious to point up the absurdity of the Jewish account, and not merely its impossibility. The idea of a non-mythological creation, taking place at the pronouncement of a magic word, must have indeed seemed foolish to a Zoroastrian, whose rationalistic religion provided him with an elaborate mythology of cosmogony and theogony. The silence of Hebrew Scriptures on points about which Zoroastrian teachings were most elaborate could only be ridiculed, not criticized, and explains the polemical quality of these lines. *Creatio e nihilo*, widely believed in the philosophical theology of this time to be the presupposition of the biblical account, yielded no extensive explanation for the processes by which the world emerged from nothingness. Having demolished the credibility of *creatio e nihilo* from evidence found within the Scriptures themselves, the author can do no more than to ridicule the inadequacy of the account of Genesis.

The author turns (XIII, 106-148) to the story of Adam and Eve. Through this story, he intends to show the harmful character of Jewish theology. It is not enough to question its metaphysical foundation. Here he shows that its theology contains not only contradictory, but also pernicious, evil statements.

He begins with a general introduction (XIII, 106). Why did Adonu make Adam and Eve? He was obviously malicious, for while he apparently wanted them to do his will (XIII, 107), he nonetheless so created them that they did not naturally keep it. Further, he was unreasonable, for if he had foreknowledge of Adam's sin and nonetheless created him (XIII, 108), then he had no reason to be angry with him. This proves that Adonu was inconsistent. On the other hand, if he did not know what would happen, then he is ignorant (XIII, 110). The dialectic is as follows: God is inconsistent within himself for (1) if he foresaw the sin of Adam and nonetheless made him, then he ought not to have angry when he sinned (XIII, 108); (2) if he did not forsee his sin, then he was ignorant (XIII, 109-110); (3) if he really did not want Adam to obey him, then why give an order at all (XIII, 111)?

The author then introduces the distinction between will and command which flows from his earlier analysis, and holds (XIII, 115) that God's will and command either contradict one another (following from XIII, 111), or Adam's power and desire were stronger than God's (XIII, 116-117).

On the other hand, it may be maintained that God actually willed that Adam and Eve obey, and that he also knew in advance they would disobey. If such was the case, however, what choice did poor Adam have, for he was in a situation in which he was of necessity to do what would bring upon his head divine wrath. It was foreknown, hence foreordained, that Adam would disobey. He had no freedom of action at all. If the original command were disobeyed, then the original command is made a lie, but if it were obeyed, then God's foreknowledge would have been faulty (XIII, 118-120).

A similar argument is adduced concerning the garden and the tree (XIII, 121-122). Here again, God's will seems divided against itself, and one may only conclude that he is malicious. If the tree was to be a snare of sin to Adam, then why create it at all? And since the tree provided knowledge, and man was commanded not to eat from it, it is clear that God did not want man to attain knowledge (XIII, 123-131), tried to prevent it, and was angry when he acquired it. Man acquired knowledge, according to this story, only through the deceit of a lowly serpent.

Thus Adonu himself was confused, unreasonable, malicious, and preferred ignorance to knowledge. In the following lines (132-134), the author summarizes his argument by showing the contradiction between God's giving man dominion over all creation and at the same time creating a source of injury to man.

The author presses his point home with an exegesis of the confrontation between Adam, Eve, the snake, and God (XIII, 134-140). God was obviously ignorant, for he had to ask Adam where he was (XIII, 136), and if Adam had not replied (physically), then God would have remained ignorant (XIII, 137-139). The extended interrogation proves this fact (XIII, 139-140).

A parallel argument to that concerning the tree proves the maliciousness of God. He created a snake, and ought, if he were benevolent, to have prevented enemies from reaching Adam (XIII, 141-142). Further exegesis yields that he was a liar as well, for he had told Adam he would die if he ate of the fruit, and yet did not put him to death (XIII, 143).

In summary, then, God is (XIII, 145-147) inconsistent, for what he *knows* will happen contradicts both what he *wants* to happen and what he *commands*.

Finally (XIII, 148), the author asks why the curse of Adam extended to his descendants. This, he says, is simply unlawful.

Thus, he concludes (XIII, 149-150) that the Genesis account contains senseless statements (that is, those applying to the proposition of *creatio e nihilo*) and ignorant and stupid statements (those dealing with Adam and Eve).

In Chapter Fourteen, the author proceeds to cite a series of Scriptures and *aggadot* which ascribe to God qualities wholly incongruent to the divinity according to Zoroastrian rationalism. The citations are frequently difficult to locate in Scripture, and the *aggadic* passages are completely garbled. An example of the former is the size of Sennacherib's army, given in Scripture as 185,000 and here as 600,000, obviously a confusion with the generation of the wilderness (compare XIV, 19-20, 29, and 30). An example of the latter is the story of Ḥanina b. Dosa; in the Talmudic account, the heavenly furniture has three legs—here, four, etc. The author obviously has heard and reshaped stories useful to his polemical purpose.

After a brief introduction (XIV, 1-3), the author emphasizes that Adonu says about his own essence that he is vengeful (XIV, 5-8), angry and harsh (XIV, 10), possessed of unpleasant physical qualities (XIV, 10-13; 15-17), a creature of darkness (XIV, 14), wrathful (XIV, 18-20), and deceitful even to those who serve him best (XIV, 22-24; 37-39). Likewise he is warlike and cruel, capricious and mean to men (XIV, 25-28), and engages in bloody battles against them (XIV, 29-31)—a veritable murderer. Furthermore, he really is not sure what he is doing, for in the end (as above), he comes to regret his creation (XIV, 32-33).

A brief reference to the *merkavah* tradition follows (XIV, 34-35), in which the sheer anthropomorphism of the *merkavah* images is ridiculed.

Four expositions of *aggadot* follow:

I. One has a right to expect that divinity will support the morality of society, and repay good deeds with goodness, and evil deeds with perdition. Divine consistency and concern must underlie society. Yet the Scriptural God pays back respect, obedience, and good deeds with punishment, meted out upon good and evil alike and even upon the angels (XIV, 37-39).

II. An elision of two *midrashim* follows, concerning Abraham and Isaac (XIV, 40-57). The story is expounded after a brief epitome (XIV, 40-50).

The author then asks how such a story is congruent to divinity. As above
(XIV, 10-13; 15-17; 34-35), he ridicules the corporeal attributes. As in
Chapter XIII, 109, he asks why the omnipotent God must commiserate
with the afflicted, and holds that obviously Adonu did not create the
sickness from which Abraham was suffering, for if he had, he would not
have commiserated with him (XIV, 53). He was, moreover, not only *not*
omnipotent, but also not omniscient, for he knew nothing of the origin of
the wine (XIV, 54); and was deceitful as well, for he changed his mind
(XIV, 55; compare XIV, 32-33). Thus the author proves once again that
the faith is not only metaphysically unsound, but theologically pernicious,
for it teaches stories about an undesirable being who would scarcely deserve
a place in human society, let alone in heaven—a liar, a murderer, stupid,
indecisive, physically repulsive and destructive, a true creature of darkness.

III. Furthermore, Adonu really does not, by his own testimony, govern
the affairs of men, for he himself had to admit that the division of the stars
was completed and a whole new creation would be required to alter it; and
yet such a new creation might not conform, in the end, to his will and
purpose. This is the point of the long Talmudic citation (XIV, 59-70),
which indicates that Adonu's angel does not divide up men's daily portions
and cannot alter their fate. He, like them, is subordinate to reality, and does
not control the zodiac (XIV, 71-73), or determine fate.[1]

IV. He is, finally, wholly unprincipled, unreasonable, and not amenable
to protest or human entreaty. This fact is clear in the reference to divine
destruction of righteous and ignorant (XIV, 75-78) together, and his rejection of the angelic protest. So the author repeats the point of XIV, 37-39.

The closing sentences (XIV, 82-86) summarize the argument of the
chapter that:
1. truth is far from him—as in XIV, 22-24; 32-33; 55; 75-78;
2. forgiveness is a stranger to him—as in XIV, 5-8; 10; 18-20; 25-28;
   29-31;
3. knowledge has not been bestowed upon him—as in XIV, 32-33; 54;
4. and he is truly the prince of dark devils—as in XIV, 10-13; 15-17; 14;
   29-31.

Thus, having in Chapter XIII challenged the metaphysical foundations
of Judaism, the author succeeds in Chapter XIV in showing that it is not
only a false religion, but also a dangerous and destructive creation of the
devil, teaching truths contrary to good order, good sense, and good taste,'
and presenting a wholly unacceptable theology, even by its own testimony.[2]

---

[1] See above, pp. 332-334.

[2] It seems to me that Chapter XIII is devoted to the Written Torah, and Chapter
XIV to the Oral Torah, thus recognizing the Jews' belief in a dual revelation, and
arguing that both Torot were equally false.

APPENDIX TWO

BIBLIOGRAPHICAL REFLECTIONS

i. Introduction

David Winston, "The Iranian Component in the Bible, Apocrypha, and Qumran: A Review of the Evidence," *History of Religions* 5, 2, 1966, 183-216 (to which I have replied briefly in the same place, 5, 3, 1966, 176-8) has provided a partial summary of the extensive literature which deals with the Iranian influence upon Palestinian Judaism. Just what one means by Iranian "influence" remains to be more closely defined.[1] Many have supposed that any evidence of dualism, such as a reference to light and darkness, or Jewish conceptions similar to Mazdean ones of any period, for example concerning Satan, Gayomart and Adam, eschatology, angelology, demonology, and the like, indicate Iranian influence. For instance, Winston supposes the undeniable similarity between Zurvanite and Qumranian dualism is proof of "interpenetration." It might, however, be the result of parallel, independent developments. We must try to determine the circumstances which may have led to the introduction of Iranian religious ideas or forms into Judaism. Who were the intermediaries on each side? When and where did they meet? Is there no other explanation for the existence in each culture of parallel concepts, institutions, beliefs, or structures, but "inter-

---

[1] All the more so Babylonian Jewish "influence" on Palestinian Judaism. For example, C. S. Mann, "The Jerusalem Church in Acts," Appendix IV, in Johannes Munck, *The Acts of the Apostles* (N.Y., 1967: The Anchor Bible, Vol. 31, edited by William Foxwell Albright and David Noel Freedman), p. 282, stated, "The Parthian invasions about 140 B.C., with the resulting disruption of ordered life, meant that the old irrigation systems could no longer be maintained, and the complex system of retaining dikes ... quickly broke. As a result, the Euphrates and Tigris rivers both changed their courses. This disastrous break with previously ordered ways of life ... must have brought with it wholesale emigration of Jews." I do not know the basis for Mann's allegation. In his Diyala studies (*Land Behind Baghdad. A History of Settlement on the Diyala Plains*, Chicago, 1965, pp. 61ff.) Robert McC. Adams does not refer to such widespread destruction in the nearby Diyala basin. It is true that Babylonia changed hands several times between 140 and 120, but evidence of destruction *so* widespread as to lead to forced migration, let alone emigration, is not known to me. In any event *no* source refers to such an emigration, and while an argument from silence may not be impressive, it is still stronger than an allegation based upon no direct, pertinent evidence whatever. (The only substantial attempt at emigration from Babylonia to Palestine, excluding the small band of Zamaris [Zimri], took place about 362-3, in consequence of Julian's promise to rebuild the Temple, when a passing Messiah urged Jews to return. According to Christian Syriac hagiographical sources, many thousands of Maḥozan Jews did in fact try to emigrate, but were slaughtered by the troops of Shapur II. But this has no relevance whatever to Mann's point.)

penetration," "influence" of one upon the other? If, as between Qumran and Zurvanism, we find striking similarities, we may satisfactorily account for them without positing reciprocal influence. Both constitute dualisms within monotheist systems. Zurvanism was a Zoroastrian monotheist "heresy," following R. C. Zaehner, *Zurvan, A Zoroastrian Dilemma* (Oxford, 1955), and the Qumran sectarians were a Jewish dualist "heresy" within monotheism. Both therefore represent dualistic structures within a monotheist framework. Indeed, the sources within Israelite monotheism from which such a dualism may have emerged have hardly been explored. One hardly needs to turn to Iran to account for Israelite ethical, anthropological, or metaphysical dualism. It would, by contrast, be simple enough to argue that Achemenid political domination of Palestine from ca. 540 to 333 B.C. made a profound impact upon Palestinian Judaism. But if so, what were the means by which such influence was mediated? Was Palestine so inundated by Persian officials, tradesmen, priests, and the like, that the Jews were likely to have had intimate contact with, and knowledge of, their traditions? Morton Smith's forthcoming volume on *The Formation of Palestinian Judaism. To the Age of the Maccabees*, to be published by Columbia University Press, contains substantial data which suggest that both Achemenid and Israelite life had come under Hellenistic influence long before Alexander's conquest of the Near and Middle East.

A further issue is, What was the state of Iranian religion in Parthian and Sasanian times? Are the contents of Avestan, Pahlavi, and Pazend texts cited as evidence for Zoroastrian beliefs valid evidence for the earlier periods? A view of the severe problem of dating Book-Pahlavi texts will be found in W. B. Bailey, *Zoroastrian Problems in the Ninth Century Books* (Oxford, 1943), 149-77, which should be compared to Jacques Duchesne-Guillemin, "La Fixation de l'Avesta," *Indo-Iranica: Mélanges Presentés à Georg Morgenstierne à l'Occasion de son Soixante-Dixieme Anniversaire* (Wiesbaden, 1964), 62-7, and P.-J. de Menasce, *Une Encyclopedie Mazdéenne, Le Denkart* (Paris, 1958), 56ff. The best recent critical studies of Achemenid and Sasanian religion include Duchesne-Guillemin, *La Religion de l'Iran Ancien* (Paris, 1964), R. C. Zaehner, *Dawn and Twilight of Zoroastrianism* (London, 1961) and Geo Widengren, *Die Religionen Irans* (Stuttgart, 1964), to mention only three important works. But for Zoroaster himself, studies begin, I think with W. B. Henning, *Zoroaster: Politician or Witchdoctor?* (Oxford, 1951).

The broader issue of Judaic-Mazdean relationships is this: If we discover a significant parallel, such as the perfectly obvious one between Judaic and Mazdean eschatology, as traced by R. H. Charles, *A Critical History of the Doctrine of Future Life in Israel, in Judaism, and in Christianity* (London, 1899, reprinted N.Y., 1963, with introduction by George W. Buchanan), what are we to make of it? Who borrowed from whom? Or, have both borrowed from a single anterior source? The usual answer given in recent times is that Israel must have borrowed from Iran, though Moulton, J. Darmesteter, Scheftelowitz, and others earlier thought that Israel had influenced Iran. The question of an anterior source is almost never raised to begin with. Both probably drew, however, from common Middle Eastern sources. The Babylonian roots in cuneiform culture of post-biblical Judaism have never been fully examined. We have helpful studies by philologists, tracing relationships between Hebrew and Akkadian words, and by biblical and cuneiform scholars on the earlier period, such as J. J. Finkelstein, "Bible and Babel," *Commentary* 26, 1958, 431-44. Qualified Assyriologists, however, have yet systematically to explain what was *Babylonian* about Babylonian Judaism, and what was Babylonian about the syncretistic Babylonian-Iranian-Hellenistic culture of later times. Scholars of ancient Near Eastern Law, such as Yoḥanan Muffs, *Studies in Elephantine Papyri* (Leiden, 1969) and Baruch A. Levine, "Mulugu Melug: The Origins of a Talmudic Legal Institution" (to appear in *JAOS*) have persuasively shown the Babylonian roots of some Talmudic legal forms and expressions. But broader cultural phenomena have yet to be traced. It seems to me premature to try to decide the relation of Iranian to Talmudic law or religion, before an extended preliminary inquiry into the roots of both in cuneiform law has been undertaken. A helpful example of what can be accomplished is W. W. Hallo, "Akkadian Apocalypses," *Israel Exploration Journal* 16, 4, 1966, 231-242. Similarly, is it not equally premature to try to decide the relationships between other aspects of Iranian and Jewish culture? Parallels may indicate a common root, or a common response to a shared condition, rather than a reciprocal influence. This is not to suggest that informed and specific accounts of Iranian words, ideas, and institutions do not illuminate Babylonian Talmudic data. Quite to the contrary, works such as Ezra Spicehandler, "*Dina de Magista* and *Be Davar*: Notes on Gentile courts in Talmudic Babylonia," *HUCA* 26, 1955, 333-54, are all too rare.

If we must make premature hypotheses, let me here hypothecate that *Iranian* "influences" on the culture and religion of Babylonian Jewry, and all the more so, of Palestinian Jewry, have been for the most part exaggerated and overrated. Examining just what the Talmudic rabbis actually knew about Iranian culture, we can hardly be impressed by the depth of their knowledge. Some could understand Pahlavi when it was spoken, but could not read it. The Talmud preserves a thoroughly garbled account of Persian festivals, and two of the three Mazdean holidays the rabbis mention were in fact days upon which taxes had to be paid, so their knowledge does not prove to have been very profound. The exchanges between various third-century rabbis and Magi recorded in the Talmud center upon astrology and medicine, the two indigenous, autochthonous sciences of Babylonia, cultivated in the Babylonian schools down to the first century A.D. and studied by sages of other groups settled in the region.

I do not know how much the Talmudic rabbis knew about, or inherited from, cuneiform law and other aspects of Babylonian civilization. Babylonian Jewry lived side by side with the ancient Semitic peoples of the region, so that by the turn of the fourth century, more than nine hundred years of symbiosis had gone by. One should therefore expect to find many examples of borrowing. But I know of no comprehensive work providing such examples. Even the legal data have been rather fragmentarily and unsystematically considered.

Attention has focused upon Iranian and Jewish relationships, but most of those who studied such matters knew little about the problems of working with Book-Pahlavi and other Iranian sources. The great philologians, W. and B. Geiger were exceptional. The latter's signed articles in the revised printing of A. Kohut's edition of *Arukh Completum* (N.Y. 1956) are of primary importance, as are his scattered articles in the *Wiener Zeitschrift für die Kunde des Morgenländes*. His "The Synagogue, Middle Iranian Texts," in *Excavations at Dura Europos, Final Report*, VIII, 1, ed. C. H. Kraeling, *The Synagogue* (New Haven, 1956), 283-317, provides a model for such studies. Among the cultural historians, Geiger has no counterpart. Most contemporary historians of religion and theologians normally have considerable training in Semitic and Hellenistic languages and culture, but are usually quite uninformed about problems of Iranology, which facilitates their reaching neat and easy conclusions. By contrast, one may note Richard N. Frye, "Reitzenstein and Qumran Revisited by an Iranian," *Harvard Theological Review* 55, 1962, 261-8.

ii. Histories of the Jews in Babylonia

The writing of the history of the Jews under Parthian and Sasanian rule began with Naḥman Zvi Gezav, '*Al Naharot Bavel* (Warsaw, 1876), a work which in general has been curiously neglected. Gezav studied Iranian history and culture as best he could, and given the primitive state of knowledge in his day, he made a singular contribution. But he had no successors. The next really *historical* work, not merely collecting clever exegeses of Talmudic texts, or providing a kind of secular hagiography listing leading rabbis and recounting as history Talmudic stories of their careers and virtues, is Salo W. Baron, *A Social and Religious History of the Jews* (Philadelphia, 1952), vol. II. Baron's contribution to this subject has never received adequate appreciation. It was Baron who transformed a literature mostly used for exegesis into a historically useful body of documents, who redefined "Talmudic history" in coherent and significant sociological and historical categories.

Previous historians, such as H. Graetz, *History of the Jews* (reprinted, Philadelphia, 1948), II, Salomon Funk, *Die Juden in Babylonien* (Berlin, 1902) I-II, I. H. Weiss, *Dor Dor veDorshav* (4th ed., Vilna, 1904), III, Z'ev Yavetz, *Sefer Toledot Yisrael* (Tel Aviv, 1935), VI & VII, and I. Y. Halevy, *Dorot HaRishonim* (Vienna and Berlin, 1923), I, 3, 5, and II, saw Babylonian Jewish history under the Arsacids and Sasanians as "Talmudic history." That is to say, they used a literary category to define a *historical* period. Such was the method of 19th century German historiography in the path of Hegel and Kant. The underlying philosophy assumed that what was *historical* about history was politics and the creations of the 'spirit.' 'Spiritual creations' were enshrined in the literature produced by great minds. The doings of ordinary people as preserved in social and economic history, the development of other than political institutions—these were not worthy of the historian's attention.

Since politics was understood as the affairs of nations, the Jews were not supposed to possess a political life, for they had no national government; therefore all that was left for them was literature. And it was more than sufficient. The presupposition that whatever was important had been recorded in the Babylonian Talmud and other rabbinic documents, moreover, conformed to the theological conviction that the Pharisees and their Tannaitic and Amoraic heirs had constituted "normative Judaism." What they said *was* Judaism, and whoever diverged represented heresy. The question was hardly asked, What was the relationship between a rabbinic law or saying and the actualities of everyday life? It was assumed that merely describing rabbinical laws and sayings would constitute satisfactory history. Describing the rabbis not as striking examples of religious and political leadership but rather as authoritative teachers and embodiments of Judaism was the content of that history. Since the Talmud and cognate literature had *become* normative over the centuries, it was assumed that they represented all that was important in Judaism during the period in which they took shape. Hence "Talmudic history."

Talmudic history was understood to extend roughly from Ezra to the Moslem conquest, for historians found in the Talmudic stories, whether verifiable or not, data relevant to those centuries. The great dividing points, such as the destruction of the Temple in Jerusalem, or the Bar Kokhba War, or the conversion of Constantine, or the rise of the Sasanians, were noted to be sure. But history was divided into "the biblical period" and "the Talmudic period." Within "Talmudic history," the nineteenth and early twentieth historians naturally focussed upon what seemed to them historically interesting materials in Talmudic and cognate literature. They were, excepting Halevy, not well-trained in legal studies, nor did they find much of merit in theological or exegetical lore. But the Talmud contains many stories about rabbis. So "Talmudic history" was written in terms of generations, of rabbis, of academies, and in a limited measure, of the character of the ideas and literature produced in a given place and time.

Both the need to criticize and verify sources and the task of recovering some sort of sustained narrative lay beyond the concern and methodological capacity of the earlier historians. Whatever the text said happened actually did happen. One had to compare and contrast various accounts, where available, but the sources were never subjected to searching criticism of either lower or higher varieties. In the positivist tradition, the earlier historians supposed they could report what had "really" happened. Since the sources contain many details contrary to what rational, modern men expect to happen—such as letters dropped from heaven into the laps of academicians, resurrections of the dead, and other exceptional events—the historians would simply omit reference to such details, and use the rest of the account as if they did not exist to begin with. The philological historians imagined that once they had properly established, understood, and interpreted a text in its own setting, they then knew pretty much what happened. I cannot think of a less likely supposition. On the other hand, the weaving of various stories into paragraphs and chapters required a sort of historical exegesis of texts, which in Graetz's and Yavetz's hands turned into out-and-out sermonizing. Halevy's exegesis was far more impressive, in my opinion. He concerned himself mostly with the misconceptions of earlier historians, whom he called contemptuously "German sages," and in the midst of his fiery polemic, he produced many thorough and penetrating accounts of specific problems. He is by far the hardest to follow, however. One needs to read a given section four or five times before the train of thought emerges clearly.

Before Baron, therefore, most historians conceived Talmudic history as a category of Talmudic literary studies. They *rarely* consulted non-Jewish sources, and when they did, they merely read popular-scientific accounts, as in the cases of Gezav, Graetz, and Yavetz. The Jews were people who suffered, wrote books, and produced great and holy leaders. They lived inside a test-tube, and the history and culture of the "surrounding peoples" played no role in their development. And most strikingly, the Jews and the rabbis were one and the same. That the rabbis' laws did not necessarily describe the social life of ordinary people, that their theological and moral dicta did not fill the mind of the common folk, that the academy and the street were not one and the same—these possibilities are not considered. So "Talmudic history," "the history of the Jews," and "Judaism" were identified with one another in the mind of the historians.

Baron is the first major Jewish historian to see the historical task in this period as a social scientific one. In studying Talmudic and cognate documents, he raised basically social scientific questions, and answered these questions as best he could according to the canons of critical inquiry, rather than the convictions of theologians. He is not an exegete of texts, though he knows texts, nor a defender of the faith. He sees the Jews as they were, living among various peoples and governments, developing institutions of politics and culture, responding to contemporary issues and challenges. Each of his notes is a bibliographical study of a problem. In studying specific matters, I have found it invariably useful to see first of all what Baron read. After considerably more detailed study than was necessary for his purposes, I have normally found he read everything he "should" have read and noted nothing inconsequential or superfluous. He very frequently points out subjects for further study, and given his grand knowledge of the scholarly literature, no one can give better guidance about what we do and do not know. The beginning of the study of the Jews and Judaism under Parthian and Sasanian rule is close and careful reading of Baron, *A Social and Religious History of the Jews*, vol. II, text *and* notes. His is the best account of the state of our knowledge up to 1952 known to me.

One would want, however, a secure knowledge of the framework of political history. For this purpose, N. C. Debevoise, *Political History of Parthia* (Chicago, 1938), remains most satisfactory. Jozef Wolski of Cracow is presently writing a new Parthian history. Anyone familiar with his recent articles, for example, "L'État Parthe des Arsacides," *Palaeologia* 7, 1959, 91ff., and "Decay of the Iranian Empire of the Seleucids and the Chronology of the Parthians' Beginnings," *Berytus* 12, 1956, 35-52, will anticipate a definitive statement. For Sasanian times, Arthur Christensen *L'Iran sous les Sassanides* (Copenhagen, 1936, 2nd ed., 1944) is basic. I find George Rawlinson, *Seventh Great Oriental Monarchy* (London, 1876) of continuing value. Rawlinson extensively quotes the Greek and Latin historians. For the Persian, Arabic, Armenian, Manichaean, and Christian-Syriac sources Christensen is, of course, of greater use.

Some Iranists working in pre-Islamic materials take a keen interest in Jewish data, though few are adequately trained to make much use of them. Among these latter, Geo Widengren, "The Status of the Jews in the Sassanian Empire," *Iranica Antiqua* 1, 1961, 117-162, and his *Iranisch-Semitisch Kulturbegegnung in Parthischer Zeit* (Cologne, 1958) and "Quelques Rapports entre Juifs et Iraniens à l'époque des Parthes," *Supplements to Vetus Testamentum IV*, (Leiden, 1957), *Volume du Congrès, Strasbourg*, 1956, 197-242 are of greatest importance. Widengren's contribution is to bring to bear a wide range of knowledge of Babylonian and Iranian data upon specific Jewish issues. In his *Iranica Antiqua* paper, he surveys Pahlavi and Oriental Christian sources in Syriac, Armenian, and Greek, providing a compendium of references to the Jews and Judaism. Some of the material was known before his time, but he called attention to many items previously not properly appreciated. Apart from philologists, only one other Iranist has consistently attended to Jewish materials, and done so with appropriate care, Otakar Klima. He makes excellent use of the German translation of the Talmud, and the original texts as well. His work shows continuing interest in questions of Jewish cultural and religious history, both in *Mazdak: Geschichte einer Sozialen Bewegung im Sassanidischen Persien* (Prague, 1957) and in the accompanying "Mazdak und die Juden," *Archiv Orientální* 24, 1956, 420-31. Similarly, his *Manis Zeit und Leben* (Prague, 1962), is exceptional among books on Mani and Manichaeism for its careful use of relevant Jewish sources. Many Iranists cite the well-known data in Graetz, and some refer to J. Newman (below), to the exclusion of weightier studies. Their discussion of the Jews and Judaism reflects a rather passing concern at best, as in M.-L. Chaumont, "Les Sassanides et la christianisation de l'Empire iranien au IIIè siècle de notre ère," *Revue de l'Histoire des Religions* 165, 1964, 165-202. Were Judaism not mentioned, it would hardly matter. Since Chaumont does raise the question of why Kartir persecuted the Jews ca. 272-292 (on pp. 192-3) it is deplorable that she has apparently not read important monographs on the subject. Her reference to the exilarch does not even indicate knowledge of Lazarus (below), nor of the excellent *Jewish Encyclopedia* article of W. Bacher ("Exilarch", *JE* V, 294ff.) Iranists quickly recognize the limitations of non-specialists attempting to make use of Iranian data. It is time they perceived how superficially they have studied so rich a resource of information on Sasanian Iran as the Talmud. It constitutes a document of *more* than narrowly philological interest for Iranian studies.

III. SPECIAL SUBJECTS

The monographic literature on Babylonian Jewish history in Arsacid and Sasanian times is not rich. We are nonetheless fortunate in having some excellent, entirely reliable guides to geographical and political data. Let us note, first of all, the truly definitive works. One must begin with Jacob Obermeyer, *Die Landschaft Babylonien im Zeitalter des Talmuds und des Gaonats* (Frankfurt a/M., 1929), which rendered obsolete all former work on the geography of Jewry in Babylonia, and has never been superseded. Obermeyer's researches involved travel throughout the region, conversation with local inhabitants and careful study of sites as well as of literary evidences, prepared while working as tutor for a Persian pretender. Two other works of exceptional value are Felix Lazarus, "Die Haüpter der Vertriebenen. Beiträge zu einer Geschichte der Exilfurst in Babylonien unter den Arsakiden und Sassaniden," *Jahrbücher für Jüdische Geschichte und Literatur* 10, 1890, 1-183, and N. Brüll, "Adiabene," in the same journal, 1, 1874, 58-86; both provide a thorough account of the sources. M. Beer's article on the Exilarchate in *Ziyyon*, 28, 1963, 1-33 represents an important supplement to Lazarus, and his as yet unpublished dissertation on the *Social and Economic Status of the Babylonian Amoraim*, in Hebrew, (Ramat Gan, 1963, in mimeographed form) will, when published, represent a major and lasting contribution. What I find most useful in Lazarus's monograph is his thorough and systematic presentation of the primary sources, and careful study of Geonic traditions. Beer copiously cites evidence on the economic, political, and administrative aspects of the exilarchate and rabbinate. Neither work fully elucidates the relationship between the rabbi and the exilarch or the political theories underlying their conflicting claim to rule Jewry. And unfortunately Lazarus and Beer both suppose that evidence pertaining to one period applies equally to the whole three or more centuries under study. So neither describes the development, growth, and change of the exilarchate over a long period of time.

We have no systematic philological study, showing the Iranian background of Talmudic language, but the nearest thing to a full catalogue of Persian words in the Talmud is found in S. Telegdi, "Essai sur la phonétique des emprunts iraniens en Araméen Talmudique," *Journal Asiatique* 226, 1935, 177-257. The Geigers' contributions, noted above, cannot be overestimated.

Economic history remains to be written. Julius Newman's volumes, *The Agricultural Life of the Jews in Babylonia*, 200-500 (London, 1932), and the mimeographed pamphlet, *Commercial Life of the Jews in Babylonia*, provide an arrangement by topic of whatever data Newman found of interest. No one supposes that they provide, or replace, rigorous and thorough economic history, for they are merely neat arrangements of relevant sayings. F. M. Heichelheim, "Roman Syria," in Tenney Frank, ed., *An Economic Survey of Ancient Rome* (Baltimore, 1938), IV, 121-258, contains much important information and has been unaccountably ignored. Just now, we are gaining access to the brilliant work of Soviet Iranists, in particular through N. Pigulevskaja, *Les Villes de l'État Iranien aux Époques Parthe et Sassanide* (Paris, 1963). Those unfortunates who, like myself, do not yet know Russian will be glad, also, for the occasional remarks on social and economic history found in Vladimir G. Lukonin, *Persia II* (N.Y. and Cleveland, 1967), which is mainly devoted to archaeological and artistic issues.

An exemplary recent work in legal history is R. Yaron, *Gifts in Contemplation of Death in Jewish and Roman Law* (Oxford, 1960). Yaron helpfully stresses aspects of legal development and change. A. Gulak, *Yesodei Ha-Mishpat Ha'Ivri* (Berlin, 1922, I-IV) and Boaz Cohen's collected essays,

Jewish and Roman Law, A Comparative Study (N.Y., 1966, I-II) provide accounts of Jewish law. None of these works concentrates specifically upon Babylonian Jewish law, nor would it have been possible to do so. I do not know why the interest in comparative law has centered upon the Mediterranean, and not the Middle Eastern world. Since Babylonian Talmudic data are used, one would suppose that the *Mātigān-i Hazār Datistān*, studied by C. Bartholomae in *Zum sasanidischen Recht, Sitzungsberichte der Heidelberger Akademie der Wissenschaften*, I, 1918, II, 1918, III, 1920, IV, 1922, V, 1923, and also reprinted in an unscientific edition and translation by Sohrad Jamshedjee Bulsara as *The Laws of the Ancient Persians* (Bombay, 1937), would have been at least as interesting for comparative purposes as Justinian's Code. J.-P. de Menasce has published a brief study of it in his *Feux et Fondations Pieuses dans le Droit Sassanide* (Paris, 1964, *Travaux de l'Institut d'Études Iraniennes de l'Université de Paris*). A. G. Perikhanian, the Soviet Iranist, will soon publish a complete edition and translation. Jozef Wolski recently published a bibliographical account, "Elam, Perse, Arménie (Achéménides, Arsacides, Sassanides)," in *Introduction bibliographique à l'histoire du droit et à l'ethnologie juridique*, A/5, Brussels, 1965, where many other important items are listed. In his *HUCA* 1955 article, mentioned above Spicehandler cites (p. 334, note; 336, note 6) the studies of Antonio Pagliaro, in *Rivista degli studi Orientali* 10, 1910, 15, 1935, 19, 1941, 22, 1946, 23, 1948, 26, 1951; and calls attention to A. Christensen, "Introduction bibliographique à l'histoire du droit de l'Iran ancien," *Archives d'histoire du droit oriental* 2, 1938, 243-57.

Babylonian Jewish literature, meaning the Babylonian Talmud, has been studied for many centuries, but only in the present age have literary historians begun to undertake the task of form- and traditions-criticism. This is the first step toward a systematic, historical appreciation of the literature. Y. N. Epstein's *Mevo'ot leSifrut Ha'Amora'im* (in Hebrew, Jerusalem, 1962) is especially relevant to the historian's interest, though he does not spell out the historical consequences of his literary inquiry, and indeed seems to have had slight, if any, interest in history. Babylonian Talmudic literature cannot be studied apart from contemporary Palestinian documents, and so S. Lieberman's *Tosefta Kifshuta* (N.Y., 1956 et seq. in eleven volumes to date) and other modern scientific works require close attention. (Lieberman's *Greek in Jewish Palestine* [N.Y., 1942], *Hellenism in Jewish Palestine* [N.Y., 1950] and "Palestine in the Third and Fourth Centuries," *Jewish Quarterly Review* n.s. 36, 1946, 329-70, and 37, 1947, 31-54, contain much important information on Babylonia as well.) The several volumes of Abraham Weiss, such as *Hithavut HaTalmud b'Shelemuto* (N.Y., 1943) focus upon problems of literary history. In my view, the articles of Hyman Klein on the Saboraic strata of Talmudic literature, such as *"Gemara and Sebara," Jewish Quarterly Review*, n.s. 38, 1947, 67-91, (and see *JQR* 43, 1953, 341-63, and *Journal of Semitic Studies*, 3, 1958, 363-372), provide a very important key to understanding the formation of the Talmudic *sugya*. Nonetheless we are at the very beginning of historical criticism of Talmudic literature, including the study of how it reached its present form. All of our studies of the history of Babylonian Judaism and Jewry, based as they are upon Talmudic evidences, must therefore be seen as tentative and primitive, for only when we fully comprehend both the way in which our sources took shape and the later concerns which have selected and shaped traditions about earlier figures, will we be able to criticize, if not to verify, our historical sources. We are a very long way from such a critical understanding of Talmudic literature as a historical source, perhaps a century behind equivalent studies of New Testament and cognate literature.

IV. HISTORY OF JUDAISM IN BABYLONIA

The history of *Judaism* in Babylonia is yet to be written. I know of not a single systematic, methodologically sophisticated, and historically reliable account. Indeed, what would constitute such a history is still by no means clear to me. It would certainly have to include attention to the development of academic, rabbinical ideas from one generation to the next. Babylonian data are mixed indiscriminately with Palestinian ones in the various accounts of "Talmudic Judaism." These provide little insight into the thought peculiar to the *Babylonian* academies in any one age or place, or in all of them put together. We are however fortunate to have a number of very helpful biographical studies, upon the basis of which the history of Babylonian *rabbinic* Judaism may eventually be constructed. The most important, comprehensive, and useful work is A. Hyman, *Toledot Tanna'im ve'Amora'im* (London, 1909, I-III), which is far more thorough than the brief entries in the *Jewish Encyclopedia*. Monographs on specific rabbis include David Hoffman, *Mar Samuel* (Leipzig, 1873), and Y. S. Zuri, *Rav* (Paris, 1925). Zuri's rather tendentious works on the relationship between Judean and Galilean culture with Sura and Nehardea, such as *Tarbut HaDeromim* (Tel Aviv, 1924) and *Toledot Darkhei HaLimud bishivot Darom, Galil, Sura, ve-Neharde'a'* (Jerusalem, 1914) remain interesting, and frequently his ideas about differing methods of study in various schools bear rich fruit. A compendium of sayings, *Abbayye veRava* was published by Y. L. Maimon (Jerusalem, 1965), for what purpose I cannot fathom. Wilhelm Bacher, *Die Agada der Babylonischen Amoräer. Ein Beitrag zur Geschichte der Agada und zur Einleitung in den Babylonischen Talmud* (Frankfurt 1913) provides brief accounts of some of the aggadic sources, arranged by generations, and frequently adds important observations. But that work is not of the same depth or value as his studies of the Palestinians. I do not yet know how to make sense of the data he provides in *Tradition und Tradenten in den Schulen Palästinas und Babyloniens* (Leipzig, 1914), on which see J. Z. Lauterbach in *Jew sh Quarterly Review* n.s. 8, 1917, 101-12. One also may note S. Baer, "Leben und Wirken des Tannaiten Chija," *Magazin für die Wissenschaft des Judentums* 17, 1890, 28-49, 119-135, one of the *very* small number of monographs dealing with specific Babylonian masters. The first modern effort at writing a history of the schools was that of M. D. Judelovitz, "The City of Nersh in Babylonia in the Time of the Talmud," in Hebrew, *Sinai* 15, 1945, 93ff.; "The City of Sura," in Hebrew, *Sinai* 1, 1937, 168ff; *Ha'Ir Pumbedita bimei ha'Amora'im* (Jerusalem, 1939), and other works. This latter work was subjected to a searching, but unusually kindly, review by G. Allon, now reprinted in his *Meḥqarim beToledot Yisra'el*, (Tel Aviv, 1958), II, 298-302. A history of the Talmudic academies ought to pay attention to the differing emphases and principles of Mishnah-study and biblical exegesis, following Ẓuri; to the various results of such study of the Bible, following Bacher; to the external setting of the schools as well as to their personnel, following Judelovitz; but most important, to their contributions to the formation of the Babylonian Talmud.

Among the many works on the relationship between "Talmudic Judaism" and Mazdaism, I should list, for bibliographical completeness only, the following of special interest: James Darmesteter, "Les Six Feux dans le Talmud et dans le Bundehesh," *Revue des Études Juives* 1, 1880, 186-96; Moses Gaster, "Parsism in Judaism," *Encyclopedia of Religion and Ethics*, 9, 64ff.; Alexander Kohut, "Parsic and Jewish Literature on the First Man," *Jewish Quarterly Review*, o.s., 3, 1890-1, 231-50, and his "Über die jüdische Angelologie und Dämonologie in ihrer Abhängigkeit vom Parsismus," *Abhandlungen für die Kunde des Morgenländes*, IV, 3, 1866; S. Krauss, *Paras veRomi beTalmud uwaMidrash* (Jerusalem, 1947); A. Marmorstein, "Iranische und Jüdische Religion," *Zeitschrift für Neutestamentliche Wissenschaft* 26, 1927, 231-42; and S. H. Taqizadeh's definitive, "Iranian Festivals Adopted by the Christians and Condemned by the Jews," *Bulletin of the School of Oriental Studies* 10, 1939-40, 632-53, as well as the works of Geo Widengren cited above. So while we have no history of rabbinic Judaism in the Babylonian academies, for which our data are so abundant, we do have a few *vorstudien* on relevant issues of rabbinic Judaism and its relationship to Mazdean religion, as well as biographical and academic studies of value.

The other forms of Judaism are still less accessible. The religion of the ordinary Jews left only a few, mostly negative remains in Talmudic sources. The rabbinical elite preserved the religion of common folk only by criticizing it. On the other hand, the Dura synagogue contains a vast, if mute testimony to what occupied the minds and souls of a small, but cosmopolitan frontier community. Kraeling's report (cited above) is definitive for all but the interpretation of the art. Erwin R. Goodenough devoted volumes IX, X, and XI of his *Jewish Symbols in Greco-Roman Times* (N.Y., 1952 et eq., Vols. I-XII) to that question, emphasizing the Hellenistic and Iranian motifs to be uncovered. I do not believe that E. J. Bickerman, "Symbolism in the Dura Synagogue," *Harvard Theological Review* 58, 1, 1965, 127-152, has said the last word on Goodenough's researches. Morton Smith's "Goodenough's *Jewish Symbols* in Retrospect," *Journal of Biblical Literature* 86, 1, 1967, 53-68 provides a list of some of the more important reviews of Goodenough's work, a careful and penetrating critique of his conclusions, and a very thoughtful appreciation of his lasting achievements. I do not know of a more persuasive or comprehensive assessment. A more constructive approach to the broader issue of the Hellenization of Judaism, with important implications for Babylonian Judaism, is Morton Smith, "The Image of God: Notes on the Hellenization of Judaism, with Especial Reference to Goodenough's Work on Jewish Symbols," *Bulletin of the John Rylands Library* 40, 2, 1958, 473-512.

A further testimony concerning popular religion is to be found in the

Mandaean incantation bowls, of which some were prepared for Jews. The classic text is James A. Montgomery, *Aramaic Incantation Texts from Nippur* (Philadelphia, 1913); Cyrus H. Gordon published many articles on the subject, including "Aramaic and Mandaic Magical Bowls," *Archiv Orientálni* 9, 1937, 95-106; and we are now fortunate to have the comprehensive dissertation of Edwin Masao Yamauchi *Mandaean Incantation Texts* (Ann Arbor, 1964, in microfilm, now published in the American Oriental Society monograph series). The bowls' implications for the history of religions and for Judaism have yet to be explored.

Finally, one notes the Book-Pahlavi testimonies concerning what the Mazdeans thought of Judaism, found in the *Denkart* and in the *Škand Gumanik Vičar*, and translated by Lewis H. Gray, "The Jews in Pahlavi Literature," *Actes du XIV Congrès International des Orientalistes* (Paris, 1906, 161-192, reprinted in the *Jewish Encyclopedia*). My translation, printed above, was based upon P.-J. de Menasce, *Une Apologétique Mazdéene du IXè Siècle* (Fribourg in Switzerland, 1945).

How accurately the Zoroastrian text observed the faith of ordinary Jews *before* the ninth century we do not know. But its stress upon fatalism and astrology certainly contradicts what we should have expected if we only had Talmudic evidences and the later philosophical writings to go on. So the Iranian and archaeological sources are not unequivocal. The former are late, and the latter as yet not wholly explicated for the history of religions. I think it likely that significant numbers of Babylonian Jews converted to Christianity in the second half of the third century, despite the persecutions of the latter community at that time. About Judaism in Mesopotamia (Edessa, Nisibis), Adiabene, Armenia, Mesene, Khuzistan, Elam, Khorrasan, and other satrapies of the Western Iranian Empire in Sasanian times where Jews lived, we know practically nothing. All we know is that there *were* Jews in these satrapies.

All our literary evidence (except scattered references in Christian Syriac literature) pertains to Babylonia; and most of it derives from, and testifies concerning the state of, the rabbinical academies alone. Indeed, the Babylonian Talmud, which makes possible a study of Babylonian Judaism, presents a grand impediment to the study of that very history. It is mostly a commentary upon the Mishnah, and the historically useful data are limited by the concentration on what was relevant to Mishnah and other legal-study, interpretation, and application. So the available literature leads us to suppose that we know more than we actually do.

v. BIBLIOGRAPHIES

I have by no means attempted to offer a full bibliography of relevant works, as is obvious to the reader. Many of the books and articles cited here contain long bibliographies as well, at least as extensive on specific problems as are mine. I call attention, for example, to the extraordinary bibliographies on oriental Christianity of Arthur Vööbus, *History of Asceticism in the Syrian Orient, I. The Origin of Asceticism. Early Monasticism in Persia* (Louvain, 1958); *II. Early Monasticism in Mesopotamia and Syria*

(Louvain, 1960), and his *History of the School of Nisibis* (Louvain, 1965).
W. B. Henning published *A Bibliography of Important Studies on Old Iranian
Subjects* (Tehran, 1950). Of Jewish bibliographies containing references to
our subject there is no end. I found very helpful Moise Schwab, *Repertoire
des Articles rélatifs à l'histoire et à la littérature juives parus dans les périodiques
de 1665 à 1900* (Paris, 1914-1923).

SUPPLEMENTARY BIBLIOGRAPHY

N.B. *Items listed in Vol. I, pp. 191-213, Vol. II, pp. 291-301,
and Vol. III, pp. 359-365 have not been repeated here.*

Adams, Robert M., "Agriculture and Urban Life in Early Southwestern Iran,"
Science 136, 1962, 109-122.
Alföldi, Andrew, *The Conversion of Constantine and Pagan Rome*, trans. H. Mattingly,
Oxford, 1948.
Altheim, Franz, "Arsakiden und Sasaniden," *Historia Mundi*, ed. F. Kern, Bern,
1956, Vol. IV, 516-541.
— —, "Mazdak and Porphyrios," *HR* 3, 1, 1963, 1-20.
Antakolski, Moshe Simon, "LeToledot Rava," *He'Assif* 3, 1884, 194-201.
Asmussen, Jes P., "Der Manichäismus als Vermittler literarischen Gutes,"
Temenos 2, 1966, 5-21.
Avi-Yonah, Michael, with Samuel Safrai, *Carta's Atlas of the Period of the Second
Temple, the Mishnah, and the Talmud*, in Hebrew, Jerusalem, 1966.
— —, "Lucius Valerius Valerianus, Governor of Syria Palestine," *IEJ* 16, 2, 1966,
135-41.

Bacher, Wilhelm, "The Church Father, Origen, and Rabbi Hoshaya," *JQR*, o.s.,
3, 1891, 357-60.
Baker, G. P., *Constantine the Great and the Christian Revolution*, N.Y., 1930.
Barnard, L. W., *Studies in the Apostolic Fathers and their Background*, Oxford, 1966.
Barr, Stringfellow, *The Mask of Jove. A History of Graeco-Roman Civilization from
the Death of Alexander to the Death of Constantine*, Philadelphia and N.Y., 1966.
Bauer, W., *A Greek-English Lexicon of the New Testament and Other Early Christian
Literature*, trans. and ed. by W. F. Arndt and F. W. Gingrich, Chicago, 1957.
Baynes, Norman H., "Athanasiana," *Journal of Egyptian Archaeology* 11, 1925, 58-69.
— —, "Constantine's Successors to Jovian: And the Struggle with Persia,"
Cambridge Medieval History [Hereinafter: *CMH*], I, 55-86.
— —, *Constantine the Great and the Christian Church*, London, 1924, [From the
Proceedings of the British Academy, Vol. 15.]
— —, "The Death of Julian the Apostate in a Christian Legend," *JRS* 27, 1937,
22-9.
— —, "The Early Life of Julian the Apostate," *JHS* 45, 251-254.
Benveniste, E., "Sur la terminologie iranienne du sacrifice," *JA* 252, 1, 1964, 45-58.
— —, *Titres et noms propres en iranien ancien*, Paris, 1966.
Bert, Georg, *Aphrahat's des Persischen Weisen Homilien, aus dem Syrischen Übersetzt
und Erläutert*, Leipzig, 1888.
Bidez, J., *La Vie de l'Empereur Julien*, Paris, 1930.
Bieler, Ludwig, ΘΕΙΟΣ ANHP. *Das Bild des "göttlichen Menschen" in Spätantike
und Frühchristentum*, Vienna, I, 1935, II, 1936.
Blau, Ludwig, "Amulets," *JE* 1, 546.
— —, "Angelology," *JE* 1, 583-589.
— —, "Astrology," *JE* 2, 241-3.
— —, "Magic," *JE* 8, 255-7.
Boulnois, Luce, *The Silk Road*, trans. Dennis Chamberlain, N.Y., 1966. [French
ed. is listed in vol. II, p. 292.]

Boyce, Mary, "Some Reflections on Zurvanism," *BSOS* 19, 1957, 304-16.
— —, "Ātaš zōhr and Āb-zōhr," *JRAS*, Oct. 1966, 100-118.
Braun, Oskar, *Ausgewählte Akten Persischer Märtyrer*, Munich, 1915.
Brecher, Gideon, *Das Transcendentale, Magie, und magische Heilarten im Talmud*, Vienna, 1850.
Brooks, E. W., "The Eastern Provinces from Arcadius to Anastasius," *CMH* 1, 457-486.
Budge, Ernest A. Wallis, trans., *The Chronography of Gregory Abu'l Faraj ... commonly known as Bar Hebraeus*, London, 1932, vol. 1.
Bultmann, Rudolf, *The History of the Synoptic Tradition*, trans. John Marsh, Oxford, 1963.
Burckhardt, Jacob, *The Age of Constantine the Great*, trans. Moses Hadas, N.Y., 1956.
Burkitt, F. Crawford, *Early Eastern Christianity*, N.Y., 1904.

Chabot, J. B., "Trois Épisodes concernant les Juifs," *REJ* 28, 1888, 290-94.
Charlesworth, Martin P., "The Fear of the Orient in the Roman Empire," *The Cambridge Historical Journal* 2, 1926, 9-16.
Chaumont, M.-L., "Le culte de la déesse Anāhitā (Anahit) dans la religion des monarques d'Iran et d'Arménie au Ièr siecle de notre ère," *JA* 253, 1965, 167-182.
— —, "Où les rois sassanides étaient-ils couronnés," *JA* 252, 1, 1964, 59-76.
Conybeare, F. C., trans.,"Antiochus Strategus, 'The Capture of Jerusalem by the Persians in the Year 614,'" *English Historical Review* 25, 1910, 502-517.

DeFries, Benjamin, *Mevo Kelali leSifrut HaTalmudit*, Tel Aviv, 1966.
Delahaye, H., "Les Actes grècs des martyrs persans sous Sapor II," *Pat. Or.*, 2, 1905, 454-55.
Dembitz, Lewis N., "Babylon in Jewish Law," *JQR*, o.s., 19, 1906-7, 109ff.
Der Nersessian, Sirarpie, *Armenia and the Byzantine Empire*, Cambridge, 1945.
De Vries, Jan. *The Study of Religion, A Historical Approach*, trans. K. W. Bolle, N.Y., 1967.
Diakonoff, I. M., and V. A. Livshitz, "New Documents from Old Nisa," in Переднеазиатский Сборник, II, Moscow, 1966, 169-173 [English summary only].
Dibelius, Martin, *From Tradition to Gospel*, trans. B. L. Woolf, N.Y., 1935.
Downey, Glanville, "The Perspective of the Early Church Historians," *Greek, Roman, and Byzantine Studies* 6, 1, 1965, 57-70.
Dunlop, D. M., *The History of the Jewish Khazars*, Princeton, 1954.

Ensslin, W., "Kaiser Julians Gesetzgebungswerk und Reichsverwaltung," *Klio* 18, 104-199.
Evans-Pritchard, E. E., "Anthropology and History," in his *Essays in Social Anthropology*, N.Y., 1963, 46-65.
— —, *Witchcraft, Oracles, and Magic among the Azande*, Oxford, 1937.

Feldblum, M. S., *Diqduqé Soferim: Gittin*, N.Y., 1966.
Fontenrose, Joseph, *The Ritual Theory of Myth*, Berkeley and Los Angeles, 1966.
Forbes, R. J., *Studies in Ancient Technology*, Leiden, 1956, Vol. 4.
Fox, Douglas A., "Darkness and Light: The Zoroastrian View," *Journal of the American Academy of Religion* [Formerly, *JBR*, hereinafter: *JAAR*] 35, 2, 1967, 129-137.
Frend, W. H. C., *The Donatist Church*, Oxford, 1952.
— —, *Martyrdom and Persecution in the Early Church*, N.Y., 1967.

Gagé, Jean, "Comment Sapor a-t-il 'triumphé' de Valérien?" *Syria*, 1965 [Not used.]

Gardner, Alice, "Religious Disunion in the Fifth Century," *CMH* 1, 487-520.

Gavin, Frank, "Rabbinic Parallels in Early Church Orders," *HUCA* 6, 1929, 55-68.

Geffcken, Johannes, *Kaiser Julianus*, Leipzig, 1914.

Gibbon, Edward, *The History of the Decline and Fall of the Roman Empire*, ed. J. B. Bury, London, 1896, Vol. 2.

Ginzberg, Louis, "Aphraates, The Persian Sage," *JE* 1, 663-65.

Glover, Terrot Reaveley, *Life and Letters in the Fourth Century*, Cambridge, 1901.

Goldberg, Avraham, "R. Zera' uMinhag Bavel b'Erez Yisra'el," *Tarbiz* 36, 1967, 319-341.

Goodenough, Erwin R., "The Greek Garments on the Jewish Heroes in the Dura Synagogue," *Biblical Motifs*, ed. A. Altmann, Cambridge, 1966, 221-237.

Gordon, Cyrus H., "Leviathan, Symbol of Evil," *Biblical Motifs*, ed. A. Altmann, Cambridge, 1966, 1-9.

Guidi, B. I., "Ostsyrische Bischöfe und Bischofssitze im V, VI, und VII Jahrhundert," *ZDMG* 43, 1889, 397ff.

Gwatkin, H. M., and J. P. Whitney, eds., *The Cambridge Medieval History, I. The Christian Roman Empire and the Foundation of the Teutonic Kingdoms*, Cambridge, 1911.

— —, "Constantine and His City," *CMH* 1, 1-23.

Gwynn, John, ed., *Selections ... from the Hymns and Homilies of Ephraim the Persian Sage*, in Philip Schaff and Henry Wace, eds., *A Select Library of Nicene and Post-Nicene Fathers*, 2nd series, Vol. 13, Grand Rapids, 1956.

Hartranft, Chester D., trans., *The Ecclesiastical History of Sozomen*, in Philip Schaff and Henry Wace, eds., *Select Library of Nicene and Post-Nicene Fathers*, 2nd series, Vol. 2, Grand Rapids, 1957.

Heinemann, Joseph, "One Benediction Comprising Seven," *REJ* 125, 1966, 101-111.

Higger, Michael, *Masekhtot Kallah*, N.Y., 1936.

Higgins, M. J., "Aphraates' Dates for the Persian Persecution," *Byzantinische Zeitschrift* 41, 1951, 265-71.

Hillkowitz, K., "The Participation of the Jews in the Conquest of Jerusalem by the Persian in 614 A.D.," in Hebrew, *Ziyyon* 4, 1939, 307-316.

Hirshberg, Hayyim Ze'ev, *Yisra'el Ba'Arav. Qorot HaYehudim beHimyar veHijaz Lemin Hurban Bayit Sheni ve'Ad Masa'ei HaZelav*, (In Hebrew: Israel in Arabia. History of the Jews in Himyar and Hijaz from the Destruction of the Second Temple to the Crusades), Tel Aviv, 1946.

Hoenig, S. B., "Origins of the Rosh Hashanah Liturgy," *JQR* n.s. 75, 1967, 312-31.

Hoffman, Georg, *Auszüge aus Syrischen Akten Persischer Märtyrer*, Leipzig, 1880, *Abhandlungen für die Kunde des Morgenländes* 7, 3, reprinted in Liechtenstein, 1966.

Hoffman, Johan G.E., *Iulianos der Abtrünnige*, Leiden, 1880 [Not used.]

Honigmann, Ernst, *Die Ostgrenze des byzantinischen Reiches von 363 bis 1071*, Brussels, 1935.

Hussey, J. M., *The Byzantine World*, N.Y., 1961.

Jacobsen, Thorkild, and Robert M. Adams, "Salt and Silt in Ancient Mesopotamian Agriculture," *Science* n.s. 128, 1958, 1251-1258.

Junge, P. J., "Hazarapatiš, Zur Stellung des Chiliarchen der Köninglichen Leibgarden im Achaemenidenreich," *Klio* 33, 1940, 3-38.

Kahle, Paul E., *The Cairo Geniza*, 2nd ed., Oxford, 1959.

Kilpatrick, George D., "Dura-Europos: The Parchments and the Papyri" (Review), *Greek, Roman, and Byzantine Studies* 5, 1964, 215-225.

Klima, Otakar, "Mazdak und die Juden,"*Arch. Or.*, 24, 1956, 420ff.

Kohler, K., "Angelology, Historical Development," *JE* 1, 589-97.

Krappe, A. H., "Observations sur une variante malaise de la légende de Jezdeguerd I," *JA* 229, 1937, 607-615.

Krauss, Samuel, "Ägyptische und syrische Götternamen im Talmud," in George Alexander Kohut, ed., *Semitic Studies in Memory of Rev. Dr. Alexander Kohut*, Berlin, 1897, 339-353.

Laeuchli, Samuel, *The Serpent and the Dove. Five Essays on Early Christianity*, Nashville, 1966.

Lagier, C., *L'Orient Chrétien des Apôtres jusqu'à Photius*, Paris, 4th ed., 1935.

Lang, David Marshall, *The Georgians*, London, 1966.

Laufer, Berthold, *Sino-Iranica. Chinese Contributions to the History of Civilization in Ancient Iran*, Chicago, 1919.

Lebeau, Charles, with M. de Saint-Martin, *Histoire du Bas-Empire*, Paris, 1824, Vol. 1.

Lees, G. M. and N. L. Falcon, "The Geographical History of the Mesopotamian Plains," *Geographical Journal* 118, 1952, 24-39.

Leipoldt, Johannes, "Frühes Christentum im Orient," in B. Spuler, ed., *Handbuch der Orientalistik*, Leiden, 1961, 8, 2, 3-42.

Levine, Philip, "The Continuity and Preservation of the Latin Tradition," in Lynn White, jr., ed., *Transformation*, [See below] 206-231.

Levy, Reuben, trans., *The Epic of the Kings. Shāh-nāma*, Chicago, 1967.

Lewin, B. M., *Ozar HaGeonim, Thesaurus of the Gaonic Responsa and Commentaries*, I, Haifa, 1928; II, 1930; III, Jerusalem, 1930; IV, 1931; V, 1932; VI, 1936; VII, 1938; VIII, 1940; IX, 1940; X, 1941; XI, 1942; XII, 1943; XIII, no date or place listed.

Lukonin, Vladimir G., *Persia II*, trans. by James Hogarth, N.Y. & Cleveland, 1967.

Maimon, Y. L. HaKohen, *Abbaye veRava. Toldotēhem uMasekhet Ma'amarēhem veSugyotēhem baHalakhah uvaAgadah*, Jerusalem, 1965.

Malinowski, Bronislaw, "The Language of Magic," in Max Black, ed., *The Importance of Language*, Engelwood Cliffs, 1962, 72-90.

Margaliot, Mordecai, ed., *Sefer HaRazim, A Newly Recovered Book of Magic from the Talmudic Period* in Hebrew, Jerusalem, 1966.

Marmorstein, Avraham, "LeQorot HaYehudim b'Erez Yisra'el beMe'ah Ha-Ḥamishit leMisparam," in I. Press and E. L. Sukenik, ed., *Yerushalayim, Journal of the Jewish Palestine Exploration Society, in Memory of A. M. Luncz*, Jerusalem, 1928, 41-50.

Martin, Edward J., *The Emperor Julian. An Essay on His Relations with the Christian Religion*, London, 1919.

Mattingly, H., *Christianity in the Roman Empire*, N.Y., 1967.

— —, "The Imperial Recovery," *CAH* 12, 297-351.

McEvedy, Colin, *The Penguin Atlas of Ancient History*, Baltimore, 1967.

McNeill, William, *The Rise of the West*, N.Y., 1965.

Meeks, Wayne A., *The Prophet-King*, Leiden, 1967.

Minorsky, V., "Roman and Byzantine Campaigns in Atropatene," *BSOS* 11, 1943-1946, 243-265.

Misch, Georg, *A History of Autobiography in Antiquity*, Cambridge, 1951.

Momigliano, A. D., *Studies in Historiography*, N.Y., 1966.

Moore, George F., "Intermediaries in Jewish Theology," *HTR* 15, 1922, 41-86.

Moss, H. St. L. B., "From A.D. 330 to the Fourth Crusade," in N. H. Baynes and H. Moss, eds., *Byzantium. An Introduction to East Roman Civilization*, Oxford, 1948, 1-33.

Muehsam, Alice, *Coin and Temple. A Study of the Architectural Representation on Ancient Jewish Coins*, Leeds, 1966.

Müller, Werner, "Mazdak and the Alphabet Mysticism of the East," *HR* 31, 1963, 72-82.

Munck, Johannes, "The New Testament and Gnosticism," *Studia Theologica* 15, 1961, 181-195.

Negri, Gaetano, *Julian the Apostate*, trans. Duchess Litta-Viconti-Arese, N.Y., 1905, 1-2.

Nöldeke, Theodor, *Sketches from Eastern History*, repr. Beirut, 1963.

Ort, L. J. R., *Mani, A Religio-Historical Description of his Personality*, Leiden, 1967.

Ostrogorsky, George, *History of the Byzantine State*, trans. Joan Hussey, New Brunswick, 1957.

Peeters, Paul, "L'Intervention politique de Constance II dans la Grande Arménie en 338," *Académie Royale de Belgique. Bulletins de la Classe des Lettres...*5th Series, 17, 1931, 10-47.

— —, "La prise de Jérusalem par les perses,"*Mélanges de l'Université Saint Joseph*, Beirut, 1923, 9, 1.

Phillips, E. D., *The Royal Hordes: Nomad Peoples of the Steppes*, London, 1965.

Pines, Shlomo, "The Jewish Christians of the Early Centuries of Christianity according to a New Source," *Israel Academy of Sciences and Humanities, Proceedings* 2, 13, 1966.

Preisendanz, Karl, *Greek Magical Papyri*, Leipzig, 1928 [Not used.]

Rice, David Talbot, *The Byzantines*, London, 1962.

— —, "Persia and Byzantium," in A. T. Arberry, ed., *The Legacy of Persia*, Oxford, 1953, 39-59.

Rolfe, John C., trans., *Ammianus Marcellinus*, Cambridge, I, 1935; II, 1937; III, 1939.

Rosenthal, Judah, "Ra'yon Bitul HaMiẓvot b'Eskatologia HaYehudit," *Jubilee Volume for Meir Waxman*, Jerusalem, 1967, 217-233.

Runciman, Steven, *Byzantine Civilization*, N.Y., 1956.

— —, "Some Remarks on the Image of Edessa," *The Cambridge Historical Journal*, 3, 1929-31, 238-252.

Sachau, Eduard, "Von den rechtlichen Verhältnissen der Christen im Sasanidenreich," *Mitteilungen des Seminars für Orientalische Sprachen an der köninglichen Friedrich-Wilhelms-Universität zu Berlin*, 10, 1907, 69-96.

Schacht, Joseph, *An Introduction to Islamic Law*, Oxford, 1964.

Scharf, A., "Jews in Byzantium," in B. Netanyahu ed., *The World History of the Jewish People*, 2nd series, Vol. 2, Cecil Roth, ed. *The Dark Ages. Jews in Christian Europe, 711-1096* New Brunswick, 1966, 49-68.

Schwabe, Moshe, "Chapters on Hellenistic Palestine in the Time of the Editing of the Palestinian Talmud" in Hebrew, *Tarbiz* 5, 1933-34, 35-69.

Simpson, W. Douglas, *Julian the Apostate*, Aberdeen, 1930.

Smith, Morton, *Tannaitic Parallels to the Gospels*, Philadelphia, 1951.

Stein, Ernst, *Geschichte des Spätrömischen Reiches*, I. *Vom Römischen zum Byzantinischen Staate*, Vienna, 1928.

Spuler, Berthold, "Die Nestorianische Kirche," in B. Spuler, ed., *Handbuch der Orientalistik*, 8, 2, Leiden, 1961, 120-169.

Tannenblatt, M. A., *Peraqim Ḥadashim leToledot 'Erez Yisra'el uBavel b'Tequfat HaTalmud*, Tel Aviv, 1966.

Taubes, Ḥaim Zvi, *Oẓar HaGeonim leMasekhet Sanhedrin*, Jerusalem, 1966.

Thompson, E. A., *The Historical Work of Ammianus Marcellinus*, Cambridge, 1947.

Thorndike, Lynn, *A History of Magic and Experimental Science*, N.Y., 1923, Vol. 1.

Tisserant, Eugene, *Eastern Christianity in India*, Westminster, 1957.

Umanski, Yosef, *Ḥokhmei HaTalmud. Sefer Rav*, Tarnow, 1931.

Vajda, Issachar Dov," 'Inyanim Talmudiim leQorot HaZ'man," *Emlékhönyv Bloch Mozes*, Budapest, 1905.

Vansina, Jan, *Oral Tradition, A Study in Historical Methodology*, trans. H. M. Wright, London, 1965.

Vasiliev, A. A., *History of the Byzantine Empire*, Madison, 1958, Vol. 1.

Vinogradoff, Paul, "Social and Economic Conditions of the Roman Empire in the Fourth Century," *CMH* 1, 542-567.

Vogt, Joseph, *Kaiser Julian und das Judentum*, Leipzig, 1939.

Wallace, Antony F. C., *Religion: An Anthropological View*, N.Y., 1966.

White, Lynn, jr., ed., *The Transformation of the Roman World*, Berkeley and Los Angeles, 1966.

Widengren, Geo, "Iran and Israel in Parthian Times with Special Regard to the Ethiopic Book of Enoch," *Temenos, Studies in Comparative Religion* 2, 1966, 139-177.

Wiessner, Gernot, *Untersuchungen zur syrischen Literaturgeschichte I: Zur Martyrerüberlieferung aus der Christenverfolgung Schapurs II, Abhandlungen der Akademie der Wissenschaften in Göttingen, Philologisch-Historische Klasse*, 3rd series No. 67, Göttingen, 1967.

Wolski, Jósef, "Les Achéménides et les Arsacides: Contribution à l'histoire de la formation des traditions iraniennes," *Syria* 43, 1966, 65-89.

— —, "Elam, Perse, Arménie (Achéménides, Arsacides, Sassanides)," in John Gillssen, ed., *Introduction bibliographique à l'histoire du droit et à l'ethnologie juridique*, A/5 Brussels, 1965.

— —, "Les recherches modernes sur l'histoire des Parthes," *Mélanges Offerts à R. Michalowski*, Warsaw, 1966, 735-740.

Wright, Wilmer Cave, trans., *The Works of the Emperor Julian*, N.Y., I, 1913; II, 1913; III, 1923.

Wulff, Hans E., *The Traditional Crafts of Persia*, Cambridge, 1966.

Yavetz Ze'ev, *Sefer Toledot Yisra'el*, Berlin, 1912, Vol. 8.

Zemos, A. C., trans., *The Ecclesiastical History of Socrates Scholasticus*, in Philip Schaff and Henry Wace, eds., *Select Library of Nicene and Post-Nicene Fathers*, 2nd series, Vol. 2, Grand Rapids, 1957.

Zernov, N., *Eastern Christendom*, London, 1961.

Zlotnick, Dov., trans and ed., *The Tractate 'Mourning,'* New Haven, 1966.

Zuri, Y. S., *The Reign of the Exilarchate and the Legislative Academies. Period of Rab Nachman bar Jizchak* (320-355). English title for *Shilton Rashut HaGolah veHa-Yeshivot. Tequfat Rav Naḥman bar Yizḥaq Rosh HaKalah veRosh HaYeshivah*, 320-355), Tel Aviv, 1939.

INDEX OF BIBLICAL AND TALMUDIC PASSAGES

i. Biblical References

ii. Talmudic Passages

GENERAL INDEX

A

Abaye, 68, 82, 84, 93-95, 97, 114, 117, 120, 184, 231, 256, 278, 373, 375, 400, 401
    Arab incursion, 44-45
    Bailments, 239-241
    Betrothal and marriage contracts, 192-194, 197
    Capital jurisdiction, 188, 189
    Court, 133-138, 141
    Court and farm, 144-146, 148
    Court and synagogue, 149, 151
    Damages, 248, 249
    Demons and angels, 334-337, 339, 340
    Divorce, 207, 208, 210
    Documents and deeds, 242-244
    Dreams and revelations, 341-345
    Family life, 200-202
    Food taboos, 152, 153, 155
    Holy days, 164, 168
    Holy objects, 161, 162
    Ifra Hormizd, 35
    Intermediate days of festivals, 169, 170
    Judaism and other religions, 56, 59
    Kallah, 384, 385
    Levirate ceremony, 204, 205
    Life of the schools, 284, 286, 289, 290, 293-306, 308, 210, 312, 314, 318-322, 325, 327-331, 333
    Litigation, 234, 235, 238
    Medicine, 363-368
    Mortgages and debts and bonds, 221-225
    Mourning rites, 156-157
    Paganism, 62, 63, 65
    Passover, 166
    Rabbi's curse, 351, 352
    Sabbath, 172-175, 177, 178
    Schools, 288
    Schools and the streets, 387-389
    Shapur and the Jews, 54
    Taxes, 40, 42
    Torah as supernatural force, 354, 356-359
    War of 363, 48
    Witchcraft, incantations and amulets, 348-350
    Workers and slaves, 246-247
    Wills and estates, 215, 216, 218, 218
'Abaye b. 'Abin, 146
'Abba, 82-84, 120, 340
'Abba b. Jacob, R., 187
'Abba b. Martha, 222, 306
'Abba Mari bar Mar, 84
'Abba Mari b. Mar 'Uqban de Zuzita, 84

C

H

J

L

Labourt, J., 20, 25
Laḥman b. Ristak, 173, 174
Langlois, Victor, 25n
Lauterbach, J. Z., 433
Lazarus, F., 82-85, 120, 430, 431
Lazarus, H. M., 156n, 307
Levi, 310
Levi b. Darga, 44
Levine, Baruch A., 426
Levirate ceremony, 204-206
Levy, Jacob, 51, 54n, 207n
Lewin, B. M., 82n, 97n, 99, 102n, 133n, 136n, 151n, 156n, 202n, 222n, 247n, 248n, 287n, 339n
Libanius, 5n
Lieberman, S., 27n, 28n, 31n, 32n, 47, 58n, 66, 330n, 349n, 354n, 406, 432
Life of the schools, 279-402
Little Kushans, 2
Liver, J., 14n
Loewe, H., 353n
Loewe, Raphael, 371n
Lot, 372, 383
Lukonin, Vladimar G., 247n, 431
Lydda, 28

M

Mabrakta, 169, 172
Macedonia, 8
Magi, 18, 19, 22, 27, 40, 51, 53, 55, 70
Magog, 35, 53, 54, 68, 319, 375
Maḥalat, 336
Maḥoza, 33, 34, 36, 46, 47, 54, 56, 59, 94, 95, 97-100, 117, 118, 123, 140, 141, 150
    156, 158, 159, 168, 169, 173, 176, 177, 185, 189, 193, 196, 200-202, 214, 226
    229, 232, 286, 287, 292, 299, 300, 305, 327, 363, 387, 388
    Southside, 163
Mahraspand, 17
Maimon, Y. L., 289n, 433
Maiozamalcha, 11, 46
Makkot, 400
    Law enforcement, 273
    Supernatural exemplification, 397
Malachi, 341
Malalas, 5n
Malkio, R., 215
Manasiah b. Taḥalifa, R., 289
Manasseh, 375
Mandelbaum, B., 87n
Mani, 17, 19, 75
Manichaeans, 55, 76, 126
Mann, C. S., 424n

Q

R

Zikonia, 152
Zoroastrian church, 18, 25, 67
Zosimus, 5n
Zucker, Moshe, 404n
Zunz, Y. L., 371n, 384n
Zuri, Y. S., 84, 95, 371n, 386n, 389n, 433, 434
Zurvan, 17, 18

Indices were prepared by Mr. Arthur Woodman, Canaan, New Hampshire under a grant from Brown University.

Date Due